Contents

Acknowledgments

We wish to acknowledge Brunner/Mazel, Inc. and The Hogarth Press for Karl Abraham, "Notes on the Psycho-Analytical Investigation and Treatment of Manic-Depressive Insanity and Allied Conditions," in SELECTED PAPERS OF PSYCHOANALYSIS.

We wish to acknowledge Basic Books, Inc., and The Hogarth Press for Sigmund Freud, "Mourning and Melancholia," in *The Standard Edition of the Complete Works of Sigmund Freud,* Volume 17.

We wish to acknowledge Basic Books, Inc., for David Rapaport, "Edward Bibring's Theory of Depression," in Merton Gill (Ed.). THE COLLECTED PAPERS OF DAVID RAPAPORT.

We wish to acknowledge *Psychiatry* for Mabel Blake Cohen, Grace Baker, Robert A. Cohen, Frieda Fromm-Reichmann, and Edith V. Weigert, "An Intensive Study of Twelve Cases of Manic-Depressive Psychosis," Vol. 17, pp. 103–137, 1954.

We wish to acknowledge Hemisphere Publishing Corporation for Peter M. Lewinsohn, "A Behavioral Approach to Depression," in R. J. Friedman and M. M. Katz (Eds.) THE PSYCHOLOGY OF DEPRESSION.

We wish to acknowledge W.H. Freeman and Company, Publishers, for William R. Miller, Robert A. Rosellini, Martin E. P. Seligman, "Learned Helplessness and Depression," in J. D. Maser and M. E. P. Seligman, PSYCHOPATHOLOGY: EXPERIMENTAL MODELS.

We wish to acknowledge *Behavior Therapy* for Lynn P. Rehm, "A Self Control Model of Depression," Vol. 8, pp. 787–804, 1977.

We wish to acknowledge *American Journal of Psychiatry* for Maria Kovacs and Aaron T. Beck, "Maladaptive Cognitive Structures in Depression," Vol. 135, pp. 525–533, 1978.

We wish to acknowledge *Journal of Abnormal Psychology* for Lyn Y. Abramson, Martin E. P. Seligman, and John D. Teasdale, "Learned Helplessness in Humans: Critique and Reformulation," 87, pp. 49–74, 1978.

We wish to acknowledge *Psychiatry* for James C. Coyne, "Toward an Interactional Description of Depression," Vol. 39, pp. 28–40, 1976.

Andrew G. Billings and Rudolf H. Moos, "Psychosocial Theory and Research on Depression: An Integrative Framework and Review," reprinted with permission from *Clinical Psychology Review,* vol. 2, pp. 213–237, copyright 1982, Pergamon Press, Ltd.

"Depression: A Comprehensive Theory," reprinted with permission of The Free Press, a Division of Macmillan, Inc., from THE REVOLUTION IN PSYCHIATRY, by Ernest S. Becker.

We wish to acknowledge Raven Press, New York, for George W. Brown, "A Three-Factor Causal Model of Depression," in J. E. Barrett et al, (Eds.), STRESS AND MENTAL DISORDERS.

We wish to acknowledge Academic Press, Inc. for Lenore Sawyer Radloff, "Risk Factors for Depression: What Do We Learn from Them?", in M. Guttentag, S. Salasin, and D. Belle (Eds.), THE MENTAL HEALTH OF WOMEN.

We wish to acknowledge Raven Press, New York, for George Winokur, "Controversies in Depression, or Do Clinicians Know Something After All?," in P. J. Clayton and J. E. Barrett (Eds.) TREATMENT OF DEPRESSION: OLD CONTROVERSIES AND NEW APPROACHES.

David L. Dunner, "Recent Genetic Studies of Bipolar and Unipolar Depression." In J. M. Davis and J. W. Maas (Eds.). AFFECTIVE DISORDERS. Washington, D. C., copyright American Psychiatric Press, Inc., 1983. Used with permission.

We wish to acknowledge *McLean Hospital Journal* for Ross J. Baldessarini, "A Summary of Biomedical Aspects of Mood Disorders," Vol. 6, pp. 1–34, 1981.

Ambiguity and Controversy:
An Introduction

Discussions of depression often start with a statement that it is the common cold of psychopathology, a ubiquitous affliction to which most all of us are subject from time to time. Such discussions may note that at any one time, one fifth of the adult population will have significant depressive symptoms, and that most of this depression goes untreated (Weissman & Meyers, 1981). It may also be suggested that whoever is most likely to become depressed is largely a matter of psychological background and social conditions; depression is a "curse of civilization," and its occurrence is linked to stress and deprivation, the disintegration of relationships, and depressing life circumstances. Thus, Pearlin (1975) has stated that depression is "intertwined with with the values and aspirations that people acquire; with the nature of the situation in which they are performing major roles, such as in occupation and family; with the location of people in broader social structures, such as age and class; and the coping devices that they use . . ." (p. 206).

At the other extreme, discussions of depression may begin with an assertion that it is one of the most serious of mental-health problems. The discussion may then go on to emphasize that it is primarily a biological disturbance, an illness, the predisposition to which lies in genes and biochemistry. While people may indeed react to their circumstances with happiness and unhappiness, this is of questionable relevance to the clinical phenomena of depression.

Advocates of each of the positions discussed above can marshal impressive evidence; yet, taken together, they present a basic contradiction. They differ not only in their view of the causes of depression but its very definition. Beck (1967) has noted, "there are few psychiatric syndromes whose clinical descriptions are so constant through successive eras of history" (p.5). However, as these opposing positions demonstrate, definitional problems continue to plague the study of depression, and they are not going to be readily resolved. There remains considerable disagreement as to what extent and for what purposes a depressed mood in relatively normal persons can be seen as one end of a continuum with the mood disturbance seen in hospitalized psychiatric patients and to what extent the clinical phenomena is distinct and discontinuous with normal sadness and unhappiness.

Should we limit the term "depression" to those people who are most distressed and seeking treatment? And what do we make of the "merely miserable" that we have defined out of the "depressed" category? If we agree to make a sharp distinction, where is it to be drawn? What of the differences *among* depressed persons? The positions on these questions that one takes have major implications for who one studies and who one treats and how, what data are going to be considered relevant, and how one organizes that data. Many of the differences in the theoretical positions to be discussed in this volume start with a fundamental difference in how depression is defined. We cannot pretend to resolve these controversies, but we can at least identify them and note some of the definitions and distinctions that are being employed currently.

One purpose of this introductory chapter is to provide an overview of the phenomena of depression and to note some of the diagnostic distinctions that are currently being made. It should become apparent that there is a tremendous heterogeneity to what falls under the broad rubric of depression and that there is an arbitariness to any boundaries that are drawn on these phenomena. There are striking differences *among* depressed persons that invite some form of subtyping. As will be seen, however, efforts to derive such subtypes are generally controversial, and any scheme is likely to be more satisfactory for some purposes than for others. Confronted with all of this ambiguity and confusion, one must be cautious and not seek more precision than the phenomena of depression afford, and one should probably be skeptical about any decisive statement about the nature of depression.

This chapter is also intended to prepare the reader for the wide diversity of theoretical perspectives that will be presented in this volume. Contemplating the phenomena of depression, one can readily detect patterns and come to a conclusion that some aspects of depression are more central than others; some are primary and causal, and others are secondary. One observer may be struck with the frequency of complaints about appetite and sleep disturbance by depressed persons and infer that some sort of biological disturbance must be the key to understanding depression. Another might find their self-derogation and pessimism irrational in a way that suggests that there must be some kind of fundamental deficit in self-esteem or cognitive distortion occurring. Still another may listen to the incessant complaining of a depressed person, get annoyed and frustrated, and yet feel guilty in a way that makes it easier to encourage the depressed person to continue to talk in this way than to verbalize these negative feelings. Cognizant of this, the observer might conclude that there is some sort of interpersonal process going on that is critical to any understanding of depression.

DEPRESSION AS MOOD

A major source of confusion is due to the fact that the term "depression" variously refers to a mood state, a set of symptoms, and a clinical syndrome. As a reference to mood, depression identifies a universal human experience. Adjectives from a standard measure of mood (*The Multiple Affect Adjective Checklist;* Zuckerman & Lubin, 1965) point to subjective feelings associated with a depressed mood: sad, unhappy, blue, low, discouraged, bored, hopeless, dejected, and lonely. Similarities between everyday depressed mood and the complaints of depressed patients have encouraged the view that clinical depression is simply an exaggeration of a normal depressed mood. However, patients sometimes indicate that their experience of depression is quite distinct from normal feelings of sadness, even in its extreme form. A patient once remarked to me that her sadness was overwhelming when her husband died but that it did not compare with her sense of emptiness and her loss of any ability to experience pleasure at the time that she entered the hospital.

The view that depressed mood in otherwise normal persons is quantitatively but not qualitatively different than the depression found in hospitalized patients has been termed the *continuity hypothesis*. Beck (1967) has provided a useful analogy to suggest the alternative to the continuity hypothesis. He notes that everyday fluctuations in body temperature can be measured on the same thermometer as the changes associated with a fever. Yet the conditions giving rise to a fever are distinct from those causing fluctuations in temperature in healthy individuals. Similarly, the conditions giving rise to clinical depression may be distinct from those producing fluctuations in normal mood.

Studies have compared the subjective mood of persons who are distressed but not seeking help to those who are seeking treatment for depression or a review, see Depue & Monroe, 1978a). The two groups may be similar in subjective mood, but they differ in other ways. Those persons who are not seeking treatment for depression tend to lack the anxiety and the physical complaints, including loss of appetite, sleep disturbance, and fatigue shown by the group seeking treatment. Still, it could be argued that there is a continuum between the two groups, with these additonal features arising when a normal depressed mood becomes more prolonged or intensified. The controversy is likely to continue until either questions about the etiology of depression are resolved or unambiguous markers for depression are identified.

Advocates of biomedical approaches to depression tend to assume that there is a discontinuity between a normal depressed mood and clinical depression, and that appropriate biological markers will be found. Yet, as the article by Winokur in this volume suggests, even if that proves to be the case, there are likely to be many individuals suffering from extremes of depressed mood who do not have these markers.

Advocates of psychoanalytic, cognitive and behavioral, and interpersonal and social perspectives on depression have generally assumed a continuum between a normal depressed mood and clinical depression. They tend to exclude psychotic and bipolar depressed persons from treatment, but, beyond that, they have tended to disregard classification issues (Gilbert, 1984). For unipolar depression, at least, they have assumed that whatever discontinuities in the biology of mild and severe moods there might be are not necessarily relevant to the psychological and social processes in which they are most interested.

SYMPTOMS OF DEPRESSION

Writers since antiquity have noted the core symptoms of depression: besides a sad or low mood, reduced ability to experience pleasure, pessimism, inhibition and retardation of action, and a variety of physical complaints. For the purposes of discussion, we can distinguish among the emotional, cognitive, motivational, and vegetative symptoms of depression, although these features are not always so neatly divisible. Beyond these symptoms, there are some characteristic interpersonal aspects of depression that are not usually considered as.formal symptoms. But they are frequent, distinctive, and troublesome enough to warrant attention.

Emotional aspects of depression

Sadness and dejection are not the only emotional manifestations of depression, although about half of all depressed patient report these feelings as their principal complaint. Most depressed persons are also anxious and irritable. Classical descriptions of depression tend to emphasize that depressed persons' feelings of distress, disappointment, and frustration are focused primarily on themselves, yet a number of studies suggest that their negative feelings, including overt hostility, are also directed at the people around them. Depressed persons are often intensely angry persons (Kahn, Coyne, & Margolin, in press; Weissman, Klerman, & Paykel, 1971).

Perhaps 10 or 15 percent of severely depressed patients deny feelings of sadness, reporting instead that all emotional experience, including sadness, has been blunted or inhibited (Whybrow, Akiskal, & McKinney, 1984). The identification of these persons as depressed depends upon the presence of other symptoms. The inhibition of emotional expression in severely depressed persons may extend to crying. Whereas mild and moderately depressed persons may readily and frequently cry, as they become more depressed, they may continue to feel like crying, but complain that no tears come.

Mildly and moderately depressed persons may feel that every activity is a burden, yet they still derive some satisfaction from their accomplishments. Despite their low mood, they may still crack a smile at a joke. Yet, as depression intensifies, a person may report both a loss of any ability to get gratification from activities that had previously been satisfying—family, work, and social life—and a loss of any sense of humor. Life becomes stale, flat, and not at all amusing. The loss of gratification may extend to the depressed persons' involvement in close relationships. Often, a loss of affection for the spouse and children, a feeling of not being able to care anymore, a sense of a wall being erected between the depressed person and others are the major reasons for seeking treatment.

Cognitive aspects of depression

In the past decade, a number of theorists, notably Beck and Abramson, Seligman, and Teasdale have given particular attention to the cognitive manifestations of depression and have assumed that these features are causal of the other aspects of the disorder. Depressed persons characteristically view themselves, their situations, and their future possibilities in negative and pessimistic terms. They voice discouragement, hopelessness, and helplessness. They see themselves as inadequate and deficient in some crucial way. There may be thoughts of death, wishing to be dead, and suicide attempts.

Depressed persons' involvement in their daily lives are interpreted by them in terms of loss, defeat, and deprivation, and they expect failure when they undertake an activity. They may criticize themselves for minor shortcomings and seemingly search for evidence that confirms their negative view of themselves. Beck (see Kovacs & Beck, this volume) suggests that they will tailor the facts to fit these interpretations and hold to them in the face of contradictory evidence. Depressed persons overgeneralize from negative experiences, selectively abstract negative details out of context, ignore more positive features of their situations, and negatively characterize themselves in absolutist and dichotimous terms. The revised learned-helplessness model (see Abramson, Seligman, & Teasdale, this volume) emphasizes that depressed persons are particularly prone to blame themselves for their difficulties and to see their defects as stable and global attributes.

Aside from these content aspects of their thinking, depressed persons frequently complain that their thinking processes have slowed down, that they are distracted, and they cannot concentrate. Decisions pose a particular problem. Depressed persons are uncertain, feel in need of more information, and are afraid of making the wrong decision. They may simply feel paralyzed, and that the work of making a choice and a commitment is an overwhelming task to be avoided at any cost.

Motivational aspects of depression

Perhaps one of the most frustrating aspects of depressed persons for those around them is their difficulty in mobilizing themselves to perform even the most simple tasks. Encouragement, expressions of support, even threats and coercion seem only to increase their inertia, leading others to make attributions of laziness, stubbornness, and malingering. Despite their obvious distress and discomfort, depressed persons frequently fail to take a minimal initiative to remedy their situations or do so only halfheartedly. To observers, depressed persons may seem to have a callous indifference to what happens to them.

Depressed persons often procrastinate. They are avoidant and escapist in their longing for a refuge from demands and responsibilities. In severe depression, the person may experience an abulia or paralysis of will, extending even to getting out of bed, washing, and dressing.

In more severe depression, there may be psychomotor retardation, expressed in slowed body movements, slowed and monotomous speech, or even muteness. Alternatively, psychomotor agitation may be seen in an inabilitiy to sit still, pacing, and outbursts of shouting.

Vegetative aspects of depression

The presence of physical or vegetative symptoms are sometimes taken as the dividing line between normal sadness and clinical depression. One of the most common and prominent vegetative symptoms is fatigue. That someone is depressed may be first recognized by the family physician who cannot readily trace the person's complaints of tiredness to other causes.

Depressed persons also often suffer sleep disturbance, and it is tempting to link their tiredness to this, but in a sample of depressed patients, the two complaints are only modestly correlated (Beck, 1967). Depressed persons generally have trouble falling asleep, they sleep restlessly, and awaken easily. Yet some depressed persons actually sleep considerably more than usual, up to 12 hours a night.

When mildly or moderately depressed, some people eat compulsively and gain considerable weight, but depression is more characteristically associated with loss of appetite and a decrease in weight. Indeed, for many depressed persons, a loss of appetite is the first sign of an incipient depression, and its return marks the beginning of recovery. Some depressed persons maintain their normal eating habits and weight, but complain that food is tasteless and eating an unsatisfying matter of habit. Besides a loss of appetite, depression is often associated with gastrointestinal disturbance, notably nausea and constipation.

Mild depression heightens sexual interest in some people, but generally depression is associated with a loss of interest in sex. In severe depression, there may be an aversion to sex. Overall, though, women who are depressed do not have sex less frequently, but they initiate it less, enjoy it less, and are less responsive (Weissman & Paykel, 1974).

Finally, depressed persons report diffuse aches and pains. They have frequent headache, and they are more sensitive to existing sources of pain, such as dental problems.

Interpersonal aspects of depression

A brief interaction with a depressed person can have a marked impact on one's own mood. Uninformed strangers may react to a conversation with a depressed person with depression, anxiety, hostility, and may be rejecting of further contact (Coyne, 1976; see Gurtman, in press, for a review). Jacobson (1968) has noted that depresed persons often unwittingly succeed in making everyone in their environment feel guilty and responsible and that others may react to the depressed person with hostility and even cruelty. Despite this visible impact of depression on others, there is a persistent tendency in the literature to ignore it and to concentrate instead on the symptoms and complaints of depressed persons out of their interpersonal context. Depressed persons can be difficult, but they may also be facing difficult interpersonal situations within which their distress and behavior makes more sense (see Coyne, this volume).

Depressed persons tend to withdraw from social activities, and their close relationships tend to be strained and conflictful. Depressed women have been more intensely studied than depressed men, in part because women are approximately twice as likely to be depressed (see Radloff, this volume). Depressed women are dependent, acquiescent, and inhibited in their communication in close relationships, and prone to interpersonal tension, friction and open conflict (Weissman & Paykel, 1974). Interestingly, the interpersonal difficulties of depressed persons are less pronounced when they are interacting with strangers than with intimates (Hinchcliffe, Hooper, & Roberts, 1975).

About half of all depressed persons report marital turmoil (Rousanville, Weissman, Prusoff, & Heraey-Baron, 1979). There is considerable hostility between depressed persons and their spouses, but often there is more between depressed persons and their children. Being depressed makes it more difficult to be a warm, affectionate, consistent parent (McLean, 1976). The children of depressed parents are more likely to have a full range of psychological and social difficulties than the children of normal or even schizophrenic parents (Emery, Weintraub, & Neale, 1982), yet one must be cautious in making causal inferences. There is evidence that the child problems are more related to a conflictful marital relationship and a stressful homelife than depression of the parent per se (Sameroff, Barocas, & Siefer, in press).

Depression thus tends to be indicative of an interpersonal situation fraught with difficulties, and this needs to be given more attention in both theorizing and planning treatment. Although depression is associated with interpersonal problems, *within* a sample of depressed persons the correlation between severity of depression and the extent of interpersonal problems tends to be modest. This may suggest that these problems are a matter not only of how depressed persons are functioning, but of the response of key people around them as well (Coyne, Kahn, & Gotlib, 1985).

THE DIAGNOSIS OF DEPRESSION

One can make a list of the symptoms of depression, and assign any person a depression score on the basis of the number of symptoms present. A number of standard self-report inventories such as the *Beck Depression Inventory* (Beck, et al., 1961), the *Center for Epidemiologic Studies Depression Scale* (Radloff, 1977), and the *Self-Rating Depression Scale* (Zung, 1965) have been validated and are widely used as research tools, screening devices, and measures of the changes associated with treatment.

Even if one assumes a continuity between normal depressed mood and clinical depression, it may still prove useful to make a distinction between the presence or absence of significant depression. One may wish to insure that a research study does not include a preponderance of persons whose depression is only mild or transient. Virtually no signs or symptoms are specific to depression, and yet in many contexts, one may need to distinguish depression from other descriptors or explanations for a person's distress and behavior. In working with the elderly, for instance, it is important to distinguish between depression and dementia. In medical patients in general, there is a high prevalence of symptoms associated with depression, both because of physical illness and the stress of hospitalization (Cavanaugh, 1984), and, whether for research or practical purposes, one may wish to establish criteria for who is to be considered depressed and who is not. Finally persons who are labeled schizophrenic or alcoholic may show considerable depression, but it would be undesirable for many purposes to lump them with those persons whose primary problem is depression. Thus, for the purposes of research, treatment, and professional communication, it proves useful to have some means of specifying some boundary conditions for the term "depression," in terms of some minimal level of severity as well as some coherence and specificity to what is included in the concept—even if one rejects the notion that it is a discrete entity, discontinuous with normal mood.

The problem of diagnosis is most critical in biomedical approaches to depression. The assumption is generally made that depression is a matter of one or more disease entities with specific etiologies and treatments. The statement, "Nosology precedes etiology" conveys the idea that the ability to identify the causes of depression depends upon the existence of an adequate diagnostic and classificatory system. For instance, to take a simplified hypothetical example, suppose that a particular biological abnormality occurs in 60 percent of all depressed persons and is specific to depression. Suppose also that, with the accepted diagnostic criteria, only 60 percent of the persons identified as such are "actually depressed." If these conditions occurred, then research might indicate that only 36 percent of depressed persons possess the abnormality.

An effective treatment for depression may also be misjudged or misapplied in the absence of an adequate diagnostic system. This was made apparent recently after a drug company had undertaken a large study to compare the effectiveness of a new drug to that of both an established drug treatment for depression and a placebo (Carroll, 1984). At five of the six research sites, the new drug proved to be no more effective than a placebo, but interpretation of this was limited by the additional finding that the estabished treatment proved no better. Patients identified as depressed by current criteria did not respond to drug treatment that had proven efficacious in a large body of past research. Either the past research was misleading, the current diagnostic criteria are invalid, or, most likely, they were misapplied by reputable investigators.

Contemporary diagnostic systems owe much to the work of Kraepelin at the turn of the century. He divided major psychopathology into two broad syndromes: dementia praecox (schizophrenia) and manic-depressive illness. The latter category included almost all serious mood disturbance, including depression in the absence of an episode of mania. As retained today, the term generally is a synonym for bipolar disorder (see below). It is also still sometimes used as a generic term for severe depression. Kraepelin considered manic-depressive illness a biological derangement. Although it might in some cases be precipitated by psychological factors, "the real cause for the malady must be sought in *permanent internal changes* which are very often, perhaps always innate" (Kraepelin, 1921, p. 180). Once started, the illness runs its course autonomously, independent of changes in the person's situation. Kraepelin also identified a group of psychogenic depressions, which were precipitated by life circumstances, but that were milder than manic-depressive illness and reactive to changes in these circumstances.

For over 30 years, the dominant diagnostic system in the United States has been the *Diagnostic and Statistical Manual of Mental Disorders* of the American Psychiatric Association, which is currently in its third edition (DSM-III). In its first edition it integrated the ideas of Kraepelin with those of Adolph Meyer and Sigmund Freud. While accepting Kraepelin's basic distinction between affective disturbance and schizophrenia, it also reflected Meyer's psychobiological view that mental disturbance represented not a simple disease entity, but the reaction of the personality to the a matrix of psychological, social, and biological factors. By its second edition, the Meyerian term "reaction" was no longer used throughout, but Meyer's influence remained. Freud's ideas about the etiology of psychopathology were built into the criteria for specific disorders. Thus, the chief defining characterisitic of neuroses was anxiety, but for purpose of diagnostic decisions, it could be manifest and observable or inferred to be operating "unconsciously and automatically" in someone who was not visibly anxious.

The authors of DSM-III attempted to avoid past controversies and answer many of the criticisms of its two predecessors. A decision was made to define diagnostic categories as precisely as possible, using descriptive data, rather than inferences about etiology. From a biomedical perspecitve, the ideal diagnostic and classificatory system would integrate knowledge about etiology with overt symptomatolgy. However, it was concluded that the present understanding of the causes of most disorders is too limited for this purpose. Furthermore, the sense was that "the inclusion of etiological theories would be an obstacle to use of the manual by clinicians of varying theoretical orientations, since it would not be possible to present all reasonable etiological theories for each disorder" (American Psychiatric Association, 1980, p. 7).

In considering depression, the authors of DSM-III attempted to sidestep a number of longstanding controversies, including that of whether there is a continuum or a discontinuity between normal mood and clinical depression, as well as that of the role of precipitating life circumstances in distinguishing among types of depression. Depressive neurosis disappeared, along with the other neuroses. Depression is now encompassed in two main categories. The first category, major affective disorder, involves the presence of a full affective syndrome, with the subcategories of bipolar and major depression distinguished by whether there has ever been a manic episode. The second category, other specific affective disorders, includes conditions in which the depression is not severe enough to warrant a diagnosis of major affective disorder, but the mood disturbance has been intermittant or chronic for at least two years.

The criteria for major depression are presented in Table 1. Major depression is subclassified as to whether it is a single episode or recurrent and also as to whether *melancholia* is present. Melancholia involves a complaint of a loss of pleasure in all or almost all activites, a lack of reactivity to pleasant events, and at least three of six symptoms: a quality of depressed mood that is distinct from grief or sadness; depression worse in the morning; early morning wakening; marked psychomotor agitation or retardation; significant weight loss; and excessive guilt. The designation was intended as an acknowledgment that some more severe depressions were characterized by a particular constellation of symptoms and might be more responsive to treatment with drugs or electroshock. This issue will be discussed further below. It should be noted, however, that there is considerable consensus that such a distinction should be made, but the exact nature of it remains controversial.

As can be seen in Table 1, a diagnosis of major depressive disorder

Table 1. DSM-III Criteria For Major Depressive Episode

A. Dysphoria or loss of interest or pleasure in all or almost all usual activites and pastimes. The dysphoric mood is characterized by symptoms such as the following: depressed, sad, blue, hopeless, down in the dumps, irritable. The mood disturbance must be prominent and relatively persistent, but not necessarily the most dominant symptom, and does not include momentary shifts from one dysphoric mood to another dysphoric mood, e.g., anxiety to depression to anger, such as are seen in states of acute psychotic turmoil. (For children under six, dysphoric mood may have to be inferred from a persistently sad facial expression.)

B. At least four of the following symptoms must have been present nearly every day for a period of at least two weeks (in children under six, at least three of the first four).

(1) poor appetite or significant weight loss (when not dieting) or increased appetite or significant weight gain (in children under six, consider failure to make expected weight gains)
(2) insomnia or hypersomnia
(3) psychomotor agitation or retardation (but not merely subjective feelings of restlessness or being slowed down) (in children under six, hypoactivity)
(4) loss of interest or pleasure in usual activities, or decrease in sexual drive not limited to a period when delusional or hallucinating (in children under six, signs of apathy)
(5) loss of energy; fatigue
(6) feelings of worthlessness, self-reproach, or excessive or inappropriate guilt (either may be delusional)
(7) complaints or evidence of diminished ability to think or concentrate, such as slowed thinking, or indecisiveness not associated with marked lossening of associations or incoherence
(8) recurrent thoughts of death, suicidal ideation, wishes to be dead, or suicide attempt

C. Neither of the following dominate the clinical picture when an affective syndrome (criteria A and B above) is not present, that is, before it developed or after it has remitted:

(1) preoccupation with a mood-incongruent delusion or hallucination
(2) bizarre behavior

D. Not superimposed on either schizophrenia, schizophreniform disorder, or a paranoid disorder.

E. Not due to any organic mental disorder or uncomplicated bereavement requires evidence of mood disturbance and at least four other symptoms lasting at least every day for two weeks. There are also exclusion criteria, including schizophrenia and what is judged to be normal or uncomplicated grief.

The criteria for depression are somewhat arbitrary. An alternative set of diagnostic criteria that is widely used in research (Spitzer, Endicott, & Robins, 1978) requires a mood disturbance lasting at least one week and at least three symptoms. Still another (Feighner, Robins, & Guze, 1972) requires four symptoms and a one month duration. While there is a consensus that such disagreement is deplorable, there is not at present a way of resolving it satisfactorily that is not itself arbitrary. In general, these diagnostic systems are viewed as significant improvements over past efforts, but there is widespread dissatisfaction with them. A prominent biologically oriented researcher has lamented

An astute observer will find little that is intellectually satisfying about the DSM-III diagnostic criteria for major depressive disorder. These criteria amount to a catalogue of symptoms, and they are in no way linked by coherent underlying constructs. They also suffer from the problem of being cast as disjunctive criteria. This means that in section B, for example, patients need to satisfy only 4 from a total of 20 possible symptoms. Therefore (and this occurs in practice), several patients may be assigned the same diagnosis without having any symptoms in common (Carroll, 1984, p. 16).

Carroll goes on to note that as the result of an inadequate diagnostic system, research studies are limited by the flaws in the diagnoses used as independent variables, and drug treatment of an individual patient tends to remain a matter of trial and error.

We are far from an adequate diagnostic system for depression. If one is to be achieved, it will have to come to terms with the enormous heterogenity in the signs and symptoms, level of severity, causal factors, and clinical course that has been subsumed under the term "depression." In the past half century, there have many efforts to bring order to this heterogenity with a variety of classificatory systems. Kendall (1976) has suggested that almost every classificatory system that is logically possible has been proposed at some point in this period, but he notes that little consensus has been achieved. Winokur (see this volume) will review some of the current controversies, but it would be useful to identify a few of the distinctions that have been made before we turn to the major theoretical perspectives on the disorder.

SUBTYPES OF DEPRESSION

Of all the distinctions that have been proposed, the most widely accepted and least controversial is that between unipolar and bipolar disorder. In its simplest form—and as it has been recognized in the DSM-III—the differential diagnosis is based on whether the patient has a personal history of mania. However, recent genetic studies have led to a familial definition of the distinction: Depressed patients who do not have a personal history of mania may still be diagnosed as being bipolar if there has been mania among first-degree relatives.

Work by Perris (1966) first established that bipolar disorder starts on the average of 15 years earlier than unipolar depression and recurs more frequently. Individual episodes are shorter, and there is a greater risk of disorder among the first-degree relatives of bipolar patients. Furthermore, there was a tendency for unipolar and bipolar disorders to breed true, with first-degree relatives of bipolar patients tending toward bipolar disorder, and first-degree relatives of unipolar patients tending to have little more risk of mania than the general population. The unipolar-bipolar distinction has proven to be clinically useful; depressed bipolar patients respond significantly better to lithium than unipolar depressed patients.

Valid though the distinction appears to be, it has some important limitations. As yet, no consistent differences in the symptomatology of bipolar and unipolar depression have been identified. Altough a bipolar diagnosis predicts a greater likelihood of response to lithium, as many as 40 percent of unipolar patients nonetheless respond positively (Depue & Monroe, 1978b). By itself, the distinction does not do justice to the heterogeneity among either bipolar or unipolar patients. Currently, persons with bipolar disorder are often subclassified as to whether either manic or depressive symptoms or both have been severe to require hospitalization (see Dunner, this volume). Unipolar depressed persons remain a large and tremendously heterogeneous group. Nonetheless, in the continuing controversies as how best to distinguish among depressed persons, the unpolar-bipolar distinction stands out in its usefulness for both clinical and research purposes.

Many issues in the study of unipolar depression have coalesced in the concept of endogenous versus nonendogenous depression. The differentiation is most often identified as being between endogenous and reactive depressions, although this has been used interchangeably with the endogenous-neurotic and psychotic-neurotic distinctions. The hope for the distinction has often been that it would prove to be the boundary between biological versus psychological and social concerns. Traditionally, the term "endogenous" has been invoked to differentiate depressions that are purportedly biological in etiology, without environmental precipitants, and that are less amenable to psychotherapy. Also, endogenous depressions are expected to be more responsive to somatically oriented interventions, notably electroconvulsive shock therapy and antidepressant medication. "Reactive" has referred to depressions that are viewed as understandable reactions to some precipitating stress and that are both more suitable for psychotherapy and less responsive to somatic therapies. The distinction was originally based on the supposition that some depressions are related to precipitating events and others seem to appear without them and that this would predict response to treatment and clinical course.

Controlled studies have not found that the endogenous-reactive distinction predicts response to psychotherapy (Blackburn, et al., 1981; Kovacs, 1980; Rush, 1984). The presence or absence of precipitating stress has not proved to be a good predictor of response to treatment (Leff, Roatch, & Bunney, 1970), and the endogenous-reactive distinction has been found to be deficient in a number of ways. Yet it retains considerable utility. Reactivity to changes in life circumstances *during* a depressive episode have been found to predict response to electroconvulsive shock and antidepressant medication (Fowles & Gersh, 1979). Other symptoms that have been associated with a positive response to somatic treatment include quality of mood and whether there has been a loss of the ability to experience pleasure; psychomotor retardation; feeling worse in the morning after than the evening; and sleep and appetite disturbance. Such symptoms are now more accepted as criteria for endogenous depression than is the absence of precipitating stress.

This consensus about the features of endogenous depression still leaves questions about its polar opposite, reactive or neurotic depression. In clinical practice, it tends to be defined in terms of milder mood disturbance, a preponderance of psychological rather than vegetative symptoms, and the presence of a precipitating stress, although there are particular doubts about the validity of this last feature. Akiskal et al. (1978) found that reactive or neurotic depression was the single most common diagnosis in inpatient and outpatient settings, but they raised the issue of whether it was useful to consider it a unified entity or type. In about a quarter of all the cases of such depression studied, it appeared to be truly reactive, in the sense that it developed in the face of overwhelming stress in persons who had previously seemed reasonably well functioning. In another quarter of the cases, it seemed to reflect a more or less chronic tendency to respond to normative stress with depressed mood and to experience social difficulties. Many of these patients were described as dependent, manipulative, hostile, and unstable. Follow-up revealed overall that only 40 percent of the total sample was considered to be have been suffering primarily from an affective disturbance in the absence of some of other condition. Some of the subsample who had faced a clear precipitating stress developed endogenous features. In 10 percent of the sample, the depression seemed secondary to a medical-surgical illness. In 38 percent of the sample, the depression was secondary to some nonaffective disorder, ranging from an anxiety disorder to schizophrenia. In these patients with medical-surgical or nonaffective psychiatric conditions, intermittent depression seemed to follow the course of the other difficulties. A final 10 percent of the sample remained undiagnosed, but depression was considered the probable diagnosis. The work of Akiskal et al. (1978) is further evidence of the problems in attempting to draw any sharp distinctions in the classification and diagnosis of depression. Beyond this, it suggests both the utility and the difficulty of distinguishing between depression that is primary and that which is secondary to other conditions. Furthermore, the work suggests the usefulness of attempting to understand depression in terms of the presence or absence of characterological or life-style difficulties. (See Winokur, this volume, for further development of this point.)

Thus, the endogenous pole of the endogenous-reactive distinction is more clearly defined than its counterpart. After a long history of debate and controversy, there is a growing consensus that the differentiation of endogenous and reactive depression is useful but that they represent points along a continuum, rather than two distinct forms of disorder. It is sometimes suggested that endogenous depressions are simply more severe, but this leaves unanswered questions about differences in etiology or the determinants of one depressive episode progressing to an endogenous course and another not. Biomedically oriented researchers look to the identification of familial patterns of affective disturbance, the development of biological markers, and the refinement of diagnostic laboratory tests as the solution to the ambiguity and confusion. Baldessarini (see this volume) notes the promise of recent developments such as the dexamethasone suppression test, but he cautions that

While there has been considerable progress toward a biologically and clinically robust diagnostic scheme, and in understanding some characteristics that can help to guide treatment, search for primary causes has been unsuccessful so far. Indeed, virtually all of the biological characteristics of [severely depressed] patients that have been identified are "state-dependent" (that is, they disappear with recovery) and are not stable biological traits or markers of a possible heritable defect.

DUALISM AND REDUCTIONISM

In dicussions of the diagnosis and subtyping of depression, it is easy to detect the suggestion that biology plays an obvious or central role in some depressions more than others, in bipolar more then unipolar, and endogenous more than nonendogenous. Useful though this insight is, it tends to be accepted too rigidly and simplistically. Too often it becomes a way of summarily resolving complex issues in the study and treatment of depression, namely, that there are some depressions that are biological and others that are psychological and social in nature or some that are illnesses and some that are not. Indeed, the goal of being able to make such a clean distinction has often been behind efforts to develop classificatory systems.

The acceptance of a such a mind-body dualism and reductionism is widespread, but it is a distortion of available data and a barrier to both effective treatment and the development of a model that does justice to the complexities of depression. The biological dysfunctions associated with depression are well recorded and can no longer be ignored. Yet, even where biological vulnerability factors are well established, as in the case of bipolar disturbance, psychological,and social factors may determine whether an episode actually occurs; its severity, course, and outcome; and its costs to the individual, the immediate family, and the larger society. Whether we choose to to focus on the biological, the psychological, or the social, we are isolating only one of a set of factors in a complex matrix. Gilbert (1984) has suggested further:

Moreover, the interdependence of the structure of the matrix makes selection of one group of factors as etiological agents arbitrary. In other words, it is not particularly helpful, at the macro-level, to view the causes of depression as due only [for example] to cognitive changes, or only to biological changes. Rather, these factors are locked together in complex relationships, and it is the change of the whole person, determined by the relationship of factors within the person, which provides the most useful conceptualization (p.105).

Increasingly, theoretical statements about the nature of depression start with an acknowledgment of its heterogeneity and the complexity and interdependence of causal factors now presumed to play a role in it. Yet beyond that, authors tend to lapse into a singular frame of reference that is predictable from their discipline and their indoctrination.

The study of depression is thoroughly fragmented and efforts at integration have been few and generally feeble and unsatisfactory. Investigators in genetics, biochemistry, experimental psychopathology, and epidemiology generally do not stay abreast of developments in other fields that have direct bearing on their own work. Dualistic thinking about the relationship between biological and psychosocial variables has tended to leave psychologists phobic about possible advances in the understanding of the biology of depression, while biologically oriented psychiatrists remain ignorant about the necessity of considering the psychological background and current interpersonal circumstances of depressed persons.

Any successful effort at integration has to confront enormous differences in terminology, interpretation, and emphasis. In a manner that was anticipated by Thomas Kuhn (1970), proponents of the various perspectives on depression are always somewhat at cross-purposes when they attempt to discuss their differences. As will be seen, methods and data are not detachable from theory. To take a simple and basic difference as an example, the cognitive theorist has a commitment to accept the self-report of depressed persons as indicating what these persons are experiencing and wish to convey. The psychodynamic theorist, however, is likely to find such interpretations superficial and would instead be interested in underlying meanings and processes. To the cognitive theorist, "I feel unlovable" is taken at face value, whereas for some psychodyamic theorists, it is probably best understood as a thinly veiled accusation directed at somebody else.

What is considered most crucial is always determined in light of some theoretical interpretation, and the facts themselves must be reconstituted in terms of this. There is no neutral language in which theoretical differences can be discussed to the satisfaction of proponents of differing viewpoints. These viewpoints are not distinct from the data their proponents muster; they are the way in which the data are seen. One might insist that the perspectives be compared in terms of accuracy, consistency, scope, simplicity, and fruitfulness. These criteria are vital; however, there are often disagreements about how they are to be applied, and the criteria themselves are often in conflict with each other (Kuhn, 1977).

It may be that it is currently too much to expect a successful wholesale integration of the perspectives that we are going to consider. Dyrud (1974) has cautioned that if we attempt a premature smoothing of differences in terms and concepts, we will lose whatever precision has been achieved. Perhaps what will prove most fruitful for now is development and refinement *within* these perspectives.

REFERENCES

Akiskal, H. S., et al. (1978). The nosological status of neurotic depression. *Archives of General Psychiatry*. 35:756–766.

American Psychiatric Association (1980). *Diagnostic and Statistical Manual of Mental Disorders,* third edition. Washington, D.C.: American Psychiatric Association.

Beck, A. T. (1967). *Depression: Clinical, Experimental, and Theoretical Aspects*. NY: Harper and Row.

Beck, A. T., et al. (1961). An inventory for measuring depression. *Archives of General Psychiatry*. 4:561–571.

Blackburn, I. M., et al. (1981). The efficacy of cognitive therapy in depression: a treatment trial using cognitive therapy and pharmacotherapy, each alone and in combination. *British Journal of Social and Clinical Psychology*. 19:353–363.

Carroll, B. J. (1984). Problems with diagnostic criteria for depression. *Journal of Clinical Psychiatry*. 45:14–18.

Cavanaugh, S. V. (1984). Diagnosing depression in the hospitalized patient with chronic medical illness. *Journal of Clinical Psychiatry*. 44:13–18.

Coyne, J. C. (1976). Depression and the response of others. *Journal of Abnormal Psychology*. 85:186–193.

Coyne, J. C., Kahn, J. and Gotlib, I. H. (1985). Depression. In T. Jacob (Ed.). *Family Interaction and Psychotherapy*. NY: Pergamon.

Depue, R. A. and Monroe, S. M. (1978a) Learned helplessness in the perspective of the depressive disorders: Conceptual and definitional issues. *Journal of Abnormal Psychology*. 87:3–20.

Depue, R. A. and Monroe, S. M. (1978b) The unipolar-bipolar distinction in the depressive disorders. *Psychological Bulletin.* 85:1001–1029.

Dyrud, J. E. (1974). On translating concepts across disciplines. In R. J. Friedman and M. M. Katz (Eds.). *The Psychology of Depression: Contemporary Theory and Research.* Washington, D.C.: V.H. Winston.

Emery, R., Weintraub, S., and Neale, J. (1982). Effects of marital discord on the school behavior of children of schizophrenic, affective disordered, and normal parents. *Journal of Abnormal Child Psychology.* 16:215–225.

Feighner, J. P., et al. (1972). Diagnostic criteria for use in psychiatric research. *Archives of General Psychiatry.* 26:57–63.

Fowles, D. C. and Gersh, F. S. (1979). Neurotic depression: The endogenous-reactive distinction. In R. A. Depue (Ed.). *The Psychobiology of Depressive Disorders.* NY: Academic Press.

Gilbert, P. (1984). *Depression: From Psychology to Brain State.* Hillsdale, NJ: Lawrence Erlbaum.

Gurtman, M. B. (in press). Depression and the response of others: re-evaluating the re-evaluation. *Journal of Abnormal Psychology.*

Hinchcliffe, M., et al. (1975). A study of the interaction between depressed patients and their spouses. *British Journal of Psychiatry.* 126:164–176.

Jacobson, E. (1968). Transference problems in the psychoanalytic treatment of severely depressive patients. In W. Gaylin (Ed.). *The Meaning of Despair.* NY: Science House.

Kahn, J., Coyne, J. C., and Margolin, G. (in press). Depression and marital conflict: The social construction of despair. *Journal of Social and Personal Relationships.*

Kendall, R. E. (1976). The classification of depression: A review of contemporary confusion. *British Journal of Psychiatry.* 194:352–356.

Kovacs, M. (1980). Cognitive therapy of depression. *Journal of the American Academy of Psychoanalysis.* 8:127–144.

Kraepelin, E. (1921). *Manic-depressive Illness and Paranoia.* Edinburgh: E. & S. Livingstone.

Kuhn, T. S. (1970). *The Structure of Scientific Revolutions,* second edition. Chicago: University of Chicago Press.

Kuhn, T. S. (1977). *The Essential Tension: Selected Studies in Scientific Tradition and Change.* Chicago: University of Chicago Press.

Leff, M., Roatch, J., and Bunney, L. E. (1970). Environmental factors preceding the onset of severe depression. *Psychiatry.* 33:298–311.

McLean, P. D. (1976). Parental depression: Incompatable with effective parenting. In E. J. Marsh, C. Handy, and L. A. Hammerlynck (Eds.). *Behavior Modification Approaches to Parenting.* NY: Brunner/Mazel.

Paykel, E. S., et al. (1969). Life events and depression: A controlled study. *Archives of General Psychiatry.* 21:753–757.

Pearlin, L. I. (1975). Sex roles and depression. In N. Datan and L. Ginsburg (Eds.). *Life-span Developmental Psychology: Normative Life Crises.* NY: Academic Press.

Perris, C. (1966). A study of bipolar (manic-depressive) and unipolar recurrent depressive psychoses. *Acta Psychiatrica Scandinavica.* 42 (Supplement No. 203):1–189.

Radloff, L. S. (1977). The CES-D scale: A self-report depression scale for research in the general population. *Applied Psychological Measurement.* 1:385–401.

Rousanville, B. J., et al. (1979). Marital disputes and treatment outcome in depressed women. *Comprehensive Psychiatry.* 20:483–490.

Rush, A. J. (1984). A phase II study of cognitive therapy for depression. In J. B. W. Williams and R. L. Spitzer (Eds.). *Psychotherapy Research: Where Are We and Where Should We Go?* NY: Guilford Press.

Sameroff, A. J., Barocas, R., and Seifer, R. (in press). The early development of children born to mentally ill women. In N. F. Watt, et al. *Children at Risk for Schizophrenia*. NY: Cambridge University Press.

Spitzer, R. L., Endicott, J., and Robins, E. (1978). Research diagnostic criteria: Rationale and reliability. *Archives of General Psychiatry*. 35:773–782.

Weissman, M. M., Klerman, G. L., and Paykel, E. S. (1971). Clinical evaluation of hostility in depression. *American Journal of Psychiatry*. 128:261–266.

Weissman, M. M., and Meyers, J. K. (1981). Depression and its treatment in a U. S. urban community 1975–1976. *Archives of General Psychiatry*. 38:417–421.

Weissman, M. M., and Paykel, E. S. (1974). *The Depressed Woman*. Chicago: University of Chicago Press.

Whybrow, P. C., Akiskal, H. S., and McKinney, W. T. (1984). *Mood Disorder: Toward a New Psychobiology*. New York: Plenum Press.

Zuckerman, M., and Lubin, B. (1965). *Manual for the Multiple Affect Adjective Checklist*. San Diego: Educational and Industrial Testing Service.

Zung, W. W. K. (1965). A self-rating depression scale. *Archives of General Psychiatry*, 12:63–70.

PART I

PSYCHODYNAMIC APPROACHES

The psychodynamic perspective was developed earlier than the others presented in this volume, and this is reflected in the style of the articles that represent it. They were written in a period "chiefly characterized by boldly speculative theoretical formulations and by insightful clinical studies. It was a richly productive era in which sensitive and intuitive observers mapped out whole continents of the mind that had previously been unexplored. It was a era of large scale conceptualizations and generalizations" (Mendelson, 1960, p. 145). In Mendelson's words, these papers were part of a "Great Debate" about such matters as which period in childhood is most critical for the development of a vulnerability to depression, what roles are to be assigned to aggression and dependency, and what significance is to be attached to depressed persons' self-reproach. In the absence of any body of independent research data to which appeals could be made, the debate was often rhetorical and even polemical.

The articles in this section were written over a period of almost half a century. Levenson (1972) has described the progress in psychodynamic thinking in this period in terms of the succession of stages defined by the dominance of one of three basic metaphors, and each of these metaphors is represented in the selections of this section. With their emphasis on libido, drives, repression, and fixation, the Freud and Abraham articles included in this volume adopt an *energy* metaphor. The article by Rapaport discusses how Bibring's theory of depression downplays any consideration of the vicissitudes of drives and libido. Instead, it adopts an *information* metaphor, in focusing on the ego's awareness of discrepancies between goals and what can possibly be attained. The article by Mabel Cohen and her colleagues employs a radically different *organismic* metaphor. Some old terms are dropped, but even where they are retained, they are used quite differently. There is less of an emphasis on the relationships among intrapsychic elements and more on the relationship between the person and the environment. The concept of superego is discarded in favor of focusing on the parent-child relationship. Transference no longer refers to the projections by the patient onto the blank screen of the therapist but rather the transformation of the therapist through the therapist's involvement with the patient. There is a reality to the patient's experience.

Freud had made some tentative comments in an early paper (1896), but the paper by Abraham (see this volume) was the first major contribution to a psychodynamic understanding of depression. In it, Abraham gave critical importance to the role of repressed hostility in the disorder. "In every one of these cases it could be discovered that the disease proceeded from an attitude of hate which was paralzying the patient's capacity to love." Abraham sketched out the dynamics by which this hostility could become turned inward by the depressed person. The depressive's basic attitude is "I cannot love people; I have to hate them." This is repressed and out of awareness, but projected outward as "People do not love me, they hate me . . . because of my inborn defects. Therefore, I am unhappy and depressed." This attitude is first projected onto the depressive's parents, but it is later generalized to the wider environment. It becomes detached from its roots in the depressive's hostility and experienced as a deep sense of inferiority. Such a fundamentally negative attitude makes it difficult for the depressed person to become invested in the external world in a positive way, and the libido that is absorbed in this way is unavailable for other purposes. The depressed persons is thus inhibited and depleted.

Freud (see this volume) accepted and enlarged upon Abraham's formulation in developing his comparison of grief and depression. The tentativeness with which Freud presented his views should be noted. He was doubtful whether depression was a single, well-defined entity; he believed that at least some depression was primarily biological, rather than psychogenic. He denied any claim that his formulation had a general validity, and raised the possibilty that it might fit only a subgroup of depressions.

Freud started his formulation by noting that both grief and depression involve a dejected mood, a loss of both interest in the world and the capacity to love, and an inhibition of activity. What distinguishes depression, however, is that the depressed person has suffered a loss of self-regard, and this expresses itself in self-criticism and even self-vilification. Freud's observations on depressed persons' self-criticism provide an interesting contrast to the cognitive (see Part III of this volume) and interpersonal (see Part IV of this volume). The pathological nature of this self-criticism was not seen as a matter of inaccuracy. Indeed, when the depressed person

describes himself as petty, egoistic, dishonest, lacking in independence, one whose sole aim is to hide the weakness of his own nature, it may be, so far as we know, that he has come pretty near to describing himself; we only wonder why a man has to be ill before he can be accessible to a truth of this kind.

Freud suggested a depressed person might actually have a "keener eye for the truth" than those who are not depressed. What is pathological is that anyone would make such a self-evaluation, whether or not it is true or accepted by others. Furthermore, rather than being ashamed by such an opinion, the depressed seems to find a satisfaction in inflicting it on others.

Freud went on to note that if one listens carefully to a depressive's self-criticisms, one often discovers that the most extreme of the complaints are less applicable to the depressed person than to someone that the depressed person loves, once loved, or should love. This was a key observation for Freud: The self-criticisms of a depressed person had been shifted back from a loved object. Thus, the woman who complains that she is utterly unlovable and challenges her husband as to why he would stay with her may actually be chastizing him for not being more lovable.

The dynamics that are described seem complicated and circuitous. In reading Freud's account, it should be remembered that he had not yet articulated the concept of the superego, and so the "self-critical faculty" that he wished to invoke had to be relegated to the ego. The process of becoming depressed starts with a real or imagined loss, rejection, or disappointment. In normal grief, this would entail a painful withdrawal of libidinal investment and an eventual displacement of it onto a new object.

However, in a depressive process, the ego refuses to accept the loss. The ego becomes enraged and regresses to an oral sadistic level. Here, as in Abraham's formulation, aggression has a key role. There is a split in the ego, and part of it regresses further to the oral receptive stage.

The lost object becomes an ego loss, as it is incorporated into the ego. The ego identifies with the lost object, and the conflict between the ego and the lost object becomes a conflict within the ego. Hostility that cannot be expressed directly to the lost object is heaped upon the portion of the ego that is identified with it, and this is reflected in a loss of self-esteem and punishing self-criticism. Freud argued that this process did not happen in just anyone facing a loss. It requires a predisposition that lies in a basic ambivalence to the love object and an underlying tendency toward narcissistic object choices. The vulnerable person choses love objects that are similar enough to the self that they can be easily abandoned and confused with it.

The article by Rapaport was originally a presentation delivered as a memorial to Bibring in 1959. It summarizes Bibring's theory of depression, yet in many ways it presents a clearer picture of the significance of Bibring's contribution than his own writings did. Rapaport identifies the place of Bibring's work in the historical development of psychoanalytic thinking about depression and uses Bibring's work to evaluate past psychoanalytic formulations. In doing so, he highlights the importance of Bibring's work for both the development of ego psychology and the psychoanalytic theory of affects in a way that Bibring was too modest to do himself.

Bibring was careful to state that he did not reject outright the formulations offered by Freud and Abraham, but he suggested that they needed modification because oral and aggressive strivings may not be as universal in depression as these formulations suppose. Yet the modification that he presents proves to be quite radical. For Bibring, what was most fundamental about depression is a fall in self-esteem due to "the ego's shocking awareness of its helplessness in regard to its aspirations." Depression occurs when the person *both* feels powerless to achieve some narcissistically important goal and the goal is not relinquished.

Irrespective of their unconscious implications, one may roughly distinguish between three groups of such persisting aspirations of the person: (1) the wish to be worthy, to be loved, to be appreciated, not to be inferior or unworthy; (2) the wish to be strong, superior, great, secure, not to be weak and insecure; and (3) the wish to be good, to be loving not to be aggressive, hateful and destructive. It is exactly from the tension between these highly charged narcissistic aspirations on the one hand, and the ego's acute awareness of its (real or imaginary) helplessness and incapacity to live up to them on the other hand, that depression reults (Bibring, 1953, p. 27).

The vulnerability to particular frustrations is acquired as a result of trauma that occur in early childhood and that produce a fixation to a state of helplessness. This state can be reactivated when the person is confronted with a situation resembling the original trauma. Bibring agreed with earlier writers that depression is more likely to occur in orally dependent persons who need "narcissistic supplies" from the outside, but he also argued that severe frustrations could produce a fixation at another stage. Importantly, depression did not depend upon the aggressive and dependent strivings of the oral stage. Rather than producing depression, such strivings might *result* from the awareness of helplessness.

Whybrow, Akiskal, and Mckinney (1984) have noted some of the most important implications of Bibring's reformulation of the classical psychodynamics of depression:

To define depression in this way is to define it as psychosocial phenomenon. The concept of the ego, unlike that of the id, is rooted in social reality, and the ego ideal is composed of socially learned symbols and motives. A breakdown of self-esteem may involve, in addition to object loss, man's symbolic possessions, such as power, status, social role, identity, values, and existential purpose. Depression, therefore, falls particularly upon the overambitious, the conventional, the individual with upward mobility, and the woman who strongly identifies with a passive social role . . . Bibring's conceptualization provides broad links with man's existential, sociological, and cultural worlds (p. 35).

The article by Cohen and her colleagues represents another important conceptual transition. Like the other psychodynamic writers, Cohen and her coauthors devote considerable attention to the early childhood experiences of depressives but emphasis is on the patterning of interpersonal relationships rather than intrapsychic functioning. They demonstrate the Sullivanian conceptualization of personality as the recurring patterning of significant relationships.

The enduring interpersonal climate in the family is given more attention than any single traumatic experience, and the family's position in the community is identified as an important determinant of what this climate will be. Specifically, the families of depressed persons tend to stand out as different from the families around them. Parents tend to have an overriding concern with fitting in, conforming to "what the neighbors think," and upward mobility. The child in the family who is most likely to be depressed later is likely to be the one who most accepted the burden of winning acceptance and prestige for the family.

This child absorbs parental attitudes in a "peculiar combination of lack of conviction of worth . . . coupled with an intense devotion to conventional morality and what people think." The child may show a strong concern with what authority expects, but a conviction that these expectations are beyond what can be achieved.

The adult relationships of depressives tend to perpetuate the patterning of their family relationships in childhood. Even when not suffering from any mood disturbance, depressives tend to have a narrow range of relationships within which they are very dependent and sensitive to signs of disapproval and rejection. As an interpersonal strategy, depressivies may undersell themselves in order to win nurturance and approval, but in doing so, actually may convince others that they lack any assets.

> At this point, they begin to hate these other people for being the cause of the vicious circle in which they are caught; and they hate themselves because they sense the fraudulence of their behavior in not their behavior in not having expressed openly their inner feelings.

This strategy and patterning of relationships becomes exaggerated and intensifed during a period of depression. The symptons of depressed persons may be seen as an appeal to those around them, but if prolonged, their main effect may be to leave the depressed persons alienated from those people upon whom they had relied and alone with their feelings of distress.

Cohen and her colleagues give an extended discussion of the therapeutic relationship with depressed persons because of the assumption that this will recapitulate other significant relationships in a way that allows the therapist to have the first hand perspective of a participant observer. The language of transference and countertransference is used, but one gets less of a sense of an ego struggling with object representations than of two people struggling with a difficult relationship. Depressed persons can be irritating and manipulative, but therapists are also implicated in the patterns that are described. They are more likely to be manipulated by depressed persons if they become overinvested in playing a benign and powerful role with their patients. This emphasis on interpersonal stategies of depressed persons and the involvement of others is developed further in the Coyne article (Part IV, this volume).

At the conclusion of his review of psychodynamic conceptions of depression, Mendelson (1960) declared that it was now time for a "responsible sober testing of theories and hypotheses" (p. 145). Yet, a vigorous, sustained research program that was explicitly psychodynamic never materialized. The richness and ambiguity of the psychodynamic conceptions of depression have resisted restatement as hypotheses that are both readily empirically testable and true to the perspective.

In the sixties, psychodynamic writings were interpreted as suggesting that when people become depressed, they are more likely to internalize or suppress hostility. Findings were generally not supportive of this hypothesis (Friedman, 1964; Schless, et al., 1974). There were also a number of examinations of whether persons who later became depressed had experienced the death of a parent in childhood. There were some well-designed studies with positive results (see Brown, this volume), but other studies found only a weak and inconsistent relationship (Crook & Elliot, 1980). Yet, as in the studies of depression and hostility, questions could be raised about the fidelity of the research to the original psychodynamic formulations. Recently, Sidney Blatt and his colleagues (Blatt, 1974; Blatt, et al., 1979) have utilized psychodynamic conceptions in developing a line of research that distinguishes between depressed persons on the basis of whether dependency or self-criticism predominate. Such a typology correlates with retrospective reports of parental behavior in childhood (McCranie & Bass, 1984).

Despite such a paucity of research, the impact of the psychodynamic perspective should not be underestimated. Ideas derived from it about the significance of early childhood experience, hostility, and self-criticism continue to have a strong influence upon clinical practice and have become a secure part of clinical folklore and laypersons' understanding of depression. Futhermore, the other psychosocial perspectives on depression remain indebted in ways that are not always obvious. Aaron T. Beck was formerly a practising psychoanalyst, and his cognitive model of depression (see Kovacs & Beck, this volume) grew out of his early work testing psyhchodynamic hypotheses about the dreams of depressed persons. The first elaborated behavioral formulation of depression (Ferster, 1973) accepted as fact psychodynamic ideas about the role of anger turned inward and fixation; it attempted to reconceptualize them in behavioral terms. Key aspects of the learned helplessness model (see Abramson Seligman, & Teasdale, this volume) were clearly anticipated in Bibring's formulation. Articles by Coyne and Becker in this volume also build upon psychodynamic formulations, but they are developed in very different directions.

REFERENCES

Bibring, E. (1953) The mechanism of depression. In P. Greenacre (ed.). *Affective Disorders*. New York: International Universities Press.

Blatt, S. J. (1974). Levels of object representation in anaclitic and introjective depression. *Psychoanalytic Study of the Child*. 29:107–157.

Blatt, S. L., et al. (1979). Experiences of depression in normal young adults. *Journal of Abnormal Psychology*. 88:388–397.

Crook, T., and Eliot, J. (1980). Parental death during childhood and adult depression: A critical review of the literature. *Psychological Bulletin*. 87:252–259.

Ferster, C. (1973). A functional analysis of depression. *American Psychologist*. 28:857–870.

Freud, S. (1896/1962). Further remarks on the neuro-psychoses of defense. *Standard Edition of the Collected Works of Sigmund Freud*. London: Hogarth.

Friedman, A. S. (1964). Hostility factors and clinical improvement in depressed patients. *Archives of General Psychiatry*. 23:524–537.

Levenson, E. A. (1972). *The Fallacy of Understanding*. NY: Basic Books.

McCranie, E. W., and Bass, J. D. (1984). Childhood family antecedents of dependency and self-criticism: Implications for depression. *Journal of Abnormal Psychology*. 93:3–8.

Mendelson, M. (1960). *Psychoanalytic Concepts of Depression*. Springfield, Ill: Thomas.

Schless, A. P., et al. (1974). Depression and hostility. *Journal of Nervous and Mental Disease*. 159:91–100.

Whybrow, P. C., Akiskal, H. S., and McKinney, W. T. (1984). *Mood Disorder: Toward a New Psychobiology*. NY: Plenum Press.

1. Notes on the Psycho-Analytical Investigation and Treatment of Manic-Depressive Insanity and Allied Conditions (1911)

Karl Abraham

Whereas states of morbid anxiety have been dealt with in detail in the literature of psycho-analysis, depressive states have hitherto received less attention. Nevertheless the affect of depression is as widely spread among all forms of neuroses and psychoses as is that of anxiety. The two affects are often present together or successively in one individual; so that a patient suffering from an anxiety-neurosis will be subject to states of mental depression, and a melancholic will complain of having anxiety.

One of the earliest results of Freud's investigation of the neuroses was the discovery that neurotic anxiety originated from sexual repression; and this origin served to differentiate it from ordinary fear. In the same way we can distinguish between the affect of sadness or grief and neurotic depression, the latter being unconsciously motivated and a consequence of repression.

Anxiety and depression are related to each other in the same way as are fear and grief. We fear a coming evil; we grieve over one that has occurred. A neurotic will be attacked with anxiety when his instinct strives for a gratification which repression prevents him from attaining; depression sets in when he has to give up his sexual aim without having obtained gratification. He feels himself unloved and incapable of loving, and therefore he despairs of his life and his future. This affect lasts until the cause of it ceases to operate, either through an actual change in his situation or through a psychological modification of the displeasurable ideas with which he is faced. Every neurotic state of depression, just like every anxiety-state, to which it is closely related, contains a tendency to deny life.

These remarks contain very little that is new to those who regard the neuroses from the Freudian point of view, although surprisingly little has been written in the literature of psycho-analysis concerning the psychology of neurotic depression. But the affect of depression in the sphere of the psychoses awaits more precise investigaton. This task is complicated by the fact that a good part of the diseases in question run a 'cyclical' course in which there is an alteration between melancholic and manic states. The few preliminary studies[1] which have hitherto been published have only dealt with one of these two phases at a time.

During the last few years I have met with six undoubted cases of this kind in my practice. Two of these were light manic-depressive cases (so-called cyclothymia), one of whom I treated only for a short time. The third, a female patient, suffered from short but rapidly recurring states of depression accompanied by typical melancholic symptoms. Two more had succumbed to a depressive psychosis for the first time, but had previously shown a tendency to slight changes of mood in a manic or depressive direction. The last patient had been overtaken by a severe and obstinate psychosis at the age of forty-five.

Most psychiatrists, following Kraepelin, do not consider states of depression as belonging to manic-depressive insanity if they come on after the patient's fortieth year. Nevertheless, as the analysis proceeded this last case disclosed such a marked similarity in its psychic structure to those cases which did undoubtedly belong to the manic-depressive insanities that I should certainly class it in that group. I do not, however, intend this as a statement of opinion concerning the line of demarcation between the two psychoses. And I do not wish to discuss states of depression occurring in dementia præcox.

Even in my first analysis of a depressive psychosis I was immediately struck by its structural similarity with an obsessional neurosis. In obsessional neurotics[2]—I refer to severe cases—the libido cannot develop in a normal manner, because two different tendencies—hatred and love—are always interfering with each other. The tendency such a person has to adopt a hostile attitude towards the external world is so great that his capacity for love is reduced to a minimum. At the same time he is weakened and deprived of his energy through the repression

---

[1] Maeder, 'Psychoanalyse bei einer melancholischen Depression' (1910). Brill, 'Elin Fall von periodischer Depression psychogenen Ursprungs' (1911). Jones, 'Psycho-Analytic Notes on a Case of Hypomania' (1910).

[2] The following brief description adheres closely to Freud's characterization in his paper, 'Notes upon a Case of Obsessional Neurosis' (1909).

of his hatred or, to be more correct, through repression of the originally over-strong sadistic component of his libido. There is a similar uncertainty in his choice of object as regards its sex. His inability to establish his libido in a definite position causes him to have a general feeling of uncertainty and leads to doubting mania. He is neither able to form a resolution nor to make a clear judgement; in every situation he suffers from feelings of inadequacy and stands helpless before the problems of life.

I will now give as briefly as possible the history of a case of cyclothymia as it appeared after a successful analysis had been made.

The patient remembered that his sexual instinct had shown itself very precociously—before he was in his sixth year—and had set in with great violence. His first sexual object at that time had been a governess whose presence had excited him. She still figured very vividly in his phantasies. His emotional excitement had led him to practise onanism, which he had done by lying on his stomach and making rubbing movements. He had been discovered doing this by his nurse (formerly his wet nurse), who expressly forbade him to do it, and whipped him whenever he disobeyed her. She also impressed upon him the fact that he would suffer for it all his life. Later, when he was at school he had been attracted in an erotic way by a school-fellow for a period of several years.

In his childhood and later he had never felt satisfied at home. He always had the impression that his parents favoured his elder brother, who was unusually clever, while he had only an average intelligence. He also believed that his younger brother, who was delicate, received greater attention from his mother than he did. The result of this was that he had a hostile attitude towards his parents, and one of jealousy and hatred towards his brothers. The intensity of this hate can be seen from a couple of impulsive acts which he carried out in his childhood. On two occasions when quarrelling over trifles he had become very violent towards his younger brother, and had knocked him down and seriously hurt him. Such violence is particularly remarkable when we learn that at school he was always the smallest and weakest among his contemporaries. He never made any real companions, but generally kept to himself. He was industrious, but had little to show for it. At puberty it became evident that his sexual instinct, which at first had shown itself so strongly, had become paralysed through repression. In contrast to his attitude in childhood he did not feel attracted to the female sex. His sexual activity was the same that he had carried out in childhood; but he did not perform it in the waking state but only in his sleep or half-asleep. He had no friends. He was quite aware of his lack of real energy when he compared himself with others. He found no encouragement at home; on the contrary, his father used to say contemptuous things about him in his presence. Added to all these depressing factors he suffered a definite psychic trauma; a teacher had the brutality to call him a physical and mental cripple in front of the whole class. His first attack of depression appeared soon after this.

Even later on he made no companions. He kept away from them intentionally, too, because he was afraid of being thought an inferior sort of person. Children were the only human beings he got on well with and liked, because with them he did not have his usual feeling of inadequacy. His life was a solitary one. He was positively afraid of women. He was capable of normal sexual intercourse, but had no inclination for it and failed to obtain gratification from it. His onanistic practices in his sleep were his chief sexual activity even in later years. He showed little energy in practical life; it was always difficult for him to form a resolution or to come to a decision in difficult situations.

Up to this point the patient's history coincided in all its details with what we find in obsessional neurotics. Nevertheless, we do not find obsessional symptoms in him but a circular parathymia that had recurred many times during the last twenty years.

In his depressive phase the patient's frame of mind was 'depressed' or 'apathetic' (I reproduce his own words) according to the severity of his condition. He was inhibited, had to force himself to do the simplest things, and spoke slowly and softly. He wished he was dead, and entertained thoughts of suicide. His thoughts had a depressive content. He would often say to himself, 'I am an outcast', 'I am accursed', 'I am branded', 'I do not belong to the world'. He had an indefinite feeling that his state of depression was a punishment. He felt non-existent and would often imagine himself disappearing from the world without leaving a trace. During these states of mind he suffered from exhaustion, anxiety and feelings of pressure in the head. The depressive phase generally lasted some weeks, though it was of shorter duration at times. The intensity of the depression varied in different attacks; he would have perhaps two or three marked states of melancholy and probably six or more slighter ones in the course of a year. His depression gradually increased during the course of an attack until it reached a certain height, where it remained for a time, and then gradually diminished. This process was conscious to him and perceptible to other people.

When the patient was about twenty-eight years old a condition of hypomania appeared, and this now alternated with his depressive attacks. At the commencement of this manic phase he would be roused out of his apathy and would become mentally active and gradually even over-active. He used to do a great deal, knew no fatigue, woke early in the morning, and concerned himself with plans connected with his career. He became enterprising and believed himself capable of performing great things, was talkative and inclined to laugh and joke and make puns. He noticed himself that his thoughts had something volatile in them; a slight degree of 'flight of ideas' could be observed. He spoke more quickly, more forcibly and louder than usual. His frame of mind was cheerful and a little elevated. At the height of his manic phase his euphoria tended to pass over into irritability and impulsive violence. If, for example, someone disturbed him in his work, or stepped in his way, or drove a motor-car quickly past him, he responded with a violent affect of anger and felt inclined to knock the offender down on the spot. While in this state he used often to become involved in real quarrels in which he behaved very unfeelingly. In the periods of depression he slept well but during the manic phase he was very restless, especially during the second half of the night. Nearly every night a sexual excitement used to overtake him with sudden violence.

Although his libido had appeared very early and with great force in his childhood, the patient had for the most part lost the capacity for loving or hating. He had become incapable of loving, in the same manner as the obsessional neurotic. Although he was not impotent, he did not obtain actual sexual enjoyment, and he used to get greater satisfaction from a pollution than coitus. His sexual activities were in the main restricted to his sleep. In this, like the neurotic, he showed an auto-erotic tendency to isolate himself from the external world. People of this kind can only enjoy pleasure in complete seclusion; every living being, every inanimate object, is a disturbing element. It is only when they have achieved the complete exclusion of every external impression—as is the case when they are asleep—that they can enjoy a gratification of their sexual wishes, by dreaming them. Our patient expressed this in the following words: 'I feel happiest in bed; then I feel as though I were in my own house.'[3]

At puberty in especial the patient was made aware that he was behind his companions of the same age in many important respects. He had never felt their equal physically. He had also been afraid of being inferior mentally, especially in comparison with his elder brother. And now the feeling of sexual inadequacy was added. It was precisely at this time that his teacher's criticism '(a mental and physical cripple') struck him like a blow. Its great effect was explained by the fact that it recalled to his memory the prophecy of his wet-nurse, when she had threatened him with lifelong unhappiness because of his masturbation. Just when he was entering upon manhood therefore, and ought to have had masculine feelings like his companions, his old feelings of inadequacy received a powerful reinforcement. It was in this connection that he had had the first state of depression he could recollect.

As we so often see in the obsessional neuroses, the outbreak of the real illness occurred when the patient had to make a final decision about his attitude towards the external world and the future application of his libido. In my other analyses a similar conflict had brought on the first state of depression. For example, one of my patients had become engaged to be married; soon afterwards a feeling of incapacity to love overcame him, and he fell into severe melancholic depression.

In every one of these cases it could be discovered that the disease proceeded from an attitude of hate which was paralysing the patient's capacity to love. As in the obsessional neuroses, other conflicts in the instinctual life of the patients as well can be shown to be factors in the psychogenesis of the illness. I should like to mention especially the patient's uncertainty as to his sexual rôle in this connection. In Maeder's case[4] a conflict of this kind between a male and female attitude was particularly pronounced; and in two of my patients I found a condition surprisingly similar to that described by him.

In their further development, however, the two diseases diverge from each other. The obsessional neurosis creates substitutive aims in place of the original unattainable sexual aims; and the symptoms of mental

---

[3] I might remark that the other male patients whose depressive psychoses I was able to analyse behaved in the same way. None of them were impotent, but they had derived more pleasure from auto-erotic behaviour all along, and to have any relations with women was a difficult and troublesome business for them.

[4] [See footnote, p. 32.]

compulsion are connected with the carrying out of such substitutive aims. The development of the depressive psychoses is different. In this case repression is followed by a process of 'projection' with which we are familiar from our knowledge of the psychogenesis of certain mental disturbances.

In his 'Psycho-Analytic Notes upon an Autobiographical Account of a Case of Paranoia (Dementia Paranoides)' Freud gives a definite formulation of the psychogenesis of paranoia. He sets out in short formulæ the stages which lead up to the final construction of the paranoic delusion. I will here attempt to give a similar formulation of the genesis of the depressive psychoses, on the basis of my analyses of depressive mental disturbances.

Freud considers that in a large portion at least of cases of paranoic delusions the nucleus of the conflict lies in homosexual wish-phantasies, *i.e.* in the patient's love of a person of the same sex. The formula for this is: 'I (a man) love him (a man)'. This attitude raises objections in the patient and is loudly contradicted, so that the statement runs: 'I do not love him, I hate him'. Since internal perceptions are replaced by external ones in paranoia, this hatred is represented as a result of the hatred endured by the patient from without, and the third formula is; 'I do not love him—I hate him—because he persecutes me'.

In the psychoses with which we are here concerned a different conflict lies concealed. It is derived from an attitude of the libido in which hatred predominates. This attitude is first directed against the person's nearest relatives and becomes generalized later on. It can be expressed in the following formula: 'I cannot love people; I have to hate them'.

The pronounced feelings of inadequacy from which such patients suffer arise from this discomforting internal perception. If the content of the perception is repressed and projected externally, the patient gets the idea that he is not loved by his environment but hated by it (again first of all by his parents, etc., and then by a wider circle of people). This idea is detached from its primary causal connection with his own attitude of hate, and is brought into association with other—psychical and physical—deficiencies.[5] It seems as though a great quantity of such feelings of inferiority favoured the formation of depressive states.

Thus we obtain the second formula: 'People do not love me, they

[5] In many cases, and particularly in the slighter ones, the original connection is only partly lost; but even so the tendency to displacement is clearly recognizable.

hate me . . . because of my inborn defects.[6] Therefore I am unhappy and depressed.'

The repressed sadistic impulses do not remain quiescent, however. They show a tendency to return into consciousness and appear again in various forms—in dreams and symptomatic acts, but especially in an inclination to annoy other people, in violent desires for revenge or in criminal impulses. These symptomatic states are not usually apparent to direct observation, because for the most part they are not put into action; but a deeper insight into the patient's mind—as afforded in the catamnesis, for instance—will bring a great deal of this kind of thing to light. And if they are overlooked in the depressive phase there is more opportunity for observing them in the manic one. I shall have more to say about this subject later on.

It is more especially in regard to such desires to commit acts of violence or revenge that the patients have a tendency to ascribe their feelings to the torturing consciousness of their own physical or psychical defects, instead of to their imperfectly repressed sadism. Every patient who belongs to the manic-depressive group inclines to draw the same conclusion as Richard III, who enumerates all his own failings with pitiless self-cruelty and then sums up:

And therefore, since I cannot prove a lover . . .
I am determined to prove a villain.

Richard cannot love by reason of his defects which make him hateful to others; and he wants to be revenged for this. Each of our patients wishes to do the same, but cannot, because his instinctual activity is paralysed by repression.

New and morbid states, such as feelings of guilt, result from the suppression of these frequent impulses of hatred and revenge. Experience so far seems to show that the more violent were the person's unconscious impulses of revenge the more marked is his tendency to form delusional ideas of guilt. Such delusions, as is well known, may attain enormous proportions, so that the patient declares that he alone has been guilty of all sins since the world began, or that all wickedness originates from him alone. In these persons an insatiable sadism directed towards all persons and all things has been repressed in the unconscious.

---

[6]Cf. with this the etymology of the German word *hässlich* ('ugly') = 'that which arouses hate'.

The idea of such an enormous guilt is of course extremely painful to their consciousness; for where there is a great degree of repressed sadism there will be a corresponding severity in the depressive affect. Nevertheless the idea of guilt contains the fulfillment of a wish—of the repressed wish to be a criminal of the deepest dye, to have incurred more guilt than everyone else put together. This, too, reminds us of certain psychic processes in obsessional neurotics, as, for instance, their belief in the 'omnipotence' of their thoughts. They frequently suffer from anxiety lest they have been guilty of the death of a certain person by having thought about his death. The sadistic impulses are repressed in the obsessional neurotic also: because he cannot *act* in conformity with his original instincts he unconsciously gives himself up to phantasies of being able to kill by means of *thoughts*. This wish does not appear as such in consciousness but it takes the form of a tormenting anxiety.

As a result of the repression of sadism, depression, anxiety, and self-reproach arise. But if such an important source of pleasure from which the active instincts flow is obstructed there is bound to be a reinforcement of the masochistic tendencies. The patient will adopt a passive attitude, and will obtain pleasure from his suffering and from continually thinking about himself. Thus even the deepest melancholic distress contains a hidden source of pleasure.

Before the actual state of depression sets in many patients are more than usually energetic in their pursuits and manner of life. They often sublimate in a forced manner libido which they cannot direct to its true purpose. They do this so as to shut their eyes to the conflict within them, and to ward off the depressive frame of mind which is tending to break into consciousness. This attitude often succeeds for long periods, but never completely. The person who has to combat disturbing influences for a long time can never enjoy peace or security within himself. Any situation which requires a definite decision in the field of the libido will cause a sudden collapse of his psychic equilibrium which he has so laboriously kept up. When the state of depression breaks out his previous interests (sublimations) suddenly cease; and this leads to a narrowing of his mental outlook which may become so pronounced as to attain to monoideism.

When the depressive psychosis has become manifest its cardinal feature seems to be a mental inhibition which renders a *rapport* between the patient and the external world more difficult. Incapable of making a lasting and positive application of his libido, the patient unconsciously seeks seclusion from the world, and his auto-erotic trend manifests itself in his inhibition. There are other means, it is true, by which neuroses and psychoses can give symptomatic expression to an auto-erotic tendency. That it should be inhibiton rather than some other symptom that appears in this case is fully explained from the fact that the inhibition is able to serve other unconscious tendencies at the same time. I refer in particular to the tendency towards a 'negation of life'. The higher degrees of inhibition in especial—*i.e.* depressive stupor—represent a symbolic dying. The patient does not react even to the application of strong external stimuli, just as though he were no longer alive. It is to be expressly noted that in the foregoing remarks only two causes of the inhibition have been considered. In every case analysis revealed still further determinants, connected with the individual circumstances of the patient.

Certain features commonly present in states of depression become comprehensible if we accept the well-founded conclusions of psychoanalytic experience. Take, for instance, the frequent ideas of impoverishment. The patient complains, let us say, that he and his family are exposed to starvation. If a pecuniary loss has actually preceded the onset of his illness, he will assert that he cannot possibly endure the blow and that he is completely ruined. These strange ideas, which often entirely dominate the patient's thoughts, are explicable from the identification of libido and money—of sexual and pecuniary 'power'[7]—with which we are so familiar. The patient's libido has disappeared from the world, as it were. Whereas other people can invest their libido in the objects of the external world he has no such capital to expend. His feeling of poverty springs from a repressed perception of his own incapacity to love.

We very frequently meet with fears or pronounced delusions centering round the same idea in states of depression connected with the period of involution. As far as my not very extensive psycho-analytical experience of these conditions goes, I have reason to believe that it is people whose erotic life has been without gratification who are liable to

---

[7] [The German word used, *Vermögen*, means both 'wealth' and 'capacity' in the sense of sexual potency.—*Trans.*]

such delusions. In the preceding decade of their life they had repressed this fact and had taken refuge in all kinds of compensations. But their repressions are not able to cope with the upheaval of the climacteric. They now pass in review, as it were, their wasted life, and at the same time feel that it is too late to alter it. Their consciousness strongly resists all ideas connected with this fact; but not being strong enough to banish them completely, it has to allow them entrance in a disguised form. They are still painful in the form of a delusion of impoverishment, but not as intolerable as before.

Viewed externally, the manic phase of the cyclical disturbances is the complete opposite of the depressive one. A manic psychotic appears very cheerful on the surface; and unless a deeper investigation is carried out by psychoanalytic methods it might appear that the two phases are the opposite of each other even as regards their content. Psycho-analysis shows, however, that both phases are dominated by the same complexes, and that it is only the patient's attitude towards those complexes which is different. In the depressive state he allows himself to be weighed down by his complex, and sees no other way out of his misery but death;[8] in the manic state he treats the complex with indifference.

The onset of the mania occurs when repression is no longer able to resist the assaults of the repressed instincts. The patient, especially in cases of severe maniacal excitation, is as if swept off his feet by them. It is especially important to notice that positive and negative libido (love and hate, erotic desires and aggressive hostility) surge up into consciousness with equal force.

This manic state, in which libidinal impulses of both kinds have access to consciousness, once more establishes a condition which the patient has experienced before—in his early childhood, that is. Whereas in the depressive patient everything tends to the negation of life, to death, in the manic patient life begins anew. The manic patient returns to a stage in which his impulses had not succumbed to repression, in which he foresaw nothing of the approaching conflict. It is characteristic that such patients often say that they feel themselves 'as though new-born'. Mania contains the fulfillment of Faust's wish:

---

[8] Some patients cling to the idea that they can be cured by the fulfillment of some external condition—usually one, however, which never can be fulfilled.

Bring back my passion's unquenched fires,
　The heavenly smart of bliss restore;
Hate's strength—the steel of love's desires—
　Bring back the youth I was once more.

The maniac's frame of mind differs both from normal and from depressive states, partly in its care-free and unrestrained cheerfulness,
partly in its increased irritability and feeling of self-importance. The
one or the other alteration can predominate according to the individu-
ality of the patient or the different stages of the disease.

The affect of pleasure in mania is derived from the same source as is
that of pleasure in wit. What I have to say about this is therefore in
close agreement with Freud's theory of wit.[9]

Whereas the melancholiac exhibits a state of general inhibition, in
the manic patient even normal inhibitions of the instincts are partly or
wholly abolished. The saving of expenditure in inhibition thus effected
becomes a source of pleasure, and moreover a lasting one, while wit
only causes a transitory suspension of the inhibitions.

Economy of inhibition is, however, by no means the only source of
manic pleasure. The removal of inhibitions renders accessible once
more old sources of pleasure which had been suppressed; and this shows
how deeply mania is rooted in the infantile.

The technique of the manic production of thoughts may be regarded
as a third source of pleasure. Abolition of logical control and playing
with words—two essential features of manic ideational processes—
indicate an extensive 'return to infantile freedom'.

Melancholic inhibition of thought finds its reverse in the manic flight
of ideas. In the melancholic phase there is a narrowing of the circle of
ideas, in the manic phase a rapid change of the content of consciousness.
The essential difference between flight of ideas and normal thinking is
that whereas in thinking or speaking the healthy person consistently
keeps in view the aim of his mental processes the manic patient very
easily loses sight of that aim.[10] This differentiation serves to characterize
the external aspect of the flight of ideas, but not its significance for the
manic subject. It is especially to be noted that the flight of ideas offers
the patient considerable possibilities for obtaining pleasure. As has

[9] *Der Witz und seine Beziehung zum Unbewussten*, 1905.
[10] Liepmann, *Über Ideenflucht* (1904).

already been said, psychic work is economized where the abolition of logical control is removed and where the sound instead of the sense has to be considered. But the flight of ideas has yet another function, and a double one: it makes it possible to glide by means of light allusions over those ideas that are painful to consciousness, for example, ideas of inadequacy; that is to say, it favours—like wit—transition to another circle of ideas. And it also permits of playful allusion to pleasurable things which are as a rule suppressed.

The similarity between the mind of the maniac and that of the child is characterized in a number of ways of which only one need be mentioned in this place. In the slighter states of manic exaltation the patient has a kind of careless gaiety which bears an obviously childish character. The psychiatrist who has had much to do with such patients can clearly see that his *rapport* with them is the same as with a child of about five years of age.

The severer forms of mania resemble a frenzy of freedom. The sadistic component-instinct is freed from its fetters. All reserve disappears, and a tendency to reckless and aggressive conduct takes its place. In this stage the maniac reacts to trifling occurrences with violent outbursts of anger and with excessive feelings of revenge. In the same way, when his exaltation had reached a certain height, the cyclothymic patient mentioned above used to feel an impulse to strike down anyone who did not at once make way for him in the street. The patients often have an excessive feeling of power, measuring it not by actual performance but by the violence of their instincts, which they are now able to perceive in an unusual degree. Fairly frequently there appear grandiose ideas which are very similar to children's boasts about their knowledge and power.

Arising from the case of cyclothymia already described at length, there is one important question which I cannot attempt to answer definitely. It remains to be explained why, when the patient was about twenty-eight, states of manic exaltation should have appeared in addition to the depressive state which had already existed for a long time. It may be that it was a case where psychosexual puberty followed a long time after physical maturity. We often see the development of instinctual life delayed in a similar manner in neurotics. On this hypothesis the patient would not have experienced an increase of his instinctual life at puberty but have been overtaken, like a woman, by a wave of repression; and it would only have been towards the end of his third decade that a certain awakening of his instincts would have occurred in the form of the first manic state. And in fact it was at the age that his sexual interests turned more to the female sex and less towards auto-erotism than before.

I must now say a few words about the therapeutic effects of psychoanalysis.

The case I have most fully reported in these pages was so far analysed at the time when I read my paper at Weimar that its structure was apparent in general. But there still remained a great deal of work to be done on it; and therapeutic results were only just beginning to be discernible. These have become more clearly visible during the last two and a half months. Naturally a definite opinion as regards a cure cannot yet be given, for after twenty years of illness, interrupted by free intervals of varying length, an improvement of two months' duration signifies very little. But I should like to record the result up to the present. In the period mentioned, no further state of depression has appeared, and the last one passed off very easily. In consequence of this the patient has been able to do continuous work. During the same period there did twice occur changed frame of mind in a manic direction, which could not escape a careful observation; but it was of a far milder character than his previous states of exaltation. And besides this, certain hitherto regularly observed phenomena were absent. Between these last two manic phases there has been no depressive one, as was usually the case, but a state which could be called normal, since no cyclothymic phenomena were present. For the rest we shall have to follow the further course of the case. There is only one more thing I should like to add: If the patient succeeds in permanently maintaining a state similar to that of the last two months, even this partial improvement will be of great value to him. In the other case of cyclothymia the period of observation has been too short to permit of an opinion regarding therapeutic results. But its pathological structure was found to be remarkably similar to that of the first case.

The third case described at the beginning of this paper showed the effectiveness of analysis in a striking manner, in spite of the fact that external circumstances obliged the treatment to cease after about forty sittings. Even in the early part of the treatment I was able to cut short a melancholic depression which had just developed in the patient, a thing which had never happened before; and as treatment proceeded its effect became more lasting and expressed itself in a distinct amelioration in the patient's frame of mind, and in a considerable increase of his capacity for work. In the months following the cessation of his analysis his state of mind did not sink back to its former level. It may be noted that in this case the preponderating attitude of hatred, the feeling of incapacity to love and the association of depression with feelings of inadequacy were clearly to be seen.

In the two above-mentioned cases of a melancholic depression occurring for the first time, a consistent analysis could not be carried out on account of external difficulties. Nevertheless, its effect was unmistakable. By the help of psycho-analytical interpretation of certain facts and connections I succeeded in attaining a greater psychic *rapport* with the patients than I had ever previously achieved. It is usually extraordinarily difficult to establish a transference in these patients who have turned away from all the world in their depression. Psycho-analysis, which has hitherto enabled us to overcome this obstacle, seems to me for this reason to be the only rational therapy to apply to the manic-depressive psychoses.

The sixth case confirms this view with greater certainty; since I was able to carry the treatment through to the end. It had a remarkably good result. The patient came to me for treatment fifteen months after the onset of his trouble. Before this, treatment in various sanatoria had had only a palliative effect in relieving one or two symptoms. A few weeks after the commencement of psycho-analytic treatment the patient felt occasional relief. His severe depression began to subside after four weeks. He said that at moments he had a feeling of hope that he would once again be capable of work. He attained a certain degree of insight and said: 'I am so egoistic now that I consider my fate the most tragic in the world'. In the third month of treatment his frame of mind was freer on the whole; his various forms of mental expression were not all so greatly inhibited, and there were whole days on which he used to feel well and occupy himself with plans for the future. At this time he once said with reference to his frame of mind: 'When it is all right I am happier and more care-free than I have ever been before'. In the fourth month he said that he had no more actual feelings of depression. During the fifth month, in which the sittings no longer took place daily, distinct variations in his condition were noticeable, but the tendency to improvement was unmistakable. In the sixth month he was able to discontinue the treatment; and the change for the better in him was noticeable to his acquaintances. Since then six months have passed without his having had a relapse.

From a diagnostic point of view the case was quite clearly a depressive psychosis and not a neurosis of the climacteric period. I am unfortunately unable to publish details of the case; they are of such a peculiar kind that the *incognito* of the patient could not be preserved if I did. There are also other considerations which necessitate a quite special discretion—a fact which is greatly to be regretted from a scientific point of view.

There is one objection that might be raised regarding the therapeutic results obtained in this case, and that is that I had begun treating it precisely at that period when the melancholia was passing off, and that it would have been cured without my doing anything; and from this it would follow that psycho-analysis did not possess that therapeutic value which I attribute to it. In answer to this I may say that I have all along been careful to avoid falling into an error of this kind. When I undertook the treatment I had before me a patient who was to all appearances unsusceptible to external influence and who had quite broken down under his illness; and I was very sceptical as to the result of the treatment. I was the more astonished when, after overcoming considerable resistances, I succeeded in explaining certain ideas that completely dominated the patient, and observed the effect of this interpretative work. This initial improvement and every subsequent one followed directly upon the removal of definite products of repression. During the whole course of the analysis I could most distinctly observe that the patient's improvement went hand in hand with the progress of his analysis.

In thus communicating the scientific and practical results of my psycho-analyses of psychoses showing exaltation and depression I am quite aware of their incompleteness, and I hasten to point out these defects myself. I am not in a position to give as much weight to my observations as I could have wished, since I cannot submit a detailed report of the cases analysed. I have already mentioned the reasons for this in one of the cases. In three other very instructive cases motives of discretion likewise prevented me from communicating any details. Nor will intelligent criticism reproach me for adopting this course. Those who take a serious interest in psycho-analysis will make good the deficiencies in my work by their own independent investigations. That further investigations are very greatly needed I am fully aware. Certain questions have not been considered at all or only barely touched upon in this paper. For instance, although we have been able to recognize up to what point the psychogenesis of obsessional neuroses and cyclical psychoses resemble each other, we have not the least idea why at this point one group of individuals should take one path and the other group another.

One thing more may be said concerning the therapeutic aspect of the question. In those patients who have prolonged free intervals between their manic or depressive attacks, psycho-analysis should be begun during that free period. The advantage is obvious, for analysis cannot be carried out on severely inhibited melancholic patients or on inattentive maniacal ones.

Although our results at present are incomplete, it is only psycho-analysis that will reveal the hidden structure of this large group of mental diseases. And moreover, its first therapeutic results in this sphere justify us in the expectation that it may be reserved for psycho-analysis to lead psychiatry out of the *impasse* of therapeutic nihilism.

2. Mourning and Melancholia

Sigmund Freud

Dreams having served us as the prototype in normal life of narcissistic mental disorders, we will now try to throw some light on the nature of melancholia by comparing it with the normal affect of mourning.[1] This time, however, we must begin by making an admission, as a warning against any over-estimation of the value of our conclusions. Melancholia, whose definition fluctuates even in descriptive psychiatry, takes on various clinical forms the grouping together of which into a single unity does not seem to be established with certainty; and some of these forms suggest somatic rather than psychogenic affections. Our material, apart from such impressions as are open to every observer, is limited to a small number of cases whose psychogenic nature was indisputable. We shall, therefore, from the outset drop all claim to general validity for our conclusions, and we shall console ourselves by reflecting that, with the means of investigation at our disposal to-day, we could hardly discover anything that was not typical, if not of a whole class of disorders, at least of a small group of them.

The correlation of melancholia and mourning seems justified by the general picture of the two conditions.[2] Moreover, the excitng causes due to environmental influences are, so far as we can discern them at all, the same for both conditions. Mourning is regularly the reaction to the loss of a loved person, or to the loss of some abstraction which has taken the place of one, such as one's country, liberty, an ideal, and so on. In some people the same influences produce melancholia instead of mourning and we consequently suspect them of a pathological dispo-

[1] [The German *'Trauer'*, like the English 'mourning', can mean both the affect of grief and its outward manifestation. Throughout the present paper, the word has been rendered 'mourning'.]

[2] Abraham (1912), to whom we owe the most important of the few analytic studies on this subject, also took this comparison as his starting point. [Freud himself had already made the comparison in 1910 and even earlier.

sition. It is also well worth notice that, although mourning involves grave departures from the normal attitude to life, it never occurs to us to regard it as a pathological condition and to refer it to medical treatment. We rely on its being overcome after a certain lapse of time, and we look upon any interference with it as useless or even harmful.

The distinguishing mental features of melancholia are a profoundly painful dejection, cessation of interest in the outside world, loss of the capacity to love, inhibition of all activity, and a lowering of the self-regarding feelings to a degree that finds utterance in self-reproaches and self-revilings, and culminates in a delusional expectation of punishment. This picture becomes a little more intelligible when we consider that, with one exception, the same traits are met with in mourning. The disturbance of self-regard is absent in mourning; but otherwise the features are the same. Profound mourning, the reaction to the loss of someone who is loved, contains the same painful frame of mind, the same loss of interest in the outside world—in so far as it does not recall him—the same loss of capacity to adopt any new object of love (which would mean replacing him) and the same turning away from any activity that is not connected with thoughts of him. It is easy to see that this inhibition and circumscription of the ego is the expression of an exclusive devotion to mourning which leaves nothing over for other purposes or other interests. It is really only because we know so well how to explain it that this attitude does not seem to us pathological.

We should regard it as an appropriate comparison, too, to call the mood of mourning a 'painful' one. We shall probably see the justification for this when we are in a position to give a characterization of the economics of pain.

In what, now, does the work which mourning performs consist? I do not think there is anything far-fetched in presenting it in the following way. Reality-testing has shown that the loved object no longer exists, and it proceeds to demand that all libido shall be withdrawn from its attachments to that object. This demand arouses understandable opposition—it is a matter of general observation that people never willingly abandon a libidinal position, not even, indeed, when a substitute is already beckoning to them. This opposition can be so intense that a turning away from reality takes place and a clinging to the object through the medium of a hallucinatory wishful psychosis. Normally, respect for realty gains the day. Nevertheless its orders cannot be obeyed at once. They are carried out bit by bit, at great expense of time and cathectic energy, and in the meantime the existence of the lost object is psychically prolonged. Each single one of the memories and expectations in which the libido is bound to the object is brought up and hypercathected, and detachment of the libido is accomplished in respect of it.[3] Why this compromise by which the command of reality is carried out piecemeal should be so extraordinarily painful is not at all easy to explain in terms of economics. It is remarkable that this painful unpleasure is taken as a matter of course by us. The fact is, however, that when the work of mourning is completed the ego becomes free and uninhibited again.

Let us now apply to melancholia what we have learnt about mourning. In one set of cases it is evident that melancholia too may be the reaction to the loss of a loved object. Where the exciting causes are different one can recognize that there is a loss of a more ideal kind. The object has not perhaps actually died, but has been lost as an object of love (e.g. in the case of a betrothed girl who has been jilted). In yet other cases one feels justified in maintaining the belief that a loss of this kind has occurred, but one cannot see clearly what it is that has been lost, and it is all the more reasonable to suppose that the patient cannot consciously perceive what he has lost either. This, indeed, might be so even if the patient is aware of the loss which has given rise to his melancholia, but only in the sense that he knows *whom* he has lost but not *what* he has lost in him. This would suggest that melancholia is in some way related to an object-loss which is withdrawn from consciousness, in contradistinction to mourning, in which there is nothing about the loss that is unconscious.

In mourning we found that the inhibition and loss of interest are fully accounted for by the work of mourning in which the ego is absorbed. In melancholia, the unknown loss will result in a similar internal work and will therefore be responsible for the melancholic inhibition. The difference is that the inhibition of the melancholic seems puzzling to us because we cannot see what it is that is absorbing him so entirely. The melancholic displays something else besides which is lacking in mourn-

---

[3] [This idea seems to be expressed already in Studies on Hysteria (1895d): a process similar to this one will be found described near the beginning of Freud's Discussion' of the case history of Fraülein Elisabeth von R. (Standard Ed., 2, 162).]

ing—an extraordinary diminution in his self-regard, an impoverishment of his ego on a grand scale. In mourning it is the world which has become poor and empty; in melancholia it is the ego itself. The patient represents his ego to us as worthless, incapable of any achievement and morally despicable; he reproaches himself, vilifies himself and expects to be cast out and punished. He abases himself before everyone and commiserates with his own relatives for being connected with anyone so unworthy. He is not of the opinion that a change has taken place in him, but extends his self-criticism back over the past; he declares that he was never any better. This picture of a delusion of (mainly moral) inferiority is completed by sleeplessness and refusal to take nourishment, and—what is psychologically very remarkable—by an overcoming of the instinct which compels every living thing to cling to life.

It would be equally fruitless from a scientific and a therapeutic point of view to contradict a patient who brings these accusations against his ego. He must surely be right in some way and be describing something that is as it seems to him to be. Indeed, we must at once confirm some of his statements without reservation. He really is as lacking in interest and as incapable of love and achievement as he says. But that, as we know, is secondary; it is the effect of the internal work which is consuming his ego—work which is unknown to us but which is comparable to the work of mourning. He also seems to us justified in certain other self-accusations; it is merely that he has a keener eye for the truth than other people who are not melancholic. When in his heightened self-criticism he describes himself as petty, egoistic, dishonest, lacking in independence, one whose sole aim has been to hide the weaknesses of his own nature, it may be, so far as we know, that he has come pretty near to understanding himself; we only wonder why a man has to be ill before he can be accessible to a truth of this kind. For there can be no doubt that if anyone holds and expresses to others an opinion of himself such as this (an opinion which Hamlet held both of himself and of everyone else[4]), he is ill, whether he is speaking the truth or whether he is being more or less unfair to himself. Nor is it difficult to see that there is no correspondence, so far as we can judge, between the degree of self-abasement and its real justification. A good, capable, conscien-

---

[4] 'Use every man after his desert, and who shall scape whipping?' (Act II, Scene 2).

tious woman will speak no better of herself after she develops melancholia than one who is in fact worthless; indeed, the former is perhaps more likely to fall ill of the disease than the latter, of whom we too should have nothing good to say. Finally, it must strike us that after all the melancholic does not behave in quite the same way as a person who is crushed by remorse and self-reproach in a normal fashion. Feelings of shame in front of other people, which would more than anything characterize this latter condition, are lacking in the melancholic, or at least they are not prominent in him. One might emphasize the presence in him of an almost opposite trait of insistent communicativeness which finds satisfaction in self-exposure.

The essential thing, therefore, is not whether the melancholic's distressing self-denigration is correct, in the sense that his self-criticism agrees with the opinion of other people. The point must rather be that he is giving a correct description of his psychological situation. He has lost his self-respect and he must have good reason for this. It is true that we are then faced with a contradiction that presents a problem which is hard to solve. The analogy with mourning led us to conclude that he had suffered a loss in regard to an object; what he tells us points to a loss in regard to his ego.

Before going into this contradiction, let us dwell for a moment on the view which the melancholic's disorders affords of the constitution of the human ego. We see how in him one part of the ego sets itself over against the other, judges it critically, and, as it were, takes it as its object. Our suspicion that the critical agency which is here split off from the ego might also show its independence in other circumstances will be confirmed by every further observation. We shall really find grounds for distinguishing this agency from the rest of the ego. What we are here becoming acquainted with is the agency commonly called 'conscience'; we shall count it, along with the censorship of consciousness and reality-testing, among the major institutions of the ego, and we shall come upon evidence to show that it can become diseased on its own account. In the clinical picture of melancholia, dissatisfaction with the ego on moral grounds is the most outstanding feature. The patient's self-evaluation concerns itself much less frequently with bodily infirmity, ugliness or weakness, or with social inferiority; of this category, it is only his fears and asseverations of becoming poor that occupy a prominent position.

There is one observation, not at all difficult to make, which leads to the explanation of the contradiction mentioned above [at the end of the last paragraph but one]. If one listens patiently to a melancholic's many and various self-accusations, one cannot in the end avoid the impression that often the most violent of them are hardly at all applicable to the patient himself, but that with insignificant modifications they do fit someone else, someone whom the patient loves or has loved or should love. Every time one examines the facts this conjecture is confirmed. So we find the key to the clinical picture: we perceive that the self-reproaches are reproaches against a loved object which have been shifted away from it on to the patient's own ego.

The women who loudly pities her husband for being tied to such an incapable wife as herself is really accusing her *husband* of being incapable, in whatever sense she may mean this. There is no need to be greatly surprised that a few genuine self-reproaches are scattered among those that have been transposed back. These are allowed to obtrude themselves, since they help to mask the others and make recognition of the true state of affairs impossible. Moreover, they derive from the *pros* and cons of the conflict of love that has led to the loss of love. The behaviour of the patients, too, now becomes much more intelligible. Their complaints are really 'plaints' in the old sense of the word. They are not ashamed and do not hide themselves, since everything derogatory that they say about themselves is at bottom said about someone else. Moreover, they are far from evincing towards those around them the attitude of humility and submissiveness that would alone befit such worthless people. On the contrary, they make the greatest nuisance of themselves, and always seem as though they felt slighted and had been treated with great injustice. All this is possible only because the reactions expressed in their behaviour still proceed from a mental constellation of revolt, which has then, by a certain process, passed over into the crushed state of melancholia.

There is no difficulty in reconstructing this process. An object-choice, an attachment of the libido to a particular person, had at one time existed; then, owing to a real slight or disappointment coming from this loved person, the object-relationship was shattered. The result was not the normal one of a withdrawal of the libido from this object and a displacement of it on to a new one, but something different, for whose coming-about various conditions seem to be necessary. The object-cathexis proved to have little power of resistance and was brought to an end. But the free libido was not displaced on to another object; it was withdrawn into the ego. There, however, it was not employed in any unspecified way, but served to establish an *identification* of the ego with the abandoned object. Thus the shadow of the object fell upon the ego, and the latter could henceforth be judged by a special[5] agency, as though it were an object, the forsaken object. In this way an object-loss was transformed into an ego-loss and the conflict between the ego and the loved person into a cleavage between the critical activity of the ego and the ego as altered by identification.

One or two things may be directly inferred with regard to the preconditions and effects of a process such as this. On the one hand, a strong fixation to the loved object must have been present; on the other hand, in contradiction to this, the object-cathexis must have had little power of resistance. As Otto Rank has aptly remarked, this contradiction seems to imply that the object-choice has been effected on a narcissistic basis, so that the object-cathexis, when obstacles come in its way, can regress to narcissism. The narcissistic identification with the object then becomes a substitute for the erotic cathexis, the result of which is that in spite of the conflict with the loved person the love-relation need not be given up. This substitution of identification for object-love is an important mechanism in the narcissistic affections; Karl Landauer (1914) has lately been able to point to it in the process of recovery in a case of schizophrenia. It represents, of course, a *regression* from one type of object-choice to original narcissism. We have elsewhere shown that identification is a preliminary stage of object-choice, that it is the first way—and one that is expressed in an ambivalent fashion—in which the ego picks out an object. The ego wants to incorporate this object into itself, and, in accordance with the oral or cannibalistic phase of libidinal development in which it is, it wants to do so by devouring it. Abraham is undoubtedly right in attributing to this connection the refusal of nourishment met with in severe forms of melancholia.[6]

The conclusion which our theory would require—namely, that the

---

[5] [In the first (1917) edition only, this word does not occur.]

[6] [Abraham apparently first drew Freud's attention to this in a private letter written between February and April, 1915. See Jones's biography (1955, 368).]

disposition to fall ill of melancholia (or some part of that disposition) lies in the predominance of the narcissistic type of object-choice—has unfortunately not yet been confirmed by observation. In the opening remarks of this paper, I admitted that the empirical material upon which this study is founded is insufficient for our needs. If we could assume an agreement between the results of observation and what we have inferred, we should not hesitate to include this regression from object-cathexis to the still narcissistic oral phase of the libido in our characterization of melancholia. Identifications with the object are by no means rare in the transference neuroses either; indeed, they are a well-known mechanism of symptom-formation, especially in hysteria. The difference, however, between narcissistic and hysterical identification may be seen in this: that, whereas in the former the object-cathexis is abandoned, in the latter it persists and manifests its influence, though this is usually confined to certain isolated actions and innervations. In any case, in the transference neuroses, too, identification is the expression of there being something in common, which may signify love. Narcissistic identification is the older of the two and it paves the way to an understanding of hysterical identification, which has been less thoroughly studied.[7]

Melancholia, therefore, borrows some of its features from mourning, and the others from the process of regression from narcissistic object-choice to narcissism. It is on the one hand, like mourning, a reaction to the real loss of a loved object; but over and above this, it is marked by a determinant which is absent in normal mourning or which, if it is present, transforms the latter into pathological mourning. The loss of a love-object is an excellent opportunity for the ambivalence in love-relationships to make itself effective and come into the open.[8] Where there is a disposition to obsessional neurosis the conflict due to ambivalence gives a pathological cast to mourning and forces it to express itself in the form of self-reproaches to the effect that the mourner himself

---

[7] [The whole subject of identification was discussed later by Freud in Chapter VII of his *Group Psychology* (1921c),*Standard Ed.*, 18, 105 ff. There is an early account of hysterical identification in *The Interpretation of Dreams* (1900a), *Standard Ed.*, 4, 149–51.]

[8] [Much of what follows is elaborated in Chapter V of *The Ego and the Id* (1923b).]

is to blame for the loss of the loved object, i.e. that he has willed it. These obsessional states of depression following upon the death of a loved person show us what the conflict due to ambivalence can achieve by itself when there is no regressive drawing-in of libido as well. In melancholia, the occasions which give rise to the illness extend for the most part beyond the clear case of a loss by death, and include all those situations of being slighted, neglected or disappointed, which can import opposed feelings of love and hate into the relationship or reinforce an already existing ambivalence. This conflict due to ambivalence, which sometimes arises more from real experiences, sometimes more from constitutional factors, must not be overlooked among the preconditions of melancholia. If the love for the object—a love which cannot be given up though the object itself is given up—takes refuge in narcissistic identification, then the hate comes into operation on this substitutive object, abusing it, debasing it, making it suffer and deriving sadistic satisfaction from its suffering. The self-tormenting in melancholia, which is without doubt enjoyable, signifies, just like the corresponding phenomenon in obsessional neurosis, a satisfaction of trends of sadism and hate which relate to an object, and which have been turned round upon the subject's own self in the ways we have been discussing. In both disorders the patients usually still succeed, by the circuitous path of self-punishment, in taking revenge on the original object and in tormenting their loved one through their illness, having resorted to it in order to avoid the need to express their hostility to him openly. After all, the person who has occasioned the patient's emotional disorder, and on whom his illness is centered, is usually to be found in his immediate environment. The melancholic's erotic cathexis in regard to his object has thus undergone a double vicissitude: part of it has regressed to identification, but the other part, under the influence of the conflict due to 'ambivalence, has been carried back to the stage of sadism which is nearer to that conflict.

It is this sadism alone that solves the riddle of the tendency to suicide which makes melancholia so interesting—and so dangerous. So immense is the ego's self-love, which we have come to recognize as the primal state from which instinctual life proceeds, and so vast is the amount of narcissistic libido which we see liberated in the fear that emerges at a threat to life, that we cannot conceive how that ego can consent to its own destruction. We have long known, it is true, that no neurotic harbours thoughts of suicide which he has not turned back upon himself from murderous impulses against others, but we have never been able to explain what interplay of forces can carry such a purpose through to execution. The analysis of melancholia now shows that the ego can kill itself only if, owing to the return of the object-cathexis, it can treat itself as an object—if it is able to direct against itself the hostility which relates to an object and which represents the ego's original reaction to objects in the external world. Thus in regression from narcissistic object-choice the object has, it is true, been got rid of, but it has nevertheless proved more powerful than the ego itself. In the two opposed situations of being most intensely in love and of suicide the ego is overwhelmed by the object, though in totally different ways.[9]

As regards one particular striking feature of melancholia that we have mentioned, the prominence of the fear of becoming poor, it seems plausible to suppose that it is derived from anal erotism which has been torn out of its context and altered in a regressive sense.

Melancholia confronts us with yet other problems, the answer to which in part eludes us. The fact that it passes off after a certain time has elapsed without leaving traces of any gross changes is a feature it shares with mourning. We found by way of explanation that in mourning time is needed for the command of reality-testing to be carried out in detail, and that when this work has been accomplished the ego will have succeeded in freeing its libido from the lost object. We may imagine that the ego is occupied with analogous work during the course of a melancholia; in neither case have we any insight into the economics of the course of events. The sleeplessness in melancholia testifies to the rigidity of the condition, the impossibility of effecting the general drawing-in of cathexes necessary for sleep. The complex of melancholia behaves like an open wound, drawing to itself cathectic energies—which in the transference neuroses we have called 'anticathexes'—from all directions, and emptying the ego until it is totally impoverished.[10] It can easily prove resistant to the ego's wish to sleep.

[9] [Later discussions of suicide will be found in Chapter V of *The Ego and the Id* (1923*b*) and in the last pages of 'The Economic Problem of Masochism' (1924*c*).]

[10] [This analogy of the open wound appears already (illustrated by two diagrams) in the rather abstruse Section VI of Freud's early note on melancholia (Freud, 1950*a*, Draft G, probably written in January, 1895).]

What is probably a somatic factor, and one which cannot be explained psychogenically, makes itself visible in the regular amelioration in the condition that takes place towards evening. These considerations bring up the question whether a loss in the ego irrespectively of the object— a purely narcissistic blow to the ego—may not suffice to produce the picture of melancholia and whether an impoverishment of ego-libido directly due to toxins may not be able to produce certain forms of the disease.

The most remarkable characteristic of melancholia, and the one in most need of explanation, is its tendency to change round into mania— a state which is the opposite of it in its symptoms. As we know, this does not happen to every melancholia. Some cases run their course in periodic relapses, during the intervals between which signs of mania may be entirely absent or only very slight. Others show the regular alternation of melancholic and manic phases which has led to the hypothesis of a circular insanity. One would be tempted to regard these cases as non-psychogenic, if it were not for the fact that the psychoanalytic method has succeeded in arriving at a solution and effecting a therapeutic improvement in several cases precisely of this kind. It is not merely permissible, therefore, but incumbent upon us to extend an analytic explanation of melancholia to mania as well.

I cannot promise that this attempt will prove entirely satisfactory. It hardly carries us much beyond the possibility of taking one's initial bearings. We have two things to go upon: the first is a psycho-analytic impression, and the second what we may perhaps call a matter of general economic experience. The impression which several psycho-analytic investigators have already put into words is that the content of mania is no different from that of melancholia, that both disorders are wrestling with the same 'complex', but that probably in melancholia the ego has succumbed to the complex whereas in mania it has mastered it or pushed it aside. Our second pointer is afforded by the observation that all states such as joy, exultation or triumph, which give us the normal model for mania, depend on the same economic conditions. What has happened here is that, as a result of some influence, a large expenditure of psychical energy, long maintained or habitually occuring, has at last become unnecessary, so that it is available for numerous applications and possibilities of discharge—when, for instance, some poor wretch, by winning a large sum of money, is suddenly relieved from chronic worry about his daily bread, or when a long and arduous struggle is finally crowned with success, or when a man finds himself in a position to throw off at a single blow some oppressive compulsion, some false position which he has long had to keep up, and so on. All such situations are characterized by high spirits, by the signs of discharge of joyful emotion and by increased readiness for all kinds of action—in just the same way as in mania, and in complete contrast to the depression and inhibition of melancholia. We may venture to assert that mania is nothing other than a triumph of this sort, only that here again what the ego has surmounted and what it is triumphing over remain hidden from it. Alcoholic intoxication, which belongs to the same class of states, may (in so far as it is an elated one) be explained in the same way; here there is probably a suspension, produced by toxins, of expenditures of energy in repression. The popular view likes to assume that a person in a manic state of this kind finds such delight in movement and action because he is so 'cheerful'. This false connection must of course be put right. The fact is that the economic condition in the subject's mind referred to above has been fulfilled, and this is the reason why he is in such high spirits on the one hand and so uninhibited in action on the other.

If we put these two indications together,[11] what we find is this. In mania, the ego must have got over the loss of the object (or its mourning over the loss, or perhaps the object itself), and thereupon the whole quota of anticathexis which the painful suffering of melancholia had drawn to itself from the ego and 'bound' will have become available. Moreover, the manic subject plainly demonstrates his liberation from the object which was the cause of his suffering, by seeking like a ravenously hungry man for new object-cathexes.

This explanation certainly sounds plausible, but in the first place it is too indefinite, and, secondly, it gives rise to more new problems and doubts than we can answer. We will not evade a discussion of them, even though we cannot expect it to lead us to a clear understanding.

In the first place, normal mourning, too, overcomes the loss of the object, and it, too, while it lasts, absorbs all the energies of the ego. Why, then, after it has run its course, is there no hint in its case of the economic condition for a phase of triumph? I find it impossible to answer

[11] [The 'psycho-analytic impression' and the 'general economic experience'.]

this objection straight away. It also draws our attention to the fact that we do not even know the economic means by which mourning carries out its task. Possibly, however, a conjecture will help us here. Each single one of the memories and situations of expectancy which demonstrate the libido's attachment to the lost object is met by the verdict of reality that the object no longer exists; and the ego, confronted as it were with the question whether it shall share this fate, is persuaded by the sum of the narcissistic satisfactions it derives from being alive to sever its attachment to the object that has been abolished. We may perhaps suppose that this work of severance is so slow and gradual that by the time it has been finished the expenditure of energy necessary for it is also dissipated.[12]

It is tempting to go on from this conjecture about the work of mourning and try to give an account of the work of melancholia. Here we are met at the outset by an uncertainty. So far we have hardly considered melancholia from the topographical point of view, nor asked ourselves in and between what psychical systems the work of melancholia goes on. What part of the mental processes of the disease still takes place in connection with the unconscious object-cathexes that have been given up, and what part in connection with their substitute, by identification, in the ego?

The quick and easy answer is that 'the unconscious (thing-) presentation[13] of the object has been abandoned by the libido'. In reality, however, this presentation is made up of innumerable single impressions (or unconscious traces of them), and this withdrawal of libido is not a process that can be accomplished in a moment, but must certainly, as in mourning, be one in which progress is long-drawn-out and gradual. Whether it begins simultaneously at several points or follows some sort of fixed sequence is not easy to decide; in analyses it often becomes evident that first one and then another memory is activated, and that the laments which always sound the same and are wearisome in their monotony nevertheless take their rise each time in some different unconscious source. If the object does not possess this

[12] The economic standpoint has hitherto received little attention in psycho-analytic writings. I would mention as an exception a paper by Victor Tausk (1913) on motives for repression devalued by recompenses.

[13] ['Dingvorstellung.']

great significance for the ego—a significance reinforced by a thousand links—then, too, its loss will not be of a kind to cause either mourning or melancholia. This characteristic of detaching the libido bit by bit is therefore to be ascribed alike to mourning and to melancholia; it is probably supported by the same economic situation and serves the same purposes in both.

As we have seen, however, melancholia contains something more than normal mourning. In melancholia the relation to the object is no simple one; it is complicated by the conflict due to ambivalence. The ambivalence is either constitutional, i.e. is an element of every love-relation formed by this particular ego, or else it proceeds precisely from those experiences that involved the threat of losing the object. For this reason the exciting causes of melancholia have a much wider range than those of mourning, which is for the most part occasioned only by a real loss of the object, by its death. In melancholia, accordingly, countless separate struggles are carried on over the object, in which hate and love contend with each other; the one seeks to detach the libido from the object, the other to maintain this position of the libido against the assault. The location of these separate struggles cannot be assigned to any system but the *Ucs.*, the region of the memory-traces of *things* (as contrasted with *word*-cathexes). In mourning, too, the efforts to detach the libido are made in this same system; but in it nothing hinders these processes from proceeding along the normal path through the *Pcs.* to consciousness. This path is blocked for the work of melancholia, owing perhaps to a number of causes or a combination of them. Constitutional ambivalence belongs by its nature to the repressed; traumatic experiences in connection with the object may have activated other repressed material. Thus everything to do with these struggles due to ambivalence remains withdrawn from consciousness, until the outcome characteristic of melancholia has set in. This, as we know, consists in the threatened libidinal cathexis at length abandoning the object, only, however, to draw back to the place in the ego from which it had proceeded. So by taking flight into the ego love escapes extinction. After this regression of the libido the process can become conscious, and it is represented to consciousness as a conflict between one part of the ego and the critical agency.

What consciousness is aware of in the work of melancholia is thus not the essential part of it, nor is it even the part which we may credit with an influence in bringing the ailment to an end. We see that the ego debases itself and rages against itself, and we understand as little as the patient what this can lead to and how it can change. We can more readily attribute such a function to the *unconscious* part of the work, because it is not difficult to perceive an essential analogy between the work of melancholia and of mourning. Just as mourning impels the ego to give up the object by declaring the object to be dead and offering the ego the inducement of continuing to live, so does each single struggle of ambivalence loosen the fixation of the libido to the object by disparaging it, denigrating it and even as it were killing it. It is possible for the process in the *Ucs.* to come to an end, either after the fury has spent itself or after the object has been abandoned as valueless. We cannot tell which of these two possibilities is the regular or more usual one in bringing melancholia to an end, nor what influence this termination has on the future course of the case. The ego may enjoy in this the satisfaction of knowing itself as the better of the two, as superior to the object.

Even if we accept this view of the work of melancholia, it still does not supply an explanation of the one point on which we were seeking light. It was our expectation that the economic condition for the emergence of mania after the melancholia has run its course is to be found in the ambivalence which dominates the latter affection; and in this we found support from analogies in various other fields. But there is one fact before which that expectation must bow. Of the three preconditions of melancholia—loss of the object, ambivalence, and regression of libido into the ego—the first two are also found in the obsessional self-reproaches arising after a death has occurred. In those cases it is unquestionably the ambivalence which is the motive force of the conflict, and observation shows that after the conflict has come to an end there is nothing left over in the nature of the triumph of a manic state of mind. We are thus led to the third factor as the only one responsible for the result. The accumulation of cathexis which is at first bound and then, after the work of melancholia is finished, becomes free and makes mania possible must be linked with regression of the libido to narcissism. The conflict within the ego, which melancholia substitutes for the struggle over the object, must act like a painful wound which calls for an extraordinarily high anti-cathexis.—But here once again, it will be well to call a halt and to postpone any further explanation of mania until we have gained some insight into the economic nature, first, of physical pain, and then of the mental pain which is analogous to it. As we already know, the interdependence of the complicated problems of the mind forces us to break off every enquiry before it is completed—till the outcome of some other enquiry can come to its assistance.

3. Edward Bibring's Theory of Depression

David Rapaport

I

Edward Bibring was one of the few systematic theoreticians of psycho-analysis. His keen awareness of the complexity of psychoanalytic theory and of the responsibility entailed by every attempt to systematize or amend it explains the fact that the range and scope rather than the volume of his writing give us the measure of his stature as a theoretician. Hence his achievement must be read not only in the lines, but also between the lines of his writing. It is such a reading of his paper on depression that I want to present tonight. Until his literary legacy is published—and perhaps even after that—such studies of his published work must serve us as the means of assessing his theoretical conceptions.

First, a word about his scope and range as a theoretician. As a historian of the theory he gave us the only broad survey of the development of the theory of instinctual drives that we have. As a systematizer he set a standard for such work in his essay on the repetition compulsion. As a critic he provided the first dispassionate analysis of Melanie Klein's theories. His contributions to the clinical theory of therapy you have heard Dr. Anna Freud discuss tonight. As a theory builder he gave us the theory of depression, which is my subject tonight.

One of Edward Bibring's central interests was to bring into the present framework of psychoanalytic theory those parts of it which were formulated before the development of the structural approach and present-day ego psychology. Of the solutions he reached he published only his theories of psychotherapy and depression, and even these were written during the struggle with his paralyzing illness. It is hoped that some more of his solutions, or hints about the directions in which he sought solutions, will be gleaned from the study of his files: for instance, a preliminary draft of "The Mechanism of Depression" contains several such hints.

II

The theory Edward Bibring presents in "The Mechanism of Depression" (1953) is deliberately limited to the ego of psychology depression. He wrote: ". . . the conception of depression presented here does not invalidate the accepted theories of the role which orality and aggression play in the various types of depression" (p. 41). Yet his theory points up the inadequacy of the accepted theory. Bibring stated his view as follows: ". . . the oral and aggressive strivings are not as universal in depression as is generally assumed and . . . consequently the theories built on them do not offer sufficient explanation, but require . . . modification" (p. 41).

As we shall see, he relegated to a peripheral rôle the factors which are central to the accepted theory of depression: in his theory they appear as precipitating or complicating factors, and indeed at times even as consequences of that ego state which, according to Bibring, is the essence of depression.

The basic proposition of Bibring's theory is akin to the proposition on which Freud built his structural theory of anxiety. Freud wrote: ". . . the ego is the real seat of anxiety . . . Anxiety is an affective state which can of course be experienced only by the ego" (1926, p. 80). Bibring wrote: "Depression is . . . primarily an ego phenomenon" (1953, p. 40); "[it] represents an affective state" (p. 27). "[Anxiety and depression are] both . . . frequent . . . ego reactions . . . [and since] they cannot be reduced any further, it may be justified to call them basic ego reactions" (p. 34).

Bibring thus set out to explore the structure of depression as an ego state. He used Freud's theory of anxiety, Fenichel's theory of boredom, and some general observations on depersonalization as his points of departure.

How decisive a step this was becomes obvious if we remember that B. D. Lewin's (1950) monograph on elation, for instance, still rests exclusively on id psychology, on the oral triad.

III

Bibring searched the literature of the accepted theory for evidence pertaining to depression as an ego state. Freud had pointed out that both grief and depression involve an inhibition of the ego. Bibring saw this inhibition as a ubiquitous characteristic of the depressive ego state. Abraham (1924) had derived from his clinical observation a concept of primal depression ("primal parathymia"); he found that all subsequent depressive episodes "brought with [them] . . . a state of mind that was an exact replica of . . . [the] primal parathymia" and asserted that "It is this state of mind that we call melancholia" (1924, p. 469). Abraham's observations and formulation indicated to Bibring that the regression in depressions is not simply a regression of the libido to an oral fixation point, but primarily an ego regression to an ego state, implying that the depressive state is not produced *de novo* every time by regression, but is a *reactivation* of a primal state. Here again we see the parallel to Freud's theory of anxiety. Freud wrote: ". . . anxiety is not created *de novo* in repression, but is reproduced as an affective state" (1926, p. 20). Bibring wrote: "Whatever . . . [the precipitating conditions], the mechanism of depression will be the same" (p. 42), and " . . . depression can be defined as the emotional expression . . . of a state of helplessness . . . of the ego, irrespective of what may have caused the breakdown of the mechanisms which established self-esteem" (p. 24). He saw in Fenichel's simple neurotic depressions, in E. Weiss's simple depressions, and in E. Jacobson's mild, blank depression further evidence for the existence of an affective ego state common to and basic to all depressions. The essence of this—as indeed of any—structural conception is that the phenomenon to be explained—in this case depression—is not conceived of as created *de novo* by dynamic factors. Since it is the reactivation of a persisting structure, the fact that it appears in essence unaltered, upon various precipitating conditions and in the most varied dynamic contexts, requires no further explanation. We shall see later that Bibring's structural theory of depression, just like Freud's structural theory of anxiety, involves a signal function.

IV

What are the descriptive characteristics of this basic affective state? According to Freud, depression is characterized by *ego inhibition* and lowered *self-esteem*. Bibring adds to these a third characteristic: *helplessness*. He wrote: ". . . depression represents an affective state, which indicates . . . [the] state of the ego in terms of [lowered self-esteem] helplessness and inhibition of functions" (p. 27).

This formulation raised several problems. First, the various clinical forms of depression had to be explained, and were explained by Bibring as complications of the basic state of depression by those factors which accounted for depression in the commonly accepted theory. Second, since the concept of helplessness had already been used by Freud in the theory of anxiety, Bibring had to clarify the relationship between depression and anxiety. Third, the term self-esteem was not defined explicitly by Freud, nor by anyone else, including Bibring. The central rôle Bibring gave it in his theory leaves us with the necessity to define this term explicitly within the conceptual framework of the psychoanalytic theory, but it also provides an indication of how this defining can be done. We will return to these problems, but first we must consider the genetics and dynamics of the ego state of depression.

V

What are the genetics of this state? Bibring wrote:

Frequent frustrations of the infant's oral needs may mobilize at first anxiety and anger. If frustration is continued, however, in disregard of the "signals" produced by the infant, the anger will be replaced by feelings of exhaustion, of helplessness and depression. This early self-experience of the infantile ego's helplessness, of its lack of power to provide the vital supplies, is probably the most frequent factor predisposing to depression. . . . the emphasis is not on the oral frustration and subsequent oral fixation, but on the infant's or little child's shock-like experience of and fixation to the feeling of helplessness [pp. 36-37].

By the phrase "this early self-experience" Bibring meant the experience of helplessness resulting from frustration of oral needs, and his apparent reservation expressed in the phrase "the infantile ego's helplessness . . . is probably the most frequent fact predisposing to depression" intends to convey that not only the oral but all continued early frustrations are such predisposing factors. His references to Abraham and Erikson corroborate this explanation: "Similar reactions may be established by any severe frustration of the little child's vital needs in and beyond the oral phase, e.g., of the child's needs for affection (Abraham), or by a failure in the child-mother relationship of mutuality (Erikson, 1950)" (pp. 39–40).

What is bold and new in this theory is the assertion that *all* depressions are affective states and as such are *reactivations* of a structured infantile ego state of helplessness. Bibring's conception of the origin of this helplessness is in accord with that of Freud concerning grief in *The Problem of Anxiety*. But Freud does not apply this conception of helplessness to all depressions nor does he imply that grief is the reactivation of a structured state. Freud wrote:

[The Infant] is not yet able to distinguish temporary absence from permanent loss; . . . it requires repeated consoling experiences before he learns that . . . a disappearance on his mother's part is usually followed by her reappearance . . . Thus he is enabled, as it were, to experience longing without an accompaniment of despair.

The situation in which he misses his mother is . . . owing to his miscomprehension . . . a traumatic one if he experiences at that juncture a need which his mother ought to gratify; it changes into a danger situation when this need is not immediate . . . . Loss of love does not yet enter into the situation.

. . . [Subsequently] repeated situations in which gratification was experienced have created out of the mother the object who is the recipient, when a need arises, of an intense cathexis, a cathexis which we may call "longingful." It is to this innovation that the reaction of grief is referable. Grief is therefore the reaction specific to object loss, anxiety to the danger which this object loss entails [1926, pp. 118–119].

It should be re-emphasized that Freud here derives this conception of helplessness from the phenomena of *grief,* while Bibring generalized it to all depressions and—as we shall see—implied that grief is a genetically late, "tamed" reactivation of this helplessness. We might add here that Spitz's observations on the so-called anaclitic depressions seem to support this part of the genetic aspect of Bibring's theory.

VI

Before we pursue further the genetics of this ego state, we must turn first to the experiences which reactivate it in adult life, and then to its dynamics. Bibring wrote:

In all these instances [described], the individuals . . . felt helplessly exposed to superior powers, fatal organic disease, or recurrent neurosis, or to the seemingly inescapable fate of being lonely, isolated, or unloved, or unavoidably confronted with the apparent evidence of being weak, inferior, or a failure. In all instances, the depression accompanied a feeling of being doomed, irrespective of what the conscious or unconscious background of this feeling may have been: in all of them a blow was dealt to the person's self-esteem, on whatever grounds such self-esteem may have been founded [pp. 23–24].

Thus the conditions precipitating the reactivation of this state are those which undermine self-esteem. Here again Bibring is close to Freud's observations, which he quotes:

... the melancholiac displays ... an extraordinary fall in his self-esteem, an impoverishment of his ego on a grand scale [Freud, 1917, p. 155].

The occasions giving rise to melancholia for the most part extend beyond the clear case of a loss by death, and include all those situations of being wounded, hurt, neglected, out of favour, or disappointed ... [p. 161].

VII

If the crucial dynamic factors of the accepted theory—oral fixation, ambivalence, incorporation, aggression turned round upon the subject—are relegated by Bibring's theory to the peripheral rôle of factors which complicate the basic affective ego state of depression, how are we to understand the dynamics of the reactivation of that state?

Bibring's explanation is based on two assumptions: first, that a blow is dealt to the subject's self-esteem, second, that this occurs while "certain narcissistically significant, i.e., for the self-esteem pertinent, goals and objects are strongly maintained" (p. 24). He formulates: "It is exactly from the tension between these highly charged narcissistic aspirations on the one hand, and the ego's acute awareness of its (real and imaginary) helplessness and incapacity to live up to them on the other hand, that depression results" (pp. 24–25).

He enumerates these aspirations: "(1) the wish to be worthy, to be loved, to be appreciated, not to be inferior or unworthy; (2) the wish to be strong, superior, great, secure, not to be weak and insecure; and (3) the wish to be good, to be loving, not to be aggressive, hateful and destructive" (p. 24).

Protagonists of the accepted theory may argue that all these aspirations are but derivatives of instinctual goals and superego demands; that the conflict is one between the ego and the superego, and involves oral fixation, ambivalence, incorporation, and aggression turned round upon the subject. This argument, however, disregards the core of Bibring's theory. His assumptions that in depression we are faced with an intra-ego conflict and that the dynamic factors of the accepted theory play only a precipitating or complicating rôle, imply that the ego processes involved must be studied and understood in their own right, because the observed commonality of depressions cannot be explained by assuming that depression is created *de novo* every time from the basic ingredients—instinct, superego, etc. This implication of Bibring's theory is also implied by Hartmann and Erikson, and it should be illuminating to cite one of Freud's formulations which also implies it and is directly pertinent to Bibring's theory.

According to Bibring, to be loved and to be loving are among the narcissistic aspirations whose rôle in depressions is crucial. In "Instincts and Their Vicissitudes" Freud defined loving as "the relation of the ego to its sources of pleasure" (1915, p. 78), and he wrote: ". . . the attitudes of love and hate cannot be said to characterize the relations of instincts to their objects, but are reserved for the relations of the ego as a whole to objects" (p. 80). Thus Bibring's approach to the dynamics of the reactivation of the affective ego state of depression has a precedent in Freud's theorizing. The relationships implied in Freud's formulation have not been explored, and one of the merits of Bibring's theory is that it makes the exploration of them a patent and urgent necessity. The same urgency applies to the necessity of defining self-esteem, and to that of redefining narcissism in ego-psychological terms, since originally it was defined in what we would now call id terms.

Bibring summarized the dynamic aspect of his theory as follows:

Though the persisting aspirations are of a threefold nature, the *basic mechanism of the resulting depression appears to be essentially the same* . . . depression is primarily not determined by a conflict between the ego on the one hand and the id, or the superego, or the environment on the other hand, but stems primarily from a tension within the ego itself, from an inner-systemic "conflict." Thus depression can be defined as the emotional correlate of a partial or complete collapse of the self-esteem of the ego, since it feels unable to live up to its aspirations . . . [which] are strongly maintained [pp. 25–26].

More generally:

. . . everything that lowers or paralyzes the ego's self-esteem without changing the narcissistically important aims represents a condition of depression [p. 42].

This conception is in accord with Hartmann's theory of the "intra-systemic conflict'' and with Erickson's theory of the crises in psycho-social epigenesis.

VIII

Now we can turn to tracing the fate of the basic depressive state in the course of development.

Bibring's formulation of the epigenesis of narcissistic aspirations is an important step toward specifying the conception of autonomous ego development, which was introduced by Hartmann. It will be worth-while to remind ourselves that Freud already implied such a conception in "Formulations Regarding the Two Principles in Mental Functioning":

. . . the decision as regards the form of subsequent illness (election of neurosis) will depend on the particular phase of ego-development and libido-development in which the inhibition of development has occurred. The chronological char-acteristics of the two developments, as yet unstudied, their possible variations in speed with respect to each other, thus receive unexpected significance [1911, pp. 19–20].

Bibring formulated the epigenesis of narcissistic aspirations as follows: The narcissistic aspirations originating on the oral level are: (1) to get affection; (2) to be loved; (3) to be taken care of; (4) to get supplies. The corresponding defensive needs are: (1) to be independent; (2) to be self-supporting. Depression then follows the discovery of: (1) not being loved; (2) not being independent (p. 27).

The narcissistic aspirations originating on the anal level refer to mas-tery over the body, over drives, and over objects, and they are: (1) to be good; (2) to be loving; (3) to be clean. The corresponding defensive needs are: (1) not to be hostile; (2) not to be resentful and defiant; (3) not to be dirty. Depression then follows the discovery of: (1) lack of control over libidinal and aggressive impulses; (2) lack of control over objects; (3) feelings of weakness (entailing the former two); (4) feelings of guilt (I will never be good, loving, will always be hateful, hostile, defiant, therefore evil).

The narcissistic aspirations originating on the phallic level refer to the exhibitionistic and sadistic competitive oedipal needs, and they are: (1) to be admired; (2) to be the center of attention; (3) to be strong and victorious. The corresponding defensive needs are: (1) to be modest;

(2) to be inconspicuous; (3) to be submissive. Depression follows the discovery of: (1) fear of being defeated; (2) being ridiculed for short-comings and defeats; (3) impending retaliation.

These steps in the development of narcissistic aspirations correspond to the first three phases of Erikson's psychosocial epigenesis: the aspirations originating on the oral level correspond to Erikson's phase of basic trust vs. mistrust (mutuality); those originating on the anal level to his phase of psychosocial autonomy vs. shame and doubt, and those originating on the phallic level to his phase of initiative vs. guilt.

If these formulations should be found wanting in inclusiveness or exclusiveness, they are as rich and thoughtful a collation of what Freud must have meant when he spoke of ego interests, and what we mean when we speak of them or of values, as any in psychoanalytic writing except Erikson's and possibly Horney's.

These genetic formulations use the concept of narcissistic aspirations and bring sharply into focus the need to redefine the concept of narcissism in structural and particularly ego-psychological terms. Hartmann and subsequently Jacobson have made an attempt to reformulate this concept, assuming that narcissism involves the cathecting of the self-representations rather than the cathecting of the ego. Bibring's formulations seem to require a more radical redefinition of narcissism.

IX

We have here a structural theory which treats depression as the reactivation of a structured state. The universal experiences of grief and sadness, ranging from passing sadness to profound depression, indicate that such an ego state exists in all men. We may infer that individual differences in the relative ease of and intensity of the reactivation of this state are determined by: (a) the constitutional tolerance for continued frustration; (b) the severity and extent of the situations of helplessness in early life; (c) the developmental factors which increase or decrease the relative ease with which this state is reactivated and modulate its intensity; (d) the kind and severity of the precipitating conditions. As for the dynamic aspect of this theory: the depressive ego state is reactivated by an intra-ego conflict. The factors involved in this conflict, however, are not yet precisely defined. As for the genetic aspect of the theory: the origin of the depressive ego state is clear and so is the epigenesis of the "narcissistic aspirations" involved.

The economic and adaptive aspects of the theory, however, are not directly treated by Bibring. It is in regard to these aspects that much work is still ahead of us. I shall not attempt to infer from Bibring's theory the directions this work might take.

X

Freud made several attempts to account for various aspects of the economics of depression.

For instance, he wrote: ". . . the ego's inhibited condition and loss of interest was fully accounted for by the absorbing work of mourning" (1917, p. 155). Or for instance:

The conflict in the ego [meaning at that time the conflict between the ego and the superego], which in melancholia is substituted for the struggle surging round the object, must act like a painful wound which calls out unusually strong anti-cathexes (p. 170).

But Freud also indicated that these assumptions are insufficient and we need "some insight into the economic conditions, first, of bodily pain, and then of the mental pain" (p. 170) before we can understand the economics of depression; and that:

. . . we do not even know by what economic measures the work of mourning is carried through; possibly, however, a conjecture may help us here. Reality passes its verdict—that the object no longer exists—upon each single one of the memories and hopes through which the libido was attached to the lost object, and the ego, confronted as it were with the decision whether it will share this fate, is persuaded by the sum of narcissistic satisfactions in being alive to sever its attachment to the non-existent object [p. 166];

and that:

This character of withdrawing the libido bit by bit is . . . to be ascribed alike to mourning and to melancholia; it is probably sustained by the same economic arrangements and serves the same purpose in both [p. 167];

and finally:

Why this process of carrying out the behest of reality bit by bit . . . should be so extraordinarily painful is not at all easy to explain in terms of mental economics [p. 154].

Though it is clear that the phenomenon from which the economic explanation must start is the inhibition of the ego, the economics of depression is still not understood. Bibring quotes Fenichel's formulation: ". . . the greater percentage of the available mental energy is used up in unconscious conflicts, [and] not enough is left to provide the normal enjoyment of life and vitality" (Bibring, 1953, p. 19). But he finds this statement insufficient to explain depressive inhibition, and proceeds to reconsider the nature of inhibition. He writes:

Freud (1926) defines inhibition as a "restriction of functions of the ego" and mentions two major causes for such restrictions: either they have been imposed upon the person as a measure of precaution, e.g., to prevent the development of anxiety or feelings of guilt, or brought about as a result of exhaustion of energy of the ego engaged in intense defensive activities [p. 33].

Bibring concludes:

The inhibition in depression . . . does not fall under either category . . . It is rather due to the fact that certain strivings of the person become meaningless— since the ego appears incapable ever to gratify them [p. 33].

Bibring implies his own explanation in his comparison of depression to anxiety:

Anxiety as a reaction to (external or internal) danger indicates the ego's desire to survive. The ego, challenged by the danger, mobilizes the signal of anxiety and prepares for fight or flight. In depression, the opposite takes place, the ego is paralyzed because it finds itself incapable to meet the "danger." [In certain instances] . . . depression may follow anxiety, [and then] the mobilization of energy . . . [is] replaced by a decrease of self-reliance [pp. 34–35].

Thus Bibring's search for an economic explanation of depressive inhibition ends in the undefined term "decrease of self-reliance," which, as it stands, is not an economic concept.

Bibring followed his observations and constructions regardless of where they led him, and had the courage to stop where he did. Yet he opened up new theoretical possibilities. It is to the discussion of these that I will turn now.

XI

What does it mean that "the ego is paralyzed because it finds itself incapable to meet the 'danger'"? Clearly "paralyzed" refers to the state of helplessness, one of the corollaries of which is the "loss of self-esteem." The danger is the potential loss of object; the traumatic situation is that of the loss of object, "helplessness" as Bibring defines it is the persisting state of loss of object. The anxiety signal anticipates the loss in order to prevent the reactivation of the traumatic situation, that is, of panic-anxiety. Fluctuations of self-esteem anticipate, and initiate measures to prevent, the reactivation of the state of persisting loss of object, that is, of the state of helplessness involving loss of self-esteem. Thus the relation between fluctuations of self-esteem and "helplessness" which is accompanied by loss of self-esteem is similar to the relation between anxiety signal and panic-anxiety. Fluctuations of self-esteem are then structured, tamed forms of and signals to anticipate and to preclude reactivation of the state of helplessness. Yet, according to the accepted theory, fluctuations of self-esteem are the functions of the superego's relation to the ego, just as anxiety was considered, prior to 1926, as a function of repression enforced by the superego. In 1926, however, superego anxiety was recognized as merely one kind of anxiety and the *repression hence anxiety* relationship was reversed into *anxiety signal hence repression*. Bibring achieves an analogous reversal when he formulates: ". . . it is our contention, based on clinical observation, that it is the ego's awareness of its helplessness which in certain cases forces it to turn the aggression from the object against the self, thus aggravating and complicating the structure of depression" (p. 41). While in the accepted theory it is assumed that the aggression "turned round upon the subject" *results* in passivity and helplessness, in Bibring's conception it is the helplessness which is the *cause* of this "turning round."

Thus Bibring's theory opens two new vistas. One leads us to consider self-esteem as a signal, that is, an ego function, rather than as an *ad hoc* effect of the relation between the ego and the superego. The other suggests that we reconsider the rôle of the ego, and particularly of its helplessness, in the origin and function of the instinctual vicissitude called turning round upon the subject.

The first of these, like Freud's structural theory of anxiety and Fenichel's of guilt (1945, p. 135), leads to a broadening of our conception of the ego's apparatuses and functions. The second is even more far-reaching: it seems to go to the very core of the problem of aggression. We know that "turning round upon the subject" was the basic mechanism Freud used before the "death-instinct theory" to explain the major forms in which aggression manifests itself. It was in connection with this "turning round upon the subject" that Freud wrote:

. . . sadism . . . seems to press towards a quite special aim:—the infliction of pain, in addition to subjection and mastery of the object. Now psycho-analysis would seem to show that infliction of pain plays no part in the original aims sought by [sadism] . . . : the sadistic child takes no notice of whether or not it inflicts pain, nor is it part of its purpose to do so. But when once the transformation into masochism has taken place, the experience of pain is very well adapted to serve as a passive masochistic aim . . . Where once the suffering of pain has been experienced as a masochistic aim, it can be carried back into the sadistic situation and result in a sadistic aim of *inflicting pain* . . . [1915, pp. 71–72].

Thus Bibring's view that "turning round upon the subject" is brought about by helplessness calls attention to some of Freud's early formulations, and prompts us to re-evaluate our conception of aggression. Indeed, it may lead to a theory of aggression which is an alternative to those which have so far been proposed, namely Freud's death-instinct theory, Fenichel's frustration-aggression theory, and the Hartmann-Kris-Loewenstein theory of an independent aggressive instinctual drive.

XII

Let us return once more to the relation between helplessness (involving loss of self-esteem) and the simultaneously maintained narcissistic aspirations, noting that their intra-ego conflict assumed by Bibring may have been implied by Freud when he wrote in "Mourning and Melancholia": "A good, capable, conscientious [person] . . . is more likely to fall ill of [this] . . . disease than [one] . . . of whom we too should have nothing good to say" (1917, pp. 156–157).

Fenichel's summary of the accepted view of the fate of self-esteem in depression is:

. . . a greater or lesser loss of self-esteem is in the foreground. The subjective formula is "I have lost everything; now the world is empty," if the loss of self-esteem is mainly due to a loss of external supplies, or "I have lost everything because I do not deserve anything," if it is mainly due to a loss of internal supplies from the superego [1945, p. 391].

Fenichel's implied definition of supplies reads: "The small child loses self-esteem when he loses love and attains it when he regains love . . . children . . . need . . . narcissistic supplies of affection . . ." (1945, p. 41).

Though the term *supplies* has never been explicitly defined as a concept, it has become an apparently indispensable term in psychoanalysis, and particularly in the theory of depression. In Bibring's theory, supplies are the goals of narcissistic aspirations (p. 37). This gives them a central rôle in the theory, highlighting the urgent need to define them. Moreover, Bibring's comparison of depression and boredom hints at the direction in which such a definition might be sought by alerting us to the fact that there is a lack of supplies in boredom also. "Stimulus hunger"[1] is Fenichel's term for the immediate consequence of this lack: "Boredom is characterized by the co-existence of a need for activity and activity-inhibition, as well as by stimulus-hunger and dissatisfaction with the available stimuli" (1934, p. 349). Here adequate stimuli are the lacking supplies. Those which are available are either too close to the object of the repressed instinctual drive and thus are resisted, or they are too distant from it and thus hold no interest.

Bibring's juxtaposition of depression and boredom suggests that narcissistic supplies may be a special kind of adequate stimuli and narcissistic aspirations a special kind of stimulus hunger. The implications of this suggestion become clearer if we note that it is the lack of narcissistic supplies which is responsible for the structuralization of that primitive state of helplessness, the reactivation of which is, according to Bibring's theory, the essence of depression.

The conception which emerges if we pursue these implications of Bibring's theory is this: (1) The development of the ego requires the presence of "adequate stimuli," in this case love of objects; when such stimuli are consistently absent a primitive ego state comes into existence, the later reactivation of which is the state of depression. (2) Normal development lowers the intensity of this ego state and its potentiality for reactivation, and limits its reactivation to those reality situations to which grief and sadness are appropriate reactions. (3) Recurrent absence of adequate stimuli in the course of development

---

[1] [Also translated as "craving for stimulus" (Fenichel, 1922–36, p. 292)—Ed.]

works against the lowering of the intensity of this ego state and increases the likelihood of its being reactivated, that is to say, establishes a predisposition to depression.

This conception is consonant with present-day ego psychology and also elucidates the economic and the adaptive aspects of Bibring's theory. The rôle of stimulation in the development of ego structure is a crucial implication of the concept of adaptation. At the same time, since psychoanalytic theory explains the effects of stimulation in terms of changes in the distribution of attention cathexes, the rôle of stimulation in ego-structure development, to which I just referred, might well be the starting point for an understanding of the economics of the ego state of depression.

XIII

This discussion of the structural, genetic, dynamic, economic, and adaptive aspects of Edward Bibring's theory gives us a glimpse of its fertility, but does not exhaust either its implications or the problems it poses. An attempt to trace more of these would require a detailed analysis of those points where Bibring's views shade into other findings and theories of psychoanalytic ego psychology, and is therefore beyond our scope tonight.

Instead, I would like to dwell in closing on three roots of Edward Bibring's theory which are less obvious than the observations and formulations so far discussed.

The first is its root in the technique of psychoanalysis. Bibring wrote:

From a . . . therapeutic point of view one has to pay attention not only to the dynamic and genetic basis of the persisting narcissistic aspirations, the frustrations of which the ego cannot tolerate, but also the dynamic and genetic conditions which forced the infantile ego to become fixated to feelings of helplessness . . . [the] major importance [of these feelings of helplessness] in the therapy of depression is obvious.[2]

This formulation seems to say nothing more than the well-known technical rule that "Analysis must always go on in the layers accessible to the ego at the moment" (Fenichel, 1938–39, p. 44). But it does say

---

[2] This is to some degree in agreement with Karen Horney (1945) who stressed the necessity of analyzing not only the "conflicts," but also the hopelessness [p. 43].

more, because it specifies that it is the helplessness, the lack of interest, and the lowered self-esteem which are immediately accessible in depression. It is safe to assume that the clinically observed accessibility of these was one of the roots of Bibring's theory.

A second root of the theory is in Bibring's critique of the English school of psychoanalysis. A study of this critique shows that on the one hand Bibring found some of this school's *observations* on depression sound and, like his own observations, incompatible with the accepted theory of depression; but on the other hand he found this school's *theory* of depression incompatible with psychoanalytic theory proper. It seems that Bibring intended his theory of depression to account for the sound observations of this school *within* the framework of psychoanalytic theory.

Finally, a third root of Bibring's theory seems to be related to the problems raised by the so-called "existential analysis." So far the only evidence for Edward Bibring's interest in and critical attitude toward "existential analysis" is in the memories of those people who discussed the subject with him. Though his interest in phenomenology is obvious in his paper on depression, his interest in existentialism proper is expressed in only a few passages, like "[Depression] is—essentially—'a human way of reacting to frustration and misery' whenever the ego finds itself in a state of (real or imaginary) helplessness against 'overwhelming odds'" (p. 36). Bibring's intent seems to have been to put the sound observations and psychologically relevant concepts of "existential analysis" into the framework of psychoanalytic ego psychology.

XIV

The measures of a theoretician's stature are the range of his interests; his simultaneous reponsiveness to empirical evidence, to theoretical consistency, and to existing alternative theories; his courage to follow his constructions even if they cannot entirely bridge the chasm over which he extends them; and the originality and stimulating power of his thought. By these measures Edward Bibring is one of the few real psychoanalytic theoreticians.

In presenting this discussion of "The Mechanism of Depression"— which I organized on the metapsychological pattern—I intended to demonstrate not only the importance of Edward Bibring's theory of depression, and not only its place in the contemporary developments of psychoanalytic theory. I intended also to reflect the multiplicity of observations, theories, historical and general considerations which Edward Bibring responded to and integrated in his theory of depression.

Our picture of Edward Bibring's achievement would, however, be inadequate if we did not take account of his human achievement, which pervades all the rest. Scientific achievements are human achievements. Psychoanalysts, when looking at a psychological theory as a human achievement, discover its motivation and hence are prone to suspect its objective validity. If this were justified there could be no valid theory: all our theories are the products of motivated human thought. There is little doubt about what provided the immediate motivation for Edward Bibring's theory of depression. He faced the devastating blows of a destructive illness and transformed them into scientific discovery. The motivation of valid theory need not be different from that of an invalid theory. What they do differ in is the control the theorist has over his motivation. The scientist who develops an invalid theory takes a short cut to the goal of his motivation: he indulges in wishful thinking. The scientist who develops a valid theory takes the detours which are necessary to test and to modify the goals he is motivated to pursue in accordance with observation and existing theory:

Edward Bibring was aware of his motivation and tested it by choosing the detour. His work is a major contribution to psychoanalytic theory and his human achievement is a monument to the power of the human mind.

REFERENCES

Abraham, K. (1924). A Short Study of the Development of the Libido, Viewed in the Light of Mental Disorders. *Selected Papers*. London: Hogarth Press, 1948, pp. 418–501.

Bibring, E. (1953). The Mechanism of Depression. In *Affective Disorders,* ed. P. Greenacre. New York: International Universities Press, pp. 13–48.

Erikson, E. H. (1950). *Childhood and Society*. New York: Norton.

Fenichel, O. (1922–36). *Collected Papers,* Vol. I. New York: Norton, 1953.

——(1934). On the Psychology of Boredom. In *Organization and Pathology of Thought,* ed. & tr. D. Rapaport. New York: Columbia University Press, 1951, pp. 349–361.

——(1938–39). *Problems of Psychoanalytic Technique*. Albany, N.Y.: Psychoanalytic Quarterly, Inc., 1941.

——(1945). *The Psychoanalytic Theory of Neurosis*. New York: Norton.

Freud, S. (1911). Formulations Regarding the Two Principles in Mental Functioning. *Collected Papers,* 4:13–21. New York: Basic Books, 1959.

——(1915). Instincts and Their Vicissitudes. *Collected Papers,* 4:60–83. New York: Basic Books, 1959.

——(1917 [1915]). Mourning and Melancholia. *Collected Papers,* 4:152–170. New York: Basic Books, 1959.

——(1926 [1925]). *The Problem of Anxiety,* tr. H. A. Bunker. New York: Psychoanalytic Quarterly & Norton, 1936.

Horney, K. (1945). *Our Inner Conflicts*. New York: Norton.

Lewin, B. D. (1950). *The Psychoanalysis of Elation*. New York: Norton.

4. An Intensive Study of Twelve Cases of Manic-Depressive Psychosis

Mabel Blake Cohen, Grace Baker, Robert A. Cohen, Frieda Fromm-Reichmann, and Edith V. Weigert

The purpose of this study is to examine the manic-depressive character by means of the intense psychoanalytic psychotherapy of a number of patients. We feel this to be potentially useful, since, the newer understanding of interpersonal processes and of problems of anxiety has not hitherto been brought to bear on this group of patients. The older psychoanalytic studies of the psychopathology of the manic depressive have largely described the intrapsychic state of the patient and left unexplained the question of how the particular pattern of maladjustive behavior has arisen. Thus, to use a simple example, the manic depressive is said to have an oral character. However, the question of how or why he developed an oral character is left unconsidered except that such factors as a constitutional overintensity of oral drives, or overindulgence or frustration during the oral phase, are mentioned. Our purpose is to delineate as far as possible the experiences with significant people which made it necessary for the prospective manic depressive to develop the particular patterns of interaction which comprise his character and his illness. To this end, neither constitutional factors nor single traumata are stressed in this report, although we do not deny their significance. Rather, we have directed our attention to the interpersonal environment from birth on, assuming that it has interacted with the constitutional endowment in such a way as to eventuate in the development of a manic-depressive character in the child. In other words, the personality of the parents, the quality of their handling of the child, and the quality of the child's response to this handling have played an important part in the development of a characteristic pattern of relating to others and reacting to anxiety-arousing situations which we call typical of the manic-depressive character.

Such a study has many implications for the improvement of the therapeutic approach to the patient. We follow the basic premise of psychoanalytic theory—that in the transference relationship with the therapist the patient will repeat the patterns of behavior which he has developed with significant figures earlier in his life. By studying the transference, we can make inferences about earlier experiences; conversely, by understanding the patient historically, we can make inferences about the transference relationship. As our grasp of the patient's part of the pattern of interaction with his therapist improves, we can gain some concept of what goals of satisfaction he is pursuing, as well as of what sort of anxieties he is striving to cope with. We may then intervene through our part in the interaction to assist him more successfully to achieve his goals of satisfaction and to resolve some of the conflicts which are at the source of his anxiety.

In this research project, a total of twelve cases were studied. They were all treated by intensive psychoanalytic psychotherapy for periods ranging from one to five years. Nine of the cases were presented and discussed in the original research seminar from 1944 to 1947. During 1952 and 1953, the present research group studied three additional cases in great detail; the members of the group met in three-hour sessions twice monthly during that period. All twelve of the cases are referred to in brief throughout the report, and extracts are used from the last three cases (namely, Miss G, Mr. R, and Mr. H) to illustrate various points.

SURVEY OF THE LITERATURE

At the end of the last century, Kraepelin[1] attempted to classify the psychiatric syndromes, including the manic-depressive or circular psychosis, as nosological entities. While his classification in general brought some order into the exisiting confusion, he was unable to establish a pathological substratum or a specific etiological factor for either dementia praecox or the manic-depressive psychosis, and this situation still exists. Nevertheless typical cases of manic-depressive psychosis, as Kraepelin first described it, do exist as well as a great number of atypical cases.

Manic or depressive syndromes have been found in exogenous psy-

[1] E. Kraepelin, *Psychiatrie* (7th ed.); Leipzig Barth, 1904.

choses, general paresis, brain injuries, involutional and epileptic illnesses, as well as in hysteric and obsessional neuroses. It is particularly difficult to make a differentiation between schizophrenia and manic-depressive psychosis, and this has frequently become a controversial issue between different psychiatric schools. Lewis and Hubbard, and P. Hoch and Rachlin[2] have all noted that a certain number of patients originally diagnosed as manic depressives have later had to be reclassified as schizophrenics. More infrequent is a reversal of the diagnosis of schizophrenia into that of manic-depressive psychosis.

The apparent lack of specificity of etiological factors in manic-depressive psychosis stimulated Bellak[3] to propose a "multiple factor psychosomatic theory of manic-depressive psychosis"; he felt that anatomical, endocrine, genetic, infectious, neurophysiological, and psychological factors might contribute to the provocation of manic and depressive syndromes. Sullivan [4] has also subscribed to this general approach to manic-depressive psychosis, stressing the importance of physical factors; this is particularly interesting since he has stressed dynamic psychogenic factors in the schizophrenic. The importance of genetic factors in the determination of the ego strength[5] of the manic-depressive has been rather generally recognized and studied. For example, studies have been made of the high incidence of manic-depressive illness in the same family, which cannot be explained entirely in terms of environmental influences;[6] other studies have been made to

[2] N. D. C. Lewis and L. D. Hubbard, "The Mechanisms and Prognostic Aspects of the Manic-Depressive-Schizophrenic Combinations," *Proc. Assn. Research N. and M. Disease* (1931) 11:539–608. P. Hoch and H. L. Rachlin, "An Evaluation of Manic-Depressive Psychosis in the Light of Follow-Up Studies," *Amer. J. Psychiatry* (1941) 97:831–843.

[3] L. Bellack, *Manic-Depressive Psychosis and Allied Conditions;* New York, Grune & Stratton, 1952.

[4] Harry Stack Sullivan, unpublished lectures given at Chestnut Lodge, Rockville, Maryland, 1944. See also *Conceptions of Modern Psychiatry;* Washington D. C., The William Alanson White Psychiatric Foundation, 1947; p. 51.

[5] Bellack has pointed out that the quality of an illness depends on the quantity of the integrating forces from within and without (reference footnote 4). In addition, as Freud has noted, "we have no reason to dispute the existence and importance of primal, congenital ego variations." (See "Analysis Terminable and Interminable," in *Collected Papers* 5:316–357; London, Hogarth Press, 1925.)

[6] There has accumulated a considerable body of evidence suggesting that constitutional factors may play a larger role in the manic depressive than in the schizophrenic, such as Kallman's studies on familial incidence. See, for instance, F. J. Kallman, "The Genetic Theory of Personality," *Amer. J. Psychiatry* (1946) 103:309–322.

validate E. Kretschmer's[7] thesis of the relation between what he terms the pyknic body shape and the manic-depressive type; and there has been some research done on identical twins who have manic-depressive psychoses.

In our study, we have been particularly interested in pursuing the part that psychodynamic factors play in bringing about the manic-depressive illness. But we agree with Rado[8] that the multiplicity of etiological factors calls for the close collaboration of the pathologist, the neurophysiologist, the endocrinologist, the geneticist, the psychiatrist, and the psychoanalyst. In the long run, better teamwork by all of these specialists may improve the method of therapy which at present varies from custodial care with sedation, to prolonged narcosis,[9] different forms of shock therapy, lobotomy, and occasionally various forms of psychotherapy. The prevailing ignorance about the etiology of manic-depressive psychosis is reflected in the haphazard application of shock therapy and lobotomy, the effects of which still remain in the realm of speculation. There are many speculative elements in the psychotherapeutic approach, too, as evidenced in this study. But psychotherapeutic experimentation abides, or tries to abide, by the medical standard of "nihil nocere."

Psychoanalytic Research

Abraham, in 1911,[10] was first to systematically apply the psychoanalytic method to the treatment of the circular psychoses. He concluded that manic and depressive phases are dominated by the same complexes, the depressive being defeated by them, the manic ignoring and denying them. Some of his ideas on depression might be summarized as follows: the regression to the oral level of libido development brings out the

[7] E. Kretchmer, "Heredity and Constitution in Aetiology of Psychic Disorders," *British Med. J* (1937) 2:403–406.

[8] S. Rado, "Recent Advances of Psychoanalytic Therapy," *Proc. Assn. Research N. and M. Disease* (1953) 31:42–57. "Psychosomatics of Depression from the Etiologic Point of View," *Psychosomatic Med.* (1951) 13:51–55.

[9] J. Klaesi, "Uber die therapeutische Anwendung der 'Dauernarkose' mittels Somnifen bei Schizophrenen," *Ztschr. f. d. ges. Psychiat. u. Neurol. (1922) 74:557.*

[10] K. Abraham, *Selected Papers on Psychoanalysis; New York, Basic Books, 1953. See the following articles in this book: "Notes on the Psycho-Analytical Investigation and Treatment of Manic-Depressive Insanity and Allied Conditions" (1911), "The Influence of Oral Erotism on Character-Formation" (1924), "A Short Study of the Development of the Libido" (1924).*

characterological features of impatience and envy, increased egocentricity, and intense ambivalence; the capacity to love is paralyzed by hate, and this inability to love leads to feelings of impoverishment; and the depressive stupor represents a form of dying. Abraham thought that the indecision of ambivalence is close to the doubts of the compulsive neurotic, and that in the free interval, the manic depressive is an obsessional neurotic. He recommended psychoanalysis in the free interval, since, in the acute phases of the psychosis, it is very difficult to establish rapport.

In 1921, Dooley continued Abraham's experiment in this country by studying, psychoanalytically, five manic-depressive patients in St. Elizabeths Hospital.[11] Like Abraham, she found considerable resistance in her patients' extraverted egocentricity, for which she accepted White's concept of "flight into reality."[12] According to White, this tendency toward extraversion of libido makes the prognosis of manic-depressive psychosis more favorable, in terms of spontaneous recovery, than that of schizophrenia. He felt that because of the dominance of his egocentric wishes, the manic-depressive patient can make "use of every object in range of his sense." But Dooley found that the resistances of the manic depressive against analysis are even stronger than those of schizophrenics. Dooley suggested that the manic attack is a defense against the realization of failure. The patient cannot look at himself in the mirror of psychoanalysis; he cannot hear the truth. "Patients who manifest frequent manic attacks are likly to be headstrong, self-sufficient, know-it-all types of person, who will get the upper hand of the analyst. . . . The analyst is really only an appendage to a greatly inflated ego." Since the life conditions of the manic depressive are often no more unsatisfactory than those of many a normal person, there must be a lack of integration which keeps the manic depressive from achieving the sublimations which he is potentially capable of. Dooley came to the conclusion that the manic and depressive episodes are due to deep regressions to the sadomasochistic level of the child. "Autoerotic wishes were satisified by hypochondriacal complaints." In a much later paper

[11] L. Dooley, "A Psychoanalytic Study of Manic-Depressive Psychosis," *Psychoanalytic Rev.* (1921) 8:37–72, 144–167.

[12] W. A. White, "Personality, Psychogenesis and Psychoses," *J. N. and M. Disease (1936) 83:645–660.*

on "The Relation of Humor to Masochism,"[13] Dooley mentioned a manic-depressive patient who began to develop humor in the analysis as she became aware that she "could neither hurt me, nor wrangle me into loving her." Dooley considered this kind of insightful humor to be a milestone in the healing process of the excessive mood swings; it indicates that the superego is losing its tragically condemning cruelty and is permitting laughter at the overweening, pestering child-ego.

In 1916–1917, Freud compared melancholia to normal mourning[14] as follows: The loss of a love object elicits the labor of mourning, which is a struggle between libido attachment and detachment—love and hate. In normal mourning this struggle of ambivalence under pressure of confrontation with reality leads to gradual rechannelization of the libido toward new objects. In the case of melancholia, the loss which, may take the form of separation, disappointment, or frustration, remains unconscious, and the reorientation exacted reality elicits strong resistances, since the narcissistic character of the disturbed relation does not permit detachment. In this way, an intensified identification with the frustrating love object in the unconscious results. "The shadows of the object has fallen on the Ego." The whole struggle of ambivalence is internalized in a battle with the conscience. The exaggerated self-accusations are reproaches against the internalized object of love and hate; the self-torture is a form of revenge, and simultaneously, an attempt at reconciliation with the internalized partner. The narcissistic, ambivalent character of the relation to the lost love object either is the result of transitory regression or is constitutionally conditioned. Thus the loss of self-esteem and the intense self-hate in the melancholic become understandable.

In 1921, Freud added some statements about mania to his earlier interpretation of depression.[15] He suggested that the mood swings of normal and neurotic persons are caused by the tensions between ego and ego ideal. These mood swings are excessive in the case of manic-depressive illness because after the frustrating of lost object has been re-established by identification in the ego, it is then tormented by the

[13] L. Dooley, "The Relation of Humor to Masochism," *Psychoanalytic Rev.* (1941) 28:37–47

[14] S. Freud, "Mourning and Melancholia," in *Collected Papers* 4:152–170; reference footnote 7.

[15] S. Freud, *Group Psychology and the Analysis of the Ego;* London, Hogarth Press, 1922.

cruel severity of the ego ideal, against which, in turn, the ego rebels. According to Freud, the manic phase represents a triumphant reunion between ego and ego ideal, in the sense of expansive self-inflation, but not in the sense of a stabilized equilibrium.

Abraham, in 1924,[16] pursued his interest in biological development and tried to find specific fixation points for mental illness in different phases of libido development. He interpreted character traits as being highly symbolized derivatives of pregenital instinctual impulses that were, in the case of the mentally ill person, hampered in their normal development by frustration or overindulgence. Because of Abraham's influence, psychoanalytic research in ego development has for a long time been dependent on highly schematized concepts of libido development and its symbolizations. Abraham located the fixation to which the manic depressive periodically regresses as being at the end of the second biting oral phase and the beginning of the first expelling anal phase. This assumption could explain the frequent preoccupation of the manic depressive with cannibalistic phantasies as well as his phantasies of incorporation in the form of coprophagia; his character trends of impatience, envy and exploitativeness, dominating possessiveness, and exaggerated optimism or pessimism; his intense ambivalence; and his explosive riddance reactions. The object loss that precedes the onset of a depression is mostly not conscious but, according to Abraham, repeats a primal depression, a frustration at the time of transition from the oral to the anal phase, when the child was disappointed in the mother. The oral dependence may be constitutionally overemphasized in the manic depressive, Abraham suggested.

In 1927 Rado[17] went a step further in the theory of identification. Freud's and Abraham's theories imply an incorporation of the lost or frustrating object, in both the tormented ego and the punishing ego-ideal or superego. This double incorporation, Rado postulated, corresponds to an ambivalent splitting into a "good"—that is, gratifying—object, and a "bad" or frustrating object; at an early stage of development, when the synthetic function of the ego is still weak, both of these

---

[16] K. Abraham, "A Short Study of the Development of the Libido"; reference footnote 10.

[17] S. Rado, "Das Problem der Melancholie," *Internat. Ztschr. f. Psa. (1927) 13:439–455.*

are the mother. The good parent by whom the child wants to be loved is incorporated in the superego, endowed with the privilege of punishing the bad parent who is incorporated in the ego. This bad object in the ego may be punished to the point of total destruction (suicide). But the ultimate goal of this raging orgy of self-torture is expiation, reconciliation, synthesis.[18] Rado described the manic phase as an unstable reconcilation reached on the basis of denial of guilt. The automatized cycle of guilt, expiation, and reconciliation is patterned after the sequence of infantile oral experience: rage, hunger, drinking. The drinking, which resembles the state of reunion of reconciliation, culminates in a satiated pleasure experience, which Rado called the "alimentary orgasm." In a paper published in 1933,[19] Rado described the way in which the drug addict, in the artifically produced intoxication, expresses the same yearning for reconciliation and blissful reunion with the gratifying mother.

In the same year, 1933, Deutsch[20] illustrated the theory of manic-depressive psychoses, as developed up to that time, by several abbreviated case presentations. She agreed with Rado that the melancholic phase is sometimes introduced by a phase of rebellion of the ego against the cruel superego. After the ego succumbs to the superego's punishment with the unconscious intention of bribing the superego and of gaining forgiveness by such submission, the ego may rescue itself from the dangerous introjection by projecting the threatening enemy onto the outside world; aggression can then be directed against the projected superego, which has become an external persecutor. Another form of escape from the melancholic predicament is the denial of any narcissistic deprivation—be it the loss of mother's breast or the absence of a penis—in a glorious triumph of manic or hypomanic excitement. Deutsch regarded mania and paranoia as alternative defenses against the intense danger to survival to an ego oppressed by melancholia. In

[18] Alexander has elaborated on this idea in his discussion of the bribing of the superego by self-punishment. See F. Alexander, *Psychoanalysis of the Total Personality;* New York, Nervous and Mental Disease Publ. Co., 1935.

[19] S. Rado, "The Pschoanalysis of Pharmacothymia (Drug Addiction)," *Psychiatric Quart.* (1933) 2:1–23.

[20] H. Deutsch, "Zur Psychologie der manisch-de-pressiven Zustaende, insbesondere der chronischen Hypomanie," *Internat. Ztschr. f. Psa.* (1933) vol. 19.

the hypomanic patient, the underlying depression has to be lifted into consciousness if therapy is to be successful. In 1938, Jacob[21] made a similar observation on a periodically manic patient.

Gero illustrated "The Construction of Depression" (1936)[22] by two case presentations. One was of a woman patient with an obsessional character structure built up as a defense against the painful ambivalence in her family relations. Only after these character defenses yielded to analysis could this patient see avenues of realistic satisfactions and therewith surmount her depressions. The other case was a male patient, who had identified with an overambitious, overexacting father, and a rejecting mother, and had repressed the rage against both frustrating parents by withdrawal into an apathetic regression, punishing therewith the internalized objects of his hate and rage. After his father's death, he had himself changed into a sick old man. The liberation of rage and hate in the transference freed the genital aggressiveness from the odium and guilt of sadomasochistic distortions. In both cases the analyst succeeded in winning the patients back from a hopeless negativism to a hopeful confirmation of life.

Jacobson described in 1943[23] a severely depressed patient, with strong suicidal urges, intense experiences of depersonalization and "Weltuntergang" phantasies–a case on the borderline between manic depressive psychosis and schizophrenia. Jacobson was able to uncover a primal depression in this patient at the age of three and a half, when the birth of a brother coincided with a disruption of the parental marital relation. Turning from mother to father and back to mother left the patient empty. Threatened by complete loss of objects, she maintained a masochistic dependence on her mother. As substitutes for the disappointing parents, she built up phantasies of idealized, perfect parents who endowed her superego with cruel severity, so that she lived in constant danger of complete desertion and in horror of punishment.

Weiss in 1944[24] pursued a slighty different approach. He postulated

---

[21] Gertrud Jacob, "Notes on a Manic-Depressive," Washington-Baltimore Psychoanalytic Society, 1938 (unpublished lecture).

[22] G. Gero, "The Construction of Depression," *Internat. J. Psychoanal.* (1936) 17:423–461.

[23] Edith Jacobson, "Depression, the Oedipus Complex in the Development of Depressive Mechanisms," *Psychiatric Quart.* (1943) 12:541–560.

[24] E. Weiss, "Clinical Aspects of Depression,"*Psychoanalytic Quart.* (1944) 13:445–461.

that melancholic episodes are a reaction to the realization of antisocial, dishonest, or egotistical aspects of the personality. The inability of the patient to reach an integration between his antisocial wishes and his moral standards causes a tension in his "ego feeling" so that the patient hates himself. The exaggerated guilt reaction maintains the split between persecuting and persecuted "introjects." Identifications with hated objects may make the task of ego integration very difficult indeed. In the manic phase, the passive objectionable introject is projected, and the ego assumes the active role of the persecuting superego against objects of condemnation in the outside world. Weiss points out that in paranoia, the ego does not cling strongly to the superego, and the *persecuting* introject, the superego, is projected; in mania, however, the *persecuted* introject is projected. The paranoiac, by this projection, succeeds in preserving his narcissistic position, while the melancholic fails; the result of his inner persecution may be self-destruction.

To turn to more recent material, Bibring[25] has summed up all the features that different kinds of depression have in common, including not only the depressions of circular psychosis, but also the reactive depressions and depressions in the course of physical illness and in states of fatigue or exhaustion. A common factor is the lowering of self-esteem, the loss of self-love, which, in melancholia, is intensified into self-hate. Bibring compares depression with states of depersonalization and boredom. In the mildly depressed person, there is not so much hate turned against the self as there is an exhaustion of the narcissistic supply of self-love. The mildly depressed person is less inclined to kill himself than to *let* himself die.

Frank in a lecture on "The Defensive Aspects of Depression"[26] follows a line of thought similar to Bibring's. He compares unspecific depressions to the hibernation of animals–a defensive response to frustrating life conditions. Depression as a defense tunes down the desires and expectations to a lower key, so that the shock of unavoidable frustration is reduced to a minimum.

The manic aspect of the manic-depressive psychosis has on the whole elicited less attention on the part of psychoanalysts than has the depressed aspect, probably because the manic patient does not so fre-

[25] E. Bibring, "Das Problem der Depression," *Psyche (Stuttgart)* (1952) 5:81–101.
[26] R. Frank, "The Defensive Aspects of Depression," American Psychopathological Association, 1952 (unpublished lecture).

quently seek therapeutic help. B. Lewin, in a monograph on *The Psychoanalysis of Elation*[27] regards elation as a defense of denial against depression. During the analytic process, Lewin suggests, normal mourning increases insight into the self and may terminate in a sense of heightened well-being, increased sexual potency, and capacity for work and sublimation. But elation or depression resist the testing of reality; they produce negative therapeutic reactions in the face of insight that cannot at the time be emotionally assimilated. The depressed and the elated ego are not trying to separate the true from the false, but the good from the bad; reality-testing is replaced by morality-testing. Lewin compares mania to sleep: in sleep the ego disappears; in mania the superego vanishes. Sleep stems from oral satisfaction—the infant drops asleep when he is satiated with nursing at the mother's breast. But the manic patient is a notoriously poor sleeper, and he is haunted by "the triad of oral wishes,"—to devour, to be devoured, and to sleep. The wish-fear to be devoured transforms the wish to sleep into a fear of dying. The yearning for the gratifying maternal breast–the wish to sleep–may be transmuted into a desire for union with the superego. In the artist this union is accomplished, as a result of the inspiration and the actualization of this inspiration in the creative process, which satisfies both the superego and the world of the artist's contemporaries.

In several papers on suicide,[28] Zilboorg emphasizes that suicide is frequent in manic-depressive psychoses. "A number of suicides occur when the depressed person appears to be convalescing and all but recovered from his depressed state." In pathologic depressions the patient is identified with a person toward whom his feelings have been highly ambivalent. Zilboorg says of such a patient: "He feels detached from reality and therefore experiences a sense of poverty of the Ego. The unconscious sadism originally directed against the object, reinforced by a sense of guilt, produces the singular phenomenon of the person becoming sadistic toward himself." Frequently, the identification with a close relative who died at the time when the patient went through the Oedipus conflict or puberty contributes to the suicidal

[27] B. Lewin, *The Psychoanalysis of Elation;* New York, W. W. Norton & Co., 1950.
[28] G. Zilboorg, "Differential Diagnostic Types of Suicide," *Arch. Neurol. and Psychiat.* (1936) 35:270–291. "Suicide among Civilized and Primitive Races," *Amer. J. Psychiatry* (1936) 92:1347–1369. "Considerations on Suicide, with Particular Reference To That of the Young," *Amer. J. Orthopsychiatry* (1937) 7:15–31.

tendency in later years. Zilboorg stresses the observation that suicide may occur in a variety of other psychopathologic conditions on the basis of different motivations, such as spite and fear.

Early Parent-Child Relationships

Since all authors who have studied depressive and manic syndromes point to a primal depression or serious disturbances in the early parent-child relation, we have been interested in learning what the child psychoanalysts have to say. Two of Spitz's[29] papers are interesting in this connection. Spitz defines anaclitic depression as the state of dullness unresponsiveness, and arrest of emotional development that can be observed in a baby removed from his mother's care and left in a hospital, so that the baby's dependency relation with his mother is interrupted. In this state, Spitz observed that the baby showed tension, anxieties, excitement, increased autoerotic activities, and increased demandingness toward the environment. When the deprivation does not last more than three months, Spitz notes that the baby recovers once his emotional needs are again met. When the deprivation lasts longer, however, irreversible changes take place, and permanent physical and psychological damage occurs; the adaptation breaks down; there is arrest of appetite and sleep, loss of weight, morbidity, decreased motility, and facial rigidity; excitement changes into depression; learning is arrested; and autoerotic activities disappear. Social responsiveness—demandingness toward the environment—is the last of the compensatory efforts to disappear, Spitz observes; indeed the life of the baby who suffers from hospital marasmus is seriously endangered.

Melanie Klein's[30] contribution to the understanding of the psychoses is based on her observation of babies in the preverbal stage and by her empathic understanding of children with whom she has worked therapeutically in the early verbal stages. In this paper we shall be concerned

[29] R. Spitz, "Anaclitic Depression"; in *The Psychoanalytic Study of the Child;* New York, Internat. Univ. Press, 1946; vol. 2. "Depression—A Psychological Disturbance of the General Adaptation Syndrome," American Psychopathological Association, 1959 (Unpublished lecture).

[30] Melanie Klein, *Contributions to Psycho-Analysis,* 1921–1945; London, Hogarth Press, 1950. See especially, "A Contribution to the Psychogenesis of Manic-Depressive States," pp. 282–310, and "Mourning and Its Relation to Manic-Depressive States," pp. 311–338. *The Psycho-Analysis of Children;* London, Hogarth Press, 1932.

with examining only that part of her thinking which is contributory to an interpretation of manic-depressive psychosis. In approaching Klein's work it is well to keep in mind that her theories place a great deal of emphasis on the theory of the death instinct. Although Freud in his last formulation of the instinct theory postulated the death instinct, many psychoanalysts have maintained a certain reserve in relation to this concept. Freud himself, with a certain caution, has called the instinct theory "our mythology," and the instincts "mythical beings, superb in their indefiniteness."[31]

In contrast to Freud, Klein assumes that the infant from birth on is never merely autoerotically or narcissistically oriented, and that from the start of the extrauterine existence, there are object relations of an introjective, projective type, although the ego boundaries are still very fluid. The ego is built up on early introjection, according to Klein; but since the synthetic function of the ego is still weak, the infant is endangered by disruptive projections and disintegration, indicated by his readiness for the alarm reaction of anxiety. According to Klein, these early months of labile integration contain the fixation points to which the psychotic individual regresses under stress and strain. Constitutional weakness in the synthetic function of the ego permits such regression even under lesser degrees of stress. Klein calls these fixation points the "paranoid" and the "depressive position." She does not mean by this that the infant passes through the major psychoses, but that the potentialities of psychotic desintegration are implied in the early ego weakness.

The paranoid position develops first, Klein says, as automatic defense against pain or displeasure in the form of projection. In the earliest phase when the infant's behavior is centered around the oral zone and swallowing and spitting are his main life-preserving activities, he learns a reflexive discrimination between pleasure and displeasure. The pleasurable object is automatically incorporated, the unpleasurable spat out or eliminated. The infantile organism tends to maintain automatically a "purified pleasure ego" by splitting pleasure and pain; Sullivan[32] has referred to this phenomenon as me and not-me, since pleasure is incor-

[31] S. Freud, *New Introductory Lectures on Psycho-Analysis;* New York, W. W. Norton & Co., 1933; p.131.

[32] H. S. Sullivan, *The Interpersonal Theory of Psychiatry;* New York, W. W. Norton & Co., 1953.

porated as me and displeasure ejected as not-me. The not-me—the strange, the unfamiliar, and the uncanny—elicits in the infant the response of dread even in the first weeks of life. Klein has defined the ejected not-me as "bad," the persecutor, and has called the infant's dread-reaction, "persecutory anxiety."

The depressive position which develops at about the time of weaning—around the first half year of life is the second fixation point in Klein's theory. It is at this time that the mother is first recognized as one person, whether she is at the moment gratifying or depriving, "good" or "bad." This marks the beginnings of recall and foresight in the baby. Even if the mother is absent at a given moment, or does not feed or care for the child satisfactorily, there is no longer the desperate quality of "never again," nor complete desertion; that is, there is some hope and trust in her return. This hope and trust is based, according to Klein, on the internalization of good experience, "internal good objects." But the beginning durability of the ego and its relation to the object is constantly endangered by the automatic splitting processes "good mother—bad mother" and "good me—bad me." Only the gratifying, good mother elicits good feelings of fulfillment, and the good internal object makes the gratified child feel good himself. But an excess of bad experience with a frustrating mother makes the child hateful, enraged, bad, and fills him with bad emotional content that he tries to get rid of by elimination or denial. The bad internal object threatens the good internal object with destruction. [In this inner conflict, which characterizes the depressive position, Klein sees the first guilt feelings arise as predecessors of what is subsequently conscience or superego formation.] Because of the synthetic function of the ego, the dependence on the mother as a whole person so needed for survival and the guilty anxiety prompt the child into repair actions, magically designed to transform the bad mother into a good mother, to protect the good inner object against the onslaught of the bad one. One is here reminded of the words of Orestes after he had murdered his mother: "Save me, ye Gods, and save your image in my soul."[33] The guilty anxiety uses the magic of self-punishment, excessive crying spells, and rage directed against the child's own body.

According to Klein, this depressive position is constantly in danger

[33] See Goethe's *Iphigenie auf Tauris*.

of being reversed into the earlier "paranoid position," in which the infant was solely dominated by the urge to rid himself of bad inner and outer objects by projection or by manic denial and usurpation of self-sufficient omnipotence. Thus the depressive position is still dominated by the all-or-none principle. The good mother on whom the child depends for survival is idealized into perfection without blemish; and the bad mother appears disproportionately dreadful because of the child's helpless dependency. Only gradually these contrasts are melted into the unity of one realistic mother. Warm consistency on the part of both parents supports this natural process of integration. But parental incompetence, overindulgence, or excessive deprivations, as well as the child's constitutional oversensitivity or intensity of drives, his physical illness, and external pressures—such as a new pregnancy or hostile envy on the part of older siblings—might interfere with the secure harmony which guarantees the optimum in the child's integration with the family. Disrupting, disintegrating experiences are, according to Klein, accompanied by psychotic fears of phantastic proportions, since the lack of grasp on reality in the young child delivers him as a helpless victim to uncanny powers; this is reflected in his early nightmares and later in his fairy tales, his animal phobias, and other phobias.

According to Klein, paranoiac and depressive anxieties in early childhood are closely related. The more primitive persecutory anxiety is solely centered around the preservation of the ego and the object remains a partial object, incorporated as far as it is "good" or gratifying; but the object is eliminated, projected, and there with experienced as persecutor as far as it is frustrating or "bad." The later depressive anxiety is centered around the need to preserve the good object as a whole person, and it indicates a broadening of the child's horizon. The badness of his love object in this position spells to the child his own badness on the basis of introjection. The depressive anxiety is a guilty anxiety, coupled with the need to preserve the good object, with the tendency to make amends, to achieve magic repair. This tendency to repair, to make amends, stands in the service of the synthetic function of the ego. When separation anxieties can be surmounted, when repair succeeds, it contributes to a broadening integration of the child's ego and to a more realistic cementing of his labile object relations. Successful repair actions are the basis of sublimation—of all those creative activities by which the growing person maintains his own wholeness and his hopeful, trusting, integrative relations to his objects. One can say that without the stimulus of depressive anxieties, the child would never outgrow his early egocentricity, his fearful withdrawal, and his tendencies toward hostile projections. But an excess of depressive anxieties without successful experience of repair produces a fixation to the depressive position. It is this position to which the adult regresses whenever frustrating life experiences tax his integrative functions to such a degree that a creative conflict solution appears impossible. The manic reaction presents itself in this context as a pseudo-repair action, since a reconciliation with frustrating objects or goals is manipulated by the manic with the inadequate means of primitive defense—the splitting of good and bad, the phantastic idealization of the goal or object to be reached, and the hasty incorporation and contemptuous denial of the negative, frustrating aspect of the object or goal.

Many psychoanalysts have expressed doubts about Klein's observation that the child has Oedipus experiences in the first year of life. But there is much agreement with Klein's theory that there is no period of narcissistic self-sufficiency, that the infant is object-related from the start by introjection and projection, and that his claim for exclusive appropriation of his love object which guarantees his security in a world of unknown dangers makes him intensely anxious when he witnesses any intimacy between the parents that excludes him. Such intimacies jeopardize his equilibrium and elicit rage reactions which, in turn, are intensely alarming to the child because of his anxious cannibalistic destructiveness. In such early stages of Oedipus conflict as Klein sees it, the destructive possessiveness, and not the incestuous wishes, gives rise to guilty anxiety.

Although Klein's theories are partially deviant from psychoanalytic theory and may even sound fantastic to the psychiatrist who is reluctant to engage in any speculation on what is going on in the preverbal child, one cannot dismiss her empathic understanding of infantile emotions, impulses, and phantasies, which in the child's early verbal phase are expressed symbolically in his play. Her intuitive understanding is at least a working hypothesis for explaining the similarities between infantile and psychotic states of mind. The latter may seem enigmatic because of this very regression to early patterns unsuccessful integration.

Rado,[34] too, sees depression as a process of miscarried repair in his more recent work on manic-depressive psychoses. The depressive phase, he says, has a hidden pattern of meaning, and the observer must penetrate into the "unconscious"—the "nonreporting" parts of the patient's experience. The depresive spell is a desperate cry for love precipitated by loss of emotional or material security, an expiatory process of self-punishment, to reconcile and regain the aim-image of the gratifying mother's breast. The intended repair miscarries, Rado believes, because the dominant motivation of repentance is complicated by strong resentment. The depressed person wants to force his object to love him. The love-hungry patient's coercive rage has oral, biting, and devouring features. Fasting—the earliest and most enduring form of expiation—springs from the fear of having destroyed mother forever. Rado thinks that coercive rage increases self-esteem and pride, but that repentance makes the ego feel weak. Thus merciless rage, turned against the self, complicates repentance, since the absurdity of self-reproaches betrays the rage against the lost object. The patient is torn between coercive rage and submissive fear. If rage dominates, the patient has an agitated depression; if fear and guilt prevail, the patient experiences a retarded depression. These opposite tensions compete for discharge; and the phenomenon of "discharge-interference" leads to an interminable struggle. In therapy the physician may be inclined to treat the patient with overwhelming kindness in order to meet the patient's craving for affection. But when guilty fear and retroflexed rage are alarming in the sense of the danger of suicide, harsh treatment may provoke a relieving outburst of rage.

In general, Rado's work shows a commendable disinclination to engage in speculation. In addition, he strives to make psychoanalytic terminology understandable to scientists in related disciplines, and we agree that this kind of collaboration is needed if the goal of improved therapy is to be reached.

To summarize, the literature seems to show a wide divergency of opinion on the etiology of the manic-depressive psychosis. In surveying the literature we have laid particular stress on the development of the psychoanalytic literature since it is this approach which represents the

[34] S. Rado, "Psychosomatics of Depression from the Etiologic Point of View," reference footnote 8.

area of our interest. We have discussed at some length the work of Melanie Klein, since it is her approach which has proved to be closest to our own thinking.

FAMILY BACKGROUND AND CHARACTER STRUCTURE

Family Background

For all of the twelve patients studied, a consistent finding was made in regard to the family's position in its social environment. Each family was set apart from the surrounding milieu by some factor which singled it out as "different." This factor varied widely. In many instances it was membership in a minority group such as the Jews, as in the case of Mr. H. In others it was economic; for example, one patient's family had lost its money and was in a deteriorating social position, and in Mr. R's case, the father's illness and alcoholism had put the family in poor economic circumstances and in an anomalous social position. In another case, the difference resulted from the mother's being hospitalized for schizophrenia.

In every case, the patient's family had felt the social difference keenly and had reacted to it with intense concern and with an effort, first, to improve its acceptability in the community by fitting in with "what the neighbors think," and, second, to improve its social prestige by raising the economic level of the family, or by winning some position of honor or accomplishment. In both of these patterns of striving for a better social position, the children of the family played important roles; they were expected to conform to a high standard of good behavior, the standard being based largely on the parents' concept of what the neighbors expected. Thus Mr. R's mother was greatly overconcerned that he not walk in front of company in the living room, and Mr. H's mother threatened him with severe punishment when he misbehaved while out on the street with her. One mother described her early attitudes toward her child as follows:

I was always an independently minded person, not very demonstrative, so therefore most affection I may have had for anyone wasn't exactly worn on my sleeve. Kay I always loved and there was nothing I didn't try to get for her. My first thought, in most all my selfish material gains, was to get her things I had wanted or didn't have; to go places that I always longed to go to. Hasn't she ever told you of all the good times she has had? College proms, high school parties, dances, rides, silly girl incidents? I can remember so many she has had. Those were the things I had worked for her to have, and believe me, I had to fight to get them. . . . If you could have just an inkling of the unhappiness I have had trying to give her the material things I thought she wanted, for she never showed any love to me, perhaps you would understand my part. I always tried to protect her from the hurts that I had. . . .

These attitudes on the part of the parents—chiefly the mother— inculcated in the child a strict and conventional concept of good behavior, and also one which was derived from an impersonal authority— "they." The concept seemed to carry with it the connotation of parents whose own standards were but feebly held and poorly conceptualized, but who would be very severe if the child offended "them."

In addition to the depersonalization of authority, the use of the child as an instrument for improving the family's social position again acted as a force devaluing the child as a person in his own right. Not "who you are" but "what you do" became important for parental approval. Getting good grades in school, winning the approval of teachers and other authorities, receiving medals of honor, winning competitions, and being spoken of as a credit to the parents were the values sought by the parents from the child. In a few cases the family's isolation seemed to stem from the fact that they were "too good" for the neighboring families, due to the fact that they had more money or greater prestige. But here, too, the child's role was seen as being in service of the family's reputation.

In a number of cases, the child who was later to develop a manic-depressive psychosis was selected as the chief carrier of the burden of the winning prestige for the family. This could be because the child was the brightest, the best looking, or in some other way the most gifted, or because he was the oldest, the youngest, or the only son or only daughter.

The necessity for winning prestige was quite frequently inculcated most vigorously by the mother. She was usually the stronger and more determined parent, whereas the father was usually the weakling, the failure who was responsible for the family's poor fortunes. This was not invariably the case; thus one patient's mother had been hospitalized with schizophrenia from the patient's babyhood on. However, in the more typical cases, the mother an intensely ambitious person, sometimes directly aggressive, at other times concealing her drive beneath a show of martyrdom. She tended to devalue the father and to blame his weakness, lack of ambition, or other fault for the family's ill fortune. The mother of the patient referred to as Kay wrote in the following terms:

> About Kay's father, I'm afraid I can't tell you too much about him, because I was away a good deal, and didn't see too much of him. But as I remember him, I guess he was sort of a pathetic person, or at least I always had a feeling of pity. He had no real home; no immediate family; no decent jobs, at least on my opinion, and no real character.

This blaming of the father for the family's lack of position is in all likelihood due to the fact that in this culture the father is customarily the carrier of prestige, as well as being due to the peculiarities of the mother's relationship with him. The mother was usually thought of by the child as the moral authority in the family, and his attitudes toward her was usually cold and unloving, but fearful and desirous of approval. Blame was also leveled at the mothers by the fathers for their coldness and contemptuousness. It seemed that the consistent use of blaming attitudes was of importance in establishing the child's patterns of self-evaluation.

The fathers in the cases studied were thought of by their children as weak but lovable. Two fathers were unsuccessful doctors, one an unsuccessful lawyer, one an unsuccessful tailor, another simply a ne'er-do-well, and so on. By and large they earned some kind of a living for their families and did not desert them but they were considered failures because of their *comparative* lack of success in relation to the standard the family *should* have achieved. The fathers usually were dependent on their wives, although they sometimes engaged in rather futile rebellious gestures against the pressures put on them—as when Mr. H's father spent the evenings playing pool and gambling with his men friends instead of at home listening to his wife's nagging. But, on the whole, they apparently accepted the blame visited upon them and thus implied to their children, "Do not be like me." Each patient, in general, loved his father much more warmly than his mother, and often attempted to defend and justify the father for his lack of success; but in the very defense of the father the patient demonstrated his acceptance of his mother's standards. This pattern was seen to occur regardless of the patient's sex.

Another important contrast in the child's attitude toward his parents was that in his eyes the mother was the reliable one. Thus the child faced the dilemma of finding the unreliable and more-or-less contempt-ible parent the lovable one, and the reliable, strong parent the disliked one. This pattern also was quite consistent in most of the families of these patients, whether the patient was a boy or a girl. The attitude of the mother toward the father served in addition as a dramatic example of what might happen to the child should he fail to achieve the high goals set by the mother.

Early Development of the Child

Present-day concepts of the development of personality in infancy and early childhood no longer assume that the infant has no relationships with the people around him until he has reached the age of a year or so. Rather, it is believed that object relations develop from birth on, although it is obvious that early relationships must be quite different in quality from those experienced later on. Much evidence on infantile development in the early postnatal period[35] demonstrates that the infant reacts selectively to various attitudes in the mothering one. He thrives in an atmosphere of warmth, relaxation, and tenderness while he ex-periences digestive disorders, shows a variety of tension disorders, and even may die of marasmus in an atmosphere of tension, anxiety, and physical coldness. Under these circumstances, a vague, chaotic, and somewhat cosmic concept of another person—the mothering one—very soon begins to develop, and to this person the infant attributes his feelings of well-being or ill-being; this person is experienced as being extremely powerful.

We have compared the reports of the inner experiences of manic-depressives with those given by schizophrenic patients in regard to the times of greatest anxiety in each. While it is manifestly impossible to make specific constructions on the basis of such accounts, it is never-theless our impression that they support the conception that the major unresolved anxiety-provoking experiences of the manic-depressive pa-tient occur at a later stage in the development of interpersonal relation-

[35] See particularly Margaret Ribble, *The Rights of Infants;* New York, Columbia Univ. Press, 1943. See also Spitz, reference footnote 29.

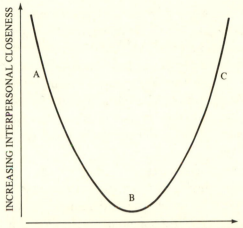

Figure 1.

ships than is the case with the schizophrenic. In the schizophrenic, a conception of self clearly differentiated from the surrounding world does not seem to have been developed, and the patient in panic believes that others are completely aware of his feelings, and that their actions are undertaken with this knowledge. The manic depressive seems not to experience this breaking down of the distinction between himself and others in times of intense anxiety; rather, he mobilizes defenses which preserve the awareness of self as distinct from others. This formulation has much in common with that of Melanie Klein.[36]

The common experience of therapists with the two disorders is to find the manic depressive much more irritating but much less frightening to work with than the schizophrenic. This may be related to the different concepts of self and others that the two groups of patients have.[37]

Figure 1 is intended to show pictorially the difference in interpersonal closeness and object relations between the schizophrenic and the manic-depressive characters.

Points A, B, and C represent successive stages in development. At and soon after birth (A), other persons—chiefly the mother—are hardly recognized as such; interpersonal closeness is great but is based upon

[36] Klein, reference footnote 30.
[37] For further discussion of this point see a later section of this paper on Differential Diagnosis of the Manic Depressive.

the intense dependence of the infant upon his mother. As relationships develop, the primary closeness based upon identification diminishes (B). Later, a more mature closeness begins to develop (C), in which the self is at last perceived as distinct and separate from other persons. It is evident that a critical phase in development (point B on the graph) occurs when the closeness with the mother based upon identification has begun to disappear, but the more mature type of relationship based on recognition of others as whole, separate persons has not as yet developed to any great degree.

We conceive of the major unresolved anxiety-provoking experiences of the schizophrenic patient as occurring at point A. At this phase of personality development, closeness is based upon identification, and relationships are partial in character. In the manic-depressive patient, these experiences would occur at point B, at a time when identification is less frequently used, but when the ability to relate to others as individuals distinct from one's self is in the earliest stage of development. Consequently, although relationships at point B are more mature than at point A, the individual in another sense is in a more isolated position, since he no longer employs the mechanism of identification to the degree that he did in earlier infancy but has yet to develop the capacity for a higher level of interpersonal relatedness. At this time, therefore, the developing child could be expected to feel peculiarly alone and consequently vulnerable to any threat of abandonment. We would conceive of the neurotic individual as having experienced his major unresolved anxiety experiences at point C, when interpersonal relatedness is more advanced than at B.

While reliable data about infancy are extremely difficult to gather, our series of manic-depressive patients shows a preponderance of normal infancies, with one major exception, Mr. R, who was a feeding problem and was malnourished and fretful for the first several months of his life. The mothers of these patients appear to have found the child more acceptable and lovable as infants than as children, when the manifold problems of training and acculturation became important. Our impression is that it was the utter dependence of the infant which was pleasurable to the mother, and that the growing independence and rebelliousness of the early stage of childhood were threatening to her. Unconforming or unconventional behavior on the part of the child was labelled as "bad" by the mother, and she exerted great pressure to stamp it out. Thus, the heretofore loving and tender mother would rather abruptly change into a harsh and punishing figure, at about the end of the first year. The child, under the stress of anxiety, would have difficulty integrating the early good mother and the later bad mother into a whole human being, now good, now bad. While a similar difficulty in integration may face all children, this split in attitude toward authority, in the more fortunate, is eventually resolved as the personality matures; but it remains with the manic depressive for the rest of his life unless interrupted by life experience or therapy. An important authority is regarded as the source of all good things, provided he is pleased; but he is thought of as a tyrannical and punishing figure unless he is placated by good behavior. These early experiences probably lay the groundwork for the manic-depressive's later ambivalence.

Later Development of the Child

In later childhood, when the child's personality traits and role in the family have begun to crystallize, the manic depressive may be likened to Joseph in the Bible story. Joseph was his father's favorite son. The envy of his eleven brothers was aroused by his father's giving him a multicolored coat, and was increased after they heard of two of Joseph's dreams. The first dream was about eleven sheaves bent down, and one standing upright; everybody knew that this represented Joseph with his eleven brothers bowing to him. In the other dream, eleven stars, the sun, and the moon were bowing to the twelfth star, and everybody agreed that this represented the mother, the father, and the eleven brothers bowing before Joseph. His envious brothers decided to kill him, but one of them, finding himself unable to agree to killing his own flesh and blood, influenced the others to throw him into a pit in the wilderness, and finally to sell him to a passing merchant from a foreign land. After his separation from his family, and his arrival in the foreign land, Joseph immediately grew in stature, and quickly rose to the position of the Pharaoh's first adviser. By his skill and foresight, he averted the evil effects of a threatening famine, not only in Egypt, but also in the neighboring countries.

This story can be used to illustrate some aspects of the manic-depressive's relationship to his family. Many of these patients are the best-endowed members of their families, excelling in some cases in specific creative abilities over their siblings, and over one or both of their parents. Some of them have a special place in the family as a result of their own ambitious strivings as, for example, Mr. H. Others are the favorites of one or both parents for other reasons, sometimes because they are the only one of their sex among the siblings, as in one of our patients. All this makes for their enviously guarding their special position in the family group, despite their being burdened with great responsibilities in connection with their special position. It also subjects them to the envy of their siblings, and, quite often, to the competition of one or both parents. Neither the patients themselves nor the family members are, generally speaking, aware of their mutual envy and competition. Mr. H's difficulties with envy were particularly acute. His therapist reported as follows:

Mr. H suffers from extreme feelings of envy toward his male contemporaries who have been more successful than he. The envy is so acute and painful that it is for the most part kept out of awareness. It occasionally forces itself upon his attention, particularly at times when someone of his contemporaries has received a promotion or other sign of success. The patient always feels that he deserves the promotion more than the other person and believes that his illnesses are the stumbling block in the way of his receiving it, or, at times, that the lack of recognition is due to anti-Semitism. While he is an extremely intelligent and able person who does his work adequately, except in periods of emotional disturbance, he does not visualize himself as succeeding on the basis of his productivity, and he makes little effort to succeed on the basis of doing a better job than his competitors. His efforts toward success are directed toward getting to be the friend of the boss, becoming a companion of the boss in sports or games, or going to the races with the boss. By getting the boss to like him especially or find him pleasant and agreeable to be with, he hopes to interest the boss in promoting his future. During his psychotic episodes this pattern increases in its scope and becomes a grandiose fantasy in which he is being groomed for the Presidency of the United States or in which the eye of some mysterious person is watching over him. He once said, for instance, "There is an organization, the FBI, which is set up to find the bad people and put them where they can't do any harm. Why should there not be a similar organization which has been set up to find the good people and see to it that they are put in a position of importance?"

As mentioned previously, manic depressives usually come from families who are in minority groups because of their social, economic, ethnic, or religious status. The family members in these minority groups cling together in group-conscious mutual love and acceptance, and in the wish and need to maintain and raise their family prestige in their groups, and their group prestige before an adverse outer world. There is little room for, or concern with, problems of interpersonal relatedness. Under the all-important requirement of seeking and maintaining high prestige, it seldom occurs to any member of these groups to think in terms other than "we belong together." This, then, is a background in which neither the active nor the passive participants in developments of envy and competition are aware of these developments. Yet, without being aware of it, the best-endowed children will spend quite a bit of energy to counteract the envy of the siblings, of which they are unconsciously afraid. Often the children are brought up, not only by their parents, but also by the joint endeavor of several other important older members of the clan. In spite of all this supervision, there is rarely an individual on whom a child can rely with confidence in a one-to-one relationship. In fact, it is frequently the case that the family group has a number of authority figures in it—grandparents, uncles, aunts, and so on—so that the child's experiences of authority are with multiple parent figures. In this setting, the manic depressive in very early childhood is frequently burdened with the family's expectation that he will do better than his parents in the service of the prestige of the family and the clan; consequently, he may feel, or be made to feel, responsible for whatever hardship or failure occurs in the family. For example, one of our patients was held responsible by her sisters for her mother's death when the patient was eighteen months old—"Mother would still be here had you not been born"; for the failure of her father's second marriage, which had been made to provide a mother for the patient; and for her father's "ruined" feet, the result of tramping the streets as a salesman after his position of considerable prominence had ended in bankruptcy. Another patient at the age of three felt that he had to take over certain responsibilities toward the clan, sensing that his parents had failed in the fulfillment of these.

The special role in the family group which these patients hold is accentuated by the fact that they are, as a rule, pushed very early into unusual responsibility, or else themselves assume this role. As a result, their image of the significant people in the family usually differs considerably from that of the other siblings. With their different appraisal of one or both of their parents, from early childhood they are extremely lonely, in spite of growing up in the group-conscious atmosphere which we have described, where there is little feeling for privacy, and where the little-differentiated experiences of the various family members are considered in the light of the common good of the whole family, or the whole clan. In many cases these people are unaware of their loneliness, as long as they are well, because the sentiment of "we belong together" is fostered by their family.

As these people grow up, they remain extremely sensitive to envy and competition. They know what it is like to harbor it themselves and to be its target. One means of counteracting this envy, which early becomes an unconscious pattern, is to undersell themselves to hide the full extent of their qualifications. Another pattern which many of these patients develop to counteract feelings of envying and being envied is to be exceptionally helpful to their siblings, to other members of the early group, and, later on, to other people with whom they come in contact in various ways. They often use their talents for promoting other persons and their abilities. The price they unconsciously demand for this is complete acceptance and preference by the others. These traits are repeated in the transference situation during treatment

For instance, a patient was brought to the hospital against her will, without any insight into her mental disturbance. Much to everybody's surprise, she most willingly entered treatment with one member of our group. Everything seemed to run in a smooth and promising way until suddenly, after about two weeks, the patient declared vehemently that she would continue treatment no longer. When she was asked for her reasons, she said that she had been under the impression that she might help her doctor, who was an immigrant, to establish herself professionally in the new country by allowing the doctor to treat her successfully. But during the two weeks she had been at the hospital, she had found that the doctor had already succeeded in establishing herself, and therefore the patient's incentive for treatment was gone.

The Adult Character

As adults, persons with cyclothymic personalities continue to manifest many of the same traits that they exhibited in childhood. During the 'healthy' intervals between attacks, they appear from a superficial point of view to be relatively well adjusted and at ease with other people. A certain social facility is typical of the hypomanic, although it is not seen so clearly in the depressive person in his 'healthy' intervals. For instance, the hypomanic typically has innumerable acquaintances with whom he appears to be on most cordial terms. On closer scrutiny of these relationships, however, it becomes apparent that they cannot be considered to be in any sense friendships or intimacies. The appearance of closeness is provided by the hypomanic's liveliness, talkativeness, wittiness, and social aggressiveness. Actually, there is little or no communicative exchange between the hypomanic and any one of his so-called friends. He is carrying out a relatively stereotyped social performance, which takes little or no account of the other person's traits and characteristics, while the other person, quite commonly, is allowing himself to be entertained and manipulated.

Both the hypomanic and the depressive share in their tendency to have one or a very few extremely dependent relationships. In the hypomanic this dependency is concealed under all his hearty good humor and apparent busyness, but it is quite clear in the depressive. The hypomanic or the depressive is extremely demanding toward the person with whom he has a dependent relationship, basing his claim for love and attention upon his need of the other, and making it a *quid pro quo* for his self-sacrifice. Demands are made for love, attention, service, and possessions. The concept of reciprocity is missing; the needs of the other for similar experiences are not recognized.[38] Yet the failure to recognize the needs of the other does elicit unconscious guilt which may be manifested by the manic depressive's consciously thinking of himself as having given a great deal. What the giving seems to amount to is a process of underselling himself. In the relationship the devaluation and underselling also indicate to the partner the person's great need of him, and serve to counteract the old, unconscious, fearful expectation of competition and envy from the important person. The cyclothymic person's own envy and competition, too, are hidden from his awareness, and take the form of feelings of inferiority and great need. The person conceives of himself as reaching success, satisfaction, or glory through the success of the other rather than by efforts of his own. Thus Mr. H made himself the stooge of the president of the class in high

----

[38] This formulation is similar to that made by O. Spurgeon English, who states, "Closely tied up with the matter of love is the patient's self-esteem or love of himself. The manic-depressive does not seem to have much feeling of love to give, and what he has he is afraid to give." English, "Observation of Trends in Manic-Depressive Psychosis," Psychiatry (1949) 12:125–133; p. 129.

school, receiving as his reward the political plums that the president was able to hand out, and failing to recognize that what he actually wanted was to be class president himself. He continued this kind of relationship with some important figure—usually male—in every free period afterward, while in his psychotic attacks the wish to be president himself came to consciousness, and he made futile efforts to achieve it.

Thus, the process of underselling themselves, both for the sake of denying envy and in order to become the recipient of gifts from the other, often reaches the point where these persons actually paralyze the use of their own endowments and creative abilities. They themselves frequently believe that they have lost their assets or that they never had any. The process of underselling themselves, especially in depressives, also may convince other people in their environment of their lack of ability. At this point, they begin to hate these other people for being the cause of the vicious circle in which they are caught; and they hate themselves because they sense the fraudulence of their behavior in not having expressed openly all their inner feelings.

One patient said time and again during his depression, "I'm a fraud, I'm a fraud; I don't know why, but I'm a fraud." When he was asked why he felt fraudulent, he would produce any number of rationalizations, but at last it was found that the thing he felt to be fraudulent was his underselling of himself. This same patient got so far in his fraudulent attempt at denying his total endowment that he was on the verge of giving up a successful career—which, while he was well, held a good deal of security and satisfaction for him—in order to regain the love of an envious friend, which he felt he was in danger of losing because of his own greater success.

We see then, in the adult cyclothymic, a person who is apparently well adjusted between attacks, although he may show minor mood swings or be chronically overactive or chronically mildly depressed. He is conventionally well-behaved and frequently successful, and he is hard-working and conscientious; indeed at times his overconscientiousness and scrupulousness lead to his being called obsessional. He is typically involved in one or more relationships of extreme dependence, in which, however, he does not show the obsessional's typical need to control the other person in for the sake of power, but instead seeks to control the other person in the sense of swallowing him up. His inner feeling, when he allows himself to notice it is one of emptiness and need. He is extremely stereotyped in his attitudes and opinions, tending to take over the opinions of the person in his environment whom he regards as an important authority. Again this contrasts with the outward conformity but subtle rebellion of the obsessional. It should be emphasized that the dependency feelings are largely out of awareness in states of well-being and also in the manic phase; in fact, these people frequently take pride in being independent.

His principal source of anxiety is the fear of abandonment. He is afraid to be alone, and seeks the presence of other people. Abandonment is such a great threat because his relationships with others are based upon utilizing them as possessions or pieces of property. If he offends them, by differing with them or outcompeting them, and they withdraw, he is left inwardly empty, having no conception of inner resources to fall back on. Also, if they offend him and he is compelled to withdraw, this leaves him similarly alone. In this situation of potential abandonment, the anxiety is handled by overlooking the emotional give-and-take between himself and others, so that he is unaware of the other person's feelings toward himself or of his feelings toward the other. This is clearly seen in the well-known difficulty which therapists have in terminating an hour with a depressive. Regardless of what has gone on during the hour, at the end of it the depressive stands in the doorway, plaintively seeking reassurance by some such question as "Am I making any progress, Doctor?" An attempt to answer the question only leads to another or to a repetition of the same one, for the patient is not seeking an answer—or rather does not actually believe there is an answer—but instead is striving to prolong his contact with the doctor. In carrying out this piece of sterotyped behavior, he is unaware of the fact of the doctor's mounting impatience and irritation, and overlooks its consequence—namely, that instead of there being increasing closeness between patient and doctor, a situation has now been set up in which the distance between them is rapidly increasing.

This character structure can be seen to have a clear-cut relationship to the infantile development which we have hypothesized for the manic depressive. According to this hypothesis, interpersonal relations have been arrested in their development at the point where the child recognizes himself as being separate from others, but does not yet see others as being full-sized human beings; rather he sees them as entities who are now good, now bad, and must be manipulated. If this is the case, then the adult's poorness of discrimination about others is understandable. His life and welfare depend upon the other's goodness, as he sees it, and he is unable to recognize that one and the same person may be accepting today, rejecting tomorrow, and then accepting again on the following day. Nor can he recognize that certain aspects of his behavior may be acceptable while others are not; instead, he sees relationships as all-or-none propositions. The lack of interest in and ability to deal with interpersonal subtleties is probably also due to the fact that the important persons in the child's environment themselves deal in conventional stereotypes. The child, therefore, has little opportunity at home to acquire skill in this form of communication.

We have said little in this report about the manic depressive's hostility. We feel that it has been considerably overstressed as a dynamic factor in the illness. Certainly, a great deal of the patient's behavior leaves a hostile impression upon those around him, but we feel that the driving motivation in the patient is the one we have stressed—the feeling of need and emptiness. The hostility we would relegate to a secondary position: we see hostile feelings arising in the patient as the result of frustration of his manipulative and exploitative needs. We conceive of such subsequent behavior, as demandingness toward the other or self-injury, as being an attempt to restore the previous dependent situation. Of course, the demandingness and exploitativeness are exceedingly annoying and anger-provoking to those around the patient—the more so because of the failure of the patient to recognize what sort of people he is dealing with. But we feel that much of the hostility that has been imputed to the patient has been the result of his annoying impact upon others, rather than of a primary motivation to do injury to them.

The Psychotic Attack

The precipitation of the depressive attack by a loss is well known. However, there have been many cases in which attacks have occurred where there has been no loss. In some it has seemed that a depression occurred at the time of a promotion in job or some other improvement in circumstances. On scrutiny it can be seen that in those patients where a depression has occurred without an apparent change in circumstances of living, the change which has actually occurred has been in the patient's appraisal of the situation. The patient incessantly hopes for and strives for a dependecy relationship in which all his needs are met by the other. This hope and the actions taken to achieve it are for the most part out of awareness since recognition of them would subject the person to feelings of guilt and anxiety. After every depressive attack, he set forth upon this quest anew. In the course of time, it becomes apparent to him that his object is not fulfilling his needs. He then gets into a vicious circle: he uses depressive techniques—complaining or whining—to elicit the gratifications he requires. These become offensive to the other who becomes even less gratifying; therefore, the patient redoubles his efforts and receives still less. Finally, he loses hope and enters into the psychotic state where the pattern of emptiness and need is repeated over and over again in the absence of any specific object.

As to the person who becomes depressed after a gain rather than a loss, we interpret this as being experienced by the patient himself as a loss, regardless of how it is evaluated by the outside world. Thus a promotion may remove the patient from a relatively stable dependency relationship with his co-workers or with his boss, and may call upon him to function at a level of self-sufficiency which is impossible for him. Also, being promoted may involve him in a situation of severe anxiety because of the envious feelings which he feels it will elicit in others, the fear occurring as a result of his unresolved childhood pattern of envying those more successful than himself and, in return, expecting and fearing the envy of others at his success. Having made them envious, he may believe that he can no longer rely on them to meet his needs, whereupon he is again abandoned and alone. For example, an episode from Mr. R's life was described by his analyst as follows:

After about a year of treatment it was suggested to the patient by one of his fellow officers that he ought to apply for a medal for his part in the war and he found the idea very tempting. When this was discussed with me, I attempted to discourage it, without coming out directly with a strong effort to interfere, and the discouraging words I said were unheard by the patient. He went ahead with a series of manipulative acts designed to win the medal, and it was awarded to him. No sooner had he received it than he became acutely anxious and tense. He began to suspect his compeers of envying him and plotting to injure him in order to punish him for having taken advantage of them by getting a medal for himself, and he thought that his superior officers were contemptuous of him for his greediness. His life became a nightmare of anxiety in which he misinterpreted the smiles, glances, gestures, hellos, and other superficial behavior of his fellow officers as signifying their hatred and disapproval of him.

The manic attack is similar to the depressive in following a precipitating incident which carries the meaning of a loss of love. It often happens that there is a transient depression before the outbreak of manic behavior. For instance, Mr. H was mildly depressed at Christmas time; his behavior from then on showed increasing evidence of irrationality which, however, was not striking enough to cause alarm until June, when he developed a full-blown manic attack. We believe, from our experience with patients who have had repeated attacks, that the presence of depressive feelings prior to the onset of the manic phase is very common, and perhaps the rule.

It is well known that many manic patients report feelings of depression during their manic phase. As one of our patients put it, while apparently manic:

I am crying underneath the laughter. . . . Blues all day long—feelings not properly expressed. Cover up for it, gay front while all the time I am crying. Laughing too much and loud hurts more. Not able to cry it complete and full of hell. All pinned up inside but the misery and hatred is greater than the need to cry. Praying for tears to feel human. Wishing for pain in hopes that there is something left. Fright is almost indescribable.

We agree with Freud, Lewin, and others that dynamically the manic behavior can best be understood as a denfensive structure utilized by the patient to aviod recognizing and experiencing in awareness his feelings of depression. The timing of the manic behavior varies widely: it may either precede the depression, in which case it can be understood as a defense which has eventually failed to protect the patient from his depression; or it may follow the depressive attack, when it represents an escape from the unbearable depressive state into something more tolerable. Subjectively, the state of being depressed is one more intolerable discomfort than the state of being manic, since the patient in effect is threatened with loss of identity of his self.

There are personalities who are able to lead a life of permanent hypomania, with no psychotic episodes. Of course, many chronic hypomanics do have psychotic episodes, but there are some who never have to be hospitalized. Such a patient was Mr. R, who had a very narrow escape from hospitalization when he became agitatedly depressed at a time when several severely anxiety-producing blows occurred in rapid succession. On the whole, however, he maintained what appeared to be an excellent reality adjustment. Subjectively, he was usually constrained to avoid thinking of himself and his feelings by keeping busy, but when he did turn his attention inward, then intense feelings of being in an isolated, unloved, and threatened position would arise.

We have noted in our private practices a trend in recent years for an increased number of persons who utilize rather typical hypomanic defense patterns to enter into analytic therapy. These people tend in general to be quite successful in a material sense and to conceal their sense of inward emptiness and isolation both from themselves and from others. Probably their entering analysis in increasing numbers has some correlation with the popular success achieved by psychoanalysis in recent years in this country. Once committed to treatment, these so-called extraverts rapidly reveal their extreme dependency needs, and, on the whole, our impression has been that psychoanalysis has proven decidedly beneficial to them.

In the light of the above discussion of the manic and depressive attacks, we have come to the conclusion that they need to be differentiated psychodynamically chiefly on the score of what makes the manic defense available to some patients while it is not so usable by others. Some investigators postulate a constitutional or metabolic factor here, but in our opinion adherence to this hypothesis is unjustified in the present state of our knowledge. We feel that further investigation of the manic defense is indicated before a reliable hypothesis can be set up.

We feel that the basic psychotic pattern is the depressive one. The onset of a depression seems understandable enough in the light of the patient's typical object-relation pattern described earlier. That is, becoming sick, grief-stricken, and helpless is only an exaggeration and intensification of the type of appeal which the manic depressive makes to the important figures in his life in the healthy intervals. When this type of appeal brings rejection, as it usually does when carried beyond a certain degree of intensity, then the vicious circle mentioned earlier can be supposed to set in, with each cycle representing a further descent on the spiral. At the end, the patient is left with his severely depressed feelings and with no feeling of support or relatedness from the people whom he formerly relied on. At this point, where the feelings of depression and emptiness are acute, the patient may follow one of three courses: he may remain depressed; he may commit suicide; or he may regress still further to a schizophrenic state.

If he remains depressed, he carries a chronic, largely fantastic acting-out of the pattern of dependency. There is no longer a suitable object. The members of the family who have hospitalized him are now only present in fantasy. The patient does, however, continue to address his complaints and appeals to them as though they were still present and powerful. In addition, he rather indiscriminately addresses the same appeal to all of those around him in the hospital. The appeal may be mute, acted out by his despair, sleeplessness, and inability to eat, or it may be highly vociferous and addressed verbally to all who come in contact with him, in the form of statements about his bowels being blocked up, his insides being empty, his family having been bankrupted or killed, and so on. The same pattern is developed with his therapist: instead of a therapeutic relationship in which he strives to make use of the doctor's skill with some confidence and notion of getting somewhere, the same empty pattern of mourning and hopelessness is set up, in which he strives to gain help by a display of his misery and to receive reassurance by repeatedly requesting it. It is notable and significant that his ability to work on or examine the nature of his relationships is nonexistent; that difficulties with others are denied and self-blame is substituted. the major therapeutic problem with the depressive is actually the establishment of a working relationship in which problems are examined and discussed. Conversely, the major system of defenses which have to be overcome in order to establish such a working relationship lie in the substitution of the stereotyped complaint or self-accusation for a more meaningful kind of self-awareness. There seems to be a sort of clinging to the hope that the repetition of the pattern will eventually bring fulfillment. Relinquishing the pattern seems to bring with it the danger of suicide on the one hand, or disintegration on the other. It is our opinion that, in the situation in which the patient has given up his habitual depressive pattern of integration and has as yet not developed a substitute pattern which brings some security and satisfaction, he is in danger of suicide. The suicide as has been well demonstrated by previous workers, has the meaning of a further, highly irrational attempt at relatedness. It can be thought of as the final appeal of helplessness. "When they see how unhappy I really am, they will do something." This fits in with the almost universal fantasy indulged in by most people in moments of frustration and depression of what "they" will say and do when I am dead. Along with this magical use of death to gain one's dependent ends, goes a fantasy of recapturing the early relationship by dying and being born again.

For instance, Miss G took an overdose of barbiturates as a last resort after her failure to persuade her father to accede to a request by other means. It appeared that in this case there was little intent to die, but that the action was resorted to because lesser means of convincing him had failed. Probably in this instance of a conscious suicidal gesture the manipulative goal is much more apparent and more clearly in awareness than with the majority of cases. On the other hand, self-destruction also has a more rational element; that is, it is the final expression of the feeling that all hope is lost, and the wish to get rid of the present pain. We are inclined to believe that the element of hopelessness in the act of suicide has not been given sufficient weight in previous studies.

Sullivan, at the end of a great many years of studying the obsessional neurotic, came to the conclusion that many of the more severely ill cases were potentially schizophrenic in situations where their habitual and trusted obsessional defenses proved inadequate to deal with anxiety. This statement also applies to the depressive: if the defensive aspects of the depression become ineffectual, then a collapse of the personality structure can occur with an ensuing reintegration on the basis of a schizophrenic way of life rather than a depressive one.

Guilt and the Superego

We have avoided using the term superego in this report, and have not involved the cruel, punishing superego in our attempted explanation of the depression. It is our opinion that utilization of the term superego in this way merely conceals the problem rather than explains it. There are several basic questions regarding the problems of conscience and guilt in the manic depressive. First, what influences account for the severe and hypermoral standards of these people? And second, what is the dynamic function of the self-punishing acts and attitudes which are engaged in during the periods of illness?

The overcritical standards of manic depressives are not explicable as a direct taking-over of the standards of the parents, since these patients in childhood have usually been treated with rather exceptional overindulgence. However, in the section on Family Background and Character Structure we have mentioned the peculiar combination of lack of conviction of worth and a standard of behavior in the family coupled with an intense devotion to conventional morality and to what other people think. It is logical that a child raised by an inconsistent mother who is at times grossly overindulgent and at others severely rejecting would be unable to build up a reasonable code of conduct for himself, and that his code—focused around what an impersonal authority is supposed to expect of him and based on no concept of parental reliability or strength—would be both over severe and frightening in its impersonality. In all probability, much of his moral code is based on the struggle to acquire those qualities of strength and virtue which he finds missing in his parents. Later in this report we will return to the problem of authority in the manic depressive. Suffice it to say here that in dealing with authority this type of patient shows a rigid preconception of what authority expects of him as well as a persistent conviction that he must fit in with these expectations which are beyond the reach of reason or experience. The authority appears, in our experience, at times as an incorporated superego and at other times as a projected, impersonal, but tyrannical force. Or rather, every significant person in the patient's social field is invested with the quality of authority.

In this relationship with authority, the self-punitive acts and experiencing of guilt can be understood as devices for placating the impersonal tyrant. The guilt expressed by the depressive does not carry on to any genuine feeling of regret or effort to change behavior. It is, rather, a means to an end. Merely suffering feelings of guilt is expected to suffice for regaining approval. On the other hand, it may also be seen that achieving a permanent, secure, human relationship with authority is regarded as hopeless. Therefore, no effort to change relationships or to integrate on a better level of behavior is undertaken, and the patient merely resorts to the magic of uttering guilty cries to placate authority.

DIFFERENTIAL DIAGNOSIS OF THE MANIC DEPRESSIVE

Some observers have stated that in the intervals between attacks, the manic depressive has a character structure similar to that of the obsessional neurotic.[39] It has also been asserted that in the psychotic phase the manic-depressive illness is essentially schizophrenic. This

[39] See Abraham, reference footnote 10.

latter statement is supported by the fact that many manic depressives do, in the course of time, evolve into chronic schizophrenic psychoses, usually paranoid in character, and that there are many persecutory ideas present both in manic attack and in the depression. In general, there has always been much uncertainty as to who should be diagnosed manic depressive—an uncertainty which is reflected in the widely differing proportions of manic depressives and schizophrenics diagnosed in different mental hospitals.

What, then, is the point of singling out a diagnostic category called manic depressive? In our opinion, the manic-depressive syndrome does represent a fairly clear-cut system of defenses which are sufficiently unique and of sufficient theoretical interest to deserve special study. We feel that equating the manic-depressive character with the obsessional character overlooks the distinguishing differences between the two. The obsessional, while bearing many resemblances to the manic depressive, uses substitutive processes as his chief defense. The manic, on the other hand, uses the previously mentioned lack of interpersonal awareness as his chief defense, together with the defensive processes which are represented by the manic and the depressive symptoms themselves. The object relations of the obsessional are more stable and well developed than those of the manic depressive. While the obsessional's relations are usually integrations in which there is an intense degree of hostility, control, and envy, they do take into consideration the other person as a person. The manic depressive, on the other hand, develops an intensely dependent, demanding, oral type of relationship which overlooks the particular characteristics and qualities of the other.

According to Sullivan's conceptualization of the schizophrenic process, the psychosis is introduced typically by a state of panic, in which there is an acute break with reality resulting from the upsurge of dissociated drives and motivations which are absolutely unacceptable and invested with unbearable anxiety. Following this acute break, a variety of unsuccessful recovery or defensive processes ensue, which we call paranoid, catatonic, or hebephrenic. These represent attempts of the personality to deal with the conflicts which brought about the panic: the paranoid by projection; the catatonic by rigid control; the hebephrenic by focussing on bodily impulses. According to this conception, the manic depressive can be differentiated from the schizophrenic by the fact that he does not exhibit the acute break with reality which is seen in the schizophrenic panic. On the other hand, his psychotic processes of depression, or of mania, can be thought of as serving a defensive function against the still greater personality disintegration which is represented by the schizophrenic state. Thus, in persons whose conflicts and anxiety are too severe to be handled by depressive or manic defenses, a schizophrenic breakdown may be the end result.

Contrasting the schizophrenic and the manic depressive from the point of view of their early relationships, we see that the schizophrenic has accepted the bad mother as his fate, and his relation to reality is therefore attenuated. He is inclined to withdraw into detachment. He is hypercritical of family and cultural values. He is sensitive and subtle in his criticisms, original but disillusioned. He is disinclined to rely on others and is capable of enduring considerable degrees of loneliness. His reluctance to make demands on the therapist makes the therapist feel more sympathetic, and therefore the therapist is frequently more effective. In addition, the schizophrenic patient is more effective in his aggression; he can take the risk of attacking, for he is less afraid of loneliness. He is more sensitively aware of the emotions of the therapist, since the boundaries between ego and environment are more fluid. The schizophrenic is not inclined to pretend, and is not easily fooled by other people's pretenses. Dream and fantasy life are nearer to awareness, and guilt feelings are also more conscious than unconscious.

The typical manic depressive, on the other hand, has not accepted the "bad mother" as his fate. He vacillates between phases in which he fights with the bad mother, and phases in which he feels reunited with the good mother. In the manic phase, his relationship with reality is more tenuous; he shows a lack of respect for other people, and all reality considerations are dismissed for the sake of magic manipulation to make the bad mother over into a good mother. The manic depressive is, therefore, mostly a good manipulator, a salesman, a bargaining personality. He is undercritical instead of being hypercritical. He easily sells out his convictions and his originality in order to force others to love him, deriving from this a borrowed esteem. In the depressive phase, he sacrifices himself to gain a good mother or to transform the bad mother into a good one. In order to do this, he calls himself bad, and suffers to expiate his sins. But these guilt feelings are, in a sense, artificial or expedient, utilized in order to manipulate the bad mother into becoming a good mother. The depressive does not come to terms with realistic guilt feelings. Instead, he uses his self-accusations, which frequently sound hypocritical, to convince the mother or a substitute that his need to be loved has absolute urgency. He denies his originality because he is terribly afraid of aloneness. He is more of a follower than a leader. He is dependent on prestige, and is quite unable to see through the pretense of his own or other people's conventionalities. He shows a high degree of anxiety when his manipulations fail. His denial of originality leads to feelings of emptiness and envy. His lack of subtlety in interpersonal relationships is due to his overruling preoccupation with exploiting the other person in order to fill his emptiness. This operates as a vicious circle: he has to maintain his claims for the good fulfilling mother, but his search for fullness via manipulation of another makes him feel helpless and empty. This incorporation of another person for the purpose of filling an inward emptiness, of acquiring a borrowed self-esteem, is very different from the lack of ego boundaries in the schizophrenic. The schizophrenic is in danger of losing his ego, and he expresses this danger in fantasies of world catastrophe. The manic depressive is threatened by object loss, since he habitually uses the object to patch up his ego weakness. Object relations in the manic depressive are, therefore, clouded by illusions, but even when he wails, demands, and blames the frustrating object, he is—by this very agitated activity in behalf of his own salvation, ineffective as it may be—defended against the loss of the ego. When the manic depressive becomes schizophrenic, this defense breaks down.

It should be noted that the infantile dependency and manipulative exploitativeness seen in the manic depressive are not unique to this type of disorder. They occur, in fact, in many forms of severe mental illness. The hysteric, for instance, exemplifies infantile dependency and exploitativeness as dramatically as the manic depressive, and in *la belle indifférence* one may see a resemblance to the euphoria of the manic or hypomanic. However, the combination of the dependent and exploitative traits with the other outstanding characteristics of the cyclothymic personality—particularly the communicative defect and the accompanying inability to recognize other persons as anything but good-bad stereotypes and the conventional but hypermoralistic values—does become sufficiently distinct and unique to distinguish these patients characterologically from other types.

PROBLEMS IN THERAPY

Transference

The diagnosis of manic-depressive character has, in the past, been made largely on the basis of the patient's exhibiting the classic manic and depressive symptomatology. It can, however, be as validly made on the basis of the transference-countertransference pattern, which is set up between the patient and the therapist. The transference pattern is particularly characteristic; the countertransference pattern would, of course, vary considerably according to the personality of the therapist, although it, too, shows a number of quite typical features.

The transference pattern shows two outstanding characteristics which could be labeled (1) the exploitative clinging dependency, and (2) the stereotyped approach to other persons, who are not seen as personalities in their own right.

(1) The dependency. Other workers in the field of the study of manic-depressive illnesses have amply documented the deep-seated dependency of this type of person (Abraham, Freud, Rado, Klein). The dependency attitudes toward the object are highly ambivalent. Gratification is demanded,[40] but not accepted or experienced as such, and the patient feels that attention, care, and tendernes must be forced from the other person. The force applied is that of demonstrating to the other person how miserable he is making one, how much the depressed one needs the other, and how reponsible and culpable the other is if he fails to meet the depressive's needs. The demands are not directly verbalized

---

[40] We use the term "demand" to denote unrealistic and inappropriate requests as distinguished from those requests which are appropriate in the treatment situation. The "demand" type of request seems to spring from a need which is essentially unfulfillable. That is, there is no realistic action the therapist can take which will make the patient feel satisfied. When the things asked for—such as extra time, reassurance, and so on—are granted, they do not lead to a feeling of satisfaction on the patient's part.

but rather consist of a wordless exploitation; the reactive hostility is not experienced as such, but instead is experienced as depression.

In the depths of the depression, it seems impossible to satisfy the patient's dependency needs. As one therapist put it, the patient seems to be saying, "I am starving, and I won't get what I need." The amount of time and attention the patient receives does not suffice to give him a sense of satisfaction. He remains depressed, crying out for more. We have not tried the experiment of spending the major portion of each day with a depressive person. Certainly 24-hour-a-day nursing does not suffice to give the patient a sense of gratification. Whether unlimited time from a therapist would have more effect is debatable in the light of our experience with Mr. R, which will be discussed in more detail in the section on Therapeutic Techniques. This type of demandingness is typical of the depressive aspects of the illness. When the patient is in a period of relative mental health, these needs are less apparent. This raises the question of what becomes of these needs during such periods: Are they not present and only stirred up again when some unusual deprivation or threat to security occurs, or are they successfully kept in repression during the healthy phases? We have commented on this question in the section on The Adult Character.

In the manic phase, the demandingness is much more open but is seen by the patient as demanding his rights rather than as asking for favors. Rejection of the demands is met with overt hostility rather than with a depressive response. The manic, of course, shows, in addition to the demandingness, the tendency to take what he needs by force, if necessary, and he will use direct aggression—in contrast to the depressive, who uses reproaches against the other person as a forcing maneuver.

(2) *The stereotyped response.* The manic-depressive personality shows a highly characteristic tendency to look upon others as stereotyped repetitions of parental figures. This has been described elsewhere in this report as "a lack of interpersonal sensitivity." The therapist is regarded (a) as an object to be manipulated for purposes of getting sympathy and reassurance, (b) as a moral authority who can be manipulated into giving approval, and (c) as, in actuality, a critical and rejecting authority figure who will not give real approval but can be counted on only for token approval which can be achieved by proper

behavior or manipulation. This uncritical categorization of the therapist results in the patient's inability to use the therapist to provide himself with a fresh point of view. Everything that the therapist says is reworked into the old pattern of concealed disapproval covered over with the sugar of artificial reassurance. This impenetrability to the reception of new ideas from the therapist represents one of the great obstacles in therapy with this type of patient, who will give lip service to the role of the therapist as a noncritical authority without a feeling of conviction that this is so. However, the lip service itself then becomes incorporated into the set of manipulative acts which will receive approval and adds another bukwark to the defense.

Early in the study of these patients, it was felt that the lack of ability to appraise the therapist as a person represented a real learning defect in the patient and that one of the therapeutic tasks therefore was a somewhat educational one of showing the patient how one person could be different from another. On further study we have come to the conclusion that the defect is not an educational one, evidence for this being that as the anxiety diminishes in an interpersonal relation, the sensitivity increases. Mr. R is an excellent illustration of this point. His therapist spoke of him as follows:

When the patient first entered treatment, I would have described him as being without the ability to empathize with another. During the subsequent years of treatment, it became apparent that the patient was acutely sensitive to nuances in the attitude of others to him, but that his interpretation of these attitudes was extremely static and stereotyped. Finally, at the end of treatment, he retained much of his sensitivity but had also gained in his ability to respond with accuracy in interpersonal situations.

Mr. R's sensitivity is illustrated by the following incident:

The patient wished to make a change in his Army assignment. The therapist was, he believed, in a position to use her influence to get him the new assignment. He did not ask the therapist to use her influence except by implication; that is, he wrote a letter stating what his plans were about getting the new assignment, and, reading between the lines, it became apparent to the therapist that she was expected to offer to use what influence she had to bring this about. This indirect request was answered indirectly by the therapist with an encouraging letter in which no offer was made to intervene on the patient's behalf. The patient became depressed in a matter of weeks, and when he next saw the therapist, his statement was that the therapist obviously did not approve of his new plans and believed him to be incapable of the change of job which he had wished for. The interpretation was promptly made that these were projections which had been precipitated by his unverbalized request and his unconscious resentment when his request was not met. The patient accepted the interpretation without hesitation and the projected hostile belittling attitudes attributed to the therapist were immediately dropped and the patient's further discussion continued on a more realistic basis.

Another therapist expressed her experience with a patient in the following way:

The discontinuity between what she thinks and how she acts, and the impression of routinization or mimicry in both, seems to come from deficiency in the function of empathy from the rest of her activity, so that the rest of her activity, both thinking and acting, is without a dimension which seems to give it depth, at least in communicating about it . . . The schizophrenic, in contrast, seems to have adequate development of the function of empathy. He has had his experiences in that medium, and utilized them, and the patient-physician communication in the medium is much as with any so-called normal person, except for the patient's abnormal sensitivity and his misinterpretations. . . . I extend myself actively to engage empathically with these [manic-depressive] patients. I keep in mind that I am talking to the patients not so much verbally as preverbally. I use the verbal communication as a means of carrying inflection and an accompaniment of facial expression and postural components. And with such patients at the end of an hour I often find I have the greatest difficulty recollecting what the verbal exchanges as such have been, because my concentration has been so much on the empathic component.

In this discussion, the therapist is using the term "empathic exchange" to signify an essentially nonverbal communication of affect or meaning. We have used a variety of descriptive phrases, including "a lack of interpersonal sensitivity" and "the stereotyped response." These two terms attempt to describe the same phenomenon as the therapist is describing in terms of a maldevelopment of the empathic function. The phenomenon is observed by a multitude of therapists but not yet satisfactorily understood, as witness the multiplicity of descriptive phrases. We feel that it is closely related dynamically to the difficulty in object relationships mentioned in the section on Early Development of the Child. There the developmental defect in the child who will later become a manic depressive is described as a failure to integrate the early part-objects into wholes and instead the retention of the concept of a separate good and bad mother. Approaching the problem from the point of view of present-day relationships, we suggest that it is anxiety-arousing for the manic depressive to recognize others as persons, as well as to conceive of himself as a person in his own right. It is probable that the intolerable aspect of this is the recognizing of good and bad traits in one and the same person; this requires a certain amount of independence—that is, the ability to deal with the good and put up with the bad. The manic depressive's recognition of bad or unacceptable traits in another person would interfere with his dependency on him; it would be necessary for him to abandon the other person for his badness, and this would then leave him alone. In order to avoid this anxiety, the manic depressive avoids the recognition and identification of the medley of attractive and unpleasant traits in others, and thereby avoids the exchange of a variety of complex feelings. Thus, as is so often true in psychopathology, what begins as a developmental defect ends up as an anxiety-avoiding defense.

Technical Problems

There are two major technical problems in dealing with the manic-depressive patient which derive logically from the transference picture as developed above. These are the technical problems related to meeting the dependency needs and the technical problems related to breaking through the stereotyped characterization of the therapist. The dilemma with regard to dependency can be stated as follows: Attempts to meet the dependency needs and to permit the type of manipulation that the patient characteristically engages in merely support the present way of relating. Our experience has shown us that the assumption of the classical passive and accepting role of the therapist tends to imply to the patient that his dependency needs are being met or will be met. There is, of course, considerable frustration for the patient in the therapist's non-intervention in any active way in the direction of meeting the patient's needs when the classical psychoanalytic technique is used. However, this does not seem to suffice to interfere with patient's fantasy that the therapist will be, or can be induced to be, the sort of giving parental figure whom the patient is looking for, and it therefore seems that something more active is needed in terms of a denial by the therapist that he will play the role the patient wishes him to play. The opposite tactic of actively rejecting the patient's demands is equally or even more undesirable, since this then reinforces the patients belief that he is bad, and tends to push him in the direction of redoubling his efforts to please the harsh authority and thereby receive the blessings of approval, and so on. Furthermore, in both of these types of therapeutic approach, the threat of suicide is an ever present, although perhaps not verbalized, obstacle. In our experience suicide during therapy frequently occurs under the following conditions: The patient establishes his characteristic dependency relationship and enters into his characteristic fantasies of gratification. He then experiences something in the relationship which he interprets as a rejection. Following this he becomes hopeless about achieving his goal and then he becomes suicidal. In other words, as long as the patient hopes that he can get the gratification from the object, the danger of suicide is less. Consequently, any therapeutic situation which implicitly promises to the patient that he can get his need gratified is running the risk of the patient's finally discovering the hopelessness of this search and becoming suicidal.

Following these considerations a step further, it seems logical to suppose that a relatively active denial of the role in which the patient casts the therapist must be present from the beginning of treatment. This is extremely difficult to achieve. One of the countertransference difficulties, which will be discussed later, is the fact that the therapist unconsciously frequently falls into a variety of ways of meeting the patient's demands without being fully aware of the fact that he has been manipulated.

The second major technical difficulty—that of breaking through the patient's stereotyped response sufficiently to introduce new concepts to the patient, and to free his own feelings—is not, of course, unique to the treatment of the manic depressive, although it does represent quantitatively a greater obstacle with these patients. It has become a truism of psychotherapy that a patient with a distorted attitude toward others tends to relate himself to new persons in such a way as to perpetuate his own problem. This process has been named *selective inattention* by Sullivan. Thus one who believes in his own unlovability will observe and react only to the rejecting elements in the attitude of the people around him, utilizing his observations to continually confirm the "fact" that people don't like him. The rigidity with which such a point of view is maintained varies with the severity of the illness and the strength of the anxiety, and is much more difficult to deal with in the psychoses than in the neuroses. However, in the manic depressive, the problem is reinforced by the stereotyped defense mentioned earlier.

This is in contrast to the schizophrenic, who notices nuances of expression and inflection, frequently in clear awareness, and then distorts their meaning. Thus a schizophrenic patient will note his therapist's tension as manifested, perhaps, by his swinging his leg during the interview. Having noticed it as tension, he will then attach a meaning to it which is inappropriate. For instance, he may interpret it as meaning that the therapist is sexually attracted to him. The manic or depressed patient will not take note of the tension phenomenon in the therapist; there may be a subliminal noticing of what goes on, but it is not sufficiently in awareness to be given a meaning. If the patient has such an occurrence called to his attention and is asked to put a meaning to it, the interpretation will fall into the category of the therapist's expressing boredom or disapproval of him. With the schizophrenic, therefore, the problem boils down to correcting a misinterpretation of an observed event; with the manic depressive, both the observation and the interpretation are awry. Once the awareness of signals from other persons is more accessible to the manic depressive, the misinterpretation is more easily corrected than in the schizophrenic.

Countertransference

While countertransference problems in the treatment of manic depressives must necessarily vary with the personality of the therapist, there are a number of quite general responses generated in therapists which are deserving of notice. Perhaps the most striking one of these is the fact that of those psychoanalysts who are working with psychotics, the large majority prefer working with schizoid and schizophrenic patients and tend to avoid those in the manic-depressive category. This preference has been thought by us to relate to the type of character structure found in the therapists. Such persons are usually schizoid or obsessional in character themselves and as such are rather subtle, introverted persons who are interested in the observation of their own and others' reactions. The extraverted, apparently unsubtle manic depressive is a threat to such therapists in several ways. In the first place, communicative efforts are a strain because of the lack of response. Secondly, the so-called healthy extraverted approach to reality is likely to fill the more sensitive, introspective person with self-doubts as to the possibility that he makes mountains out of molehills, reads meanings in where none were meant, and so forth; one of our therapists had particular difficulty in speaking of feelings with a manic patient, on the basis that the patient would regard all that as foolishness. Thirdly, the therapist tends to dislike this sort of person and to think of him as "shallow." And, finally, the patient's difficulty in recognizing or discussing his or another's feelings or meanings throws the therapist into a situation of helplessness, since these things are the coin in which he deals. An interpretation which is highly meaningful to the therapist, and which he would expect to have a tremendous impact on one of his obsessional or schizoid patients, is hardly noticed by his manic-depressive patient. One therapist describes this difficulty with a patient as follows:

The outstanding therapeutic problem during this period was that of getting the patient to think in terms of "psychic causality"; that is, recognize that there was a connection between what he experienced in his dealings with others and the way he felt. He was unable to recognize, for instance, that when someone did something to slight him, this would lead to his having hurt feelings. His feeling-response to the happenings of his life was out of awareness. This can be illustrated by an incident: He was doing some part-time teaching in a night law school, and at Christmas time the students gave presents to the various members of the faculty. Since the patient had been a faculty member for only a very short time, he received a small present, a necktie, while some of the other teachers received much more magnificent ones. Following this event, the patient came to his hour and complained of not feeling well. As he went through his account of the happenings of his life during the previous few days, the fact that he had received a Christmas present was mentioned. He did not, however, mention any comparison between the size of his gift and that of others, or any feeling of being wounded that he had not received a finer gift. Largely by chance, I inquired in more detail about the Christmas giving at this school, and as I did so, I heard the full story. It was still not apparent to the patient that he had felt hurt and did not become apparent to him until I asked him whether he had felt hurt. When I asked the question, he then realized that he had been hurt. He was then able to go on and see that his feeling of depression had been initiated by this episode. However, without actually having his feeling experience identified for him and named by me, he was unable spontaneously to recognize it.

We have wondered whether, on the basis of these facts, a more appropriate choice of therapist for the manic-depressive could not be made from among the psychiatrists who have, character-wise, something in common with them. Our data on this point is largely impressionistic, but among the therapists who have participated in this seminar there has seemed to be some tendency for greater success and greater preference for this type of patient among those with characters more nearly approaching the manic depressive than the schizoid. It should also be noted, however, that as our familiarity with the problems of the manic-depressive person increased and some, however vague, conceptions of how to meet them came into being, the general feeling of dislike or distaste diminished and was replaced by interest.

Many of the therapists had countertransference difficulties with the patients' demandingness. This is illustrated by the therapeutic difficulties with the patients Mr. H and Mr. R both of whom were treated by the same therapist. In the initial stage of treatment, the therapist tended to permit herself to be manipulated into meeting or promising to meet the demands of the patient. This is a rather characteristic personal problem of the therapist who is somewhat overinvolved in playing a benign and powerful role with patients. the second phase of the difficulty occurred when the therapist became aware of how she had been manipulated and then became overhostile and overrejecting. In treating both of these patients the whole treatment process was affected by these countertransference difficulties. The process in both patients show a similar course, in that treatment for the first year, or year and a half, was relatively smooth, but relatively unproductive of improvement. During this time the "honeymoon" was going on and the therapist was permitting herself to be manipulated in a variety of ways into fulfilling or seeming to fulfill the patient's needs. Following this phase in both patients there occurred a crisis in which the patients' symptoms became more severe, on the one hand; and on the other hand, the therapist became consciously hostile and rejecting toward the patients. These crises came about through a recognition on the part of the therapist of the lack of progress in the patients, a recognition of the manipulative aspects of the relationships, and an increasing resentment of being so manipulated. This led to a fairly abrupt and unkind rejection of the patients. Following the crises, during which the therapist worked through some of her resentful attitudes toward the patients, therapy in one case went on to a much more productive relationship, with consequent improvement and insight developing in the patient. In the other more severely sick patient, the improvement was missing.

Another therapist consciously set the goal of meeting the patient in empathic communication. The patient was severely depressed and the therapist undertook the exhausting task of providing such a bridge between them. The approach proved very useful during the patient's depression; indeed, it was sufficiently successful to remove the necessity for hospitalizing the patient, a step which had been necessary in previous depressions. However, after the depression lifted and the patient became hypomanic, the treatment was disrupted. The patient became hostile and dismissed the therapist. At this time the therapist commented:

She had developed a type of behavior which actually got under my skin— the telephone calls. When she first talked about the transference [the patient accused the doctor of "throwing the transference out of the window"], I think that she was talking about the hostility and frustration in me when I wasn't able to protect my own life. A further element was the change in my attitude as I watched her move from depression into elation, the change in my evaluation of potentialities in this person. During the depression the sense of depth that attends this affect leads one to feel that there must be considerable to this character. When the depression lifted and, in the period prior to the elation, I began to see the range of her interests and the smallness of the grip that her interests had on her, my feeling about her changed. I came to question the notion that I had had about what treatment would amount to. I believe that she had reacted to my hopes for the treatment and to a process going on in me of giving them up.

Another therapist found herself protected in refusing to meet the patient's dependency demands by the reflection that since it was commonly accepted that no one knew how to treat manic depressives successfully, her professional prestige would not be threatened if she failed with the patient. Apparently this point gave her sufficient security to deny the patient's demands without experiencing too much uneasiness. She did, however, show some vulnerability to the patient's demanding attitude in that on one occasion she felt that the patient was justified in being angry at her for an unavoidable tardiness. And on several other occasions when the therapist had to be away from town for a day, she made the probably meaningful arrangement of making up the missed hour with the patient *in advance*. We concluded that even though the therapist was relatively secure in the face of the patient's demandingness, a certain degree of apprehensiveness remained of which she was unaware.

Therapeutic Techniques

Many of the topics covered throughout this report carry therapeutic implications, since rational therapy must be based primarily upon an understanding of the patient's dynamics and specifically upon an understanding of the transference and countertransference patterns.

All of the members of the seminar agreed that the first step in therapy with these patients should be the establishment of a communicative relationship, in the ordinary sense of the term, in which thoughts, feelings, and meanings are noticed and talked about. A variety of maneuvers were suggested for the accomplishment of this goal: (1) One suggestion was that the emphasis in communication with the manic depressive be nonverbal, chiefly using tone of voice and gesture rather than emphasis on the intellectual content of the exchange, with a view toward development of more facility for noticing nonverbal experiences. This was done by one therapist largely by assuming this sort of role herself. (2) Another therapist felt that the usual technique, applied with more patience and more intenseness, would suffice, with the addition that it would be necessary for the therapist to realize that the patient's seemingly good contact and ability to tell a great deal about himself should not deceive the therapist into assuming that meaningful communication exists when it does not. A further point made by this therapist is that the presence of strong feelings of envy and competitiveness with the therapist keeps the patient focussed on "who is better" and prevents him from working on his problems. She would use this interpretation quite consistently in the early stages of treatment. (3) Another suggested maneuver was to press the patient in an insistent manner to look for and give the emotionally meaningful material, on the basis of the assumption that the material is present and available if the therapist demands it. This would involve treating the stereotypy of the patient as a defense from the outset. (4) Another approach suggested was summed up under the name "relationship therapy," by which is meant the substitution of action for words. This would include the nonverbal technique mentioned above, and it could also include the various shock or startle experiences which have seemed to help in shaking the stereotypy defense of these patients. This latter has been explained as being effective because it was sufficiently intense and spontaneous to loosen the defensive armor of the patient momentarily and involve him in a more genuine emotional interchange. It is of course, highly speculative whether such a sudden, spontaneous eruption of the therapist could be fashioned into a planned technical approach. However, the point remains that the conventionalized verbal psychoanalytic approach may be quite an undesirable one for the conventionalized manic-depressive patient. As one member of the seminar expressed it: "Words become very easily stereotyped, whether you use Freudian language or Sullivanian language; whatever language you use, it becomes stereotyped and doesn't convey any feeling. When you want to get at the feeling, there has to be some startle reaction."

The consensus of the seminar was that the *first and foremost problem is that of getting beyond the conventionalized barrier into the area of emotional exchange.* The variety of methods suggested for approaching this goal are a reflection of the variety of personalities in the seminar group. In addition to the various approaches suggested, however, there appeared to be general agreement that looking at the stereotyped or conventional behavior as a defense against anxiety and making interpretations of it as such is a therapeutically fruitful approach.

A second point of general agreement in the treatment of these patients had to do with the handling of the demands. From the material in the section on countertransference it can be seen that there are dangerous pitfalls in this aspect of the relationship, especially since too great or impossible demands on the part of the patient are likely to mobilize countertransference anxieties in the therapist. While numerous speculations were entered into as to the feasibility of meeting some or all of the patient's demands, the experience of the years seemed to indicate that it is more desirable to *take a firm and consistent attitude of refusing to attempt to meet irrational demands from the beginning.* To this must be added a certain watchfulness, lest one be outmaneuvered by the patient and, while saying "no" to one demand, be simultaneously trapped into meeting another. This seemed to be the case with the therapist who was impelled to make up missed hours in advance. And, of course, this is an area where the manipulative ingenuity of the patient is particularly spectacular. We also agreed that since the manipulative aspects of the relationship are prone to involve the therapist in various degrees of unspoken or even unrecognized resentment, great care and alertness should be exercised (a) to get the demandingness out into the open and (b) to resolve the tensions which come into the relationship by a full discussion of the reactions of both patient and therapist.

Another therapeutic difficulty which is closely related to the demandingness is the problem of acting-out. In the manic, this takes the form either of ill-advised acts which do the patient's reputation or economic security real damage, or of making decisions at a time of poor judgment which seriously alter the course of life. In the depressive, the acting-out takes the form either of failure in job or life situation due to apathy and hopelessness, or of suicide. These dangers seem to imply the need for firmness and guidance in dealing with both the manic and the depressive aspects of the illness. However, as soon as the therapist begins to play a guiding role with the patient, he seems to meet one of the patient's most basic demands and opens himself up to receiving more and more demands which are presented as necessary to prevent injurious acting-out. The therapist is soon in a situation where the patient is able to re-enact with him his old pattern of dependency, and the therapist does not know where or how to draw the line. Numerous almost humorous tales are told by psychiatrists about how they have handled suicidal threats from patients. One psychiatrist, in response to a sucidal threat told the patient, "Well, please don't do it on my doorstep." Another, when telephoned by a patient who threatened to kill himself, said, "Well, what did you wake me up to tell me that for?" A third therapist told the patient that it was against the rules for him to commit suicide, and if he did so, she would discontinue the treatment! Laughable as these illustrations are, their effectiveness in reducing the danger of suicide nonetheless makes a point regarding the dynamics of the patient. On the one hand, a denial of responsibility for the continued existence of the patient seems vitally necessary in order to prevent the use of suicide as a weapon to enforce the patient's dependency demands. However, implicit in each statement is the doctor's admission to the patient that he is meaningful or important to him; this aspect of the problem has been referred to before. We feel that an air of blandness or indifference is quite undesirable in dealing with these patients; that a condition of *involvement* of the patients with their therapists, and vice versa, is necessary for their progress and even survival. The patient seems to need recognition of his importance from the therapist in order to attain even a minimal degree of security in the therapeutic relationship. This is usually sought for in terms of dependency—the patient endeavors to see the therapist as dependent on him—for his reputation, if for nothing else. This often leads the patient to use suicidal threats as a means of testing the therapist's dependency. It seems probable that the patient's underlying fear is that he will be unable to keep the therapist's interest and therefore that the therapeutic relationship will dissolve unless the therapist needs him. This fear can often be modified if the therapist can make the distinction to the patient that the patient can be *important* to him as a person without the therapist's necessarily having to be dependent on him.

This problem is illustrated in the management of Mr. R's acute depression. In order to avoid the necessity of hospitalizing him, the therapist was seeing him six or seven times a week. In addition, the patient was referred to an internist for help with his insomnia and saw him about twice a week. And, beyond this, a psychiatrist friend of the patient made himself available and spent an evening or two a week listening to the patient's complaints. All this attention was ineffective; the patient's tension continued to rise and his suicidal threats increased in number. It was not until his therapist grew angry and scolded him thoroughly that the patient's tension began to subside. On reconsideration of this episode we concluded that it was the fact that the therapist cared enough to grow angry that made the episode significant to the patient. Her anger startled the patient sufficiently to push his stereotyped defense aside for a moment and permit a real exchange of feeling to occur. It seems to have been the first time the therapist ever appeared to be a human being to him, and following this first experience, later recognition of her humanness became more easily achieved.

Not only in dealing with the depressive, but also with the manic, it is manifestly impossible for the therapist's denial of the patient's dependency demands to go to the length of passive indifference. In treating a manic, either within or outside of a hospital, restrictions on his activity are necessary to prevent both his destructive impact on his environment and his destroying himself. Such restrictions are also necessary for the sake of the therapist. That is, exploitation beyond the particular level of tolerance of any individual therapist will inevitably lead to nontherapeutic resentment, and the manic will characteristically attempt to find the limits and then go beyond them.

We have concluded, on the basis of these considerations, that the manic depressive can best be treated in a situation where certain rules are laid down for him in an active, vigorous, and "involved" way by the therapist. We feel that his irrational demands should be recognized, labeled, and refused. We feel that the therapist should not make decisions for the patient nor attempt to give him advice on how to behave; in fact, the therapist's pressure should be in the opposite direction— that of the patient's working through his conflicts to the point of being able to make his own decisions. The rules should be laid down in terms of setting up a structure or frame of reference within which the patient would then be responsible for working out his own personal choices and decisions. We conceive of the making of rules or setting of limitations as conveying to the patient, not only guidance, but also a sense of his own importance. To illustrate: In dealing with a depressive who was unable to eat or dress, the therapist would convey much more a sense of the patient's importance by setting up a rule that the patient must eat a certain minimum number of meals a day than by allowing the patient to starve or undernourish himself until he "worked out his conflict" about eating.

The patient's sense of his own meaningfulness to the therapist is, we believe, also promoted by the therapist's continuous attempt to convey to the patient some sense of the therapist's own feeling attitudes. Thus we would advocate the expression of resentment to a manic or depressive patient when it was genuinely and warmly felt. In the treatment of Mr. R, after the initial change for the better occurred, his therapist found that his stereotyped defenses would be dropped if she *complained* that she did not know what he was talking about. This can be considered to be an interpretation that he was now using a defensive maneuver, plus an expression of feeling—annoyance—about it.

As in any other analysis, the working through of the transference and countertransference with the manic depressive constitutes the most important part of the analysis. The particular defenses in this kind of illness make these problems unusually acute and probably contribute to the feeling among many therapists that manic-depressive patients are the most difficult of all patients to treat. We feel that the difficulty in communication resulting from the stereotyped response of these patients is by all odds the greatest technical problem to be solved in their therapy.

SUMMARY AND CONCLUSIONS

An intensive study of twelve manic-depressive patients was made in order to reformulate and further develop the dynamics of the character structure of these patients in terms of their patterns of interpersonal relationships. In addition to further developing our knowledge of their psychodynamics, we hoped to arrive at therapeutic procedures which would prove more useful in interrupting the course of this kind of illness.

A comprehensive survey of the literature was made in order to determine the present state of development of psychopathological theory in regard to manic-depressive states.

The manic-depressive character was investigated from the point of view of (1) the patterns of interaction between parents and child and between family and community; (2) the ways in which these patterns influenced the character structure of the child and affected his experiencing of other people in his subsequent life; and (3) the way in which these patterns are repeated in therapy and can be altered by the processes of therapy.

Psychopathology

Among the significant parent-child interactions, we found that the family is usually in a low-prestige situation in the community or socially isolated in some other way and that the chief interest in the child is in his potential usefulness in improving the family's position or meeting the parent's prestige needs. A serious problem with envy also grows out of the importance of material success and high prestige. We also found that the child is usually caught between one parent who is thought of as a failure and blamed for the family's plight (frequently the father) and the other parent who is aggressively striving, largely through the instrumentality of the child, to remedy the situation. And finally, the serious disturbance in the child's later value system (superego) is in part attributable to the lack of a secure and consistent authority in the home and to the tremendous overconcern of the parents about what "they" think.

A study of the major unresolved anxiety-provoking experiences of the manic depressive indicates that the crucial disturbance in his interpersonal relationship occurs at a time in his development when his closeness (identification) with his mother has diminished but his ability to recognize others as whole, separate persons has not yet developed. This accounts for the perpetuation of his response to important figures in his later life as either good or bad, black or white, and his inability to distinguish shades of grey.

Therapy

As a result of our study of these patients, we found that our ability to intervene successfully in the psychosis improved. While all of the factors which contributed to successful therapy with these patients are by no means understood, we concluded that certain areas could be isolated, as follows:

Communication. The primary problem in therapy is establishing a communicative relationship, which is, of course, a reflection of the patient's basic life difficulty. The most characteristic aspect of the manic depressive's defenses is his ability to avoid anxiety by erecting conventional barriers to emotional interchange. We have learned to interpret this as a defense rather than a defect in the patient's experience, and we have found that when it is interpreted as a defense, he responds by developing a greater ability to communicate his feelings and to establish empathic relationships.

Dependency. A second major problem is that of handling the patient's dependency needs, which are largely gratified by successful manipulation of others. Since the manic depressive's relationships with others are chiefly integrated on the basis of dependency, the therapist is in a dilemma between the dangers of allowing himself to fit into the previous pattern of the dependency gratification patterns of the patient and of forbidding dependency *in toto*. Furthermore, the therapeutic relationship in itself is a dependent relationship. The therapist must be alert to the manipulative tendencies of the patient and must continually bring these into open discussion rather than permit them to go on out of awareness.

Transference-countertransference. The most significant part of treatment is, as always, the working through of the transference and countertransference problems. The patient's main difficulties with the therapist are those of dealing with him as a stereotype and as a highly conventionalized authority figure who is either to be placated or manipulated, and by whom all of his dependency needs are to be met. The main difficulties of the therapist are in the frustrations and helplessness of trying to communicate with the patient through his defensive barriers and the strain of constantly being the target for the manipulative tendencies. These problems inevitably involve the therapist in a variety of feelings of resentment and discouragement which must be worked through. We have found that a recognition of the ways in which transference-countertransference patterns manifest themselves and vary from the patterns found with other types of patients makes the working through of this problem possible.

Problem of authority and defining limits. One of the great risks in therapy with the manic depressive is the danger of suicide when he is depressed or of the patient's damaging his economic and social security when he is in a manic phase. Much of the success in handling this destructive element must, of course, depend on successful therapy. However, we have found that a careful definition of limits and an appropriate expression of disapproval when the limits are violated is helpful.

Further Areas for Study

We feel that the conclusions derived from our intensive study of twelve patients require confirmation by further investigatin of a larger series. A thorough statistical study of the families of manic depressives is desirable in order to confirm and elaborate the picture of the family patterns as we have developed it. And finally, a more intensive study of psycho-therapeutic interviews with manic-depressive patients is needed in order to define more clearly the characteristic patterns of communication and interaction between patient and therapist, and to contrast these with the interactions in other conditions. This is a logical next step in advancing our knowledge of the psychopathology of all mental disorders.

PART II

BEHAVIORAL AND COGNITIVE APPROACHES

Behavioral models of depression are relatively new, compared to the psychodynamic formulations that have just been presented. The behavioral perspective on psychopathology developed later, but it is also true that behaviorists at first neglected the subject of depression. A few papers appeared in the late sixties (Burgess, 1968; Lazarus, 1968), but they were highly speculative and lacked any rigorous definition or analysis of depressive behavior.

The behavioral perspective emphasizes the analysis of psychopathology in terms of observable behavior in relation to preceding and consequential events in the environment—controlling stimuli and reinforcement consequences. Yet a behavioral definition of depression has remained rather elusive. Depression does not refer to a single response class; at least, as it has traditionally been defined, its primary symptom is a state of subjective distress. It is often the case that depressed persons do not exhibit any marked changes in overt behavior despite their considerable distress and sense of personal inadequacy. As a group, depressed persons do not share much in common in terms of specific behavioral excesses or deficiencies. Furthermore, depression often seems to involve change in behaviors without any apparent change in the conditions that have previously maintained them (Costello, 1972). For instance, upon learning that his former girl friend back home has become engaged to someone else, a college student might stop eating regularly, withdraw from his friends on campus, and neglect his studying.

Of necessity, the two most influential behavioral formulations of depression (see Lewinsohn; Miller, Rosellini & Seligman, this volume) involved the introduction of some concepts that go substantially beyond the usual analysis of reinforcement contingencies. Consistent with more general trends is psychology, they both also were later modified to include an emphasis on cognition.

Lewinsohn developed a model of depression that was an extension of an earlier model presented by Ferster (1973, 1974), in which the central feature of the disorder was identified as a reduction in the emission of positively reinforced behavior. A major innovation in the Lewinsohn formulation was its emphasis on the concept of total amount of response-contingent positive reinforcement "resconposre". The emission of some given adaptive behavior is seen as not being merely a function of specific rewards available for it. Rather, it is also a function of the *overall* amount of positive reinforcement that is available as consequences for any available response. It is not a matter of this reinforcement being available but of its being contingent upon the person making a response. Thus, according to Lewinsohn, a retired person who receives a paycheck without having to work may emit less adaptive behavior and become depressed.

Depression is conceptualized as a low rate of behavior and a state of dysphoria that occur when there is a low rate of resconposre. There is a potential for a vicious cycle to develop, with a lower rate of positive reinforcement leading to a lower rate of adaptive behavior, leading to a further reduction in reinforcement, and so on. Expression of distress may be met with reassurance, and in this way depressive behavior can become the primary way of obtaining reinforcement.

The rate of response-contingent reinforcement available is dependent upon three sets of factors: the events that are potentially reinforcing to a person; of these, those that are available in the immediate environment; and the extent to which the person possesses the necessary skills to receive this reinforcement. Events that precipitate depression may do so by affecting one or more of these factors. For instance, for a man who has just become divorced, the availability of reinforcing events has been changed, and if he may lack the skills to meet someone new and to form a relationship, he may become depressed.

The Lewinsohn model has been the basis for the development of an extensive research program and a behavioral approach to therapy for depression that includes a self-treatment course (Lewinsohn, et al., 1978). The article in this volume reviews some of the early research on the relationship between positive events and mood, as well as the assessment of social skills. Lewinsohn subsequently posited a relationship between the total number of aversive events in a person's life and depression, and developed an instrument assessing unpleasant events that paralleled the earlier *Pleasant Events Schedule* (Lewinsohn & Takington, 1979). In his most recent work, Lewinsohn has become more eclectic in both his model of therapy and his research program (Lewinsohn & Hoberman, 1982) and has given attention to the role of cognition in depression. However, he has assumed that the complaints of depressed persons are not necessarily distortions and that they may instead reflect depressed persons' inability to obtain valued rewards. His research has even been interpreted as suggesting that depressed persons are more accurate in their self-perceptions than nondepressed persons are (Lewinsohn, et al., 1980).

Lewinsohn cites one study in particular as a major reason for his shift to a more eclectic and a more cognitive model. Zeiss, Lewinsohn, and Munoz (1979) compared social skills training, the scheduling of pleasant activities, and cognitive therapy as treatments for depression. The results of the study indicated that not only were these treatments equally effective in reducing depression, but that they were not specific (i.e., cognitive therapy had as much effect on pleasant activities as did the scheduling of these activities).

By now, it should have become apparent that the phenomena of depression are vaguely delineated and poorly understood. Seligman and his colleagues (see Miller, Rosellini, & Seligman, this volume) have provided a fine example of a strategy for dealing with this problem: the construction of a laboratory model or analogue, within which greater precision can be achieved.

The term "learned helplessness" was first used in connection with laboratory experiments in which dogs were exposed to shock from which they could not escape (Overmier & Seligman, 1967). After repeated trials, the dogs tended to sit passively when the shock came on. Exposed to a new situation from which they could escape a shock by jumping over a barrier, they failed to initiate the appropriate response. Some would occasionally jump over the barrier and escape, but they would generally revert to taking the shock passively. For the purposes of constructing an analogue of clinical depression, the behavior of the dogs is significant in suggesting that exposure to uncontrollable aversive events may lead to a failure to initiate appropriate responses in new situations and an inability to learn that responding is effective.

The linchpin of the analogy to depression is the view of the disorder as being fundamentally a matter of depressed persons being passive— i.e., as failing to initiate appropriate responses to cope with their predicaments—and unable to perceive that their responses make a difference. Thus, whereas Lewinsohn invoked the concept of the total amount of response-contingent reinforcement to explain the rather generalized problems of depressed persons, Seligman and his colleagues introduce the notions of a generalized inhibition of response and an acquired perception of response-reinforcement independence.

The analogy to depression was bolstered by initial findings that in a variety of task situations, depressed human subjects resembled nondepressed subjects who had received repeated failure experiences. For instance, compared to nondepressed subjects who had not received repeated failure experiences, these two groups of subjects took longer to solve anagrams and apparently failed to perceive the pattern underlying their successful solution (Klein & Seligman, 1976). As described in the article by Miller, Rosellini, and Seligman, other research suggested that the parallels between laboratory learned helplessness and depression were not limited to similarities in behavior. Promising leads were also established with regard to etiology, treatment, and prevention.

The original learned helplessness model stimulated a large body of research and considerable controversy (Buchwald, Coyne, & Cole, 1978; Costello, 1978). Ultimately, the accumulated research led to questions about both the adequacy of the learned-helplessness explanation for the behavior of nondepressed subjects who had been exposed to failure as well as the appropriateness of learned helplessness as an analogue of depression. For instance, it was shown that the performance deficits of subjects who had been given a typical learned helplessness induction were very much situation-specific (Cole & Coyne, 1977), and that these deficits might better be explained as the result of anxious self-preoccupation, rather than the perception of response-reinforcement independence (Coyne, Metalsky, & Lavelle, 1980). Furthermore, the characterization of depressed persons as passive and lacking in aggression was challenged. Difficulties with the original learned helplessness model led to a major reformulation (see Abramson, Seligman, & Teasdale, this volume) that will be discussed below.

Rehm's (this volume) self-control model of depression is less developed than either of the preceding two models, but it adds an additional dimension to the discussion of the role of cognition in depression. Rehm draws on the work of Kanfer (1970) and others in suggesting that depression is a matter of some interrelated problems in self-control. Briefly, the self-control model assumes that people may regulate their own behavior in a way that allow them to be somewhat independent of their immediate environment and the controlling stimuli and reinforcement contingencies that it offers. *Self-monitoring* involves attending to one's own behavior and its antecedents and consequences. *Self-evaluation* is a matter of interpreting one's behavior and comparing it to internal standards. Attributional processes are one set of determinants of the evaluations that are made. *Self-reinforcement* involves administering reinforcement to oneself, just as one could administer a reinforcement to someone else. Furthermore, self-reinforcement can be covert or cognitive, in the sense that one can praise or criticize one's own behavior privately or to oneself.

Depression may be seen as a reflection of deficiencies in one or more of these self-control processes. First, the self-monitoring of depressed persons may be maladaptive in that they selectively attend to negative aspects of their own behavior and ignore positive accomplishments. Their self-evaluations may involve an attributional bias so that they are excessively blamed for failures and take insufficient credit for successes. They may employ overly harsh or stringent standards in evaluating themselves. Finally, they may be stingy in rewarding themselves or overly self-punishing.

Rehm is explicit in his indebtedness to other cognitive and behavioral models of depression. However, this model can go beyond the more behavioral models in providing an alternative way of explaining depression in the absence of substantial changes in the immediate environment. Furthermore, the identification of deficiencies in self-control processes suggest specific therapeutic interventions to alter them that would not be suggested by the other approaches. In addition to the work reported by Rehm in this article, a number of studies have produced results consistent with hypotheses derived from the model (see Kanfer & Zeiss, 1983), although questions have been raised as to whether deficits in self-monitoring, self-evaluation, and self-reward are specific to depression (Gotlib, 1981).

In his 1967 book, Beck noted that there was a lack of systematic psychological research on depression. The cognitive model that he presented in that book did much to change that situation. A recent review (Coyne & Gotlib, 1983), cited over 100 studies generated by the prevailing cognitive models alone. Cognitive models of depression have a strong intuitive appeal. The self-deprecating and pessimistic talk of depressed persons and their apparent failure to take obvious steps to remedy their situations readily invite the suggestion that they suffer from distorted cognitive processes.

In the model presented by Kovacs and Beck (this volume), three sets of interrelated cognitive concepts are used to explain the psychological phenomena of depression: the cognitive triad, schemata, and cognitive distortion or faulty information processing. These cognitive factors are seen as having a causal primacy over the affective, motivational, and behavioral features of depression.

The cognitive triad consists of thinking patterns that lead depressed persons to construe themselves, their current situations, and their future possibilities in negative terms. The concept of schemata is used to explain why depressed persons persist in these negative and self-defeating attitudes even in the face of contradictory evidence. Cognitive schema are stable, organized representations of past experience that provide for the screening, differentiating, and encoding of information from the environment. In depression, prepotent dysfunctional schema dominate information processing so that depressed persons may not even be able to consider alternative interpretations of their experience that are more positive or optimistic. They overgeneralize from negative experiences, selectively abstract negative details out of context, and negatively characterize themselves in absolutist terms—"always," "never," "nothing but," etc.

These cognitive processes are activated in the depressed person by stressful experiences, but they exist before a depressive episode in a latent state. In explaining how a vulnerability to these thinking processes comes about, Beck (1974) has offered an account that bears a strong resemblance to psychodynamic formulations:

In the course of his development, the depression-prone person may become sensitized by certain unfavorable types of life situations such as the loss of a parent or chronic rejection by peers. Other unfavorable conditions of a more insidious nature may similarly produce vulnerability to depression. These traumatic experiences predispose the individual to overreact to analogous situations later in life. He has a tendency to make extreme, absolute judgments when such situations occur (p. 7).

Beck's work has done much to bring the "cognitive revolution" to the study of psychopathology and to revitalize the psychological study of depression. He and his colleagues have also developed a cognitive therapy for depression that in controlled studies has been shown to produce a greater reduction in depressive symptoms with fewer drop-outs and relapses than treatment with conventional tricyclic antide-pressant medication (Rush, et al., 1977).

Although the original learned-helplessness model could also be said to be cognitive in the sense that it invoked the concept of a perception of response-reinforcement independence, it defined this perception in terms of its environmental antecedents and behavioral consequences. Overall, the model gave little attention to higher cognitive processes. In the reformulated model (Abramson, Seligman & Teasdale, this volume) it was no longer that mere exposure to uncontrollability was sufficient for helplessness to develop. Instead, the additional require-ment was that the person must come to expect that future outcomes would also be uncontrollable, and higher cognitive processes were assumed to mediate the development of this expectation. "When a person finds that he is helpless, he asks *why* he is helpless. The casual attributions he makes determine the generality and chronicity of his helpessness deficits as well as his later self-esteem."

According to the reformulated model, the vulnerability of depression-prone persons lies in their negative attributional style, their tendency to interpret negative events in internal, global, and stable terms. Attri-butions of negative events to internal causes a reduction in self-esteem; attribution to global factors lead to a generalization of deficits across situations; and attributions to stable factors lead to a persistence of deficits over time. Thus, the reformulation integrated the original model with attribution theory.

It was possible to contrast predictions made from the original learned-helplessness model with those derived from Beck's model (Rizley, 1978). The original model seemed to suggest that depressed persons saw a lack of control over key outcomes, whereas Beck's model indi-cated that their problem was that they blamed themselves excessively. However, with the reformulation of the helplessness model, it became more difficult to specify what types of data would support one model while contradicting the other. At this point, the two models are probably best seen as complementary (Coyne & Gotlib, 1983). Beck's model focuses on how past exerience is organized, and this organization shapes the processing of new experiences. The revised learned-helplessness model focuses on how this experience is explained and how such explanations determine subsequent cognition, behavior, and affect.

The two models are undeniably the dominant psychological formulations of depression at the present time. Together, they have given rise to a huge body of research examining depressed persons' expectations and evaluations of performance, their perception of information from the environment, recall of information, cognitive biases, and attributions for laboratory and naturalistically occurring events. Coyne and Gotlib's review of this literature (1983) concluded that depressed persons do make negative, self-deprecating, and pessimistic responses to laboratory, hypothetical, and actual life situations. However, depressed-nondepressed differences on cognitive measures have not been as strong or consistent as either model would predict. Furthermore, the strongest evidence has been correlational in nature. Depressed persons show evidence of negative cognitive processes, but there has been little success in demonstrating any measurable cognitive vulnerability in these persons before they become depressed or after they have fully recovered. Research continues, but it may be that such cognitions are best seen as an aspect of being depressed, rather than an identifiable antecedent. Yet, current work is showing some promise in the development of new methods for studying attributional style when vulnerable persons are not depressed (Peterson & Seligman, 1984), as well as schematic processing and enduring dysfunctional attitudes (Kuiper & Higgins, 1985). Further research is needed to determine whether these new methods will overcome the problems of past efforts to identify cognitive markers for depression that are not state dependent.

REFERENCES

Beck, A. T. (1967). *Depression: Clinical, experimental, and theoretical aspects.* New York: Harper & Row.

Beck, A. T. (1974). The development of depression. In R. J. Friedman, & M. M. Katz (Eds.). *The Psychology of Depression.* NY: Winston-Wiley.

Buchwald, A. M., Coyne, J. C., and Cole, C. S. (1978). A critical evaluation of the learned helplessness model. *Journal of Abnormal Psychology.* 87:180–193.

Burgess, E. (1968). The modification of depressive behavior. In R. Rubin and C. Franks (Eds.). *Advances in Behavior Therapy.* NY: Academic Press.

Cole, C. S., and Coyne, J. C. (1977). Situational specificity of laboratory induced learned helplessness. *Journal of Abnormal Psychology.* 86:615–623.

Costello, C. G. (1972). Depression: Loss of reinforcers or loss of reinforcer effectiveness? *Behavior Therapy.* 240–247.

Costello, C. G. (1978). A critical review of Seligman's laboratory experiments on learned helplessness and depression in humans. *Journal of Abnormal Psychology.* 87:21–31.

Coyne, J. C., and Gotlib, I. H. (1983). The role of cognition in depression. *Psychological Bulletin.* 94:472–505.

Coyne, J. C., Metalsky, G., and Lavelle, T. L. (1980). Learned helplessness as experimenter-induced failure and its alleviation with attentional redeployment. *Journal of Abnormal Psychology.* 89:350–357.

Ferster, C. (1973). A functional analysis of depression. *American Psychologist.* 28:857–870.

Ferster, C. S. (1974). Behavioral approaches to depression. In R. J. Friedman and M. M. Katz (Eds.). *The Psychology of Depression: Contemporary Theory and Research.* Washington, D.C.: V. H. Winston.

Gotlib, I. H. (1981). Self-reinforcement and recall: Differential deficits in depressed and nondepressed psychiatric patients. *Journal of Abnormal Psychology.* 90:521–530.

Kanfer, F. H. (1970). Self-regulation: Research issues and speculations. In C. Neuringer and J. L. Michael (Eds.). *Behavior Modification in Clinical Psychology.* NY: Appleton-Century-Crofts.

Kanfer, R., and Zeiss, A. M. (1983). Depression, interpersonal standard setting, and judgment of self-efficacy. *Journal of Abnormal Psychology.* 92:319–330.

Klein, D. C., and Seligman, M. E. P. (1976). Reversal of performance deficits and perceptual deficits in learned helplessness and depression. *Journal of Abnormal Psychology.* 85:508–516.

Kuiper, N. A., and Higgins, E. T. (1985). Social cognition and depression: A general integration. *Social Cognition.* 3:1–15.

Lazarus, A. A. (1968). Learning theory in the treatment of depression. *Behavior Research and Therapy.* 6:83–89.

Lewinsohn, P. M., and Hoberman, H. M. (1982). Depression. In A. S. Bellack, M. Hersen, and A. E. Kazdin (Eds.). *International Handbook of Behavior Modification and Therapy.* NY: Plenum Press.

Lewinsohn, P. M., et al. (1980). Social competence and depression: The role of illusory self-perceptions? *Journal of Abnormal Psychology.* 89:203–212.

Lewinsohn, P. M., et al. (1978). *Control Your Depression.* Englewood Cliffs, NJ: Prentice-Hall.

Lewinsohn, P. M., and Takington, J. (1979). Studies on the measurement of unpleasant events and relations with depression. *Applied Psychological Measurement.* 3:83–101.

Overmier, J. B., and Seligman, M. E. P. (1967). Effects of inescapable shock upon subsequent escape and avoidance responding *Journal of Comparative and Physiological Psychology.* 63:23–33.

Peterson, C., and Seligman, M. E. P. (1984). Causal explanations as a risk factor for depression: Theory and evidence. *Psychological Review.* 91:347–374.

Rizley, R. (1978). Depression and distortion in the attribution of causality. *Journal of Abnormal Psychology.* 87:32–48.

Rush, A. J., et al. (1977). Comparative efficacy of cognitive therapy and pharmacotherapy in the treatment of depressed outpatients. *Cognitive Therapy and Research.* 1:17–37.

Zeiss, A. M., Lewinsohn, P. M., and Munoz, R. F. (1979). Nonspecific improvement effects in depression using interpersonal skills training, pleasant activity schedules, or cognitive training. *Journal of Consulting and Clinical Psychology.* 47:427–439.

5. A Behavioral Approach to Depression[1]

Peter M. Lewinsohn

The purpose of this paper is threefold: (1) to explicate the major theoretical assumptions and premises that have been guiding the design of our research; (2) to present our empirical findings, which are consistent with these assumptions; and (3) to describe studies now in progress that are designed to test hypotheses about the relationship between positive reinforcement and depression. Intervention strategies that have been found useful for the treatment of depressed individuals within a behavioral framework have been presented elsewhere (Lewinsohn, Shaffer, & Libet 1969; Lewinsohn, Weinstein, & Shaw 1969; Lewinsohn & Atwood 1969; Lewinsohn & Shaw 1969; Lewinsohn, Weinstein, & Alper 1970; Lewinsohn & Shaffer 1971; Johannson, Lewinsohn & Flippo 1969).

OPERATIONAL DEFINITION OF DEPRESSION AND A METHODOLOGICAL POINT

We use the term "depression" to refer to the syndrome of behaviors that have been identified in descriptive studies of depressed individuals (e.g., Grinker, et al., 1961). It includes verbal statements of dysphoria, self-depreciation, guilt, material burden, social isolation, somatic complaints, and a reduced rate of many behaviors. We assume depression to be a continuous variable which can be conceptualized as a "state" which fluctuates over time as well as a "trait" (some people are more prone to becoming depressed than others). Being depressed does not exclude other psychopathological conditions such as schizophrenia, psychosis, sexual deviation, or alcoholism. For research purposes a patient (subject) is defined as "depressed" if he meets certain experi-

[1] The author gratefully acknowledges the helpful suggestions he received from Richard Diller and Douglas MacPhillamy in writing this paper.

mental criteria (e.g., Lewinsohn & Libet 1972) based on selected MMPI scales and on the interview factors identified by Grinker (1961).

It would seem important that any study relying on differences between depressed and nondepressed *groups* for its conclusions have a normal control as well as a "psychiatric control" group (i.e. patients for whom anxiety or other neurotic symptoms but not depression constitute the major psychopathology) if any observed group differences are to be attributed to depression (depressed $\neq$ psychiatric control, normal) and not to the deviation hypothesis (depressed, psychiatric control $\neq$ normal control).

THE MAJOR ASSUMPTIONS OF THE BEHAVIORAL THEORY OF DEPRESSION

We make the following three assumptions: (1) A low rate of response-contingent positive reinforcement (resconposre) acts as an eliciting (unconditioned) stimulus for some depressive behaviors, such as feelings of dysphoria, fatigue, and other somatic symptoms. (2) A low rate of resconposre constitutes a sufficient explanation for other parts of the depressive syndrome such as the low rate of behavior. For the latter the depressed person is considered to be on a prolonged extinction schedule. (3) The total amount of resconposre received by an individual is presumed to be a function of three sets of variables: (a) The number of events (including activities) that are potentially reinforcing (PotRe) for the individual. PotRe is assumed to be a variable subject to individual differences, influenced by biological (e.g., sex and age) and experiential variables. (b) The number of potentially reinforcing events that can be provided by the environment, i.e., the availability of reinforcement in the environment (AvaiRe). (c) The instrumental behavior of the individual, i.e., the extent to which he possesses the skills and emits those behaviors that will elicit reinforcement for him from his environment.

A schematic representation of the theory is shown in Figure 1.

The behavioral theory requires that (a) the total amount of resconposre received by depressed persons be less than that received by nondepressed persons, and similarly, it will be less when the individual is depressed than when he is not depressed; (b) the onset of depression be accompanied by a reduction in resconposre; (c) intensity of depression covary with rate of resconposre; and (d) improvement be accom-

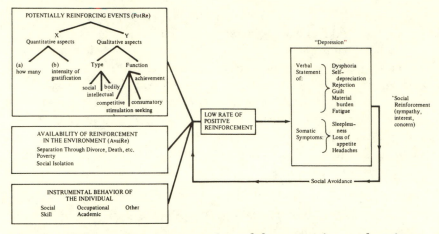

Figure 1. Schematic representation of the causation and maintenance of "depressive" behavior.

panied by an increase in resconposre. Before proceeding to an examination of relevant empirical studies several additional clarifications and
hypotheses are offered.

First, even were such predictions affirmed, further data would be
needed to ascertain whether the differences between depressed and
non-depressed individuals in regard to resconposre are due to: (a) differences in the number and kinds of activities and events which are
potentially reinforcing (PotRe); (b) and/or the possibility that depressed
individuals may be more likely to be in situations which lack reinforcement for them (AvaiRe); (c) and/or differences between depressed and
non-depressed individuals in those skills which are necessary to obtain
reinforcement from one's environment.

Second, the degree to which the individual's behavior is maintained
(followed) by reinforcement is assumed to be the critical antecedent
condition for the occurrence of depression, rather than the total amount
of reinforcement received. It is a well-known clinical fact that "giving"
(i.e., noncontingently) to depressed individuals does not decrease their
depression. We assume that the occurrence of behavior followed by
positive reinforcement is vital if depression is to be avoided. We predict
depression when the probability is low that the individual's behavior
will be followed by reinforcement, and also when the probability is high
that the individual will be "reinforced" when he does not emit the

behavior (e.g., the retired person receiving his paycheck regardless of what he does). Under both conditions the probability of the individual emitting behavior is reduced.

BEHAVIORAL VIEW OF OTHER ASPECTS OF DEPRESSION

1. *Low self-esteem, pessimism, feelings of guilt, and other related phenomena.* These cognitive changes are commonly observed in depressed individuals, even though the specific manifestations vary considerably from individual to individual. Thus there are depressed patients who do not have low self-esteem and there are many who lack feelings of guilt. Theorists such as Aaron T. Beck (1967) assign primary causal significance to these cognitive changes. A behavioral theory assumes these to be secondary elaborations of the feeling of dysphoria, which in turn is presumed to be the consequence of a low rate of resconposre. The first thing that happens when an individual becomes depressed is that he is experiencing an unpleasant feeling state (dysphoria). He *is* feeling bad. This feeling state is difficult for the individual to label and a number of alternative "explanations" are available to him including, "I am sick" (somatic symptoms), "I am weak or otherwise inadequate" (low self-esteem), "I am bad" (feelings of guilt), or "I am not likeable" (feelings of social isolation). The research of Stanley Schachter (Schachter & Singer 1962) may contain important implications for this aspect of the behavior of depressed individuals and for treatment as well (cognitive relabeling). If the depressed individual can be helped to relabel his emotion (e.g., "I am worthless" into "I am feeling bad because I am lacking something that is important to my welfare"), he may be in a much better position to do something about his predicament.

2. *Relationship between hostility and depression.* The role of hostility which is so central to psychodynamically-oriented theories of depression (i.e., depression is caused by internalized hostility) is hypothesized to be secondary to the low rate of resconposre. In a manner analogous to the way in which aggressive behavior is elicited by an aversive stimulus in Azrin's (1966) studies, aggressive behavior may be assumed to be elicited by a low rate of resconposre in the depressed individual. When these aggressive responses are expressed, they serve to alienate other people and therefore contribute even further to the social isolation

of the depressed individual. He therefore learns to avoid expressing hostile tendencies by suppressing (or repressing) them.

3. *Role of precipitating factors in occurrence of depression.* In a substantial number of depressed patients, the depression can be shown to have begun after certain environmental events (e.g., Paykel, et al. 1969). Many of these events involve a serious reduction of positive reinforcement in that the event deprives the individual of an important source of reinforcement (e.g., death of spouse) or of an important set of skills (e.g., spinal cord injuries or brain disease). The relationship between the occurrence of such events and depression is consistent with the behavioral theory of depression. There are, however, also instances of depression following "success" experiences (e.g., promotions or professional success). It is also not at all uncommon for an individual to become depressed following the attainment of some important and long-sought goal (e.g., award of Ph.D. degree). The existence of such precipitating factors would seem at first glance to contradict the notion of a relation between a reduction in positive reinforcement and depression. Two considerations would seem relevant: (a) That the individual is judged to be a "success" by external criteria (e.g., is promoted), does not necessarily mean that the number of potentially reinforcing events available to him has increased. Thus, for example, a promotion may *actually* involve a serious reduction in the amount of social reinforcement obtained by the individual. (b) The behavioral theory would predict depression for an indvidual who attains a goal for which he has worked long and hard *if* the reward (e.g., award of degree) turns out to be a weak reinforcer for him. In that case he has worked hard for little; i.e., his rate of resconposre is low.

EMPIRICAL FINDINGS CONSISTENT WITH THE THEORY AND STUDIES IN PROGRESS

Relationship Between Rate of Positive Reinforcement and Depression

A critical test of the major hypothesis requires a two-step strategy. (1) One must first functionally identify events that act as reinforcement for individuals who may be characterized as either depressed, psychiatric controls, or normal controls, and (2) one must then compute the rate of response contingent reinforcement for these subjects. Holding activity level constant, the theory predicts a lower rate of reinforcement for the depressed individuals. This crucial test has not so far been performed, but a study now in progress with Julian Libet based on home observation and group interaction data will do just that.

Another prediction derived from the theory will be tested in a study being conducted by Douglas MacPhillamy and the author which will compare the total amount of positive reinforcement received by depressed and nondepressed subjects. The operational measure of "total amount of positive reinforcement obtained" for this study will be represented by the sum of the products of the intensity and frequency ratings for each of the 320 items of the Pleasant Events Schedule (MacPhillamy & Lewinsohn 1971). (The Pleasant Events Schedule consists of 320 events and activities which were generated after a very extensive search of the universe of "Pleasant Events." The Ss are asked to rate each item in the schedule on a three-point scale of pleasantness and again on a three-point scale of frequency of occurrence.)

To date the results of several studies are consistent with the major tenet of the behavioral theory of depression, i.e., that there is an association between rate of positive reinforcement and intensity of depression. First, depressed individuals elicit fewer behaviors from other people than control subjects (Shaffer & Lewinsohn 1971; Libet & Lewinsohn 1973). Assuming that it is reinforcing to be the object of attention and interest, this finding suggests that depressed persons receive less social reinforcement. The studies forming the basis for this conclusion are discussed in greater detail below. There is also a significant association between mood and number of "pleasant" activities engaged in (Lewinsohn & Libet 1972).

Three groups of ten subjects (depressed, psychiatric controls, and normal controls) were used. Subjects rated their mood on the Depression Adjective Check List (Lubin 1965) and also indicated the number of "pleasant" activities engaged in each day on a check list over a period of 30 days. The correlation between the mood ratings and the activity scores was computed separately for each subject. The null hypothesis of no association between mood and pleasant activities was strongly rejected ($t = 9.3$, $df = 29$, $p < .001$). There were large individual differences with respect to the magnitude of the correlations between mood and activity, the highest correlation being—.66. For 10 of the 30 subjects, however, the correlation was not significantly different from 0. Future research might address itself to the hypothesis that there are important individual difference variables moderating the relationship between mood and activity.

Depressed individuals have a significantly larger number of events associated with their mood (Lewinsohn & Libet 1972). The number of activities negatively correlated (at the .05 level of statistical significance) with mood ratings was counted for each subject. The depressed group had a significantly larger number of mood-related activities than the psychiatric and normal control groups ($F = 7.67$, $df = 2/24$, $p < .05$). Also, the correlation between depression level (as measured by the MMPI D scale) and the number of "related" activities was computed across all subjects ($N = 30$), and was found to be statistically significant at the .01 level ($r = .46$). The finding suggests a greater vulnerability of depressed individuals to the vicissitudes of everyday experiences, a notion that has been central to a great deal of previous theorizing (Fenichel 1945).

Many of the individual activities that are correlated with mood across subjects involve social reinforcement (Lewinsohn & Libet 1972).

The number of subjects for whom each activity was significantly associated with mood was also tabulated. Those items that correlated with mood for four or more subjects are listed in Table 1.

An important qualitative aspect of this list appears to be that many of them involve social interactions.

Relation Between PotRe and Depression

Our general hypothesis is that there are qualitative and quantitative differences between depressed and nondepressed groups in regard to the number and kinds of potentially reinforcing events.

Any attempt to study positive reinforcement with human subjects (e.g., determination of the amount of positive reinforcement received by the individual or identification of what are potentially reinforcing events for him) is handicapped by the fact that there is no psychometrically sound instrument for the assessment of responses to potentially reinforcing events. Direct observation of behavior is very expensive and often practically impossible. The closest equivalent, the Reinforcement Survey Schedule (Cautella & Kastenbaum 1967), was primarily

Table 1. Rank Order List of Items Correlating More Than .30 with DACL Mood Ratings for at Least Four Persons (From Lewinsohn & Libet 1972)

Items	No. of Ss out of 30
Being with happy people	12
Being relaxed	10
Having spare time	9
Laughing	8
Having people show interest in what you have said	8
Looking at the sky or clouds	7
Saying something clearly	6
Talking about philosophy or religion	6
Meeting someone new (opposite sex)	6
Watching attractive girls or men	6
Reading stories or novels	5
Taking a walk	5
Seeing beautiful scenery	5
Sleeping soundly at night	5
Amusing people	5
Having coffee or a coke with friends	5
Having someone agree with you	4
Petting	4
Being with someone you love	4
Traveling	4
Breathing clean air	4
Having a frank and open conversation	4
Having sexual relations with a partner of the opposite sex	4
Watching people	4

designed to assess the valence of reinforcers potentially available for clinical or laboratory manipulation rather than to provide a systematic survey of the events potentially reinforcing for a given individual. The Pleasant Events Schedule (MacPhillamy & Lewinsohn 1971) was constructed to provide quantitative and qualitative information about what is potentially reinforcing for a given individual. Normative data about the instrument and its psychometric properties and dimensional structure are presented elsewhere (MacPhillamy & Lewinsohn 1971).

The design of a study now under way (MacPhillamy & Lewinsohn) is outlined in Table 2. The general expectation is that depressed and

Table 2. General Design of Study of Relationship of PotRe with Depression and with Age

Group		Depressed		Nondepressed Psychiatric	Normal Controls
Age	Sex	Endogenous	Reactive		
20-39	M				
	F				
40-59	M				
	F				
60-79	M				
	F				

nondepressed groups, and the three age groups, can be discriminated by the number and kind of items rated as pleasant, as well as by the frequency with which the person engages in those activities.

In addition to being interested in possible differences between depressed and nondepressed groups as to potentially positively reinforcing events, we have also been interested in collecting data about the hypothesis that depressed individuals are more sensitive to aversive stimuli (i.e., negative reinforcers) than nondepressed subjects.[2] Since most "real-life" situations contain both positive (approach) and negative (avoidance) components, confirmation of the hypothesis would predict greater avoidance by the depressed individual in many situations. The short-term consequence would be greater isolation and the long-term consequence of less skill acquisition for the depressed individual.

Stewart, in a study conducted in our laboratory (Stewart 1968), hypothesized that "the behavior of depressed subjects is more influenced by the quality (positive or negative) of social reinforcement elicited than is the behavior of nondepressed subjects" (p. 2). Stewart found that depressed individuals generally had a longer latency of response (operationally defined as the amount of time between the reaction by another person to the subject's verbalization and a subsequent action by that subject in a group situation). The largest differences between

---

[2] While this hypothesis is not "discoverable" from the major assumptions of the theory as stated earlier, its affirmation would be consistent with them.

depressed and nondepressed subjects were associated with the occurrence of a negative social reaction (e.g., being ignored, criticized, disagreed with).

We have since tried to expand the hypothesis to the autonomic level. Specifically, a study was conducted (Lewinsohn, Lobitz, & Wilson 1973) to test the following predictions:

H-1: Aversive stimuli elicit a greater autonomic response in depressed subjects.

H-2: Aversive stimuli elicit a greater autonomic anticipatory response in depressed subjects.

H-3: Return to base level following an aversive stimulus is less complete in depressed subjects.

H-4: The autonomic responses of depressed subjects shows less habituation over repeated trials.

The hypotheses about the autonomic reactivity of depressed persons postulate a reaction pattern opposite to that described by Hare (1965) for the psychopath. Psychopaths and depressed individuals are conceptualized as being located at opposite ends of an autonomic response continuum; one is thought to be overresponsive, whereas the other is considered underresponsive to aversive stimuli.

The experimental subjects were classified, using the previously described two-stage selection procedure, into three groups: depressed (D), psychiatric controls (PC), and normal controls (NC). Twelve D, 12 PC, and 12 NC Ss were used, there being an equal number of males and females in each group.

Data were collected during one experimental session which lasted approximately 45 minutes, with the S seated in a comfortable chair. The procedure consisted of the following eight standardized steps: (1) The Depression Adjective Check List (DACL) (Lubin 1965) was administered. (2) The GSR electrodes were attached. (3) Partially to allow time for hydration, the Ss were administered the Subjective Interpretation of Reinforcement Scale (Stewart 1968). The statements from the Subjective Interpretation of Reinforcement Scale had been tape-recorded, and the Ss were asked to rate their reaction to each one on an 11-point scale with +5 indicating the most pleasant and −5 indicating the most negative reaction. (4) The S's threshold for electric shock delivered to the finger was determined. The intensity of the shock was controlled by E by a calibrated dial which had 10 positions. The Method of Ascending Limits was used to determine each S's threshold. (5) The shock level for the S was set at one arbitrary unit above the threshold. The shock apparatus delivered a shock of short duration (approximately 2 msec.) with a spike of approximately 500 volts. Shock was delivered by means of electrodes attached to the index and ring fingers. (6) The Ss on this and all subsequent shock administrations rated their reactions on an 11-point scale. The mean shock level and the mean subjective shock ratings for the three groups were comparable. (7) In the next phase the S was told that E would be counting along with an automatic print-out mechanism which was set to print every three seconds. S was told that E would start with 5 and count down 4-3-2-1-0 and then count up 1-2-3-4-5 and that the S would receive one shock when E said "0". This constituted one trial. (8) The procedure was repeated five times.

Skin resistance was measured by passing a constant 7 microamps of current through the S's hand, using zinc zinc-sulphate electrodes. The resistance was measured directly in K-ohms on a digital volt meter and with a print-out occurring every 3 seconds. Following standard psycho-physiologic procedure, the scores were converted into log conductance units.

The autonomic data can be thought of as comprising a $36 \times 5 \times 11$ element three-dimensional matrix where one dimension consists of 36 subjects, the second consists of five trials, and the third consists of 11 count-down measures within each trial. The 36 subjects are nested within two orthogonal factors, groups (D, PC, NC) and sex (male, female). The study may be conceptualized as a four-factor experiment with repeated measures on two of the four factors, i.e., trials (T) and countdown measures (M) (Winer 1962).

The entire experiment, using identical procedures and Ns, was repeated with another group of Ss (Study No. 2).

Figures 2 and 3 show the groups' mean log skin conductance levels, averaged across all five trials. Points -5 through -2 reflect the anticipatory phase, points -1 through $+1$ indicate the Ss' response to the occurrence of the shock, and points $+2$ through $+5$ reflect the Ss' recovery.

Results of the ANOVAs for the two studies are shown in Table 3.

Our first concern is with the effectiveness of the aversive stimulus in producing *change* in skin conductance. The main effect due to *measurements* is highly significant in both studies. There is also a significant

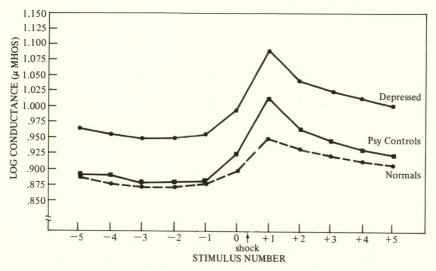

Figure 2. Skin conductance as a function of anticipated shock (shock between 0 and 1) averaged over the five trials. (From Lewinsohn, Lobitz, & Wilson 1973.)

decrease in skin conductance level as a function of the repeated administration of the experimental procedure (*trials*). It may thus be concluded that the experimental manipulations were successful in eliciting an autonomic response and that adaptation occurred as a function of repeated exposure to the shock.

In both studies the overall skin conductance level is highest (suggesting greater arousal) for the depressed Ss. Due to large differences in conductance level between Ss within the groups, however, the differences between groups do not attain statistical significance.

Hypotheses 1, 2, and 3 demand greater *change* on the part of the depressed group during the anticipatory phase, in response to the shock, and during the recovery phase. The interaction of Groups × Measurements is statistically significant in both studies. To explicate the basis for this interaction, the three time segments, i.e., anticipatory phase (-5 through -2), response to shock (-1 through $+1$), and recovery phase ($+2$ through $+5$), were subjected to separate ANOVAs. The results suggest that, contrary to H_2, the depressed Ss do not show a greater anticipatory response in Study No. 1 ($F<1$) and actually decrease slightly in skin conductance during this period in Study No. 2 (F

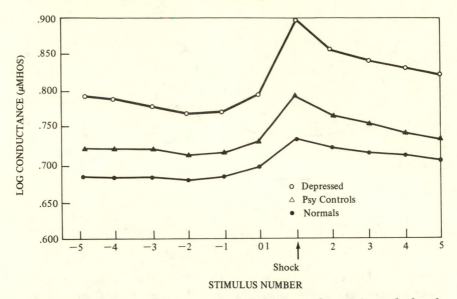

Figure 3. Skin conductance as a function of anticipated shock (shock between 0 and 1) averaged over the five trials (Study 11). (From Lewinsohn, Lobitz, & Wilson 1973.)

$= 2.7$, $df = 6$, 90, $p < .02$). Consistent with H_1, depressed Ss show a greater increase in skin conductance in response to the shock ($F = 1.8$, $p < .2$; $F = 2.9$, $p < .05$, for Studies 1 and 2 respectively). Contrary to H_3, there is a slight tendency for the normal control group to show less change in skin conductance during the recovery phase, but the differences between groups do not attain statistical significance.

There was a significant Groups × Trials interaction in Study No. 1($F = 2.3$, $df = 8$, 120, $p < .05$). However, this interaction is caused by the fact that both the depressed and the psychiatric control groups show less adaptation than the normal control group. The marginally significant Groups × Trials interaction in Study No.2 is caused by the fact that the psychiatric control group adapts less than the other two groups.

The statistically significant Groups × Sex × Trials interaction in Study No. 1 is also relevant to H_4. Inspection of the data indicates that the female depressed Ss adapt less than the psychiatric and normal Ss, but this effect is not revealed in the data for males. This triple interaction, however, is not replicated in Study No.2.

Table 3. Results of ANOVAS of Skin Conductance Data for Studies No. 1 and No. 2

Source of Variance	df	F Study No. 1	F Study No. 2	p Study No. 1	p Study No. 2
Groups (G)	2	0.5	0.6	NS	NS
Sex (S)	1	0.0	0.1	NS	NS
Trials (T)	4	7.2	23.6	0.01	0.001
Measurements (M)	10	69.5	51.0	0.001	0.001
$G \times S$	2	0.0	0.1	NS	NS
$G \times T$	8	2.3	1.6	0.05	0.20
$S \times T$	4	3.0	8.5	0.05	0.01
$G \times M$	20	1.7	2.2	0.05	0.01
$S \times M$	10	2.4	3.5	0.01	0.01
$T \times M$	40	1.9	2.4	0.01	0.01
$G \times S \times T$	8	3.2	0.6	0.01	NS
$G \times S \times M$	20	0.6	0.4	NS	NS
$G \times T \times M$	80	0.6	0.9	NS	NS
$S \times T \times M$	40	1.3	1.2	NS	NS
$G \times S \times T \times M$	80	0.6	0.8	NS	NS

Taken in their totality, the findings provide strong support for H_1. In both studies the depressed group was found to be more responsive to the aversive stimulus. Our results are consistent with those obtained by Zuckerman, Persky, and Curtis (1968), who also found that greater autonomic responsivity to a different aversive situation, namely the Cold Pressor Test, was associated with depression. Within the limits of these experimental manipulations and measurements, the results also suggest that the greater sensitivity of the depressed individual is restricted to the actual occurrence of the aversive stimuli and does not extend backward or forward in time.

Even though three out of the four predictions were not confirmed, the fact that the depressed individuals respond more to an aversive stimulus would still lead one to expect them to show a greater tendency to avoid and to withdraw from unpleasant situations. Hence, desensitization to aversive situations may be therapeutically useful with depressed individuals. The findings also suggest the hypothesis that the increased latency of response following the incidence of a negative social reaction from another person found in Stewart's study (1968) may be due to the emotional disruption experienced by the depressed individual in situations involving negative consequences.

Relationship Between Social Skill and Depression

In testing the hypothesis about the instrumental behavior of depressed individuals, we have tended to focus on social skill. The general hypothesis has been that depressed persons as a group are less socially skillful than nondepressed individuals. It is conceivable and not incompatible with the above that depression further reduces the person's social skill.

The first study of the social skill hypothesis was conducted by Rosenberry and coworkers (1969). The hypothesis being tested was that the depressed person's *timing* of social responses is deviant. In the experiment, subjects listened to tape-recorded speeches and responded by pressing a button whenever they would normally say or do something to maintain rapport with the speaker. The depressed subjects, as a group, responded less predictably and less homogeneously than did the control group.

Another unpublished study (Lewinsohn, Golding, Johannson, & Stewart 1968) had subjects talking to each other via teletypewriters. Pairs of subjects took turns talking to each other and each subject could say as much or as little as he wanted to before ending his turn. Subjects from two groups, depressed and nondepressed, were randomly assigned to one of three types of dyadic pairings; depressed-depressed; depressed-normal; normal-normal. Each pair of subjects was tested in front of the teletype machines. The subjects were able to communicate with each other via the teletypewriters, which were connected through a wall between the two rooms in which the subjects were seated. There was thus no visual contact between the subjects and they were unable to talk to each other except via the teletypewriters. For all subjects the number of words typed per person increased over the 45-minute session, but for depressed subjects the increase in output was much less than for nondepressed subjects ($F = 3.86$; $df = 1, 26$; $p < .05$ for one-tailed test). The data are graphically shown in Figure 4.

We have since then been concerned with more systematic comparisons between the interpersonal behavior of depressed and nondepressed individuals in small group situations and in the home.

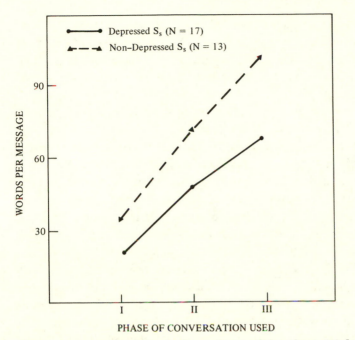

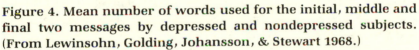

Figure 4. Mean number of words used for the initial, middle and final two messages by depressed and nondepressed subjects. (From Lewinsohn, Golding, Johansson, & Stewart 1968.)

Operational Measures of Social Skill

Social skill is defined as the ability to emit behaviors that are positively reinforced by others. This definition involves sequences of behavior consisting of actions emitted by an individual together with the reactions he elicits from the social environment. An individual is considered to be skillful to the extent that he elicits positive (and avoids negative) consequences from the social environment. A behavior sequence may elicit positive reactions in situation *A* but not in situation *B*. A second behavior sequence may elicit positive reactions in situation *B* but not in situation *A*. The socially skillful individual is the one who emits sequence 1 in situation *A* and sequence 2 in situation *B*. By definition, lack of social skill is associated with a low rate of positive reinforcement.

As a result of investigating the behavior of depressed and nondepressed persons in group therapy situations (Lewinsohn, Weinstein, & Alper 1970; Libet & Lewinsohn 1973) and in their home environment (Lewinsohn & Shaffer 1971; Shaffer & Lewinsohn 1971), a number of different measures of social skill have evolved. The measures differ in

that they focus on various aspects of an individual's interpersonal behavior. Nevertheless, they embody a common rationale. Consistent
with the definition of social skill, each measure of social skill is assumed
to be related to the amount of positive reinforcement an individual
elicits from the environment.

A system for coding the interactional behavior of people serves as an
operational basis for the measures of social skill. The system is shown
schematically in Figure 5. Behavior interactions are seen as having a
"source" and an "object". "Actions" are followed by "reactions"
which can be coded as either positive (i.e., expressions of affection,
approval, interest) or negative (criticism, disapproval, ignore, etc.). A
simplified illustration of an interaction involving four people might be
as follows: A makes a statement (an action) which is responded to by
B (a reaction). B continues talking (an action) and this is followed by a
reaction on the part of C, which in turn is followed by some new action
on the part of D, etc. Data so generated allow one to focus on any one
individual in terms of the actions which he emits and the kinds of
reactions he elicits. Two observers code all interactional behaviors. The
observers pace themselves with an automatic timer which delivers an
auditory and visual signal simultaneously every 30 seconds. Differences
between raters are conferenced. Interjudge agreement for the major
scoring categories has been quite high, and is shown in Table 4. A
manual for the coding system has been developed (Lewinsohn, et al.
1968).

1. *The amount of behavior emitted by the individual.* A very simple but
very important aspect of social skill is represented by the activity level
of the individual defined as the total number of actions emitted by him
(expressed as a rate per hour). We have found (Libet & Lewinsohn
1973; Shaffer & Lewinsohn 1971) that depressed individuals emit interpersonal behaviors at about half the rate of nondepressed control
subjects.

2. *Interpersonal efficiency.* One may conceptualize the "efficiency"
with which an individual interacts with other people in two different
ways. *Interpersonal Efficiency-Actor* is represented by the ratio of the
number of behaviors directed toward the individual (return, income),
divided by the number of behaviors he emits towards other people
(work, effort). If individuals X and Y each emit 100 actions during a
session and X is the object of 80 actions while Y is the object of 120

Action		Reaction			
Interactional Categories		Positive		Negative	
Psychol. Complaint	Psy C	Affection	Aff	Criticism	Crit
Somatic Complaint	Som C	Approval	App	Disapproval	Disapp
Criticism	Crit.	Agree	Agr	Disagree	Disagree
Praise	Pr	Laughter	L+	Ignore	Ign
Information Request	I–	Interest	Int	Change Topic	Ch T
Information Giving	I+	Continues talking	Con T	Interrupts	Inter
Request for Help	Req H	about topic		Physical Punishment	Pun
Personal Problem	PP	Physical Affection	Phys Aff		
Instrument Problem	IP				
Other People's Problems	OP < $\frac{I}{E}$				
Talking about abstract impersonal general, etc.					

Content–Topics	
School	Sch
Self	X, Y, Z
Other People (group, family)	X, Y, Z
Treatment	Rx
Therapist	T
Sex	Sx

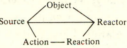

Figure 5. Behavior rating scale.

actions, then Y gets more for what he does than X. Interpersonal Efficiency-Actor looks at the individuals efficiency from the point of view of what he has to do relative to what he gets. A low Interpersonal Efficiency-Actor ratio would imply that the individual is on a low schedule of reinforcement.

Another way of looking at interpersonal efficiency is from the vantage point of the other person, wondering what he "gets" for interacting

Table 4. Estimated Spearman-Brown Reliability Coefficients for One Conferenced Rating Based on 3-way ANOVAS[a] (10 Persons, Categories, Two Conferenced Ratings) (From Libet & Lewinsohn 1973)

Source	Actions		Reactions	
	Emit	Elicit	Emit	Elicit
(A) Persons	0.995	0.774	0.956	0.973
(B) Categories	0.800	0.763	0.890	0.893
(AB) Profiles	0.851	0.634	0.956	0.914

[a]Winer (1962, pp. 124–132, 289) discusses the statistical basis of and outlines the computational procedures for estimation of reliability using an analysis of variance model.

with our subject (e.g., a depressed individual). For example, if *B* (the other person) emits 10 actions to *A* (a nondepressed) person and 10 actions to *C* (a depressed patient), and if he elicits 20 actions from *A* but only 5 from *C* then clearly it is more "efficient" for *B* to interact with *A* than it is for him to interact with *C*. *C* might be said to be less reciprocal (his *Interpersonal Efficiency-Other* ratio is lower), and holding other things constant, one would over a period of time expect *B* to reduce his interactions with *A* and to increase his interactions toward *C*. We have not been able to find systematic differences between depressed and nondepressed individuals in either Interpersonal Efficiency-Actor or in Interpersonal Efficiency-Other (Libet & Lewinsohn 1973; Shaffer & Lewinsohn 1971).

A post hoc analysis (Shaffer & Lewinsohn 1971) indicated, however, that while it was impossible to predict the direction of lack of reciprocity, the relationships of depressed individuals tended to be less reciprocal overall, i.e., the depressed individual either did much more for the other person than the other person did for him or vice versa. We intend to examine this emergent (or revised) hypothesis again with new data. One might hypothesize that to the extant relationships lack reciprocity, they would tend to be less stable over longer times.

3. *Interpersonal range.* Another aspect of social skill, interpersonal range, concerns the number of individuals with whom a person interacts, i.e., the ones to whom he emits behaviors and from whom he elicits behaviors.

To quantify the degree to which an individual distributes his actions equally to other members, a measure was derived from information theory (Attneave 1959). The interpersonal range measure [Relative Uncertainty Value (R)] varies from 0 to 1. If an individual emits actions to one other group member, $R = 0$, which indicates a minimum unpredictability and minimum interpersonal range. Conversely, if a person distributes his actions equally among his peers, $R = 1$, which indicates maximum unpredictability of the targets of his actions or maximum interpersonal range. Procedural details on how to compute R have been provided elsewhere (Libet & Lewinsohn 1973). On the basis of small-group interaction data, the prediction that depressed individuals have restricted interpersonal range is supported for males but not for females (Libet & Lewinsohn 1973).

4. *Use of positive reactions.* Another aspect of social skill involves

reinforcing the behavior of others toward the subject. The number of positive reactions emitted per session (holding activity level constant) is used to measure this aspect of social skill. The depressed subjects emitted a smaller proportion of positive reactions than did the nondepressed persons (Libet & Lewinsohn 1973).

5. *Action latency.* Another operational measure of social skill is represented by action latency, which is defined as the lapse of time between the reaction of another person to the subject's verbalization, and another subsequent action by that subject. In order to maintain the behavior of others, it is not merely sufficient to reinforce their behavior, but this has to be done at the appropriate time, namely, in close temporal proximity to the other person's behavior. Also, the individual who delays (has a long action latency) is more likely to "lose the floor". We have found (Stewart 1968; Libet & Lewinsohn 1973) significant differences that reflect a 3:1 ratio in latency for depressed and nondepressed.

6. *General comments about social skill and depression.* Though the data support the hypothesis that measures of social skill discriminate between depressed and nondepressed groups, there remain many unanswered questions such as, Does the social skill of an individual when he is depressed differ systematically from that when he is not depressed? Clinically, one can find individuals who show extreme manifestations of one or more of the above-mentioned measures of social skill. The advantage of the social skill measure is that they are quantitative and can easily be used to define goals for behavior change (Killian 1971; Lewinsohn, Weinstein, & Alper 1970). New hypotheses that have suggested themselves to us and which can be tested empirically but for which we have as yet no data are as follows:

H-1. The social skill of depressed persons is more adversely affected by size of group than that of nondepressed persons.

H-2. Being unfamiliar to others in the group has a more negative effect on social skill of depressed than of nondepressed persons.

THE RELEVANCE OF THE BEHAVIORAL THEORY OF DEPRESSION TO THE PHENOMENA OF AGING

Within a behavioral framework, depression is conceptualized as an extinction phenomena. On reading the gerontological literature one is struck by the many behavioral similarities between the depressed and the elderly person: (1) One of the most striking features of both old age and depression is a progressive reduction in the rate of behavior. The concept of "disengagement" has been advanced to account for this reduction of behavior. It is assumed to be a natural process which the elderly person accepts and desires, and which is thought to have intrinsic determinants (Cumming & Henry 1961). From a behavioral framework, the elderly person's reduced rate of behavior suggests that his behavior is no longer being reinforced by his environment, i.e., that he, like the depressed person, is on an extinction schedule. (2) Other aspects of the depressive syndrome (feeling rejected, loss of self-esteem, loss of interest, psychophysiological symptoms, etc.) are quite common among the elderly (Wolf 1959). (3) Motivation is a critical problem in the elderly, as it is in the depressed patient. It is hard to find effective reinforcers for either. The number of potentially reinforcing events seems reduced. (4) The elderly person and the depressed person are turned inward, and focus on themselves, their memories, fantasies, and the past. The hypothesis immediately suggests itself that a reduction in the response contingent rate of positive reinforcement is a critical antecedent condition for many of the behavioral changes described in the elderly person.

We are in the process (Lewinsohn & MacPhillamy 1972) of collecting data about the following hypotheses:

H-1. The number of events and activities with reinforcement potential diminishes with age.

H-2. The availability of reinforcement in the elderly individual's environment has diminished because of separation from children, former friends, business associates, and generally those people who have been maintaining the individual's behavior.

H-3. There are systematic differences between groups differing in age on the social skill measures, with increasing age being associated with decreasing social skill.

CONCLUDING REMARKS

The hypotheses and the conclusions that have been presented are meant to be very tentative. Our conceptualization of depression and the kinds of questions we have been asking are in a state of flux. New possibilities suggest themselves continuously and undoubtedly the hypotheses will have to be revised and new ones developed.

We do think that we are developing methods for studying depression. Perhaps this constitutes progress.

REFERENCES

Attneave, F. *Application of information theory of psychology*. New York: Holt, Rinehart, & Winston, 1959.

Azrin, N. H., Hutchinson, R. R., & Hake, D. F. Extinction-induced aggression. *Journal of the Experimental Analysis of Behavior*, 1966, **9**, 191–204.

Beck, A. T. *Depression: Clinical, experimental, and theoretical aspects*. New York: Harper & Row, 1967.

Cautela, J., & Kastenbaum, R. A reinforcement survey schedule for use in therapy, training, and research. *Psychological Reports*, 1967, **20**, 1115–1130.

Cumming, E., & Henry, W. *Growing old: The process of disengagement*. New York: Basic Books, 1961.

Fenichel, O. The psychoanalytic theory of neurosis. New York: W. W. Norton, 1945.

Grinker, R. R., Miller, J., Sabshin, M., Nunn, R. J., & Nunnally, J. C. *The phenomena of depression*. New York: Harper & Row, 1961.

Hare, R. D. A conflict and learning theory analysis of psychopathic behavior. *Journal of Research in Crime and Delinquency*, 1965, **2**, 12–19.

Johansson, S. L., Lewinsohn, P. M., & Flippo, J. R. *An application of the Premack Principle to the verbal behavior of depressed subjects*. Paper presented at the meeting of the Association for the Advancement of Behavior Therapy, 1969. Mimeo. University of Oregon, 1969.

Killian, D. H. *The effect of intructions and social reinforcement on selected categories of behavior emitted by depressed persons in a small group setting*. Unpublished doctoral dissertation. University of Oregon, 1971.

Lewinsohn, P. M., et al. *Manual of instruction for the behavior rating use for the observation of interpersonal behavior*. Unpublished manuscript. University of Oregon, 1968. Revised, 1971.

Lewinsohn, P. M., & Atwood, G. E. Depression: A clinical-research approach. *Psychotherapy: Theory, Research, & Practice*, 1969, **6**, 166–171.

Lewinsohn, P. M., Golding, S. L., Johansson, S. L., & Stewart, R. C. Patterns of communication in depressed and nondepressed subjects. Unpublished data, 1968.

Lewinsohn, P. M., & Libet, J. Pleasant events, activity schedules, and depression. *Journal of Abnormal Psychology*, 1972, **79**, 291–295.

Lewinsohn, P. M., Lobitz, C., & Wilson, S. "Sensitivity" of depressed individuals to aversive stimuli. *Journal of Abnormal Psychology*, 1973, **81**, 259–263.

Lewinsohn, P. M., Shaffer, M., & Libet, J. *Depression: A clinical-research approach*. Paper presented at the meeting of the Western Psychological Association, 1969; Mimeo, University of Oregon, 1969.

Lewinsohn, P. M., & Shaffer, M. The use of home observation as an integral part of the treatment of depression: Preliminary report and case studies. *Journal of Consulting and Clinical Psychology*, 1971, **37**, 87–94.

Lewinsohn and P. M., & Shaw, D. A. Feedback about interpersonal behavior as an agent of behavior change: A case study in the treatment of depression. *Psychotherapy & Psychosomatics*. 1969, **17**, 82–88.

Lewinsohn, P. M., Weinstein, M. S., & Shaw, D. A. Depression: A clinical-research approach. In Rubin, R. D., & Frank, C. M. (Eds.) *Advances in Behavior Therapy*, 1968, New York: Academic Press, 1969.

Lewinsohn, P. M., Weinstein, M. S. & Alper, T. A behaviorally oriented approach to the group treatment of depressed persons: A methodological contribution. *Journal of Clinical Psychology*, 1970, **4**, 525–532.

Libet, J., & Lewinsohn, P. M. The concept of social skill with special reference to the behavior of depressed persons. *Journal of Consulting and Clinical Psychology*, 1973, **40**, 304–312.

Lubin, B. Adjective checklists for the measurement of depression. *Archives of General Psychology*, 1965, **12**, 57–62.

MacPhillamy, D. J., & Lewinsohn, P. M. *Pleasant Events Schedule*, 1971.

MacPhillamy, D. J., & Lewinsohn, P. M. The structure of reported reinforcement. In preparation.

Paykel, E. S., Meyers, J. K., Dicnett, M. N., Klerman, G. L., Lindenthall, J. J., & Pepper, M. P. *Life events and depression: A controlled study*. Mimeo. Yale University, 1969.

Rosenberry, C., Weiss, R. L., & Lewinsohn, P. M. *Frequency and skill of emitted social reinforcement in depressed and nondepressed subjects*. Paper presented at Meeting of Western Psychological Association, 1969. Mimeo. University of Oregon, 1969.

Schachter, S., & Singer, J. E. Cognitive, social, and physiological determinants of emotional state. *Psychological Review*, 1962, **69**, 379–399.

Shaffer, M., & Lewinsohn, P. M. *Interpersonal behaviors in the home of depressed versus nondepressed psychiatric and normal controls: A test of several Hypotheses*. Paper presented at meeting of the Western Psychological Association, 1971. Mimeo, University of Oregon, 1971.

Stewart, R. C. *The differential effects of positive and negative social reinforcement upon depressed and nondepressed subjects*. Unpublished Masters thesis. University of Oregon, 1968.

Winer, B. J. *Statistical principles in experimental design*. New York: McGraw-Hill, 1962.

Wolf, K. *The biological, sociological, and physiological aspects of aging*. Springfield, Ill.: Charles Thomas, 1959.

Zimet, C. N., & Schineider, C. Effects of group size on interaction in small groups. *Journal of Social Psychology*, 1969, **77**, 177–187.

Zuckerman, M., Persky, S., Curtis, G. C. Relationships among anxiety, depression, hostility, and autonomic variables. *Journal of Nervous and Mental Disease*, 1968, **146**, 481–487.

DISCUSSION

Dr. Seligman: I find Dr. Lewinsohn's data very rich and significant, particularly in view of my own research focus. However, I would like to address myself to the theoretical basis and particularly to the hypothesis that a low rate of positive reinforcement explains the findings. I will try to outline the reasons leading me to believe that the hypothesis of a low rate of positive reinforcement does not serve as an adequate explanation for the data at hand.

When one takes a concept such as a low rate of positive reinforcement, which after all emerges from the animal literature, there should be an empirical basis in this literature indicating that a low rate of reinforcement corresponds to his findings. That is, in the animal one should see low activity level and low latency following a decrease in positive reinforcement before any of his clinical findings can be meaningful.

There are three lines of evidence indicating that this correspondence is not to be found in the animal literature. One is that changing the rate of reinforcement from a high to a low rate is the whole basis not of the depression literature but of the frustration literature. Indeed, that is a perfect way to generate more behavior in an animal, at least transiently and occasionally over long periods of time. One might retort in response to this contention that a low rate of reinforcement produces a chronic extinction schedule, but then I would point out that what you are describing is not truly a low rate of reinforcement but is rather intermittent reinforcement. Despite Dr. Ferster's remarks about the maintenance of the repertoire, it simply cannot be denied that animals on an intermittent schedule (or as Dr. Lewinsohn states, a low rate of reinforcement) are emitting absolutely large quantities of behavior and not low rates of behaviors similar to the depressed state. It is a well-known and documented fact that intermittent schedules are very effective in obtaining large quantities of behavior in animals. Note, if one hypothesizes that the depressed person is on an extinction schedule, he generates a paradoxical prediction. If the person were being maintained on an intermittent reinforcement schedule (a low rate of reinforcement), and then were to be experimentally shifted to a real extinction schedule consisting of no reinforcement at all, the hypothesis forces the prediction that a depressed person would persist much longer than a nondepressed person. I suspect one would not be able to verify this experimentally or clinically, because the principles coming from the animal literature clearly tell us that intermittent reinforcement causes greater persistence.

Finally, I would suggest that the hypothesis stating that there is a lack of contingency between responding and reinforcement in the depressed subjects best explains Dr. Lewisohn's findings.

Dr. Lewinsohn: I would like to address myself to Dr. Seligman's final point. Of course, it is the temporal relationship between the behavior of a person and positive reinforcement which I assume to be of critical importance for the occurrence of "depression". It is essential that the reinforcement be contingent upon behavior. I think it is a clinical fact that giving (noncontingently) to the depressed person does not reduce his depression; for it is not the absolute amount of attention or other "goodies" received that is critical but the fact that the environment provides consequences sufficient to maintain the individual's behavior. One might say that the depressed person is not getting paid much for what he is doing, and that it is being paid for what one does that is critical and not just being given a check. For example, in the case of the elderly person who recieves his Social Security check regardless of what he does, his behavior is not being maintained by the check.

Dr. Lasky: I would appreciate some clarification on the investigation of the interpersonal range of the depressed person, which appears to me to be desirable research. Could you elaborate briefly on your work and the assumptions underlying the experiments you have done?

Dr. Lewinsohn: We define "social skill" in a circular way, i.e., as those behaviors that elicit positive reinforcement from others. We assume there are a wide variety of behaviors used by individuals to elicit positive reinforcement from others, and we have been searching for quantitative measures with which to define social skill operationally. Our major hypothesis is that individuals who are prone to depression are less "skillful" in social, interactional situations. One of our measures (interpersonal range) was generated by the clinical observation that some depressed individuals are clearly overinvolved with one significant person to the exclusion of most other potential relationships. We are collecting data in group therapy situations about this hypothesis and certainly observe depressed individuals with extremely restricted interpersonal ranges. Our observations have also led us to hypothesize that as the size of the group increases, the participation of depressed individuals diminishes. Depressed patients appear to be more comfortable in dyadic relationships, and their behavior begins to drop off when they are in groups of more than three people.

Dr. Lasky: In your research program do you actually set up dyads or do you study dyads within a larger group setting?

Dr. Lewinsohn: Not yet. We plan to manipulate group size. On occasion we have subdivided some of our groups, which typically consist of either eight or twelve individuals, for specific tasks.

Dr. Ekman: Are you measuring verbal behavior only or verbal behavior plus nonverbal behavior?

Dr. Lewinsohn: Our data are based on verbal behavior only.

Dr. Ekman: Do you have any data to suggest that patients who interact primarily with one or two other persons in a group receive less total positive reinforcement than others who spread their interaction around among a larger number of group members?

Dr. Lewinsohn: We have the data but I cannot answer that question at this time.

Dr. Chodoff: Clinically, we know that it is not only depressive patients but almost all psychiatric patients who show deficits in their interpersonal skills and reduced interpersonal fossae. It is also the paranoid as well as the depressive who produces negative reactions in the people in his environment and who has a negative cognitive set which purports that the world is against him.

There are two aspects to Dr. Lewinsohn's research that I would like to question. The first concerns the sample selection. The portion of the sample of "depressed" people that troubles me comes from classrooms where Dr. Lewinsohn has selected those students who scored high on a rating scale which he administered.

I'm not sure that I could clinically consider these people depressed; it seems they are, at the best, mild or borderline depressives. The other portion of the sample is composed of patients who are more obviously depressed, but, again, only mildly so, for none of them are hospitalized and they are all living at home and indeed are clinic patients. I have great difficulty accepting findings based on the college students and also some reservations about the findings based on the depressed outpatient sample as indicative of the more serious "clinical" depressions.

My second question concerns the use of a rating scale as the primary criterion of depression. There are, as you know, many other ways to diagnose depressive illness in addition to the patient's own report and evaluation of his feeling state. Findings such as anorexia, weight loss, and other somatic concerns, as well as clinical judgments, may often be entirely at variance with the mood the patient ascribes to himself.

In addition to the methodological problems, I see a historical redundancy in this approach. Dr. Lewinsohn states that depression is maintained by a lack of contingent positive reinforcement and, although the language is new, at least to me, it seems that he is talking about a phenomenon clinicians, patients, and their families have been aware of for years. This approach also has a long history as a therapeutic device. Depressed patients are told to "get out there and find something you enjoy." Or, "Go out and do it—you are not as bad as you think you are." Depressed patients receive plenty of positive encouragement and they get it until it comes out their ears, but most of them cannot use it! That depressed patients lack and want positive reinforcement is perhaps an assumption that may not be true. Profoundly depressed individuals no longer enjoy doing anything. If you force them to engage in activity, they will tell you they do not derive much satisfaction from it. This seems to be a common-sense approach which everyone takes in dealing with depressed patients, and I might add that it is not just the families of depressed people who try this method. Every psychiatrist, whether he admits it or not, generally tries to get depressed people to engage in activity and to enjoy themselves. It usually does not work very well, however. I conclude that Dr. Lewinsohn is really systematizing, in a rather elaborate way, a type of approach which—at least in my experience—has been tried and has not proved very effective.

Dr. Lewinsohn: Dr. Chodoff focuses on an extremely important methodological point, namely, the selection of subjects in research studies on depression. As we all know, depression rarely exists in "pure" form and different researchers' operational definitions of depression and of depressed patients vary widely. In our research we employ a two-stage selection strategy using an abbreviated MMPI to screen very large samples, and then conduct semistructured interviews with those whose MMPI scores exceed certain critical levels. On the basis of the interview, the subjects are rated on some of the factors identified by Grinker. To be included as a depressed subject, a person has to have an intensity of depression exceeding a certain cut-off score, and depression must constitute his major presenting psychopathology. In absolute terms I would place the depression level of our subjects from mild to moderate.

I would also like to address myself to the other issue raised by Dr. Chodoff, namely, the similarities and the differences between our approach and what might be called the "common sense" approach to the management of the depressed patient. I believe our approach differs in two ways. In the first place we attempt to identify those events and activites likely to be reinforcing (meaningful) for the patient and we do not assume we know beforehand which these might be. For example, we are beginning to use the Pleasant Events Schedule to pinpoint specific activities for individual patients because they are functionally related to his being or not being depressed.

The second point of departure from a strictly common-sense approach is to be found in our systematic efforts to apply reinforcement principles. We are well aware that the depressed patient often receives a great deal of advice and encouragement and that, more often than not, he is unable to use it. In fact, depressed patients are very resistant to suggestions and sensitive about being controlled. We employ a reinforcement paradigm designed to increase the depressed person's activity level. For example, we have been using the amount of time the patient can talk about his depression, as well as the total amount of therapy time, as a reinforcement for becoming more active. Our results confirm Dr. Beck's research findings that once the person actually begins to engage in activities, he does receive reinforcement and his mood changes. The difficulty is to get the depressed person to begin to engage in activities, even though intellectually he appreciates that he should.

Dr. Friedman: Dr. Lewinsohn, if I understand you correctly you are maintaining that depression is a state of the organism and that you are addressing in your research what we might call depression of affect rather than what some of us have labeled earlier in this conference as the "clinical condition of depression." In other words, you do not see a qualitative difference between the "clinical state" and depression that sometimes occurs in every human being.

Dr. Lewinsohn: We do define depression in our research as a state that can occur in any of us in different degrees or intensities and under given circumstances.

Dr. Goodwin: The theoretical notion that depression exists as a continuum from everyday sadness to the severe "clinical state" is easier to maintain if one refrains from studying hospitalized patients. I find it an appealing construct, but I believe that future research will not bear it out.

Dr. Tabachnick: I would also like to respond to the criticism Dr. Chodoff raises and suggest an alternative way of viewing the situation. I agree with Dr. Chodoff's observation that much of the activity described by Dr. Lewinsohn and other clinicians is precisely what most human beings have been doing to other human beings who are called "depressed" for centuries. However, I think we are hasty in assuming that such activity by concerned friends and relatives is ineffective; after all, depressions do end. Human beings do not live outside a social milieu, and the intervention of that milieu may be one of the factors that brings a depression to a close. Perhaps our assumption that intervention of this type is ineffective is hasty, because we are expecting the results to be direct and obvious instead of indirect and part of a general picture of improvement. Perhaps all of the cajolery and encouragement which the depressed person receives has a cumulative effect and is *the* significant variable in shortening or terminating the depression.

Both Dr. Chodoff's contention and my counter suggestion are only hypotheses at present, and one of the values of Dr. Lewinsohn's research is that it does represent an approach to the problem that may allow us to choose more intelligently between such widely varying explanations.

Dr. Lewinsohn: I could not agree more!

Dr. Chodoff: So far our discourse has been based on hypotheses generated on the basis of behavior only. We really have not taken into account a hypothetical construct of immense value in psychology, namely, the unconscious. In reality we discover that behavior is rather complicated and that superficial explanations are often undermined by more contradictory unconscious determinants. A person may agree that some activity or some input would be reinforcing to him, and yet at a deeper level he may be forced to reject this input because it arouses unconscious conflicts. We do not do the complexity of human nature justice if we cling to the idea of rational man only.

Dr. Lewinsohn: There are obviously many different levels at which one can approach personality. We have found it useful to focus mainly on the depressed person's behavior.

Dr. Beck: Dr. Tabachnick has touched one of the truly positive aspects of Dr. Lewinsohn's research—the fact that it is a systematic application of positive reinforcement. I have research data to corroborate the finding that the systematic application and tailoring of treatment to the individual patient works. We have found improvement in mood after giving depressed patients "positive informational feedback," a form of reinforcement which demonstrates to the patient that he can succeed on a task which he previously predicted would end in failure.

Dr. Friedman: I would like to draw on Dr. Seligman's findings about the control issue. Dr. Seligman has demonstrated that the control of trauma is critical in the etiology of depression, and in a similar vein Dr. Beck explained that the expression of hostility seems to be effective in depressive states because it shows the person that he can exercise control over his environment. From the therapeutic standpoint I believe we all agree that we must *give* the depressed person something, and I hope we can agree that the "quality" of what we give is essential.

I believe Dr. Chodoff is equating positive reinforcement with positive encouragement or with other signs of something "positive." We all know that doesn't do much good, and I believe the strategy advocated by Drs. Lewinsohn and Beck is a tribute to the necessity for showing the depressed person that he can control his world. It is not enough to sit down with the depressed person and determine with him what he thinks he would like. That can only be the first step. The second step is to devise a method to show him that he can obtain what he wants because of the power or ability or control he has. In other words, he can earn it.

Dr. Lewinsohn: Dr. Friedman not only points to some of the underlying similarities between our positions which might otherwise be obscured by semantic differences, but he also focuses on the importance of having the depressed individual learn that he can control his environment by his own actions.

Dr. Klerman: I would like to advance the hypothesis that Dr. Lewinsohn's research sample consists of two groups. One is a group of relatively "normal" people who have a mood fluctuation as part of "normal" life. I believe it is very important to study the depressive mood as part of a person's interaction with his environment. A second group is composed of people who are suffering from an "ambulatory depression." The determinants of the relationship between external events and mood in the latter group probably are determined more by internal factors than they are among the normal people of the first group.

I hypothesize that in the first group, in which the mood seems to follow a behavior or an event, we are dealing with relatively normal people because that is indeed what we consider normal, namely, that contingent positive reinforcement promotes a sense of well-being. The second group, in whom the mood disturbance appears to precede the activity, seems to me to characterize what empathically I feel is the condition we are observing in the clinical state of depression. Earlier I used the label "endogenous" to refer to the second group. I realize this may not be the best descriptive term for this subsample because, historically, "endogenous" has connoted biological or constitutional determination. Perhaps the concept of "depressive character" would be more appropriate than "endogenous," but I must admit I am uncertain whether the concept of the depressive character actually refers to a specific personality organization in which we see dependency, excessive requirements for reassurance, and low self-esteem, or whether it refers to a person who is perking along at a low grade of clinical depression.

I urge Dr. Lewinsohn to examine his clinical population as admixtures of these group and admixtures of depression as a normal state and as a clinical entity.

Dr. Dyrud: I am troubled that we are employing what is really a very precise language in a loose way. I believe the study which Dr. Lewinsohn has described represents more of an empirical, Meyerian type of research than it does a Skinnerian study.

I think it might be more appropriate to use the term "response" instead of "reinforcement." The term "reinforcement" has great precision when we are looking at schedules of reinforcement, and I find it part of an interesting and challenging area of research. However, I'm not sure that the clinical field is ready for research which purports to employ the precision of the animal laboratory.

My plea to Dr. Lewinsohn and others is to use terms such as "response" and "pleasant event" instead of "reinforcement" because they are not of the same order. Perhaps when the data are more refined, we can go back and begin to study the phenomena more precisely, using a language consistent with greater precision and control.

6. Learned Helplessness and Depression

William R. Miller, Robert A. Rosellini,
Martin E. P. Seligman

Each year, 4 to 8 million people in the United States suffer from debilitating depression, which is possibly the most common major mental disorder. Many people recover from depression, but unlike most other forms of psychopathology it can be lethal. One out of every 100 persons afflicted by a depressive illness dies by suicide (Williams, Friedman, and Secunda, 1970). The economic cost is also enormous. Loss of productivity and cost of treatment among adults in the United States amount to between $1.3 and $4 billion a year (Williams, Friedman, and Secunda).

Most of us have experienced some sort of depression—we are sad, we cry without knowing why, we feel helpless, worthless, or unsure, we lose interest in our own lives. Yet in spite of being a universal experience, depression has remained a mystery. This chapter highlights qualities that depression and the phenomenon of learned helplessness have in common. It suggests that learned helplessness can provide a model for understanding *reactive* depression, or depression caused by environmental rather than internal events.

The term *learned helplessness* describes what happens when prior exposure to uncontrollable aversive experiences interferes with escape and avoidance learning (Overmier and Seligman, 1967; Seligman and Maier, 1967). The main behavioral symptoms of learned helplessness—deficits in response initiation and in association of reinforcement with responding—are seen as resulting from learning that reinforcement and responding are independent. Such learning is said to lower performance by reducing the incentive for instrumental responding, which results in lowered response initiation. In addition, learning that reinorcement and responding are independent interferes with learning that responses later control reinforcement (Seligman, Maier, and Solomon, 1971).

In order to compare learned helplessness and depression, let us look at their similarities in four areas: symptoms, cause, treatment, and prevention. Learned helplessness and depression have not been convincingly demonstrated to be similar in all four areas as yet, but making the form of the argument explicit has two virtues: it enables us to test the model and it can help us to narrow the definition of depression. As the two phenomena overlap in one area, we can then test the model by looking for other similarities. Say, for example, that learned helplessness in animals and men presents similar symptoms to reactive depression. If the etiology of the two is similar, and if we find that learned helplessness can be cured by forcibly exposing subjects to responding that produces relief, we can make a prediction about the cure of depression. The recognition that responding is effective in producing reinforcement should be the central issue in successful therapy. If this is tested and confirmed, the model is strengthened. Strengthening our model is a two-way street: if Imipramine (a trycyclic drug) helps reactive depression, does it also relieve learned helplessness in animals?

In addition to being easier to test, the model can help sharpen the definition of depression. The laboratory phenomenon of learned helplessness is well defined. Depression is not so easily defined. Rather, it is a convenient diagnostic label that denotes a constellation of symptoms, not one of which is necessary. The relationship among phenomena called depression is perhaps best described as a family resemblance (See Wittgenstein, 1953, paragraphs 66–77). Depressed people often report feeling sad, but sadness is not a necessary symptom of depression. Consider a patient who does not feel sad, but who experiences verbal and motor retardation, cries a lot, is anorexic, and whose symptoms can be traced to his wife's death. Depression is the appropriate clinical label for his condition. Some of these symptoms may be absent in different types of depression; other symptoms may take their place. Clinical labels can best be seen as denoting "a complicated network of similarities overlapping and crisscrossing" (Wittgenstein, 1953). A well-defined laboratory model does not mirror the openendedness of the clinical label; rather it imposes necessary conditions on it. Thus if a particular model of depression is valid, some phenomena formerly classified as depression may be excluded. We as psychologists are engaged in an attempt to refine the classification: learned helplessness does not model all phenomena now called depression. Rather, we think there will some day come to be "helplessness depressions"—embodied in passive people who have negative cognitive sets about the effects of their own actions, who become depressed upon the loss of an important source of gratification. The disorder will have a given prognosis, a preferred set of therapies, and perhaps a given physiology. Some phenomena not now called depression—such as the catastrophe syndrome (Wallace, 1957)—will be included. Others, now called depressions, will be excluded—manic depression, for example. Learned helplessness attempts to understand depressions like that of the man whose wife had died. His slowness in initiating responses, his belief that he was powerless and hopeless, his negative outlook on the future all began as a reaction to having lost his control over gratification and relief of suffering.

Let us now examine learned helplessness in the laboratory and depression in nature.

SYMPTOMS

Learned Helplessness

When an experimentally naive dog receives escape-avoidance training in a shuttle box, it usually responds in this way: at the onset of the first traumatic electric shock, the dog runs frantically about until it accidentally scrambles over the barrier and so escapes the shock. On the next trial, the dog, running and howling, crosses the barrier more quickly than before. Eventually, the dog learns to avoid shock altogether. Overmier and Seligman (1967) and Seligman and Maier (1967) found a striking difference between this pattern of behavior and the pattern exhibited by dogs first given inescapable electric shocks in a Pavlovian hammock. Those dogs resemble a naive dog in their first reactions to shock in the shuttle box. In dramatic contrast to a naive dog, a dog that has experienced uncontrollable shocks before avoidance training usually soon stops running and sits or lies, quietly whining, until shock terminates. The dog does not cross the barrier and escape from shock. Rather, it seems to give up resisting and to passively accept the shock. On succeeding trials, the dog continues to fail to make escape movements and it accepts as much shock as the experimenter chooses to give.

Dogs that have first experienced inescapable shock demonstrate another peculiar characteristic. They occasionally jump the barrier early in training and escape, but then they revert to taking the shock; they appear to learn nothing by jumping the barrier and so avoiding the shock. In naive dogs a successful escape response is a reliable predictor of future successful escape responses.

We studied the escape-avoidance behavior of over 150 dogs that had received prior inescapable shocks. Two-thirds of these dogs did not escape shock; the other third escaped and avoided shock in normal fashion. Clearly, failure to escape is highly maladaptive—it means that the dog is experiencing 50 seconds of severe, pulsating shock on each trial. In contrast, only 6 percent of experimentally naive dogs fail to escape in the shuttle box. Dogs either fail to escape on almost any trial or learn normally; an intermediate outcome is rare.

We use the term *learned helplessness* to describe the interference with adaptive responses produced by inescapable shock and also as a short-hand to describe the process that we believe underlies the behavior (this will be discussed further later in this model.) Learned helplessness in the dog is defined by two types of behavior: (1) dogs that have had experience with uncontrollable shock *fail to initiate responses* to escape shock or are slower to make responses than naive dogs, and (2) if the dog does make a response that turns off shock, it has *more trouble than a naive dog learning that responding is effective*.

This example of learned helplessness is not an isolated phenomenon. In addition to the reports of Overmier and Seligman (1967), and Seligman and Maier (1967), such interference was also reported in dogs by Carlson and Black (1957), Leaf (1964), Seligman, Maier, and Geer (1968), Overmier (1968), Maier (1970), and Seligman and Groves (1970). Nor is it restricted to dogs: deficits in escaping or avoiding shock after experience with uncontrollable shock has been shown in rats (Seligman and Beagley, 1975; Katzev and Miller, 1974; and Shurman and Katzev, 1975), cats (Seward and Humphrey, 1967), dogs (Overmier and Seligman, 1967), fish (Behrend and Bitterman, 1963), chickens (Maser and Gallup, 1974), and mice (Braud, Wepmann, and Russo, 1969). Similar deficits are found in humans following experience with uncontrollable noise (Hiroto and Seligman, 1975).

We have worked extensively with rats and have found one procedure to be successful (Seligman and Beagley, 1975; Seligman, Rosellini, and Kozak, 1975). We expose them to 80 trials of 15 seconds of inescapable shock. Twenty-four hours later we test them to see whether they will press a bar to escape shock on a Fixed-Ratio 3 (FR-3) schedule. The behavior of a rat that has experienced inescapable shock is very much like that of a similarly shocked dog. Even though it may successfully escape shock on the first few trials of the test, the rat eventually sits passively in one corner of the experimental chamber and receives the total amount of scheduled shock. Maier, Albin, and Testa (1973) have also found similar behavior in rats. After 64 exposures to 5 seconds of inescapable shock while restrained, their rats showed a deficit in acquiring a shuttling escape response. Rats were required to cross from one side of the two-way shuttlebox to the other and then back again (Fixed Ratio-2) to terminate shock. Few of them could complete the task. In addition, the more trials of inescapable shock (Looney and Cohen, 1972), or the higher the intensity of the inescapable shock (Seligman and Rosellini, unpublished data) the poorer was the subsequent performance.

When inescapable shock is given to weanling rats, the rats also exhibit escape learning deficits as adults (Hannum, Rosellini, and Seligman, 1976). Both our research and that of Maier and his coworkers have indicated that only a relatively difficult voluntary testing response yields large deficits in rats (Maier, Albin, and Testa, 1973; Seligman and Beagley, 1975). Helplessness does not seem to undermine reflexive responses.

However, if we are to propose a model of depression in man, we must have proof that learned helplessness occurs in man. And it does.

Hiroto (1974) used an analogue of the shuttlebox, a finger shuttle, to test for the symptoms of learned helplessness in human subjects. A finger shuttle is a rectangular box with a handle protruding out from the top. With one finger a subject can move the handle from one end of the box to the other to stop noise. Hiroto found that subjects who had listened to inescapable loud noise were severely impaired in their ability to learn to shuttle to escape noise. Groups who had experienced escapable noise and no noise showed no impairment. It is important to realize that a well-designed helplessness experiment always consists of these three groups: one that experiences some inescapable event, a second that experiences exactly the same event but can do something to control it, and a third that does not experience the event. The symptoms of helplessness, as opposed to the symptoms produced by the event itself, occur only in the first group. Interestingly, impairment in learning was greater among subjects who were instructed that the task was a chance rather than a skill task and for subjects who perceived that their lives were determined by outside forces (Externals) rather than caused by their own actions (Internals).

Racinskas (1971) has also reported such impairment in human responses following inescapable electric shock. Hiroto and Seligman (1975) reported that people who had experienced inescapable noises or who had worked unsolvable problems were impaired both in learning to finger shuttle to escape noise and in solving five-letter anagrams such as EBNOL. Subjects who had listened to escapable noise or who had worked solvable problems and subjects who had no experience were unimpaired in shuttlebox and anagram performance.

These findings have been replicated (Miller and Seligman, 1975), as has the Hiroto and Seligman (1975) study of unsolvable problems and anagrams (Klein, Fencil-Morse, and Seligman, 1976). Klein and Seligman (1976) replicated the inescapable noise-shuttlebox observation. These replications make us confident that our findings for humans are not due only to chance.

Miller and Seligman (1976) and Klein and Seligman (1976) found that subjects who had been exposed to inescapable noise perceived reinforcement in a skill task as more response independent than subjects who had been exposed to escapable noise or no noise. Roth and Bootzin (1974) and Roth and Kubal (1975) have also found deficits in learning and tendency to continue trying to solve cognitive problems following noncontingent reinforcement with concept formation problems. These authors have also found improved performance (facilitation), on cognitive problems following noncontingent reinforcement. Roth and Kubal (1975) identified two factors that seem to determine whether helplessness or facilitation occurs: task importance and amount of helplessness pretreatment. Subjects who have performed seemingly trivial tasks or who have received small amounts of noncontingent reinforcement are likely to experience facilitation. Helplessness seems to result when the pretreatment task is defined as important and when subjects receive noncontingent reinforcement over many trials.

Inability to control trauma not only disrupts shock escape in a variety of species, but also interferes with many types of adaptive behavior. Both Powell and Creer (1969) and Maier, Anderson, and Lieberman (1972) found that rats that had received inescapable shocks responded to pain with less aggression toward other rats. McCulloch and Bruner (1939) reported that rats given inescapable shocks were slower to learn to swim out of a water maze, and Braud, Wepmann, and Russo (1969) reported similar findings in mice. Brookshire, Littman, and Stewart (1961) reported that when inescapable shocks were given to weanling rats, their food-getting behavior was still disrupted when they were adults, even when the rats were very hungry. And we have found that rats that had experienced inescapable shock failed to hurdle-jump escape from frustration (Rosellini and Seligman, 1975).

Uncontrollable events other than shock can produce effects that may be related to failure to escape shock. Escape deficits can be produced by inescapable tumbling (Anderson and Paden, 1966), as well as by unsolvable problems, loud noise (Hiroto and Seligman, 1975), and by defeat in fighting (Kahn, 1951). Harlow, Harlow, and Suomi (1971) reported that 45-day old monkeys that were confined from birth to a narrow pit showed deficits later in locomotion, exploration, and social behavior. A more detailed discussion of the generality of the effects of various inescapable USs across species is presented by Seligman (1975).

Besides passivity and retarded response-relief learning, four other characteristics associated with learned helplessness are relevant to depression in man. First, helplessness has a time course. In dogs, inescapable shock produces transient as well as permanent interference with escape (Overmier and Seligman, 1967) and avoidance (Overmier, 1968): 24 hours after *one* session of inescapable shock, dogs are helpless; but after 48 hours their response is normal. This is also true of goldfish (Padilla et al., 1970). After multiple sessions of inescapable shock, helplessness is not transient (Seligman and Groves, 1970; Seligman, Maier, and Geer, 1968). Weiss (1968) found a parallel time course for weight loss in rats given uncontrollable shock, but other than this no time course has been found in rats or in other species (e.g., Anderson, Cole, and McVaugh, 1968; Seligman, Rosellini, and Kozak, 1975).

In spite of the fact that permanent learned helplessness does occur in dogs and rats, one session of inescapable shock may produce a physiological depletion that is restored in time. Weiss, Stone, and Harrell (1970) and Weiss, Glazer, and Pohorecky (1976) found smaller amounts of whole-brain norepinephrine in rats when shock was inescapable than when they had experienced escapable shock or not shock. Thomas and DeWald, (1977), found that blocking cholinergic activity with atropine, which released inhibited noradrenergic neurons, broke up learned helplessness in cats. Weiss, Glazer, and Pohorecky (1976) hypothesized that depletion of norepinephrine may partly cause the transient form of helplessness by creating a "motor activation deficit." According to this hypothesis, as a consequence of norepinephrine depletion, which occurs following inescapable shock, the amount of activity an animal is capable of is lowered. Reduced activity results in the failure to perform or learn the escape-avoidance response required on a subsequent test. Weiss and his coworkers have performed a series of studies to test the applicability of this hypothesis to the learned helplessness phenomena. They report a deficit in FR-1 shuttlebox escape after treatment either with a very large amount of inescapable shock or with exposure to a cold (2° C) swim task, both of which produce norepinephrine depletion. In an interesting study reported by Weiss, Glazer, and Pohorecky (1976) rats failed to show a deficit in escape-avoidance after repeated exposure to stress. Rats were given either a cold swim or 15 sessions of intense shock. Control rats received one session of shock. As expected, the controls showed the typical deficit in escape-avoidance learning. However, no deficit was found in the rats that had experienced repeated exposure to the stress. Weiss says that such a finding is not expected in view of other evidence about learned helplessness. This result is seen as supportive of the motor activation deficit hypothesis, since the noradrenergic system is known to recover after repeated exposure to a stress. We have recently replicated this procedure using our own means for producing helplessness. Rats were exposed to 15 sessions (one per day) of 80 trials of 1.0 mA of inescapable shock and were subsequently tested in FR-3 bar press shock escape. In direct contrast to Weiss, we found that repeated exposure to inescapable shock does produce a profound escape deficit (Rosellini and Seligman, 1976). This finding, the lack of a time course of helplessness in the rat, and Maier's repeated failure to obtain helplessness on an FR-1 shuttle response indicate that the escape-avoidance deficit obtained by Weiss, Glazer, and Pohorecky (1976) may not be a representative result. Thus, although norepinephrine depletion may be a consequence of uncontrollability, there is no strong evidence that such depletion causes the behavioral deficits of learned helplessness. The interested reader should consult Maier and Seligman (1976) for the details of this and other hypotheses.

Weiss (1968a, b) reported that uncontrollable shock retarded weight gain more than controllable shock in rats. Mowrer and Viek (1948), and Lindner (1968) reported more cases of anorexia in rats given inescapable shock than in rats given escapable shock.

In summary, uncontrollable trauma produces a number of effects found in depression. The two basic effects are these: animals and humans become *passive*—they are slower to initiate responses to alleviate trauma and may not respond at all; and animals and humans are *retarded in learning* that their behavior may control trauma. If a response is made that does produce relief, they often have trouble realizing that one causes the other. This maladaptive behavior has been observed in a variety of species over a range of tasks that require voluntary responding. In addition, this phenomenon dissipates in time in the dog, and it causes lowered aggression, loss of appetite, and *norepinephrine depletion*.

Depression

Depression is not well defined; for this reason it needs a model. The clinical "entity" has multifaceted symptoms, but let us look at those that seem central to the diagnosis *and* that may be related to learned helplessness. The symptoms of learned helplessness that we have discussed all have parallels in depression.

Lowered Response Initiation. The word "depressed" as a behavioral description denotes a reduction or depression in responding. It is, therefore, not surprising that a prominent symptom of depression is failure or slowness of a patient to initiate responses. In a systematic study of the symptoms of depression, Grinker, Miller, Sabishin, Nunn, and Nunally (1961, pp. 166, 169, 170) described this in a number of ways:

Isolated and withdrawn, prefers to remain by himself, stays in bed much of the time . . .
Gait and general behavior slow and retarded . . .
Volume of voice decreased, sits alone very quietly . . .
Feels unable to act, feels unable to make decisions . . .
[They] give the appearance of an "empty" person who has "given up . . ."

Mendels (1970, p. 7) describes the slowdown in responding associated with depression as:

Loss of interest, decrease in energy, inability to accomplish tasks, difficulty in concentration, and the erosion of motivation and ambition all combine to impair efficient functioning. For many depressives the first signs of the illness are in the area of their increasing inability to cope with their work and responsibilities.

Beck (1967) describes "paralysis of the will" as a striking feature of depression:

In severe cases, there often is complete paralysis of the will. The patient has no desire to do anything, even those things which are essential to life. Consequently, he may be relatively immobile unless prodded or pushed into activity by others. It is sometimes necessary to pull the patient out of bed, wash, dress, and feed him.

The characteristic passivity and lowered response initiation of depressives have been demonstrated in a large number of studies (see Miller, 1975, for a review of these studies). Psychomotor retardation differentiates depressives from normal people and is a direct example of reduced voluntary response initiation. In addition, depressives engage in fewer activities and they show reduced interpersonal responding and reduced nonverbal communication. Finally, the intellectual slowness and learning, memory, and IQ deficits found in depressed patients may be viewed as resulting from reduced motivation to initiate cognitive actions such as memory scanning and mental arithmetic. These deficits all parallel the lowered response initiation in learned helplessness.

Recent experiments in our laboratory demonstrate a striking similarity between the lowered response initiation of learned helplessness and depression (Klein, Fencil-Morse, and Seligman, 1976; Miller and Seligman, 1975). In each of these studies, depressed and nondepressed students were first divided into three groups: group 1 experienced inescapable loud noise (or unsolvable concept formation problems), group 2 heard the loud noise but could turn it off by pressing a button (or was provided with a solvable problem); group 3 heard no noise (or did not work on any problems). All subjects then worked on a series of patterned anagrams. Half of all subjects were depressed; half were not depressed. As in the earlier study by Hiroto and Seligman (1975), nondepressed subjects in group 1, who had previously been exposed to inescapable noise or unsolvable problem, showed response initiation deficits on the anagrams, while nondepressed subjects in groups 2 and 3 exhibited no deficit. Moreover, depressed subjects in all groups, including those in group 3 who had no pretreatment, showed poorer response initiation on the anagrams than the nondepressed subjects in group 3. Nondepressed subjects given a helplessness pretreatment showed response initiation deficits wholly parallel to those found in naturally occurring depression. Klein and Seligman (1976) showed the same parallel deficits between depressed subject and nondepressed helpless subjects on tasks involving noise escape.

Negative Cognitive Set. Depressives not only make fewer responses, but they interpret their few responses as failures or as doomed to failure. This negative cognitive set directly mirrors the difficulty that helpless subjects have in learning that responding produces relief from an aversive situation.

Beck (1967, pp. 256–257) considers this negative cognitive set to be the primary characteristic of depression:

The depressed patient is peculiarly sensitive to any impediments to his goal-directed activity. An obstacle is regarded as an impossible barrier, difficulty in dealing with a problem is interpreted as a total failure. His cognitive response to a problem or difficulty is likely to be an idea such as "I'm licked," "I'll never be able to do this," or "I'm blocked no matter what I do . . ."

Indeed, Beck views the passive and retarded behavior of depressed patients as stemming from their negative expectations of their own effectiveness:

The loss of spontaneous motivation, or paralysis of the will, has been considered a symptom *par excellence* of depression in the classical literature. The loss of motivation may be viewed as the result of the patient's hopelessness and pessimism: as long as he expects a negative outcome from any course of action, he is stripped of any internal stimulation to do anything.

This cognitive set crops up repeatedly in experiments with depressives. Friedman (1964) observed that although a patient was performing adequately during a test, the patient would occasionally reiterate this original protest of "I can't do it," or "I don't know how." This is also our experience in testing depressed patients.

Experimental demonstrations of negative cognitive set in depressed college students were provided by Miller and Seligman (1973) and Miller, Seligman, and Kurlander (1975). These studies showed that depressed students view their skilled actions very much as if they were only chance actions. In other words, depressed subjects, more than nondepressed subjects, tend to perceive reinforcement in a skill task as independent of their behavior. Miller, Seligman, and Kurlander (1975) found this perception to be specific to depression: anxious and nonanxious students matched for extent of depression did not differ in their perceptions of reinforcement contingencies.

Miller and Seligman (1975; 1976), Klein, Fencil-Morse, and Seligman (1976), and Klein and Seligman (1976) more directly demonstrated the parallel between the negative cognitive set in learned helplessness and depression. While replicating the findings of Miller and Seligman (1973) and Miller et al. (1975) mentioned before, Miller and Seligman (1976) and Klein and Seligman (1976) found that nondepressed subjects who had been exposed to inescapable noise perceived reinforcement as less response contingent than did nondepressed subjects who had been exposed to either escapable or no noise during a skilled task. Pretreatment had no effect on perception of reinforcement in chance tasks. So, the effects of learned helplessness and depression on perception of reinforcement are parallel.

Cognitive deficits were also found in the previously mentioned studies of Miller and Seligman (1975), Klein et al. (1976), and Klein and Seligman (1976). These studies measured the degree to which subjects were able to benefit form successful anagram solutions or escapes from shuttlebox noise. As with response initiation, depressed subjects in the untreated groups showed cognitive deficits relative to nondepressed subjects, and nondepressed subjects who had experienced inescapable noise or unsolvable problems exhibited cogitive deficits relative to nondepressed subjects in the control groups. So, learned helplessness and depression produce similar effects on measures of cognitive functioning.

Some studies indicate that negative cognitive set may also explain poor discrimination learning by depressives (Martin and Rees, 1966), and may be partly responsible for their lowered cognitive abilities (Payne, 1961; Miller, 1975).

Time Course. Depression, like learned helplessness, seems to have its time course. In discussing the "disaster syndrome," Wallace (1957) reported that people experience a day or so of depression following sudden catastrophes, and then they again function normally. It seems possible that multiple traumatic events intervening between the initial disaster and recovery might exacerbate depression in humans considerably, as they do in dogs. We should also note that endogenous or process depression is characterized by fluctuations of weeks or months between depression and mania. Moreover, it is commonly thought that almost all depressions dissipate in time, although whether they last days, weeks, months, or years is a matter of some dispute (see Paskind, 1929; 1930; Lundquist, 1945; Kraines, 1957).

Lack of Aggression. According to psychoanalysts, the lowered aggression of depressives is due to introjected hostility. In fact, psychoanalysts view introjection of hostility as the primary mechanism producing symptoms of depression. We do not believe that the increased self-blame in depression results from hostility turned inward, but it seems undeniable that hostility, even in dreams (Beck and Hurvich, 1959; Beck and Ward, 1961), is reduced among depressives. This symptom corresponds to the lack of aggression in learned helplessness.

Loss of Libido and Appetite. Depressives commonly show reduced interest in food, sex, and interpersonal relations. These symptoms correspond to the anorexia, weight loss, and sexual and social deficits in learned helplessness.

Norepinephrine Depletion and Cholinergic Activity. According to the catecholamine hypothesis of affective disorders, depression is associated with a deficiency of norepinephrine (NE) at receptor sites in the brain, whereas elation may be associated with its excess. This hypothesis is based on evidence that imipramine, a drug that increases the NE available in the central nervous system, causes depression to end. Klerman and Cole (1965) and Cole (1964) experimented with imipramine and placebos on depressed patients and reported positive results of imipramine over placebos. Monoamineoxidase (MAO) inhibitors, which prevent the breakdown of NE, also may be useful in relieving depression (Cole, 1964; Davis, 1965). Reserpine, an antihypertensive medication that depletes NE, often produces depression as a side-effect in man (Beck, 1967). There is also some suggestion of cholinergic mediation of depression. Janowsky et al. (1972) reported that physostigmine, a cholinergic stimulator, produced depressive affect in normal people. Atropine, a cholinergic blocker, reversed these symptoms. So NE depletion and cholinergic activation are implicated in both depression and learned helplessness (Thomas and DeWald, 1977). However, Mendels and Frazer (1974) reviewed the behavioral effects of drugs that deplete brain catecholamines and they contend that the behavioral changes associated with reserpine are better interpreted as a psychomotor retardation-sedation syndrome than as depression. Moreover, selective depletion of brain catecholamines by alpha-methyl-para-tyrosine (AMPT) fails to produce some of the key features of depression, despite the fact that this drug produces a consistently greater reduction in amine metabolate concentration than occurs in depression. So depletion of catecholamines in itself may not be sufficient to account for depression.

Feelings of Helplessness, Hopelessness, and Powerlessness. Although this is a discussion of the behavioral and physiological symptoms of depression, we cannot avoid mentioning the subjective feeling states and self-evaluations that accompany the passivity and negative expectations of depressed people. Depressed people say they feel helpless, hopeless, and powerless, and by this they mean that they believe they are unable to control or influence those aspects of their lives that are significant to them.

Grinker and coworkers (1961) describe the "characteristics of hopelessness, helplessness, failure, sadness, unworthiness, guilt and internal suffering" as the "essence of depression."

Melges and Bowlby (1969) also characterize depressed patients in this way and Bibring (1953) *defines* depression "as the emotional expression [indicative] of a state of helplessness and powerlessness of the ego."

There clearly are considerable parallels between the forms of behavior that define learned helplessness and major symptoms of depression.

Differences. But there are substantial gaps.

First, there are two symptoms found with uncontrollable shock that may or may not correspond to symptoms of depression. Stomach ulcers occur more frequently and severely in rats receiving uncontrollable shock than in rats receiving controllable shock (Weiss, 1968b; 1971a, b, c). We know of no study examining the relationship of depression to stomach ulcers. Second, uncontrollable shock produces more anxiety, measured subjectively, behaviorally, and physiologically, than controllable shock (see Seligman and Binik, 1976). The question of whether depressed people are more anxious than nondepressed people does not have a clear answer. Beck (1967) reported that although both depression and anxiety can be observed in some people, only a small positive correlation was found in a study of 606 patients. Yet, Miller et al. (1975) found very few depressed college students who were not also anxious. We can speculate that anxiety and depression are related in the following way: when a man or animal is confronted with a threat or a loss, he initially responds with fear or anxiety. If he learns that the threat is wholly controllable, anxiety, having served its function, disappears. If he remains uncertain about his ability to control the threat, his anxiety remains. If he learns or is convinced that the threat is utterly uncontrollable, depression emerges.

A number of facts about depression have been insufficiently investigated for parallels in learned helplessness. Preeminent among these are the depressive symptoms that cannot be investigated in animals: dejected mood, feelings of self-blame and self-dislike, loss of mirth, suicidal thoughts and crying. Now that learned helplessness has been reliably produced in man (Hiroto, 1974; Hiroto and Seligman, 1975; Klein et al., 1976; Klein and Seligman, 1976; Miller and Seligman, 1975; 1976; Racinskas, 1971; Roth and Kubal, 1975; Thornton and Jacobs, 1970; Dweck and Reppucci, 1973), we can determine whether any of these states occur in helplessness.

Finally, we know of no evidence that *disconfirms* the correspondence of symptoms in learned helplessness and depression.

ETIOLOGY

Learned Helplessness

The cause of learned helplessness is reasonably well understood: it is not a trauma itself that produces interference with later adaptive responses but rather trauma that we cannot control. The distinction between controllable and uncontrollable reinforcement is central to the phenomenon and theory of helplessness, so let us now examine it.

Learning theorists usually use a line depicting the conditional probability of reinforcement following a response, designated p (RFT/R), to

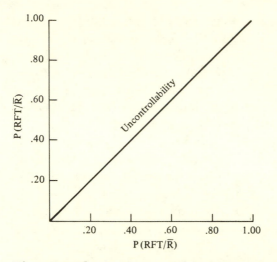

Figure 1. The instrumental training space. The ordinate and abscisa represent the relationships between the subject's response and a reinforcer. They are conditional probabilities or contingencies arranged by the experimenter. The 45-degree line represents a special condition in which the reinforcer is uncontrollable because the probability of reinforcement for responding is equal to the probability of reinforcement for not responding.

explain the relationship between instrumental responses and outcomes about which organisms could learn. This line ranges from 0 to 1. At 1, every response produces a reinforcement (continuous reinforcement). At 0, a response never produces a reinforcement (extinction). Intermediate points on the line represent various degrees of partial reinforcement.

However, a single line does not exhaust relations between response and outcomes to which organisms are sensitive. Rewards or punishments sometimes occur when no specific response has been made. Only a woefully maladaptive S could not learn about such a contingency. Rather than representing instrumental learning as occurring along a single dimension, we can better describe it using the two-dimensional space shown in Figure 1. The x-axis (p[RFT/R]) represents the traditional dimension, conditional-probability of reinforcement, following a response.

At a right angle to the conditional probability of reinforcement, given a response, is the conditional probability of reinforcement, given the absence of *that* response (p[RFT/R]). This dimension is represented along the y-axis. We think that Ss learn about variations along *both* dimensions at the same time. Thus, S may learn the extent to which relief occurs when it does not make a specific response at the same time as it learns the extent to which relief occurs when it makes the specific response. Systematic changes in behavior occur with systematic changes along both dimensions.

There is considerable convergence of opinion and evidence among learning theorists today that organisms can learn about the contingencies within this instrumental training space, including the crucial 45-degree line (e.g., Catania, 1971; Church, 1969; Gibbon, Berryman, and Thomson, 1974; Maier, Seligman, and Solomon, 1969; Poresky, 1970; Premack, 1965; Rescorla, 1967, 1968; Seligman, Maier, and Solomon, 1971; Wagner, 1969; Watson, 1967; and Weiss, 1968a).

The traditional training line has been thoroughly explored (e.g., Ferster and Skinner, 1957; and Honig, 1966). The points in the line that are of special concern in the study of helplessness are those that line along the 45-degree line, (where x = y). Whether or not the organism responds, it still gets the same amount of reinforcement. The conditional probability of reinforcement, given a specific response, *does not differ* from the conditional probability of reinforcement in the absence of that response. Responding and reinforcement are independent.

The concept of control is defined within this instrumental training space. Any time there is something the organism can do or refrain from doing that changes what it gets, it has control. Specifically, a response, stands in control of a reinforcer *if and only if:*

$$p(RFT/R) \neq p(RFT/\bar{R})$$

That is, the probability of reinforcement given a response is different from the probability of reinforcement in the absence of that response. Furthermore, when a response does not change what S gets, the response and reinforcement are independent. Specifically, when a response is independent of a reinforcer, $p(RFT/R) = p(RFT/\bar{R})$. When this is true of all responses, S cannot control the reinforcer, the outcome is uncontrollable, and nothing the organism does matters.

The passivity of dogs, rats and men in the face of trauma and their difficulty in benefiting from response-relief contingencies result, we

believe, from their having learned that responding and trauma are independent—that trauma is uncontrollable. This is the heart of the
learned helplessness hypothesis. The hypothesis states that when shock
is inescapable, the organism learns that responses and shock termination are independent (the probability of shock termination given any
response doesn't differ from its probability in the absence of that response). Learning that trauma is uncontrollable has three effects.

(1) A motivational effect. It reduces the probability that the subject
will initiate responses to escape, because part of the incentive for
making such responses is the expectation that they will bring relief. If
the subject has previously learned that its responses have no effect on
trauma, this contravenes the expectation. Thus the organism's motivation to respond is undermined by experience with reinforcers it cannot control. We think this motivational effect underlies passivity in
learned helplessness, and, if the model is valid, in depression.

(2) A cognitive effect. Learning that responses and shock are independent makes it more difficult to learn that responses do produce relief
when the organism makes a response that actually terminates shock.
In general, if we have acquired a cognitive set in which As are irrelevant
to Bs, it will be harder for us to learn that As produce Bs when they
do. By the helplessness hypothesis, this mechanism is responsible for
the difficulty that helpless organisms have in learning that responding
produces relief, even after they respond and successfully turn off shock.
Further, if the model is valid, this mechanism produces the "negative
expectations" of depression.

(3) An emotional effect. Although it does not follow directly from the
helplessness hypothesis, we have mentioned that uncontrollable shock
also has an emotional impact on animals. Uncontrollable shock produces more conditioned fear, ulcers, weight loss, defecation, and pain
than controllable shock.

We have tested and confirmed this hypothesis in several ways. We
began by ruling out alternative hypothesis. It is unlikely that our dogs
have either become adapted (and therefore not motivated enough to
escape shock) or sensitized (and therefore too disorganized to escape
shock) by pretreatment with shock; because making the shock very
intense or very mild in the shuttle box does not attenuate the phenomenon. Further, it is unlikely that the dogs have learned during inescapable shock, by explicit or superstitious reinforcement or by punishment,

some motor response pattern that competes with barrier jumping in the shuttle box because interference occurs even if the dogs are paralyzed by curare and can make no overt motor responses during shock. Seligman and Maier (1967) performed a direct test of the hypothesis that not the shock itself but rather its uncontrollability causes helplessness. Three groups of eight dogs were used. Dogs in the escape group were trained in the hammock to press a panel with their noses or heads to turn off shock. Dogs in a yoked group received shocks identical to the shocks delivered to the escape group. The yoked group differed from the escape group only with respect to the degree of instrumental control it had over shock; pressing the panel in the yoked group did not affect the programmed shocks. Dogs in a naive control group received no shock in the hammock.

Twenty-four hours following the hammock treatment all three groups received escape-avoidance training in the shuttle box. The escape group and the naive control group suffered no impairment in shuttle box performance. In contrast, the yoked group showed significantly slower defenses than the naive control group. Six of the eight Ss in the yoked group failed to escape shock. It was not the shock itself but, rather not being able to control the shock that produced failure to escape.

Maier (1970) provided more dramatic confirmation of the hypothesis in response to the criticism that what is learned during uncontrollable trauma is not a cognitive set as we have proposed, but rather some motor response, reinforced by shock termination, that antagonizes barrier jumping. Maier reinforced the most antagonistic response he could find. One group of 10 dogs (passive-escape) was tied down in the hammock and panels were pushed to within one-fourth inch of the sides and top of their heads. Only by *not* moving their heads, by remaining passive and still, could these dogs terminate shock. Another group of 10 (yoked) received the same shock in the hammock, but the shock was independent of their responses. A third group received no shock. A response-learning theory of helplessness would predict that when the dogs were later tested in the shuttle box, a test situation requiring active responding for successful escape, the passive-escape group should be the most helpless since it had been explicitly reinforced for not moving during shock. The cognitive-set view made a different prediction: these dogs could control shock, even though it required a passive response. Some response, even one that competed with barrier jumping, produced relief, and they should not learn response-reinforcement independence. As predicted by the cognitive-set theory, dogs in the yoked group were predominantly helpless in the shuttle box escape, and the naive controls escaped normally. The passive-escape group at first looked for "still ways of minimizing shock in the shuttle box: failing to find these, they began to escape and avoid. Thus it was not trauma itself nor interfering motor habits that produced failure to escape, but having learned that no response at all could control trauma.

Maier and Testa (1975) have shown that the escape deficit seen in rats after exposure to inescapable shock partly results from associative interference and not from a motor deficit. In a lucid series of studies, they have found that it is the contingency between the response and shock termination that is crucial in determining the effect of prior inescapable shock, and not the amount of motor response required of the animal to execute the response. In the first experiment, they simplified the typical FR-2 shuttling contingency by briefly terminating shock after the first response of the FR-2. Rats that had experienced inescapable shock showed no learning deficit. In a second experiment, they made the escape contingency more difficult to see, but not to perform, by interposing a delay between shuttling and shock termination. Only one crossing of the barrier (FR-1) was required of the rats (usually, inescapably shocked rats do not show a deficit in FR-1 shuttling). However, a deficit was obtained when shock termination was delayed after escape. Changing the complexity of the escape contingency in no way altered the amount of motor response required of the animals but it drastically affected the animals' behavior. (See Maier and Seligman, 1976, for a more exhaustive discussion of motor response theories of learned helplessness.)

Learning that responses and reinforcement are independent causes retarded reponse initiation, but does it also cause a negative cognitive set that interferes with later formation of associations? Evidence from four different areas in recent literature supports the idea that independence between events retards learning that events are correlated: Seligman (1968) reported that when stimulus and shock were presented independently, rats were later retarded in learning that a second stimulus preceded shock. Bresnahan (1969), and Thomas et al. (1970) reported that experience with the value of one stimulus dimension, presented independently of food, retarded a rat's ability to discriminate among other dimensions of the stimulus. MacKintosh (1965) reviewed substantial discrimination learning literature and concluded that when stimuli are presented independent of reinforcement, animals are retarded at discrimination learning when these same stimuli are later correlated with reinforcement (see also Kemler and Shepp, 1971, and MacKintosh, 1973. N. Maier (1949) reviewed a set of related results.) Gamzu and Williams (1971) reported that when pigeons are exposed to independence between a lighted key and grain, they later are retarded in learning when the lighted key signals grain. Engberg, Hansen, Welker, and Thomas (1972) found that noncontingent food presentations produced deficits in the pigeon's ability to autoshape, a phenomenon they referred to as *learned laziness*. This result is an unsatisfactory demonstration of learned laziness, however, because autoshaping may be under Pavlovian as well as operant control. Welker (1974) also reported rats were deficient in learning to bar press for food after the rats had prolonged exposure to bar pressing which was independent of food. Recently, we have obtained some preliminary data that suggest that prolonged presentation of noncontingent food may produce a deficit in learning to escape shock (Rosellini, Bazerman, and Seligman, 1976).

In summary, one cause of laboratory-produced helplessness seems to be learning that one cannot control important events. Learning that responses and reinforcement are independent results in a cognitive set that has two effects: fewer responses to control reinforcement are initiated, and associating successful responses with reinforcement becomes more difficult.

Depression

The etiology of depression is less clear than are its symptoms. A dichotomy exists between kinds of depression and it will be useful for our purposes: the "exogenous-endogenous" or "process-reactive" distinction (e.g., Kiloh and Garside, 1963; Kraepelin, 1913; and Partridge, 1949). Without agreeing that a dividing line can be clearly drawn, we can observe that one type of depression occurs cyclically with no identifiable external event precipitating it (e.g., Kraines, 1957), and that it may swing regularly from mania to depression. This so-called *endogenous* or *process* depression and its immediate etiology are presumably biochemical or genetic or both. On the other hand, depression is also sometimes clearly precipitated by environmental events. This form of depression—*reactive* or *exogenous*—is the primary concern of this paper. It is useful to regard the process-reactive distinction as a continuum rather than a dichotomy. On the extreme of the reactive side, strong events of the kind discussed in following passages are necessary. In between may lie a continuum of preparedness to become depressed when faced with helplessness-inducing external events. The most mild events set off depression at the extreme process end.

Let us enumerate some of the events that typically precipitate depression: failure in work or school; death or loss of loved ones; rejection by or separation from loved ones; physical disease, and growing old. What do all of these have in common?

Four recent theories of depression seem to be largely in agreement about the etiology of depression, and what they agree on is the centrality of helplessness and hopelessness. Bibring (1953), arguing from a dynamic viewpoint, sees helplessness as the cause of depression:

What has been described as the basic mechanism of depression, the ego's shocking awareness of its helplessness in regard to its aspirations, is assumed to represent the core of normal, neurotic,and probably also psychotic depression.

Melges and Bowlby (1969) see a similar cause of depression:

Our thesis is that while a depressed patient's goals remain relatively unchanged his estimate of the likelihood of achieving them and his confidence in the efficacy of his own own skilled actions are both diminished . . . the depressed person believes that his plans of action are no longer effective in reaching his continuing and long range goals . . . From this state of mind is derived, we believe, much depressive symptomology, including indecisiveness, inability to act, making increased demands on others, and feelings of worthlessness and of guilt about not discharging duties.

Beck (1967, 1970a, b) sees depression as resulting primarily from a patient's negative cognitive set, largely about his abilities to change his life.

A primary factor appears to be the activation of idiosyncratic cognitive patterns which divert the thinking into specific channels that deviate from reality. As a result, the patient perseverates in making negative judgements and misinterpretations. These distortions may be categorized within the triad of negative interpretations of experience; negative evaluations of the self; and negative expectations of the future.

Lichtenberg (1957) sees hopelessness as the defining characteristic of depression:

Depression is defined as a manifestation of felt hopelessness regarding the attainment of goals when responsibility for the hopelessness is attributed to one's personal defects. In this context hope is conceived to be a function of the perceived probability of success with respect to goal attainment.''

We believe what joins these views and lies at the heart of depression is this: the depressed patient has learned or believes that he cannot control those elements of his life that relieve suffering or bring him gratification. In short, he believes that he is helpless. Consider a few of the common precipitating events. What is the meaning of job failure or incompetence at school? Frequently it means that all of a person's efforts have been in vain, his responses have failed to bring about the gratification he desires: he cannot find responses that control reinforcement. When a person is rejected by someone he loves, he can no longer control this significant source of gratification and support. When a parent or lover dies, the bereaved person is powerless to produce or influence love from the dead person. Physical disease and growing old are obvious helplessness experiences. In these conditions, the person's own responses are ineffective and he must rely on the care of others. So, we would predict that it is not life events per se that produce depression (cf. Alarcon and Cori, 1972), but uncontrollable life events.

The previously mentioned studies by Miller and Seligman (1975, 1976) and Klein, Fencil-Morse, and Seligman (1976) are of interest here. These studies all involved the same 3 (controllability) $\times$ 2 (depression) design—depressed and nondepressed subjects were first exposed to controllable reinforcement, uncontrollable reinforcement, or no pretreatment and then asked to perform on a test task where reinforcement was controllable. In all three studies, strikingly similar test task performance deficits were found for depressed subjects who had no pretreatment and for nondepressed subjects who had uncontrollable pretreatment. With a slightly different design, Klein and Seligman (1976) obtained parallel results. Clearly, the fact that noncontingent reinforcement results in behavioral deficits similar to those of naturally occurring depression does not *prove* that the depression was also produced by experiences with uncontrollable reinforcement. However, if experiments using the 3 $\times$ 2 design continue to demonstrate a variety of similarities in the effects of helplessness and depression, the hypothesis that learned helplessness and depression are parallel phenomena with the same etiology will be strengthened.

Ferster (1966, 1973), Kaufman and Rosenblum (1967); McKinney and Bunney (1969); and Liberman and Raskin (1971) have suggested that depression is caused by extinction procedures or the *loss* of reinforcers. There is no contradiction between the learned-helplessness and extinction views of depression; helplessness, however, is more general. Extinction commonly denotes a set of contingencies in which reinforcement is withdrawn, so that the subjects' responses (as well as lack of responses) no longer produce reinforcement. Loss of reinforcers, as in the death of a loved one, can be viewed as an extinction procedure. In conventional extinction procedures the probability of the reinforcer occurring is zero whether or not the subject responds. Extinction is a special case of independence between responding and reinforcement. Reinforcement, however, may also be presented with a probability greater than zero, and still be presented independent of responding. This occurs in the typical helplessness paradigm and causes responses to decrease in probability (Rescorla and Skucy, 1969). Therefore, a view that talks about independence between responses and reinforcement assumes the extinction view and, in addition, suggests that situations in which reinforcers still occur independent of responding also will cause depression.

Differences. Both learned helplessness and depression may be caused by learning that responses and reinforcement are independent. But this view runs into several problems. Can depression actually be caused by situations other than extinction in which reinforcements still occur but are not under the individual's control? To put it another way, "Is a net loss of reinforcers necessary for depression, or can depression occur when there is only loss of control without loss of reinforcers?" Would a Casanova who made love with seven new women every week become depressed if he found out that women wanted him not because of his amatory prowess but because of his wealth or because his fairy godmother wished it? We can only speculate.

It seems appropriate to mention "success" depression in this context. When people finally reach a goal after years of striving—being promoted or getting a PhD—many become depressed. This puzzling phenomenon is clearly a problem for a loss of reinforcement view of depression. From a helplessness view, success depression may occur because reinforcers are no longer contingent on present responding: After years of goal-directed instrumental activity, the reinforcement automatically changes. One now gets his reinforcement because of who he is rather than what he is doing. The common clinical impression that many beautiful women become depressed and attempt suicide also presents problems for the loss of reinforcement theory: positive reinforcers abound not because of what they do but because of how they look. Would a generation of children raised with abundant positive reinforcers that they received independently of what they did become clinically depressed?

We do not wish to maintain that helplessness is the only cause of reactive depression. The absolute quality of life also alters mood. Holding the quality of one's life constant, even when events are uncontrollable, will push mood in the *direction* of euphoria or dysphoria. Controllable events will be less depressing or more cheering than uncontrollable ones, and uncontrollable events more depressing or less cheering (Klinger, 1975).

CURE

Learned Helplessness

We have found one behavioral treatment that cures helplessness in dogs and rats. According to the helplessness hypothesis, the dog makes no attempt to escape because he expects that no instrumental response will produce shock termination. By forcibly demonstrating to the dog that responses produce reinforcement, you can change this expectation. Seligman, Maier, and Geer (1968), moreover, found that forcibly dragging the dog from one side of the shuttle box to the other so that changing compartments terminated shock for the dog cured helplessness. The experimenters pulled three chronically helpless dogs back and forth across the shuttle box with long leashes. This was done during CS and shock, with the barrier removed. After being pulled across the center of the shuttle box (thus terminating shock and CS) 20, 35, and 50 times respectively, each dog began to respond on its own. Then the barrier was replaced, and the subject continued to escape and avoid. Recovery from helplessness was complete and lasting, a finding that has been replicated with more than two dozen helpless dogs.

The behavior of animals during the time they were pulled by a leash was noteworthy. At the beginning of the procedure, a good deal of force had to be exerted to pull the dog across the center of the shuttle box. Less and less force was needed as training progressed. Generally, a stage was reached in which a slight nudge of the leash would drive the dog into action. Finally, each dog initiated its own response, and thereafter failure to escape was very rare. The problem seemed to be one of motivating the dog.

We first tried other procedures with little success. Merely removing the barrier, calling to the dog from the safe side, dropping food into the safe side, kicking the dangerous side of the box—all failed. Until the correct response occurred repeatedly, the dog was not effectively exposed to the response-relief contingency. It is significant that so many forced exposures were required before the dogs responded on their own. A similar "therapy" procedure has also been successfully used with rats (Seligman, Rosellini, and Kozak, 1975). Helpless rats were forcibly exposed to FR-3 bar press escape by being dragged onto the operant lever. After many forced exposures, the rats began to escape on their own. Their behavior was much like that of the dogs. During the early part of training, a fair amount of force was needed to drag the rat to the lever. As therapy progressed, less and less force was required to induce the animal to escape. Finally, after repeated exposure to escape, the rats started escaping without any intervention from the experimenter. This observation supported the twofold interpretation of the effects of inescapable shock: (1) the motivation to initiate responses during shock was low, and (2) the ability to associate successful responses with relief was impaired.

Time (Overmier and Seligman, 1967), electroconvulsive shock (Dorworth, 1971), atropine (Thomas and DeWald, 1977), and the antidepressant drug pargyline (Weiss, Glazer, and Pohorecky, 1976) have all been reported successful in alleviating learned helplessness.

Depression

According to the helplessness view, the central theme in successful therapy should be having the patient discover and come to accept that his responses produce the gratification that he desires—that he is, in short, an effective human being. Some therapies that reportedly alleviate depression are consonant with a learned helplessness model. However, it is important to note that the success of a therapy often has little to do with its theoretical underpinnings. So, with the exception of Klein and Seligman (1976), the following "evidence" should not be regarded as a test of the model, but merely as a set of examples that seem to have exposure to response-produced success as a cure for depression.

Consonant with their helplessness-centered views of the etiology of depression, Bibring (1953), Beck (1967), and Melges and Bowlby (1969) all stressed that reversing helplessness alleviates depression. For example, Bibring (1953) has stated:

The same conditions which bring about depression (helplessness) in reverse serve frequently the restitution from depression. Generally one can say that depression subsides either (a) when the narcissistically important goals and objects appear to be again within reach (which is frequently followed by a temporary elation) or (b) when they become sufficiently modified or reduced to become realizable, or (c) when they are altogether relinquished, or (d) when the ego recovers from the narcissistic shock by regaining its self-esteem with the help of various recovery mechanisms (with or without any change of objective or goal).

In their review of therapies for depression, Seligman, Klein, and Miller (1976) indicated that most of the therapies have strong elements of inducing the patient to discover that responses produce the reinforcement he desires. In antidepression milieu therapy (Taulbee and Wright, 1971), for example, the patient is *forced* to emit one of the most powerful responses people have for controlling others—anger—and when this response is dragged out of his depleted behavior repertoire, he is powerfully reinforced. Beck's (1970a) cognitive therapy is aimed at similar goals. He sees success manipulations as changing the negative cognitive set ("I'm an ineffective person") of the depressive to a more positive set, and argues that the primary task of the therapist is to change the negative expectations of the depressed patient to more optimistic ones. In both Burgess's (1968) therapy and the graded task assignemnt (Beck, Seligman, Binik, Schuyler, and Brill, unpublished data), the patient makes instrumental responses of gradually increasing complexity, and each is reinforced. Similarly, all instrumental behavior therapy for depression (Hersen, Eisler, Alford, and Agras, 1973; Reisinger, 1972), by definition, arranges the contingencies so that responses control the occurrence of reinforcement; the patient's recognition of this relationship should alleviate depression. Lewinsohn's therapy also has this element: participation in activity and other nondepressed behavior controls therapy time (Lewinsohn, Weinstein, and Shaw, 1969). In assertive training (Wolpe, 1968), the patient must emit social responses to bring about a desired change in his environment.

As in learned helplessness, the passage of time has been found to alleviate depression. Electroconvulsive therapy, which alleviates helplessness, probably alleviates endogenous depression (Carney, Roth and Garside, 1965), but its effects on reactive depression are unclear. The role of atropine is largely unknown (see Janowsky et al., 1972).

In a recent series of human helplessness studies, Klein and Seligman (1976) demonstrated that the behavioral deficits of both depression and learned helplessness are reversed if subjects are exposed to success experiences. Three groups of college students were used—nondepressed students who had experienced inescapable noise, and depressed and nondepressed groups, both of whom had experienced no noise. Following the pretreatment, subjects were allowed to solve 0, 4, or 12 discrimination problems. Then, subjects performed in either the noise escape task of Hiroto (1974) or the skill and chance tasks of Miller and Seligman (1973). As in the human helplessness studies reviewed above, the nondepressed subjects that had experienced inescapable noise and depressed subjects who had experienced no noise showed similar deficits on noise escape and skill expectancy changes relative to the nondepressed subjects that had experienced no noise when the subjects were not allowed to solve the discrimination problems. However, when subjects successfully solved 4 or 12 discrimination problems following the pretreatment, those groups did not exhibit test task deficits relative to the nondepressed subjects who had experienced no noise. Experience in controlling reinforcement reversed the behavioral deficits of both learned helplessness and mild depression,

We think that the study provides a useful method for testing the effectivness of *any* therapy for depression in the laboratory. Because we can bring depression into the laboratory both in its naturally occurring state and in the form of learned helplessness, we can see what reverses it in the laboratory. Will assertive training, emotive expression, or atropine given to helpless and depressed subjects in the laboratory reverse the symptoms of depression and helplessness?

Some comment is in order on the role of *secondary gain* in depression;

that is, on the tendency to use symptoms for inducing others to display sympathy and affection. In order to explain depression, Burgess (1968) and others have relied heavily on the reinforcement the patient gets for his depressed behaviors. It is tempting to seek to remove this reinforcement during therapy, but caution is in order here. Secondary gain may explain the persistence or maintenance of *some* depressive behaviors, but it does not explain how they began. Helplessness suggests that failure to initiate active responses originates in the perception that the patient cannot control reinforcement. Thus, there can be two sources of a depressed patient's passivity: 1) patients are passive for instrumental reasons, because they think staying depressed brings them sympathy, love and attention, and 2) patients are passive because they believe that *no* response at all will be effective in controlling their environment. In this sense, secondary gain, although a practical hindrance to therapy, may be a hopeful sign in depression: it means that there is at least some response (albeit passive) that the patient believes he can effectively perform. Maier (1970) found that dogs who were reinforced for being passive by shock termination were not nearly as debilitated as dogs for whom all responses were independent of shock termination. Similarly, patients who use their depression as a way of controlling reinforcement are less helpless than those who have given up.

Psychologists can cause learned helplessness to end by forcing the passive dog or rat to see that his responses produce reinforcement. A variety of techniques and theories suggest that therapy aimed at breaking up depression should center on the patient's sense of efficacy: Depression may be directly antagonized when patients come to see that their own responses are effective in alleviating their suffering and producing gratification.

Difficulties. Many therapies, from psychoanalysis to T-groups, claim to be able to cure depression. The evidence presented here is selective: only those treatments that seemed compatible with helplessness were discussed. It is possible that when other therapies work it is because they reinstate the patient's sense of efficacy. However, evidence on the effectiveness of therapy in depression that is less anecdotal and selective is sorely needed. The recent study of Klein and Seligman (1976) may provide a laboratory procedure for evaluating the effectiveness of *any* therapy suggested for learned helplessness and depression.

PREVENTION

Learned Helplessness

Dramatic success in medicine has come more frequently from prevention than from treatment, and we would hazard a guess that inoculation and immunization have saved many more lives than any cure. Psychotherapy is almost exclusively limited to use as a cure, and preventive procedures rarely play an explicit role. In our studies of animals we found that behavioral immunization provided an easy and effective means of preventing learned helplessness.

The helplessness viewpoint suggested a way to immunize animals against inescapable shocks. Initial experience with escapable shocks should do two things: it should interfere with learning that responses and shock termination are independent, and it should allow the animal to discriminate between situations in which shocks are escapable and those in which they are inescapable. The relevant experiment was done by Seligman and Maier (1967). One group of dogs was given 10 escape-avoidance trials in the shuttle box before it received inescapable shocks in the hammock. The dogs that began by learning to escape shock in the shuttle box pressed the panels four times as often in the hammock during the inescapable shocks as did naive dogs, even though pressing panels had no effect on shock. Such panel pressing probably measures the attempts of the dog to control shock. Seligman, Marques, and Radford (unpublished data) extended these findings by first letting the dogs escape shock by panel pressing in the hammock. This was followed by inescapable shock in the same place. Experience with control over shock termination prevented the dogs from becoming helpless when they were later tested in a new apparatus, the shuttle box.

Other findings from our laboratory support the idea that experience in controlling trauma may protect organisms from the helplessness caused by inescapable trauma. Recall that among dogs of unknown history, helplessness is a statistical effect. Approximately two-thirds of dogs given inescapable shock become helpless, and one-third respond normally. Only 6 percent of naive dogs become helpless in the shuttle box without any prior exposure to inescapable shock. Why do some dogs become helpless and others not? Could it be that those dogs that become helpless even without any inescapable shock have had a history of uncontrollable trauma? Seligman and Groves (1970) tested this hypothesis by raising dogs singly in cages in the laboratory. Relative to dogs of variegated history, these dogs had very limited experience controlling anything. Cage-reared dogs proved to be more susceptible to helplessness; although it took four sessions of inescapable shock to produce helplessness in dogs of unknown history, only two sessions of inescapable shock in the hammock were needed to cause helplessness in the cage-reared dogs. Lessac and Solomon (1969) also reported that dogs reared in isolation seemed prone to experience interference with escape. Thus, dogs that are deprived of natural opportunities to master reinforcement in their developmental history may be more vulnerable to helplessness than naturally immunized dogs. We have been able to immunize rats against the debilitating effects of inescapable shock. Rats first exposed to one session of escapable shock did not become helpless when subsequently exposed to inescapable shock (Seligman, Rosellini, and Kozak, 1975). More recently we have found lifelong immunization against helplessness: rats, given inescapable shock at weaning, did not become helpless when given inescapable shock as adults (Hannum, Rosellini, and Seligman, 1976).

Even less is known about the prevention of depression than about its physiology or cure. Almost everyone at some time loses control over the reinforcements that are significant to him—parents die, loved ones reject us. Everyone also becomes at least mildly and transiently depressed in the wake of such events. But why are some people emotionally paralyzed and others resilient? We can only speculate about this, but the data on immunization against helplessness guide our speculations in a definite direction. The life histories of those persons who are particularly resistant to depression may have been filled with mastery. These people may have had extensive experience controlling and manipulating the sources of reinforcement in their lives, and they may therefore perceive the future more optimistically. Those people who are particularly susceptible to depression may have had lives relatively devoid of *mastery*. Their lives may have been full of experiences in which they were helpless to influence their sources of suffering and gratification.

The relationship of depression in adults to loss of parents in youth seems relevant. It seems likely that children who lose their parents experience helplessness and may be more vulnerable to later depression. The findings on this topic are mixed. So it is possible, although not established, that losing a parent in youth may make one more vulnerable to depression.

A caveat is in order here, however. Although it seems reasonable that extensive experience controlling reinforcement might make one more resilient from depression, how about the person who has met *only* with success? Is a person whose responses have always met with success more susceptible to depression when confronted with situations beyond his control? It seems reasonable that too much experience controlling reinforcers might not allow the development and use of coping responses against failure, just as too little control might prevent the development of ability to cope.

One can also look at successful therapy as preventive. After all, therapy is usually not focused just on undoing past problems. It also should arm the patient against future depressions. Would therapy for depression be more successful if it were explicitly aimed at providing the patient with a wide repertoire of coping responses that he could use in future situations where he found he could not control reinforcement by his usual responses?

Finally, we can speculate about child rearing. What kinds of experience can best protect our children against the debilitating effect of helplessness and depression? A tentative answer follows from the learned helplessness view of depression: a childhood of experiences in which one's own actions are instrumental in bringing about gratification and removing annoyances. Seeing oneself as an effective human being may require a childhood filled with powerful synchronics between responding and its consequences.

Testing the learned helplessness model of depression requires the demonstration of similarities in symptoms, etiology, cure and prevention of learned helplessness. The current evidence, reviewed in this model, indicates that in many respects the major symptoms of helplessness parallel those of depression. In addition, we have suggested that the cause of both reactive depression and learned helplessness is the belief that responses do not control important reinforcers. Finally, we have speculated that the methods that succeed in curing and preventing learned helplessness have their parallels in the cure and prevention of depression. Much remains to be tested, but we believe that a common theme has emerged: both depression and learned helplessness have at their core the belief in the futility of responding.

REFERENCES

Alarcon, R. D., and Cori, L. The precipitating event in depression. *Journal of Nervous and Mental Disease*, 1972, *155*, 379–391.

Anderson, D. C., and Cole, J. O., and Mc Vaugh, W. Variations in unsignaled inescapable preshock as determinants of responses to punishment. *Journal of comparative and Physiological Psychology* (Supplement), 1968, *65*, 1–17.

Anderson, D. C., and Paden, P. Passive avoidance response learning as a function of prior tumblime trauma. *Psychonomic Science*, 1966, *4*, 129–130.

Beck, A. T. *Depression: Clinical, experimental, and theoretical aspects.* New York: Hoeber, 1967.

Beck, A. T. Cognitive therapy: Nature and relation to behavior therapy. *Behavior Therapy*, 1970, *1*, 184–200. (a)

Beck, A. T. The phenomena of depression: A synthesis. In D. Offer and D. X. Freedman (Eds.), *Clinical research in perspective: Essays in honor of Roy R. Grinker, Sr.* New York: Basic Bookds, 1970. (b)

Beck, A. T., and Hurvich, M. S. Psychological correlates of depression: I. Frequency of masochistic dream content in a private practice sample. *Psychosomatic Medicine*, 1959, *21*, 50–55.

Beck, A. T., and Ward, C. H. Dreams of depressed patients: Characteristic themes in manifest content. *Archives of General Psychiatry*, 1961, *5*, 462–467.

Behrend, E. R. and Bitterman, M. E. Sidman Avoidance in the fish. *Journal of the Experimental Analysis of Behavior*, 1963, *13*, 229–242.

Bibring, E. The mechanism of depression. In Greenacre, P. (Ed.), *Affective disorders.* New York: International Universities Press, 1953.

Braud, W. G., Wepmann, B., and Russo, D. task and species generality of the "helplessness" phenomenon. *Psychonomic Science*, 1969, *16*, 164–165.

Bresnahan, E. L. Effects of intradimensional and extradimensional equivalence training, and extradimensional discrimination training upon stimulus control. (Paper presented at the meeting of the American Psychological Association, Washington, D.C., September, 1969.)

Brookshire, K. H., Littman, R. A., and Stewart, C. N. Residue of shock trauma in the white rat: A three factor theory. *Psychological Monographs*, 1961, *75* 10.

Burgess, E. The modification of depressive behavior. In R. Rubin and C. Franks (Eds.), *Advances in behavior therapy.* New York: Academic Press, 1968.

Carlson, M. J., and Black, A. H. Traumatic avoidance learning: The effects of preventing escape responses. *Canadian Journal of Psychology*, 1957, *14*, 21–28.

Carney, M. W. P., Roth, M., and Garside, R. F. The diagnosis of depressive syndromes and the prediction of E. C. T. response. *British Journal of Psychiatry*, 1965, *111*, 659–674.

Catania, A. C. Elicitation, reinforcement, and stimulus control. In R. Glaser, (Ed.), *The Nature of reinforcement.* New York: Academic Press, 1971, pp. 196–220.

Church, R. M. Response suppression. In B. A. Campbell and R. M. Church (Eds.), *Punishment and aversive behavior*. New York: Appleton-Century-Crofts, 1969. Pp. 111–156.

Cole, J. O. Therapeutic efficacy of antidepressant drugs. *Journal of the American Medical Association*, 1964, *190*, 448–455.

Davis, J. Efficacy of tranquilizing and antidepressant drugs. *Archives of General Psychiatry*, 1965, *13*, 552–572.

Dorworth, T. R. The effect of electroconvulsive shock on "helplessness" in dogs. (Unpublished doctoral dissertation, University of Minnesota, 1971.)

Dweck, C. S., and Reppucci, N. D. Learned hslplessness and reinforcement responsibility in children. *Journal of Personality and Social Psychology*, 1973, *25*, 109–116.

Engberg, L. A., Hansen, G., Welker, R. L., and Thomas, D. R. Acquisition of key-peeking via autoshaping as a function of prior experience. *Science*, 1972, *178*, 1002–1004.

Ferster, C. B. Animal behavior and mental illness. *Psychological records*, 1966, *16*, 345–346.

Ferster, C. B. A functional analysis of depression. *American Psychologist*, 1973, *28*, 857–870.

Ferster, C. B., and Skinner, B. F. *Schedules of reinforcement*. New York: Appleton-Century-Crofts, 1957.

Friedman, A. S. Minimal effects of severe depression on cognitive functioning. *Journal of Abnormal Psychology*, 1964, *69*, 237–243.

Gamzu, E., and Williams, D. R. Classical conditioning of a complex skeletal response, *Science*, 1971, *171*, 923–925.

Gibbon, J., Berryman, R., and Thompson, R. L. Contingency spaces and measures in classical and instrumental conditioning. *Journal of the Experimental Analysis of Behavior*, 1974, *21*, 585–605.

Grinker, R., Sr., Miller, J., Sabishin, M., Nunn, R. J., and Nunally, J. C. *The phenomena of depression*. New York: Hoeber, 1961.

Hannum, R. D., Rosellini, R. A., and Seligman, M. E. P. Retention of learned helplessness and immunization in the rat from weaning to adulthood. *Developmental Psychology*, 1976, *12*, 449–454.

Harlow, H. F., Harlow, M. K., and Suomi, S. J. From thought to therapy: Lessons from a primate laboratory. *American Scientist*, 1971, *59*, 538–549.

Hersen, M., Eisler, R. M., Alford, G. S., and Agras, W. S. Effects of token economy on neurotic depression: An experimental analysis. *Behavior Therapy*, 1973, *4*, 392–397.

Hiroto, D. S. the relationship between learned helplessness and the locus of control. *Journal of experimantal Psychology*, 1974, *102*, 187–193.

Hiroto, D. S., and Seligman, M. E. P. Generality of learned helplessness in man. *Journal of Personality and Social Psychology*, 1975, *31*, 311–327.

Honig, W. H. (Ed.). *Operant behavior: Theory and research*. New York: Appleton-Century-Crofts, 1966.

Janowsky, D. S., El-Yousef, M. K., Davis, J. M., Hubbard, B., and Sekerke, H. J. cholinergic reversals of manic symptoms. *Lancet*, 1972, *1*, 1236–1237.

Kahn, M. W. The effect of severe defet at various age levels on the aggressive behavior of mice. *Journal of Genetic Psychology*, 1951, *79*, 117–130.

Katzev, R. D., and Miller, S. V. Strain differences in avoidance conditioning as a function of the classical CS-US contingency. *Journal of Comparative and Physiological Psychology*, 1974, *87*, 661–671.

Kaufman, I. C., and Rosenblum, L. A. The reaction to separation in infant monkeys: Anaclitic depression and conservation-withdrawal. *Psychosomatic Medicine*, 1967, *29*, 648–675.

Kemler, D., and Shepp, B. the learning and transfer of dimensional relevance and irrelevance in children. *Journal of Experimental Psychology*, 1971, *90*, 120–127.

Kiloh, L. C., and Garside, R. F. The independence of neurotic depression and endogenous depression. *British Journal of Psychiatry*, 1963, *109*, 451–463.

Klein, D. C., Fencil-Morse, E., and Seligman, M. E. P. Learned helplessness, depression, and the attribution of failure. *Journal of Personality and Social Psychology*, 1976, *33*, 508–516.

Klein, D. C. and Seligman, M. E. P. Reversal of performance deficits and perceptual deficits in learned helplessness and depression. *Journal of Abnormal Psychology*, 1976, *85*, 11–26.

Klerman, G. L., and Cole, J. O. Clinical and pharmacology of imipramine and related antidepressant compounds. *Pharmacological Revies*, 1965, *17*, 101–141.

Klinger, E. Consequences of commitment to and disengagement from incentives. *Psychological Review*, 1975, *82*, 1–25.

Kraepelin, E. Manic-depressive insanity and paranoia. In his *Textbook of psychiatry* (Trans. R. M. Barclay). Edinburgh: Livingstone, 1913.

Kraines, S. H. *Mental depressions and their treatment*. New York: Macmillan, 1957.

Leaf, R. C. Avoidance response evocation as a function of prior discriminative fear conditioning under curare. *Journal of Comparative and Physiological Psychology*, 1964, *58*, 446–449.

Lessac, M., and Solomon, R. L. Effects of early isolation on the later adaptive behavior of beagles: A methodological demonstration. *Developmental Psychology*, 1969, *1*, 14–25.

Lewinsohn, P. M., Weinstein, M. S., Shaw, D. Depression: A clinical research approach, in R. D. Rubin and C. M. Franks (Eds.) *Advances in behavior therapy*. New York: Academic Press, 1969. Pp. 231–240.

Liberman, R. P., and Raskin D. E. Depression: A behavioral formulation. *Archives of General Psychiatry*, 1971, *24*, 515–523.

Lichtenberg, P. A definition and analysis of depression. *Archives of Neurology and Psychiatry*, 1957, *77*, 516–527.

Linder, M. *Hereditary and environmental influences upon resistance to stress*. (Doctoral dissertation, University of Pennsylvania, 1968.)

Looney, T. A., Cohen, P. S. Retardation of jump-up escape responding in rats pretreated with different frequencies of noncontingent electric shocks. *Journal of Comparative and Physiological Psychology*, 1972, *78*, 317–322.

Lundquist, G. Prognosis and course in manic-depressive psychosis. *Acta Psychiatrica Neurologica* (Supplement), 1945, *35*.

MacKintosh, N. J. Selective attention in animal learning. *Psychological Bulletin*, 1965, *64*, 124–150.

MacKintosh, N. J. Stimulus selection: Learning to ignore stimuli that predict no change in reinforcement. In R. A. Hinde and J. Stevenson-Hinde (Eds.). *Constraints on learning*. New York: Academic Press, 1973, pp. 75–100.

Maier, N. R. F. *Frustration*. Ann Arbor: University of Michigan Press, 1949.

Maier, S. F. Failure to escape traumatic shock: Incompatible skeletal motor responses or learned helplessness? *Learning and Motivation*, 1970, *1*, 157–170.

Maier, S. F., Albin, R. W., and Testa, T. J. Failure to learn to escape in rats previously exposed to inescapable shock depends on the nature of the escape response. *Journal of Comparative and Physiological Psychology*, 1973, *85*, 581–592.

Maier, S. F., Anderson, C., and Lieberman, D. A. Influence of control of shock on subnsequent shock-elicited aggression. *Journal of Comparative and Physiological Psychology,* 1972, *81,* 94–100.

Maier, S. F., and Seligman, M. E. P. Learned helplessness: Theory and evidence. *Journal of Experimental Psychology: General,* 1976, *105,* 3–46.

Maier, S. F., Seligman, M. E. P., and Solomon, R. L. Pavlovian fear conditioning and learned helplessness. In B. A. Campbell and R. M. Church, *Punishment and aversive behavior.* New York: Appleton-Century-Crofts, 1969. Pp. 299–342.

Maier, S. F., and Testa, T. J. Failure to learn to escape by rats previously exposed in inescapable shock is partly produced by associative interference. *Journal of Comparative and Physiological Psychology,* 1975, *88,* 554–564.

Martin, I., and Rees, L. Reaction time and somatic reactivity in depressed patients. *Journal of Psychosomatic Research,* 1966, *9,* 375–382.

Maser, J. D., and Gallup, G. G. Jr. Tonic immobility in the chicken: Catalepsy potentiation by uncontrollable shocks and alleviation by imipramine. *Psychosomatic Medicine,* 1974, *36,* 199—205.

McCulloch, T. L., and Bruner, J. S. The effect of electric shock upon subsequent learning in the rat. *Journal of Psychology,* 1939, *7,* 333—336.

McKinney, W. T., and Bunney, W. E. Animal model of depression: Review of evidence and implications for research. *Archives of General Psychiatry,* 1969, *21,* 240—248.

Melges, F. T., and Bowlby, J. Types of hopelessness in psychopathological process. *Archives of General Psychiatry, 21,* 1969, 240—248.

Mendels, J. *Concepts of depression.* New York: Wiley, 1970.

Mendels, J., and Frazer, A. Brain biogenic amine depletion and mood. *Archives of General Psychiatry,* 1974, *30,* 447—451.

Miller, W. R. Psychological deficit in depression. *Psychological Bulletin,* 1975, *82,* 238—260.

Miller, W. R., and Seligman, M. E. P. Depression and the perception of reinforcement. *Journal of Abnormal Psychology.* 1973, *82,* 62—73.

Miller, W. R. and Seligman, M. E. P. Learned helplessness and depression in man. *Journal of Abnormal Psychology,* 1975, *84,* 228—238.

Miller, W. R., and Seligman, M. E. P. Learned helplessness, depression, and the perception of reinforcement. *Behaviour Research and Therapy,* 1976, *14,* 7—17.

Miller, W. R., Seligman, M. E. P., and Kurlander, H. M. Learned Helplessness, depression, and anxiety. *Journal of Nervous and Mental Disease,* 1975, *161,* 347—357.

Mowrer, O. H. and Viek, P. An experimental analogue of fear from a sense of helplessness *Journal of Abnormal Social Psychology,* 1948, *43,* 193—200.

Overmier, J. B. Interference with avoidance behavior: Failure to avoid traumatic shock. *Journal of Experimental Psychology,* 1968, *78,* 340—343.

Overmier, J. B., and Seligman, M. E. P. Effects of inescapable shock upon subsequent escape in avoidance responding. *Journal of comparative and Physiological Psychology,* 1967, *63,* 23—33.

Padilla, A. M., Padilla, C., Ketterer, T., and Giacalone, D. Inescapable shocks and subsequent avoidance conditioning in goldfish, *Carrasius avaratus. Psychonomic Science,* 1970, *20,* 295—296.

Partridge, M. Some reflections on the nature of affective disorders arising from the results of prefrontal leucomoty. *Journal of Mental Science,* 1949, *20,* 295—296.

Paskind, H. A. Brief attacks of manic-depressive depression. *Archives of Neurological Psychiatry,* 1929, *22,* 123—124.

Paskind, H. A. Manic-depressive psychosis in private practice: Length of attack and length of interval. *Archives of Neurological Psychiatry*, 1930, *23*, 789—794.

Payne, R. W. Cognitive abnormalities. In H. J. eysenck (Ed.), *Handbook of abnormal psychology*. New York, Basic Books, 1961, pp. 193—261.

Poresky, R. Noncontingency detection and its effects. (Paper presented at Eastern Psychological Association, Atlantic City, April 1970.)

Powell, P. A., and Creer, T. L. Interaction of developmental and environmental variables in shock-elicited aggression. *Journal of comparative and Physiological Psychology*, 1969, *69*, 219—225.

Premack, D. Reinforcement theory. In D. Levine, (Ed.), *Nebraska Symposium on Motivation*, (Vol. 13). Lincoln: University of Nebraska Press, 1965. Pp. 123—188.

Racinskas, J. R. Maladaptive consequences of loss or lack of control over aversiv events. (Doctoral dissertation, Waterloo University, Ontario, Canada, 1971.)

Reisinger, J. J. The treatment of "anxiety-depression" via positive reinforcement and response cost. *Journal of Applied Behavior Analysis*, 1972, *5*, 125—130.

Rescorla, R. A. Pavlovian conditioning and its proper control procedures. *Psychological Review*. 1967, *74*, 71—80.

Rescorla, R. A. Probability of shock in the presence and absence of the CS in fear conditioning. *Journal of Comparative and Physiological Psychology*, 1968, *66*, 1—5.

Rescorla, R. A., and Skucy, J. Effect of response independent reinforcers during extinction. *Journal of Comparative and Physiological Psychology*, 1969, *67*, 381—389.

Rosellini, R. A., Bazerman, M. H., and Seligman, M. E. P. Exposure to noncontingent food interferes with the acquisition of a response to escape shock. *Journal of Experimental Psychology: Animal Behavior Processes*, unpublished manuscript (1976).

Rosellini, R. A., and Seligman, M. E. P. Frustration and learned helplessness. *Journal of Experimental Psychology: Animal Behavior Processes*, 1975, *104*, 149—157.

Rosellini, R. A., and Seligman, M. E. P. Failure to escape shock after repeated exposure to inescapable shock. *Bulletin of the Psychonomic Society*, 1976, *7*, 251—253.

Roth, S., and Bootizin, R. R. The effects of experimentally induced expectancies of external control: An investigation of learned helplessness. *Journal of Personality and Social Psychology*, 1974, *29*, 253—264.

Roth, S., and Kubal, L. The effects of noncontingent reinforcement on tasks of differing importance: Facilitation and learned helplessness effects. *Journal of Personality and Social Psychology*, 1975, *32*, 680—691.

Seligman, M. E. P. Chronic fear produced by unpredictable shock. *Journal of Comparative and Physiological Psychology*, 1968, *66*, 402—411.

Seligman, M. E. P. *Helplessness*. San Francisco: W. H. Freeman and Company, 1975.

Seligman, M. E. P., and Beagley, S. Learned helplessness in the rat. *Journal of Comparative and Physiological Psychology*, 1975, *88*, 534—541.

Seligman, M. E. P. and Binik, Y. Safety signal hypothesis. In H. Davis and H. Hurwitz (Eds.), *Pavlovian and Operant Interactions*. Hillsdale, New Jersey: Lawrence Erlbaum Associates, 1976.

Seligman, M. E. P., and Groves, D. Non-transient learned helplessness. *Psychonomic Science*, 1970, *19*, 191—192.

Seligman, M. E. P., Klein, D. C., and Miller, W. R. Depression. In H. Leitenberg (Ed.), *Handbook of behavior modification and behavior therapy*. Englewood Cliffs, N. J.: Prentice-Hall, 1976.

Seligman, M. E. P., and Maier, S. F. Failure to escape traumatic shock. *Journal of Experimental Psychology*, 1967, *74*, 1—9.

Seligman, M. E. P., Maier, S. F., and Geer, J. The alleviation of learned helplessness in the dog. *Journal of Abnormal Psychology*, 1968, *73*, 256—262.

Seligman, M. E. P., Maier, S. F., and Solomon, R. L. Unpredictable an uncontrollable aversive events. In F. R. Brush (Ed.), *Aversive conditioning in learning.* New York, Academic Press, 1971.

Seligman, M. E. P., Rosellini, R. A., and Kozak, M. J. Learned helplessness in the rat: time course, immunization and reversibility. *Journal of Comparative and Physiological Psychology*, 1975, *88*, 542—547.

Seward, J. P., and Humphrey, G. L. Avoidance learning as a function of pretraining in the cat. *Journal of Comparative and Physiological Psychology*, 1967, *63*, 338—341.

Shurman, A. J., and Katzev, R. D. Escape avoidance responding in rats depends on strain and number of inescapable reshocks. *Journal of Comparative and Physiological Psychology*, 1975, *88*, 548—553.

Taulbee, E. S. and Wright, H. W. A psycho-social-behavioral model for therapeutic intervention. In C. D. Speilberger (Ed.), *Current topics in clinical and community psychology III.* New York: Academic Press, 1971.

Thomas, D. R., Freeman, F., Sviniki, J. G., Burr, D. E., and Lyons, J. Effects of extradimensional training on stimulus generalization. *Journal of Experimental Psychology*, 1970, *83*, 1—22.

Thomas, E. and DeWald, Louise. Experimental neurosis: Neuropsychological analysis. In J. D. Maser and Martin E. P. Seligman (Eds.), *Psychopathology: Experimental Models.* San Francisco: Freeman, 1977, pp. 214—231.

Thornton, J. W., and Jacobs, P. D. Learned helplessness in human subjects. *Journal of Experimental Psychology*, 1970, *83*, 1—22.

Wagner, A. R. Stimulus selection and a "modified continuity theory." In G. H. Bower, and J. T. Spence, (Eds.), *The psychology of learning and motivation, III.* New York: Academic Press, 1969.

Wallace, A. F. C. Mazeway disintegration: The individual's perception of socio-cultural disorganization. *Human Organization*, 1957, *16*, 23—27.

Watson, J. S. Memory and "contingency analysis" in infant learning. *Merrill-Palmer Quarterly Behavioral Development*, 1967, *13*, 55—67.

Weiss, J. M. Effects of coping responses on stress. *Journal of Comparative and Physiological Psychology*, 1968, *65*, 251—260. (a)

Weiss, J. M. Effects of predictable and unpredictable shock on development of gastrointestinal lesions in rats. In *Proceedings, 76th Annual Convention, American Psychological Association*, 1968, pp. 263—264. (b)

Weiss, J. M. Somatic effects of predictable and unpredictable shock. *Psychosomatic Medicine*, 1970, *32*, 397—408.

Weiss, J. M. Effects of coping behavior in different warning-signal conditions on stress pathology in rats. *Journal of Comparative and Physiological Psychology*, 1971, *77*, 1—13. (a)

Weiss, J. M. Effects of coping behavior with and without a feedback signal on stress pathology in rats. *Journal of Comparative and Physiological Psychology*, 1971, *77*, 22—30. (b)

Weiss, J. M. Effects of punishing the coping response (conflict) on stress pathology in rats. *Journal of Comparative and Physiological Psychology*, 1971, *77*, 14—21. (c)

Weiss, J. M., Glazer, H. I. and Pohorecky, L. A. Coping behavior and neuro-chemical changes: and alternative explanation for the original "learned helplessness" experiments. In G. Serban and A. Ling (Eds.), *Animal models of human psychobiology.* New York: Plenum Press, 1976, pp. 141—173.

Weiss, J. M., Stone, E. A., and Harrell, N. Coping behavior and brain norepinephrine levels in rats. *Journal of Comparative and Physiological Psychology,* 1970, *72,* 153—160.

Welker, R. L. Acquisition of a free-operant-appetitive response in pigeons as a function of prior experience. (Doctoral dissertation, University of Colorado, 1974).

Williams, T. A., Friedman, R. J., and Secunda, S. K. *The depressive illness.* (Special report.) Washington D.C.: National Institute of Mental Health, 1970.

Wittgenstein, L. *Philosophical investigations.* New York: Macmillan, 1953.

Wolpe, J. The practice of behavior therapy. New York: Pergamon Press, 1968.

7. A Self-Control Model of Depression

Lynn P. Rehm

This paper outlines a behavioral self-control model for the study of depression. Contemporary models focus on different subsets of depressive phenomena. The self-control model organizes and relates these phenomena and has its own implications for symptomatology, etiology, and therapy.

CONTEMPORARY MODELS OF DEPRESSION

Depression has certain properties which make the development of a model particularly difficult. In the clinical literature, the term depression refers to a syndrome which encompasses a broad set of symptoms with diverse behavioral referents (cf. Beck, 1972; Levitt & Lubin, 1975; Mendels, 1970; Woodruff, Goodwin, & Guze, 1974). Especially notable is the diversity among cognitive symptoms. Aside from manifest subjective sadness, depressed persons show clinical symptons such as guilt, pessimism, low self-esteem, self-derogation, and helplessness. Accounting for these distinctive cognitive behaviors and integrating them with the various overt-motor behaviors characteristic of depression are desirable features of any model of depression. At this time, a focus limited to verbal-cognitive and overt-motor variables is appropriate since no reliable physiological index has been clearly identified as a symptom of depression (cf. Bruder, Note 1; Mendels, 1970). A model should also provide a framework for hypotheses about causes of depression and should serve as a heuristic device for the development of means of treating the disordered behavior.

A recent resurgence of interest in psychological aspects of depression has become evident in the last 5 to 10 years and, with it, new and innovative models have been advanced. Behavioral and cognitive models proposed by Lewinsohn (1974a, 1974b), Seligman (1974), and Beck (1974) have been most prominent and influential in behavioral research and clinical application.

Lewinsohn

Lewinsohn (1974a, 1974b; Lewinsohn, Weinstein, & Shaw, 1969) has developed a clinical and research program which looks at depression as an extinction phenomenon. A loss or lack of response contingent positive reinforcement results in reduced rates of common overt-motor behaviors and also elicits a basic dysphoria. All other cognitive-verbal symptoms of depression are secondary elaborations of this basic dysphoria. Susceptibility to depression and ability to overcome depression are related to social skill, the range of events which are potentially reinforcing to the person, and reinforcement availability. The etiology of depression is therefore the joint function of external environmental changes and individual differences in reinforcement potential and social skills. Therapy procedures are aimed at identifying potential sources of reinforcement in the person's environment and developing strategies to increase their frequency of occurrence (Lewinsohn, 1976; Lewinsohn & Shaffer, 1971; Robinson & Lewinsohn, 1973a, 1973b). In other instances, therapy consists of isolating deficits in social interaction and training subjects in modifying these social skill behaviors (Lewinsohn, Biglan, & Zeiss, 1976; Lewinsohn & Shaw, 1969; Lewinsohn, Weinstein, & Alper, 1970).

Seligman

Seligman has proposed a model of depression based on a laboratory paradigm of learned helplessness (Seligman, 1974, 1975). A situation in which the probability of the consequence given a response is equal to the probability of the consequence given no response produces the phenomenon of learned helplessness. Noncontingent punishment has been the situation most studied. Learned helplessness has properties which parallel the symptoms of depression: (1), lowered response initiation (passivity); (2), negative cognitive set (belief that one's actions are doomed to failure); (3), dissipation over time; (4), lack of aggression; (5), loss of libido and appetite; and (6), norepinephrine depletion and cholinergic activity (Seligman, Klein, & Miller, 1974). Cognition is given a central position in this model in that "depressive retardation is caused by a brief in response-reinforcement independence" (Seligman et al.,

1974, p. 48). Other cognitive symptoms are held to be elaborations on this central belief. No therapy studies have been directly generated by this model to date, but Klein and Seligman (1976) have demonstrated the reversability of learned helplessness and depression following experience with solvable problems.

Beck

From a different perspective, Beck (1970, 1972, 1974) has evolved a cognitive model of depression which holds that depression consists of a primary triad of cognitive patterns or schema: (1), a negative view of the world; (2), a negative view of the self; and (3), a negative view of the future. These views are maintained by distorted modes of cognition such as selective abstraction, arbitrary inference, and overgeneralization. The overt-behavioral symptoms of depression follow from cognitive distortion. Distorted schema develop in early childhood and leave individuals susceptible to depression in the face of stress. Therapy involves the identification of distortions and their confrontation with the evidence of objective experience. Case studies employing these methods have been described by Beck (1972) and Rush, Khatami, and Beck (1975). Group studies have shown that therapy based on a Beck's cognitive behavior modification model is superior to a program based on Lewinsohn's model, a nondirective control therapy and a waiting list control (Shaw, Note 2) and is more effective than treatment with imipramine hydrochloride (Rush, Beck, Kovacs, & Hollon, Note 3).

Each model focuses on a different set of behaviors or symptoms of depression and each presents a different perspective on the relationship between cognitive and over-behavioral processes, on etiology, and on therapy. It may be argued that a behavioral model of self-control provides a broader framework for considering depression and in doing so subsumes many of the conceptions contained in the prior models, but first it is necessary to outline a specific behavioral model of self-control.

A SELF-CONTROL MODEL

Self-control has recently become an important focus of behavioral research (Goldfried & Merbaum, 1973; Mahoney & Thoresen, 1974; Thoresen & Mahoney, 1974). Models of self-control have been used to analyze various forms of normal and deviant behavior and have generated self-administered behavior change programs applicable to various target behaviors. With slight modification the model used in this paper is one described by Kanfer (1970, 1971; Kanfer & Karoly, 1972). Kanfer sees self-control as those processes by which an individual alters the probability of a response in the relative abscence of immediate external supports. Three processes are postulated in a feedback loop model: self-monitoring, self-evaluation, and self-reinforcement.

Self-Monitoring

Self-monitoring involves observations of one's own behavior along with its situational antecedents and its consequences. For instance, in self-control therapy procedures, smokers may note the places in which they smoke, socially anxious males may record the number of contacts they have with females, and overweight persons may count calories. Internal events in the form of proprioceptive, sensory, and affective responses may also be self-monitored. For example, smokers may be asked to rate their anxiety level at the time of smoking a cigarette. Self-monitoring invovles not only a passive perceptual awareness of events but a selective attention to certain classes of events and the ability to make accurate discriminations. Deficits in self-control may therefore exist in the manner in which individuals customarily self-monitor. Specific deficits in self-monitoring behavior represent on potential form of maladaptive self-control.

Self-Evaluation

Self-evaluation refers to a comparison between an estimate of performance (which derives from self-monitoring) and an internal criterion or standard. For example, the dieter compares the day's calorie count to a goal and judges whether or not the criterion has been met. Standards may be derived from a variety of sources (cf. Kanfer, 1970; Bandura, 1971). Individuals may set their internal criteria by adopting externally imposed standards (e.g., a diet calorie chart based on sex and height), or they may self-impose criteria which are more stringent than external standards (e.g., not just an A but 100% correct on every test). Criteria may or may not be realistic and, thus, inappropriately selected internal criteria may represent another specific type of deficit in self-control behavior.

Self-attribution and self-evaluation attributional processes play a role in self-evaluation and can be incorporated into Kanfer's model. Bandura (1971) notes that in self-evaluation research, judgement that a response is accurate or successful is often confounded with judgement that the response is commendable. In fact, these judgements are not always equivalent. Adults might perceive themselves as accurate and successful on a child's task and not evaluate their performance as commendable in any way. Similarly, people might perceive themselves as inaccurate and failing on a task outside their own area of expertise and not condemn themselves for it. Bandura suggests selecting tasks which minimize these confounding effects, but there are further implications of the problem.

The larger issue is that positive or negative self-evaluation implies more than a comparison of performance to criteria of success or failure. Such comparisons are modified by the manner in which people perceive themselves as capable of, and responsible for the behavior. That is, the cause of the behavior must be internally attributed. In that Kanfer (1970, 1971) refers to self-control as occurring in the relative absence of external control, efforts to control one's behavior are premised on at least the perception of internal control.

Thus, self-evaluation should be considered to be the comparison of *internally attributed* performance to a standard or criterion. Performance is commendable only if it is both attributed internally *and* judged to exceed a criterion of success. Performance is condemnable only if it is both attributed internally *and* judged to fall below a criterion for failure. Degree of internal attribution interacts with perceived success or failure to determine the value of self-evaluation. Weiner, Heckhausen, Meyer, and Cook (1972) demonstrated this relationship in a correlational study of the tendency to make internal attributions and magnitude of self-reward and self-punishment in normal subjects. Because individual differences in making internal attributions exist, self-attributional deficits are another potenial type of maladaptive self-control behavior.

Self-Reinforcement

A basic assumption in behavioral conceptions of self-control is that individuals control their own behavior by the same means that one organism might control a second organism and that the same principles apply. Thus, the administration of covert or overt contingent reward or punishment to oneself is postulated as a mechanism of self-control. The self-control model suggests that self-reinforcement supplements external reinforcement in controlling behavior, As Bandura (1976) has argued, self-reinforcement must be conceptualized in a context of external reinforcement. That is, while behavior must generally be seen as directed by and toward gaining external reinforcement, self-reinforcement (overt or covert) functions to maintain consistency and bridge delay when external reinforcers are delayed and immediate reinforcement for alternative behavior is available.

Self-reinforcement has been a major focus of self-control research and many clinical uses of self-administered reward and punishment programs have been described (cf. Thoresen & Mahoney, 1974). Rates of self-reward and self-punishment yield relatively stable individual differences (Kanfer, Duerfeldt, & LePage, 1969; Marston, 1964) and do not necessarliy correlate with one another (Kanfer er al., 1969). Self-control may be maladaptive in terms of either self-reward or self-punishment patterns.

SELF-CONTROL IN DEPRESSION

The model of self-control which has been outlined above can serve as a heuristic model for studying depression in regard to its symptoms, etiology, and therapy. Specific deficits at different stages of self-control may be seen as the basis for specific manifestations of depression.

Self-Monitoring in Depression

There are at least two ways in which the self-monitoring of depressed persons can be characterized. First, depressed persons tend to attend selectively to negative events, and second, depressed persons tend to attend selectively to immediate versus delayed outcomes of their behavior. The term "negative event" is intended to include stimuli which are aversive and other stimuli which are perceived as cues for aversive stimuli. The term has a converse correspondence to Lewinsohn's (1974a) "pleasant event." From complex experience including both positive and negative events, depressed persons selectively attend to negative (unpleasant) events to the relative exclusion of positive (pleasant) events. Ferster (1973) has argued that depressed persons devote disproportionate time to avoidance of or escape from aversive events. This behavior precludes positively reinforced behavior. Beck (1972) includes in his discussion of cognitive distortions the concepts of "selective abstraction" and "arbitrary inference," both of which describe similar processes of attention to negative events. Selective abstraction involves focusing on a detail taken out of a more salient context and using it as a basis for conceptualizing an entire experience. In depression, the detail attended to is usually a negative event embedded in an array of more positive or neutral events. Arbitrary inference involves a personal interpretation of an ambiguous or personally irrelevant event. In depression, a negative quality of the event is selectively attended to. An inappropriate attribution may also be involved.

Although no research has been aimed at this specific formulation as yet, there are studies which are interpretable in these terms. The negative perceptions which occur in response to projective stimuli (e.g., Weintraub, Segal, & Beck, 1974) could easily be seen as due to selective attention. Wener and Rehm (1974) found that depressed persons underestimated the percentage of positive feedback they received. A relative inattention to these positive events could be inferred.

Selective attention to immediate versus delayed outcomes is related to Lewinsohn's (1974a) concept that depressed behavior functions to elicit immediate reinforcement from the social environment at the expense of more important forms of delayed reinforcement. Also related is Lazarus' (1968, 1974) suggestion that depressed persons lose their future perspective. They may be seen as attending to immediate outcomes instead.

Correlational evidence consistent with this deficit was obtained by Rehm and Plakosh (1975) who found a greater expressed preference for immediate as opposed to delayed rewards among depressed as compared to nondepressed undergraduates and by Wener and Rehm (1975) who found that depressed persons were influenced to a greater extent by both high and low rates of immediate reinforcement.

Self-Evaluation in Depression

The self-control of depressed persons can be characterized as maladaptive in two ways within the self-evaluation phase. First, depressed persons frequently fail to make accurate internal attributions of causality. Second, depressed persons tend to set stringent criteria for self-evaluation.

From an attributional point of view a depressed person can be "helpless" in either of two ways. In the first, the person makes excessive external attributions of causality and thus generally believes that there is a high degree of independence between performance and consequences. Such a person is helpless in Seligman's sense of the word and would seldom engage in self-control behavior even in an aversive environment. Such a person would be passive and apathetic but would not necessarily be self-derogating. Since aversive consequences are seen as uncontrollable, performance is neither commendable nor condemnable. In the second form of helplessness, the person makes accurate or even excessively internal attributions of causality but perceives himself or herself to be lacking in ability to obtain positive consequences. Thus, the person believes that the world does contain lawful performance-consequence relationships but that she or he is incompetent and ineffective. This person would be self-derogatory and would express inappropriate guilt, i.e., excessive internal attribution of causality for past aversive consequences. The use of the term helpless in this latter instance is somewhat different from Seligman's use of the term.

The work on learned helplessness in depression can be interpreted as support for either type of inaccurate attribution. For example, Miller and Seligman (1973) found that following success on a skill-defined task, depressed students did not raise their expectancies of success as the nondepressed students did. No differences in expectancy change were found after failure or in chance-defined tasks. The authors interpret this finding in terms of a generalized perception by depressed persons that reinforcement is response independent. From an attributional framework subjects either perceived the task outcome to have been due to external causes (i.e., chance, not skill) or perceived themselves as incapable of repeating or sustaining their success (i.e., lacking skill). The data admit equally to either interpretation.

Stringent self-evaluative criteria as a characteristic of depression has been previously suggested by Marston (1965) and Bandura (1971). Self-evaluative standards may be stringent in more than one sense. Criteria for positive self-evaluation may be stringent in the sense of a high threshold requiring great quantitative or qualitative excellence for self-approval. Golin and Terrel (Note 4) found that depressed college students tend to set higher goal levels for themselves. This deficit together with selective monitoring of negative events results in very few perceived successes. Depressed persons may also have low thresholds for negative self-evaluation. Although these criteria may be relatively independent, clinical observation (e.g., Beck, 1972) suggests that for some depressed persons they may be almost reciprocals. Depressed persons may have "all or none" self-evaluative criteria, i.e., an effort is either a smashing success or a dismal failure.

Self-evaluative criteria may also be stringent in the sense of excessive breadth. Failure in one instance is taken as failure in the entire class of behavior. For example, failure on one exam is taken as evidence for failure as a student and, perhaps, as a person. Beck (1972) describes overgeneralization as one of the primary mechanisms of cognitive distortion in depression.

Self-Reinforcement in Depression

The self-reinforcement phase of self-control is particularly important in accounting for depressive behavior. Depression can be characterized by the self-administration of relatively low rates of self-reward and of high rates of self-punishment. Low rates of self-reward can be associated with the slowed rates of overt behavior which typify depression. Lower general activity level, few response initiations, longer latencies, and less persistence may all be interpreted as resulting from low rates of self-reward.

Self-punishment in normals serves to control behavior by reducing undesirable behavior, often in the presence of external reward (e.g., "kicking oneself" for going off a diet). Self-punishment may also serve as a cue for initiating alternative behavior for approaching a goal (Kanfer & Karoly, 1972). Because the depressed individual may selectively monitor negative feedback and set stringent self-evaluative criteria, potenially effective behavior may also be suppressed by excessive self-punishment. Vacillation between responding strategies may also result because each alternative is self-punished early in the response chain (i.e., indecisiveness).

Correlational evidence for self-reinforcement deficits in depression was obtained by Rozensky, Rehm, Pry, and Roth (Note 5). Their study demonstrated differences in rates of self-reward and self-punishment between depressed and nondepressed hospital patients. General medical VA patients who were referred for psychological evaluation were separated into high and low depression groups on the basis of the Beck Depression Inventory and were given a word recognition memory task. Depressed patients (scores of 20 and over) gave themselves fewer self-rewards and more self-punishments for their responses than either the low depression group (referred patients with Depression inventory scores of 19 or less) or a normal group of patients who were solicited from the hospital recreation room. The groups did not differ in correct responses. Roth, Rehm, and Rozensky (Note 6) replicated this procedure with college students varying in degree of depression. Depressed students gave themselves more self-punishment and less self-reward than nondepressed students although only the former difference obtained statistical significance. The failure to replicate the self-reward finding may be due to the fact that the latter population was by definition a relatively active group of normals capable of working for long term rewards.

In summary, depression can be accounted for in terms of six deficits in self-control behavior: (1), selective monitoring of negative events; (2), selective monitoring of immediate as opposed to delayed consequences of behavior; (3), stringent self-evaluative criteria; (4), inaccurate attributions of responsibility; (5), insufficient self-reward; and (6), excessive self-punishment.

IMPLICATIONS OF THE MODEL

Symptomatology

The diverse symptoms of depression are accounted for as either direct or indirect reflections of self-control deficits. Monitoring negative events is reflected in the pessimism and negative view of the world, the future, and the self which characterize depression. Self-monitoring of immediate consequences to the exclusion of delayed consequences is reflected in what Lazarus (1968) talks about as an inability to contemplate future reinforcement. Reports of lack of motivation and hopelessness about the future also reflect this deficit.

Stringent self-evaluative criteria are directly reflected in setting unrealistic goals and result in attitudes of lack of self-esteem and negative self-evaluation. Inappropriate attribution of internal responsibility is reflected in helplessness, the belief in the independence of behavior and consequence, or the belief in one's inability to produce change. Guilt can be thought of as the internal attribution of responsibility for failure.

Lack of self-reward may be directly observed in depression but is most important in accounting for the overt-motor symptomatology of depression. Lack of self-reward results in psychomotor retardation, lowered activity level, and lack of initiative, all of which are associated with depression. In addition, many of the so-called "neurovegetative signs" of depression may be understood in terms of reduced frequency of behavior. Loss of appetite, loss of "libido," and fatiguability can be translated into reduced frequency of eating, sexual, and work behaviors. In that self-reinforcement can be thought of as supplementing external reinforcement in the pursuit of delayed goals, lack of self-reward can result in an inability to sustain effort and a tendency to be self-indulgent with regard to immediate reinforcement. Emotional lability can be thought of as oversusceptibility to external reinforcement because of lack of self-reinforcement, i.e., the person's mood is affected by whatever external events are occurring without the more consistent effect of self-reward to act as a functional supplement to maintain behavior. Excessive self-punishment may be directly reflected in negative self-statements and other forms of self-directed hostility. It may also result in the suppression or inhibition of thoughts, speech, and actions.

Different individuals may show different combinations or degrees of these symptoms as a function of their specific patterns of self-control habits and/or deficits. The model does imply relationships among the underlying mechanisms and thus among symptoms. As an example of these relationships, Kirshenbaum (cited in Kanfer, Note 7) demonstrated that monitoring incorrect responses (negative events) on a learning task led to a less favorable self-evaluation and a decrease in reported self-reward in comparison to monitoring correct responses. Thus, depressed persons showing negative self-monitoring should also show a negative self-image and depressed overt behavior. On the other hand, depressed overt behavior does not necessarily imply a negative monitoring but might also result from attributional or evaluative deficits alone.

Etiology

The self-control model provides a framework for studying various etiological events and mechanisms in depression. Since self-reinforcement is considered to be a supplement to external reinforcement, a loss or lack of either may produce depressed behavior. Loss of external reinforcement would characterize a reactive depression. Adaptive self-control skills in such cases would function to reorient the person to alternative sources of reinforcement and thus aid in overcoming the depression with time. Poor self-control skills and thus a lack of self-reward would make it more difficult for a person to overcome depression normally, and would make the person more susceptible to depression. Unless she or he encountered a particularly beneficent environment, a person with severe self-control deficits would be chronically depressed. Such persons would be characterized by a dependence on others and a "need" for external reinforcement, direction, and reassurance.

Variables which affect self-control are implicated in the etiology of depression. For example, several studies have demonstrated that self-evaluative criteria can be influenced by modeling (e.g., Bandura & Kupers, 1964; Bandura & Whalen, 1966; Marston, 1965). Marston (1969) demonstrated that self-reinforcement may be influenced directly by external reinforcement contingent on self-reinforcement. The histories of depressed persons may reflect maladaptive modeling or reinforcement schedules. Bandura (1971) pointed out how self-punishment may be reinforced under certain social contingencies. These processes could be examined in the environments and social histories of depressed persons.

Single external events may have multiple effects on self-control behavior. An intense, noncontingent aversive event might lead an individual to monitor negative events in an attempt to avoid a recurrence and/or it might lead to a perception of noncontingency in the environment and thus to helplessness. Further basic research is necessary to elucidate possible influences on self-control behavior and thus depression. The model suggests a number of directions which might fruitfully be pursued.

Therapy

The model has a number of implications for psychotherapy with depression. Different behavior therapy techniques may focus on each of the separate self-control deficits. Selective attention to negative events could be modified by increasing the self-monitoring of positive events. Behavioral techniques have been described which appear to function in this manner. Rush et al. (1975) describe three case studies in which clients kept records of specific classes of behavior. The self-monitoring records were used as a basis for therapy discussion aimed at modifying the clients' distortions of their own behavior. Presumably, part of these distortions related to accurate refocusing of attention on positive behavior and accomplishments. Lewinsohn (1976) has described the use of activity schedules in therapy with depression. Attempts are made to increase the number of pleasant events which occur. Simply self-monitoring pleasant (positive) events may have the effect of refocusing attention as a mechanism through which mood change ultimately occccurs.

Refocusing depressed clients' self-monitoring on delayed as well as immediate consequences could also be accomplished by methods analogous to those used in other self-control therapy programs. Weight loss and smoking reduction programs have advocated a variety of methods for making long-range goals more immediately salient. Such techniques as photos of obese persons taped to the refrigerator door or lists of reasons for quitting smoking inserted in cigarette packs are intended to focus attention on delayed sources of reinforcement. The specification of explicit long-range goals in some concrete form which would allow their frequent presentation in association with desired behavior could be adapted for depression therapy.

Self-attribution behavior has not been the direct target of behavior modification research but basic research in self-attribution may suggest variables related to the modification of self-attributional deficits in depression. For instance, attributions of causality vary as a function of observed covariance between events (Kelley, 1971). It would be expected that systematic self-monitoring of one's behavior and its outcomes might lead to more accurate attributions. Klein and Seligman (1976) demonstrated the reversal of learned helplessness in both cognitive and overt-behavioral aspects following a series of experiences with solvable problems. More accurate attributions of responsibility are presumed to mediate these changes.

Basic research in self-evaluation behavior also suggests therapy applications. Rehm and Marston (1968) employed procedures for modifying self-evaluative criteria in an instigation therapy program for socially anxious college males. Subjects were aided in constructing behavioral criteria for social interaction with females. Specific obtainable goals not dependent on the behavior of others were stressed. Implicit in the procedure was an attempt to make criteria for success less stringent (and thus increase positive self-reinforcement) and to relate small steps to long-term goals.

Self-reinforcement procedures have been used fairly extensively in behavior modification (cf. review by Thoresen & Mahoney, 1974). Jackson (1972) reported a case study in which depression was explicitly conceptualized as a deficiency in self-reinforcement. A systematic program was developed using contingent self-administered reinforcement.

A behavioral treatment program for depression based on the self-control model has been developed and evaluated in a doctoral dissertation by Carilyn Fuchs (Fuchs & Rehm, 1977). A self-control program consisting of didactic presentations of self-control concepts and behavioral assignments was offered to volunteer depressed subjects in group sessions. In the first phase of the program the homework assignment consisted of monitoring positive activities with immediate or delayed reinforcement value. In the second phase, subject-clients used their monitoring data to specify goals in behavioral terms. They then developed realistic and obtainable subgoals which were within their power to carry out. These subgoals then became the primary activities which the subjects self-monitored. In the third phase, subjects were helped to set up self-administered reinforcement programs including overt and covert self-reinforcement for subgoal activities. Results on self-report and behavioral measures favored the self-control therapy over placebo therapy and waiting list controls.

COMPARISON OF THE SELF-CONTROL MODEL WITH OTHER CONTEMPORARY MODELS

Lewinsohn

The self-control model differs from Lewinsohn's model in three major respects. First, it adds consideration of covert reinforcement processes. In addition to external sources of reinforcement, self-reinforcement is implicated in the schedule changes which may account for depressed overt behavior. This addition has greater explanatory power with regard to depressions where the external environment remains constant. For instance, depression following the news of some distant event may produce no objective change in external reinforcement schedules. In such cases, changes in self-monitoring, self-evaluation, and thus self-reinforcement may better explain depressed overt behavior.

Second, the self-control model adds considerations of the role of punishment, overt or covert, in producing depressions. Not only loss or lack of positive reinforcement but also an excess of overt punishment may produce depression by actively suppressing behavior. Covert self-punishment is asserted to play an analogous role in depression.

Third, the self-control model provides a means of differentiating cognitive symptoms and relating them systematically to the overt behavior changes observable in depression. Cognitive symptoms are viewed as reflections of self-control deficits which are interrelated and which affect overt behavior. Individual differences in self-control habits produce differential susceptibility to depression following losses of external reinforcement.

Although overlapping in many ways, the self-control perspective has several heuristic implications which go beyond the Lewinsohn model. One major implication is that intervention can be aimed directly at covert self-control processes as well as at overt behavior. For instance, Lewinsohn uses activity schedules (the Pleasant Events Schedule) to choose targets for modification. The self-control model suggests that this procedure may be an intervention in and of itself redirecting attention to positive events. Fuchs (Fuchs & Rehm, 1977) employed just such a procedure in her dissertation study.

Interventions aimed at modifying self-evaluational criteria also follow from the self-control model, where they would not follow from Lewinsohn's model. Again, Fuch's dissertation provides a demonstration of this possibility. The model suggests that behavior which produces external reinforcement (Lewinsohn's goal) can be increased through modification of self-control mechanisms.

Beck

Beck has made a major contribution to depression research and theory by focusing on and identifying cognitive distortions in depression. The self-control model deals with the same phenomena in a way which specifies the distortion processes in operational terms and places them in a theoretical context with other factors in depression. For instance, Beck's concepts of *arbitrary inference* and *selective abstraction* can be translated into the self-control concept of selective attention to negative events. The latter puts the issue into a more testable and quantifiable form. Similarly, Beck's *overgeneralization* is handled in the self-control model as an issue of excessively broad self-evaluative criteria. Beck's *magnification and minimization* and *inexact labeling* could be interpreted as covert self-punishment with stringent criteria. The self-control model postulates specific relationships among covert cognitive processes and the overt symptomatology seen in depression.

Seligman

The phenomena on which Seligman's theory focuses are accounted for within the more comprehensive self-control model. From the self-control perspective, Seligman's model describes how noncontingent punishment produces inaccurate attributions of causality. These inaccurate attributions lead to a lessening of cues for self-reinforcement and thus the passivity which Seligman has demonstrated.

Considering learned helplessness in attributional terms suggests a more detailed analysis of certain points. Individuals may be helpless either by (1) perceiving a noncontingent relationship between response and consequence or by (2) perceiving themselves incapable or unskilled in producing positive consequences in situations where contingencies actually exist. These two forms of helplessness may be associated with different forms of depressed behavior. For example, it would be inconsistent for depressed people to perceive noncontingency and still set high goals for themselves. It would be more consistent for them to set high goals for themselves if they believed they should be able to do something and yet found themselves incapable. Thus, a self-control analysis resolves some inconsistancies while integrating the phenomena into a broader framework.

CHARACTERISTICS AND LIMITATIONS OF THE MODEL

The self-control model as applied to depression serves as a framework for analysis and intergration and provides a framework for distinguishing among various depression symptoms, each of which can be logically associated with a particular aspect of self-control. The model encompasses and integrates a range of behaviors on which available models focus exclusively. The model also suggests interrelationships among these behaviors, which have an empirical basis in self-control research (e.g., Kirshenbaum, cited in Kanfer, Note 7; Weiner et al., 1972). The model specifies relationships between covert, cognitive behavior and overt-motor behavior in depression.

As a heuristic framework, some parts of the model are only suggested in outline and require further refinement and validation. Although the model is consistent with certain empirical findings, the evidence is largely correlational and further research is clearly needed. The products of research specifically directed by the model will determine its ultimate value.

The self-control model is applied here to a particular form of psychopathology, namely depression. The deficits postulated here may not be exclusive to depression. For instance, Clark and Arkowitz (1975) found stringent self-evaluative criteria among socially anxious college students who rated their own behavior in an interaction with a confederate. On the other hand, self-control deficits of other kinds may be more characteristic of other forms of psychopathology. Sociopaths may show some of the deficits of depression in reverse: lenient self-evaluative criteria, excessive self-reward, and insufficient self-punishment. The self-control model may have wider applicability as a model of psychopathology.

Finally, the model may have some limitations as to causes and types of depression. Recent evidence in genetic and biochemical researach on depression strongly points to a biological component in some forms of depression. Biological factors and self-control deficits may represent separate sources of variance in accounting for the occurrence of depression or they may interact. Akiskal and McKinney (1973, 1975) have argued for a broad interaction model. In any case, the relative contributions of biological and psychological factors to the etiology, symptomatology, and therapy of depression is an extremely complex set of questions, the answers to which will depend upon a great deal of additional basic research on the separate factors. It is hoped that the self-control model may diret inquiries toward these final solutions.

REFERENCE NOTES

1. Bruder, G. E. Psychophysiology. In B. Lubin (Chairperson), *Recent advances in diagnosis and treatment of affective disorders*. Symposium presented at the meeting
2. Shaw, B. F. A systematic investigation of three treatment approaches to the psychotherapy of depression. In A. T. Beck (Chairperson), *Current developments in the psychotherapy of depression*. Symposium at the meetings of the Eastern Psychological Association, New York, April 1976.
3. Rush, A. J., Beck, A. T., Kovacs, M., & Hollon, S. *Comparative efficacy of cognitive therapy and pharmacotherapy in the treatment of depressed outpatients*. Manuscript submitted for publication, 1976.
4. Golin, S., & Terrell, F. *Motivational and associative aspects of depression in skill and chance tasks*. Unpublished manuscript, University of Pittsburgh, 1974.
5. Rozensky, R. A., Rehm, L. P., Pry, G., & Roth, D. *Depression and self-reinforcement behavior in hospital patients*. Unpublished manuscript, University of Pittsburgh, 1974.
6. Roth, D., Rehm, L. P., & Rozensky, R. A. *Depression and self-reinforcement*. Unpublished manuscript, University of Pittsburgh, 1975.
7. Kanfer, F. H. *The many faces of self-control, or behavior modification changes its focus*. Paper presented at the Eighth International Banff Conference, Banff, Alberta, Canada, March 1976.

REFERENCES

Akiskal, H. S., & McKinney, W. T., Jr. Depressive disorders: Toward a unified hypothesis. *Science,* 1973, **182,** 20–29.

Akiskal, H. S., & McKinney, W. T., Jr. Overview of recent research in depression. *Archives of General Psychiatry,* 1975, **32,** 285–305.

Bandura, A. Vicarious and self-reinforcement processes. In R. Glaser (Ed.), *The nature of reinforcement*. New York: Academic Press, 1971.

Bandura, A. Self-reinforcement: Theoretical and methodological considerations. *Behaviorism,* 1976.

Bandura, A., & Kupers, C. J. The transmission of patterns of self-reinforcement through modeling. *Journal of Abnormal and Social Psychology,* 1964, **69,** 1–9.

Bandura, A., & Whalen, C. K. The influence of antecedent reinforcement and divergent modeling cues on patterns of self-reward. *Journal of Personality and Social Psychology,* 1966, **3,** 373–382.

Beck, A. T. The core problem in depression: The cognitive triad. *Science and Psychoanalysis,* 1970, **17,** 47–55.

Beck, A. T. *Depression: Causes and treatment*. Philadelphia: University of Pennsylvania Press, 1972.

Beck, A. T. The development of depression: A cognitive model. In R.M. Friedman & M. M. Katz (Eds.), *The psychology of depression: Contemporary theory and research*. New York: Wiley, 1974.

Clark, J. V., & Arkowitz, H. Social anxiety and self-evaluation of interpersonal performance. *Psychological Reports,* 1975, **36,** 211–221.

Ferster, C. B. A functional analysis of depression. *American Psychologist,* 1973, **28,** 857–870.

Fuchs, C. Z., & Rehm, L. P. A self-control behavior therapy program for depression. *Journal of Consulting and Clinical Psychology,* 1977.

Goldfried, M. R., & Merbaum, M. (Eds.) *Behavior change through self-control.* New York: Holt, Rinehart & Winston, 1973.

Jackson, B. Treatment of depression by self-reinforcement. *Behavior Therapy,* 1972, **2,** 298–307.

Kanfer, F. H. Self-regulation: Research issues and speculations. In C. Neuringer & J. L. Michael (Eds.), *Behavior Modification in Cinical Psychology.* New York: Appleton-Century-Crofts. 1970.

Kanfer, F. H. The maintenance of behavior by self-generated stimuli and reinforcement. In A. Jacobs & L. B. Sachs (Eds.), *The psychology of private events: Perspectives on covert response systems.* New York: Academic Press, 1971.

Kanfer, F. H., Duerfeldt, P. H., & LePage, A. L. Stability of patterns of self-reinforcement. *Psychological Reports,* 1969, **24,** 663–670.

Kanfer, F. H., & Karoly, P. Self-control: A behavioristic excursion into the lion's den. *Behavior Therapy,* 1972, **2,** 398–416.

Kelley, H. H. *Attribution in social interaction.* Morristown, NJ: General Learning Press, 1971.

Klein, D. C., & Seligman, M. E. P. Reversal of performance deficits and perceptual deficits in learned helplessness and depression. *Journal of Abnormal Psychology,* 1976, **85,** 11–26.

Lazarus, A. A. Learning theory and the treatment of depression. *Behaviour Research and Therapy,* 1968, **6,** 83–89.

Lazarus, A. A. Multimodal behavioral treatment of depression. *Behavior Therapy,* 1974, **5,** 549–554.

Levitt, E. E., & Lubin, B. *Depression: Concepts, controversies and some new facts.* New York: Springer, 1975.

Lewinsohn, P. M. A behavioral approach to depression. In R. M. Friedman & M. M. Katz (Eds.), *The psychology of depression: Contemporary theory and research.* New York: Wiley, 1974. Pp. 157–185.(a)

Lewinsohn, P. M. Clinical and theoretical aspects of depression. In K. S. Calhoun, H. E. Adams, & K. M. Mitchell (Eds.), *Innovative treatment methods of psychopathology.* New York: Wiley, 1974. (b)

Lewinsohn, P. M. Activity schedules in treatment of depression. In J. D. Krumboltz & C. E. Thoresen, *Counseling methods.* New York: Holt, Rinehart & Winston, 1976.

Lewinsohn, P. M., Biglan, A., & Zeiss, A. M. Behavioral treatment of depression. In P. O. Davidson, (Ed.), *The behavioral management of anxiety, depression and pain.* New York: Brunner/Mazel, 1976.

Lewinsohn, P. M., & Shaffer, M. The use of home observation as an integral part of the treatment of depression: Preliminary report and case studies. *Journal of Consulting and Clinical Psychology,* 1971, **37,** 87–94.

Lewinsohn, P. M., & Shaw, D. A. Feedback about interpersonal behavior as an agent of behavior change: A case study in the treatment of depression. *Psychotherapy and Psychosomatics,* 1969. **17,** 82–88.

Lewinsohn, P. M., Weinstein, M. S., & Shaw, D. Depression: A clinical-research approach. In R. D. Rubin & C. M. Franks (Eds.), *Advances in behavior therapy,* 1968. New York: Academic Press. 1969.

Lewinsohn, P. M., Weinstein, M. S., & Alper, T. A behavioral approach to the group treatment of depressed persons: Methodologicl contributions. *Journal of Clinical Psychology*, 1970, **26**, 525–532.

Mahoney, M. J., & Thoresen, C. E. *Self-control: Power to the person*. Monterey, CA: Brooks/Cole, 1974.

Marston. A. R. Variables affecting incidence of self-reinforcement. *Psychological Reports*, 1964, **14**, 879–884.

Marston, A. R. Self-reinforcement: The relevance of a concept in analogue research to psychotherapy. *Psychotherapy: Theory, Research and Practice*, 1965, **2**, 1–5.

Marston, A. R. Effect of external feedback on the rate of positive self-reinforcement. *Journal of Experimental Psychology*, 1969, **80**, 175–179.

Mendels. J. *Concepts of depression*. New York: Wiley, 1970.

Miller. W. R., & Seligman, M. E. P. Depression and the perception of reinforcement. *Journal of Abnormal Psychology*, 1973, **82**, 62–73.

Rehm, L. P., & Marston, A. R. Reduction of social anxiety through modification of self-reinforcement: An instigation therapy technique. *Journal of Consulting and Clinical Psychology*, 1968, **32**, 565–574.

Rehm, L. P., & Plakosh, P. Preference for immediate reinforcement in depression. *Journal of Behavior Therapy and Experimental Psychiatry*, 1975, **6**, 101–103.

Robinson, J. C., & Lewinsohn, P. M. An experimental analysis of a technique based on the Premack principle for changing the verbal behavior of depressed individuals. *Psychological Reports*, 1973, **32**, 199–210. (a)

Robinson, J. C., & Lewinsohn, P. M. Behavior modification of speech characteristics in a chronically depressed man. *Behavior Therapy*, 1973, **4**, 150–152. (b)

Rush, A. J., Khatami, M., & Beck, A. T. Cognitive and behavior therapy in chronic depression. *Behavior Therapy*, 1975, **6**, 398–404.

Seligman, M. E. P. Depression and learned helplessness. In R. J. Friedman & M. M. Katz (Eds.), *The psychology of depression: Contemporary theory and research*, New York: Winston-Wiley, 1974.

Seligman, M. E. P. *Helplessness: On depression, development, and health*. San Francisco: Freeman, 1975.

Seligman, M. E. P., Klein, D. C., & Miller, W. R. Depression. In H. Leitenberg (Ed.), *Handbook of behavior modification and behavior therapy*. Englewood Cliffs, NJ: Prentice-Hall, 1974.

Thoresen. C. E., & Mahoney, M. J. *Behavioral self-control*. New York: Holt, Rinehart & Winston, 1974.

Weiner, B., Heckhausen, H., Meyer, W., & Cook, R. E. Causal ascriptions and achievement behavior. *Journal of Personality and Social Psychology*, 1972, **21**, 239–248.

Weintraub, M., Segal, R. M., & Beck, A. T. An investigation of cognition and affect in the depressive experiences of normal men. *Journal of Consulting and Clinical Psychology*, 1974, **42**, 211.

Wener, A., & Rehm, L. P. Depressive affect: A test of behavioral hypotheses. *Journal of Abnormal Psychology*, 1975, **84**, 221–227.

Woodruff, R. A., Jr., Goodwin. D. W., & Guze. S. G. *Psychiatric diagnosis*. London: Oxford University Press, 1974.

8. Maladaptive Cognitive Structures in Depression

Maria Kovacs and Aaron T. Beck

Depression (or melancholia) has been recognized for thousands of years. The Book of Job, for example, illustrates the profound mood alteration, loss of interest, social withdrawal, self-deprecation, self-blame, and sleep disturbance that characterize the depressions. A 3,900-year-old Egyptian manuscript provides a distressingly accurate picture of the sufferer's pessimism, his loss of faith in others, his inability to carry out the everyday tasks of life, and his serious consideration of suicide (1). Such historical descriptions are congruent with current accounts of the phenomenology of clinical depressions (2–5).

In spite of considerable agreement of the phenomenology of the clinical syndrome of depression, no completely satisfactory explanation has yet been offered to account for the mechanisms underlying the wide variations in symptomatology and course. The number of competing viewpoints and nosological systems (2, 3, 6–12) clearly mirrors the incomplete knowledge of etiological and contributory factors in the depressive disorders. Nevertheless, as Akiskal and McKinney's "pluralistic" view of depression (6) suggests, most explanatory models, including psychological and biological models, provide a unique perspective that can contribute to a fuller understanding of these clinical syndromes.

In this paper we will present the cognitive approach to the description and treatment of depression. The cognitive approach focuses on the psychological and behavioral aspects of the depressive syndrome and highlights typical cognitive distortions that occur in all of the nosological categories of depression (2).

THE COGNITIVE VIEW OF BEHAVIOR AND PSYCHOPATHOLOGY

The cognitive view of behavior assigns primary importance to the self-evident fact that people *think*. It assumes that the nature and characteristics of thinking and resultant conclusions determine what people feel and do and how they act and react. This view of behavior and psychopathology has a long history that bridges the disciplines of clinical psychiatry, clinical and academic psychology, and philosophy (2, 13–19). The increasing emphasis on the role of cognition in behavior has been termed the "cognitive revolution" (20).

"Cognition" is a broad term that refers to both the content of thought and the processes involved in thinking (15, 16). Ways of perceiving and processing material, the mechanisms and content of memory and recall, and problem-solving attitudes and strategies are all aspects of cognition (16). In short, cognition encompasses the processes of knowing, as well as the products of knowing (16, 21). Many of the complex processes subsumed under the term "cognition" are still poorly understood. In the absence of a comprehensive theory of memory that would help to explain the consistencies in individual behavior over time, the existence of "cognitive structures" or "schemata" has been postulated (12, 14, 16, 22, 23).

Cognitive structures are relatively enduring characteristics of a person's cognitive organization. They are organized representations of prior experience; different aspects of experience are organized through different schemata (16, 22). The concept of cognitive structures or schemata can be used to explain why people react differently to similar or identical situations, while a particular individual may show the same type of response to apparently dissimilar events.

A schema allows a person to screen, code, and assess the full range of internal or external stimuli and to decide on a subsequent course of action. When a person is confronted with a particular situation, it is assumed that a schema is activated that is relevant to that stimulus configuration (2, 14). The different schemata in the cognitive organization may vary in their specificity and detail and the range of stimuli or patterns to which they apply. For example, a person may have a complex, multifaceted, and well-developed cognitive schema to deal with problems in mathematics, but a simple, narrow schema to deal with sexual encounters. In our use of the term, schemata encompass systems for classifying stimuli that range from simple perceptual configurations to complex stepwise reasoning processes.

The cognitive approach to behavior and psychopathology is different in many ways from previous psychological perspectives. Previous models have used motivational or adaptational concepts that are so elaborate and remote from clinically observable phenomena as to preclude empirical validation (2). As we shall demonstrate, hypotheses derived from the cognitive approach to depression are readily testable, and many of them have been supported by empirical evidence.

Contrary to common belief among clinicians, the cognitive approach to depression and psychopathology does *not* assume that a well-adjusted individual is one who thinks logically and solves problems rationally (2, 13, 14). What is assumed is that to understand and correct maladaptive behavior, the idiosyncratic meaning people ascribe to their experiences must be uncovered. Within this framework, we do not try to alter or remove all idiosyncratic evaluations but only those that are dysfunctional or maladaptive. The evaluations or idiosyncratic views that are pathogenic of depression are generally associated with negative value judgements. For example, a woman's belief that she is unattractive may not be consensually validated, and thus it may reflect an idiosyncratic cognition. Nonetheless, if the cognition did not interfere with her emotional well-being and general functioning, it would not be considered maladaptive. On the other hand, if the woman attached a negative value to her opinion of her appearance and considered appearance to be an important aspect of her desirability as a person, she would be likely to progress to inaccurate *and* dysfunctional conclusions, such as "Nobody could love me because I am ugly" or "I might as well give up in life since I don't have much going for me."

THE COGNITIVE VIEW OF DEPRESSION

Beck (2, 24–27) has provided the most comprehensive exposition of the cognitive view of depression. In contradistinction to current emphases that mood alteration is central in depressive syndromes (28), the cognitive approach focuses on self-castigation, exaggeration of external problems, and hopelessness as the most salient symptoms.

According to Beck (2, 26), the depressed person's thinking and preoccupation represent erroneous and exaggerated ways of viewing oneself and events. The depressed person is overly sensitive to obstacles to goal-directed activity, interprets trivial impediments as substantial, reads disparagement into innocuous statements by others, and, at the same time, devalues himself or herself. The characteristic depressive preoccupations are stereotypical and are evident in self-report, fantasy, and dream content. Moreover, the cognitions are frequently irrelevant and inappropriate to the reality of the situation and mirror a consistent negative bias against oneself (2, 24, 25).

Profuse negative cognitions inevitably lead to dysphoria, reduced desire to provide for one's pleasure or welfare, passivity, and ultimately to giving up. The specific cognitive content is "chained" to a particular affect (25). Thus concern about an anticipated threat is connected with feelings of anxiety; thoughts about being unloved and abandoned are associated with depressive feelings. Depressive cognitive content generally relates to notions of loss or perceived subtractions from what Beck refers to as one's "personal domain." The personal domain includes the individual, significant others, valued objects and attributes, and ideals, principles, and goals held to be important (25). Thus if professional accomplishment is a central and cherished goal, a temporary setback may be magnified out of proportion and seen as having devastating implications about one's abilities and one's prospects for future achievement. As a consequence of such an overgeneralized negative interpretation, the depressed person is likely to experience increased dysphoria, dejection, and discouragement.

In the clinical depressions, the patient's perceptions, interpretations, and evaluations are not consensually validated, and the pervasive, negative bias against oneself remains relatively immune to conventional corrective feedback. This negative view of oneself and the future also militates against the reality testing of one's ideas, active exploration of problem solving alternatives, and appropriate use of other people as resources.

Beck's approach to depression and its derivative treatment, cognitive therapy (2, 26), is targeted on selected aspects of the patient's thinking and behavior. In a recent review (29) we summarized the content and process peculiarities of depressive cognitions and their relationship to affect.

DEPRESSIVE COGNITIONS: CONTENT AND PROCESS

The content of depressive cognitions is predominantly negative in tone and self-referential in direction; the individual is preoccupied with self-derogatory and self-blaming thoughts. Moreover, the depressed patient projects into the future his or her notions of real or imagined loss. He or she becomes pessimistic and hopeless and believes that the current discomfort is unending and unalterable. Beck (2) has referred to the thematic content of depressive cognitions as the "negative cognitive triad," a negative, demeaning view of oneself, the world, and the future. A number of empirical investigations support the common clinical observation that depression is associated with negative, self-referential cognitive content (30–33).

Much of our knowledge about ourselves and the world is meaningful only when considered in a time dimension. In addition, most of our actions implicitly reflect future goal-orientation (13, 16, 17, 34). It has long been noted that a disturbance in time orientation, such as a constricted time perspective, is indicative of psychopathology (13, 34). In the clinical interview the depressed patient's highly constricted time perspective is evident in statements that he or she has "no future" or "nothing to look forward to." In other words, in depression the future loses its meaning as a portent for prospective solutions (35); in the patient's eyes the future becomes a singular state of unending pain and despair rather than a multiplicity of experiences and opportunities.

A number of studies have documented the fact that distorted construction of temporal experience is indeed one of the characteristics of depressive cognitions. Compared with both nondepressed "normal" people and nondepressed psychiatric patients such as schizophrenic and manic individuals, depressed patients manifest specific distortions of temporal schemata (35-38).

Recall, an additional aspect of cognitive functioning, is also characteristically skewed in depression. Depressed individuals selectively recall material with negative content or implication at the expense of neutral or positively toned material. In the clinical interview they usually paint the bleakest picture of their background; positive material can be elicited only by the most pointed and specific questioning. Lloyd and Lishman (39, 40) reported empirical data that depressive recall is biased toward negatively toned material; the extent of negative recall is related to the severity of the depression and to depression as a diagnosis. The characteristically biased recall was also documented by the work of Nelson and Craighead (41), who showed that depressed subjects tend to remember more experimental punishment and less positive experimental reinforcement than nondepressed subjects do.

Other studies (42, 43) have indicated that depressed subjects underestimate the amount of positive experimental reinforcement they receive.

Our clinical observations of depressed patients also disclose that they have a strong tendency to assign negative global and personalized meanings to events. For example, one of our patients, who repeatedly called friends and sought advice when he was in distress, wrote in his diary, "I am despicable for asking opinions." He believed that his multiple phone calls to friends reflected his inability to handle his own problems. Moreover, he was convinced that this alleged weakness detracted from his "worth" as a person and actually made others think unfavorably of him.

The depressed patient is especially prone to disqualify prior positive experiences and to personalize experiences of failure. The latter are often interpreted as indicative of his or her blameworthiness. For example, a patient was not pleased when a short story she had written was accepted for publication because she attributed the acceptance to sheer luck. However, she regarded a rejected article as proof of her incompetence and felt distraught. A similar phenomenon was reported by Stuart (38), who found that depressive tendencies correlate with evaluative rather than classificatory associations, i.e., associating the word "apple" with "sweet" (evaluation) rather than "fruit" (classification). Empirical work (44, 45) has documented the fact that depressed subjects personalize failure; they ascribe failure in an experimental task to lack of ability, while they do not attribute success to internal factors.

The depressed patient's characteristic stereotypical conclusions and assessments reflect a combination of negative cognitive themes and certain systematic errors of thinking (2, 26). A characteristic error in depressive thinking is drawing conclusions in the absence of or contrary to evidence. This process of arbitrary inference is illustrated by the following cognition: "John didn't call tonight. . . . He probably doesn't want to see me anymore." When depressed patients are confronted with a negative event or attribute they typically magnify its importance; however, the implications of a pleasant event or positive attribute are minimized. For instance, a patient evaluated a slight increase in her dysphoria to mean that she was "deteriorating," while she viewed a well-done task as quite insignificant. In clinical work we typically find that the patient selectively abstracts isolated elements of a situation that are most consistent with his or her negative and pessimistic world view and ignores other salient cues. A depressed patient decided that her boss's failure to say hello was ominous; she completely ignored the fact that he was under considerable pressure and preoccupied. As Beck and Shaw (27) have noted, the depressed patient's invariant method of information processing results in overgeneralization and the ignoring of fine discriminations.

Hammen and Krantz (30), Weintraub and associates (33), and Beck (2) have reported empirical data that document the presence and preponderance of erroneous cognitive processes in depressed college students and depressed patients. The depressive tendency to magnify negative experiences is reflected in depressed subjects' hypersensitivity to experimentally manipulated failure, compared with the reactions of nondepressed subjects. Loeb and associates (46) and Hammen and Krantz (30) have documented the fact that such manipulations lead to increased dysphoria and pessimism, decreased levels of aspiration, and less positive predictions of one's performance on subsequent tasks.

DEPRESSOGENIC PREMISES AND SCHEMATA

It is clear that a concept is needed to integrate the various cognitive distortions that characterize depressed thought. This integrative concept should also help explain why, given certain internal or external events, some people develop a clinical depression and others do not. Two concepts, namely, "premises" and "schemata," nicely fulfill the integrative function we seek.

Premises are implicit or explicit statements of fact that form the basis or cornerstone of an argument, conclusion, evaluation, or problem-solving strategy. Wason and Johnson-Laird (18) have suggested that everyday problem solving is best understood as a function of "emotional decisions to accept or reject premises." We have already noted the patient who evaluated the missed phone call from her boyfriend as a rejection and pointed out her arbitrary inference and personalized, negatively referential meaning. From a clinical viewpoint, her conclusion that her boyfriend did not want to see her any more was erroneous because it was not based on any evidence. The conclusion was also *maladaptive* because it led to increased dysphoria, lack of activity for the duration of the evening, and continued rumination about her allegedly poor interpersonal skills. Nevertheless, the interpretation was a natural function of the patient's basic premise, namely, "If I am not important to everyone, I can't go on living." This patient defined being "important to others" as other people attending to her, worrying about her, and always following through with promises and commitments.

We use the terms "silent assumptions," "formulas," and "basic equations" to refer to the premises that are crucial in depression. While depressive premises can be described in terms of common themes or leitmotifs, each depressed patient has a distinctly personal set of rules or formulas that he or she uses to integrate experiences. These formulas are generally unarticulated. Nevertheless, their content can be inferred vis-à-vis the patient's goals, self-evaluations, and the meanings he or she assigns to the raw data of his or her experiences. In addition, the depressed patient's stereotypical and rigid notions and directives are often the "surface" manifestations of an underlying depressogenic premise.

For example, depressed patients tend to make excessive use of the directives "should" and "must." Compared with the "shoulds" of nonsymptomatic people, the depressed patients' directives are generally unreasonable, rigid, and unyielding; the goal, which reflects the depressive premise, is usually unattainable. One of our patients was preoccupied with how she "should" and "must" study every day, contact her family regularly, be undemanding of others, and always present a neat, organized appearance. The profuse, content-specific use of "should" eventually revealed her underlying premise: "I have to be perfect at everything." Another patient repeatedly and stereotypically concerned herself with themes that reflected her dependence on other people; one of her basic premises concerning herself was "I need the continuous presence of others for survival." Depressed patients also frequently use premises such as "I should be able to endure any hardship with grace," "I should always be generous, dignified, and courageous," "I should be smart and capable all the time."

"Either-or" assumptions that treat two separate premises as having equivalent meanings are also common among depressed individuals, for example, "Either I am one hundred percent successful in everything or I am a failure," "If I am not a success, life has no meaning," "If I am not loved by everyone, I cannot go on living." In collaboration with us, Weissman constructed the Dysfunctional Attitude Scale (DAS), which contains statements reflecting a variety of both adaptive and maladaptive attitudes and beliefs. The maladaptive statements had been found to be characteristic of depressed patients in therapy but generally uncharacteristic of nondepressed patients. A high DAS score indicates endorsement of a large number of items that reflect depressogenic attitudes. In a pilot study with 35 depressed psychiatric outpatients, Weissman found a correlation coefficient of .58 between the DAS score and level of depression. Weissman is currently analyzing the reliability and validity of the DAS using large samples of college students and psychiatric patients.

Silent assumptions or premises, bits of information and conclusions provide the content of a cognitive schema. A schema is a relatively enduring structure that functions like a template; it actively screens, codes, categorizes, and evaluates information. By definition, it also represents some relevant prior experience (16).

CHARACTERISTICS AND DEVELOPMENT OF DEPRESSOGENIC SCHEMATA

Although we cannot offer proof that certain schemata predispose to depression, clinical experience indicates an abundance of typical cognitions that help to maintain the patient's depression. The preponderant characteristic cognitions presumably reflect the operation of distinct cognitive schemata. We postulate that the schemata which are active in depression are previously latent cognitive structures. They are reactivated when the patient is confronted with certain internal or external stimuli. Once reactivated, the depressogenic schemata gradually replace more appropriate ways of organizing and evaluating information.

As the depressogenic schemata become more active in the patient's cognitive organization, they can be evoked by a wide range of stimuli through the process of stimulus generalization (2). In the initial stages of depression the patient tends to ruminate over a few characteristic ideas, such as "I'm a complete failure" or "My depression is a punishment for my sins." As the depression progresses, the patient gradually loses control over his or her thinking; even when he or she tries to focus on other material, the depressive cognitions intrude and occupy a central place in his or her thoughts. In the more severe depressions, the depressive schemata and associated ideas gradually become so potent that the patient cannot even consider that his or her ideas or interpretations may be erroneous. Such loss of reasonable thinking and reality testing may be best understood in terms of the "hyperactivity" of the depressive schemata and their consequent interference with the operation of other cognitive structures (2). From a clinical point of view, the hyperactive, idiosyncratic schemata produce cognitions that are exceptionally compelling, vivid, and plausible to the patient. Their intensity noticeably affects the patient's interpretations and information processing.

In our clinical experience, the schemata that predispose to and become overly active in a depressive episode have several characteristics. First, they relate to and organize those aspects of the person's experience that concern self-evaluation and relationships with other people. Specifically, depressogenic schemata code and organize information about life situations or events that the individual perceives as real or potential subtractions from his personal domain. Since people's perceptions are idiosyncratic and variable, it is not possible to foresee the specific stimulus conditions that can reactivate a depressogenic schema.

Depressogenic schemata have a number of additional characteristics that may help explain that, while everyone has schemata that relate to self-assessment and interpersonal relationships, not everyone gets depressed. One defining characteristic is inflexible or absolute rules of conduct and evaluation that become manifest in the patient's language as rigid quantifiers (e.g., "all," "always," "never"), categorical imperatives ("must," "ought," "have to"), and preemptive class assignments ("nothing but").

Although one of our patients, a Ph.D. in history, was still capable of employing appropriate constructs in most of her everyday business, a gradually eroding marriage and recent interpersonal rejection reactivated her phenomenologically more primitive cognitive schema that related to interpersonal disapproval and loss. The inflexibility of her depressogenic schema is evident in the following cognitions: "I *must* make my life meaningful every day or else my life is worthless. . . . To make my life worthwhile, I *have to* make *every* hour count. I have to be productive and please *everyone* around me. . . . If people leave me or disapprove of me, I haven't pleased them; therefore I'm *nothing but* a failure—a parasite, a useless creature" (italics added). In this set of cognitions, the idiosyncratic evaluation is clearly maladaptive because

of the final, devastating value judgment and the bizarre overgeneralization. The rigidity and absoluteness built into this patient's schema
inevitably led to the exaggerated, overgeneralized conclusions. In the
beginning of her treatment this patient ruminated primarily about her
worthlessness and did not report the sequence of cognitions noted
above.

During their development and maturation people develop a large
number of schemata that organize different aspects of experience. The
schemata ostensibly undergo modification as a result of living, learning,
and experiencing. The formal characteristics of most depressogenic
schemata, including the psychologically simplistic and "childish" content of the premises, the rigid directives, and their apparent lack of
differentiation, all combine to create the impression that we are dealing
with relatively stable, developmentally early constructions. In other
words, it appears that most of these schemata contain erroneous conclusions which stem from the patient's earlier years and which have
remained fairly constant through years of living. The functional utility
of these schemata apparently has not been systematically tested against
the changing reality of the maturing person. Their content and their
process characteristics have not been modified to parallel the increasing
flexibility and complexity of other (nondepressogenic) schemata.

Depressogenic schemata are specific to and most likely to be activated
by conditions that resemble the circumstances under which they developed. However, eventually their range probably extends to stimulus
conditions that are only marginally similar to the original one. For
example, a schema that originally developed as a consequence of the
death of a close relative during the patient's childhood may be readily
reactivated by any death the patient confronts during adulthood. The
schema may also be reactivated by conditions that the adult *interprets*
as constituting irrevocable loss, such as the disruption of an interpersonal relationship.

In repeated episodes of depression the same negative cognitive schemata can be discerned in the profusion of distorted cognitions and in
blatant expressions of regret over unattainable goals or expectations.
When the patient is confronted with a perceived anticipated rejection,
failure, or loss, the reactivation of the depressogenic schemata gradually
leads to the other classic symptoms of depression (2). Insofar as these
schemata appear to be long-term psychological templates associated

with fairly stereotypical attitudinal and behavioral responses under certain stimulus conditions, they may well constitute a cognitive dimension of the depression-prone individual's personality. The central assumption of the cognitive approach to depression, namely, that cognition can determine affect, is supported by a growing body of literature. The literature documents that even in laboratory settings, mood and behavior changes can be induced through cognitive manipulations (47–51).

Patients' self-reports appear to support the clinical observation that depressogenic schemata are probably long-term, characteristic attitudes and problem-solving approaches. More to the point is a recent study by Hauri (52), supporting earlier work by Beck (2), both of which document that the content of depressed patients' dreams is consistent with their waking cognitions, i.e., the dreams are dominated by themes of being rejected, thwarted, abandoned, ill, punished, undesirable, and ugly. Using a dream laboratory to collect dreams from normal subjects and remitted depressed patients, Hauri (52) also found that, compared with the dreams of control subjects, even the dreams of *remitted* patients showed a preponderance of negative themes. Moreover, *remitted* depressed patients dreamed more about the past than normal controls did, which reflects the depressive tendency for selective focus on past events.

Thus certain cognitive processes seem chronically atypical among depressed patients and may represent a stable characteristic of their personality. This hypothesis is partly supported by data on the relative stability of cognitive factors compared with affective factors. These data were reported by Weintraub and associates (33), who investigated cognition and affect over a two-month period. Cognitive content that was assessed through multiple-choice responses to a story completion task was found to be significantly intercorrelated over five testings. On the other hand, affect (assessed through the Multiple Affect Adjective Check List) was considerably less consistent over time. Furthermore, changes in cognitive content appeared to precede changes in affect.

What factors and situations potentiate the development of depressogenic schemata? It has been suggested that the loss of a parent during one's childhood may have etiological significance (2). A set of premises may evolve to guide the person's eventual interpretation of losses as irreversible and traumatic. Data which show that depressed patients more often experienced childhood bereavement than comparison groups did may lend some credence to this assumption (2). However, since these findings describe only a small number of all depressed patients, it is obvious that other predisposing factors need to be explored.

Other factors important in the development of depressogenic schemata may include a parent whose own belief system revolves around personal inadequacy or a parent whose constructive system encompasses inflexible and rigid rules of conduct. Thus a young person may learn and develop some maladaptive schemata on the basis of modeling and social identification. Such social processes can be reinforced by the parent or parenting one. For example, in family therapy sessions it is not uncommon to observe a parent who derogates herself or himself for self-perceived inadequacies and later expresses love for the child by saying, "He is just like me."

As already noted, according to our clinical experience the negative schemata that are dramatically operative in the depressive episode seem to have been refractory to ordinary change and reality testing. Thus what makes these schemata remarkable is probably not their uniqueness in the depression-prone person's development, but the individual's lack of opportunity or lack of experience in submitting them to examination.

Since depressogenic cognitive structures generally relate to interpersonal conduct and evaluation, a number of factors can militate against reality-testing them. A deficit in the child's or young person's social skills or negative interactions with peers or siblings may militate against social testing and reassessment of early interpretations. A young person's self-construction of "differentness," derived from an actual or imagined physical defect, childhood obesity, natural shyness, or the like, may also hinder the testing or modification of socially and interpersonally oriented schemata.

CLINICAL MODIFICATION OF MALADAPTIVE COGNITIVE SCHEMATA

Although cognitive structures appear to have some of the characteristics of personality traits, they *can* be modified. In fact, since normal maturation encompasses increasing knowledge and awareness of oneself and time milieu, the modification of cognitive schemata and modulation of behavior are probably the norm rather than the exception.

We have effectively used short-term cognitive therapy (2, 26) to treat outpatients with both minor and major (nonpsychotic) unipolar depression. Cognitive therapy is structured and directive, yet requires the patient's active collaboration. It encompasses the use of both verbal and behavioral techniques to alleviate depressive symptoms. In the initial treatment sessions we often employ behavioral techniques such as listkeeping, planning productive activities, and scheduling potentially enjoyable events. These techniques help to "break into" the depressive circle. Moreover, they not only focus the patient's attention on relevant, productive activity and *away* from his or her depressive preoccupations, but also provide him with experiences of accomplishment. The therapist can also use behavioral assignments to challenge the validity of the depressed patient's belief that he cannot do anything at all or cannot help himself to feel better.

The patient and therapist then work together to pinpoint the content and process characteristics of the patient's distorted cognitions, question their "sense," and reality-test their appropriateness in the patient's life. Later, the treatment focuses on the identification and modification of the dysfunctional beliefs that derive from the patient's depressogenic schemata. From the patient's habitual thinking errors, stereotypical preoccupations, or repeated allusions to what makes other people happy or miserable, the therapist gradually infers the patient's "silent assumptions."

The following case briefly illustrates the chain of negative cognitions, assumptions, and premises uncovered in the cognitive therapy of a middle-aged married scientist.

CASE REPORT

The patient, Mr. D., sought treatment because of a severe depression, confirmed by high scores on both self and clinical rating scales of depression. Diagnostically, he satisfied the criteria for primary depression of the major unipolar (nonpsychotic) type. Mr. D. had a 10-year history of chronic depression with periodic exacerbations. His current depressive episode coincided with a promotion and was reinforced by long-standing marital problems.

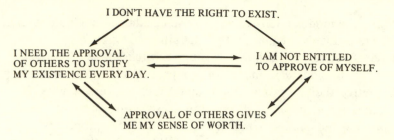

Figure 1. Model of the Patient's Assumptions and Premises

In the first phase of treatment the patient learned to monitor and record his negative automatic thoughts associated with dysphoria. The following three self-observations were typical: "I'm unable to respond to my wife emotionally," "I'm alienated from my family," "I'm responsible for my wife's depression." In the next phase of treatment these kinds of negative thoughts were grouped in order to abstract general cognitive themes. As the cognitions cited above reflect, one theme concerned Mr. D.'s self-perceived inadequacy in the roles of husband and father. As therapy progressed the therapist sought to elicit the *meaning* of Mr. D.'s presumed inadequate performance in the family. According to the patient, the above observations indicated that he was "emotionally empty" and a miserable person who had "nothing to give," The theme of interpersonal self-derogation was subsequently also abstracted from his distorted cognitive responses to his relationships with other people in various settings. To be interpersonally incompetent meant that he was "unworthy." Underlying all of the patient's depressive cognitions was the basic formula that if he did not live up to his own idiosyncratic expectations of perfection (which he unquestioningly believed everyone shared), other people "would not approve" of him.

After considerable questioning and trial-and-error "fitting," the therapist and patient were able to derive a meaningful chain of assumptions and premises (see figure 1).

The patient's underlying belief that he did not have "the right to exist" was apparently related to his discovery, about age 10, that he was an unplanned child. Mr. D.'s highly negative interpretation of this information and its concomitant affective impact was conveyed by the fact that even at age 55, he was able to state with conviction, "I *am* an unwanted baby." This basic belief seemed to underlie Mr. D.'s other assumptions, e.g., "I need the approval of others to justify my existence."

The assumptions relevant to interpersonal disapproval could also be used to explain the preponderance of negative depressive cognitions in response to different stimulus conditions. For example, at work Mr. D. was preoccupied with the recurrent negative cognitions "I have no opinion on anything," "My mind is sluggish . . . I can't speak up at meetings." The possibility of being called upon at a meeting activated Mr. D.'s interpersonal schema concerned with disapproval, which led, in turn, to the cognition that if he did speak up, he would make a fool of himself. Subsequent to the uncovering of Mr. D.'s depressogenic schemata, treatment focused on questioning their relevance and plausibility and having Mr. D. test out new, alternative behaviors and interpretations.

By testing and modifying the dysfunctional premises, the patient was helped to process, in a more realistic way, information regarding other people's reactions to him. One technique that demonstrated the inappropriateness of his system of assumptions consisted of Mr. D.'s adopting behaviors that were contrary to his dysfunctional beliefs, for example, behaving as if the assumption that he needed the approval of other people were untrue. The consequences of such "new" behaviors led to an increase in more reality-oriented adaptive cognitions.

EFFICACY OF COGNITIVE THERAPY

A recent empirical study by Rush and associates (53) assessed the efficacy of cognitive therapy, compared with pharmacotherapy, in the treatment of depressed outpatients. Forty-one unipolar depressed outpatients randomly assigned to either cognitive therapy (N = 19) or imipramine treatment (N = 22) were seen over a period of 12 weeks. As a group, the patients had a long history of repeated episodes of depression and multiple past attempts at treatment. Analysis of self-ratings and clinical ratings of depression revealed that while both treatments were highly effective in decreasing depressive symptoms, the group receiving cognitive therapy showed statistically greater clinical improvement. These findings were essentially replicated at 3- and 6-month follow-up. Moreover, significantly more pharmacotherapy than cognitive therapy patients dropped out of treatment. Among the patients who completed treatment, a significantly greater number of pharmacotherapy patients reentered treatment of depression in the follow-up phase.

COMMENT

While at the present time we have no definitive data on exactly *how* cognitive therapy works, the relatively low posttreatment relapse rate may well indicate that there has been some modification of the patient's depressogenic cognitive schemata. Although the cognitive approach seems to "fit" the observable clinical phenomena, a definitive test of its theoretical rigor will have to await further analyses and detailed inquiry.

REFERENCES

1. Thacker TW: A dispute over suicide, in Documents from Old Testament Times. Edited by Thomas DW. New York, Harper & Row, 1958, pp. 162–167
2. Beck AT: Depression: Clinical, Experimental, and Theoretical Aspects. New York, Harper & Row, 1967
3. Becker J: Depression: Theory and Research. New York, John Wiley & Sons, 1974
4. Grinker RR, Miller J, Sabshin M, et al: The Phenomena of Depressions. New York, Hoeber, 1961
5. Mendels J: Concepts of Depression. New York, John Wiley & Sons, 1970
6. Akiskal HS, McKinney WT: Depressive disorders: toward a unified hypothesis. Science 182:20–29, 1973
7. Akiskal HS, McKinney WT: Overview of recent research in depression. Arch Gen Psychiatry 32:285–305, 1975
8. Klein DF: Endogenomorphic depression. Arch Gen Psychiatry 31:447–454, 1974
9. Klerman GL: Clinical research in depression. Arch Gen Psychiatry 24:305–319, 1971
10. Rush AJ: The why's and how's of diagnosing the depressions. Biological Psychology Bulletin 4:47–62, 1975
11. Secunda SK, Katz MM, Friedman RJ, et al: The Depressive Disorders. DHEW Publication 73–9157. Washington, DC, US Government Printing Office, 1973
12. Wing JK: The functional psychoses and neuroses. Psychiatric Annals 6:393–403, 1976
13. Adler A: The Science of Living. Edited by Ansbacher HL. Garden City, NY, Doubleday, 1969
14. Kelly GA: The Psychology of Personal Constructs. New York, Norton, 1955
15. Broadbent DE: Cognitive psychology: introduction. Br Med Bull 27:191–194, 1971
16. Neisser U: Cognitive Psychology. New York, Appleton-Century-Crofts, 1967
17. Staudenmeyer H: Understanding conditional reasoning with meaningful propositions, in Reasoning: Representation and Process. Edited by Falmagne RJ. Hillsdale, NJ, Erlbaum, 1975, pp 55–78
18. Wason PC., Johnson-Laird PN: Psychology of Reasoning. Cambridge, Mass, Harvard University Press, 1972

19. Craik KJW: The Nature of Explanation. Cambridge, England, Cambridge University Press, 1952
20. Dember WN: Motivation and the cognitive revolution. Am Psychol 29:161–168, 1974
21. Mahoney MJ: Reflections on the cognitive-learning trend in psychotherapy. Am Psychol 32:5–13, 1977
22. Inhelder B. Piaget J: The Early Growth of Logic in the Child. New York, Norton, 1969
23. Johnson-Laird PN: Models of deduction, in Reasoning: Representation and Process. Edited by Falmagne RJ. Hillsdale, NJ, Erlbaum, 1975, pp 7–52
24. Beck AT: Thinking and depression: I. Idiosyncratic content and cognitive distortions. Arch Gen Psychiatry 9:324–333, 1963
25. Beck AT: Cognition, affect, and psychopathology. Arch Gen Psychiatry 24:495–500, 1971
26. Beck AT: Cognitive Therapy and the Emotional Disorders. New York, International Universities Press, 1976
27. Beck AT, Shaw BF: Cognitive approaches to depression, in Handbook of Rational Emotive Theory and Practice. Edited by Ellis A. Grieger R. New York, Springer (in press)
28. American Psychiatric Association: Diagnostic and Statistical Manual of Mental Disorders, 2nd ed. Washington, DC, APA, 1968
29. Kovacs M, Beck AT: Cognitive-affective process in depression, in Emotions, Confict, and Defense. Edited by Izard CE. New York, Plenum (in press)
30. Hammen CL, Krantz S: Effect of success and failure on depressive cognitions. J Abnorm Psychol 85:577–586, 1976
31. Laxer RM: Self concept changes of depressive patients in general hospital treatment. J Consult Psychol 28:214–219, 1964
32. Melges FT. Bowlby J: Types of hopelessness in psychopathological process. Arch Gen Psychiatry 20:690–699, 1969
33. Weintraub M, Segal RM, Beck AT: An investigation of cognition and affect in the depressive experiences of normal men. J Consult Clin Psychol 42:911, 1974
34. May R. Angel E, Ellenberger HF (eds): Existence. New York, Simon and Schuster, 1958
35. Dilling CA. Rabin AI: Temporal experience in depressive states and schizophrenia. J Consult Psychol 31:604–608, 1967
36. Andreasen NJC, Pfohl B: Linguistic analysis of speech in affective disorders. Arch Gen Psychiatry 33:1361–1367, 1976
37. Rey AC. Silber E, Savard RJ, et al: Thinking and language in depression. Presented at the 130th annual meeting of the American Psychiatric Association, Toronto, Ont, Canada, May 2–6, 1977
38. Stuart JL: Intercorrelations of depressive tendencies, time perspective, and cognitive style variables. Dissertation Abstracts International 23:696, 1962
39. Lloyd GG, Lishman WA: Effect of depression on the speed of recall of pleasant and unpleasant experiences. Psychol Med 5: 173–180, 1975
40. Lishman WA: Selective factors in memory: part 2: affective disorder. Psychol Med 2:248–253, 1972
41. Nelson RE, Craighead WE: Selective recall of positive and negative feedback, self-control behaviors, and depression. J Abnorm Psychol 86:379–388, 1977
42. DeMonbreun BG, Craighead WE: Distortion of perception and recall of positive and neutral feedback in depression. Cognitive Therapy and Research 1:311–329, 1977

43. Wener AE, Rehm LP: Depressive affect: a test of behavioral hypotheses. J Abnorm Psychol 84:221–227, 1975
44. Rizley RC: The perception of causality in depression: an attributional analysis of two cognitive theories of depression. New Haven, Yale University Department of Psychology, 1976 (doctoral dissertation)
45. Klein DC, Fencil-Morse E, Seligman MEP: Learned helplessness, depression, and the attribution of failure. J Pers Soc Psychol 33:508–516, 1976
46. Loeb A, Beck AT, Diggory J: Differential effects of success and failure on depressed and nondepressed patients. J Nerv Ment Dis 152:106–114, 1971
47. Coleman RE: Manipulation of self-esteem as a determinant of mood of elated and depressed women. J Abnorm Psychol 84:693–700, 1975
48. Ludwig LD: Elation-depression and skill as determinants of desire for excitement. J Pers 43:1–22. 1975
49. Moore BS, Underwood B, Rosenhan DL: Affect and altruism. Developmental Psychology 8:99–104, 1973
50. Natale M: Effects of induced elation-depression on speech in the initial interview. J Consult Clin Psychol 45:45–52, 1977
51. Velten E: A laboratory task for induction of mood states. Behavior Res Ther 6:473–482, 1968
52. Hauri P: Dreams in patients remitted from reactive depression. J Abnorm Psychol 85:1–10, 1976
53. Rush AJ, Beck AT, Kovacs M, et al: Comparative efficacy of cognitive therapy and pharmacotherapy in the treatment of depressed outpatients. Cognitive Therapy and Research 1:17–37, 1977

9. Learned Helplessness in Humans: Critique and Reformulation

Lyn Y. Abramson, Martin E. P. Seligman, and John D. Teasdale

Over the past 10 years a large number of experiments have shown that a variety of organisms exposed to uncontrollable events often exhibit subsequent disruption of behavior (see Maier & Seligman, 1976, for a review of the infrahuman literature). For example, whereas naive dogs efficiently learn to escape shock by jumping over a barrier in a shuttle box, dogs that first received shocks they could neither avoid nor escape show marked deficits in acquisition of a shuttle escape response (Overmier & Seligman, 1967; Seligman & Maier, 1967). Paralleling the experimental findings with dogs, the debilitating consequences of uncontrollable events have been demonstrated in cats (Masserman, 1971; Seward & Humphrey, 1967; Thomas & Dewald, 1977), in fish (Frumkin & Brookshire, 1969; Padilla, 1973; Padilla, Padilla, Ketterer, & Giacolone, 1970), and in rats (Maier, Albin, & Testa, 1973; Maier & Testa, 1975; Seligman & Beagley, 1975; Seligman, Rosellini, & Kozak, 1975). Finally, the effects of uncontrollable events have been examined in humans (Fosco & Geer, 1971; Gatchel & Proctor, 1976; Glass & Singer, 1972; Hiroto, 1974; Hiroto & Seligman, 1975; Klein, Fencil-Morse, & Seligman, 1976; Klein & Seligman, 1976; Krantz, Glass, & Snyder, 1974; Miller & Seligman, 1975; Racinskas, 1971; Rodin, 1976; Roth, 1973; Roth & Bootzin, 1974; Roth & Kubal, 1975; Thornton & Jacobs, 1971; among others). Hiroto's experiment (1974) is representative and provides a human analogue to the animal studies. College student volunteers were assigned to one of three groups. In the controllable noise group, subjects received loud noise that they could terminate by pushing a button four times. Subjects assigned to the uncontrollable noise group received noise that terminated independently of subjects' responding. Finally, a third group received no noise. In the second phase of the experiment all groups were tested on a hand shuttle box. In the shuttle box, noise termination was controllable for all subjects; to turn off the noise, subjects merely had to move a lever from one side of the box to the other. The results of the test phase were strikingly similar to those obtained with animals. The group receiving prior controllable noise as well as the group receiving no noise readily learned to shuttle, but the typical subject in the group receiving prior uncontrollable noise failed to escape and listened passively to the noise.

Although a number of alternative hypotheses (see Maier & Seligman, 1976, for a review) have been proposed to account for the debilitating effects of experience with uncontrollability, only the learned helplessness hypothesis (Maier & Seligman, 1976; Maier, Seligman, & Solomon, 1969; Seligman, 1975; Seligman et al., 1971) provides a unified theoretical framework integrating the animal and human data. The cornerstone of the hypothesis is that learning that outcomes are uncontrollable results in three deficits: motivational, cognitive and emotional. The hypothesis is "cognitive" in that it postulates that mere exposure to uncontrollability is not sufficient to render an organism helpless; rather, the organism must come to expect that outcomes are uncontrollable in order to exhibit helplessness. In brief, the motivational deficit consists of retarded initiation of voluntary responses and is seen as a consequence of the expectation that outcomes are uncontrollable. If the organism expects that its responses will not affect some outcome, then the likelihood of emitting such responses decreases. Second, the learned helplessness hypothesis argues that learning that an outcome is uncontrollable results in a cognitive deficit since such learning makes it difficult to later learn that responses produce that outcome. Finally, the learned helplessness hypothesis claims that depressed affect is a consequence of learning that outcomes are uncontrollable.

Historically, the learned helplessness hypothesis was formulated before helplessness experiments were performed with human subjects. In the main, early studies of human helplessness attempted to reproduce the animal findings in humans and were rather less concerned with theory building. Recently however, investigators of human helplessness (e.g., Blaney, 1977; Golin & Terrell, 1977; Wortman & Brehm, 1975; Roth & Kilpatrick-Tabak, Note 2) have become increasingly disenchanted with the adequacy of theoretical constructs originating in animal helplessness for understanding helplessness in humans. And so have we. We now present an attributional framework that resolves several theoretical controversies about the effects of uncontrollability in humans. We do not know whether these considerations apply to infra humans. In brief, we argue that when a person finds that he is helpless, he asks *why* he is helpless. The causal attribution he makes then determines the generality and chronicity of his helplessness deficits as well as his lowered self-esteem. In developing the attribution framework, we find it necessary to refine attribution theory (cf. Heider, 1958; Weiner 1972, 1974). Finally, we discuss the implications of the reformulation for the helplessness model of depression (Seligman, 1972, 1975; Seligman, Klein, & Miller, 1976).[1]

PERSONAL HELPLESSNESS VERSUS UNIVERSAL HELPLESSNESS

Inadequacy 1 of the Old Theory

Several examples highlight a conceptual problem encountered by the existing learned helplessness hypothesis when applied to human helplessness. consider a subject in Hiroto's experiment (1974) who is assigned the group that received uncontrollable noise. The experimenter tells the subject there is something he can do to turn off the noise. Since the noise is actually uncontrollable, the subject is unable to find a way to turn off the noise. After repeated unsuccessful attempts the subject may come to believe the problem is unsolvable; that is, neither he nor any other subject can control noise termination. Alternatively, the subject may believe that the problem is solvable but that he lacks the ability to solve it; that is, although he can't control noise termination, other subjects could successfully control the noise. The old helplessness hypothesis does not distinguish these two states, either of which could be engendered by the procedure of presenting uncontrollable outcomes.

In a recent publication, Bandura (1977) discussed a similar distinction:

Theorizing and experimentation on learned helplessness might well consider the conceptual distinction between efficacy and outcome expectations. People can give up trying because they lack a sense of efficacy in achieving the required behavior, or, they may be assured of their capabilities but give up trying because they expect their behavior to have no effect on an unresponsive environment

---

[1] Ivan Miller (Note 1) has proposed an almost identical reformulation. We believe this work to have been done independently of ours, and it should be so treated.

or to be consistently punished. These two separable expectancy sources of futility have quite different antecedents and remedial implications. To alter efficacy-based futility requires development of competencies and expectations of personal effectiveness. By contrast, to change outcome-based futility necessitates changes in prevailing environmental contingencies that restore the instrumental value of the competencies that people already possess. (pp. 204–205)

A final way of illustrating this inadequacy concerns the relation between helplessness and external locus of control. Early perspectives of learned helplessness (Hiroto, 1974; Miller & Seligman, 1973; Seligman, Maier, & Geer, 1968) emphasized an apparent similarity between the helplessness concept of learning that outcomes are uncontrollable and Rotter's (1966) concept of external control. Rotter argued that people's beliefs about causality can be arrayed along the dimension of locus of control, with "internals" tending to believe outcomes are caused by their own responding and "externals" tending to believe outcomes are not caused by their own responding but by luck, chance, or fate. Support for this proposed conceptual similarity of externals and helpless individuals was provided by studies of verbalized expectancies for success in tasks of skill (Klein & Seligman, 1976; Miller & Seligman, 1975). Helpless subjects gave small expectancy changes, which suggests a belief in external control, whereas subjects not made helpless gave large expectancy changes, which suggests a belief in internal control. These findings indicated that helpless subjects perceived tasks of skill as if they were tasks of chance. A puzzling finding, however, was consistently obtained in these studies. On postexperimental questionnaires, helpless and nonhelpless subjects rated skill as playing the same large role in a person's performance on the skill task. Both helpless and nonhelpless subjects said they viewed the skill task as a skill task. Thus, the relation between the concepts of external control and uncontrollability may be more complex than implied by the old hypothesis.

Taken together, these examples point to one conceptual problem concerning the notions of uncontrollability and helplessness. Recall the distinction made by the old helplessness hypothesis between controllable and uncontrollable outcomes. An outcome is said to be uncontrollable for an individual when the occurrence of the outcome is not related to his responding. That is, if the probability of an outcome is the same whether or not a given response occurs, then the outcome is independent of that response. When this is true of all voluntary responses, the outcome is said to be uncontrollable for the individual (Seligman, 1975; Seligman, Maier, & Solomon, 1971). Conversely, if the probability of the outcome when some response is made is different from the probability of the outcome when the response in not made, then the outcome is dependent on that response: The outcome is controllable. The early definition, then, makes no distinction between cases in which an individual lacks requisite controlling responses that are available to other people and cases in which the individual as well as all other individuals do not possess controlling responses. These three examples all illustrate the same inadequacy. In the next section we outline a framework that resolves this inadequacy, and we discuss the implications of this framwork.

Resolution of Inadequacy 1

Suppose a child contracts leukemia and the father bends all his resources to save the child's life. Nothing he does, however, improves the child's health. Eventually he comes to believe there is nothing he can do. Nor is there anything anyone else can do since leukemia is incurable. He subsequently gives up trying to save the child's life and exhibits signs of behavioral helplessness as well as depressed affect. This example fits the specification of the old learned helplessness hypothesis. The parent believed the course of the child's disease was independent of all of his responses as well as the responses of other people. We term this situation *universal helplessness*.

Suppose a person tries very hard in school. He studies endlessly, takes remedial courses, hires tutors. But he fails anyway. The person comes to believe he is stupid and gives up trying to pass. This is not a clear case of uncontrollability according to the old model, since the person believed there existed responses that would contingently produce passing grades although he did not possess them. Regardless of any voluntary response the person made, however, the probability of this obtaining good grades was not altered. We term this situation *personal helplessness*.

Before discussing the distinction between universal and personal helplessness, it is usefull to spell out the flow of events leading to symptoms of helplessness in both examples. First, the person perceived

Objective noncontingency → *Perception of* present and past noncontingency → *Attribution* for present or past noncontingency → *Expectation* of future noncontingency → *Symptoms* of helplessness.

Figure 1. Flow of events leading to symptoms of helplessness.

that all of his acts were noncontingently related to the desired outcome; regardless of what the father did, the child's illness did not improve, and the student continued to do poorly no matter how hard he tried. The person then made an attribution for the perceived noncontingency between his acts and the outcome; the father came to believe leukemia was incurable and the student came to believe he was stupid. In each case, the attribution led to an expectancy of noncontingency between future acts of the individual and the outcome. Finally, the symptoms of helplessness were a consequence of the person's expectancy that his future responses would be futile in obtaining the outcome. The usual sequence of events leading from objective noncontingency to the helplessness is diagrammed in Figure 1.

Both the old and reformulated hypotheses hold the expectation of noncontingency to be the crucial determinant of the symptoms of learned helplessness. Objective noncontingency is predicted to lead to symptoms of helplessness only if the expectation of noncontingency is present (Seligman, 1975, pp. 47–48). The old model, however, was vague in specifying the conditions under which a perception that events are noncontingent (past or present oriented) was transformed into an expectation that events will be noncontingent (future oriented). Our reformulation regards the attribution the individual makes for noncontingency between his acts and outcomes in the here and now as a determinant of his subsequent expectations for future noncontingency. These expectations, in turn, determine the generality, chronicity, and type of his helplessness symptoms. In the context of this general account of the role of attribution in the production of symptoms, the distinction between universal and personal helplessness can now be clarified.

Table 1 explicates the distinction between universal helplessness and personal helplessness and ultimately serves to define our usage of the

Table 1. Personal Helplessness and Universal Helplessness

	Self	
Other	*The person expects the outcome is contingent on a response in his repertoire.*	*The person expects the outcome is not contingent on any response in his repertoire.*
The person expects the outcome is contingent on a response in the repertoire of a relevant other.	1	personal helplessness 3 (internal attribution)
The person expects the outcome is not contingent on a response in the repertoire of any relevant other.	2	universal helplessness 4 (external attribution)

attributional dimension of internality. We take the self–other dichotomy as the criterion of internality. When people believe that outcomes are more likely or less likely to happen to themselves than to relevant others, they attribute these outcomes to internal factors. Alternatively, persons make internal attribution for outcomes that they believe are as likely to happen to themselves as to relevant others.

In the table, the x-axis represents the person's expectations about the relation between the desired outcome and the responses in his repertoire.[2] The person expects the outcome either to be contingent on some response in his repertoire. The y-axis represents his expectations about the relation between the desired outcome and the responses in the repertoires of relevant others. The person expects the outcome to

[2]For the purpose of exposition, dichotomies rather than continua are used. The person expects that the controlling response is or is not available to him and that the controlling response is or is not available to others. These two dichotomies allow for four possible belief states. Strictly speaking, however, the x-axis is a continuum. At the far right, the person expects there is a zero probability that the desired outcome is contingent on any response in his repertoire. Conversely, on the far left he expects there is a probability of one that the desired outcome is contingent on a response in his repertoire. Similar considerations apply to the y-axis as a continuum.

be either contingent on at least one response in at least one relevant other's repertoire or not contingent on any response in any relevant other's repertoire. Cell 4 represents the universal helplessness case and includes the leukemia example, and Cell 3 represents the personal helplessness case and includes the school failure example. Because the person does not believe he is helpless in Cells 1 and 2, these cells are not relevant here and are not discussed. It should be pointed out, however, that a person in Cell 2 would be more likely to make an internal attribution for his perceived control than would a person in Cell 1.

In Table 1, the y-axis represents the person's expectations about whether someone else, a relevant other, had the controlling response in his repertoire. The following example makes it clear why we use a "relevant other" rather than a "random other" or "any other": It is of no solace to a floundering graduate student in mathematics that "random others" are unable to do topological transformations. Crucial to the student's self-evaluation is his belief that his peers, "relevant others," have a high probability of being able to do topological transformations. Nor is it self-esteem damaging for a grade school student to fail to solve mathematical problems that only professional mathematicians can solve, although he may have low self-esteem if his peers can solve them. Therefore, the y-axis is best viewed as representing the person's expectations about the relation between the desired outcome and the responses in the repertoires of relevent others.[3]

[3] Our formulation of "internal" and "external" attributions resembles other attributional frameworks. Heider (1958), who is generally considered the founder of attribution theory, made a basic distinction between "factors within the person" and "factors within the environment" as perceived determinants of outcomes. Similarly, in the locus of control literature, Rotter (1966) distinguished between outcomes that subjects perceive as causally related to their own responses and personal characteristics and outcomes that subjects perceive as caused by external forces such as fate. Unlike these previous formulations that ask whether a factor resides "within the skin" or "outside the skin" to determine whether it is internal or external, we define the self–other dichotomy as the criterion of internality. Although these two formulations may appear to be at odds, analysis reveals strong similarities. For example, Heider (1958) argued that in making a causal attribution, individuals hold a condition responsible for an outcome if that condition is present when the outcome is present and absent when the outcome is absent. Likewise, Kelley (1967) suggested that the procedure individuals use in determining the cause of events is similar to an analysis of variance procedure employed by scientists. The factor that consistently covaries with an outcome is considered to be its cause.

Implications

The distinction between universal and personal helplessness resolves the set of inadequacies with which we began the article. Situations in which subjects believe they cannot solve solvable problems are instances of personal helplessness according to the reformulated hypothesis. Alternatively, situations in which subjects believe that neither they nor relevant others can solve the problem are instances of universal helplessness. Similarly, Bandura's (1977) conceptual distinction between efficacy and outcome expectancies relates to the reformulation in the following way: Personal helplessness entails a low efficacy expectation coupled with a high outcome expectation (the response producing the outcome is unavailable to the person), whereas universal helplessness entails a low outcome expectation (no response produces the outcome). Finally, the reformulation regards "external locus of control" and "helplessness" as orthogonal. One can be either internally or externally helpless. Universally helpless individuals make external attributions for failures, whereas personally helpless individuals make internal attributions. The experimental finding that helpless individuals view skill tasks as skill tasks, not as chance, is no longer puzzling. The task is one of skill (relevant others can solve it), but they do not have the relevant skill. These subjects view themselves as personally rather than universally helpless.

The distinction between universal helplessness and personal helplessness also clarifies the relation of uncontrollability to failure. In the literature these two terms have often been used synonymously. Tennen (Note 3), arguing from an attributional stance, suggested that the terms are redundant and that we abandon the concept of uncontrollability for the simpler concept of failure. We believe this suggestion is misguided both from the point of view of attribution theory and from common usage of the term *failure*.

Let us examine the leukemic child and the school failure examples from the perspective of Kelley and Heider. The responses of no person are consistently associated with improvement of the leukemic child's disease. If the father performed Kelley or Heider's causal analysis, he would conclude that his failure was due to some external factor (e.g., leukemia is incurable). Alternatively, in the school example, failing is consistently associated with the student and not associated with his peers. Here, the student would conclude that some internal factor (e.g., studpidity) was the cause of his failure. Thus, Heider and Kelley also rely on social comparison as a major determinant of internality.

In current attribution theories (e.g., Weiner, 1972) success and failure refer to outcomes. Success refers to obtaining a desired outcome and failure to not obtaining a desired outcome. According to this framework, then, the term *failure* does not embrace all cases of uncontrollability. Thus, from a strict attributional point of view, failure and uncontrollability are not synonymous: Failure is a subset of uncontrollability involving bad outcomes. Early theoretical accounts of helplessness suggested that good things received independently of responding should lead to helplessness deficits. Recent evidence bears this out: Uncontrollable positive events produce the motivational and cognitive deficits in animals (Goodkin, 1976; Welker, 1976) and in humans (Griffiths, 1977; Eisenberger, Mauriello, Carlson, Frank, & Park, Note 4; Hirsh, Note 5; Nugent, Note 6; but see Benson & Kennelly, 1976, for contrary evidence) but probably do not produce sad effect. Similarly Cohen, Rothbart, and Phillips (1976) produced helplessness effects in the absence of perceived failure. In the future, such studies should measure perception of noncontingency as well as performance, since Alloy and Abramson (Note 7) found than noncontingency is more difficult to perceive when one is winning than when one is losing. So the notion of uncontrollability means more than just failure, and it makes predictions concerning both failure and noncontingent success.

In ordinary language, failure means more than merely the occurrence of a bad outcome. People say they have failed when they have tried unsuccessfully to reach a goal and attribute this to some internal factor. Obtaining poor grades in school is considered failure, but being caught in a flash flood is generally considered misfortune. The concepts of trying and personal helplessness are both necessary to analyze failure in the ordinary language sense. According to the reformulated model, then, failure, seen from the individual's point of view, means the subset of personal helplessness involving unsuccessful trying.

The final ramification of the distinction between universal and personal helplessness is that it deduces a fourth deficit of human helplessness—low self-esteem. A major determinant of attitudes toward the self is comparison with others (Clark & Clark, 1939; Festinger, 1954; Morse & Gergen, 1970; Rosenberg, 1965). Our analysis suggests that individuals who believe that desired outcomes are not contingent on acts in their repertoires but are contingent on acts in the repertoires of relevant others, will show lower self-esteem than individuals who believe that desired outcomes are neither contingent on acts in their repertoires nor contingent on acts in the repertoires of relevant others. That is, an unintelligent student who fails an exam his peers pass will have lower self-esteem than a student who fails an exam that all of his peers fail as well.

The dichotomy between universal and personal helplessness determines cases of helplessness (and depression, see below) with and without low self-esteem. But it is neutral with regard to the cognitive and motivational deficits in helplessness. It is important to emphasize that the cognitive and motivational deficits occur in both personal and universal helplessness. Abramson (1977) has demonstrated this empirically while showing that lowered self-esteem occurs only in personal helplessness. According to both the old and the new hypotheses, the expectation that outcomes are noncontingently related to one's own responses is a sufficient condition for motivational and cognitive deficits.

We now turn to the second set of inadequacies. The old hypothesis was vague about when helplessness would be general across situations and when specific, and when it would be chronic and when acute. We now formulate this inadequacy and develop an attributional framework that resolves it.

GENERALITY AND CHRONICITY OF HELPLESSNESS

Inadequacy 2 of the Old Theory

A second set of examples point to the other inadequacy of the old helplessness hypothesis. Consider debriefing in a typical human helplessness study: The subject is presented with an unsolvable problem, tested on a second solvable task, and finally debriefed. The subject is told that the first problem was actually unsolvable and therefore no one could have solved it. Experimenters in human helplessness studies seem to believe that telling a subject that no one could solve the problem will cause helplessness deficits to go away. The prior discussion suggests that convincing a subject that his helplessness is universal rather than personal will remove self-esteem deficits suffered in the experiment. Neither the old nor the new hypothesis, however, predicts that such debriefing will remove the cognitive and motivational deficits. What does debriefing undo and why?

A second way of illustrating this inadequacy is the following: A number of investigators (Hanusa & Schulz, 1977; Tennen & Eller, 1977; Wortman & Brehm, 1975) have emphasized those cases of learned helplessness in which a person inappropriately generalizes the expectation of noncontingency to a new, controllable situation. It is important to point out that the old hypothesis does not require an inappropriate generalization for helplessness. Helplessness exists when a person shows motivational and cognitive deficits as a consequence of an expectation of uncontrollability. The veridicality of the belief and the range of situations over which it occurs are irrelevant to demonstrating helplessness. But the old hypothesis does not specify where and when a person who expects outcomes to be uncontrollable will show deficits. In keeping with the resolution of the first inadequacy, an attributional framework is now presented to resolve the second inadequacy by explaining the generality and chronicity of deficits associated with helplessness.

A Resolution: The Attributional Dimensions of Stability and Generality

Helplessness deficits are sometimes highly general and sometimes quite specific. An accountant, fired from his job, may function poorly in a broad range of situations: he cannot get started on his income tax, he fails to look for a new job, he becomes impotent, he neglects his children, and he avoids social gatherings. In contrast, his helplessness may be situation specific: He does not do his income tax and fails to look for a new job, but he remains an adequate lover, father, and party-goer. When helplessness deficits occur in a broad range of situations, we call them *global*; when the deficits occur in a narrow range of situations, we call them *specific*.

The time course of helplessness (and depression, see below) also varies from individual to individual. Some helplessness deficits may last only minutes and others may last years. Helplessness is called chronic when it is either long-lived or recurrent and *transient* when short-lived and nonrecurrent.

The old hypothesis was vague about generality and chronicity. The helpless person had learned in a particular situation that certain responses and outcomes were independent. The deficits resulting could crop up in new situations if either the responses called for or the outcomes desired were similar to the responses and outcomes about which original learning had occurred. Helplessness was global when it depressed responses highly dissimilar to those about which original learning had occurred or when it extended to stimuli highly dissimilar to those about which original learning had occurred. No account was given about why helplessness was sometimes specific and sometimes global.

When helplessness dissipated in time, forgetting produced by interference from prior or later learning was invoked (e.g.; Seligman, 1975, pp. 67–68). Forgetting of helplessness could be caused either by earlier mastery learning or by subsequent mastery learning.

Again, the explanation was largely post hoc. Helplessness that dissipated rapidly was assumed to have strong proactive or retroactive interference; that which persisted was not.

The reformulated hypothesis makes a major new set of predictions about this topic: The helpless individual first finds out that certain outcomes and responses are independent, then he makes an attribution about the cause. This attribution affects his expectations about future response-outcome relations and thereby determines, as we shall see, the chronicity, generality, and to some degree, the intensity of the deficits. Some attributions have global, others only specific, implications. Some attributions have chronic, others transient, implications. Consider an example: You submit a paper to a journal and it is scathingly rejected by a consulting editor. Consider two possible attributions you might make. "I am stupid" and "The consulting editor is stupid." The first, "I am stupid," has much more disastrous implications for your future paper-submitting than the second. If "I am stupid" is true, future papers are likely to be rejected as well. If "The editor is stupid" is true, future papers stand a better chance of being accepted as long as you do not happen on the same consulting editor. Since "I" is something I have to carry around with me, attributing the cause of helplessness internally often but not always (see below) implies a grimmer future than attributing the cause externally, since external circumstances are usually but not always in greater flux than internal factors.

Recent attribution theorists have refined the possible attribution for outcomes by suggesting that the dimension "stable–unstable" is orthogonal to "internal–external" (Weiner, 1974; Weiner, Frieze Kukla,

Reed, Rest, & Rosenbaum, 1971). Stable factors are thought of as long-lived or recurrent, whereas unstable factors are short-lived or intermittent. When a bad outcome occurs, an individual can attribute it to (a) lack of ability (an internal–stable factor), (b) lack of effort (an internal–unstable factor), (c) the task's being too difficult (an external-stable factor), or (d) lack of luck (an external-unstable factor).

While we applaud this refinement, we believe that further refinement is necessary to specify the attributions that are made when an individual finds himself helpless. In particular, we suggest that there is a third dimension—"global–specific"—orthogonal to internality and stability, that characterizes the attributions of people. Global factors affect a wide variety of outcomes, but specific factors do not.[4] A global attribution implies that helplessness will occur across situations, whereas a specific attribution implies helplessness only in the original situation. This dimension (like those of stability and internality) is a continuum, not a dichotomy; for the sake of simplicity, however, we treat it here as a dichotomy.

Consider a student taking graduate record examinations (GREs) measuring mathematical and verbal skills. He just took the math test and believes he did very poorly. Within the three dimensions, there are eight kinds of attribution he can make about the cause of his low score (Internal–External × Stable–Unstable × Global–Specific). These attributions have strikingly different implications for how he believes he will perform in the next hour on the verbal test (generality of the helplessness deficit across situations) and for how he believes he will do on future math tests when he retakes the GRE some months hence (chronicity of the deficit over time in the same situation). Table 2 describes the formal characteristics of the attributions and exemplifies them. Table 1 relates to Table 2 in the following way: Table 2 uses the attributional dimensions of stability and generality to further subdivide

[4] In principle, there are a large number of dimensions on which attributions can be specified. Weiner (Note 8) suggested that the criterion for a dimension, as opposed to a mere property, of attribution be that we can sensibly ask, Does it apply to all the causes that we assign to behavior? So stable–unstable is a dimension because we can sensibly ask, Is ability a factor that persists stably over time? Is patience a factor that persists stably?, and so on. Similarly, global–specific qualifies as a dimension since we can ask sensibly, Is ability a factor that affects many situations or only few? Is patience a factor that affects many situations?, and so on.

Table 2. Formal Characteristics of Attribution and Some Examples

Dimension	Internal		External	
	Stable	Unstable	Stable	Unstable
Global				
Failing student	Lack of intelligence	Exhaustion	ETS gives unfair tests.	Today is Friday the 13th.
	(Laziness)	(Having a cold, which makes me stupid)	(People are usually unlucky on the GRE.)	(ETS gave experimental tests this time which were too hard for everyone.)
Rejected woman	I'm unattractive to men.	My conversation sometimes bores men.	Men are overly competitive with intelligent women.	Men get into rejecting moods.
Specific				
Failing student	Lack of mathematical ability	Fed up with math problems	ETS gives unfair math tests.	The math test was from No. 13.
	(Math always bores me.)	(Having a cold, which ruins my arithmetic)	(People are usually unlucky on math tests.)	(Everyone's copy of the math test was blurred.)
Rejected woman	I'm unattractive to him.	My conversation bores him.	He's overly competitive with women.	He was in a rejecting mood.

Note: ETS = Educational Testing Service, the maker of graduate record examinations (GRE).

the cases of personal helplessness (Cell 3—internal attribution) and universal helplessness (Cell 4—external attribution) in Table 1.

According to the reformulated hypothesis, if the individual makes any of the four global attributions for a low math score, the deficits observed will be far-reaching: Global attributions imply to the individual that when he confronts new situations the outcome will again be independent of his responses. So, if he decides that his poor score was caused by his lack of intelligence (internal, stable, global) or his exhausted condition (internal, unstable, global) or that the Educational Testing Service (ETS; the creator of GREs) gives unfair tests (external, stable, global) or that it is an unlucky day (external, unstable, global), when he confronts the verbal test in a few minutes, he will expect that here, as well, outcomes will be independent of his response, and the helplessness deficits will ensue. If the individual makes any of the four specific attributions for a low math score, helplessness deficits will not necessarily appear during the verbal test: i.e., lack of mathematical ability (internal, stable, specific) or being fed up with math problems (internal, unstable, specific) or that ETS asks unfair math questions (external, stable, specific) or being unlucky on that particular math test (external, unstable, specific).

In a parallel manner, chronicity of the deficits follows from the stability dimension. Chronic deficits (he will be helpless on the next math GRE when he retakes it at a later time) will ensue if the attribution is to stable factors: Lack of intelligence, lack of mathematical ability, ETS gives unfair tests, ETS gives unfair math tests. Attribution to stable factors leads to chronic deficits because they imply to the individual that he will lack the controlling response in the future as well as now. If the attribution is to an unstable factor—exhaustion, fed up with the math problems, unlucky day, or unlucky on the math tests—he will not necessarily be helpless on the next math GRE. If he makes any of the internal attributions—lack of intelligence, lack of math ability, exhaustion, or fed up with math problems—the self-esteem deficits will occur. In contrast, none of the external attributions will produce self-esteem deficits.[5]

[5] A critical remark is in order on the adequacy of abilility, effort, task difficulty, and luck as embodying, respectively, internal–stable, internal–unstable, external–stable, external–unstable attributions (Weiner et al., 1971). While we find the orthogonality of internality and stability dimensions useful and important, we do not believe that

Because so much real-life helplessness stems from social inadequacy and rejection, Table 2 illustrates a social example. Here a woman is rejected by a man she loves. Her attribution for failure will determine whether she shows deficits in situations involving most other men (global) and whether she shows deficits in the future with this particular man or with other men (chronic). She might select any of four types of global attributions: I'm unattractive to men (internal, stable, global); my conversation sometimes bores men (internal, unstable, global); men are overly competitive with intelligent women (external, stable, global); men get into rejecting moods (external, unstable, global). All four of these attributions will produce helplessness deficits in new situations with most other men. The four specific attributions will produce deficits only with this particular man: I'm unattractive to him (internal, stable, specific); my conversation sometimes bores him (internal, unstable, specific); he is overly competitive with intelligent women (external, stable, specific); he was in a rejecting mood (external, unstable, specific). Any of the four stable attributions will produce chronic deficits either with that man (if specific) or with most men (if global); the four unstable attributions will produce transient deficits. The four internal attributions will produce self-esteem deficits; the four external attributions will not.

Having stated what we believe are the determinants of the chronicity and generality of helplessness deficits, a word about intensity or severity is in order. Severity is logically independent of chronicity and generality; it refers to how strong a given deficit is at any one time in a particular situation. We believe that the intensity of the motivational

---

the ability–effort/task difficulty–luck distinctions map into these dimensions. Table 2 presents (in parentheses) attributions that systematically violate the mapping. An internal–stable attribution for helplessness need not be to lack of ability; it can be to lack of effort: laziness (global), math always bores me (specific). An internal–unstable attribution need not be to lack of effort, it can be to (temporary) inabilities: I have a cold, which makes me stupid (global); I have a cold, which ruins my arithmetic ability (specific). An external–stable attribution need not be to task difficulty; it can be to lack of luck: Some people are always unlucky on tests (global); people are always unlucky on math tests (specific). An external–unstable attribution need not be to bad luck; it can be to task difficulty: ETS gave experimental tests this time that were difficult for everyone (global); everyone's copy of the math test was blurred (specific). So, ability and effort are logically orthogonal to internal–stable and internal–unstable attributions, and luck and task difficulty are orthogonal to external–stable and external–unstable attributions.

and cognitive deficits increases with the strength or certainty of the expectation of noncontingency. We speculate that intensity of self-esteem loss and affective changes (see Implications of the Reformulated Model for the Helplessness Model of Depression below) will increase with both certainty and importance of the event the person is helpless about. We also speculate that if the attribution is global or stable, the individual will expect to be helpless in the distant future (both across areas of his life and across time) as well as in the immediate future. The future will look black. This expectation will increase the intensity of the self-esteem and affective deficits. If the attribution is internal, this may also tend to make these deficits more severe, since internal attributions are often stable and global.

Attribution and Expectancy

In general, the properties of the attribution predict in what new situations and across what span of time the expectation of helplessness will be likely to recur. An attribution to global factors predicts that the expectation will recur even when the situation changes, whereas an attribution to specific factors predicts that the expectation need not recur when the situation changes. An attribution to stable factors predicts that the expectation will recur even after a lapse of time, whereas an attribution to unstable factors predicts that the expectation need not recur after a lapse of time. Whether or not the expectation recurs across situations and with elapsed time determines whether or not the helplessness deficits recur in the new situation or with elapsed time. Notice that the attribution merely *predicts* the recurrence of the expectations but the expectation *determines* the occurrence of the helplessness deficits. New evidence may intervene between the initial selection of an attribution and the new and subsequent situation and change the expectation. So the person may find out by intervening successes that he was not as stupid as he thought, or he may gather evidence that everyone obtained low scores on the math GRE and so now ETS is under new management. In such cases, the expectation need not be present across situations and time. On the other hand, if the expectation is present, then helplessness deficits must occur (see Weiner, 1972, for a related discussion of achievement motivation).

Implications

The attributional account of the chronicity and generality of the symptoms of helplessness explains why debriefing ensures that deficits are not carried outside the laboratory. The debriefing presumably changes the attribution from a gobal (and potentially harmful outside the laboratory) and possibly internal (e.g., I'm stupid) one to a more specific and external one (e.g., psychologists are nasty: They give unsolvable problems to experimental subjects). Since the attribution for helplessness is to a specific factor, the expectation of uncontrollability will not recur outside the laboratory anymore than it would have without the experimental evidence.

These attributional dimensions are also relevant to explaining when inappropriate, broad generalization of the expectation of noncontingency will occur. Broad transfer of helplessness will be observed when subjects attribute their helplessness in the training phase to very global and stable factors. Alternatively, attributing helplessness to very specific and unstable factors predicts very little transfer of helplessness.

A final question concerns the determinants of what particular attribution people make for their helplessness. Attribution theorists (e.g., Heider, 1958; Kelley, 1967; Weiner, 1974) have discussed situational factors that influence the sort of attribution people make. In addition, Heider and Kelley pointed to systematic biases and errors in the formation of attributions. Later, we discuss an "attributional style" that may characterize depressed people.

VALIDITY OF THE REFORMULATED MODEL

The validity of the new hypothesis must ultimately be assessed by its ability to generate novel predictions that survive attempts at experimental disconfirmation. As it is a new hypothesis, no results from such attempts are yet available. However, a minimum requirement is that this hypothesis should be consistent with the available experimental evidence. Although such consistency can lend only limited support to the hypothesis (as the available evidence has been one factor shaping the hypothesis), inconsistency might seriously embarrass the hypothesis.

Is the Reformulated Hypothesis Consistent with the Experimental Evidence on Learned Helplessness in Humans?

Three basic classes of evidence are covered: (a) deficits produced by learned helplessness, (b) attributional evidence, and (c) skill/chance evidence.

Deficits Produced by Learned Helplessness

Nondepressed students given inescapable noise or unsolvable discrimination problems fail to escape noise (Glass, Reim, & Singer, 1971; Hiroto & Seligman, 1975; Klein & Seligman, 1976; Miller & Seligman, 1976), fail to solve anagrams (Benson & Kennelly, 1976; Gatchel & Proctor, 1976; Hiroto & Seligman, 1975; Klein et al., 1976), and fail to see patterns in anagrams (Hiroto & Seligman, 1975; Klein et al., 1976). Escapable noise, solvable discrimination problems, or no treatment does not produce these deficits. Both the old and the reformulated hypothesis explain these deficits by stating that subjects expect that outcomes and responses are independent in the test situation. This expectation produces the motivational deficit (failure to escape noise and failure to solve anagrams) and the cognitive deficit (failure to see patterns). The reformulated hypothesis adds an explanation of why the expectation for the inescapability of the noise or the unsolvability of the discrimination problems must have been global enough to transfer across situations (e.g., I'm unintelligent; problems in this laboratory are impossible) and stable enough to survive the brief time interval between tests. The data are ambiguous about whether the global, stable attribution is internal (e.g., I'm stupid) or external (e.g., laboratory problems are impossible); self-esteem changes would have been relevant to this determination. Nondepressed students who escape noise, solve problems, or receive nothing as pretreatment do not perceive response–outcome independence and do not, of course, make any attribution about such independence.

For a control procedure, subjects have been told to listen to noise (which is inescapable) but not to try to do anything about it, (Hiroto & Seligman, 1975); similarly, subjects have been given a panic button that "will escape noise if pressed" but have been successfully discouraged from pressing ("I'd rather you didn't, but it's up to you"); (Glass &

Singer, 1972). These subjects do not become helpless. Both the old and reformulated hypotheses hold that these subjects do not perceive non-contingency (in this latter case they perceive potential response–outcome contingency; in the first case, they have no relevant perception) and so do not form the relevant expectations and attributions.

A number of studies on human helplessness have obtained findings that are difficult to explain with the old helplessness hypothesis. Examination of these studies suggests that investigators may have tapped into the attributional dimensions of generality and stability. For example, Roth and Kubal (1975) tested helplessness across very different situations: Subjects signed up for two separate experiments that happened to be on the same day in the same building. They failed on the task in Experiment 1 (pretraining) and then wandered off to Experiment 2 (the test task). When subjects were told in Experiment 1 that they had failed a test that was a "really good predictor of grades in college" (important), they showed deficits on the cognition problem of Experiment 2. When told that Experiment 1 was merely "an experiment in learning" (unimportant), they did better in Experiment 2. In the case of "good prediction of grades," subjects probably made a more global, internal, and possibly more stable attribution (e.g., I'm stupid enough to do badly on this, therefore on college exams as well). The expectation therefore recurred in the new situation, producing deficits. In the unimportant condition, subjects probably made a more specific and less stable attribution, so the expectation of failure was not present in Experiment 2. (See Cole and Coyne, 1977, for another way of inducing a specific, rather than a global, attribution for failure.)

Similarly, Douglas and Anisman (1975) found that failure on simple tasks produced later cognitive deficits but that failure on complex tasks did not. It seems reasonable that failure on simple tasks should produce a more global and internal attribution (e.g., I'm stupid) whereas failure on the complex tasks could be attributed to external and more specific factors (e.g., these problems are too difficult).

An important advantage of the reformulation is that it better explains the effects of therapy and immunization than does the old hypothesis. The key here is the attributional dimension of generality. Helplessness can be reversed and prevented by experience with success. Klein and Seligman (1976) gave nondepressed people inescapable noise and then did "therapy," using 4 or 12 cognitive problems, which the subjects solved. (Therapy was also performed on depressed people given no noise.) Therapy worked: The subjects (both depressed and nondepressed) escaped noise and showed normal expectancy changes after success and failure. Following inescapable noise the subjects presumably made an attribution to a relatively global factor (e.g., I'm incompetent, or laboratory tasks are unsolvable), wich was revised to a more specific one after success on the next task (e.g., I'm incompetent in only some laboratory situations, or, only some laboratory tasks are difficult). The new test task, therefore, did not evoke the expectation of uncontrollability. Teasdale (1978) found that real success experiences and recalling similar past successes are equally effective in shifting attribution for initial failure from internal to external success. Only real success, however, reversed helplessness performance deficits. This suggests success does not have its effect by shifting attribution along the internal–external dimension. Although the relevant data were not collected, it is likely that real, but not recalled, success modifies attribution along the global–specific dimension. Immunization (Thornton & Powell, 1974; Dyck & Breen, Note 9) is explained similarly: Initial success experience should make the attribution for helplessness less global and therefore less likely to recur in the new test situation.

A number of human helplessness studies have actually shown facilitation in subjects exposed to uncontrollable events (Hanusa & Schulz, 1977; Roth & Kubal, 1975; Tennen & Eller, 1977; Wortman et al., 1976). While such facilitation is not well understood (see Wortman & Brehm, 1975; Roth & Kilpatrick-Tabak, Note 2, for hypotheses), it seems reasonable that compensatory attempts to reassert control might follow helplessness experiences, once the person leaves the situations in which he believes himself helpless (see Solomon & Corbit, 1973, for a relevant rebound theory). Such compensatory rebound might be expected to dissipate in time and be less strong in situations very far removed from the original helplessness training. When the "facilitation" effect of helplessness is brought under replicable, experimental control, the compensatory rebound hypothesis can be tested. People may also show facilitation of performance in uncontrollable situations when they cannot find a controlling response but have not yet concluded that they are helpless.

The reformulated hypothesis accounts for the basic helplessness results better than does the old hypothesis. The explanations given by the reformulated hypothesis are necessarily post hoc, however. Relevant measures of the generality, stability, and internality of attribution were not made. Helplessness studies can, in principle, test the hypothesis either by measuring the attributions and correlating them with the deficits that occur or by inducing the attributions and predicting deficits. We now turn to the few studies of helplessness that have induced or measured attribution.

Attributional evidence. Dweck and her associates (Dweck, 1975; Dweck & Reppucci, 1973; Dweck, Davidson, Nelson, & Enna, Note 10; Dweck, Goetz, & Strauss, Note 11) have demonstrated the differential effects of attribution for failure to lack of ability versus lack of effort. When fourth-grade girls fail, they attribute their failure to lack of ability (consonant with their teachers' natural classroom criticisms of girls) and perform badly on a subsequent cognitive test. Lack of ability is a global attribution (as well as internal and stable) and implies failure expectation for the new task. Fourth-grade boys, on the other hand, attribute failure to lack of effort or bad conduct (also consonant with the teachers' natural classroom criticisms of boys) and do well on the subsequent test. Lack of effort is unstable and probably more specific (but also internal). Boys, having failed and attributed failure to lack of effort, put out more effort on the test task and do adequately. Similarly, when students are told to attribute failure on math problems to not trying hard enough, they also do better than if they attribute it to lack of ability (Dweck, 1975).

Effort is not only "unstable," but it is readily controllable by the subject himself, unlike being bored, for example, which is also unstable, specific, and internal, or unlike lack of ability. It should be noted that the dimension of controllability is logically orthogonal to the Internal × Global × Stable dimensions (although it is empirically more frequent in the internal and unstable attribution), and as such it is a candidate for a 2 × 2 × 2 × 2 table of attributions. While we do not detail such an analysis here, we note that the phenomena of self-blame, self-criticism, and guilt (a subclass of the self-esteem deficits) in helplessness (and depression) follow from attribution of failure to factors that are controllable. Lack of effort as the cause of failure probably produces more self-blame than does boredom, although both are internal and unstable attributions. Similarly, a failure caused by not speaking Spanish attributed to lack of ability to speak Spanish, which might have been corrected by taking a Berlitz course, probably causes more self-blame than a less correctable lack of ability, such as ineptitude for foreign languages, even though both are internal and stable.

According to the reformulation, performance deficits should occur in cases of both universal and personal helplessness. In these cases people expect that outcomes are independent of their responses. In addition, attribution of helplessness to specific or unstable factors should be less likely to lead to performance deficits than attribution to stable or global factors. To date, four studies have manipulated attribution for helplessness in adults. In line with the reformulation, Klein et al. (1976) found that relative to groups receiving solvable problems or no problems in all, nondepressed students did poorly on anagrams task following experience with unsolvable discrimination problems regardless whether they attributed their helplessness to internal factors (personal helplessness) or external factors (universal helplessness).

Tennen and Eller (1977) attempted to manipulate attribution by giving subjects unsolvable discrimination problems that were labeled either progressively "easier" or progressively "harder." The authors reason that failure on easy problems should produce attribution to lack of ability (internal, stable and more global) whereas failure on harder problems should allow attribution to task difficulty (external, unstable, and more specific. Subjects then went to what they believed was a second, unrelated experiment (see Roth & Kubal, 1975) and tried to solve anagrams line with the reformulation, attribution to the ability (easy problems) produced deficits. Attribution to task difficulty (hard problems resulted in facilitation of anagram solving. The most likely explanation for lack of performance deficits in the task-difficulty group is that their attributions for helplessness were too specific to produce an expectation of noncontingency in the test task.

Finally, two studies (Hanusa & Schulz 1977; Wortman et al., 1976) found that respective to a group exposed to contingent events, neither a group instructed to believe they were personally helpless nor a group instructed to believe they were universally helpless on a training task showed subsequent performance deficits on a test task. While results appear contrary to the reformulation they are difficult to interpret. The problem is that in both studies, the typical helplessness group (a group exposed to noncontingency events in the training task but given no explicit attribution) did not show performance deficits on the test task.

Thus, the test task may not have been sensitive to helplessness deficits. (For a discussion of the relative sensitivity of tasks to helplessness in animals, see Maier and Seligman, 1976.) It is interesting that Wortman et al. (1976) found that personally helpless subjects showed more emotional distress than universally helpless subjects.

Overall, then, the few helplessness studies directly assessing and manipulating attribution provide some support for the reformulation. Because of the methodological problems in some of these studies, future research that manipulates attribution is necessary. Care must be taken to ensure that one attributional dimension is not confounded with another. Past studies, for example, have confounded externality with specificity and internality with generality.

Helpless subjects show dampened expectancy changes in skill tasks. In skill tasks, expectancy for future success increases less following success and/or decreases less following failure for helpless subjects than for subjects not made helpless (Klein & Seligman, 1976; Miller & Seligman, 1976; Miller, Seligman, & Kurlander, 1975; see also Miller & Seligman, 1973, and Abramson, Garber, Edwards & Seligman, 1978, for parallel evidence in depression). The old hypothesis interpreted these results as a general tendency of helpless subjects to perceive responding and outcomes on skill tasks as independent, and it was assumed that this index measured the central helplessness deficit directly. In other words, it had been suggested that such subjects perceive skill tasks as if they were chance tasks. The rationale for this interpretation was derived from the work of Rotter and his colleagues (James, 1957; James & Rotter, 1958; Phares, 1957; Rotter, Liverant, & Crowne, 1961). These investigators argued that reinforcements on previous trials have a greater effect on expectancies for future success when the subject perceives reinforcement as skill determined than when he perceives it as chance determined. According to this logic, subjects will show large expectancy changes when they believe outcomes are chance determined.

Recent developments in attribution theory suggest that expectancy changes are not a direct index of people's expectations about response–outcome contingencies. Weiner and his colleagues (1971) argued that the attributional dimension of stability rather than locus of control is the primary determinant of exepectancy changes. According to Weiner (Weiner, 1974; Weiner, Heckhausen, Meyer, & Cook, 1972) people give small expectancy changes when they attribute outcomes to unstable factors and large expectancy changes when they attribute outcomes to stable factors. The logic is that past outcomes to stable factors. The logic is that past outcomes are good predictors of future outcomes only when they are caused by stable factors.

In the absence of knowledge about individual attributions, the reformulated helplessness hypothesis cannot make clear-cut predictions about expectancy changes and helplessness, since belief in response–outcome dependence or independence is orthogonal to stable–unstable. For example, suppose a person makes an internal attribution to lack of ability for his helplessness, i.e., he believes in response outcome independence for himself. When confronted with the skill task, he may show very large expectancy changes after failure since he believes he lacks the stable factor of ability for the task. Alternatively, when contronted with the 50% success rate typically used in helplessness studies, he may maintain his belief that he lacks the stable factor of ability but conclude that ability is not necessary for success on the task. After all, he succeeded sometimes in spite of his perceived lack of ability. Under such conditions, the person will believe outcomes are a matter of chance (unstable factor) for himself but not for others. Accordingly, he will give small expectancy changes. Moreover, a nonhelpless person (who perceives response–outcome dependency) may believe unstable factors, such as effort, cause his outcomes and show little expectancy change; alternatively, if he believes a stable factor is responsible for response–outcome dependence, he will show large shifts.

Rizley (1978) similarly argued that expectancy changes on chance and skill tasks do not directly test the learned helplessness model of depression. We agree. As argued in the previous paragraph, small expectancy changes need not imply belief in independence between responses and outcomes, and large expectancy changes need not imply belief in dependence between responses and outcomes. Nor does belief in response–outcome independence imply small expectancy changes, or belief in dependence imply large changes. The fact that depressives often show smaller expectancy changes than nondepressed people (Abramson et al., 1978; Klein & Seligman, 1976; Miller & Seligman, 1973, 1976; Miller et al., 1975) is intriguing but provides only limited support for the learned helplessness model. In order for expectancy changes to be used as a way of inferring perception of response–outcome independence, the particular attribution and its stability must also be known. None of the studies to date that measured expectancy shifts also measured the relevant attributions, so these studies do not tell us unambiguously that helpless (or depressed) people perceive response–outcome independence. They support the model only in as far as these two groups show the same pattern of shifts, but the pattern itself cannot be predicted in the absence of knowledge about the accompanying attribution.

To conclude this section, examination of expectancy changes on chance and skill tasks is not a direct way of testing helplessness, since such changes are sensitive to the attributional dimension of stability and not to expectations about response–outcome contingencies. Recent failures to obtain small expectancy changes in depressed people (McNitt & Thornton, 1978; Willis & Blaney, 1978) are disturbing empirically, but less so theoretically, since both depressed and helpless subjects show the same pattern, albeit a different pattern from the one usually found.

IMPLICATIONS OF THE REFORMULATED MODEL FOR THE HELPLESSNESS MODEL OF DEPRESSION

This reformulation of human helplessness has direct implications for the helplessness model of depression. The cornerstone of previous statements of the learned helplessness model of depression is that learning that outcomes are uncontrollable results in the motivational, cognitive, and emotional components of depression (Seligman, 1975; Seligman et al., 1976). The motivational deficit consists of retarded initiation of voluntary responses, and it is reflected in passivity, intellectual slowness, and social impairment in naturally occurring depression. According to the old model, deficits in voluntary responding follow directly from expectations of response outcome independence. The cognitive deficit consists of difficulty in learning that responses produce outcomes and is also seen as a consequence of expecting response–outcome independence. In the clinic, "negative cognitive set" is displayed in depressives' beliefs that their actions are doomed to failure. Finally, the model asserts that depressed affect is a consequence of learning that outcomes are uncontrollable. It is important to emphasize that the model regards expectation of response–outcome independence as a sufficient, not a necessary, condition for depression. Thus, physiological states, postpartum conditions, hormonal states, loss of interest in reinforcers, chemical depletions, and so on may produce depression in the absence of the expectation of uncontrollability. According to the model, then, there exists a subset of depression—helplessness depressions—that is caused by expectation of response–outcome independence and displays the symptoms of passivity, negative cognitive set, and depressed affect.

We believe that the original formulation of the learned helplessness model of depression is inadequate on four different grounds: (a) Expectation of uncontrollability per se is not sufficient for depressed *affect* since there are many outcomes in life that are uncontrollable but do not sadden us. Rather, only those uncontrollable outcomes in which the estimated probability of the occurrence of a desired outcome is low or the estimated probability of the occurrence of an aversive outcome is high are sufficient for depressed affect. (b) Lowered self-esteem, as a symptom of the syndrome of depression, is not explained (c) The tendency of depressed people to make internal attributions for failure is not explained. (d) Variations in generality, chronicity, and intensity of depression are not explained. All but the first of these shortcomings are directly remedied by the reformulation of human helplessness in an attributional framework.

Inadequacy 1: Expectation of Uncontrollability Is Not Sufficient for Depressed Affect

We view depression, as a syndrome, to be made up of four classes of deficits: (a) motivational, (b cognitive, (c) self-esteem, and (d) affective (but see Blaney, 1977, for a review that contends that only affective changes are relevant to depression). Whereas the first three deficits are the result of uncontrollability, we believe the affective changes result from the expectation that bad outcomes will occur, not from their expected uncontrollability.

Everyday observation suggests that an expectation that good events will occur with a high frequency but independently of one's responses is not a sufficient condition for depressed affect (see Seligman, 1975 (p. 98), versus Maier & Seligman, 1976 (p. 17), for previous inconsistent accounts). People do not become sad when they receive $1,000 each month from a trust fund, even though the money comes regardless of what they do. In this case, people may learn they have no control over the money's arrival, become passive with respect to trying to stop the money from arriving (motivational deficit), have trouble relearning should the money actually become response contingent (cognitive deficit), but they do not show dysphoria. Thus, only those cases in which the expectation of response–outcome independence is about the loss of a highly desired outcome [6] or about the occurrence of a highly aversive outcome are sufficient for the emotional component of depression. It follows, then, that depressed affect may occur in cases of either universal or personal helplessness, since either can involve expectations of uncontrollable, important outcomes.

At least three factors determine the intensity of the emotional component of depression. Intensity of affect (and self-esteem deficits) increases with desirability of the unobtainable outcome or with the aversiveness of the unavoidable outcome, and with the strength or certainty of the expectation of uncontrollability. In addition, intensity of depressed affect may depend on whether the person views his helplessness as universal or personal. Weiner (1974) suggested that failure attributed to internal factors, such as lack of ability, produces greater negative affect than failure attributed to external factors, such as task difficulty. The intensity of cognitive and motivational components of depression, however, does not depend on whether helplessness is universal or personal, or, we speculate, on the importance of the event.

Perhaps the expectation that one is receiving positive events noncon-

---

[6] One problem remains. It is a "highly desired" outcome for us that the editor of this journal give us each one million dollars, and we believe this to have a very low probability and to be uncontrollable. Yet, we do not have depressed affect upon realizing this. Some notion, like Klinger's (1975) "current concerns," is needed to supplement our account. We feel depressed about the nonoccurrence of highly desired outcomes that we are helpless to obtain only when they are "on our mind," in the realm of possibility," "troubling us now," and so on. Incidentally, the motivational and cognitive deficits do not need current concerns, only the affective deficit. We take this adequacy to be general not only to the theory stated here but to much of the entire psychology of motivation, which focuses on behavior, and we do not attempt to remedy it here. We find Klinger's concept heuristic but in need of somewhat better definition. We, therefore, use the notion of "loss of a highly desired outcome" rather than "nonoccurrence." Loss implies that it will probably be a current concern. Since this is only part of a sufficiency condition, we do not deny that nonoccurrence can also produce depressed affect.

tingently contributes indirectly to vulnerability to depressed affect. Suppose a person has repeatedly learned that positive events arrive independently of his actions. If the perception or expectation of response–outcome independence in future situations involving loss is facilitated by such a set, the heightened vulnerability to depression will occur.

Inadequacy 2: Lowered Self-Esteem as a Symptom of Depression

A number of theoretical perspectives (Beck, 1967, 1976; Bibring, 1953; Freud, 1917/1957) regard low self-esteem as a hallmark symptom of depression. Freud has written, "The melancholic displays something else besides which is lacking in mourning—an extraordinary diminution in his self-regard, an impoverishment of his ego on a grand scale" (p. 246). A major shortcoming of the old model of depression is that it does not explain the depressive's low opinion of himslef. Our analysis of universal and personal helplessness suggests that depressed individuals who believe their helplessness is personal show lower self-esteem than individuals who believe their helplessness is universal. Suppose two individuals are depressed because they expect that regardless of how hard they try they will remain unemployed. The depression of the person who believes that his own incompetence is causing his failure to find work will feel low self-regard and worthlessness. The person who believes that nationwide economic crisis is causing his failure to find work will not think less of himself. Both depressions, however, will show passivity, negative cognitive set, and sadness, the other three depressive deficits, since both individuals expect that the probability of the desired outcome is very low and that it is not contingent on any responses in their repertoire.

It is interesting that psychoanalytic writers have argued that there are at least two types of depression, which differ clinically as well as theoretically (Bibring, 1953). Although both types of depression share motivational, cognitive, and affective characteristics, only the second involves low self-regard. Further paraleling our account of two types of depression is recent empirical work (Blatt, D'Afflitti, & Quinlan, 1976) suggesting that depression can be characterized in terms of two dimensions: dependency and feelings of deprivation, and low self-esteem and excessively high standards and morality.

Inadequacy 3: Depressives Believe They Cause Their Own Failures

Recently, Blaney (1977) and Rizley (1978) have construed the finding that depressives attribute their failures to internal factors, such as lack of ability, as disconfirming the learned helplessness model of depression. Similarly, aware that depressives often blame themselves for bad outcomes, Abramson and Sackeim (1977) asked how individuals can possibly blame themselves for outcomes about which they believe they can do nothing. Although the reformulation does not articulate the relation between blame or guilt and helplessness, it clearly removes any contradiction between being a cause and being helpless. Depressed individuals who believe they are personally helpless make internal attributions for failure, and depressed individuals who believe they are universally helpless make external attributions for failure. A personally helpless individual believes that the cause of the failure is internal (e.g., I'm stupid) but that he is helpless (No response I could make would help me pass the exam).

What are the naturally occurring attributions of depressives? Do they tend to attribute failure to internal, global, and stable factors, and success to external, specific, and unstable factors?[7]

Hammen and Krantz (1976) looked at cognitive distortion in depressed and nondepressed women. When responding to a story containing "being alone on a Friday night," depressed women selected more depressed–distorted cognitions ("upsets me and makes me start to imagine endless days and nights by myself"), and nondepressed women selected more nondepressed–nondistorted cognitions ("doesn't bother me because one Friday night alone isn't that important; probably everyone has spent nights alone"). Depressed people seem to make more global and stable attributions for negative events. When depressed women were exposed to failure on an interpersonal judgment task, they lowered their self-rating more than did nondepressed women. This

---

[7]The literature on the relation between internal locus of control and depression might be expected to yield direct information about internal attribution in depression. It is, however, too conflicting at this stage to be very useful. Externality, as measured by the Rotter scale, correlates weakly (.25–.30) with depression (Abramowitz, 1969; Miller & Seligman, 1973), but the external items are also rated more dysphoric and the correlation may be an artifact (Lamont, 1972).

indicates that the depressed women are systematically generating more internal as well as global and stable attributions for failure.[8]

Rizley (1978) caused depressed and nondepressed students to either succeed or fail on a cognitive task and then asked them to make attributions about the cause. Depressed students attributed failures to incompetence (internal, global stable), whereas nondepressed students attributed their failures to task difficulty (external, specific, stable). Similarly, depressed students attributed success to the ease of the task (external, specific, stable), whereas nondepressed students attributed their success to ability (internal, global, stable). Although inconsistent with the old model, Rizley's results are highly consistent with the reformulation.

Klein et al. (1976) assessed the attribution depressed and nondepressed college students made for failure on discrimination problems. Whereas depressed students tended to attribute failure to internal factors, nondepressed students tended to attribute failure to external factors. These findings parallel those of Rizley on attribution in achievement settings.

Garber and Hollon (Note 12) asked depressed and nondepressed subjects to make predictions concerning their own future success as well as the success of another person in the skill/chance situation. The depressed subjects showed small expectancy changes in relation to their own skilled actions; however, when they predicted the results of the skilled actions of others, they showed large expectancy changes, like those of nondepressives rating themselves. These results suggest that depressives believe they lack the ability for the skill task but believe others possess the ability, the internal attribution of personal helplessness.

---

[8] Alloy and Abramson (Note 7) also examined distortion, not in attributions but in perception of contingency between depressed and nondepressed students. The subjects were exposed to different relations between button pushing and the onset of a green light and were asked to judge the contingency between the outcome and the response. Depressed students judged both contingency and noncontingency accurately. In contrast, nondepressed students distorted: When the light was noncontingently related to responding but occurred with a high frequency, they believed they had control. So there was a net difference in perception of contingency by depressed and nondepressed subjects, but the distortion occurred in the nondepressed, who picked up noncontingency less readily (see also Jenkins & Ward, 1965).

Taken together, the studies examining depressives' attributions for success and failure suggest that depressives often make internal, global, and stable attributions for failure and may make external, specific, and perhaps less stable attributions for their success. Future research that manipulates and measures attributions and attributional styles in depression and helplessness is necessary from the standpoint of our reformulated hypothesis.

Inadequacy 4: Generality and Chronicity of Depression

The time course of depression varies greatly from individual to individual. Some depressions last for hours and others last for years. "Normal" mourning lasts for days or weeks; many severe depressions last for months or years. Similarly, depressive deficits are sometimes highly general across situations and sometimes quite specific. The reformulated helplessness hypothesis suggests that the chronicity and generality of deficits in helplessness depressions follow from the stability and globality of the attribution a depressed person makes for his helplessness. The same logic we used to explain the chronicity and generality of helplessness deficits above applies here.

The reformulation also sheds light on the continuity of miniature helplessness depressions created in the laboratory and of real-life depression. The attributions subjects make for helplessness in the laboratory are presumably less global and less stable than attributions made by depressed people for failure outside the laboratory. Thus, the laboratory-induced depressions are less chronic and less global and are capable of being reversed by debriefing, but, we hypothesize, they are not different in kind from naturally occurring helplessness depressions. They differ only quantitatively, not qualitatively, that is, they are mere "analogs" to real helplessness depressions.

Do depressive deficits occur in situations that have nothing to do with the expectation of noncontingency? After failing a math GRE, the student goes home, burns his dinner, cries, has depressive dreams, and feels suicidal. If this is so, there are two ways our reformulation might explain this: (a) He is still in the presence of the relevant cues and expectations, for even at home the expectation that he will not get into graduate school is on his mind, and (b) the expectation, present earlier but absent now, has set off endogenous processes (e.g., loss of interest in the world, catecholamine changes) that must run their course. Remember that expectations of helplessness are held to be sufficient, not necessary, conditions of depression.

Finally, does the attributional reformulation of helplessness make depression look too "rational"? The chronicity, generality, and intensity of depression follow inexorably, "rationally" from the attribution made and the importance of the outcome. But there is room elsewhere for the irrationality implicit in depression as a form of psychopathology. The particular attribution that depressed people choose for failure is probably irrationally distorted toward global, stable, and internal factors and, for success, possibly toward specific, unstable, and external factors. It is also possible that the distortion resides not in attributional styles but in readiness to perceive helplessness, as Alloy and Abramson (Note 7) have shown: Depressed people perceive noncontingency more readily than do nondepressed people.

In summary, here is an explicit statement of the reformulated model of depression:

1. Depression consists of four classes of deficits: motivational, cognitive, self-esteem, and affective.

2. When highly desired outcomes are believed improbable or highly aversive outcomes are believed probable, and the individual expects that no response in his repertoire will change their likelihood, (helplessness) depression results.

3. The generality of the depressive deficits will depend on the globality of the attribution for helplessness, the chronicity of the depression deficits will depend on the stability of the attribution for helplessness, and whether self-esteem is lowered will depend on the internality of the attribution for helplessness.

4. The intensity of the deficits depends on the strength, or certainty, of the expectation of uncontrollability and, in the case of the affective and self-esteem deficits, on the importance of the outcome.

We suggest that the attributional framework proposed to resolve the problems of human helplessness experiments also resolves some salient inadequacies of the helplessness model of depression.

VULNERABILITY, THERAPY, AND PREVENTION

Individual differences probably exist in attributional style. Those people who typically tend to attribute failure to global, stable, and internal factors should be most prone to general and chronic helplessness depressions with low self-esteem. By the reformulated hypothesis, such a style predisposes depression. Beck (1967) argued similarly that the premorbid depressive is an individual who makes logical errors in interpreting reality. For example, the depression-prone individual overgeneralizes; a student regards his poor performance in a single class on one particular day as final proof of his stupidity. We believe that our framework provides a systematic framework for approaching such overgeneralization: It is an attribution to a global, stable, and internal factor. Our model predicts that attributional style will produce depression proneness, perhaps the depressive personality. In light of the finding that women are from 2 to 10 times more likely than men to have depression (Radloff, Note 13), it may be important that boys and girls have been found to differ in attributional styles, with girls attributing helplessness to lack of ability (global, stable) and boys to lack of effort (specific, unstable; Dweck, 1976).

The therapeutic implications of the reformulated hypothesis can now be schematized. Depression is most far-reaching when (a) the estimated probability of a positive outcome is low or the estimated probability of an aversive outcome is high, (b) the outcome is highly positive or aversive, (c) the outcome is expected to be uncontrollable, (d) the attribution for this uncontrollability is to a global, stable, internal factor. Each of these four aspects corresponds to four therapeutic strategies.

1. Change the estimated probability of the outcome. Change the environment by reducing the likelihood of aversive outcomes and increasing the likelihood of desired outcomes.

2. Make the highly preferred outcomes less preferred by reducing the aversiveness of unrelievable outcomes or the desirability of unobtainable outcomes.

3. Change the expectation from uncontrollability to controllability when the outcomes are attainable. When the responses are not yet in the individuals repertoire but can be, train the appropriate skills. When the responses are already in the individual's repertoire but cannot be made because of distorted expectation of response–outcome independence, modify the distored expectation. When the outcomes are unattainable, Strategy 3 does not apply.

4. Change unrealistic attributions for failure toward external, unstable specific factors, and change unrealistic attributions for success toward internal, stable, global factors. The model predicts that depression will be most far-reaching and produce the most symptoms when a failure is

attributed to stable, global, and internal factors, since the patient now expects that many future outcomes will be noncontingently related to his responses. Getting the patient to make an external, unstable, and specific attribution for failure should reduce the depression in cases in which the original attribution is unrealistic. The logic, of course, is that an external attribution for failure raises self-esteem, an unstable one cuts the deficits short, and a specific one makes the deficits less general.

Table 3 schematizes these four treatment strategies.

Table 3. Treatment, Strategies, and Tactics Implied by the Reformulated Hypothesis

A. Change the estimated probability of the relevant event's occurrence: Reduce estimated likelihood for aversive outcomes and increase estimated likelihood for desired outcomes.

    a. Environmental manipulation by social agencies to remove aversive outcomes or provide desired outcomes, for example, rehousing, job placement, financial assistance, provision of nursery care for children.

    b. Provision of better medical care to relieve pain, correct handicaps, for example, prescription of analgesics, provision of artificial limbs and other prostheses.

B. Make the highly preferred outcomes less preferred.

    a. Reduce the aversiveness of highly aversive outcomes.

        1. Provide more realistic goals and norms, for example, failing to be top of your class is not the end of the world—you can still be a competent teacher and lead a satisfying life.

        2. Attentional training and/or reinterpretation to modify the significance of outcomes perceived as aversive, for example, you are not the most unattractive person in the world. "Consider the counter-evidence" (Beck, 1976; Ellis, 1962).

        3. Assist acceptance and resignation.

    b. Reduce the desirability of highly desired outcomes.

        1. Assist the attainment of alternative available desired outcomes, for example, encourage the disappointed lover to find another boy or girl friend.

        2. Assist reevaluation of unattainable goals.

        3. Assist renunciation and relinquishment of unattainable goals.

C. Change the expectation from uncontrollability to controllability.

a. When responses are not yet within the person's repertoire but can be, train the necessary skills, for example, social skills, child management skills, skills of resolving marital differences, problem-solving skills, and depression-management skills.

b. When responses are within the person's repertoire, modify the distorted expectation that the responses will fail.

1. Prompt performance of relevant, successful responses, for example, graded task assignment (Burgess, 1968).
2. Generalized changes in response–outcome expectation resulting from successful performance of other responses, for example, prompt general increase in activity; teach more appropriate goal-setting and self-reinforcement; help to find employment.
3. Change attributions for failure from inadequate ability to inadequate effort (Dweck, 1975), causing more successful responding.
4. Imaginal and miniaturized rehearsal of successful response–outcome sequences: Assertive training, decision-making training, and role playing.

D. Change unrealistic attributions for failure toward external, unstable, specific; change unrealistic attributions for success toward internal, stable, global.

a. For failure

1. External: for example, "The system minimized the opportunities of women. It is not that you are incompetent."
2. Unstable: for example, "The system is changing. Opportunities that you can snatch are opening at a great rate."
3. Specific: for example, "Marketing jobs are still relatively closed to women, but publishing jobs are not" (correct overgeneralization).

b. For success

1. Internal: for example, "He loves you because you are nurturant not because he is insecure."
2. Stable: for example, "Your nurturance is an enduring trait."
3. Global: for example, "Your nurturance pervades much of what you do and is appreciated by everyone around you."

Although not specifically designed to test the therapeutic implications of the reformulated model of depression, two studies have examined the effectiveness of therapies that appear to modify the depressive's cognitive style. One study found that forcing a depressive to modify his cognitive style was more effective in alleviating depressive symptoms than was antidepressant medication (Rush, Beck, Kovacs, & Hollon,

1977). A second study found cognitive modification more effective than behavior therapy, no treatment, or an attention–placebo therapy in reducing depressive symptomatology (Shaw, 1977). Future research that directly tests the therapeutic implications of the reformulation is necessary.

The reformulation has parallel preventive implications. Populations at high risk for depression—people who tend to make stable, global, and internal attributions for failure—may be identifiable before onset of depression. Preventive strategies that force the person to criticize and perhaps change his attributional style might be instituted. Other factors that produce vulnerability are situations in which highly aversive outcomes are highly probable and highly desirable outcomes unlikely; here environmental change to less pernicious circumstances would probably be necessary for more optimistic expectations. A third general factor producing vulnerability to depression is a tendency to exaggerate the aversiveness or desirability of outcomes. Reducing individuals' "catastrophizing" about uncontrollable outcomes might reduce the intensity of future depressions. Finally, a set to expect outcomes to be uncontrollable—learned helplessness—makes individuals more prone to depression. A life history that biases individuals to expect that they will be able to control the sources of suffering and nurturance in their life should immunize against depression.

REFERENCE NOTES

1. Miller, I. *Learned helplessness in humans: A review and attribution theory model.* Unpublished manuscript, Brown University, 1978.
2. Roth, A., & Kilpatrick-Tabak, B. *Developments in the study of learned helplessness in humans: A critical review.* Unpublished manuscript, Duke University, 1977.
3. Tennen, H. A. *Leaving helplessness and the perception of reinforcement in depression: A case of investigator misattribution.* Unpublished manuscript, State University of New York at Albany, 1977.
4. Eisenberger, R., Mauriello, J., Carlson, J., Frank, M., and Park, D. C. *Learned helplessness and industriousness produced by positive reinforcement.* Unpublished manuscript, State University of New York at Albany, 1976.
5. Hirsch, Kenneth A. *An extension of the learned helplessness phenomenon to potentially negatively punishing and potentially positively reinforcing stimuli non-contingent upon behavior.* Unpublished manuscript, 1976. (Available from K. A. Hirsch, Galesburg Mental Health Center, Galesburg, Illinois.)
6. Nugent, J. *Variations in non-contingent experiences and test tasks in the generation of learned helplessness.* Unpublished manuscript, University of Massachusetts.
7. Alloy, L. B., & Abramson, L. Y. *Judgment of contingency in depressed and non-*

depressed students: A nondepressive distortion. Unpublished manuscript, University of Pennsylvania, 1977.

8. Weiner, B. Personal communication to M. E. P. Seligman, 1977.
9. Dyck, D. G., & Breen, L. J. *Learned helplessness, immunization and task importance in humans.* Unpublished manuscript, University of Manitoba, 1976.
10. Dweck, C. S., Davidson, W., Nelson, S., & Enna, B. *Sex differences in learned helplessness: (11) The contingencies of evaluative feedback in the classroom and (III) An experimental analysis.* Unpublished manuscript, University of Illinois at Urbana-Champaign, 1976.
11. Dweck, C. S., Goetz, T., & Strauss, N. *Sex differences in learned helplessness: IV. An experimental and naturalistic study of failure generalization and its mediators.* Unpublished manuscript, University of Illinois at Urbana-Champaign, 1977.
12. Garber, J., & Hollon, S. *Depression and the expectancy of success for self and for others.* Unpublished manuscript, University of Minnesota, 1977.
13. Radloff, L. S. *Sex differences in helplessness—with implication for depression.* Unpublished manuscript, Center for Epidemiologic Studies, National Institute of Mental Health, 1976.

REFERENCES

Abramowitz, S. I. Locus of control and self-reported depression among college students. *Psychological Reports,* 1969, *25,* 149–150.

Abramson, L. *Universal versus personal helplessness: An experimental test of the reformulated theory of learned helplessness and depression.* Unpublished doctoral dissertation, University of Pennsylvania, 1977.

Abramson, L. Y., Garber, J., Edwards, N. B., & Seligman, M. E. P. Expectancy changes in depression and schizophrenia, *Journal of Abnormal Psychology,* 1978, *87,* 102–109.

Abramson, L. Y., & Sackeim, H. A. A paradox in depression: Uncontrollability and self-blame. *Psychological Bulletin,* 1977, *84,* 838–851.

Bandura, A. Self-efficacy: Toward a unifying theory of behavioral change. *Psychological Review,* 1977, *84,* 191–215.

Beck, A. T. *Depression: Clinical, experimental and theoretical aspects.* New York: Hoeber, 1967.

Beck, A. T. *Cognitive therapy and emotional disorders.* New York: International Universities Press, 1976.

Benson, J. S., & Kennelly, K. J. Learned helplessness: The result of uncontrollable reinforcements or uncontrollable aversive stimuli? *Journal of Personality and Social Psychology,* 1976, *34,* 138–145.

Bibring, E. The mechanism of depression. In P. Greenacre (Ed.), *Affective disorders: Psychoanalytic contributions to their study.* New York: International Universities Press, 1953.

Blaney, P. H. Contemporary theories of depression: Critique and comparison. *Journal of Abnormal Psychology,* 1977, *86,* 203–223.

Blatt, S. J., D'Afflitti, J. P., & Quinlan, D. M. Experiences of depression in normal young adults. *Journal of Abnormal Psychology,* 1976, *85,* 383–389.

Burgess, E. P. The modification of depressive behaviors. In R. D. Rubin & C. M. Franks (Eds.), *Advances in behavior therapy.* New York: Academic Press, 1968.

Clark, K. B., & Clark, M. P. The development of consciousness of self and the emergence of racial identification in Negro preschool children. *Journal of Social Psychology*, 1939, *10*, 591–599.

Cohen, S., Rothbart, M., & Phillips, S. Locus of control and the generality of learned helplessness in humans. *Journal of Personality and Social Psychology*, 1976, *34*, 1049–1056.

Cole, C. S., & Coyne, J. C. Situational specificity of laboratory-induced learned helplessness. *Journal of Abnormal Psychology*, 1977, *86*, 615–623.

Douglas, D., & Anisman, H. Helplessness or expectation incongruency: Effects of aversive stimulation on subsequent performance. *Journal of Experimental Psychology: Human Perception and Performance*, 1975, *1*, 411–417.

Dweck, C. S. The role of expectations and attributions in the alleviation of learned helplessness. *Journal of Personality and Social Psychology*, 1975, *31*, 674–685.

Dweck, C. S. Children's interpretation of evaluative feedback: The effect of social cues on learned helplessness. In C. S. Dweck, K. T. Hill, W. H. Reed, W. M. Steihman, & R. D. Parke, The impact of social cues on children's behavior. *Merrill-Palmer Quarterly*, 1976, *22*, 83–123.

Dweck, C. S., & Reppucci, N. D. Learned helplessness and reinforcement responsibility in children. *Journal of Personality and Social Psychology*, 1973, *25*, 109–116.

Ellis, A. *Reason and emotion in psychotherapy*. New York: Lyle Stuart, 1962.

Festinger, L. A theory of social comparison processes. *Human Relations*, 1954, *7*, 117–140.

Fosco, F., & Geer, J. H. Effects of gaining control over aversive stimuli after differing amounts of no control. *Psychological Reports*, 1971, *29*, 1153–1154.

Freud, S. Mourning and melancholia. In J. Strachey (Ed. and trans.), *Standard edition of the complete psychological works of Sigmund Freud* (Vol. 14). London: Hogarth Press, 1957. (Originally published, 1917.)

Frumkin, K., & Brookshire, K. H. Conditioned fear training and later avoidance learning in goldfish. *Psychonomic Science*, 1969, *16*, 159–160.

Gatchel, R. J., & Proctor, J. D. Physiological correlates of learned helplessness in man. *Journal of Abnormal Psychology*, 1976, *85*, 27–34.

Glass, D. C., Reim, B., & Singer, J. R. Behavioral consequences of adaptation to controllable and uncontrollable noise. *Journal of Experimental Social Psychology*, 1971, *7*, 244–257.

Glass, D. C., & Singer, J. E. *Urban stress: Experiments on noise and social stressors*. New York: Academic Press, 1972.

Golin, S., & Terrell, F. Motivational and associative aspects of mild depression in skill and chance. *Journal of Abnormal Psychology*, 1977, *86*, 389–401.

Goodkin, F. Rats learn the relationship between responding and environmental events: An expansion of the learned helplessness hypothesis. *Learning and Motivation*, 1976, *7*, 382–393.

Griffiths, M. Effects of noncontingent success and failure on mood and performance. *Journal of Personality*, 1977, *45*, 442–457.

Hammen, C. L., & Krantz, S. Effect of success and failure on depressive cognitions. *Journal of Abnormal Psychology*, 1976, *85*, 577–586.

Hanusa, B. H., & Schulz, R. Attributional mediators of learned helplessness. *Journal of Personality and Social Psychology*, 1977, *35*, 602–611.

Heider, F. *The psychology of interpersonal relations*. New York: Wiley, 1958.

Hiroto, D. S. Locus of control and learned helplessness. *Journal of Experimental Psychology*, 1974, *102*, 187–193.

Hiroto, D. S. & Seligman, M. E. P. Generality of learned helplessness in man. *Journal of Personality and Social Psychology,* 1975, *31,* 311–327.

James, W. H. *Internal versus external control of reinforcement as a basic variable in learning theory.* Unpublished doctoral dissertation, Ohio State University, 1957.

James, W. H., & Rotter, J. B. Partial and one hundred percent reinforcement under chance and skill conditions. *Journal of Experimental Psychology,* 1958, 55, 397–403.

Jenkins, H. M., & Ward, W. C. Judgment of contingency between responses and outcomes. *Psychological Monographs,* 1965, *79*(1, Whole No. 594).

Kelley, H. H. Attribution theory in social psychology. In D. Levine (Ed.), *Nebraska Symposium on Motivation* (Vol. 15). Lincoln: University of Nebraska Press, 1967.

Klein, D. C., Fencil-Morse, E., & Seligman, M. E. P. Learned helplessness, depression, and the attribution of failure. *Journal of Personality and Social Psychology,* 1976, *33,* 508–516.

Klein, D. C., & Seligman, M. E. P. Reversal of performance deficits in learned helplessness and depression. *Journal of Abnormal Psychology,* 1976, *85,* 11–26.

Klinger, E. Consequences of commitment to and disengagement from incentives. *Psychological Review,* 1975, *82,* 1–25.

Krantz, D. S., Glass, D. C., & Snyder, M. L. Helplessness, stress level, and the coronary prone behavior pattern. *Journal of Experimental Social Psychology,* 1974, *10,* 284–300.

Lamont, J. Depression, locus of control, and mood response set. *Journal of Clinical Psychology,* 1972, *28,* 342–345.

Maier, S. F., Albin, R. W., & Testa, T. J. Failure to learn to escape in rats peviously exposed to inescapable shock depends on nature of escape response. *Journal of Comparative and Physiological Psychology,* 1973, *85,* 581–592.

Maier, S. F., & Seligman, M. E. P. Learned helplessness: Theory and evidence. *Journal of Experimental Psychology: General,* 1976, *105,* 3–46.

Maier, S. F., Seligman, M. E. P., & Solomon, R. L. Pavlovian fear conditioning and learned helplessness. In B. A. Campbell & R. M. Church (Eds.), *Punishment.* New York: Appleton-Century-Crofts, 1969.

Maier, S. F., & Testa, T. J. Failure to learn to escape by rats previously exposed to inescapable shock is partly produced by associative interference. *Journal of Comparative and Physiological Psychology,* 1975, *88,* 554–564.

Masserman, J. H. The principle of uncertainty in neurotigenesis. In H. D. Kimmel (Ed.), *Experimental psychopathology.* New York: Academic Press, 1971.

McNitt, P. C., & Thornton, D. W. Depression and perceived reinforcement: A reconsideration. *Journal of Abnormal Psychology,* 1978, *87,* 137–140.

Miller, W. R., & Seligman, M. E. P. Depression and the perception of reinforcement. *Journal of Abnormal Psychology,* 1973, *82,* 62–73.

Miller, W. R., & Seligman, M. E. P. Depression and learned helplessness in man. *Journal of Abnormal Psychology,* 1975, *84,* 228–238.

Miller, W. R., & Seligman, M. E. P. Learned helplessness, depression, and the perception of reinforcement. *Behaviour Research and Therapy,* 1976, *14,* 7–17.

Miller, W. R., Seligman, M. E. P., & Kurlander, H. M. Learned helplessness, depression, and anxiety. *Journal of Nervous and Mental Disease,* 1975, *161,* 347–357.

Morse, S., & Gergen, K. J. Social comparison, self-consistency,and the concept of self. *Journal of Personality and Social Psychology,* 1970, *16,* 148–156.

Overmier, J. B., & Seligman, M. E. P. Effects of inescapable shock upon subsequent escape and avoidance learning. *Journal of Comparative and Physiological Psychology,* 1967, *63,* 28–33.

Padilla, A. M. Effects of prior and interpolated shock exposures on subsequent avoidance learning by goldfish. *Psychological Reports*, 1973, *32*, 451–456.

Padilla, A. M., Padilla, C., Ketterer, T., & Giacolone, D. Inescapable shocks and subsequent avoidance conditioning in goldfish *(Carrasius auratus)*. *Psychonomic Science*, 1970, *20*, 295–296.

Phares, E. J. Expectancy change in chance and skill situations. *Journal of Abnormal and Social Psychology*, 1957, *54*, 339–342.

Racinskas, J. R. *Maladaptive consequences of loss or lack of control over aversive events*. Unpublished doctoral dissertation, Waterloo University, Ontario, Canada, 1971.

Rizley, R. Depression and distortion in the attribution of causality. *Journal of Abnormal Psychology*, 1978, *87*, 32–48.

Rodin, J. Density, perceived choice, and response to controllable and uncontrollable outcomes. *Journal of Experimental Social Psychology*, 1976, *12*, 564–578.

Rosenberg, M. *Society and the adolescent self-image*. Princeton, N. J.: Princeton University Press, 1965.

Roth, S. *The effects of experimentally induced expectancies of control: Facilitation of controlling behavior or learned helplessness?* Unpublished doctoral dissertation, Northwestern University, 1973.

Roth, S., & Bootzin, R. R. Effects of experimentally induced expectancies of external control: An investigation of learned helplessness. *Journal of Personality and Social Psychology*, 1974, *29*, 253–264.

Roth, S., & Kubal, L. Effects of noncontingent reinforcement on tasks of differing importance: Facilitation and learned helplessness. *Journal of Personality and Social Psychology*, 1975, *32*, 680–691.

Rotter, J. B. Generalized expectancies for internal versus external control of reinforcement. *Psychological Monographs*, 1966, *80*(1, Whole No. 609).

Rotter, J. B., Liverant, S., & Crowne, D. P. The growth and extinction of expectancies in chance controlled and skilled tasks. *Journal of Psychology*, 1961, *52*, 161–177.

Rush, A. J., Beck, A. T., Kovacs, M., & Hollon, S. Comparative efficacy of cognitive therapy and pharmacotherapy in the treatment of depressed outpatients. *Cognitive Therapy and Research*, 1977, *1*, 17–37.

Seligman, M. E. P. Learned helplessness. *Annual Review of Medicine*, 1972, *23*, 407–412.

Seligman, M. E. P. *Helplessness: On depression, development, and death*. San Franciso: Freeman, 1975.

Seligman, M. E. P., & Beagley, G. Learned helplessness in the rat. *Journal of Comparative and Physiological Psychology*, 1975, *88*, 534–541.

Seligman, M. E. P., Klein, D. C., & Miller, W. R. Depression. In H. Leitenberg (Ed.) *Handbook of behavior modification and behavior therapy*. Englewood Cliffs, N.J.: Prentice-Hall, 1976.

Seligman, M. E. P., & Maier, S. F. Failure to escape traumatic shock. *Journal of Experimental Psychology*, 1967, *74*, 1–9.

Seligman, M. E. P., Maier, S. F., & Geer, J. The alleviation of learned helplessness in the dog. *Journal of Abnormal and Social Psychology*, 1968, *73*, 256–262.

Seligman, M. E. P., Maier, S. F., & Solomon, R. L. Unpredictable and uncontrollable aversive events. In F. R. Brush (Ed.) *Aversive conditioning and learning*. New York: Academic Press, 1971.

Seligman, M. E. P., Rosellini, R. A., & Kozak, M. Learned helplessness in the rat: Reversibility, time course, and immunization. *Journal of Comparative and Physiological Psychology*, 1975, *88*, 542–547.

Seward, J. P., & Humphrey, G. L. Avoidance learning as a function of pretraining in the cat. *Journal of Comparative and Physiological Psychology*, 1967, *63*, 338–341.

Shaw, B. F. Comparison of cognitive therapy and behavior therapy in the treatment of depression. *Journal of Consulting and Clinical Psychology*, 1977, *45*, 543–551.

Solomon, R. L., & Corbit, J. D. An opponent-process theory of motivation: II. Cigarette addiction. *Journal of Abnormal Psychology*, 1973, *81*, 158–171.

Teasdale, J. D. Effects of real and recalled success on learned helplessness and depression. *Journal of Abnormal Psychology*, 1978, *87*, 155–164.

Tennen, H., & Eller, S. J. Attributional components of learned helplessness and facilitation. *Journal of Personality and Social Psychology*, 1977, *35*, 265–271.

Thomas, E., & Dewald, L. Experimental neurosis: Neuropsychological analysis. In J. D. Maser & M. E. P. Seligman (Eds.), *Psychopathology: Experimental models*. San Francisco: Freeman, 1977.

Thornton, J. W., & Jacobs, P. D. Learned helplessness in human subjects. *Journal of Experimental Psychology*, 1971, *87*, 369–372.

Thornton, J. W., & Powell, G. D. Immunization and alleviation of learned helplessness in man. *American Journal of Psychology*, 1974, *87*, 351–367.

Weiner, B. *Theories of motivation: From mechanism to cognition*. Chicago: Rand McNally, 1972.

Weiner, B. (Ed.). *Achievement motivation and attribution theory*. Morristown, N. J.: General Learning Press, 1974.

Weiner, B., Frieze, I., Kukla, A., Reed, L., Rest, S., & Rosenbaum, R. M. *Perceiving the causes of success and failure*. Morristown, N. J.: General Learning Press, 1971.

Weiner, B., Heckhausen, H., Meyer, W., & Cook, R. E. Causal ascriptions and achievement behavior: A conceptual analysis of locus of control. *Journal of Personality and Social Psychology*, 1972, *21*, 239–248.

Welker, R. L. Acquisition of a free operant appetitive response in pigeons as a function of prior experience with response-independent food. *Learning and Motivation*, 1976, *7*, 394–405.

Willis, M. H., & Blaney, P. H. Three tests of the learned helplessness model of depression. *Journal of Abnormal Psychology*, 1978, *87*, 131–136.

Wortman, C. B., & Brehm, J. W. Responses to uncontrollable outcomes: An integration of reactance theory and the learned helplessness model. In L. Berkowitz (Ed.), *Advances in experimental social psychology* (Vol. 8). New York: Academic Press, 1975.

Wortman, C. B., Panciera, L., Shusterman, L., & Hibscher, J. Attributions of causality and reactions to uncontrollable outcomes. *Journal of Experimental Social Psychology*, 1976, *12*, 301–316.

PART III

INTERPERSONAL AND SOCIAL APPROACHES

The articles in this section are diverse, but they share an assumption that depression must be understood in its social context. The article by Coyne is concerned with the interpersonal dynamics in the close relationships of depressed persons and is more clinical in nature than the other articles of the section. The article by Billings and Moos deals with the social environment in terms of stress and coping processes and social support. Both Brown and Becker are sociologists, and in different ways each set about to do what C. Wright Mills (1959) has identified as the proper task of social science: to demonstrate the connection of "personal troubles" to the social structure. Our consideration of interpersonal and social approaches to depression would be incomplete without some acknowledgment of the greater risk for depression that Western industrialized society has for women, and Radloff explores this issue in the final article of the section.

The article by Coyne builds upon earlier work by Mabel Cohen and her colleagues. Its point of departure is a greater focus on the contemporary relationships of adult depressed persons, with a conceptualization of depression as an emergent interpersonal system of depressive behavior and the response of others. According to this model, the symptoms of depression are powerful in their ability to arouse guilt in others and to inhibit the direct expression of anoyance and hostility from them. Intitially, the depressed persons' distress engages others and shifts the interactional burden onto them. Yet the persistence of the depressed persons' distress may soon prove incomprehensible and aversive to them. Members of the social environment attempt to control this aversiveness and alleviate their guilt by manipulating depressed persons with nongenuine reassurance and support. At the same time, these persons may come to reject and avoid the depressives. As these feelings become apparent, the depressed persons are confirmed in their suspicions that they are not accepted or valued by others, and that future interactions cannot be assured. In an attempt to maintain themselves in this increasingly insecure situation, the depressed persons may display more distress, thereby strengthening this interpersonal pattern.

Coyne's model suggests that depressed persons' self-complaints are not merely a matter of cognitive distortion, as they are construed by the cognitive models, but rather that they reflect in part the confusing but negative reactions that they are receiving from others. Like other people, depressed people form expectations and interpret ambiguous situations in terms of frequent and salient recent experiences, and their negative social involvements may provide a background for interpreting new experiences. Furthermore, voicing their self-complaints may become a way of avoiding or inhibiting negative responses from others, even if the long-term effect of such a strategy is rejection.

Laboratory studies have found that in a short interaction, depressed persons induce negative affect in others and get rejected (Coyne, 1976; Gurtman, in press; Strack & Coyne, 1983). In just three minutes, there are identifiable changes in the nonverbal bahavior of persons talking to someone who is depressed (Gotlib & Robinson, 1982), and in a debriefing, subjects admit to being less honest with a depressed partner (Strack & Coyne, 1983). Coyne (1976) proposed that the negative mood that depressed persons induce in others has the effect of making any positive behavior they display less rewarding. It is not just that depressed persons lack social skills, as Lewinsohn suggested, but that they lack the *special* skills required by their situations.

Recent work derived from this model has centered on the marital and family relationships of depressed persons (Coyne, Kahn, & Gotlib, 1986). In marital interation, the inhibited and inhibiting quality of depressed behavior is seen in terms of a self-perpetuating pattern of (1) avoidance of conflict in a way that allows unresolved issues to accumulate, (2) negative exchanges with no problem resolution, and (3) withdrawl into inhibition and conflict avoidance again (Kahn, Coyne, & Margolin, in press). Both laboratory and home observations of depressed persons reveal that they face more hostility from family members than do nondepressed persons, but that their display of symptoms may indeed inhibit expression of these negative feelings (Biglan, et al., in press; Hops, et al., 1984). Therapeutic applications of this model are seen in the refinement of a brief strategic martial therapy for depressed persons (Coyne, 1983), but systematic outcome studies have not yet been conducted. Overall, the model is newer than the cognitive and behavioral formulations of depression, and it has not yet been subject to the critical scrutiny that these models have.

Billings and Moos sumarize recent developments in the conceptualization of depression in terms of stress and coping process. A considerable body of research has documented the relationship between major life events and the onset of depression. (For a review, see Dohrenwend & Dohrenwend, 1974.) In particular, events involving interpersonal losses have been shown to result in depression, but the association between negative life events and depression have been weaker than originally anticipated. This has led theorists and researchers to consider broader definitions of stress, as well as the personal and environmental resources and coping that might mediate the stress-depression connection.

As noted by Billings and Moos, stressful life circumstances leading to depression may include not only major life events, but chronic life strains such as financial problems and poor working conditions, and the accumulation of microstressors or daily hassles. Personal resources may make the difference as to whether such stress occurs or actually results in depression. Under this rubric, Billings and Moos include cognitive factors such as a sense of mastery or control and attributional style, as well as interpersonal orientation.

Social support is perhaps the most critical environmental resource, and its possible stress-buffering role has received considerable attention. Work by Brown (see below) has singled out the availability of a close confiding relationship as an important protection against depression. However, Billings and Moos note that close relationships are also one of the most important sources of stress, and that in particular, marital conflict and disruption frequently result in depression.

Personal and environmental resources shape how a person appraises and copes with stress. Appraisal refers to the person's continually reevaluated judgments about the demands and constraints in ongoing transactions with the environment and the options for meeting them (Coyne & Lazarus, 1980). Appraisal processes determine coping, consistent with the person's agenda. Billings and Moos note that three subdomains of coping are generally recognized: efforts to define or redefine the personal significance of a situation, efforts to deal with the source of stress, and efforts to reduce or manage one's distress. Billings and Moos raise the interesting issue of whether support-seeking is an effective form of coping with stress. Consistent with the results of a number of studies Coyne, Aldwin, & Lazarus, 1981; Pearlin & Schooler, 1978), they suggest that support-seeking may have a detrimental effect upon relationships, particularly in the face of chronic stressors. Apparently, support-seeking is an ineffective form of coping, and those who actively seek support are not those who receive it.

The model presented by Billings and Moos is less of a theoretical formulation than a heuristic device for organizing some of the findings emerging from a growing number of recent studies of the stress, support, and coping processes associated with depression. They are careful to emphasize that the model is a simplification as it is presented, and that many of the unicausal pathways that they identify are best seen as aspects of more complex, mutually causative relationships. The Moos group has noted this in its own empirical work. For instance, Mitchell, Cronkite, and Moos (1983) proposed that stress faced by members of a social network has both a direct effect on individual levels of depression and an indirect effect by way of a reduction in the support available.

Brown (this volume) attempts to explain social class differences in depression among women in terms of more proximal psychosocial variables. In developing and testing his model with six samples of depressed women, he also succeeds in providing a precise empirical statement about the relationship of stress and support to depression.

He employed an intensive interview to discover the characteristics of life events most related to depression. Not all major life events increase the risk for depression, only the most severe and typically those involving loss. These severe events were designated *provoking agents*. A second class of provoking agents, ongoing life difficulties, also proved important, but less potent.

The presence of a provoking agent was related to class background and to depression, but it did little to explain class differences in depression. Brown then set out to identify a set of factors leading to a vulnerability to provoking agents. By far, the most important *vulnerability factor* was the lack of an intimate, confiding relationship with a husband or boyfriend. Other significant, but less important vulnerability factors were the presence of three or more children in the home under age 14, being unemployed, and having lost a mother in childhood. The greater likelihood of working-class women becoming depressed was more related to their having one or more these vulnerability agents than it was to their greater risk of experiencing a provoking agent. In the article, Brown develops this model further and also distinguishes a third class of factors influencing the formation of symptoms (see also Brown & Harris, 1978, for an extended discussion).

Brown's work is proving highly influential in terms of his method for exploring the contextual determinants of the stress-depression relationship, as well as the specific findings he obtained. In particular, his findings about the importance of the absence of a single confiding relationship with an intimate and of having extensive childrearing responsibilities as vulnerability factors sparked considerable interest in the social determinants of depression. Brown's model is more limited than the heuristic one presented by Billings and Moos, but within those limits, it is developed more precisely. Yet unlike Billings and Moos, Brown's model lacks any consideration of coping. Brown and Harris (1978) have acknowledged this as setting the agenda for future work:

Future research will need to focus on the role of the immediate social context, on individuals and their households, and on how they get caught up in a crisis or difficulty, try to cope with it, and the resources they have for this. But at the same time the possibilty of spelling out broader links must be pursued. . . . Both individual-oriented and society-oriented studies are required. . . . It is too easy for the broader approach to ignore the complexities of the individual's immediate social milieu and for the more detailed approach to get lost in the intricacies of the individual personality (p. 293).

Ernest Becker's work on depression has thus far received more attention in Europe than in the United States (Freden, 1982). The lively, irreverent style of the Becker article contrasts sharply with the scholarly tone of other articles in this volume. His presentation of the psycho-dynamic perspective borders on satire. Yet, we should not let this distract us from the serious points that he makes.

Becker draws on Szasz (1961) in suggesting that depression is more properly seen as a loss of a "game" rather than the mere loss of an object, with game referring to the norms or rules that structure one's life and give it meaning. In light of this, the puzzling self-accusations of depressed persons are seen as an effort to claim a meaning or identity or a meaning when these have been lost or damaged. "The individual gropes for a language with which to supply a meaning to his life-plot when all other props for meaning are pulled away." Being depressed is the game that one plays when one is frustrated in attempts to play another meaningful game.

Despite his diatribe against psychodynamic formulations of depression, Becker accepts and builds upon Bibring's suggestion that depression is a result of a threat to self-esteem. Yet, for Becker, self-esteem is a matter of social symbols and social motives even more than it was for Bibring. It is not just an inner experience, it is a social construction, and depends upon what society and culture provide. "Nothing less than a full sweep of culture activity is brought into consideration in the single case of depression."

The risk for depression lies in having too limited a range of games to play. Like Brown, Becker raises the possibility that culture creates the opportunity for depression. A culture may provide only a narrow range of objects and games. In the case of Western industrialized society, women are given access to a "limited range of monopolizing interpersonal experiences." Becker's intent and style are quite different than Brown's, but reading the two articles together one gets a sense of a rich and creative way of making sense of Brown's findings concerning the determinants of depression among working class women.

Radloff examines some possible reasons for persistent findings that in both community surveys and clinical samples, women are 1.6 to 2 times more likely to be depressed than are men (Boyd & Weissman, 1981; Weissman & Klerman, 1977). These sex differences do not appear to be due to women's greater tendencies to acknowledge, report, or seek help for depressive symptoms. The main exceptions to these generally consistent findings of a sex difference in depression come from studies conducted in developing countries or Finland and Norway or with the American Amish.

The Radloff goes beyond simple efforts to demonstrate a sex difference in depression and uses data from two epidemiological surveys to explore the social conditions in which this difference does or does not occur. Marriage proves to be an important factor. In Radloff's combined sample, women are more depressed than are men, but this is true only among the married, divorced, separated, and never-married heads who are not heads of households. Women who have never married but are heads of households are not only less depressed than married women, they are even less depressed than their male counterparts.

Radloff examines a number of demographic variables that might provide alternative explanations for her results, but her basic conclusions are sustained. These results could have profound social implications in the way that they implicate the institution of marriage. Other studies are also finding an interaction between sex and marriage in rates of depression, but the general suggestion seems to be that it is not that marriage makes women more depressed but rather that it confers less benefits on women than on men (Kessler & McRae, 1984). One provocative study found that women were more depressed than men only when children were present in the home, but that the major portion of this sex difference was due to men benefiting from being married *and* having children in the home, relative to both other men and women, rather than to women being placed more at risk by these factors (Aneshensel, Frerichs, & Clark, 1981). The debate continues, and it is likely that a host of additional variables will have to be considered to fully explain the social determinants of sex differences in depression. Yet, as Radloff notes, the findings thus far clearly indicate that this sex difference cannot be reduced to a matter of biological vulnerability.

The Radloff article is an excellent example of the uses to which such epidemiological data can be put. Such an approach represents a different level of analysis than the more psychological perspectives that we have been considering, but in principle, at least, the two should be compatible and even complementary. Indeed, valid results from both approaches should converge in suggesting how features of the social structure might make more likely the psychological conditions associated with depression. Yet, survey studies are typically conducted by epidemiologists and sociologists who give little heed to developments in psychiatry and psychology. The Radloff article is unusual in attempting an integration.

Having identified some social factors associated with depression, Radloff goes on to speculate about what psychological factors might intervene between social factors and depression. Creative use is made of the theoretical and research literature concerning both learned helplessness and sex role stereotypes.

REFERENCES

Aneshensel, C. S., Frerichs, R. R., and Clark, V. A. (1981). Family roles and sex differences in depression. *Journal of Health and Social Behavior.* 22:379–393.

Biglan, A., et al. (in press). Problem solving interactions of depressed women and their spouses. *Behavior Therapy.*

Boyd, J. W. and Weissman, M. M. (1981). Epidemiology of affective disorders. *Archives of General Psychiatry.* 38:1039–1046

Brown, B. W., and Harris, T. (1978). *Social Origins of Depression: A Study of Psychiatric Disorder in Women.* NY: Free Press.

Coyne, J. C. (1976). Depression and the response of others. *Journal of Abnormal Psychology.* 85:186–193.

Coyne, J. C. (1984). Strategic therapy with married depressed persons: agenda, themes, and interventions. *Journal of Marital and Family Therapy.* 10:53–62.

Coyne, J. C., Aldwin, C., and Lazarus, R. S. (1981). Depression and coping in stressful episodes. *Journal of Abnormal Psychology.* 90:439–447.

Coyne, J. C., Kahn, J., and Gotlib, I. H. (1986). Depression. In T. Jacob (Ed.). *Family Interaction and Psychopathology.* NY: Pergamon Press.

Coyne, J. C. and Lazarus, R. S. (1980). Cognitive style, stress perception and coping. In I. L. Kutash and L. B. Schlesinger (Eds.). Handbook on Stress and Anxiety. San Francisco: Jossey-Bass.

Dohrenwend, B. P., and Dohrenwend, B. S. (1974). *Stressful Life Events: Their Nature and Effects.* NY: Wiley.

Freden, L. (1982). *Psychosocial Aspects of Depression.* NY: Wiley.

Gotlib, I. H., and Robinson, L. A.(1982). Responses to depressed individuals: Discrepancies between self-report and observer-rated behavior. *Journal of Abnormal Psychology.* 91:231–240.

Gurtman, M. B. (in press). Depression and the response of others: re-evaluating the re-evaluation. *Journal of Abnormal Psychology.*

Hops, H., et al. (1984). Home observations of family interactions of depressed women. Paper presented at the Annual Convention of the American Psychological Association, Toronto, Canada.

Kahn, J., Coyne, J. C., and Margolin, G. (in press). Depression and marital conflict: The social construction of despair. *Journal of Social and Personal Relationships.*

Kessler, R. C., and McRae, J.A.(1984). A note on the relationships of sex and marital status to psychological distress. In J. Greenly (Ed.). *Research in Community and Mental Health,* Volume 4. Greenwich, CT: JAI Press.

Mills, C. S. (1959). *The Sociological Imagination.* NY: Oxford University Press.

Mitchell, R. E., Cronkite, R. C., and Moos, R. H. (1983). Stress, coping, and depression among married couples. *Journal of Abnormal Psychology*. 92:433–449.

Pearlin, L. I., and Schooler, C. (1978). The structure of coping. *Journal of Health and Social Behavior*. 20:2–21.

Strack, S., and Coyne J. C. (1983). Social confirmation of dysphoria: shared and private reactions to depression. *Journal of Personality and Social Psychology*. 44:806–814.

Szasz, T. (1961). *The Myth of Mental Illness*. NY. Dell.

Weissman, M. M., & Klerman, G. L. (1977). Sex differences and the epidemiology of depression. *Archives of General Psychiatry*. 34:98–111.

10. Toward an Interactional Description of Depression

James C. Coyne

Developments in the interactional description of schizophrenia have not been paralleled in the area of depression. As yet, concepts such as pseudomutuality, double-bind, schism, and skew have found no counterparts. Kubler and Stotland (1964) have argued, "emotional disturbance, even the most severe, cannot be understood unless the field in which it develops and exists is examined. The manifestations of the difficulty in the disturbed individual have meaning depending on aspects of the field. The significant aspects of the field are usually interpersonal" p. 260). Yet the study of depression has focused on the individual and his behavior out of his interactional context. To a large degree, the depressed person's monotonously reiterated complaints and self-accusations, and his provocative and often annoying behavior have distracted investigators from considerations of his environment and the role it may play in the maintenance of his behavior. The possibility that the characteristic pattern of depressed behavior might be interwoven and concatenated with a corresponding pattern in the response of others has seldom been explored. This paper will address itself to that possibility.

For the most part, it has been assumed that the depressed person is relatively impervious to the influence of others. Ruesch (1962) stated that to talk to the depressed person makes little sense; to listen, little more. Grinker (1964) conceptualized depressive symptomatology as communication to others, but argued that the depressed person is not responsive to communication from others: "The depressed person . . . cannot use information for the purpose of action; he cannot perceive the cues of reality; he makes statements but does not care if he is understood" (p. 578).

In terms of systems theory (von Bertalanffy, 1950; Allport, 1960; Miller, 1971), the usual conceptualization of the depressed person is one of a relatively closed system. Grinker (1964) was explicit in stating that the depressed person repeats his messages and behavior without reception or acceptance of resulting feedback. Beck (1964, 1967) described the cognitive distortions that dominate the information processing of the depressed person so that experiences are rigidly interpreted to maintain existing schema of personal deficiency, self-blame, and negative expectations.

The implicit assumption of these and other writers has been that the support and information available to the depressed person are incongruent with his depression, and the persistence of his symptomatology is evidence of a failure to receive or accept this information. Withdrawal, isolated intrapsychic processes, or as Beck describes (1967), interactions of depressive schema and affective structures, produce a downward depressive spiral. The present paper will adopt an alternative argument that the depressed person is able to engage others in his environment in such a way that support is lost and depressive information elicited. This in turn increases the level of depression and strengthens the pathogenic pattern of depressed behavior and response of others. If a depressive spiral develops, it is mutually causative, deviation-amplifying process (Maruyama, 1963) in the interaction of the depressed person with his environment. Thus, what is customarily viewed as some internal process is, I believe, at least in part a characteristic of interaction with the environment, and much of what is customarily viewed as cognitive distortion or misperception is characteristic of information flow from the environment. It should be noted that while the depressed persons's different interpretation of his predicament is traditionally attributed to his distortion or misperception, general disorders of thought and perception are neither defining criteria nor common among depressed patients (McPartland and Hornstra, 1964). An observer who fails to take into account the intricacies of someone's relationship to his environment frequently attributes to him characteristics that he does not possess, or leaves significant aspects of his experience unexplained (Watzlawick et al., 1967). Feedback introduces phenomena that cannot be adequately explained by reference to the isolated individual alone (Ashby, 1960, 1962). For the study of depression, identification of a pattern of depressive feedback from the environment demands a more complex conceptualization of the disorder than one explaining its phenomena with reference to the isolated depressed person.

Lemert (1962), in his study of the interpersonal dynamics of paranoia, argued that the net effect of the developing interaction pattern between the paranoid person and others is that (1) the flow of information to the person is stopped, (2) a real discrepancy between expressed ideas and affect among those with whom he interacts is created, and (3) the situation or group image becomes as ambiguous for him as he is for others. In this context of attenuated relationships, exclusion, and disrupted communication, the paranoid person cannot get the feedback on his behavior that is essential in order for him to correct his interpretations of social relationships. Lemert concluded that the paranoid person may indeed be delusional, but that it is also true that in a very real sense he is able to elicit covertly organized action and conspiratorial behavior.

The present paper will attempt to demonstrate in a similar manner aspects of the interpersonal dynamics of depression. What will be sought is an interaction and information flow pattern congruent with the established phenomena of depression, and at the same time, indications as to why this, rather than alternative patterns, persists in the apparent absence of external constraint. Existing descriptions of the interpersonal behavior of the depressed person will be examined, and an attempt will be made to reconstruct the interactional contexts in which this behavior has meaning.

It should be made clear that such a perspective does not deny the existence of important intrapersonal factors in depression. Numerous writers have pointed out that the depressed person's feelings of worthlessness and helplessness do not arise *de novo* in his immediate stimulus situation (Chodoff, 1972). McCranie (1971) has argued that there is a "depressive-core" in the personality of the depression-prone person, consisting of a tendency to feel worthless and helpless and an oversensitivity to stimuli that impinge on these feelings. Together, these are aroused from dormancy by specific situations such as loss and threat to self-esteem. However, the emphasis of this paper will be on means by which the environment comes into congruence with these feelings. The depressive's vague, generalized feeling that there is something wrong with him, and his search for this among his minor defects, imperfections, and personal attributes, may arise from a depressive core to his personality, but at the same time, the confusing response from the environment serves to validate these feelings. Likewise, conflicts about the reception of support and approval from others may be deeply rooted in the depressive's intrapersonal style, but these conflicts can only be aggravated by the mixed messages of approval and rejection received from significant others, and by their withdrawal from him despite reassurances to the contrary.

Furthermore, the present exposition does not deny the importance of possible biochemical or genetic factors in the etiology of depression. Price (1974) has argued that even in disorders in which the importance of such factors has been clearly established, there may be a large number of links in the causal chain between specific etiological factors and the symptoms displayed by an individual. Social and interpersonal variables may determine to a large degree whether a disorder occurs and the form its symptoms will take. It is assumed that to initiate the process described below, a person need only begin to display depressive behavior.

DEPRESSION AND INTERPERSONAL BEHAVIOR

Since Freud, real and imagined object losses have been given prominence in the explanation of depression, and depressive process has often been seen as miscarried restitutive work. While most early formulations focused on intrapsychic phenomena, there were implications for interpersonal behavior. As early as Abraham (1911, 1916), the overdemanding aspects of the depressive's orality were noted. Rado (1928) assigned major etiological importance to an accentuated need for dependency in the depressed person. Fenichel (1945) described the neurotically depressed person's interpersonal maneuvers—his demonstrations of his misery, his accusations that others have brought about the misery, and even his blackmailing of others for attention—as desperate attempts to force others to restore damaged self-esteem. Yet in seeking this gratification, he is at the same time afraid to receive it because of the revenge that he expects will accompany it. In the psychotically depressed person, the loss is more complete, the objects have fallen away, and the restitutive effort is aimed exclusively at the superego.

Cohen et al. (1954) described the depressed person as seeing others as objects to be manipulated for the purpose of receiving sympathy and reassurance, but also as seeing them as being critical, rejecting, and ungenuine in their support. Further, in the achievement of reassurance, the depressed person finds concealed disapproval and rejection. According to the Cohen et al. formulation, what the depressed person seeks is a dependent relationship in which all his needs are satisfied, and in his failure to obtain this, he resorts to the depressive techniques of complaining and whining. if this too fails, he may lose hope, and enter into the psychotic state, where the pattern of emptiness and need continues in the absence of specific objects.

Grinker (1964) interpreted the factor patterns obtained in an earlier study of depression (Grinker et al., 1961) as representing relatively constant patterns of communication. "What is requested or seemingly needed by the depressed patient expressed verbally, by gestures or in behavior, varies and characterizes the pattern of the depressed syndrome" (1964, p. 577).

Bonime (1960, 1966) described how the depressed person can dominate his environment with his demands for emotionally comforting responses from others. He considered depression to be a practice, an active way of relating to people in order to achieve pathological satisfactions, and he dismissed any suffering the depressed person may incur as secondary to the satisfaction of manipulative needs.

Aggression played a central role in early psychoanalytic formulations of depression (Abraham, 1911; Freud, 1917), but later writers have increasingly disputed its role. Bibring (1953) went so far as to declare that depression was an ego phenomenon, "essentially independent of the vicissitudes of aggression as well as oral drives" (p. 173).

Fromm-Reichmann(1959) argued that aggression had been considerably overstressed as a dynamic factor in depression, and that if hostile feelings were found in the depressed person, they were the result of the frustration of his manipulative and exploitative needs. Cohen et al. (1954) attributed the hostility of the depressed person to his "annoying impact on others, rather than to a primary motivation to do injury to them" (p. 121). On the other hand, Bonime found the hurting or defying of others to be essential to depressed behavior.

Renewed interest in the relationship between hostility and depression—particularly in the psychoanalytic view that depressed persons turn hostility that had orginally been directed at others (hostility-outward), against themselves (hostility-inward)—has generated a number of empirical studies. Wessman et al. (1960) suggested that relatively normal persons became hostile outward when depressed, whereas persons tending to become severely depressed were more likely to internalize or suppress this hostility. The data of Zuckerman et al. (1967) supported this view, indicating that only in the relatively normal was hostility correlated with depression on mood questionnaries or as rated by interviewers. Friedman (1964) found depressives to have more "readily expressed resentment" as shown by their endorsement of adjectives such as "bitter," "frustrated," and "sulky," yet found no greater overt hostility. In a later study, Friedman (1970) showed that feelings of depression and worthlessness were consonant with hostile and resentful feelings, even though depressed persons were not more likely to directly express these feelings to persons in the environment. Schless et al. (1974) found equal numbers of depressed patients turning hostility inward and outward, with both types of hostility increasing as depression became more severe. However, because these patients also saw other people's anger as more readily expressed and more potent, they feared retaliation, and therefore expressed hostility only in the form of resentment. In summary, recent studies have been interpreted so as to call into question classical psychoanalytic formulations of the relationship of depression, hostility-inward amd hostility-outward. On the other hand, the view that hostility may serve a defensive function against depression has been supported. That depression is preceded by increases in hostility that is directed out but cannot be expressed directly to appropriate objects in the environment, is taken as a failure of this defensive function (Friedman, 1970; McCranie, 1971; Schless et al., 1974).

Most writers who comment on the complaints and self-accusations of the depressed person have rejected the idea that they should be taken literally. Lichtenberg (1957) found that attempts to answer them directly with assurance, granting of dependency, and even punishment all increased depression and feelings of personal defect. Freud (1917) suggested that the self-accusations are actually aimed at someone else, a lost love object, and further notes, ". . . it must strike us that after all the melancholic does not behave in quite the same way as a person who is crushed by remorse and self-reproach in a normal fashion. Feelings of shame in front of other people, which would more than anything characterize this latter condition, are lacking in the melancholic, or at least they are not prominent in him. One might emphasize the presence in him of an almost opposite trait of insistent communicativeness which finds satisfaction in self-exposure" (p. 247).

In an attempt to modify depressive behavior in a family situation (Liberman and Raskin, 1971), the baseline data indicated that other family members rejected opportunities to interact with the depressed person, and that all initiations of interaction between him and his family in the baseline period were undertaken by him.

Paykel and Weissman (1973) reported extensive social dysfunction in women during depressive episodes. Interpersonal friction, inhibited communication, and submissive dependency occurred in both the initial episodes and in subsequent relapses. Onset of social difficulties was related to symptoms, but these difficulties continued months after the symptoms remitted, a fact that Paykel and Weissman argue must be taken into account in any treatment plan.

As mentioned earlier, the provocative and often annoying behavior of the depressive has distracted investigators from consideration of the role of the response of others. An exception, Jacobson (1954) noted that "however exaggerated the patients' hurt, disappointment, and hostile derogation of their partners may be, their complaints are usually more justified than may appear on the surface" (p. 129). According to her, the depressed person often makes his whole environment feel guilty and depressed, and this provokes defensive aggression and even cruelty precisely when he is most vulnerable. Depressives also have a tendency to develop an "oral interplay" with those around them, so that mutual demands and expectations are built up to inevitable disappointment and depression for everyone concerned.

Cohen et al. (1954) found therapists generally uncomfortable working with depressed patients. They identified a tendency of therapists to react to depressive manipulations with unrealistic reassurance and "seductive promises too great to be fulfilled," followed by hostility and rejection. The present author became aware of a dramatic example of this when a student therapist showed up at a Florida suicide prevention center with a recent client. The therapist had attempted to meet her client's complaints of worthlessness and rejection with explicit reassurances that she more than understood her and cared for her, she *loved* her! After weeks of such reassurance and increasingly frequent sessions, the client finally confronted the therapist with the suggestion that if the therapist really cared for her as she said, they should spend the night together. The therapist panicked and terminated the case, suggesting that the client begin applying her newly acquired insights to her daily life. The client continued to appear for previously scheduled appointments and made vague suicidal gestures, at which time her therapist brought her to the suicide prevention center. When it was suggested that the therapist should honestly confront her client with what had happened in the relationship, the therapist angrily refused to speak to her, stating that she truly loved her client and would do nothing to hurt her.

Lewinsohn and his associates (Lewinsohn and Shaw, 1969; Lewinsohn, 1969; Lewinsohn et al., 1970; Libet and Lewinsohn, 1973) have undertaken an ambitious clinical research program focusing on a social interaction of the depressed person from a behavioral point of view. In attempting to develop hypotheses about the reinforcement contingencies available to the depressed person, they have attempted a precise specification of the social behavior of the depressed person. Libet and Lewinsohn found depressed persons in group therapy to be lower than controls on a number of measures of social skill: activity level, interpersonal range, rate of positive reactions emitted and action latency. Their data are subject to alternative interpretations, however, particularly since they also found that rate of positive reactions emitted was highly correlated with rate of positive reactions elicited. While depressed persons may well be deficient in social skills, some of the observed differences in group interaction situations may be due to the fact that fewer people are willing to interact with depressed persons (which results in a narrower interpersonal range and less opportunity for activity), and in this interaction emitted fewer positive responses (thereby also reducing the positive responses elicited from the depressed). The most useful behavioral conceptualization of social interaction involving depressed persons would specify the lack of social skills of all participants, as evidenced by their inability to alter the contingencies offered or received. Behavioral interventions in the depressed person's marital and family relationships would therefore involve training all participants in these social skills, and go beyond simply altering the contingencies available to the depressed person. Behavioral observations and self-reports of a couple in the Lewinsohn study (Lewisohn and Shaw, 1969) seem to support such a view.

Studies of suicide attempts and their effects on interpersonal relationships also provide data relevant to this discussion. While suicide attempts do not have an invariable relationship to depression, there is a definite association. McPartland and Hornstra (1964) examined the effects of suicide attempts on subsequent level of depression. They conceptualized depressive symptomatology as "a set of messages demanding action by others to alter or restore the social space" (p. 254), and examined the relationships between suicide attempts and the ambiguity of the depressive message and the diffuseness of its intended audience. They were able to reliably place depressed patients at definite points along a dimension of interactive stalemate on the basis of the range of intended audience and the stridency of message in depressive communications. Patients who were farthest along this continuum, whose communication was most diffuse, nonspecific, strident, and unanswerable, were most likely to have long hospital stays and diagnoses of psychosis. Suicide attempts tended to reduce the level of depression, apparently by shifting the interactive burden onto others. Other studies (Rubenstein et al., 1958; Moss and Hamilton, 1956; Kubler and Stotland, 1964) have indicated that suicidal patients who improve following their attempts on their lives consistently have effected changes in their social fields, and those who fail to improve generally have failed to change their situation fundamentally.

THE DEPRESSED PERSON IN HIS ENVIRONMENT

Depression is viewed here as a response to the disruption of the social space in which the person obtains support and validation for his experience. This view, and a view of depressive symptomatology in terms of message value and intended audience, is similar to that of McPartland and Hornstra (1964), but the present analysis will place a greater emphasis on the contribution of the social environment to depressive drift. The interpersonal process described will be a general one, and it is assumed that the course of a specific depressive episode will be highly dependent on the structure of the person's social space. One of the implications of the approach taken here is that an understanding of the social context is vital to an understanding of depression, although traditionally it has been largely ignored.

Social stresses leading to depression include loss of significant relationships, collapse of anticipated relationships, demotions (and in some cases, promotions), retirement, missed chances, or any of a variety of other changes in a person's social structure. Depressive symptomatology is seen as a set of messages demanding reassurance of the person's place in the interactions he is still able to maintain, and further, action by others to alter or restore his loss.

Initial communications—verbal expressions of helplessness and hopelessness, withdrawal from interaction, slowing, irritability and agitation—tend to engage others immediately and to shift the interactive burden to others. The receivers of these messages usually attempt to answer the depressed person's requests directly. However, as previously noted by Grinker (1964) and Lichtenberg (1957), their literal responses present him with a dilemma. Much of the depressive's communication is aimed at ascertaining the nature of relationship or context in which the interaction is taking place; Grinker (1964) has compared this to the various "how" and "why" questions that young children direct to their parents, and has suggested that both children and depressives will be left feeling rejected, ignored, or brushed aside if provided with a literal response.

If communication took place at only one level, depression would probably be a less ubiquitous problem. However, the problem is that human beings not only communicate, but communicate about this communication, qualifying or labeling what they say by (a) the context or relationship in which the communication takes place, (b) other verbal messages, (c) vocal and linguistic patterns, and (d) bodily movement (Haley, 1963). A person may offer support and reassurances with a rejecting tone or he may offer criticism in a supportive and reassuring tone.

When messages qualify each other incongruently, then incongruent statements are made about the relationship. If people always qualified what they said in a congruent way, relationships would be defined clearly and simply even though many levels of communication were functioning. However, when a statement is made which by its existence indicates one type of relationship and is qualified by a statement denying this, then difficulties in interpersonal relations become inevitable [Haley, 1963, pp. 7–8].

It is enough that vocal and linguistic patterns and body movement are ambiguous and subject to alternative interpretations. However, a further problem for the depressed person is that the context, the nature of the relationship between the depressed person and the persons communicating to him, may require time and further messages to be clearly defined.

The depressed person's problem is to decide whether others are assuring him that he is worthy and acceptable because they do in fact maintain this attitude toward him, or rather only because he has attempted to elicit such responses. Unwilling or unable to endure the time necessary to answer this question, the depressive uses his symptoms to seek repeated feedback in his testing of the nature of his acceptance and the security of his relationships.

While providing continual feedback, these efforts are at the same time profoundly and negatively affecting these relationships. The persistence and repetition of the symptoms is both incomprehensible and aversive to members of the social environment. However, the accompanying indication of distress and suffering is powerful in its ability to arouse guilt in others and to inhibit and direct expression of annoyance and hostility from them, as observed in both the family difficulties of depressed persons (Jacobson, 1954) and the problems therapists report in their efforts to relate to depressed patients (Cohen et al., 1954).

Irritated, yet inhibited and increasingly guilt-ridden, members of the social environment continue to give verbal assurance of support and acceptance. However, a growing discrepancy between the verbal content and the affective quality of these responses provides validation for the depressive's suspicions that he is not really being accepted and that further interaction cannot be assured. To maintain his increasingly uncertain security, the depressive displays more symptoms.

At this point the first of a number of interactive stalemates may be reached. Members of the depressed person's environment who can find a suitable rationalization for their behavior may leave the field or at least reduce their interactions with him. Considerable effort may be involved in efforts to indicate that this is not in fact rejection, but given the context, these efforts do little more than reduce credibility and increase the depressive's insecurity. With those members of the social environment who remain, a self-maintaining pattern of mutual manipulation is established. Persons in the environment find that they can reduce the aversive behavior of the depressed person and alleviate the guilt that this depressed behavior has a uncanny ability to elicit, if they manipulate him with reassurance, support, and denial of the process that is taking place. The depressed person, on the other hand, finds that by displaying symptoms he can manipulate his environment so that it will provide sympathy and reassurance, but he is aware by now that this response from others is not genuine and that they have become critical and rejecting. While this situation is attractive for neither the depressed person nor members of his social enviornment, it provides a stabilization of what has been a deteriorating situation.

One alternative facing the depressed person is for him to accept the precipitating disruption of his social space and the resulting loss of support and validation. However, now that he has begun showing symptoms, he has invested portions of his remaining relationships in his recovery effort. That is, he has tested these relationships, made demands, and has been frustrated in ways that seriously call into question his conception of these relationships. If he abandons these efforts, he may have to relinquish the support and validation derived from these relationships while accepting the precipitating loss. At this point he may be too dependent on the remaining relationships to give them up. Furthermore, as a result of the mixed messages he has been receiving from others, he now has an increasingly confused and deteriorated self-concept, which must be clarified. With new desperation more symptoms may be displayed.

Various possible efforts by the depressed person to discover what is wrong with him (i.e., why he is being rejected and manipulated) and to reestablish a more normal interactive pattern are in this context indistinguishable from the mananipulations he has used to control the responses of others. Therefore they are met with the usual counterminipulation. Requesting information as to how people *really* view him is indistinguishable from symptomatic efforts. If the depressed person attempts to discuss the interpersonal process that is taking place, he touches on a sensitive issue, and is likely only to elicit denial by the others or an angry defensive response. On the other hand, efforts by others to assure the depressed person that he is really accepted and that they are not rejecting him are in this context also indistinguishable from previous manipulations that they have employed, and therefore serve to strengthen the developing system. Thus, interpersonal maneuvers directed at changing the emerging pattern become system-maintaining, and any genuine feedback to the depressed person is also indistinguishable from manipulations. Persons leaving the social field increase both the depressed person's feelings of rejection and his impetus to continue his behavior pattern. Persons just entering the social field can be quickly recruited into the existing roles, since their efforts to deal with the depressed person—even if genuine—are likely to be quite similar to those now being employed manipulatively. They therefore become subject to the compelling coantermanipulations of the depressed person, come to respond manipulatively themselves, and are inducted into the system.

Descriptions of the depressed person at this point in his career focus on the distortions and misperceptions that serve to maintain his depression. What is generally ignored is that these "distortions" and "misperceptions" are congruent with the social system in which the depressed person now finds himself. The specific content of the depressive's complaints and accusations may not be accurate, but his comments are a recognition of the attenuated relationships, disrupted communication, and lack of genuineness that he faces. These conditions serve to prevent him from receiving the feedback necessary to correct any misperceptions or distortions. He has played a major role in the creation of this social system, but the emergence of the system has also required the cooperation of others, and once established, it tends to be largely beyond the control of its participants.

Depending on characteristics of both the depressed person and his environment, a number of punishing variations on the above pattern may develop. Members of the social environment who have been repeatedly provoked and made to feel guilty may retaliate by witholding the responses for which the depressed person depends on them. The depressed person may become aware of the inhibiting influence his symptoms have on the direct expression of negative feelings, and may use these symptoms aggressively, while limiting the forms that counteraggression can take. He may also discover and exploit the interdependence of others and himself. While he is being made acutely aware of his dependence on others and the frustrations it entails, he may also become aware of the extent to which others are dependent on him, in that their own maintenance of mood and their ability to engage in varieties of activities require in some way his cooperation. Either because of outright hostility, or as a self-defeating effort to convince others of their need to renegotiate their relationship with him, the depressed person may become more symptomatic in his withholding of these minimal cooperative behaviors. While hostility may not necessarily be a major etiological factor in depression, the frustrations, provocations, and manipulations occurring in interactions between depressed persons and others would seem to encourage it.

As efforts to end the interactive stalemate fail, there may be a shift in the depressive's self-presentation to one indicating greater distress and implying that the environment has more responsibility for bringing about the necessary changes. McPartland and Hornstra (1964) found that they could unambiguously differentiate themes of hopelessness and helplessness from more disturbed themes of low energy and physical complaints in communications of depressed patients. The latter themes were associated with longer hospitalization when hospitalized depressed patients were sampled. McPartland and Hornstra give the examples of "I can't sleep and I can't stand it any longer", "I am too tired to move"; "My head and my stomach feel funny all the time." Unable to restore his life space, the depressive now implicitly demands "a suspension of the rules; a moratorium on the web of obligations under which the person lives, such as admission to the sick role" (McPartland and Hornstra, 1964, p. 256). With immediate relationships deteriorating, the depressive addresses his plea to a more general audience, but in more confusing and unanswerable terms. Literal responses to his communications may involve medical intervention for his specific complaints, but this generally fails to alleviate the problem. Any efforts to move the interactional theme back to the depressive's sense of hopelessness and helplessness threaten to reopen the earlier unfruitful and even punishing patterns of relations, and tend to be resisted. Unable to answer, or in many cases, even to comprehend the depressive's pleas, members of the social environment may withdraw further from him, increasing his desperation, and quickening the depressive drift.

With a second interactive stalemate now reached, the depressed person may attempt to resolve it by increasing his level of symptomatology and shifting the theme of his self-presentation to one of the worthlessness and evil. "I am a failure; it's all my fault; I am sinful and worthless." Unable either to restore his social space or to reduce his obligations sufficiently for him to continue to cope, the depressive now communicates his bafflement and resignation. The intended audience is now more diffuse, relationships are even more attenuated, and the new message is more obscure and perplexing. The social environment and the depressive soon arrive at another stalemate. Otherwise helpless to alleviate the situation, remaining members of the enviroment may further withdraw or, alternatively, have the depressive withdrawn through hospitalization. In the absence on any relatedness to others, the depressive may drift into delusions and frankly psychotic behavior.

DISCUSSION

Once an individual has suffered a disruption of his social space, his ability to avoid depressive drift, or to abort the process once it has begun, depends on the structure of his social space and on his interpersonal skills. With regard to the latter, it is generally ignored that the person facing this situation is dealing with a changing environment, and that the skills needed to deal with it are likely to be different from those required by a more stable, normal environment. Consequently, persons who previously have had adequate skills to deal with their life situation may lack the skills to cope with a disrupted social space. With regard to the structure of this social space, resistance to depression seems to depend on the availability of alternative sources of support and validation, particularly of the type that cannot be threatened by depressive symptomatology, (2) the availability of direct nonpunitive feedback should the person's behavior become annoying or incomprehensible; and (3) the ability of the social space to generate new sources of support and meaning that are unambiguously independent of the presence or absence of symptoms. Earlier speculative writings (Abraham, 1911) and later behavioral studies (Lewinsohn, 1969) have suggested that depressed persons tend to be quite limited in their range of interactions, and that this may be a major source of their vulnerability.

Stable relationships may generally provide a buffer against depression, but when they are stable yet low in support and validation, they may encourage a chronic depressive cycle. If, for instance, in a marriage of this type, the depressed person recognizes that his spouse is tolerating more than is reasonable from him without protest, he may begin to assume that she is staying with him out of some obligations, rather than because she accepts him and wants a relationship (Haley, 1963). The depressed person may then test whether he is really accepted by driving the other person to the point of separation with his symptoms. Yet if the spouse passes the test by continuing to tolerate the annoying behavior, the depressed person may not necessarily be reassured about his acceptance. Rather he may only be convinced that his spouse remains because she is unable to leave. On the other hand, if she makes an effort to leave the situation, she may be indicating that their relationship has been voluntary and that he had been accepted. With reconciliation the spouse may again seem too tolerant and a new series of doubts, testing, and strife may be enacted. While such a cycle may produce chronic difficulties, it may also be an alternative to a downward depressive spiral. Essentially the depressed person finds himself in the awkward situation of wanting to avoid rejection, yet at the same time fearing acceptance.

The constraints operating on the person who has suffered a disruption in his social space are his need for support and validation, and the investment of his remaining relationships in his efforts to receive such support. The symptoms of the depressed person offer a powerful constraint on the ability of members of the social environment to offer adjustive feedback, and while eliciting verbal messages of sympathy, support, and reassurance, these symptoms disrupt the relationships and cultivate hostility and rejection.

Those who resist induction into the system without rejecting the depressed person do so because they are able to resist the pressure to convey discrepant messages. A successful therapist in Cohen et al. study stated, "I keep in mind that I am talking to the patients not so much verbally as preverbally. I use the verbal communication as a means of carrying inflection and an accompaniment of facial expression and postural components" (1954, p. 129).

Several writers have suggested that the emerging communication context can be disrupted by strong affective expressions such as anger, excitement, and amusement (Lazarus, 1968), which are incompatible with the pattern of mutual manipulation that maintains the context. As early as 1820 a London physician reported the cure of a depressive episode using anger induction. He informed the patient that in Scotland there was another physician famous for his cures of the disorder, and that the patient should leave immediately in order to procure relief. The patient undertook the journey but discovered that the famed doctor did not exist. Returning home to confront his doctor about this abuse of confidence, he found "a desire to upbraid [the doctor] had engaged his entire thoughts on his way home, to the complete exclusion of his original complaint" (Williams, 1820). A modern version of this technique of constructing situations in which aggressive responses are appropriate and rewarded is being put into effect in a number of Veterans Administration hospitals (Taulbee and Wright, 1971a, 1971b). A depressed patient, even one who is severely disturbed, is assigned to monotonous, nongratifying, and repetitive tasks such as sanding wood with fine-grain sandpaper, counting tiny seashells, or bouncing a ball on a small square on the floor. Although the patient is not ridiculed or belittled, his task performance is continually criticized as not perfect. This continues—usually three or four days are needed—until the patient "blows up," refuses to follow orders, or becomes verbally (seldom physically) aggressive. At that time he is removed from the task, given hearty social approval, and assigned a more pleasant task. This anti-depression program takes place in the context of a larger Attitude Therapy Program designed to maximize the consistency of expectations and emotional expression communicated to the patient. During the dull-task phase of treatment, an attitude of kind firmness (Taulbee and Folsom, 1966) is prescribed to the entire staff. They are instructed not to give in to the patient's pleadings to be left alone to suffer, not to try to cheer him up, and not to offer sympathy or encouragement. After the patient has "blown up," a matter-of-fact attitude is prescribed to the staff members. They are instructed to communicate clearly to him their explicit expectations and to make social reinforcement contingent on his meeting these expectations. Studies of the effectiveness of this program indicate that it is more effective than a variety of alternative programs in terms of measures of depression, anxiety, interpersonal orientation, and length of hospital stay (Taulbee and Wright, 1971b).

Although many writers have indicated that a depressive reaction lifts when a patient regains his ability to express anger toward others (Friedman, 1970), some research indicates that the mobilization of anger is not necessary for symptomatic improvement (Weissman, et al., 1971; Klerman and Gershon, 1970). Interpersonally, hostility may be one of a number of means of disrupting or blocking the operation of a depressive interpersonal system. Involvement in this system is difficult to avoid once it has begun. The symptoms of depression have an ability to perpetuate themselves through the involvement of others in a system of manipulation and countermanipulation that soon gets beyond the control of its participants.

The author is presently engaged in research that examines the response of others to depression and the quality of the communications context that emerges. Preliminary results from a study involving an interpersonal behavior questionaire suggest that a person is less likely to respond in an overtly hostile manner to the behavior of another person when the second person is depressed. This inhibition persists even when it is indicated that the second person is responding hostilely. The inhibition of appropriate hostile behavior may be a characteristic of interactions involving the depressed person, and not just of the depressed person. Another study involves twenty-minute phone conversations between naive subjects and target individuals from three groups: depressed outpatients, nondepressed outpatients, and normals. Preliminary results suggests that subjects respond with unrealistic reassurance and useless advice to the depressed outpatients. They are more likely to be depressed, anxious, and hostile themselves after converstions with depressed patients, and are more likely to reject opportunities for future interaction. For the most part, changes in the a subjects' mood remain concealed during the conversation, and the depressed patients are given little direct indication of their impact on others. If the subjects do respond with any hostility, it emerges only in occasional statements, such as "You certainly seem to have had a lot a problems, but problems are what allow us to grow, and so you'll have lots of opportunity to grow in the future." Further research is needed to examine the nature of the depressive's social field so that the specific relationships that resist or perpetuate the depressive interpersonal system can be identified and described.

CONCLUSION

Depression has been conceptualized here as a self-perpetuating interpersonal system. Depressive symptomatology is congruent with the developing interpersonal situation of the depressed person, and the symptoms have a mutually maintaining relationship with the response of the social environment. Essentially, the depressed person and others within his social space collude to create a system in which feedback cannot be received, and various efforts to change become system-maintaining.

REFERENCES

Abraham, K. "Notes on the Psychoanalytic Investigation and Treatment of Manic-Depressive Insanity and Allied Conditions" [1911], "The First Pregenital Stage of Libido" [1916], in *Selected Papers on Psychoanalysis;* Basic Books, 1953.

Allport, G. "The Open System in Personality Theory," *J. Abnormal and Social Psychol.* (1960) 61:301–311.

Ashby, W. R. *Design for a Brain* (2d Ed.); Science Paperbacks, 1960.

Ashby, W. R. "Principles of the Self-Organizing Systems," in H. von Foerster and G. W. Zupf (Eds.), *Principles of Self-Organization;* Pergamon, 1962.

Beck, A. T. "Thinking and Depression: II. Theory and Therapy," *Arch. Gen. Psychiatry* (1964) 10:561–571.

Beck, A. T. *Depression;* Hoeber, 1967.

Bibring, E. "The Mechanism of Depression," in P. Greenacre (Ed.), *Affective Disorders;* Int. Univ. Press. 1953.

Bonime, W. "Depression as a Practice: Dynamics and Psychotherapeutic Considerations," *Compr. Psychiatry* (1960) 1:194–201.

Bonime, W. "The Psychodynamics of Neurotic Depression," in S. Arieti (Ed.), *American Handbook of Psychiatry,* Vol. 3; Basic Books, 1966.

Chodoff, P. "The Depressive Personality," *Arch. Gen. Psychiatry* (1972) 27:666–673.

Cohen, M. B., et al. " An Intensive Study of Twelve Cases of Manic-Depressive Psychosis," Psychiatry (1954) 17:103–137.

Fenichel, O. *The Psychoanalytic Theory of Neurosis;* Norton, 1945.

Friedman, A. S. "Minimal Effects of Severe Depression on Cognitive Functioning."*J. Abnormal and Social Psychol.* (1964) 69:237–243.

Friedman, A. S. "Hostility Factors and Clinical Improvement in Depressed Patients," *Arch. Gen. Psychiatry* (1970) 23:524–537.

Freud, S. "Mourning and Melancholia [1917]," *Standard Edition of the Complete Psychological Works,* Vol. 14; Hogarth, 1951.

Fromm-Reichmann, F. *Psychoanalysis and Psychotherapy: Selected Papers;* Univ. of Chicago Press, 1959.

Grinker, R. R. "Reception of Communications by Patients in Depressive States," *Arch. Gen. Psychiatry* (1964) 10:576–580.

Grinker, R. R., et al. *The Phenomena of Depression;* Hoeber, 1961.

Haley, J. *Strategies of Psychotherapy;* Grune & Stratton, 1963.

Jacobson, E. "Transference Problems in the Psychoanalytic Treatment of Severely Depressed Patients." *J. Amer. Psychoanal. Assn.* (1954) 2:595–606.

Klerman, G. L., and Gershon, E. S. "Imramine Effects upon Hostility in Depression," *J. Nerv. and Mental Dis.* (1970) 150:127–132.

Kubler, A. L., and Stotland, E. *The End of Hope: A Social-Clinical Study of Suicide;* Free Press, 1964.

Lazarus, A. A. "Learning Theory and the Treatment of Depression," *Behav. Res. and Ther.* (1968) 6:83–89.

Lemert, E. M. "Paranoia and the Dynamics of Exclusion," *Sociometry* (1962) 25:2–20.

Lewinsohn, P. M. "Depression: A Clinical-Research Approach," unpublished manuscript, 1969.

Lewinsohn, P. M., and Shaw, D. A. "Feedback About Interpersonal Behavior

Change: A Case Study in the Treatment of Depression," *Psychother. and Psychosom.* (1969) 17:82–88.

Lewinsohn, P. M., et al. "A Behavioral Approach to the Group Treatment of Depressed Persons: Methodological Contributions," *J. Clin. Psychol.* (1970) 26:525–532.

Liberman, R. P., and Raskin, D. E. "Depression: A Behavioral Formulation," *Arch. Gen. Psychiatry* (1971) 24:515–523.

Libet, J. M., and Lewinsohn, P. M. "Concept of Social Skill with Special Reference to the Behavior of Depressed Persons," *J. Consult. and Clin. Psychol.* (1973) 40:304–312.

Lichtenberg, P. "Definition and Analysis of Depression," *AMA Arch. Neurol. and Psychiatry* (1957) 77:519–527.

Maruyama, M. "The Second Cybernetics: Deviation-Amplifying Mutual Causative Processes," *Amer. Sci.* (1963) 51:164–179.

McCranie, E. J. "Depression, Anxiety and Hostility," *Psychiatric Quart.* (1971) 45:117–133.

McPartland, T. S., and Hornstra, R. K. "The Depressive Datum," *Compr. Psychiatry* (1964) 5:253–261.

Miller, J. "The Nature of Living Systems," *Behav. Sci.* (1971) 16:277–301.

Moss, L., and Hamilton, D. M. "The Psychotherapy of the Suicidal Patient," *Amer. J. Psychiatry* (1956) 112:814–820.

Paykel, E. S., and Weisman, M. M. "Social Adjustment and Depression," *Arch. Gen Psychiatry* (1973) 28:659–663.

Price, R. H. "Etiology, the Social Environment, and the Prevention of Psychological Dysfunction," in P. Insel and R. H. Moos (Eds.), *Health and the Social Environment;* Heath, 1974.

Rado, S. "The Problem of Melancholia," *Int. J. Psycho-Anal.* (1928) 9:420–438.

Rubenstein, R., et al. " On Attempted Suicide," *AMA Arch. Neurol. and Psychiatry* (1958) 79:103–112.

Ruesch, J. *Therapeutic Communication;* Norton, 1962.

Schless, A. P., et al. "Depression and Hostility," *J. Nerv. and Mental Dis.* (1974) 159:91–100.

Taulbee, L. R., and Folsom, J. C. "Reality Orientation for Geriatric Patients," *Hosp. and Community Psychiatry* (1966) 17:133–135.

Taulbee, E. S., and Wright, H. W. "Attitude Therapy: A Behavior Modification Program in a Psychiatric Hospital," in H. C. Rickard (Ed.), *Behavioral Intervention in Human Problems;* Macmillan, 1971. (a)

Taulbee, E. S., and Wright, H. W. "A Psychosocial-Behavioral Model for Therapeutic Intervention," in C. D. Spielberger, *Current Topics in Clinical and Community Psychology,* Vol. 3; Academic Press, 1971. (b)

von Bertalanffy, L. "The Theory of Open Systems in Physics and Biology," *Science* (1950) 111:23–29.

Watzlawick, P., et al. *Pragmatics of Human Pragmatic Communication;* Norton, 1967,

Weissman, M. M., et al. "Clinical Evaluation of Hostility in Depression," *Amer. J. Psychiatry* (1971) 128:261–266.

Wessman, A. E., et al. "Characteristics and Concomitants of Mood Fluctuation in College Women, " *J. Abnormal and Social Psychol.* (1960) 60:117–126.

Williams, J. C. *Cure of Inveterate Dejection;* London, 1820.

Zuckerman, M., et al. "A Multitrait, Multimethod Measurement Approach to the Traits (or States) of Anxiety, Depression, and Hostility," *J. Projective Techniques* (1967) 31:39–48

11. Psychosocial Theory and Research on Depression: An Integrative Framework and Review

Andrew G. Billings and Rudolf H. Moos

There is increasing theoretical and empirical concern about the etiology and treatment of depression. This concern mirrors recent confirmation that depressive disorders are a major health problem. Present estimates place the point prevalence of clinically significant depression at approximately five percent, with as much as 10 to 20% of the population reporting significant depressive symptomatology (Radloff, 1977; Weissman & Myers, 1978). A diversity of conceptual models and empirical methods have been used to explore intrapsychic, cognitive-phenomenological, social, and behavioral aspects of depression. Each of these approaches also have implications for the formulation and implementation of clinical interventions.

While psychosocial research has identified the etiologic role of stressful life events and several promising psychological treatments have been formulated, a number of important research and clinical issues have been identified. For instance, why do stressful life circumstances lead to depression among some persons but not others? How can one explain the finding that different psychosocial interventions appear to have similar affects on depression? Toward what areas should prevention efforts be targeted?

In this paper we formulate a framework to organize these questions and to explore the commonalities among diverse areas of research and treatment on depression. The framework focuses on such issues as the identification of factors that determine the occurrence of stressful events and the likelihood that they will lead to depression, as well as the stress-moderating role of coping and social resource factors. Our goal here is to review and integrate research on the interplay of a set of conceptual domains, including environmental stressors, personal and environmental resources, and appraisal and coping responses. We use

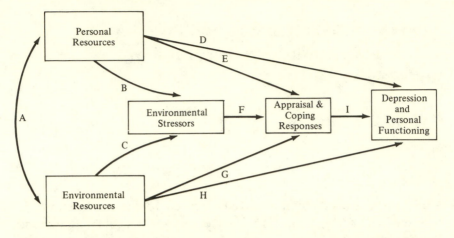

Figure 1. An integrative framework for the analysis of adaptive processes and depression.

the framework to help understand the effectiveness of conceptually different treatment strategies, to explore the recovery process, to plan interventions that maximize the durability of treatment gains, and to develop implications for designing prevention programs and clarifying the determinants of their effectiveness.

AN INTEGRATIVE FRAMEWORK

The framework presented in Figure 1 hypothesizes that the depression-related outcomes of stressful life circumstances are influenced by individuals' personal and environmental resources as well as by their appraisal and coping responses. These resources affect the occurrence of stressors, shape and nature of the coping responses selected to deal with them, and influence the adaptive outcome of the stressful episode. Thus the link between *environmental stressors* and depression is seen as mediated by individuals' personal and environmental resources, their cognitive appraisal and coping responses, and the interrelationships among these domains. Stressful life circumstances develop from personal and environmental factors and include specific events (divorce, death of a spouse, job loss), chronic life strains associated with major social roles (a stressful job, marital discord), and medical conditions and illnesses (arthritis, cancer).

Personal resources include dispositional characteristics such as self-concept, sense of environmental mastery and attributional styles, as well as social skills and problem-solving abilities. *Environmental resources* refer to the informational, material, and emotional support provided by intimates, other family members, and nonkin social network members. It is in the context of these environmental and personal resources that individuals *appraise* particular stressors; that is, perceive and interpret specific events. Along with the appraisal process, individuals use *coping responses* that are intended to minimize the adverse effects of stress. The outcome of this process influences the individual's level of *functioning* and adaptation. From this perspective, adaptation includes those cognitive, affective, and behavioral aspects of functioning that may be disrupted in the depressive syndrome.

The model highlights the interrelationships among the domains affecting depression. For instance, the impact of environmental stressors on functioning is mediated by the other domains identified. A stressor elicits appraisal and coping responses (path F), whose nature and effectiveness determine whether the stressful event leads to depression and disruptions in functioning (path I). These processes are conditioned by personal and environmental resources. Personal resources, such as high self-esteem, may mitigate depressive outcomes by reducing the occurrence of stressors (path B), by facilitating stress-reducing coping (path E), or by fostering healthy functioning even in the absence of stress (path D). Environmental resources can affect functioning in similar ways. Furthermore, personal resources can indirectly affect depression by facilitating the development of environmental resources, such as supportive interpersonal ties (path A), that also affect functioning (path H). Finally, depressed mood and related aspects of functioning can affect each of the "preceding" sets of factors. We describe existing research in terms of these paths or processes and use the model to highlight important relationships between sets of factors.

Framework Boundaries

Formulating such a framework involves certain simplifications. *First,* we recognize the presence of genetic and biologic "determinants" of depression (see Akiskal & McKinney, 1975; Maas, 1975), as well as the role of developmental factors. For example, early parental loss or death may increase the likelihood of subsequent depression by curtailing important socialization experiences that bolster adult coping resources (see Crook & Eliot, 1980; White, 1977). There are also macro-system factors, such as aspects of the physical environment (crowding, urban traffic congestion, airport noise) and social conditions (economic factors, racial prejudice, sexism), that may be distal determinants of depression. An adequate treatment of these factors is beyond the scope of this paper. However, we view all three of these sets of factors as potentially affecting depression via their influence on the domains within the framework.

Second, the model highlights the unidirectional "causal" effects typically considered in the literature, even though variables in the domains can have reciprocal effects on each other, such as when changes in coping and functioning affect personal and environmental resources. We refer to these reciprocal effects by adding a prime to the letter of the relevant path. For example, depression may lead to the use of less effective coping strategies (path I') and attributions of uncontrollability (path D'). Such strategies may alienate members of the individual's social network and thereby reduce future social support (path H'). We incorporate some findings on such effects in our presentation.

Lastly, considerable attention has been given to the diagnosis and description of depressive disorders (Endicott & Spitzer, 1978; Overall & Zisook, 1980), as well as to distinctions between depressive moods, symptoms, and syndromes. We hypothesize that the salient variables and processes that are related to depressed moods and behaviors among "healthy" individuals are isomorphic (albeit accentuated) to those involved in the development of "diagnosable" depressions, although there is as yet little research on this issue. We distinguish between clinical and nonclinical populations in reviewing the literature, but we believe that the basic nature of the framework is applicable to both groups. We also believe that the framework applies to different subtypes of depressive disorders, although the relative importance of the sets of factors may vary among subtypes (for example, life stressors may be more likely to precipitate relapse among reactive than among endogenous patients).

We turn now to a review of research on each of the domains in the framework. We attempt to indicate how variables in each domain may affect depression directly, as well as indirectly, by preventing stress and by mediating the effects of stress and of the other domains on adaptation. We later consider how much demographic factors as socioeconomic status and gender relate to depression through their influence on the components of the framework. Lastly, we consider how the framework might guide the formulation and evaluation of clinical interventions.

STRESSFUL LIFE CIRCUMSTANCES

Much of the literature on stress and depression is concerned with the effects of major life events such as divorce, job loss, and death. Recent studies indicate the need to expand the concept of stress to include continuing life strains arising from major social roles, as well as more minor but frequent stresses encountered in daily living. We consider each of these factors in examining the role of stressful life circumstances in depression. This research has focused primarily on the overall association between stressors and depression without considering the mediating factors noted in our framework.

Stressful Events

Substantial evidence implicates environmental stressors in the development and maintenance of depression (Paykel, 1979). The conceptual and methodological issues concerning life events are summarized elsewhere (Dohrenwend & Dohrenwend, 1974; Lindenthal & Myers, 1979) and will not be reviewed here. In brief, this line of inquiry has identified depressogenic effects of undesirable (negative) life changes in the areas of health, finances, and interpersonal relationships, particularly those representing exits or losses in the social field (such as deaths and separations). These events, which apparently have cumulative effects that may manifest themselves over several months, and three to six times more common among depressed individuals as compared to general population controls (Brown & Harris, 1978: Costello, in press).

Another significant source of stress derives from chronic strains associated with an individual's major social roles of spouse, parent, and provider. For example, Pearlin and Schooler (1978) found that such strains as frustration of marital role expectations, children's deviations from parental standards of behavior, and difficulty affording food and clothing were associated with greater depressive symptomatology among community residents. Physical and emotional dysfunction of one's spouse or children also create strain. Recent research has focused on the work setting as an important source of such stressors (for a review see Kasl, 1978). Work pressure, a lack of autonomy in decision making, and ambiguity about job roles and criteria of adequate performance have been associated with psychological distress and depression (Billings & Moos, in press-a). The comparability of findings on life strains (examined primarily among community samples) and stressful events (typically explored among clinical samples) suggests an underlying commonality in the role of environmental stressors in minor and major depressive outcomes.

Microstressors

Lazarus and Cohen (1977) have noted the potential impact of daily "hassles," those comparatively minor but frequent irritants and frustrations associated with both the physical and social environment (such as noise, rush hour traffic, concerns about money, family arguments). In a short-term longitudinal study of a middle-aged community sample, indices of daily hassles were better predictors of current and subsequent depression than were indices of major life events (Kanner, Coyne, Schaefer, & Lazarus, in press). Hassles may have "direct" effects on adaptation and may also be the functional subunits that comprise the stressful aspects of major life events.

Despite these conceptual and methodological advances, stressful life circumstances provide only a partial explanation for the development of serious depression or for the prevalence of depressive mood and reactions among essentially "normal" individuals. While up to three-quarters of depressed patients may have experienced a provoking stressful event or strain recently, only one person in five in a nonpatient sample will become clinically depressed after facing a severe stressor (Brown & Harris, 1978). Among general community samples, typically less than 10% of the variance in depressive symptoms can be "accounted for" by life stressors (Billings & Moos, 1981; Warheit, 1979). Stressors may act "directly" on depression or they may have "indirect" effects by reducing social resources and leading to maladaptive appraisals and ineffective coping responses. We turn our attention now toward factors that may help to explain individual variability in response to stressful circumstances.

PERSONAL RESOURCES

Personal resouces include relatively stable dispositional characteristics that affect functioning and provide a "psychological context" for coping. We focus here on several aspects of personal resources that are particularly relevant to depression: sense of environmental mastery, attributional styles relating to environmental stressors, and interpersonal orientation and skills. These resources are thought to be consistent across situations; specific appraisal and coping responses that vary according to the nature of the stressor are discussed subsequently. These stable personal resources accrue from the outcomes of previous coping episodes and may be shaped by demographic factors which we consider later.

Personal resources can affect depression in several related ways. They may have "direct" effects on functioning (path D), as supported, for instance, by the finding that individuals who enjoy high self-esteem are less likely to become depressed. In fact, there is often some conceptual overlap in measures of personal resources and depression, since low self-esteem may be considered to be one aspect of a depressive syndrome. Personal resources may have indirect effects on depression by reducing stressors (path B) and by fostering social resources (path A) and coping responses (path E) that can attenuate the effects of stress.

Sense of Environmental Mastery

A lack of global personal resources such as perceived competence and a sense of mastery is common in many disorders, particularly depression (for reviews see Becker, 1979; Sundberg, Snowden, & Reynolds, 1978; Wells & Marwell, 1976). A focal construct in this area is an internal locus of control, that is, a generalized belief in one's ability to affect the environment so as to maximize rewards and minimize unpleasant outcomes (for reviews see Lefcourt, 1976; Perlmuter & Monty, 1979). An external locus of control, a perceived inability to master one's environment either by controlling important events or in managing the consequences of events that are not controllable, has been directly associated with depression. For example, an external locus of control is associated with serious depression as well as greater frequency of dysphoria among college students (Calhoun, Cheney, & Dawes, 1974).

An internal control orientation may afford some resistance to the effects of stress. For instance, Johnson and Sarason (1978) found that negative life events were less likely to be associated with depression among college students with an internal locus of control than among those with an external locus. Similarly, in comparison to externally oriented corporative executives, internally oriented executives were more likey to remain healthy while under high stress (Kobasa, 1979). A sense of environmental mastery, along with high self-esteem and freedom from self-denigration, has also been found to attenuate the depressive effects of life strains among members of a community group (Pearlin & Schooler, 1978).

The development and maintenance of this sense of mastery has been a focus in the work of several important theorists including Bandura, Beck, and Seligman. For example, Bandura's model of adaptational behavior (1977, 1980) suggests that an internal control orientation and feelings of self-efficacy are related to the generalized expectancy of being able to cope successfully with prospective stressors. Self-efficacious persons will typically persist in active efforts to reduce stress, while those who see themselves as less efficacious tend to lack persistence and to utilize avoidance responses (path E). Active coping responses should reduce exposure to stress (path F') as well as moderate the effects of stress when it occurs (path I). Mastery of previous stressful circumstances can increase feelings of self-efficacy and reduce the use of defensive and avoidance-oriented coping styles. The effects of a sense of mastery may also extend to the development and use of social-environmental resources (path A), which themselves affect coping and depression (paths G and H).

Attributional Styles

Cognitive styles that are thought to be relatively stable and to affect perceptions of stressful circumstances have received considerable attention. Much of this work centers on the issue of perceived controllability and personal attribution of causality of the outcomes of stressful situations. The learned helplessness model hypothesizes that the lack of contingency between an individual's coping responses and environmental outcomes produces a generalized belief in the uncontrollability of the environment which relates to depression directly (path D) and indirectly by inhibiting active coping responses (path E) (Seligman, 1975). This belief, with its associated behavioral passivity (path E) and depressive affect (paths D and I), insulates the individual from future counteractive experiences of environmental control.

Beck's cognitive theory holds that persons with a strong predisposition to assume personal responsibility for negative outcomes are prone to depression (Beck, 1967, 1974). Such individuals are filled with self-blame that may cause depression (path D) and their pessimistic view of their future effectiveness can adversely affect their coping responses (path E). Beck postulates that depressives' cognitive appraisals are characterized by several distortions: arbitrary inferences—conclusions unwarranted by the situation; selective abstractions—not considering all elements of a situation; magnification/minimization—distortions of the significance of an event; and overgeneralization—drawing inappropriate conclusions given minimal evidence. Such appraisals are thought to promote attributions of failure in mastery situations to personal rather than environmental factors, thereby reinforcing depressive cognitive schemas (path E').

The learned helplessness and cognitive self-blame theories have been viewed as complementary (e.g., Akiskal & McKinney, 1975). However, Abramson and Sackeim (1977) point out that these two theories have conceptually contradictory positions on the role of perceived controllability of stressful events. Merging these models could create "the paradoxical situation of individuals blaming themselves for outcomes they believe they neither caused not controlled" (p. 843). In exploring such a paradox, Peterson (1979) found that depressives do have a tendency toward contradictory attributions, viewing stressful events as externally controlled yet blaming themselves for unsuccessful resolutions of such events. Additional theory development (see Abramson, Seligman, & Teasdale, 1978; Garber & Hollon, 1980) has suggested that depressives view themselves as personally incompetent in handling stressful situations which they perceive as being handled adequately by other persons (i.e., who are internally controlled).

While research has indicated an association between certain attributional dispositions and depression, we know little of how such factors shape the appraisal of specific environmental stressors (path E). Thus, the consistency with which these attributions will be observed across different stressful situations is unclear. We later consider specific attributional responses that have been measured within the context of particular events in discussing the appraisal and coping domain of our framework. We also explore the mechanisms whereby treatment procedures that focus on these styles may alleviate or prevent depression.

Interpersonal Skills and Orientation

Interpersonal skills and social competence are important aspects of personal resources (Heller, 1979; Tyler, 1978). Depression-prone persons are thought to display low social competence, including social passivity, inadequate verbal activity and communication skills, and an inability to serve as a source of positive reinforcement to others (Lewinsohn, 1974; McLean, 1981). The etiologic effects of impaired social skills, passivity, and dysfunctional interpersonal perceptions on depression have been noted frequently (e.g., Paykel, Weissman, & Prusoff, 1978; Sanchez & Lewinsohn, 1980; Hammen, Jacobs, Mayol, & Cochran; 1980). Effective interpersonal skills may prevent depression by fostering social resources and coping responses (paths A and E) that can help to avoid stressors or to mediate the impact of stressors that do occur. There is evidence that depressed persons have less effective social skills and that improving such skills can enhance their levels of social reinforcement, ease discomfort in social situations, and reduce their stress levels (Youngren & Lewinsohn, 1980). Furthermore, marital communication and conflict-resolution skills can preserve major sources of environmental support (path A) and reduce exposure to such stressors as marital separation and divorce (paths B and C).

Certain individuals may not be oriented toward utilizing their interpersonal skills and social resources to deal with stressors. Although there is little research on this issue among depressed patients, Tolsdorf (1976) noted that psychiatric patients are not inclined to tap the resources of their social environments. In a community sample, Brown (1978) identified subsets of nonhelpseekers who were either unaware of existing sources of informal help or viewed them as ineffective. These groups displayed lower self-esteem and less effective coping responses than self-reliant non-helpseekers and helpseekers. Coyne (1976a) found that depressive persons used help-seeking behaviors (such as soliciting support at inappropriate times and from inappropriate persons) that sharply limited the potential support available to them. In combination with a lack of interpersonal skills, a negative orientation toward help-seeking reduces the development of supportive social ties (path A). Subsequent experiences of stress and depression thus might confirm depressive persons' negative appraisal of their social environments (path G'), and thereby compound the adversity of their life circumstances.

A diverse set of personal factors has been linked to a susceptibility to depression. While we have sought to explicate some of the connections comprising the subdomains mentioned, additional integrative research is needed. For instance, what roles do self-concept factors such as self-esteem and sense of mastery play in developing and applying social skills? In what cases may deficits in certain personal resources be compensated for by attributional styles or other resources? To move beyond an examination of isolated sets of person-centered variables, researchers need to consider coping and social resources as mediators through which personal factors may affect depression. For example, we have noted that persons with an internal locus of control are less likely to become depressed given the occurrence of stressful events. In exploring how this effect is mediated, the framework suggests considering both the direct effects of this resource on functioning (path D), as well as its indirect effects via appraisal and coping (paths E and I). We also need to examine how depression can adversely affect future personal resources, as well as how successful coping with potentially depressogenic stressors can facilitate the development and maintenance of such resources (paths D' and E').

ENVIRONMENTAL RESOURCES

Supportive interpersonal relationships are a major component of a person's social-evironmental resources. These social resources provide companionship, emotional support, cognitive guidance and advice, material aid and services, and reaffirmation of normative social role expectations. Access to new sources of support may also be provided via the interpersonal relationships that characterize social networks (Mitchell & Trickett, 1980). The development of these resources is influenced by an individual's personal resources (path A). These resources are also shaped by the physical and architectural features of community settings and by the organizational and suprapersonal characteristics (that is, average characteristics of individuals inhabiting a setting) of these interpersonal contexts (Moos & Mitchell, in press). We focus here on the functional effects of environmental resources rather than on their determinants.

Social-environmental resources may have both positive and negative effects on personal functioning. Theorists have suggested that deficits in such resources may lead to depression (path H) due to the unavailability or lack of social reinforcers, or both (Costello, 1972; Lewinsohn, 1974). A direct relationship between a lack of support and depression has been noted in surveys of community samples (Andrews, Tennant, Hewson, & Vaillant, 1978; Costello, in press; Lin, Simeone, Ensel, & Kuo, 1979). Social-environmental factors may also have indirect effects. For instance, impaired communication processes and friction in interpersonal relationships can indirectly promote depressive symptomatology (Bothwell & Weissman, 1977) by fostering stress or leading to ineffective coping responses (paths C and G).

Among positive effects, the stress-buffering value of social support has been most frequently noted (Cassel, 1976; Cobb, 1976; Dean & Lin, 1977). There is evidence that social support attenuates the relationship between depressive symptomatology and stressful life events among community (Billings & Moos, 1981; Wilcox, 1981) and depressed patient respondents (Brown, 1979; Weissman & Paykel, 1974), as well as among individuals experiencing such stressors as pregnancy and childbearing (Wandersman, Wandersman, & Kahn, 1980), job strain and job loss (Gore, 1978; LaRocco, House, & French, 1980), and bereavement (Hirsch, 1980). The presence of social support may positively influence stressor-related appraisals and provide the resources necessary for effective coping that underlie the "buffering" effect (path G). Although there are many different sources of support, we focus here on family and work settings as two primary sources of environmental resources.

Family Support

Family members are a central source of emotional and material resources. Depression is associated with marital dissatisfaction (Coleman & Miller, 1975) as well as with disruption of the marital relationship (Bloom, Asher, & White, 1978). In a study of depressed patients, Vaughn and Leff (1976) found that the amount of criticism expressed toward the patient by family members at the time of hospitalization was a significant predictor of relapse during the posthospitalization period. In studies of a general community group, persons living in families that were less cohesive and expressive, and had more inter-personal conflict reported, more symptoms of depression than those living in more supportive families (Billings & Moos, in press-b). In another community survey, Pearlin and Johnson (1977) found that married persons reported less depression than did the unmarried, even after controlling for such sociodemographic factors as gender, age, and ethnicity. In probing the determinants of this difference, persons who were married were found to be less exposed to various life strains (path C) such as occupational stress and economic hard-ship. Married persons were still less depressed than the unmarried after equating for levels of strain, indicating that married persons are less vulnerable to the effects of such strains, possibly because they have more sources of available support.

Work Support

The work setting is a potential source of support and stress. Work support is highest for persons who are highly involved in their jobs, have cohesive relationships with co-workers, and have supportive su-pervisors who encourage job involvement through work innovation and participation in decision making (Cooper & Marshall, 1978). In a com-munity sample, Billings and Moos (in press-a) found that employees who perceived their work settings as high on these dimensions reported fewer symptoms of depression. These support factors also attenuated the depressive effects of work stress among men, but less so among women (see also House, 1981). A supportive work setting may diversify one's social resources by serving as an alternate source of interpersonal support. Conversely, work stress can erode family support (path C'). For instance, Billings and Moos (in press-a) noted that men whose wives were employed in stressful job settings tended to report less family support and more depression that men whose wives had non-stressful jobs.

Indirect and Reciprocal Effects

Environmental resources may affect depression by facilitating effective coping with minor stressors, thereby circumventing the occurrence of major stressors (path G; see Billings, Mitchell, & Moos, 1981). The availability of social relationships can also provide the necessary context for certain coping responses (such as help-seeking and comparing one's situation to that of others) that may be particularly effective in preventing or alleviating stress (path C). In addition, the appraised severity of a stressor may be attenuated by the awareness that supportive resources are available to resolve a problematic situation (path G). For instance, Gore (1978) found that persons with high support perceived less financial stress due to a job loss than did those with less support, even though there were no differences between high and low support groups in their objective financial hardship.

Conversely, depression may affect environmental resources by leading to an erosion of social support (path H'). Depressed persons often elicit negative reactions from friends and family members (Lewinsohn & Schaffer, 1971; McLean, 1981; Weissman & Paykel, 1974). When friends and relatives are unsuccessful in controlling and reducing the individual's distress they may become hostile, withdraw their support, and eventually avoid interaction (Coates & Wortman, 1980). Concurrent elevations in the depressive symptomatology of spouses and family members of depressed patients (Coleman & Miller, 1975; Rubenstein & Timmins, 1978) may reflect a cyclic process that reduces family support and exacerbates stress for all members. Depression can also reduce support by impairing future social initiative and social skills which are necessary to maintain social resources (via paths D' and A).

Clinicians who plan intervention efforts need to employ an expanded perspective to understand the varied aspects of social support and the different mechanisms of its effects. For instance, low social resources may be sufficient to induce depression in the absence of stress. Conversely, high stress and/or a lack of adaptive personal factors may be sufficient to cause depression even in the presence of supportive environmental resources. The framework suggests that environmental supports shape and are shaped by personal resources and levels of functioning, as well as by stressors and coping responses. Practitioners thus need to consider support in the context of these other domains. In addition, to understand the evolution of a depressive episode and plan effective treatment, clinicians must plan interventions to overcome the negative effects that depression can have on the individual's social resources.

APPRAISAL AND COPING RESPONSES

Our framework indicates that cognitive appraisal and coping responses can help an individual avoid depression by mediating the potential effects that stressors have on functioning (paths F and I), as well as by avoiding stressors (path F'). An appraisal involves the perception and interpretation of environmental stimuli. Appraisals are an iterative component of the coping process in which initial appraisals are followed by specific coping responses, and by reappraisal and possible modification of coping strategies (Lazarus, 1981). Our inclusion of appraisal and coping in a common domain reflects the interconnected and inseparable nature of these processes. We use appraisal and coping to refer to the particular cognitions and behaviors emitted in response to specific events. These specific behaviors are influenced by the "traitlike" attribution factors described earlier as personal resources and by the individual's environmental resources, which provide the context for coping. Current research has not always observed this distinction between personal resources and general attribution patterns and appraisal and coping responses to specific stressors.

While several attempts have been made to formulate a classification system for categorizing various appraisal and coping responses, no accepted method has yet emerged. We organize these dimensions into three sub-domains: (1) appraisal-focused coping—efforts to define and redefine the personal meaning of a situation; (2) problem-focused coping—behavioral responses to modify or eliminate the source of stress by dealing with the reality of the situation; and (3) emotion-focused coping—functions oriented toward managing stress-elicited emotions and maintaining affective equilibrium (Moos & Billings, 1982).

Appraisal of Stressors

Much of the research on the appraisal of stressful events has evolved from the self-blame and learned helplessness theories of depression. For example, among college students and depressed patients, Krantz and Hammen (1979) found a consistent relationship between depressive symptoms and scores on the *Cognitive Bias Questionnaire,* a measure of the distortions outlined by Beck. Hollon and Kendall (1980) have also shown that depressives score higher on an inventory of cognitive distortions and negative self-statements potentially triggered by stressful events. Although it is possible that depression may exacerbate "depressive" appraisals (path I), Golin, Sweeney, and Schaeffer (1981) found that such appraisals were more likely to preceed than to follow an increase in depressive symptomatology (i.e., path I is stronger than path I').

The attribution of causality is an important aspect of the reformulated learned helplessness model. Abramson et al. (1978) hypothesize that individual attributions of the *causes* of a stressful event and perceived coping ability vary along three dimensions: (a) internal vs. external to self, (b) stable vs. unstable, and (c) global vs. situation- or role-specific. For example, given the stressor of unemployment and unsuccessful job search, attributions might be to either internal causes such as personal characteristics like lack of employment-related skills, or to external causes such as job discrimination. Stable causal attributions imply that future job-seeking efforts are likely to result in a similar lack of success. Global causal attributions, such as a general lack of perceived self-efficacy, would involve role performances in addition to employment and job hunting. Presumably, persons are more likely to remain free of depression if they attribute causality of negative outcomes to characteristics of stressors that are external to the self, that vary across situations, and that relate to a restricted area of performance. Operationalizing these factors with their *Scale of Attributional Style,* Seligman and his colleagues (Seligman, Abramson, Semmel, & von Baeyer, 1979) found that the appraisals of depressed and nondepressed college students differed in expected directions along these dimensions.

However, several recent studies have failed to find inconsistent relationships between these three attributional dimensions (internality, stability, and globality) and depression among college student samples (e.g., Golin et al., 1981; Harvey, 1981; Pasahow, 1980). Extending research on these attributional processes to patient populations, Gong-Guy and Hammen (1980) utilized an attribution questionnaire to assess respondents' appraisals of recent stressful events as internal, stable, global, expected, and intended. Depressed and nondepressed outpatients showed expected differences along these dimensions in the appraisal of their most upsetting event, but not in their appraisals of all recent stressors (see also Hammen & Cochran, 1981). The reconciliation of these findings is complicated by divergence in the content of current measures. For example, the *Cognitive Bias Questionnaire* and the *Scale of Attributional Style* are both correlated with depressive symptoms, even though they are only moderately related to each other (Blaney, Behar, & Head, 1980).

Stressor-Appraisal Specificity

Our framework indicates that the appraisal process is at least partially determined by the type of stressor (path F). In fact, studies employing heterogeneous samples of stressors (e.g., Dohrenwend & Martin, 1979; Fontana, Hughes, Marcus, & Dowds, 1979) have indicated that appraisal may be more closely related to event characteristics (path F) than personal characteristics (path E). Clinical theories have emphasized the interaction between personal factors and predispositions to appraise stressors in characteristic ways. Much of the laboratory research, however, has focused on the appraisals and effects of success versus failure outcomes in experimental tasks, such as solving anagram problems. Thus, there is little information on the extent to which stable attributional styles are linked to specific appraisal responses (paths E and E').

While conceptual and measurement issues have received increasing attention, we as yet know little of the actual appraisals made by depressed persons in their natural environments. Observed differences between depressed and non-depressed respondents in their appraisals of questionnaire-based scenarios of stressful events may not reflect their appraisals of actual personal stressors (Hammen & Cochran, 1981) Studies are needed to examine the extent to which the attributional styles of depressed individuals are related to their appraisals of real-life stressors. Current conceptualizations also need to be reviewed and elaborated. For instance, depressed persons may be "accurate" in perceiving stressors as personally uncontrollable and their personal and environmental resources as being inadequate. In this regard, there is evidence that normals have positively biased and self-serving attributions of causality (for a review, see Miller & Ross, 1975), while depressives may have "accurate" perceptions rather than negative biases. During recovery, depressed persons' perceptions of their competence and control may become somewhat less realistic by moving toward the self-enhancing bias of nondepressed persons (Lewinsohn, Mischel, Chaplin, & Barton, 1980).

Coping Responses

We now consider the problem-focused and emotion-focused cognitions and behaviors that occur in response to appraised stressors. Relevant studies have examined the coping responses of depressed patients as well as the responses associated with depression among community groups. As with other domains, coping responses may attenuate the depressive effects of stress (paths F and I) or directly reduce or prevent the stressor (path F'). Coping patterns may also be influenced by the fact that depression can develop into a syndrome that requires coping efforts (path I'). For example, insomnia, weight loss and memory problems can influence current coping responses and may require additional coping efforts to alleviate the stress they themselves engender.

The interplay between appraisal and coping responses among a community group has been explored by Coyne, Aldwin, and Lazarus (1981). They compared the coping responses of 15 persons falling within the depressed range of the Hopkins Symptom Checklist (on two occasions) with 72 persons who did not meet this criterion at either assessment. Although the depressed and nondepressed group did not differ in the type or perceived significance of stressful events encountered, there were differences in appraisal and coping responses. Depressed persons tended to appraise situations as requiring more information before they could act, and to view fewer events as necessitating acceptance and accommodation. They were also more likely to use such responses as seeking advice and emotional support and engaging in wishful thinking. However, there were no differences in the amount of problem-focused coping or use of self-blame, as might be predicted from the learned helplessness model. These findings are consistent with the idea that depressed persons find it difficult to make decisions and wish to be completely certain prior to either taking action or electing to view the objective characteristics of the stressor as outside of their control (Beck, Rush, Shaw, & Emery, 1979).

Billings and Moos (1981) evaluated the efficacy of various classes of coping responses among a representative community sample. Coping responses to a recent stressful event were assessed according to the method (active-behavioral coping, active-cognitive coping and avoidance coping) and focus of coping (problem-focused, emotion-focused). The use of avoidance responses, which serve to avoid actively confronting a problem or to reduce emotional tension by such behavior as increased eating or smoking, was associated with greater depressive symptomatology. In contrast, the use of active-cognitive and active-behavioral coping attenuated the depressogenic effects of stressful life events.

Some investigators have examined how individuals cope with the stress of being depressed. Funabiki and his colleagues (Funabiki, Bologna, Pepping, & Fitzgerald, 1980) developed a method of assessing the thoughts and behaviors college students use in coping with a depressive episode (see also McLean, 1981). Depressed students were more likely to be preoccupied with their stress-related emotions and to seek help from other depressed persons. However, these students also reported the use of efforts to counteract depression (tell myself things to cheer me up and try something new). Self-preoccupation may not be entirely maladaptive as it may provide an opportunity to identify environmental and intrapsychic contingencies relevant to depression. In this connection, structured self-monitoring of mood and activity can be effective in treating depressed patients (Harmon, Nelson, & Hayes, 1980).

Help-Seeking

Since social resources can be an important source of protection against the depressive effects of stressful events, help-seeking behaviors that tap or generate these resources are a key class of coping responses. Indeed, over half of the individuals who experience a troubling event will seek some help (Gourash, 1978). While preliminary, there is some evidence that the nature and success of help-seeking may differentiate depressed and nondepressed groups. The nature of these differences is complex, as shown by the unexpected finding of Pearlin and Schooler (1978) that those who sought help in handling a stressful event reported more depression than those who relied on their own personal resources.

To understand the link between help-seeking responses and depression, we need to consider the impact that coping repsonses and depressive symptomatology may have on an individual's social resources (paths G' and H'). Help-seeking together with the expression of distress may have mixed effects on these resources. Howes and Hokanson (1979) found that undergraduates expressed more overt reassurance and sympathetic support to a "depressive" than to a normal role confederate. However, Coyne (1976a) found that subjects conversing with a depressed patient were themselves more depressed and anxious, and tended to covertly reject the patient. Hammen and Peters (1977, 1978) also report results indicating the covert rejection of depressed partners, although depressive behavior was more acceptable from women than from male partners. Thus, certain patterns of help-seeking may be more intense than is appropriate for the strength, intimacy, and context of the relationship.

While help-seeking in the context of depression may elicit superficial support in brief encounters with strangers, its long-term consequences on more intimate relationships may be negative. Intimates may initially offer mollifying support to aid the depressed person and to control that person's expression of hysphoria, which intimates find aversive. Intimates may suppress the direct expression of their own negative reactions to the depressives' behavior (Coyne, 1976b). However, these initial responses often fail to provide the validation that depressives seek for the appropriateness of their stress reactions. This ambiguity in the "supportive" communications of others exacerbates stress (path C), and fails to provide the feedback necessary to guide the depressive's coping responses (path G) that might effectively reduce dysphoria.

Increased help-seeking and expression of depressive behaviors, so as to draw more convincing and effective support, may lead to an increase in intimates' efforts to control and minimize depressive symptomatology (Coates & Wortman, 1980). The failure of social network members to control the expression of distress produces frustration and more negative attitudes toward the depressed person. It may be at this point that the negative and rejecting responses of intimates and family members (e.g., Salzman, 1975; McLean, 1981) are frankly expressed. Network members' expression of negative reactions and withdrawal from their relationship with the stressed individual may have adverse effects on that individual's coping and functioning (paths G and H), and may heighten susceptibility to depression by decreasing the individual's self-esteem (path A).

The effects of various help-seeking responses should be explored in the context of particular stressors. The chronicity of the stressor may be a particularly relevant dimension. For instance, obtaining help from informal sources may be most advantageous in coping with discrete, time-limited stressors. When the stressor is of a more chronic nature (e.g., long-term unemployment or physical disability), individuals may "burn-out" their social resources by overreliance on an informal social network. Professional or institutionalized sources of support may be especially important in handling chronic or major stressors that surpass the individual's social resources. Similarly, normative life stage stressors, such as marriage and childbirth, elicit institutionalized support responses while unexpected events, such as divorce, have no guides for help-seeking.

SOCIAL BACKGROUND FACTORS

Epidemiological research has shown that depression is related to such demographic factors as socioeconomic standing and gender (Radloff, 1977; Weissman & Klerman, 1977; Weissman & Myers, 1978). We view these factors as distal determinants of depression, via their influence on the other domains included in the framework.

Social Status

Individuals of lower social status (that is, those with lower education, income, and occupational levels) are more likely to become depressed. As suggested by the "social causation" and "social selection" hypotheses, social status has links to each of the domains in our framework that may help to explain its association with depression (Liem & Liem, 1978). The social causation hypothesis holds that those of lower status experience a greater number of environmental stressors. For example, such persons are exposed to unemployment, financial setbacks, poor health and a variety of other stressors (Kessler, 1979).

The social selection hypothesis holds that those of lower social status are more vulnerable to the effects of stress. Such vulnerability may be due to the lack of supportive social resources (Myers, Lindenthal, &

Pepper, 1975), to fewer personal resources, or to less effective coping responses. In this connection, Pearlin and Schooler (1978) found that less efficacious coping responses were overrepresented among those of lower social standing. In comparison to upper class women, lower class women tend to use fewer active and preparatory coping responses and more avoidance and fatalistic responses in dealing with childbearing (Westbrook, 1979). These responses were associated with greater anxiety and sense of helplessness. Our framework suggests that factors related to both social causation and social selection underlie the link between social status and depression.

Gender Differences

Depression is more common among women than among men, but the determinants of this gender difference remain controversial. While space does not permit a complete review of the extensive literature, we indicate how our framework can be used to explore this issue. In general, there is evidence that women are more exposed to environmental stressors (Dohrenwend, 1973). In addition, differences in the types of events experienced may mediate differences in the amount of stress. For example, men report more work and economic stressors, while women report more health and family-related events (Billings & Moos, 1981b; Folkman & Lazarus, 1980).

Women may also be more vulnerable to the effects of stressors (Radloff & Rae, 1979). This vulnerability may derive from gender differences in personal and environmental resources. For instance, women are more likely to be pessimistic and lack self-esteem (Altman & Wittenborn, 1980; Cofer & Wittenborn, 1980); and to favor a field dependent cognitive style that may sensitize them to social and interpersonal stressors (see Witkin & Goodenough, 1977). Furthermore, marriage per se is not as protective for women as it is for men (for a review, see Weissman & Klerman, 1977), and, conversely, marital conflict and dissatisfaction is less strongly related to depression among women than among men (Coleman & Miller, 1975; Weiss & Aved, 1978). However, women's vulnerability to depression can be reduced by the presence of an intimate and confiding relationship with a husband or male partner (Brown & Harris, 1978).

Gender differences in appraisal and coping are largely unexplored.

There is some evidence that women use coping responses that are less effective in attenuating the depressive effects of stress. In a previously described study, Billing and Moos (1981) found that women made greater use of avoidance coping, which was itself associated with depression. This difference remained even after controlling for gender differences in the source and severity of stressors. This finding is consistent with analyses of other community samples, which have identified a tendency for women to use less effective coping methods (Folkman & Lazarus, 1980; Pearlin & Schooler, 1978). Funabiki et al. (1980) also noted several gender differences among a group of depressed students. Compared to depressed men, depressed women ate more, more frequently engaged in self-deprecation, and avoided large social gatherings but sought personal contact from meetings with friends. Lastly, differences between men and women in each of the domains may interact in a synergistic process which contributes to gender differences in the incidence, duration and prevalence of depression.

IMPLICATIONS FOR RESEARCH AND PREVENTION

Having reviewed research on each of the domains in the framework, we now consider the clinical implications of our perspective. Much of the research on the treatment of depression has been concerned with evaluating and comparing the outcomes of different treatment regimens. We use our framework to interpret the results of such clinical trials. The domains we have identified also provide a means of describing the recovery and relapse process, and of evaluating the determinants of posttreatment functioning. Lastly, we consider the potential roles of these factors in the design and effectiveness of prevention programs.

Comparing the Effectiveness of Psychosocial Treatments

Current intervention programs differ in the specific sets of factors in the model that are targeted for change. Some interventions are aimed primarily at personal resources by attempting to enhance self-concept and change maladaptive cognitive styles, or to modify depressogenic attributional styles. Cognitive therapies also seek to change appraisal and coping responses by teaching the patient to identify distorted appraisals and to replace them with more realistic perceptions (Beck et al., 1979; Rush, Beck, Kovacs, & Hollon, 1977). Since depressed persons tend to exaggerate the negative aspects of their environment and bahavior, such treatment often leads to a decrease in negative and self-derogatory thoughts and an increase in positive self-statements and cognitive self-reinforcement. Other interventions have focused on other personal factors and aspects of coping, such as improving problem-solving and social skills and monitoring positive and negative environmental reinforcers (e.g., Lewinsohn, Biglan, & Zeiss, 1976). Some interventions aim to enhance environmental resources by improving the supportiveness of family and other interpersonal relationships, and by modifying how patients cope with the social consequences of their disorder (e.g., McLean, 1981; Shaw, 1977; Weissman, 1979).

A series of controlled clinical trials have demonstrated that these interventins reduce depression for a significant number of patients (Hollon & Beck, 1978). While comparisons between psychosocial interventions sometimes show differential effectiveness, the most compelling conclusion is that all treatments are more effective in alleviating depression (alone and in combination with pharmacotherapy) than placebo or non-intervention control conditions (Kovacs, 1980; Weissman, 1979). For example, Zeiss, Lewinsohn, and Munoz (1979) found that several different treatment programs, interpersonal skills training (a personal resource), cognitive modification (appraisal and coping), and pleasant events scheduling (environmental resources and coping) were equally effective in reducing depression. All three groups of treated patients increased their social skills and pleasant activities and decreased their dysfunctional cognitions. Differential improvement in the three areas was not specifically related to receiving the treatment that targeted one of these modalities.

Why are conceptually different interventions comparable in their effectiveness in alleviating depression? Zeiss and her colleagues view their results as reflecting nonspecific effects that combine to increase personal self-efficacy. Frank (1974) states that the central determinant of treatment effectiveness lies in the amelioration of clients' frustration with their unsuccessful problem-solving efforts and in the restoration of their morale. Alternatively, our framework suggests multiple sources of treatment effectiveness that can be identified in different treatment procedures.

Since there are complex linkages between the domains shown in the framework, changes in a domain targeted by a specific treatment procedures may affect, or be affected by, changes in other domains. This situation complicates inferences about the reasons for changes "resulting from" an intervention intended to affect a cluster of variables within a single domain. For example, although cognitive treatment specifically seeks to modify maladaptive cognitive schemas, this intervention may also affect appraisal and preferred coping responses (path E), and the orientation toward social resources (path A), all of which may influence depression. Similarly, interventions designed to improve social skills and increase positive events may also reduce stress (path B), increase supportive social resources (path A), and provide new coping alternatives (path E), all of which may affect depression. Different treatment procedures may thus obtain similar effects because of the interrelationships among the sets of factors involved in depression.

These considerations indicate that treatment effectiveness might be maximized by targeting multiple domains within a broad spectrum program. For example, recent efforts have combined cognitive and behavioral techniques with social resources interventions by including the functioning and attitudes of the depressed person's spouse and family members within the scope of treatment (see McLean & Hakistan, 1979; Rush, Shaw, & Khatami, 1980). Programs of training in the development of more effective cooping responses to ongoing or expected stressors can decrease the risk of stress-related relapse. Such programs may achieve their effectiveness by increasing the supportiveness of important relationships, reducing the negative attitudes that social network members have developed toward the depressed patient, and facilitating the generalization of treatment gains to a range of natural settings.

Exploring the Determinants of Posttreatment Functioning

Treatment increases the probability of recovery and even untreated depression usually shows remission. However, the longer-term outcomes of clinical depression are less positive. More than 50% of depressed patients seem to relapse within one year regardless of whether they have received either psychosocial therapy, pharmacotherapy, or a combination of the two (Keller & Shapiro, 1981; Kovacs, Rush, Beck, & Hollon, 1981; Weissman & Kasl, 1976). What factors determine whether individuals will relapse or maintain recovery? While socioeconomic status, pretreatment functioning, and treatment experiences are related to outcome, these factors typically account for less than 25% of the variance in posttreatment functioning, depending on the outcome criterion involved (e.g., McLean & Hakistan, 1979).

Given that the domains identified in our framework contribute to the onset of depression, they also warrant consideration as determinants of posttreatment functioning. For example, patients who experience stressful life events are more likely to relapse. However, those with adequate personal and environmental resources and effective coping responses may be most able to "resist" relapse-inducing influences that occur subsequent to the termination of treatment. In assessing these domains as determinants of the posttreatment functioning of alcoholic patients, Cronkite and Moos (1980) found that stressors, coping, and family resources had a strong impact on outcome. The long-term effects of pretreatment and treatment-related variables (e.g., amount and type of treatment) may be mediated by these posttreatment factors. Cross, Sheehan, and Kahn (1980) found that treated patients subsequently made more use of informal social resources for guidance and problem-solving than did untreated controls. Two treatment approaches which differed in their outcome effectiveness were also associated with differential increases in patients' use of these social resources. Thus, persons who are initially more severely depressed and receive less treatment, are likely to experience more posttreatment stressors, to use less effective coping resources, and to show poorer posttreatment functioning.

Increased understanding of the posttreatment determininants of recovery provides a basis for improving clinical assessment and intervention techniques so as to maximize treatment effects and their maintenance. Therapists need to consider the depressed persons' stress levels, social-environmental resources and coping responses to maximize positive treatment outcome. Current and future advances in assessment techniques (see Moos & Billings, 1982; Moos & Mitchell, in press) can facilitate screening for relevant deficits and disturbances in these areas. The development of an integrated battery of measures of the type and amount of environmental stress, along with assessments of the individual's relevant social environments (e.g., work, family) and methods of coping, would be particularly valuable in planning treatment and aftercare. Better understanding of extratreatment factors may also increase patient compliance and reduce the number of early dropouts. It would also be informative to study concurrent changes in stress levels and social resources that may reduce depression and lead to early termination of treatment. Assessment of such changes may clarify the differential role of formal and informal sources of assistance in recovering from depression.

Developing Prevention Programs

The effectiveness of prevention programs is often viewed as stemming from one of two sources: a reduction in exposure to stressors or an increase in individuals' resistance to such stressors (Kessler & Albee, 1977). Given the interconnectedness of the domains included in our framework, preventive interventions may simultaneously focus on both these sources. Interventions aimed at bolstering personal and social resources may decrease stressors as well as increase resistance. For example, community interventions such as block clubs and neighborhood social organizations (see Wandersman & Giamartino, 1980) facilitate neighborhood improvements in housing and safety and thereby enhance members' physical and social-environmental resources. These interventions may simultaneously reduce such stressors as the amount of actual and feared crime. Changes in work settings, such as reorganizing assembly line workers into work groups responsible for a more substantial proportion of the final product, may promote cooperation and social support from coworkers and potentially reduce such work stressors as boredom, lack of involvement in decision making, and uncontrolled work pressure.

Community groups and agents such as neighborhood and parent groups, lawyers, youth recreation leaders, hairdressers, and bartenders may provide important sources of informal social support (Gottlieb, 1981). Programs designed to foster the support-giving skills of such individuals may increase the social and coping resources in depressed persons' extended social networks, and thereby serve to enhance their adaptation. Similarly, preventive interventions may be aimed at smaller social units, such as families, and at particular stressors, such as bereavement and divorce, that are especially likely to elicit depressive outcomes. For example, a self-help program for widows might have multiple intervention foci: providing increased social support, cognitive guidance and modeling of effective coping responses to grief, and assistance in resolving economic, social, and personal stressors that can accompany the death of a spouse (Rogers, Vachon, Lyall, Sheldon, & Freeman, 1980). The framework presented here can be a guide for planning prevention programs and for developing program evaluations which yield information on the process as well as the outcomes of interventions.

SUMMARY

We have presented an integrative conceptual framework that considers both stressful life circumstances and factors that foster well-being and protect against depressive outcomes. This framework suggests that there are multiple pathways to depression. A lack of personal and environmental resources may be "sufficient" to lead to depression. While stressful circumstances may predispose to depression, the presence of supportive resources and adaptive appraisal and coping responses may moderate the adverse effects of stress, and thus prevent a serious depressive outcome. Future research and clinical interventions should benefit from considering a broad spectrum of factors that are capable of utillizing the interconnectedness of the domains we have identified. Since personal and environmental factors are often slow to change, and since the elimination of stress is neither feasible nordesirable, appraisal and coping may be a pivotal factor to be addressed by treatment and pevention programs. Most importantly, a conceptual framework such as the one we have presented here, can help clinicians and researchers to organize the rapidly expanding information on the development and treatment of depression and to formulate more integrated plans for future research and intervention.

REFERENCES

Abramson, L. Y. & Sackeim, H. A paradox in depression: Uncontrollability and self-blame. *Psychological Bulletin,* 1977, **84,** 838–851.

Abramson, L. Y., Seligman, M. E. P., & Teasdale, J. D. Learned helplessness in humans: Critique and reformulation. *Journal of Abnormal Psychology,* 1978, **87,** 49–74.

Akiskal, H. S., & McKinney, W. T. Overview of recent research in depression. *Archives of General Psychiatry,* 1975, **32,** 285–305.

Altman, J. H., & Wittenborn, J. R. Depression prone personality in women. *Journal of Abnormal Psychology,* 1980, **89,** 303–308.

Andrews, G., Tennant, C., Hewson, D., & Vaillant, G. Life event stress, social support, coping style, and risk of psychological impairment. *Journal of Nervous and Mental Disease,* 1978, **166,** 307–316.

Bandura, A. Self-efficacy: Toward a unifying theory of behavioral change. *Psychological Review,* 1977, **84,** 191–215.

Bandura, A. Self-referent thought: The development of self-efficacy. In J. H. Flavell & L. D. Ross (Eds.), *Cognitive social development: Frontiers and possible futures.* New York: Cambridge University Press, 1980.

Beck, A. T. *Depression: Clinical, experimental and theoretical aspects.* New York: Harper & Row, 1967.

Beck, A. T. The development of depression: A cognitive model. In R. Friedman & M. Katz (Eds.), *The psychology of depression: Contemporary theory and research.* Washington D. C.: Winston, 1974.

Beck, A. T., Rush, A. J., Shaw, B. F., & Emery, G. *Cognitive therapy of depression.* New York: Guilford, 1979.

Becker, J. Vulnerable self-esteem as a predisposing factor in depressive disorders. In R. A. Depue (Ed.), *The psychobiology of the depressive disorders: Implications for the effects of stress.* New York: Academic Press, 1979.

Billings, A. G., Mitchell, R. E., & Moos, R. H. *Social support and well-being: Research implications for prevention programs.* Paper presented at the Annual Meeting of the American Psychological Association, Los Angeles, 1981.

Billings, A. G., & Moos, R. H. Work stress and the stress-buffering roles of work and family resources. *Journal of Occupational Behaviour,* in press. (a)

Billings, A. G., & Moos, R. H. The role of coping responses and social resources in attenuating the impact of stressful life events. *Journal of Behavioral Medicine,* 1981, **4,** 139–157.

Billings, A. G., & Moos, R. H. Social support and functioning among community and clinical groups: A panel model. *Journal of Behavioral Medicine,* in press. (b)

Blaney, P. H., Behar V., & Head, R. Two measures of depressive cognitions: Their association with depression and with each other. *Journal of Abnormal Psychology,* 1980, **89,** 678–682.

Bloom, B., Asher, S. J., & White, S. W. Marital disruption as a stressor: A review and analysis. *Psychological Bulletin,* 1978, **85,** 867–894.

Bothwell, S., & Weissman, M. M. Social impairments four years after an acute depressive episode. *American Journal of Orthopsychiatry,* 1977, **47,** 231–237.

Brown, B. B. Social and psychological correlates of help-seeking behavior among urban adults. *American Journal of Community Psychology,* 1978, **6,** 425–439.

Brown, G. W. The social etiology of depression. In R. A. Depue (Ed.), *The psychobiology of the depressive disorders: Implications for the effects of stress.* New York: Academic Press, 1979.

Brown, G. W., & Harris, T. O. *Social origins of depression: A study of psychiatriac disorder in women.* New York: Free Press, 1978.

Calhoun, L. G., Cheney, T., & Dawes, A. S. Locus of control, self-reported depression, and perceived causes of depression. *Journal of Consulting and Clinical Psychology,* 1974, **42,** 736.

Cassel, J. The contribution of the social environment to host resistance. *American Journal of Epidemiology,* 1976, **104,** 107–123.

Coates, D., & Wortman, C. B. Depression maintenance and interpersonal control. In A. Baum & J. E. Singer (Eds.), *Advances in environmental psychology* (Vol. 2). Hillsdale, N.J.: Lawrence Erlbaum, 1980.

Cobb, S. Social support as a moderator of life stress. *Psychosomatic Medicine*, 1976, **38**, 300–314.

Cofer, D. H., & Wittenborn, J. R. Personality characteristics of formerly depressed women. *Journal of Abnormal Psychology*, 1980, **89**, 309–314.

Coleman, R. E., & Miller, A. G. The relationship between depression and marital maladjustment in a clinic population: A multitrait-multimethod study. *Journal of Consulting and Clinical Psychology*, 1975, **43**, 647–651.

Cooper, G. L., & Marshall, J. Sources of managerial and white collar stress. In C. L. Cooper & Payne (Eds.), *Stress at work*. New York: Wiley & Sons, 1978.

Costello, C. G. Depression: Loss of reinforcers or loss of reinforcer effectiveness? *Behavior Therapy*, 1972, **3**, 240–247.

Costello, C. G. Social factors associated with depression: A retrospective community study. *Psychological Medicine*, in press.

Coyne, J. C. Depression and the response of others. *Journal of Abnormal Psychology*, 1976, **85**, 186–193.(a)

Coyne, J. C. Toward an interactional descripton of depression. *Psychiatry*, 1976, **39**, 28–40.(b)

Coyne, J. C., Aldwin, C., & Lazarus, R. S. Depression and coping in stressful episodes. *Journal of Abnormal Psychology*, 1981, **90**, 439–447.

Cronkite, R. C., & Moos, R. H. The determinants of posttreatment functioning of alcoholic patients: A conceptual framework. *Journal of Consulting and Clinical Psychology*, 1980, **48**, 305–316.

Crook, T., & Eliot, J. Parental death during childhood and adult depression: A critical review of the literature. *Psychological Bulletin*, 1980, **87**, 252–259.

Cross, D. G., Sheehan, P. W., & Kahn, J. A. Alternative advice and counsel in psychotherapy. *Journal of Consulting and Clinical Psychology*. 1980, **48**, 615–625.

Dean, A., & Lin. N. The stress buffering role of social support. *Journal of Nervous and Mental Disease*, 1977, **165**, 403–417.

Dohrenwend, B. S. Social status and stressful life events. *Journal of Personality and Social Psychology*, 1973, **28**, 225–235.

Dohrenwend, B. S., & Dohrenwend, B. P. (Eds.). *Stressful life events: Their nature and effects*. New York: Wiley, 1974.

Dohrenwend, B. S., & Martin, J. L. Personal versus situational determination of anticipation and control of the occurrence of stressful life events. *American Journal of Community Psychology*, 1979, **7**, 453–468.

Endicott, J., & Spitzer, R. L. A diagnostic interview: The Schedule for Affective Disorders and Schizophrenia. *Archives of General Psychiatry*, 1978, **35**, 837–844.

Folkman, S., & Lazarus, R. S. An analysis of coping in a middle-aged community sample. *Journal of Health and Social Behavior*, 1980, **21**, 219–239.

Fontana, A. F., Hughes, L. A., Marcus, J. L., & Dowds, B. N. Subjective evaluation of life events. *Journal of Consulting and Clinical Psychology*, 1979, **47**, 906–911.

Frank, J. D. Psychotherapy: The restoration of morale. *American Journal of Psychiatry*, 1974, **131**, 271–274.

Funabiki, D., Bologna, N. C., Pepping, M., & Fitzgerald, K. C. Revisiting sex differences in the expression of depression. *Journal of Abnormal Psychology*, 1980, **89**, 194–202.

Garber, J., & Hollon, S. D. Universal versus personal helplessness in depression: Belief in uncontrollability or incompetence? *Journal of Abnormal Behavior*, 1980, **89**, 56–66.

Golin, S., Sweeney, P. D., & Schaeffer, D. E. The causality of casual attributions in depression: A cross-lagged panel correlational analysis. *Journal of Abnormal Psychology*, 1981, **90**, 14–22.

Gong-Guy, E., & Hammen, C. L. Causal perceptions of stressful events in depressed and nondepressed outpatients. *Journal of Abnormal Psychology*, 1980, **89**, 662–669.

Gottlieb, B. H. (Ed.). *Social networks and social support*. Beverly Hills: Sage Publications, 1981.

Gore, S. The effect of social support in moderating the health consequences of unemployment. *Journal of Health and Social Behavior*, 1978, **19**, 157–165.

Gourash, N. Help seeking: A review of the literature. *American Journal of Community Psychology*, 1978, **6**, 413–423.

Hammen, C. L., & Cochran, S. D. Cognitive correlates of life stress and depression in college students. *Journal of Abnormal Psychology*, 1981, **90**, 23–27.

Hammen, C. L., Jacobs, M., Mayol, A., & Cochran, S. D. Dysfunctional cognitions and the effectives of skills and cognitive-behavioral training. *Journal of Consulting and Clinical Psychology*, 1980, **48**, 685–695.

Hammen, C. L., & Peters, S. D. Differential responses to male and female depressive relations. *Journal of Consulting and Clinical Psychology*, 1977, **45**, 994–1001.

Hammen, C. L., & Peters, S. D. Interpersonal consequences of depression: Responses to men and women enacting a depressed role. *Journal of Abnormal Psychology*, 1978, **87**, 322–332.

Harmon, T. M., Nelson, R.O., & Hayes, S. C. Self-monitoring of mood versus activity by depressed clients. *Journal of Consulting and Clinical Psychology*, 1980, **48**, 30–38.

Harvey, D. M. Depression and attributional style: Interpretations of important personal events. *Journal of Abnormal Psychology*, 1981, **90**, 134–142.

Heller, K. the effects of social support: Prevention and treatment implications. In A. P. Goldstein & F. H. Kanfer (Eds.), *Maximizing treatment gains: Transfer enhancement in psychotherapy*. New York: Academic Press, 1979.

Hirsch, B. Natural support systems and coping with major life changes. *American Journal of Community Psychology*, 1980, **8**, 159–172.

Hollon, S. D., & Beck, A. T. Psychotherapy and drug therapy: Comparison and combinations. In S. L. Garfield & A. E. Bergin (Eds.), *Handbook of psychotherapy and behavior change: An empirical analysis*. (2nd ed.). New York: Wiley & Sons, 1978.

Hollon, S. D., & Kendall, P. C. Cognitive self-statements in depression: Development of an automatic thoughts questionnaire. *Cognitive Therapy and Research*, 1980, **4**, 383–395.

House, J. S. *Work stress and social support*. Reading, Mass: Addison-Wesley, 1981.

Howes, M. J., & Hokanson, J. E. Conversational and social responses to depressive interpersonal behavior. *Journal of Abnormal Psychology*, 1979, **88**, 625–634.

Johnson, J. H., & Sarason, I. G. Life stress, depression and anxiety; Internal-external control as a moderator variable. *Journal of Psychosomatic Research*, 1978, **22**, 205–208.

Kanner, A. D., Coyne, J. C., Schaefer, C., & Lazarus, R. S. Comparison of two modes of stress measurement: Daily hassles and uplifts versus major life events. *Journal of Behavioral Medicine*, in press.

Kasl, S. V. Epidemiological contributions to the study of work stress. In C. L. Cooper & R. Payne (Eds.), *Stress at work*. New York: Wiley, 1978.

Keller, M. B., & Shapiro, R. W. Major depressive disorder: Initial results from a one year prospective naturalistic follow-up study. *Journal of Nervous and Mental Disorders*, 1981, **169**, 761–768.

Kessler, R. A strategy for studying differential vulnerability to the psychological consequences of stress. *Journal of Health and Social Behavior*, 1979, **20**, 100–108.

Kessler, M., & Albee, G. W. An overview of the literature of primary prevention. In G. W. Albee & J. M. Joffe (Eds.), *Primary prevention of psychopathology: The issues* (Vol. 1). Hanover, New Hampshire: University Press of New England, 1977.

Kobasa, S. C. Stressful life events, personality, and health: An inquiry into hardiness. *Journal of Personality and Social Psychology*, 1979, **37**, 1–11.

Kovacs, M. The efficacy of cognitive and behavior therapies for depression. *The American Journal of Psychiatry*, 1980, **137**, 1495–1501.

Kovacs, M., Rush, A. J., Beck, A. T., & Hollon, S. D. Depressed outpatients treated with cognitive therapy or pharmacotherapy. *Archives of General Psychiatry*, 1981, **38**, 33–39.

Krantz, S., & Hammen, C. L. Assessment of cognitive bias in depression. *Journal of Abnormal Psychology*, 1979, **88**, 611–619.

LaRocco, J. M., House, J. S., & French, J. R. P. Social support, occupational stress, and health. *Journal of Health and Social Behavior*, 1980, **21**, 202–218.

Lazarus, R. S. The stress and coping paradigm. In C. Eisdorfer, D. Cohen, A. Kleinman, & P. Maxim (Eds.), *Theoretical bases for psychopathology*. New York: Spectrum, 1981.

Lazarus, R. S., & Cohen, J. B. Environmental stress. In I. Altman & J. F. Wohlwill (Eds.), *Human behavior and the environment: Current theory and research* (Vol. 1). New York: Plenum, 1977.

Lefcourt, H. M. *Locus of control: Current trends in theory and research*. Hillsdale, N.J.: Lawrence Erlbaum, 1976.

Lewinsohn, P. M. A behavioral approach to depression. In R. Friedman & M. Katz (Eds.), *The psychology of depression: Contemporary theory and research*. New York: Wiley, 1974.

Lewinsohn, P. M., Biglan, T., & Zeiss, A. Behavioral treatment of depression. In P. O. Davidson (Ed.), *Behavioral management of anxiety, pain, and depression*. New York: Brunner-Mazel, 1976.

Lewinsohn, P. M., Mischel, W., Chaplin, W., & Barton, R. Social competence and depression: The role of illusory self-perceptions. *Journal of Abnormal Psychology*, 1980, **89**, 203–212.

Lewinsohn, P. M., & Schaffer, M. Use of home observations as an integral part of the treatment of depression: Preliminary report and case studies. *Journal of Consulting and Clinical Psychology*, 1971, **37**, 87–94.

Liem, R., & Liem, J. Social class and mental illness reconsidered: The role of economic stress and social support. *Journal of Health and Social Behavior*, 1978, **19**, 139–156.

Lin, N., Simeone, R., Ensel, W. M., & Kuo, W. Social support, stressful life events, and illness: A model and an empirical test. *Journal of Health and Social Behavior*, 1979, **20**, 108–119.

Lindenthal, J. J., & Myers, J. K. The New Haven longitudinal study. In I. G. Sarason & C. D. Spielberger (Eds.), *Stress and anxiety* (Vol. 6). Washington, DC: Hemisphere, 1979.

Maas, J. W. Biogenic amines and depression. *Archives of General Psychiatry*, 1975, **32**, 1357–1361.

McLean, P. D. Behavioral treatment of depression. In W. E. Craighead, A. E. Kazdin, & M. J. Mahoney (Eds.), *Behavior modification: Principles, issues, and applications.* Boston: Houghton Mifflin, 1981.

McLean, P. D. & Hakistan, A. R. Clinical depression: Comparative efficacy of outpatient treatments. *Journal of Consulting and Clinical Psychology,* 1979, **47,** 818–836.

Miller, D. T., & Ross, M. Self-serving biases in the attribution of causality: Fact or fiction? *Psychological Bulletin,* 1975, **82,** 213–225.

Mitchell, R. E., & Trickett, E. J. Social networks as mediators of social support: An analysis of the effects and determinants of social networks. *Community Mental Health Journal,* 1980, **16,** 27–44.

Moos, R. H., & Billings, A. G. Conceptualizing and measuring coping resources and processes. In L. Goldberger & S. Breznitz (Eds.), *Handbook of Stress: Theoretical and clinical aspects.* New York: Macmillan, 1982.

Moos, R. H., & Mitchell, R. E. Conceptualizing and measuring social network resources. In T. A. Wills (Ed.), *Basic processes in helping relationships.* New York: Academic Press, in press.

Myers, J. K., Lindenthal, J. J., & Pepper, M. P. Life events, social integration and psychiatric symptomatology. *Journal of Health and Social Behavior,* 1975, **16,** 421–427.

Overall, J. E., & Zisook, S. Diagnosis and the phenomenology of depressive disorders. *Journal of Consulting and Clinical Psychology,* 1980, **48,** 626–634.

Pasahow, R. J. The relation between an attributional dimension and learned helplessness. *Journal of Abnormal Psychology,* 1980, **89,** 358–367.

Paykel, E. S. Recent life events in the development of the depressive disorders. In R. A. Depue (Ed.), *The psychobiology of the depressive disorders: Implications for the effects of stress.* New York: Academic Press, 1979.

Paykel, E. S., Weissman, M. M., & Prusoff, B. A. Social maladjustment and severity of depression. *Comprehensive Psychiatry,* 1978, **19,** 121–128.

Pearlin, L.I., & Johnson, J. Marital status, life strains, and depression. *American Sociological Review,* 1977, **42,** 704–715.

Pearlin, L. I., & Schooler, C. The structure of coping. *Journal of Health and Social Behavior,* 1978, **19,** 2–21.

Perlmuter, L. C., & Monty, R. A. *Choice and perceived control.* Hillsdale, N.J.: Lawrence Erlbaum, 1979.

Peterson, C. Uncontrollability and self-blame in depression: Investigation of the paradox in a college population. *Journal of Abnormal Psychology,* 1979, **88,** 620–624.

Radloff, L. S. The CES-D Scale: A self-report depression scale for research in the general population. *Applied Psychological Measurement,* 1977, **1,** 385–410.

Radloff, L. S., & Rae, D. S. Susceptibility and precipitating factors in depression: Sex differences and similarities. *Journal of Abnormal Psychology,* 1979, **88,** 174–181.

Rogers, J., Vachon, M. L., Lyall, W. A., Sheldon, A., & Freeman, S. J. A self-help program for widows as an independent community service. *Hospital and Community Psychiatry,* 1980, **31,** 844–847.

Rubenstein, D., & Timmins, J. F. Depressive dyadic and triadic relationships. *Journal of Marriage and Family Counseling,* 1978, **4,** 13–23.

Rush, A. J., Beck, A. T., Kovacs, M., & Hollon, S. D. Comparative efficacy of cognitive therapy and pharmacotherapy in the treatment of depressed outpatients. *Cognitive Therapy and Research,* 1977, **1,** 17–36.

Rush, A. J., Shaw, B. F., & Khatami, M. Cognitive therapy of depression: Utilizing the couples system. *Cognitive Therapy and Research,* 1980, **4,** 103–113.

Salzman, L. Interpersonal factors in depression. In F. F. Flach & S. C. Draghi (Eds.), *The nature and treatment of depression.* New York: Wiley, 1975.

Sanchez, V., & Lewinsohn, P. M. Assertive behavior and depression. *Journal of Consulting and Clinical Psychology,* 1980, **48,** 119–120.

Seligman, M. E. P. (Ed.). *Helplessness: On depression, development, and death.* San Francisco: Freeman, 1975.

Seligman, M. E. P., Abramson, L. Y., Semmel, A., & von Baeyer, C. Depressive attributional style. *Journal of Abnormal Psychology,* 1979, **88,** 242–247.

Shaw, B. A comparison of cognitive therapy and behavior therapy in the treatment of depression. *Journal of Consulting and Clinical Psychology,* 1977, **45,**543–551.

Sundberg, N. D., Snowden, L. R., & Reynolds, W. M. Toward assessment of personal competence and incompetence in life situations. *Annual Review of Psychology,* 1978, **29,** 179–221.

Tolsdorf, C. C. Social networks, support, and coping: An exploratory study. *Family Process,* 1976, **15,** 407–417.

Tyler, F. B. Individual psychological competence: A personality configuration. *Educational and Psychological Measurement,* 1978, **38,** 309–323.

Vaughn, C. E., & Leff, J. P. The influence of family and social factors on the course of psychiatric illness: A comparison of schizophrenic and depressed neurotic patients. *British Journal of Psychiatry.* 1976, **129,** 125–137.

Wandersman, A., & Giamartino, G. A. Community and individual difference characteristics as influences on initial participation. *American Journal of Community Psychology,* 1980, **8,** 217–228.

Wandersman, L., Wandersman, A., & Kahn, S. Social support in the transition to parenthood. *Journal of Community Psychology,* 1980, **8,** 332–342.

Warheit, G. J. Life events, coping, stress, and depressive symptomatology. *American Journal of Psychiatry.* 1979, **136,** 502–507.

Weiss, R. L., & Aved, B. M. Marital satisfaction and depression as predictors of physical health status. *Journal of Consulting and Clinical Psychology,* 1978, **46,** 1379–1384.

Weissman, M. M. the psychological treatment of depression: Evidence for the efficacy of psychotherapy alone, in comparison with, and in combination with pharmacotherapy. *Archives of General Psychiatry.* 1979, **36,** 1261–1269.

Weissman, M. M., & Kasl, S. V. Help-seeking in depressed outpatients following maintenance therapy. *British Journal of Psychiatry,* 1976, **129,** 252–262.

Weissman, M. M. & Klerman, G. L. Sex differences and the epidemiology of depression. *Archives of General Psychiatry.* 1977, **34,** 98–111.

Weissman, M. M., & Myers, J. Affective disorders in a U.S. urban community: The use of Research Diagnostic Criteria in an epidemiological survey. *Archives of General Psychiatry,* 1978, **35,** 1304–1311.

Weissman, M. M., & Paykel, E. S. *The Depressed woman: A study of social relationships.* Chicago: University of Chicago Press, 1974.

Wells, L. E., & Marwell, G. *Self-esteem: Its conceptualization and measurement.* Beverly Hills, CA: Sage Publications, 1976.

Westbrook, M. T. Socioeconomic differences in coping with childbearing. *American Journal of Community Psychology,* 1979, **7,** 397–412.

White, R. B. Current psychoanalytic concepts of depression. In W. E. Fann, I. Karacan, A. D. Pokorny, & R. L. Williams (Eds.), *Phenomenology and treatment of depression.* New York: Spectrum, 1977.

Wilcox, B. L. Social support, life stress, and psychological adjustment: A test of the buffering hypothesis. *American Journal of Community Psychology,* 1981, **9,** 371–386.

Witkin, H. A., & Goodenough, D. R. Field dependence and interpersonal behavior. *Psychological Bulletin,* 1977, **84,** 661–689.

Youngren, M. A., & Lewinsohn, P.M. The functional relationship between depression and problematic interpersonal behavior. *Journal of Abnormal Psychology,* 1980, **89,** 333–341.

Zeiss, A. M., Lewinsohn, P. M., & Munoz, R. F. Nonspecific improvement effects in depression using interpersonal skills training, pleasant activity schedules, or cognitive training. *Journal of Consulting and Clinical Psychology,* 1979, **47,** 427–439.

12. Depression: A Comprehensive Theory

Ernest S. Becker

Schizophrenia sums up man's coming of age in society. In order to understand it we have had to trace a lengthy picture of the process of becoming human. Depression is much more simple. Unlike the schizophrenic, the depressed person has not failed to learn secure answers to the four common human problems. His dilemma, if anything, is somewhat of a paradox: he has learned these answers *only too well*. He has built himself so firmly into his cultural world that he is imprisoned in his own narrow behavioral mold.

If the theory on schizophrenia has been hampered by an ingrown psychoanalysis and nearly stifled by the medical affiliations of psychiatry, what are we to say about depression? "Incredible" is the only word that comes to mind—absolutely incredible. The only thing to which the theory of depression—largely a psychoanalytic one—can be reasonably compared, is to the Eskimo explanation of *piblokto*. How else can we make sense out of the classification of "wet" and "dry" depression—depending on the amount of the patient's saliva? How else can we consider subdivisions like "shame depression," "guilt depression," and "depletion depression"? How else can we justify the magical use of electroshock, an idea inspired from slaughterhouses (Szasz, unpublished paper)—the sometimes therapeutic effects of which no one understands?

The psychoanalytic theory of depression, let it be admitted, has a certain alchemical beauty. The patient is designed on the model of a hydraulic machine, with certain outlets, and pipes which double back. There are control faucets and other "emergency dyscontrol" valves.[1] The center of the machine is a tank, with a reinforced, galvanized false bottom: It is here that the patient stores a hard core of "coercive rage." The various pipes, channels and outlets, and those that double back into the tank, transport this rage, as well as guilt, and "guilty-fear," in different directions. The depressed patient is considered to be a poorly socialized child—not fully adult. He retains, it is thought, unnatural dependencies, as well as strong aggressions created in his early years. All this is stored up in the tank. The apparatus is activated when the "overgrown child" meets a severe frustration—usually loss of a loved object, or some strong threat to his own satisfactions. It is then that he strives to make an adaptation. To avoid sketching the complex workings of the hydraulic machine, it is sufficient to note that the adaptation does not work. The various instinctive energies go off in all directions, and the patient is finally undermined by one that turns back, that can find no outlet. Thus, the primary cause of breakdown in depression is thought to be self-directed aggression. The patient bogs down into a pitiful self-accusation, whiningly protesting his worthlessness, his evil, his need to be punished. He seethes with hate, self-pity, stunted rage, and childish dependency. But this amalgam is not solvent in the tank, with the result that the mechanism can trickle to a stop. The depressed person can abandon all activity, let himself slide into the surrender of death.

For the most part, this model represents the advanced theoretical cogitations of the psychiatric profession on a perplexing human phenomenon. This much must be said: It is not easy to comprehend why anyone would opt out of life. It is understandable that we would be quick to look for some basic genetic taint, some stunted early development, that would mark such an individual off from others. But the matter is not quite so simple: The fact is that a good proportion of depressed patients have led mature and responsible lives; some have achieved notable success, financial and personal. We distort our vision if we use the above theory to explain why these people become abysmally depressed.

It is amazing that human action could have been so consistently and thoroughly conceived in instinctual and compartmentalized terms. It is to the credit of some psychoanalysts that they themselves have begun to break out of their own inherited theories, and to range more broadly for an explanation of depression.[2] This is part of the natural development of ego psychology. As the view of man as a cultural animal shaped by learning takes over from the older instinctive explanations, the way is clear for a full theoretical revolution. If the ego is the basis for action, and if a warm feeling of self-value must pervade one's acts, then it is only a step to focusing on the really crucial dynamic of a breakdown in action, namely, the undermining of the individual's sense of self-value.

Sap the individual's sense of self-righteousness and he is drained of his life-predication. This is the all-pervasive "slipping-away," the unspeakably, unbelievably "Frightful"—to use an apt word of Binswanger's.

Adler very early saw the importance of self-esteem in depression.[3] More recently, Bibring (1953) signalled a truly radical break with the older theory in psychoanalysis, by postulating that an undermining of self-esteem was the primary focus in depression, that it was principally to be understood as an ego-phenomenon, and only secondarily as a consequence of self-directed aggression.

It would be impossible to overestimate the significance of this shift in emphasis. In spite of Bibring's own protestations to the contrary, theories about the role of orality and aggression are now as outmoded as the hydraulic-tank model. If self-esteem is the primary focus of depression, then it is evident that cognition plays a larger role in its dynamics than does physiology. An ego-based theory of depression broadens the area of explanation from a purely "intra-psychic battle-field" to the entire range of social phenomena. Since the ego is rooted in social reality, since self-esteem is composed of *social* symbols and *social* motives, depression becomes a direct function of a cognitively apprehended symbolic world. Nothing less than a full sweep of cultural activity is brought into consideration in the single case of depression.

Little wonder, then, that more recently a crucial sociological dimension was added to the theory of depression—again from within psychoanalysis (Szasz, 1961, pp. 280–291). In the classical formulation of depressive, mourning and melancholic states, Freud had presented psychoanalysis with a model (1917). He postulated that since the ego grows by developing responses to and identifications with objects, the loss of an object was a threat to the ego. This, Freud reasoned, was the basic dynamic of mourning and melancholic states. The loss of an object in the real world meant a corresponding depletion in the ego; to relinquish a loved object was to subject oneself to a sometimes massive trauma. Freud theorized beautifully on the rather elaborate procedures that society sets up to ease this relinquishing of objects: the funeral rites, mourning rituals, and so on. There is nothing fundamentally wrong with Freud's view of depression[4]—it explains a good deal. Its principal drawback is that it is used to explain too much.

Szasz's objection to the traditional view of depression is precisely its insistence on the *predominant* importance of object-loss in unleashing dependency cravings and hostility. He proposes to emend this by stressing that the loss of "game" is fully as significant in depression as is the loss of object. "Game," in this context, is a series of norms or rules for significant action. And for the symbolic animal, there is nothing "playful" about significance. Szasz says:

> . . . persons need not only human objects but also norms or rules—or, more generally—games that are worth playing! [And he observes at greater length:] It is a matter of everyday observation that men suffer grievously when they can find no games worth playing, even though their object world might remain more or less intact. To account for this and similar events, it is necessary to consider the relationship of the ego or self to games. Otherwise, one is forced to reduce all manner of personal suffering to consideration of object relationships . . . Conversely, since loss of a real or external object implies the loss of a player from the game—unless a substitute who fits exactly can be found— such loss inevitably results in at least some changes in the game. It is thus evident that the words "player" and "game" describe interdependent variables making up dynamic steady states—for example, persons, families, societies, and so forth (1961, p. 282).

With this broadening out of traditional object-loss theory, there is no longer any valid pretense for keeping the phenomenon of depression within medicine. Psychoanalysis is fully linked here with social science. Since, as Szasz insists, objects and games are inseparably joined, self and society must be seen as a single phenomenon. People "create" objects by acting according to social rules. They "create" themselves as they create objects. Social rules and objects provide man with a staged drama of significance which is the theatre of his action. Man discovers himself by making appeal for his identity to the society in which he performs. To lose an object, then, is to lose someone to whom one has made appeal for self-validation. To lose a game is to lose a performance part in which identity is fabricated and sustained.

We noted before that answering the four common human problems gave the actor the one thing he needed most: the sentiment that he was an object of primary value in a world of meaning (Hallowell, 1955). Data from anthropology support this fundamental place of self-esteem in human action. It seems that nowhere on this once-vast globe has man been able to act unless he had a basic sentiment of self-value. Unless the individual feels worthwhile, and unless his action is considered worthwhile, life grinds to a halt. Whole cultures have begun to expire in this way: Melanesians, Marquesans, reservation Indians, and, for a time after 1929, the world of Wall Street.

THE FUNDAMENTAL IMPORTANCE OF MEANING

Self-value, then, and objects, are inseparable from a drama of life-significance. To lose self-esteem, to lose a "game," and to lose an object, are inseparable aspects of the loss of meaning. Meaning, we saw, is not something that springs up from within man, something born into life that unfolds like a lotus. Meaning is not embedded in some obscure "inner human nature," not something that is destined to be developed by successively "higher forms of life." There is, in short, nothing vitalistic or mysteriously emergent implied in the idea of meaning. Meaning is the elaboration of an increasingly intricate ground plan of broad relationships and ramifications. It is the establishment of dependable cause-and-effect sequences which permit ego-mastery and action. Meaning is at the heart of life because it is inseparable from dependable, satisfying action. Man embroiders his cause-and-effect action sequences with an intricate symbolism: flags, commandments, lace underwear, and secret-codes. The result is that particular kinds and sequences of action take on a life-and-death flavor. The dependable becomes the indispensable; the satisfying becomes the necessary. Man's symbolic life is an imbibing of meaning and a relentless creation of it. This symbolic elaboration of meaning is *Homo sapiens'* "home brew," so to speak, brought by him onto the evolutionary scene and manufactured solely for his use and delight. By means of it, man intoxicates himself into the illusion that his particular meaning-fabric, his culture's concoction of symbols and action, is god-given and timeless. In his imagination, man fuses symbols and action into a cohesion that has atomic tenacity.

Let us review here briefly how this comes about. Initially, meaning does not need language. We stressed that it exists in behavior. For energy-converting organisms, action is primary. Forward-momentum is enough to build meaning, and possibilities for forward-momentum exist in nature, in the animal's instinctive behavioral *umwelt,* in the world cut out for his perception and attention. Instinctive action gives experience which, in turn, provides meaning simply because it commands attention and leads to *further* action. But for the symbolic animal a complication enters: language replaces instinctive readiness. Man grows up naming objects for his attention and use. Language makes action broader and richer for the symbolic animal. But something curious occurs in this process: Language comes to be learned as a means of acting without anxiety. Each of the infant's acts comes to be dressed in words that are provided by his loved objects. As a child, lacking a word, he lacks a safe action. Action and word-prescriptions become inseparable, because they join in permitting anxiety-free conduct. Growing into adulthood, the individual has built his habits into a self-consistent scheme. To lack a word is then to lack a meaningful action: the simplest act has to take on meaning, has to point to something beyond itself, exist in a wider referential context. We become paralyzed to act unless there is a verbal prescription for the new situation.[5] Even our perceptions come to be built into a rigid framework. Man loses progressively the capacity to "act in nature," as he verbally creates his own action world. Words give man the motivation to act, and words justify the act. Life-meaning for man comes to be predominantly an edifice of words and word-sounds.

Now, the upshot of all this is crucial for our subsequent discussion of meaning-loss. It is simply this: When action bogs down—for any animal—meaning dies. For man, it suffices that verbal or purely symbolic action bogs down in order for meaning to die.[6] Having refined meaning with symbols, he is hopelessly dependent on the coherence of the symbolic meaning-framework. He is a slave to his own delicate handiwork. In other words, if the individual can keep verbal referents going in a self-consistent scheme, action remains possible and life retains its meaning. If he cannot, if the integrity of the symbolic meaning-framework is undermined, external action grinds to a halt. Let us see how this works in depression.

GUILT-LANGUAGE

Part of the reason for the grotesque nature of early psychoanalytic explanations of depression was the original grotesqueness of a major feature of the syndrome: the delusional self-accusations. That an individual would so malign himself without apparent cause seemed explainable only by postulating that he was intent on reducing himself to nothing—that his control over some deepseated aggressiveness had gone awry, and that this hate was now turned "against himself." This kind of interpretation is a blunder that we noted earlier in connection with the schizophrenic's imagined "sexuality": the patient's preoccupations are accepted at almost face value as part of an explanation of his condition. Thus, while pretending to "get behind" what is going on, the theorist actually is taken in by appearances. Perhaps this is inevitable in a complex young science. Perhaps, too, as James noted, it is difficult to back away and look clearly at data in which one is heavily invested, which strike at the core of one's own human susceptibilities.

The whole matter now has to be recast. Instead of asking "Why does the patient feel so humiliatingly guilty?" the question should be: "What is the patient trying to accomplish *with this particular language?* Two things, obviously, which everyone is always trying to accomplish, albeit with different means. They bear repeating: (1) The patient is trying to keep his identity self-consistent. (2) The patient is trying to entertain and elaborate the meanings of things. He is, in short, attempting to keep action going in the only way the human animal can. Depressive self-accusation is an attempted unplugging of action in the face of the Frightful, of the possibility that one's whole world will slip away.[7]

Take, as a direct example, a situation recently observed in Ghana by the anthropologist and psychiatrist M. J. Field (1960). Before Field's study, it used to be thought that depression was rare among the "simpler" peoples, and this for several reasons. For one thing, traditional societies enjoyed firmly institutionalized rituals and practices that provided dependable and ready "catharsis" for object-loss. Society united in working off anxieties attendant on the departure of one of its members; the bereaved person was supported by everyone in his grief. In sum, he lost an object only to gain—at least temporarily—a whole social performance world.

For another thing, it was thought that the absence of a Christian tradition of sinfulness lessened the accumulation of guilt so prominent in the depressive syndrome. And perhaps still another reason offered for the supposed rarity of depression in traditional society was the lingering myth that only industrial man was heroically subject to the psychic burdens of a complex, technological civilization.

But contrary to all this accumulated mythology, Field's study of rural Ghana shows that depression can be quite common in any disintegrating, individualistically anarchistic, or unreflective society. Depressed women in considerable number travel to Ashanti religious shrines, and there hurl accusations of vile witchcraft against themselves. They present a guilt-laden syndrome quite like that of our culture. The explanation is not far to seek and, as Field postulates, depression and witchcraft have probably had a long historical connection.[8] The self-accusation of witchcraft seems to provide the perfect justification for failure and worthlessness. In the case of the Ashanti woman the picture seems quite clear. She raises large families with extreme care, is an excellent housekeeper and businesswoman as well. There is enough significant activity in her life to provide ample self-justification. But often the fruit of her labor is lavished by the the husband on a younger bride, when the wife grows old.

This cruel turnabout is tolerated by the culture, and evidently it is a principal cause of anxiety on the part of aging wives. But the wife seems to have little say in the matter. How is she to justify this utter subversion of life-meaning? A life-plot that had consistency, integrity, and full social support is suddenly undermined. Fortunately, the culture itself provides a ready rationalization. Verbalizations are ready-made with which to construct a framework of meaning and justification; the continuity of the staged drama of one's life-experience need not be broken: the woman can simply acknowledge that *all along* she has been a witch. Thus the circle is closed: "I have become useless because I have always been evil. I deserve this fate. I deserve to be hated."

Field's observations on depression and self-accusation of witchcraft in Ghana can be safely generalized to depressive self-accusation in *any* culture. The individual gropes for a language with which to supply a meaning to his life-plot when all other props for meaning are pulled away. The alternative to this—namely, the realization that perhaps life *has no meaning*—is much more difficult to come by.[9] This apprehension is given to very few. It is even easier to speculate that *all* life may be in vain, than to admit that *one's* life has been. It may seem paradoxical that even in the extreme case of opting out of life, a meaning must be supplied: "Let me die *because* I am worthless." But this is no paradox. It is merely a continuation of the inescapable burden of fashioning a coherent identity to the very end.

The ego, after all, as we saw at some length previously, strives to create a continuity of integrated experience. As Erikson's work so eloquently shows, the identity is a painstakingly fashioned work of art.

it is symbolically constructed, and continually refashioned, never complete. In this sense, the individual can be compared to a movie director who is saddled with a lifetime job of staging a plot, the outcome of which he never knows. Indeed, he never knows what will happen in the *very next* scene, but he must strive to give the whole thing credibility and self-consistency. This he can only accomplish by reworking the previous material as new events joggle his creation. When one gets down to the last twenty years of this life drama, it becomes more and more difficult to justify abrupt changes in continuity: there is too much preceding plot for it to be remanipulated with ease. Whole portions cannot be reinterpreted with credibility, much less restaged. Hence, if the continuity is radically undermined the individual grasps at whatever straws his ingenuity can muster. No movie director would accept such an assignment, yet each individual is burdened with this ultimately and perilously creative task. This makes understandable the remark that an individual cannot know if his life has been satisfactory until the moment before he expires. It is symbolically reappraisable until the very last second. The proverbial drowning man whose life passes in review is merely exercising the last impulsion of the reclaiming artist.

When sharp changes take place in one's object world, the identity problem becomes severe: One's whole performance is in jeopardy. The identity has to be maintained even though an object which validated it is no longer available or a series of actions on which it was predicated is no longer possible or satisfying. In a desperate attempt at rearrangement, a proper framework of words is sought, which will sustain both the accustomed identity and the habitual action. Self-esteem, symbolic integrity of the identity and the life-plot, and the possibilities for continued action must all be provided for. This is no mean job, and the burden of it all is on *the proper word formula.* In the face of a frustrating problematic situation the individual has recourse to thought. The situation is juggled around, dissected, spread out, reworked, recombined— in fantasy—until a prescription for forward-momentum is hit upon. Basically, the individual has two alternatives: justify somehow a continuation of action in the old, habitual framework; or scrap the old action, habits, meanings entirely, and try to build a new framework of meaning. Obviously, this latter alternative cannot present itself as an immediate behavioral possibility; it means the abandonment of one's accustomed world, the suspension literally in a void, a plunge into the massive unknown, into the gaping chasm of anxiety.[10] Self-accusation, then, can be understood as a meaningful behavioral prescription within a *closed* behavioral world.

We know there is nothing straightforward about a rationalization. But it has taken us some time to realize that neither is there anything direct and explicit about most communication. Language grows up as a way of gently coercing others, of getting them to satisfy our needs. Primarily too, language grows up as a way of allaying anxiety of object-loss, separation, abandonment. Sullivan defined the self-system as a series of "linguistic tricks" by means of which we keep our world satisfying. But in each culture people communicate different things: the range of knowledge differs, and the kinds of things people become anxious about differ. Thus, stupidity and anxiety form a sieve through which explicit communications are filtered. Meanings tend to dwell under the surface, to explode in angry gestures, to linger in facial expressions, to be contained in an emphasis or a word arrangement that has nothing to do with the dictionary sense of the words. It almost seems as if "symbolic animal" is a misnomer: People are so inept at understanding and communicating their desires: the important problematic aspects of interpersonal situations are rarely made explicit. The reason is not far to seek: The individual doesn't know the performance style into which he has been trained; he doesn't know why he feels anxious at certain eventualities; he doesn't know why is trying to get the other person to do *just this* particular thing. In sum, most people, not knowing what has made them what they are, or made them want what they want, amble through life using hieroglyphics in a jet-age.

Jurgen Ruesch (1948) thought that the really mature person should be able to express symbolically all his desired meanings, including physiological urges. It remained for Thomas Szasz (1961) to show that when the individual does not control meanings symbolically, we call him "mentally ill." He showed that the prototype syndrome on which modern psychiatry was nourished refected a failure in communication. Hysteria is, in effect, stupidity. It bespeaks a failure to control symbolically the problematic aspects in a blocked action situation.[11] Each culture and each family unit places a burden of ingenuity on each individual they shape. Every individual has to keep action moving under sometimes severe vocabulary limitations. The rub is, that when the individual shows himself truly ingenious, we usually label him "mentally ill."[12] Thus it is with the hysteric who uses "body-language"; as well as with the depressed person who uses "guilt-language." Depressive self-accusation, in sum, amounts to a *search for a vocabulary of meaning* in the form of language substitute, a type of stupidity by someone poor in words.

Since psychiatrists as a whole do not understand what the patient is doing with this language, they often make his situation worse. They imagine that the "burden of guilt" would be relieved if he could release his "pent up anger" (remember the hydraulic-machine model). Hence, the psychiatrist explores with the patient valid reasons for hating his objects, hoping thereby to "bring up" the anger. this *may* result in bringing some critical clarity onto the situation. On the other hand, it may dissipate the guilt language, *which is the primary unplugging*. It may also fixate the patient onto his past, which is the one thing that is irrevocably lost, *because the present is so hopeless*. One patient complained that five years of talking with psychiatrists had made her illness worse precisely because it led to increased rumination about the past (Schwartz, 1961). If the psychiatrist is going to undermine the very creative efforts of the patient, then he should also take the next logical step, namely, help the patient break out of his constricted object range, and create a new life. "But the psychiatrist is not God." Let us, then, realize this and begin to act on the basis of it. In view of all damage that can be done in psychiatric consultations, perhaps after all the electroshock machine is the lesser of evils at the present time. By temporarily blotting out the patient's memory it allows him to discover to world anew (cf. Kelly, 1955, Vol. 2, pp. 905–908).

JEALOUSY-LANGUAGE

We are coming to understand that the language-thesis holds true for some forms of jealousy. Take the woman in our culture who helps her husband through college, but has to give up her own adumbrated career in order to do it. Subsequently she may find that her husband, increasingly successful, spends less and less time at home, takes her less into his confidence. She finds herself growing old, her children married, her husband distant and independent. She is in roughly the same position as the Ashanti woman, except that she has no witchcraft tradition to fall back on for ready rationalization of her sense of utter uselessness and worthlessness. However, the culture provides her with another language for protesting the gradual undermining of her self-esteem and identity, namely, the possibility that her husband is "cheating on her." To be adulterous is to fail to uphold one's part of the marriage bargain. This is obviously *the closest she can come* to adumbrating that he is "cheating *her,*" since the culture *does not give voice* to the idea that the frustrated career wife of a successful businessman *should* feel cheated when she has been well provided for. She may go to any length to imagine adulterous affairs of her husband, even in her own home while she sleeps upstairs. She senses that her world has been undermined and that she is being "defiled" literally at her very doorstep. But it is noteworthy that in these cases the woman rarely attempts to surprise "the lovers," even though ample opportunity presents itself. It is as though one fears undermining a rationalization that so perfectly sustains meaning. If the jealousy-language were to fail, one would be struck dumb.

Jealousy has manifold uses, as many investigators have determined. It can be a "defense mechanism" to cover one's own insecurities (Langfeldt, 1951). It can unplug action and bolster self-value in any number of ways (Shepherd, 1961). Minkowski, aware of the multiform uses to which jealousy can be put, made a distinction between jealousy based on the love relationship, and that based on other aspects of the interpersonal situation (1929). It is precisely this jealousy "inauthentique" that arises to unplug an intolerable situation when communication breaks down. Tiggelaar gets right to the heart of the matter: "This so-called jealousy seems to rise only from the bare personality, from the personality which is excluded from normal communication, especially owing to a fundamental change" (1956, p. 538). Inauthentic jealousy, in other words, like the body-language of the hysteric and the guilt-language of the depressed, is a pure creation of ingenuity in a hopelessly blocked situation. By means of jealousy-language the individual *draws himself* into a situation that excludes him; he creates a bond of self-reference, spans a serious and threatening breach in his world.

We are very far here from Freud's insight into the jealousy accusations of a 53-year-old woman patient (1920, pp. 213–218). One has only to read this case closely to see the possibility of a picture quite different from the one Freud imagined. He thought that the woman's delusional accusations of unfaithfulness, directed to her husband, were a mere cover for her own unconscious desires to commit infidelity with a younger man. But it seems obvious that, on the contrary, the woman's whole situation in the world was involved: her children grown up and married; her husband deciding to continue operating his factory instead of retiring and joining her at home. The young career girl with whom she imagined her husband having an affair had defied social convention, and had entered a man's world. She took business training rather than the domestic service customary to her class. Now she had a position at the factory as *a social equal* of the men, and was "even addressed as 'Miss.'"

One cannot make out, in Freud's account, any evidence for the woman's infatuation with her son-in-law—the desired infidelity that Freud claims he detected. Indeed, he says it was "unconscious." In a short two-hours of interviews with Freud, the woman had let fall only "certain remarks" which led Freud to his interpretation. Now, it is possible that this woman sensed the attractiveness of this young man, and assayed her own possible appeal to him, as women are wont to do. Perhaps this was the hint that Freud seized upon in the interview. It is possible too that at 53 she sensed the decline of her only (cultural) value to men—her physical charm. Whereupon she had only to compare herself to the girl at the factory who had chosen other means of performing in the male world. Thus, the wife, by accusing her husband of infidelity, may have been expressing a threat to her self, as well as giving oblique voice to the idea that the culture had cheated her. Now she was no longer attractive to men, *nor* could she ever have any active place in her husband's world. He had *chosen* not to retire, but instead to remain at the factory. She had no choice. As I read this woman's jealousy-language, it is a protest against cultural injustice: The world belonged to men, and to certain courageous women who opted for a career in that world.

It is typical both of psychoanalytic theory and of Freud personally, to have reduced this whole complex matter to a mere "unconscious" urge to fornication. Freud, as he demonstrated in his own life, in his actions toward his own wife (Fromm, 1959), could not have understood a female protest against inequality and a threat to self-value in a man's world. An inchoate female cry against helplessness and potential meaninglessness is thus reduced to a ubiquitous sexual motive. Reducing everthing to supposed instincts keeps the cultural world ethical and right. A real understanding of the complex human situation is sacrificed to the smug interpretations of an encapsulated theory—and to the morality of a Victorian world.

RANGES OF OBJECTS AND MEANING

It is pardonable for the theorist to make the error of narrowness when he is attempting to understand what is behind stupidity-languages. Stupidity-languages do make the person using them seem childish, whining, and somehow culpable in himself. the person provides a sorry spectacle when he tries to keep his world from caving in upon him with only the limited means at the disposal of his ingenuity. Thus it is logical to look for selfish motives in those who show themselves cognitively limited and childish. Perhaps this is another reason why theory has so long been hampered.

But people are not fated to *remain* childish, they are *kept* childish by parents and by culture. We train them to live in a certain kind of world, and to accept it dumbly. The culture, in other words, creates certain kinds of bondage from which people cannot be released without threatening others. Can a wife be released from a marriage contract when her husband begins neglecting her? Can she begin life anew at 40 when she has not previously provided herself with the werewithal? Can a factory-operator's wife suddenly join him at 53, untrained as she is, and basically unwanted in a man's world? Anthropology has provided us with the knowledge that there are any number of possible arrangements for human action, and that they all work—for better or for worse.[13] We have discovered that the word "natural" does not apply to human relationships: these are all learned. When we say that an individual's world "crumbles" we don't mean that his "natural" world crumbles—but rather that his cultural world does. If he had been taught to operate in another kind of world, it would perhaps not have crumbled. The Ashanti could have drawn up rules forbidding the taking of another wife, and the witchcraft depression syndrome would certainly be much reduced.

We saw that theorists have considered object-loss to be the principal cause for depression, and have overlooked the importance of "games" and meaning. One reason for this error of emphasis is that some cultures provide only a narrow range of objects and games. The result is that the object and the limited meaning come to be inseparable. That is to say, the more people to whom one can make appeal for his identity, the easier it is to sustain life-meaning. Object-loss hits hardest when self-justification is limited to a few objects. But object-loss is not crucial—or even necessarily important per se—when there is the possibility of sustaining one's conduct as before. Action is the basic problem in object-loss, and people devise ingenious ways to sustain it. An excellent illustration is the phenomenon of vengefulness. Harold F. Searles (1956) showed beautifully that the revenge process can serve as a way of *keeping the object*. It cannot be overstressed that an object is never an object per se, in isolation. It is a means of coming in contact with the world, it permits action. By definition, to constitute an object is to create a behavior pattern. To lose an object *is to lose the possibility of undertaking a range of satisfying action*. This is foremost. In addition, for man, the object is a private performance audience. It is a locus to which is addressed the continuing identity dialogue of the self and experience. The continued presence of the object, in other words, serves as a purchase to the symbolic elaboration of the self. The object need not be present in the outer world; one needs only to have developed behavior patterns toward it, or modeled on it, and to keep its image in mind. Thus, the object, exists on an internal-external continuum, it reflects a *process* of growth and activity in the actor. Just as the "external pole" serves as experiential contact with the outer world, so does the "internal pole" permit a continual fashioning of the identity. Hence we can see that object-loss means not only external performance loss, but inner identity loss as well. This bears repeating, because it enables us to understand the phenomenon of vengefulness. To hate and to seek revenge *is to create a continually present object*. Searles says that the vindictive person "has not really *given up* the other person toward whom his vengefulness is directed: that is, his preoccupation with vengeful fantasies about that person serves, in effect, as a way of psychologically *holding on to* him" (1956, p. 31). Vengefulness is a type of continuous performance, a way of maintaining an object that otherwise would not be there.

Initially, what we call the "superego" is the "internal pole" of our objects. We address our performance to them, by saying "See how well I am doing, as you would wish me to." Both action and identity are potentiated. The revenge-object is merely a variation on this. We keep it in order to be able to say: "See how great I have become, as you did not think I could become," etc. It has often been observed that the motif "I'll show the folks back in my home town" is a primary impetus to success. On the primitive level, revenge murders of the death of a loved one is simply a variation on this. One continues to perform *as if* the object were still there. The automatic nature of primitive revenge shows how important it is to *keep some kind of behavior pattern,* which serves in effect to keep the object. Vilification of the dead in mourning ceremonies is also a way of keeping behavior patterns toward the object. To remain silent is to be swamped by the action void.

Finally, "showing the folks back home" keeps the identity rooted in time, gives it the all-important duration and continuity. If one could not *keep* objects, the identity would have to be continuously recreated in the present. One would be in the position of Sartre's gambler: the entire past accretion of meanings would be severed. The identity owes its very existence to its rooting in the past.

We have a hard job—in our culture—in realizing how inseparable are object-range and performance-possibility. But consider the situation in traditional society. There the extended family is the rule, and not the small, tight, nuclear one that is familiar to us. The consequence of this is that the life-chances and life-meaning of the individual do not depend on a few parental objects. Meaning is generalized to a whole range of kin. The extended family provides a continuing source of esteem and affirmation for the individual actor, *even though significant figures drop out.*

In our culture we are familiar with the person who lives his life for the wishes of his parents and becomes depressed when they die and he has reached the age of forty or fifty. He has lost the only audience for whom the plot in which he was performing was valid. He is left in the hopeless despair of the actor who knows only one set of lines, and loses the one audience who wants to hear it. The extended family takes care of this problem: Even though it makes rigid prescriptions for the behavior of each individual, still each member can count on an audience for his continuing performance even after his own immediate parents die.

Thus, culture designs the action scene, and outlines the kind of crises to which the individual will have to adapt. One of the sharpest exposés of the grip in which culture holds the individual, and the breakdown which results from that grip, is Edmund Volkart's study of bereavement (1957). Volkart points out that restriction of the identity-appeal to only a few objects is a type of "psychological bondage." We train people to "love, honor, and obey" only a few others. And when death or some other train of events leaves the haplessly loyal person in the lurch, the psychiatrist is apt to hold a microscope to his body chemistry, or measure his saliva. Instead of providing for continuing life-designs, instead of training people in critical self-awareness, we actually facilitate the subversion of life-meaning. Volkart does not soft pedal this major personality issue, and I can do no better than to quote him directly:

> Any culture which, in the name of mental health, encourages extreme and exclusive emotional investments by one person in a selected few others, but which does not provide suitable outlets and alternatives for the inevitable bereavement, is simply altering the conditions of, and perhaps postponing, severe mental ill health. It may, in the vernacular, be building persons up for a big letdown by exacerbating vulnerability (1957, p. 304).

In other words, in our culture we champion limited horizons—a limited range of objects—and call people "mentally ill" when they suffer its effects. We make no provision for sustaining meaning when the bottom drops out of someone's life. When a woman's children marry, when the mirror begins to reflect the gradual and irrevocable loss of her charm, her performance as a responsible person, culturally desirable, is over. She may find herself left with no part to play, as early as her late 30's—with nothing to justify and sustain her identity. Since this utter subversion of meaning usually coincides with menopause, psychiatry has labelled the depression that may occur "involutional depression." Medical psychiatry has only recently come to focus on social role;[14] clinically, it was easier to imagine that the depression is somehow due to bodily changes. Or, the psychoanalytic theory might see this as a pampered self-pity over the imagined loss of sexual capacity, over the inevitable diminution in instinctual vigor.

Thus, in sum, we bring people up to be uncritical children, and wrench them with electroshock when their lives fail. We draw a portrait of man as a creature of instincts, and examine him pityingly and cynically. All this we do, in the name of "scientific" medical psychiatry, because most of us find the unexamined life worth living.

Students of epidemiology first took to studying the social distribution of types of illness in the hope of turning up some answers. Since clinical research did not provide any real understanding of the etiology of depression and schizophrenia, it was hoped that perhaps social research might. These early hopes proved elusive. Fact does not precede theory, and no amount of counting can ever explain. But statistics on epidemiology did provide some kind of picture. It now seems generally agreed that depression occurs more frequently among persons with cohesive family groupings; among women, who are more cohesively identified with close ingroups; in higher socio-economic statuses; in highly traditionalized groups; and among professionals.

Schizophrenia, on the other hand, presents a radically different epidemiological picture. It occurs more among men than women; in the lower socio-economic brackets; among dislocated peoples—that is, generally where group membership and identifications are weakest.

Mental illness, as we have been surveying it here, is a form of cultural and individual stupidity, an urge to meaning by those poor in command over vocabularies. If this thesis holds up we should expect some confirmation from the epidemiological picture: action varies according to class, as does awareness; possibilities for self-justification as well as degree of cultural indoctrination vary by class. Indeed, the class picture does seem to give some kind of consistent reflection of the views we have detailed.

If depression is a form of meaning-stupidity in an overwhelmingly frustrating situation, we would *expect* it to be more prevalent in the upper classes, among women, and among people in close identification with others. These are all people who feel that *they should* find their situation acceptable—but who somehow do not. The upper classes, having achieved socially approved success, have no reason to be unhappy. Women are given their status in the social structure as a matter of course, and should not question otherwise. People in close and "loving" identification with others are taught that they should derive all their life satisfactions from the quality of these relations, and from the pattern of rights and obligations which they entail. All the more reason that guilt should present itself as a natural alternative for deep-seated dissatisfaction: one can well believe himself guilty for not being content where he *should* be content. On the other hand, among the lower classes, dissatisfaction need not necessarily terminate in depressive self-accusation. Any number of scapegoats can be found and other rationalizations used, to justify failure: the rich, the boss, the low status of women in the lower class *as compared with* the upper, "bad luck," "hard times" and so on (cf. Prange and Vitols, 1962). In terms of alternative vocabularies of meaning, the lower classes, paradoxically, are less "stupid" than the upper.[15]

But the situation is quite different with the lower-class schizophrenic. He lacks even that meaning which belongs to his own class—since he has failed to learn to interact effortlessly. He joins a personal "poverty" to a class poverty; and it has been observed repeatedly that the extreme schizophrenic is more obedient and conservative in accepting ideal formulas for proper behavior than are his peers. He tends to conform to idealized behavioral standards which deprive him of the possibility of easy scapegoats available to those who flaunt standards.

The upper-class schizophrenic, on the other hand, is in a more fortunate situation. In the first place, he can effect *some measure of correspondence between his fantasy world* and certain specialized symbolic achievements provided by society. He has more of a chance of having his fantasies fed, and his identity somewhat validated. Clifford Beers, for example, could assume the identity of a mental-hygiene reformer, and create some measure of conformity between his omnipotent fantasies and the real action world.[16] Possibilities of symbolic self-justification are more available to upper- than to lower-class schizophrenics. Also, it is worth noting that the upper-class schizophrenic can usually extend his identity back in time, to include family traditions, roots in the Old World, illustrious ancestors, and so on. This socially supported extension of the self in time gives some experiential depth to the personality, and helps buffer present ineptitudes (Strauss, 1959, Chapter 6). The lower-class schizophrenic, on the other hand, has no such time depth to his identity, and must rely solely on fantasy and on the unrewarding contemporary situation. Rogler and Hollingshead observe bluntly on the extremely stressful and unrewarding nature of lower-class life: "The afflicted individual moves from an unpleasant world into an unreal world of fictions. These fictions may be equally unpleasant. Class V individuals are trapped" (1961, p. 185).

THE SYNDROMES AS STUPIDITY: A SUMMING-UP

Meaning-poverty then, depends on the type of stupidity. For the schizophrenic, shallowness of meaning, is a result of behavioral poverty; it reflects insufficient participation in interpersonal experiences. The depressed person, on the other hand, suffers instead from *a too uncritical participation in a limited range of monopolizing interpersonal experiences.* Here are two kinds of failure of the humanization process: the individual who has not been indoctrinated into his culture, and the one who has been *only too well* imbued with a narrow range of its sentiments. If both of these individuals end up in our mental hospitals, perhaps we cannot blame the psychiatrist for juggling chemicals and ignoring culture.[17] The problem seems to be individual rather than cultural. But this is only because one has a narrow medical view of human behavior. Individual and culture are inseparable. The individual finds answers to the four common problems in a cultural world. He finds himself enmeshed in the answers provided for by social institutions—by a whole accumulated tradition of cultural learning. In view of this the psychiatrist may object that it would be much too big a job for the medical practitioner to bring under critical fire the institutions of his society. How can he undertake to determine how people "should be" brought up? Quite right, he cannot. This is the task of a broad, unified human science.

Happily, after 50 years of incredible deviousness, the data of the human sciences are starting to emerge, their relationships are becoming clear. If this revolution, like any other, is to be successful, no vested institution can escape critical review. Nature—in her constitution of *Homo sapiens*—seems to have framed the four common human problems. But man—by his cultural and social world—frames the answers. Nothing done by man for man cannot be undone and redone. It suffices to design the problem.

This seems a good place, then, to round out conceptually our whole discussion of schizophrenia and depression. We might say that the stupidity of the schizophrenic lies in the fact that he *may* have simple *awareness* of multiple vocabularies of motive, but no corresponding firm and broad range of interpersonal behaviors. Hence, he has poor control over these vocabularies. The depressed person's stupidity, on the other hand, resides in the fact that he has firm patterns of interpersonal behavior, but a narrow repertory of explicit vocabularies of choice.

Now, one thing will be immediately obvious about this kind of sharp classification: it can rarely exist in reference to human nature as we have traced its complex development. Schizophrenic and depressive types merge into one another and overlap. They represent different kinds and degrees of adaptation to ranges of objects and events which are not mutually exclusive within one behavioral system. Thus we can see, at the end of this four-chapter presentation of the two major "syndromes," that they are not syndromes at all. Rather, they reflect the typical problems that man is prone to, the restrictions, coercions, the lack of control over behavior, and the confusions in symbolic reconstruction of himself and his experience. All this blends in varying proportions in the individual personality. If we can only rarely see clear "types" emerging from this, then there is all the more reason to reorient our approach to labelling the human personality.

NOTES

1. This model is reconstructed here with some artistic license. Admittedly, it is subjectively satirical, but the theoretical literature is there for all to see. For a sampling: Greenacre (1953), Hoch and Zubin (1954), and Rado (1951). For what seems to me a singularly sterile, reductionist approach conveying psychiatric scientism at its most forceful, see R. R. Grinker, Sr., *et al.* (1961). For example, buried on page 96, we find that a person becomes depressed because of object-loss and low self-esteem, which hypothesis renders completely redundant the arid tables and charts which stuff the book.

2. Among others, Mabel Cohen and her co-workers have taken steps to broaden theory. See Myer Mendelson (1960). Also, Rado's recent views (1961) tend away from the libidinal formulation.

3. But the modern Adlerian view of depression still sees the depressed patient predominantly as a spoiled child, rather than as an adult whose world may have gone wrong (Kurt Adler, 1961).

4. The sociological explanation of funeral and mourning rites is that they serve as the social dramatization of solidarity at the loss of one of society's performance members. Ceremonies of mourning serve to reaffirm social cohesiveness even though single performers drop out of the cultural action plot.

5. I am of course omitting consideration of the nondiscursive arts, and of action reduced to subconscious habit.

6. Cf. D.O. Hebb's observation that for man, cognitive processes in themselves have immediate drive value (1955), (an observation which indicates that psychology is belatedly emerging from its long scientistic moratorium; it is over eighty years since Alfred Fouillée elaborated the notion of *idées-forces*).

7. In this use, it is an inept attempt at coping—a feeble coping in Goldstein's sense—which, as previously noted, may avert a truly catastrophic breakdown.

8. Depression has also probably had a long historical connection with the self-effacement of mystics. John Custance (1951, pp. 61–62) compared his experiences during depression with the self-flagellation of Madame Guyon and St. Theresa.

9. Others make a similar observation: "Acknowledgment of personal sin or confession of guilt may sometimes be a defense against the possibility that there may be no meaning in the world . . . Guilt in oneself is easier to face than lack of meaning in life" (Lynd, 1958, p. 58). But I would not say "defense," rather, simply, *the only language* one knows. M. Schmideberg observes also that "Guilt implies responsibility; and however painful guilt is, it may be preferable to helplessness"

(1956, p. 476). For further remarks which are very much to the point of our discussion, see Charles Orbach and Irving Bieber (1957).

10. The nausea that sometimes accompanies depression may be due to the inability to place the world into meaningful interrelationships. This is the existential view— nausea as a reaction to meaninglessness. Alonzo Graves noted that he suffered attacks of nausea while engaged "in reflecting rather definitely over my situation and outlook" (1942, p. 678).

11. This is also very clear on the primitive cultural level, where hysteria is a common "syndrome." Cf. for example, Seymour Parker (1962).

12. Ingenuity in an infantile or "primitive" type of personality is often more clumsy. Cora Du Bois (1961, pp. 153–158) reports one case of "madness" from Alor that looks very much like the hysteric's "illness-language." This woman's attacks began a year after the death of her husband, when she was 35. She often repeated, in private, "This madness gives me much trouble." In view of her personal situation, and the abysmal cultural level of Alorese life, the phrase "This madness" seems very much like what Sullivan called the hysteric's "happy idea" (1956, p. 205), i.e., the ingenious language the hysteric hits upon to unplug a situation he does not understand.

13. In the light of our subsequent discussion on variations in range of objects provided by various cultures, see Seymour Parker's paper on the difference in symptomatology between the Eskimo and the Ojibwa (1962). Gien the Ojibwa's narrow range of objects and upbringing, depression, as Parker notes, is a logical reaction to frustration. The broad range of objects and the communal life among the Eskimo, on the other hand, seem literally to make impossible a depressive reaction (as we understand it here.)

14. Arnold Rose has correctly stressed the social role aspects of "involutional depression," namely, the loss of meaning (1962). His paper is part of a broad and growing attack on the narrow psychiatric jurisdiction over human failure. Its opening paragraph contains the keynote of this attack (p. 537). For some excellent case histories which reveal the restriction of interests to a few objects, the restriction of awareness, and the sudden undermining of occupational role, see: William Malamud, S. L. Sands, and Irene T. Malamud. (1941).

15. In a random observation, it seems that even the suicide notes left by individuals in the various classes vary in verbosity. A mere cursory scanning of the literature— which may be erroneous—seems to reveal that upper-class notes are invariably curt, containing little vocabulary other than that one is "tired" of living. Lower-class notes seem verbose in accusations of specific individuals, and sometimes of definite circumstances. See H. P. David and J. C. Brengelmann (1960).

16. See C. W. Beers (1960). It is noteworthy that when Beers smuggled a letter to the governor of the state, the governor read it and replied to it. Szasz opines that a letter signed "Clifford Whittingham Beers" would be attended to; whereas that of a hypothetical lower-class schizophrenic patient, say, "Joe Kowalski," would not (personal communication, cited with permission). The class difference in possibilities of self-justification made itself felt immediately in Beer's case.

17. A *note on mania:* Mania, often found to alternate with depressive states, offers a picture of such puzzling lack of control that even Harry Stack Sullivan thought it due probably to a physiochemical disorder. (This is all the more strange for one who saw schizophrenia as an interpersonal problem.) The manic, in his states of hyperactivity, seems to go out of control and will often do things that normally he

would never do. Perhaps most annoying to the others in our culture is the manic's tendency to indiscriminate sexual activity and heedless squandering of the hallowed bank account. There are various degrees of mania—in our culture it has been observed that salesmen are often recruited on the manic continuum. An individual can spend an entire lifetime as a "successful" manic, earning high achievement and recognition, and even extreme states are not recognized by others as "abnormal" (Allers, 1961, pp. 62–64). Often the manic signals himself by becoming depressed due to some setback in his plans, and then he earns a diagnosis of "manic-depressive."

All this is well known; the problem is what to make of it in behavioral terms rather than in physio-chemical ones. There are some interesting suggestions. In the first place there seems to be general agreement that the manic—like the depressed—has a very loose grip on his self-esteem. Despite the manic's appearance of boundless self-confidence, Federn (1952) noted that underneath was a weak ego. Kurt Adler says of the manic that he "intoxicates himself with false courage" (1961, p. 60). Generally, the manic seems as uncritical of his performance world as is the depressed. He is just as much caught up in it, and performs wholeheartedly on the basis of a narrow range of rules. The manic seems to intoxicate himself with an adroit, superficial performance of the rules, with the immediate stimulus of the moment (cf. Graves, 1942, pp. 672–673). He seems to carry himself along by his fluent command of the cultural fiction. This kind of immature and flighty omnipotence—not grounded in substantial ego-strength—is very much akin to the schizophrenic who is carried along to similar omnipotent feelings by mere word sounds: we seem to have here a difference between word-sound stimulus and "total organic sense". It is noteworthy that adolescents experience quick successions of omnipotence and extreme inferiority (Eissler, 1952, p. 104). This seems to indicate new behavior that does not have a firm basis in self-feeling: it seems as though the symbolic self, with a glib command over performance, is attaining to heights that the individual cannot really feel to be a part of himself. The adolescent stands torn on this very threshold: possibilities of unmeasured increase in social experience of self-value, and in new ranges of behaviors, versus the accustomed experience of low self-value in the home, and the narrow range of objects and behavior it permits. The depressed phase is merely a surrender to the narrow object range. In this sense the manic is continually juvenile; to himself he is always unproven in the world.

As for the florid end-state of mania, this is analogous to the schizophrenic end-state. It is an extreme case of lack of control of a certain kind of being-in-the-world. Mania certainly should not be explained by splitting languages, and searching for a physio-chemical explanation. Past a given point, the whole organism can go out of control *behaviorally,* as the schizophrenic loses his world behaviorally. There seems to be no more need to split mind and body in the study of mania than in any other syndrome.

REFERENCES

Bibring, Edward (1953), "The Mechanism of Depression," in *Affective Disorders,* Phyllis Greenacre (ed.) (New York: International Universities Press).

Field, M. J. (1960), *Search for Security: An Ethno-Psychiatric Study of Rural Ghana* (Evanston: Northwestern University Press).

Freud, Sigmund (1917), "Mourning and Melancholia," *Collected Papers,* Vol. 4 (London: Hogarth Press, 1946).

——(1920), *A General Introduction to Psychoanalysis* (New York: Liveright).

Fromm, Erich (1959), *Sigmund Freud's Mission* (New York: Harper).

Hallowell, A. Irving (1955), *Culture and Experience* (Philadelphia: University of Pennsylvania Press).

Kelly, George A. (1955), *The Psychology of Personal Constructs* (New York, Norton), 2 vols.

Langfeldt, Gabriel (1951), "The Hypersensitive Mind," *Acta Psychiatrica and Neurologica Scandinavica,* Supp. 73 (Copenhagen).

Minkowski, Eugene (1929), "Jalousie Pathologique sur un Fond D'Automatisme Mental," *Ann. Med. Psychol.,* Vol. 87, part 2.

Prange, Arthur J. Jr. and Vitols, M. M. (1962), "Cultural Aspects of the Relatively Low Incidence of Depression in Southern Negroes," *International Journal of Social Psychiatry,* Vol. 8, no. 2 (Spring), pp. 104–112.

Rogler, Lloyd H. and Hollingshead, August B. (1961), "Class and Disordered Speech in the Mentally Ill," *Journal of Helth and Human Behavior,* Vol. 2 (Fall), pp. 178–185.

Ruesch, Jurgen (1948), "The Invantile Personality: The Core Problem of Psychosomatic Medicine," *Psychosomatic Medicine,* Vol. 10, pp. 134–144.

Schwartz, D. A. (1961), "The Agitated Depression," *Psychiatric Quarterly,* Vol 34, no. 4 (October), pp. 758–776.

Searles, Harold F. (1956), "The Psychodynamics of Vengefulness," *Psychiatry,* Vol. 19, pp. 31–39.

Shepherd, Michael (1961), "Morbid Jealousy: Some Clinical and Social Aspects of a Psychiatric Syndrome," *Journal of Mental Science,* Vol. 107, no. 449 (July), pp. 687–704.

Strauss, Anselm (1959), *Mirrors and Masks, The Search for Identity* (New York: The Free Press of Glencoe).

Szasz, Thomas S. (1961), *The Myth of Mental Illness: Foundations of a Theory of Personal Conduct* (New York: Hoeber-Harper).

Tiggelaar, J. (1956), "Pathological Jealousy and Jealousy Delusions," *Fol. Psychiatr. Neerl.,* Vol 59, pp. 522–541.

Volkart, Edmund (1957), "Bereavement and Mental Health," in *Explorations in Social Psychiatry,* A. H. Leighton, J. A. Clausen, and R. N. Wilson (eds.) (New York: Basic Books), pp. 281–307.

13. A Three-Factor Causal Model of Depression

George W. Brown

This chapter outlines and etiological model of clinical depression developed by my colleagues and myself (for a full account, see ref. 4).

I *am* convinced that depression is largely a social phenomenon and the three main components of the model are all social—or it might be better to say psychosocial. By this I mean two tings. First, the clinical depression is a cognitive phenomenon, stemming from ideas about the world—past, present and future. Second, I can conceive of societies in which clinical depression is rare. Here, I will add a rider: I have no wish to assert that genetic, constitutional and physical factors are never involved in etiology. Existing evidence for their importance remains indirect and unimpressive: if such factors can in the future be shown to play a role they can easily be incorporated into the model. The ideas developed slowly over the last 9 to 10 years. Nonetheless, model and theory probably do not diverge much from ideas expressed elsewhere. Any claim to originality probably rests on the manner in which the three factors have been brought together in a causal model and its use to explain social class differences in the prevalence of depression. It may be of some interest to outline the main stages of the model's construction.

The research involved the study of six groups of depressed women, all aged between 18 and 65 years. Two were treated by psychiatrists, a group of inpatients and a group of outpatients, and another by general practitioners. All three lived in Camberwell in South London, a part of the Inner London borough of Southwark. There is a sizable middle-class population, but the majority are working class and the district has many of the problems of inner city populations, such as declining employment opportunities in industry. The final three groups were obtained by selecting women at random from nonpatient populations and establishing whether or not they were depressed. The first two surveys also involved women in Camberwell: in 1969 and 1974 we collected, among other things detailed information based on a clinical-type interview about the psychiatric state of 458 women. Recently, similar information has been obtained for 354 women living in the Outer Hebrides.

The six groups of depressed women, although different in origin, have given essentially similar results. For example, like Paykel and his colleagues, we found little or no evidence of an endogenous depressive group; all the forms of depression we studied appear to be equally influenced by social factors (4, Chap. 14). What differences have occurred may prove to be explicable variations of the same basic etiological process. This chapter therefore holds for all types of depression, excluding only conditions involving definite manic features, which were not studied.

At the center of the model is a particular type of life event. Given our views on the cognitive basis of depression it was, of course, essential to deal with the meaning of life events and their immediate consequences. In current research, there is a good deal of uncertainty about what is important about life events in their role as etiological agents, although the majority of accounts appear to hold that meaning is in some way crucial. Given this, the most persistent shortcoming has been to proceed as though an event such as 'pregnancy' can be interpreted or decoded in the way that an encyclopedia will tell us the meaning of a term. For some purposes—perhaps early in a research program—it may be useful to proceed as if this kind of decoding were possible: but fundamental progress surely can only come from recognizing that events in themselves do not have meaning. A pregnancy is never a pregnancy in the way it is described in an encyclopedia. It occurs to a woman with a past, present, and future and this context has in some way to be taken into account—the fact, for example, that her husband is in prison.

Our method for doing this is not uncomplicated, but it is, I believe, misrepresented when it is described in a recent commentary as requiring an acceptance of 'a certain mystification of measurement' (7). The method demands that the interviewer-investigator takes a dominant role in the measurement process and involves a lengthy training—and neither is fashionable. The debilitating grip of the standardized questionnaire on the social science research is still strong, although for the most part it is probably incapable of accurately measuring anything of complexity or emotional significance. It is in any case an approach that is only apparently 'objective'. A move from the rigidities of the questionaire to an approach in which the investigator is trained to use rating scales, and to interview flexibly, gives back some hope of accurate and unbiased measurement (2). Once the need for lengthy developmental work and training is accepted there is no mystification. We have trained workers from all parts of the world in the use of our methods. It has so far required them to visit us; but this is a common experience with new measures, not least in the natural sciences.

Our study established the date of onset of depression in the year before we saw the women and the exact date of events before this in the year. Our procedures, though relying on the skill of trained interviewers, are highly reliable. They also appear to be valid in the basic sense of considerable agreement about the occurrence of *particular* events when the accounts of respondents, seen by different interviewers, are compared. The procedures also avoid the potential bias present in instruments relying on the use of questionnaires (2). Events to be included in the study were defined in detail *before* we began. All were capable, in our judgement, of arousing significant positive or negative emotion. For instance, the admission of a husband or child to hospital was included only if it was an emergency or the stay was seven days or more. On average such women in Camberwell had three such 'events' per year (4, Chap. 10).

On the basis of substantial background information about individual women, events are characterized in terms of two contextual scales: *short-term* threat, based on its likely threat the day it occurred, and *long-term* threat, based on the situation resulting from the event about one week after it occurred. The raters are allowed to take account of everything known about a particular woman except her psychiatric condition and how she reacted to the event. Both rate the degree of threat a woman would have been likely to feel given her particular biography and present situation. One of the most remarkable results of the entire program is that it is only the most threatening events on the *long-term* scale—what we call *severe events*—that are capable of provoking onset of depression. They formed only 16 percent of the total 'events' occuring to women in Camberwell. Events severely threatening only in the *short-term* showed not the slightest association with onset however threatening they were on the day they occurred—for example, an emergency hospital admission of a child with an extremely high temperature.

The result is methodologically significant since it argues against measurement bias. It is difficult to see why such bias should be restricted to severe events alone; that is why it should not also have led to an association between depression and events severe only on *short-term* threat. The result is theoretically significant since the majority of the severe events turned out upon inspection to involve a loss, if this term is used with a certain license to include not only loss of a person but loss of a role or loss of an idea. For example, a woman who had considered she was happily married and who found that her husband had had a love affair a year before would have experienced a severe loss event in the sense she had lost a conception of her husband and her marriage. This would be so even if the affair was over and the husband was not aware of her knowledge of the affair. Loss of an idea is probably a crucial component of most 'loss' events.

The threat ratings were only two of twenty-eight measures completed for each event and the degree of change in routine involved. But, as with the shorterm threat scale, there was no suggestion that change as such or any other dimension had significance once the presence of a severe event had been taken into account.

Severe events were the major component of the first factor in our model— the *provoking agents*. The results are, of couse, comparable to those of Paykel and his colleagues in New Haven (8). Using their concept of 'exit event,' the size of the effect is a good deal smaller than in the London study. But at the same time their categorization is a less sensitive indicator of *long-term threat*, that is, the type of event that appears to be critically involved in the etiology of depression. We do not include as a matter of course the 'exit' events of a child marrying or a son drafted as *severe* events, and Paykel apparently would not include as an 'exit' event a woman finding out about a husband's love affair—a severe event or us. Nonetheless the results are clearly convergent. There is, however, a second type of provoking agent. We also recorded ongoing difficulties such as poor housing which might or might not have been associated with an event. We found that certain difficulties were capable of producing depression but not with the same freuency as severe events. Such difficulties were all markedly unpleasant, had lasted at least two years, and did not involve health problems.

When severe events and such major difficulties are considered together our search for provoking agents had been as successful as we could have reasonably hoped—a large proportion of all types of depression were preceded by one or other of the provoking agents. But just as a well-established carcinogen will not always lead to cancer, so a provoking agent does not always bring about depression. Indeed only a small minority of the women in Camberwell who experienced a provoking agent became depressed. In arithmetical terms two-thirds of women who developed depression had a provoking agent of causal importance in the year before onset. This is probably a conservative estimate and takes account of the fact that some events and difficulties will be juxtaposed with onset by chance (4, p. 120; also see Chap. 9). However, in spite of the size of this association only 1 in 5 of women in Camberwell with a provoking agent developed clinical depression. Therefore while this factor determines *when* a woman develops depression, it does not tell us *who* will break down among those with a severe event or major difficulty. This is the function of the second factor of the model, which deals with the vulnerability.

Such vulnerability proved to be intimately related to social class. Fifteen percent of the women in Camberwell were suffering from a definite affective disorder in the three months before interview, almost all of depression. We have called such women *cases*. All had disorders of a severity commonly met in a psychiatric out-patient department although few had seen a psychiatrist. Twenty-three percent of the working-class women were *cases* compared with only 6 percent of the middle-class women—a fourfold difference in prevalence.

Surprisingly, although severe events and major difficulties were more common among working-class women, this explained little of this difference in risk. If we consider only women with a severe event or major difficulty in the year before we saw them, thus controlling for class differences in the incidence of the provoking agents, there was still a large difference in risk. For example, 8 percent ($\frac{3}{36}$) of middle-class women with a child who had experienced a provoking agent developed depression compared with 31 percent($\frac{21}{67}$) of working-class women—a fourfold difference in vulnerability. For those without a provoking agent risk was only 1 percent in both groups ($\frac{1}{80}$) and ($\frac{1}{68}$), respectively.

What then is the reason for this remarkable difference in vulnerability? Anything capable of increasing risk of depression should have been

Table 1. Percentage of women in Camberwell who experienced onset of depression in year by whether they had a severe event or major difficulty and intimacy context

	Intimate relationship		
Event	Yes, with husband or boyfriend %	Yes, with someone seen regularly other than husband or boyfriend %	No %
Severe event or major difficulty	10 (9/88)	26 (12/47)	41 (12/29)
No severe event or major difficulty	1 (2/193)	3 (1/39)	4 (1/23)

revealed by our lengthy search for provoking agents. We therefore felt reasonably sure that if there were factors that increased vulnerability, they would do so *only when a woman also had* a provoking agent. We therefore began looking among these women for the second factor of our model.

Lack of an intimate, confiding relationship with a husband or boyfriend acted in exactly the way we had predicted. For the women who had had a provoking agent and who were not already depressed lack of such a tie greatly increased risk. Further, as predicted, for those *without* a provoking agent lack of intimacy was *not* associated with an increased risk of depression. (Table 1.)

'Intimacy' unfortunately is a 'soft' measure, at least in a cross-sectional survey, and we cannot altogether rule out the possibility of bias. We therefore looked for 'harder' indicators of vulnerability. We found three which, when considered together, gave much the same result as intimacy. They are having 3 or more children under 14 living at home, lacking employment away from home, and loss of a mother before the age of 11. The four vulnerability factors provide much of the reason why particular women get depressed following a provoking agent. They also provide most of the reason for the increased risk of working-class women. Such women are at greater risk largely because they more often have one or more of them.

Table 2 summarizes these results. Groups A and C in the table provide

Table 2. Proportion of women in Camberwell in whom depression developed in the year among women who experienced a severe event or major difficulty by vulnerability factors[a]

Event	Status	With event or difficulty			With event or difficulty	Without event or difficulty			Without event or difficulty
		%		%		%		%	
A. Intimate tie with husband or boyfriend regardless	Employed	9	(4/43)		10 (9/88)	1	(1/117)		1 (2/193)
	Not employed	11	(5/45)			1	(1/76)		
B. No intimate tie with husband or boyfriend, excluding early loss or 3+ children under 14 living at home	Employed	15	(6/39)			0	(0/34)		
	Not employed	30	(7/23)			11	(2/19)		
C. No intimate tie with husband or boyfriend *and* with early loss of mother or 3+ children under 14 lining at home	Employed	63	(5/8)			0	(0/7)		
	Not employed	100	(6/6)			0	(0/2)		
Total		20 (33/164)				2 (4/255)			

[a]Intimacy, employment status, early loss of mother, and 3+ children under 14 at home.

the extremes of protection and vulnerability for those with a provoking agent. Everyone with a confiding relationship with a husband or boyfriend is placed in group A and such a relationship is associated with a neutralizing of the effect of the three other factors. For women in group A not going out to work, for example, does not increase risk. Group B contains those without such a relationship but not a loss of mother before age 11 or 3 or more children under 14 at home, and C the remaining women. Compared with A, risk is increased in B and still more in C. It is only in groups B and C that work outside the home serves a protective function. In both groups it almost halves the risk of

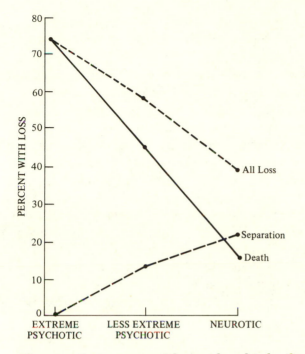

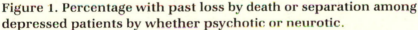

Figure 1. Percentage with past loss by death or separation among depressed patients by whether psychotic or neurotic.

depression in the presence of a severe event or major difficulty. Finally, for women without such an event or difficulty groups A, B, and C are unrelated to risk of depression.

We found nothing else that helped to explain why women developed depression. But there remained yet a further question. Provoking agent and vulnerability factor were quite unrelated to the form or the severity taken by a depressive disorder. They in no way helped to explain why some women suffered from a 'psychotic' form and others a 'neurotic' form, and why within each some were more severely disturbed than others. We therefore looked for a third, *symptom-formation* factor. We have not only found such a factor but much the most important of its components involves social experience—the past loss of a parent or other close relative, usually in childhood and adolescence (5). Among psychiatric patients loss by death of such a relative is associated with psychotic-like depressive symptoms (and their severity). Figure 1 illustrates this by dividing a group of depressed psychiatric patients into an extreme psychotic, a less extreme psychotic, and a neurotic group. The associations are large, have been replicated, and are not explained by background factors such as age.

It is important to note that loss of mother before 11 plays two roles—as a vulnerability factor it increases risk of depression, and as a symptom-formation factor it influences the form and the severity of depression according to whether the loss was by death or by separation.

This then is the outline of the model. Bearing various methodological innovations in mind, I believe a reasonable case has been made that the factors follow the temporal order specified and are involved in bringing about depression.

But what is going on? A causal model on its own, whatever its validity, is not enough. Consider employment. Is its protective role due to alleviation of boredom, greater variety of social contacts, or an enhanced sense of self-worth—or something else? The measures of a model do not have to be theoretically understandable in this sense—and at an early stage of development some at least will almost inevitably be theoretically ambiguous.

We have speculated that low self-esteem is the common feature behind all vulnerability factors and it is this that makes sense of our results. It is not loss itself that is important but the capacity once an important loss has occurred for a woman to hope for better things. In response to a provoking agent relatively specific feelings of hopelessness are likely to occur: the person has usually lost an important source of value—something that may have been derived from a person, a role, or an idea. If this hopelessness develops into a *general* feeling of hopelessness it may form the central feature of the depressive disorder itself.

We have come to see clinical depression as an affliction of a person's sense of values which leads, in Aaron Beck's terms, to a condition in which there is no meaning in the world, that the future is hopeless and the self worthless (1). It is after such generalization of hopelessness that the well-known affective and somatic symptoms of depression develop. Essential in any such generalization of hopelessness is a woman's ongoing self-esteem, her sense of her ability to control her world and her confidence that alternative sources of value will be at sometime available. If the woman's self-esteem is low before the onset of depression, she will be less likely to be able to see herself as emerging from her privation. And, of course, once depression has occurred feelings of confidence and self-worth can sink even lower.

It should not be overlooked that an appraisal of general hopelessness may be entirely realistic: the future for many women *is* bleak. It is probably here that our ideas depart most decisively from current opinion. We do not emphasize an inherent personality 'weakness.' While we do not rule out influence from the past—indeed we have demonstrated it has some importance—it is the link with the present that needs emphasis. Nor is it adversity or unhappiness or even loss that are central. They doubtless will always be with us, the inevitable precursors or consequences of whatever happiness we manage to achieve. Clinical depression is much less inevitable. It is a question of resources that allow a person to seek alternative sources of value and that allow her to hope that they can be found.

This interpretation is clearly relevant to factors of the model involving the current situation. It seems possible that loss in childhood and adolescence can also work through cognitive factors. For instance, the effect of loss of mother before 11 may be linked to the development of a sense of mastery. The earlier a mother is lost the more impeded is the growth of mastery and this may well permanently lower a woman's feeling of control and self-esteem. But, of course, there are other possibilities. Early loss of a mother might, for example, increase the chance of untoward experiences which are the direct antecedents of current vulnerability. Enduring feelings of insecurity may, for instance, increase the chance of marrying early an 'unsuitable' man.

For early loss acting as a symptom-formation factor we have suggested that women develop particular expectations about their environment as a result of past loss and these condition attitudes and behavior. Long-held perceptions of abandonment and helplessness may be linked to psychotic symptoms, and rejection and failure to neurotic symptoms.

For four years we have been developing new measures capable of exploring and testing these ideas, and we plan to use them in a prospective study. But we have also continued to use the existing material to explore the model. I have stated that only *severe* life-events are capable of provoking depression—at least in the sense of producing a disorder that would not have occurred for a long period of time or not at all without the event. (Using our index of the 'brought forward time' we call this a formative causal influence in contrast to a triggering one (see 6; and 4, pp. 121-126). But events other than those rated as *severe* do play a lesser etiological role and the way they appear to do this fits our general view of depression as a cognitive disorder.

Women often endure major difficulty and disappointment for many years before developing depression. We therefore looked to see whether there was anything to suggest some kind of triggering effect about the time of onset of depression. We found, in fact, that these women do have an increased rate of quite minor events in the 5 weeks before onset. If these events served to 'bring home' to a woman the full implications of her lot, the reason for breakdown at that particular point in time would to some extent be explicable.

We see these minor events not as provoking agents in the sense outlined, but they do appear capable of triggering a depressive disorder where there has been a major loss or disappointment. For example, one woman in Camberwell, who had a very difficult marriage and was living in poor and overcrowded conditions, developed depression four weeks after she learned of her sister's engagement to be married. The likely significance of the engagement needs no underlining. Quite trivial incidents may therefore in the context of an enduring disappointment produce feelings of profound hopelessness and swiftly the psychological and physical components of clinical depression. Such a mechanism may also help to explain the existence of the minority of severe events that do not involve obvious loss. A number of concerned incidents such as hospital admission for a threatening physical illness. It was notable that a number of the women also had major domestic difficulties, and it is again easy to see how such a brief separation from them might have 'brought home' the full implications of their position.

It has been common to study the effect of 'stress' on illness in general. The research in London, which has also involved studies of schizophrenia, anxiety states, and various physical conditions, suggests that this is a mistake. There is now a fair amount of evidence that when the likely meaning of events is considered there is considerable specificity in the sense used by Paykel in this volume. This may hold even within diagnostic groups. For example, a fifth of psychiatric patients with a severe event did not have one involving an obvious loss. Significantly more of these patients had a marked degree of anxiety associated with their depression (4, p. 228). The research indicates that specific types of experience should be related to particular psychiatric and physical consequences. While we argue that it is hopelessness that is critical in depression, usually provoked by some loss or disappointment, an important change in routine seems enough to bring about a florid relapse of schizophrenia symptoms (3). But it is not just a matter of different experiences leading to different conditions; it is possible that an experience protective for one condition may increase risk at the same time of another. A protective factor such as employment may help a woman to avoid depression because it raises feelings of self-worth and mastery; it may, however, because of the 'stress' of doing two 'jobs' be associated with risk of other kinds of disorder.

Probably quite disparate disorders will ultimately be shown to relate to comparable psychosocial precursors, but this needs to be demonstrated and not assumed.

A final and obvious point. It is effective theory that is desired. Working-class women away from Camberwell may not always experience so many vulnerability factors, and these may in other settings have different implications. Therefore 'refutation' or 'support' of our results must take into account the link of the elements in the model with background factors such as class and also the fact that theoretical implications of the measures may vary with the social setting. We have begun comparative research in the Outer Hebrides with the idea of forcing ourselves to face these kinds of possibilities. The population is largely rural and Gaelic-speaking. While the model has been supported to a surprising degree, there *are* some differences, and we trust these will lead to further development of measures, model, and theory. It is, I believe, from the struggle to resolve tensions between these three that new knowledge about etiology is likely to arise.

REFERENCES

1. Beck, A. T. (1967): *Depression: Clinical, Experimental and Theoretical Aspects:* Staples Press, London.
2. Brown, G. W. (1974): Meaning, measurement and stress. In: *Stressfulness of Life Events: Their Nature and Effects,* edited by B. S. Dohrenwend and B. P. Dohrenwend, pp. 217–243. Wiley, London.
3. Brown, G. W., and Birley, J. L. T. (1968): Crises and life changes and the onset of schizophrenia. *J. Health Soc. Behav.,* 9:203–214:
4. Brown, G. W., and Harris, T. (1978): *Social Origins of Depression: A Study of Psychiatric Disorder in Women.* Tavistock, London.

5. Brown, G. W., Harris, T., and Copeland, J. R. (1977): Depression and loss. *Br. J. Psychiatry,* 130:1–18.
6. Brown, G. W., Harris, T. O., and Peto, J. (1973): Life events and psychiatric disorders. Part 2: Nature of causal link. *Psychol. Med.,* 3:159–176.
7. Dohrenwend, B. P., and Dohrenwend, B. S. (1977): The conceptualization and measurement of stressful life events: An overview of the issues. In: *The Origins and Course of Psychopathology,* edited by J. S. Strauss, H. M. Babigian, and M. Roff. Plenum Press, New York.
8. Paykel, E. S. (1974): Recent life events and clinical depression. In: *Life Stress and Illness,* edited by E. K. E. Gunderson and R. D. Rahe. Charles C Thomas, Springfield, Illinois.

14. Risk Factors for Depression: What Do We Learn from Them?

Lenore Sawyer Radloff

The fact that depression is more common among women than men has been thoroughly documented, but it is important to go beyond this basic epidemiologic finding and ask why. Empirically, this question translates first to asking under what conditions are women more depressed, and whether there are conditions under which women are *not* more depressed than men. These conditions can then be examined for underlying commonalities related to etiologic theories of depression. In other words, the research question changes from "Why are women more depressed than men?" to "What kinds of people are most likely to be depressed?" What do they have in common, and what does this tell us about the nature of depression?

DEFINITIONS OF DEPRESSION

Klerman and Weissman have described the variety of definitions of depression and its symptoms. A diagnosis of clinical depression depends on the pattern of symptoms and on their severity and duration. One way of classifying the symptoms of unipolar depression is into a syndrome of four dimensions. The *cognitive dimension* includes hopeless, helpless beliefs—the conviction that nothing will ever get better. The irony of depression is that the person feels that nothing can help, whereas, in fact, depression can be quite effectively treated. The *motivational behavioral dimension* includes feeling apathetic, lacking in energy, not wanting to do anything, and actually doing less than usual. Depression often interferes with normal activities. It especially disrupts interpersonal relationships. The *affective dimension* includes feeling sad, blue, depressed, and taking no pleasure in the things that were formerly enjoyed. Depressed persons also often feel irritable and anxious, even quite openly angry and hostile, especially with the people closest to them (Weissman & Paykel, 1974). The trouble is that the anger is not used to communicate and to solve problems, but simply to express distress. It may be that the depressed person's low self-esteem and anger toward self comes from an awareness of his or her inadequate coping rather than from some mysterious turning of anger inward. The so-called *"vegetative" dimension* includes disturbances of appetite and sleep. Most commonly, depressed people have insomnia and do not feel like eating, but some sleep much more than usual, and overeat. These symptoms usually appear only in fairly severe depression (McLean, 1976).

There are many ways of measuring depression. In the data reported here, degree of depression will be operationally defined as the score on a depression scale, the Center for Epidemiologic Studies Depression Scale, referred to as the CES-D scale (see Table 1). The score consists of the number of symptoms of depression experienced during the past week, weighted by the frequency and duration of each symptom. A higher score indicates a higher level of depression. The scale includes many of the symptoms listed by Klerman and Weissman as characteristic of depression (for more information about the CES-D Scale, see Radloff 1977: and Weissman, Sholomskas, Pottenger, Prusoff, & Locke, 1977).

THE SURVEY DATA

The data presented in this chapter came from a mental health interview survey sponsored by the Center for Epidemiologic Studies, National Institute of Mental Health, conducted in Kansas City, Missouri in 1971–1972 and in Washington County, Maryland in 1971–1973. Individuals aged 18 years and over were randomly selected for interview from a representative sample of households. Response rates were 74.8% in Kansas City; 80.1% in Washington County.

The racial compositions of the samples reflected those of the populations. There were about 24% nonwhite in Kansas City, and only 2% nonwhite in Washington County. Preliminary analyses suggested that the whites and nonwhites should not be combined because they might differ in relationships among some variables. But the numbers of nonwhites were too small to analyze separately in detail. Therefore, we shall cover analyses of whites only, with a sample size of 876 whites in

Table 1. Center for Epidemiologic Studies Depression Scale[a,b]

During the past week	Rarely	A Little	Moderate	Most
1. I was bothered by things that usually don't bother me	0	1	2	3
2. I did not feel like eating; my appetite was poor	0	1	2	3
3. I felt that I could not shake off the blues even with help from my family or friends	0	1	2	3
4. I felt that I was just as good as other people	3	2	1	0
5. I had trouble keeping my mind on what I was doing	0	1	2	3
6. I felt depressed	0	1	2	3
7. I felt that everything I did was an effort	0	1	2	3
8. I felt hopeful about the future	3	2	1	0
9. I thought my life had been a failure	0	1	2	3
10. I felt fearful	0	1	2	3
11. My sleep was restless	0	1	2	3
12. I was happy	3	2	1	0
13. I talked less than usual	0	1	2	3
14. I felt lonely	0	1	2	3
15. People were unfriendly	0	1	2	3
16. I enjoyed life	3	2	1	0
17. I had crying spells	0	1	2	3
18. I felt sad	0	1	2	3
19. I felt that people disliked me	0	1	2	3
20. I could not get going	0	1	2	3

[a]Instructions for questions: Below is a list of the ways you might have felt or behaved. Please tell me how often you have felt this way during the past week (Hand card A): *Rarely* or none of the time less than a day); some or a *Little* of the time (1–2 days); Occasionally or a *Moderate* amount of time (3–4 days). *Most* or all of the time (5–7 days).

[b]Total score equals the sum of the 20 weighted item scores.

Kansas City and 1639 whites in Washington County. Numbers in the various analyses will differ somewhat, due to missing data.

The survey operation was managed by local organizations[1] in each site, and coordinated by the Center for Epidemiologic Studies to main-

[1]Fieldwork by Epidemiologic Field Station, Greater Kansas City Mental Health Foundation, Kansas City, Missouri; and Johns Hopkins Training Center for Public Health Research Johns Hopkins University, Hagerstown, Maryland; under contract from Center for Epidemiologic Studies, National Institute of Mental Health.

Table 2. Average Depression Scores (CES-D), by Sex and Marital Status[a]

	Male		Female		Total	
Marital Status	N	$\bar{X}$	N	$\bar{X}$	N	$\bar{X}$
Married	778	7.33	930	9.53	1708	8.53
Divorced-separated	66	7.89	145	13.71	211	11.89
Never married (not head of household)	71	10.27	61	12.79	132	11.43
Never married (head of household)	51	9.84	87	7.93	138	8.64
Widowed	45	12.78	267	10.26	312	10.62
Total	1011	7.94	1490	10.10	2501	9.23

Two Way Analysis of Variance
Interactor sex × marital status $p = .0001$ (p values rounded)
Sex $p = .03$
Marital status $p = .001$
[a]Higher score indicates more depressive symptomatology.

tain the greatest possible comparability between the sites. Previous analyses of the data indicated that there was a small difference between the sites on the depression scale, but it disappeared when adjustments were made for racial composition and socioeconomic variables (Comstock & Helsing, 1976). Relationships among variables were very similar for the two sites. Therefore, the data from the two sites have been combined for the present report.

The questionnaire used in this survey included over 300 separate questions, including the CES-D Scale. The present analyses will cover only the CES-D Scale and some of the more objective sociodemographic factors which previously have been found to relate to depression (Silverman, 1968).

Overall, the average scores on the depression scale were higher for women than for men. However, this was true only among the married, the divorced–separated, and the never-married who were not heads of their own households (mostly young people living with parents). Among the widowed and the never-married heading their own households, the men's scores were higher than the women's (see Table 2). (See also Radloff, in press and Radloff, 1975 for related analyses.)

Table 3 shows that other social factors associated with more depression for both sexes included youth (those of age 18–24 were more depressed than all other age groups), low education, low income, low status employment and physical illness (current or recent). Among males, but not females, currently employed workers were less depressed than others. For both males and females, those who had had children but were not living with them ("empty nest" parents) were less depressed than others. Note that the average depression score for females was higher than that for males throughout Table 3, except among the high-level professionals. In some cases, however, the sex difference was quite small.

The same social factors were analyzed by sex separately for each marital status, to determine whether the sex-marital status interaction might be due to differences in these factors. In general, it can be seen that this is not the case. Adjusting for the social factors did not change the original findings of Table 2. Among the married (Table 4), the women were more depressed than the men except among the high-level and low-level professionals and the unemployed. Among the divorced–separated, Table 5 shows the women were more depressed than the men except in the sales and clerical occupations. Note however, that the few men in the survey living with children had average depression scores almost as high as the many women $N = (76)$ in that situation. Men and women who had exactly high school education also had very similar scores.

Among the never-married who were not heads of households, Table 6 shows the women were more depressed than men except among midlevel professionals, unskilled laborers, the "housewife, retired and other" occupational status category, the retired, and students. All of these groups contained very small numbers of people. However, the sex difference was not significant in any of these analyses, partly because of very unbalanced designs (small numbers in some cells). Table 7's data shows that among the never-married who were heads of household, it was usually the men who were more depressed, although not significantly so. The women were more depressed than the men only among those very small numbers of subjects with less than a high school education, or who were unemployed, students, or low-level professionals; and, reflecting very small differences, among the retired and those without illness. Again, none of the sex differences were significant.

Table 8 indicates that among the widowed, the men were also usually more depressed than the women. The women were more depressed than the men only among those with a high school or higher education

Table 3. Average Depression Scores (CES-D), by Sex and Other Social Factors

	Male		Female		Total	
	N	$\bar{X}$	N	$\bar{X}$	N	$\bar{X}$
Age[a]						
18–24	146	10.51	189	13.48	335	12.19
25 & up	866	7.51	1296	9.62	2162	8.78
Education[a]						
Less than high school	375	8.27	608	11.22	983	10.09
High school	331	8.52	507	10.00	888	9.41
Beyond high school	304	6.94	369	8.44	673	7.76
Income[a]						
Less than $4000	121	10.06	311	11.58	432	11.16
$4000 or more	827	7.70	1034	9.47	1861	8.68
Occupational Status[a]						
High-level professional	45	5.76	5	2.80	50	5.40
Mid-level professional	100	6.11	69	8.14	169	6.94
Low-level professional	98	7.39	33	8.24	181	7.60
Sales & Clerical	88	7.50	181	8.73	269	8.33
Skilled manual	207	7.25	22	11.77	229	7.69
Semi-skilled manual	108	8.99	100	10.91	208	9.91
Unskilled manual	42	8.74	41	9.73	88	9.23
Housewife, retired, other	259	8.64	912	10.31	1171	9.94
Unemployed or student	64	10.98	127	11.64	191	11.42
Illness[a]						
No	307	6.61	382	8.35	689	7.38
Yes	705	8.52	1108	10.71	1813	9.80
Occupational Role[b]						
Worker	798	7.59	636	9.61	1434	8.49
Housewife	—	—	510	10.53	510	10.53
Retired	148	8.53	212	9.67	360	9.20
Unemployed	46	10.35	115	11.44	161	11.13
Student	20	12.00	17	12.41	37	12.19
Parental Status[a]						
Not living with children	288	6.81	477	9.15	765	8.27
Living with children	468	8.35	691	10.81	1159	9.12
No children	256	8.46	322	9.99	578	9.31

[a] One-way Analysis of variance overall $p < .02$ for both sexes.
[b] One way analysis of variance, overall $p < .01$ for males; not significant for females.

(with small numbers of men and very small differences in mean scores) and among the small number of those working as laborers. The sex

Table 4. Average Depression Scores (CES-D) of Married Subjects by Sex and Other Social Factors

	Male		Female		Two-way analysis of variance	
	N	X̄	N	X̄		
Age					Sex × Age	p = .510
18–24	62	9.47	109	12.39	Sex	p = .000
25 & up	717	7.14	821	9.15	Age	p = .000
Education						
Less than high school	301	7.73	335	10.90	Sex × Education	p = .095
High school	254	7.78	360	9.61	Sex	p = .000
Beyond high school	224	6.25	235	7.46	Education	p = .000
Income					Sex × Income	p = .728
Less than $4000	68	9.32	84	11.01	Sex	p = .004
$4000 or more	669	7.20	775	9.35	Income	p = .005
Occupational Status						
High-level professional	38	5.58	4	3.25	Sex × Occupation	p = .05
Mid-level professional	88	5.86	41	7.66	Sex	p = .09
Low-level professional	92	7.37	23	7.35	Occupation	p = .001
Sales and Clerical	73	6.73	104	8.01		
Skilled manual	173	7.09	14	11.79		
Semi-skilled manual	82	9.01	56	9.91		
Unskilled manual	23	5.83	19	10.68		
Housewife, retired, other	179	7.46	586	9.95		
Unemployed or student	30	12.40	83	9.33		
Illness					Sex × Illness	p = .72
No	210	6.09	257	8.45	Sex	p = .0001
Yes	544	7.87	673	9.94	Illness	p = .0003
Occupational Role						
Worker	644	7.05	381	9.01	Sex × Occupation	p = .01
Retired	105	7.59	53	9.86	Sex	p = .70
Unemployed	24	12.79	77	9.40	Occupation	p = .00
Parental status						
Not living with children	210	5.91	254	8.07	Sex × Parental status	p = .51
Living with children	458	8.21	571	10.14	Sex	p = .0001
No children	110	6.39	105	9.72	Parental status	p = .0001

difference was significant (p < .04, with the men more depressed) only in the analysis by income, where numbers were reasonably balanced.

In summary, women were more depressed than men among the married and divorced–separated. Exceptions which seem interpretable were found in those married persons who were unemployed and divorced–separated people living with children. In the other groups, the

Table 5. Average Depression Scores (CES-D) of Divorced-Separated Subjects, by Sex and Other Social Factors

	Male		Female		Two-way analysis of variance	
	N	X̄	N	X̄		
Age					Sex × Age	p = .572
18–24	4	12.25	17	20.82	Sex	p = .019
25 & up	62	7.61	128	12.80	Age	p = .030
Education						
Less than high school	25	7.28	74	14.86	Sex × Education	p = .172
High school	16	11.19	47	11.96	Sex	p = .002
Beyond high school	25	6.40	25	13.44	Education	p = .721
Income					Sex × Income	p = .118
Less than $4000	13	5.77	64	14.55	Sex	p = .002
$4000 or more	50	8.42	68	11.57	Income	p = .926
Occupational Status						
High-level professional	2	4.50	0	—	Omitting high level professionals	
Mid-level professional	6	7.33	11	11.45	Sex × Occupation	p = .78
Low-level professional	3	6.00	2	12.50	Sex	p = .01
Sales and Clerical	5	12.40	29	11.93	Occupation	p = .91
Skilled manual	15	8.93	3	13.33		
Semi-skilled manual	5	9.60	24	11.33		
Unskilled manual	4	2.50	8	13.00		
Housewife, retired, other	19	6.74	55	15.47		
Unemployed or student	7	9.71	13	17.23		
Illness					Sex × Illness	p = .23
No	20	6.65	36	9.33	Sex	p = .006
Yes	46	8.43	109	15.16	Illness	p = .02
Occupational Role						
Worker	47	8.22	94	12.36	Sex × Occupation	p = .42
Retired	12	5.58	17	11.12	Sex	p = .00
Unemployed	5	6.20	11	17.53	Occupation	p = .49
Parental status						
Not living with children	3	6.79	46	12.74	Sex × Parental status	p = .53
Living with children	6	14.17	76	14.70	Sex	p = .08
No children	17	8.47	23	12.39	Parental status	p = .16

sex difference was smaller and less consistent, with some tendency for men to be more depressed among the never-married heads of household and the widowed. The other social factors related to depression fairly consistently in all sex-marital status categories.

A variety of three-way analyses of variance were examined but they showed no dramatic departures from the patterns of Table 2. (The data are not shown on a table.) Analysis of covariance, using age, education, income, occupational status, illness, and living with children as covariates, also did not change the pattern, although it reduced the sex

Table 6. Average Depression Scores (CES-D) of Never-Married (not Head of Households), Subjects by Sex and Other Social Factors

	Male		Female		
	N	X̄	N	X̄	Two-way analysis of variance
Age					Sex × Age p = .554
18–24	58	10.76	48	14.30	Sex p = .131
25 & up	14	7.79	17	8.88	Age p = .027
Education					
Less than high school	11	9.09	10	10.30	Sex × Education p = .597
High school	37	9.57	27	13.59	Sex p = .143
Beyond high school	24	11.63	24	12.92	Education p = .554
Income					Sex × Income p = .33
Less than $4000	5	11.20	5	12.40	Sex p = .526
$4000 or more	55	9.98	41	12.49	Income p = .819
Occupational Status					
High-level professional	0	—	0	—	Omitting high-level and low-level professionals
Mid-level professional	3	9.00	4	7.50	
Low-level professional	0	—	1	4.00	Sex × Occupation p = .33
Sales & Clerical	4	10.50	9	12.11	Sex p = .55
Skilled manual	9	6.44	1	10.00	Occupation p = .50
Semi-skilled manual	11	8.82	7	14.43	
Unskilled manual	10	11.50	4	6.50	
Housewife, retired, other	19	12.63	19	12.58	
Unemployed or student	15	10.00	16	16.31	
Illness					
No	25	10.84	19	11.21	Sex × Illness p = .27
Yes	46	9.96	42	13.50	Sex p = .27
					Illness p = .63
Occupational Role					
Worker	54	10.00	35	11.86	
Retired	2	17.00	4	12.00	Sex × Occupation p = .536
Unemployed	10	8.00	8	18.75	Sex p = .600
Student	5	14.00	8	13.88	Occupation p = .327

difference in the divorced–separated and the never-married heads of household categories. For a description of regression analyses using a larger number of social factors, see Radloff and Rae (1979).

A THEORETICAL MODEL OF DEPRESSION

The sex-marital status interaction and the relationship of social factors to depression suggest that the sex difference in depression is not due entirely to biological factors. Klerman and Weissman have reviewed a

Table 7. Average Depression Scores (CES-D) of Never-Married (Head of Household) Subjects, by Sex and Other Social Factors

	Male		Female			
	N	$\bar{X}$	N	$\bar{X}$	Two-way analysis of variance	
Age					Sex × Age	p = .976
18–24	21	12.33	19	11.16	Sex	p = .526
25 & up	29	8.24	66	7.15	Age	p = .010
Education						
Less than high school	9	4.89	20	8.65	Sex × Education	p = .017
High school	13	16.38	25	7.12	Sex	p = .185
Beyond high school	28	8.61	42	8.07	Education	p = .037
Income					Sex × Income	p = .501
Less than $4000	14	10.36	25	9.88	Sex	p = .666
$4000 or more	32	10.31	53	7.51	Income	p = .518
Occupational Status						
High-level professional	5	7.60	1	1.00	Sex × Occupation	p = .07
Mid-level professional	3	8.00	11	6.00	Sex	p = .65
Low-level professional	2	4.50	4	12.00	Occupation	p = .02
Sales & Clerical	6	10.83	21	6.57		
Skilled manual	5	6.60	1	1.00		
Semi-skilled manual	8	9.38	4	5.75		
Unskilled manual	4	26.00	2	13.50		
Housewife, retired, other	7	10.86	40	8.10		
Unemployed or student	10	7.70	3	20.67		
Illness					Sex × Illness	p = .12
No	21	6.29	17	7.00	Sex	p = .27
Yes	30	12.33	70	8.16	Illness	p = .02
Occupational Role						
Worker	37	10.89	54	7.35	Sex × Occupation	p = .028
Retired	2	7.00	25	7.08	Sex	p = .094
Unemployed	4	6.00	2	22.50	Occupation	p = .346
Student	6	8.83	1	17.00		

variety of theories of depression and related them to possible explanations for the sex difference. The model presented here (see also Radloff & Rae, 1979) is closest to the "learned helplessness" explanation, but incorporates aspects of the behavioral and cognitive models, as well as a sequential "coping" model (McLean, 1976). It suggests that the sex difference in depression is related to the different learning histories of males and females, which result in different ways of coping with stress.

The epidemiologic or "disease" model assumes that the probability that an individual will develop a given disease depends on that individual's susceptibility to the disease and the exposure to the precipitating

Table 8. Average Depression Scores (CES-D) of Widowed Subjects, by Sex and Other Social Factors

	Male		Female		
	N	X̄	N	X̄	Two-way analyses of variance
Age					Sex × Age p = .56
18–64	13	15.38	108	11.22	Sex p = .14
65 & up	32	11.76	161	9.65	Age p = .08
Education					
Less than high school	29	15.38	171	10.56	Sex × Education p = .20
High school	10	9.30	49	10.84	Sex p = .110
Beyond high school	4	7.25	44	8.64	Education p = .774
Income					Sex × Income p = .857
Less than $4000	21	14.62	134	10.94	Sex p = .089
$4000 or more	21	11.81	98	8.70	Income p = .126
Occupational Status					
High-level professional	0	—	0	—	Omitting Occ. levels
Mid-level professional	0	—	2	13.00	1,2,4
Low-level professional	1	19.00	3	8.67	Sex × Occupation p = .63
Sales and Clerical	0	—	18	8.56	Sex p = .81
Skilled manual	4	11.50	3	14.33	Occupation p = .69
Semi-skilled manual	2	6.00	9	15.56	
Unskilled manual	1	4.00	8	4.88	
Housewife, retired, other	35	13.09	212	10.16	
Unemployed or student	2	18.00	12	13.08	
Illness					Sex × Illness p = .57
No	6	11.17	53	6.62	Sex p = .16
Yes	39	13.03	214	11.16	Illness p = .17
Occupational Role					
Worker	16	11.77	74	9.79	Sex × Occupation p = .89
Retired	27	13.04	113	9.92	Sex p = .30
Unemployed	1	21.00	13	14.31	Occupation p = .47
Parental Status					
Not living with children	34	12.29	176	9.77	Sex × Parental p = .68
					status
Living with children	3	20.00	41	12.22	Sex p = .10
No children	8	12.13	50	10.38	Parental status p = .27

factors which initiate the disease. In the case of depression, both susceptibility and precipitating factors may include both biological and
social factors. It is here suggested that there is a component of susceptibility that is a learned habit, which could be called a "helpless style
of coping," and that the precipitating factors which would activate this
kind of susceptibility would be problems or stresses that need to be
coped with.

General learning theory has shown that in the presence of a goal, such as obtaining a reward or avoiding a punishment, the response that succeeds in reaching the goal (i.e., is reinforced) will be "learned" (i.e., will be more likely to occur again in similar circumstances). In learning theory terms, this is known as learned instrumental behavior. The layman might call it "learning to cope." In humans, this learning may be accompanied by cognitions which could be verbalized: "In this situation, if I do this, that will happen."

Learning will not occur if any part of the sequence is absent, that is, if there is no goal, no response, no reinforcement, or no contingency between response and reinforcement. A person may not learn to cope if one or more of these factors is consistently missing. for example, extremely overprotected or "spoiled" children may learn as little as children in an extremely deprived environment. People cannot learn to obtain rewards by their own responses if rewards are either always or never available regardless of their actions, so that there is a lack of contingency. They may also fail to develop goals if they never want for anything or never have anything. If the person cannot or does not make the responses which would succeed in reaching a goal, lacking appropriate skills, there will be no learning. Or, if rewards or punishments are completely independent of a person's responses, what Seligman (1975) has called an "uncontrollable situation," the person may generalize this helplessness to new situations. This generalized "learned helplessness" is related to depression.

It is possible that a person can also learn to *not* cope, as well as fail to learn to cope. If successful responses which are rewarded are also consistently punished, the person will be in conflict and may try to solve it by avoiding the situation entirely—by, for example, giving up the goal. It is also possible that people can be directly taught not to cope by instruction or example, (e.g. discouragement or disparagement by significant others). Whatever its origin, failure to cope may lead to a generalized habit of not responding, even when there is a goal which could be reached by some possible response. Failure to cope may also be verbalized in helpless cognitions such as "nothing I do matters," "I can't cope," or "I can't do anything right." These expressions are characteristic of depression. Beck (1976) suggests that these cognitions are a basic cause of depression. McLean (1976) suggests that depression is the result of anticipation of chronic failure which is the result of feelings of lack of control resulting from repeated goal frustrations.

It is suggested here that the cognitive dimension of depression, the expectation that goals cannot be reached by any responses available to the person, is a basic factor in learned *susceptibility* to depression. Depression itself will not occur unless there is a goal actively present. In other words, the precipitating factors which activate the susceptibility are goals (rewards desired or punishments to be escaped or avoided). Given a goal situation and the expectation that nothing the person can do will influence the outcome, the person is unlikely to try to do anything. This lack of activity is like the motivational-behavioral dimension of depression. Depending on the environment and the generality of the helpless cognitions, such a person would be faced with more and more unescaped punishments and fewer and fewer rewards. This would result in pain, anxiety, sadness and lack of enjoyment—the affective dimension of depression. There is speculation and some evidence (Brenner, 1979) that the vegetative dimension of depression may follow from severe and prolonged affective disturbance.

Theoretically, then, depression develops sequentially, but in real life it is no doubt a vicious cycle. For example the inability to cope would strengthen the helpless cognitions and contribute to low self-esteem. The sleep and appetite disturbances would reduce energy level and aggravate the motivational-behavioral deficit. The sadness and apathy would interfere with social relationships, thereby reducing reinforcements still further. Depression would continue to deepen unless the cycle were interrupted. Intervention at any point in the cycle might be effective for treatment. But if this model has any validity, to prevent a relapse, the cognitive (susceptibility) dimension must be changed. Reduction in precipitating factors may also be necessary in cases where they are abnormally numerous or stressful.

APPLICATION OF THE MODEL TO THE SEX DIFFERENCE AND OTHER RISK FACTORS

The kinds of people who are most likely to be depressed include the young, the poor, and poorly educated (especially if female), those with low-status occupations, those with illness, the unemployed and students, women who are married or divorced-separated, the men who are never-married heads of households or widowed, and both sexes if they were never married but were not heads of households. Seligman (1975) has analyzed a variety of risk factors for depression, especially poverty and school failure, in terms of learned helplessness: "A child reared in . . . poverty will be exposed to a vast amount of uncontrollability [p. 159]." A background of poverty and poor education would reduce a person's chances of learning effective coping habits, and leave him or her more vulnerable to depression. Since past poverty and poor education are often correlated with current poverty and low-status occupations or unemployment, the high levels of depression in these groups is understandable. They would be more susceptible due to past experiences and also currently exposed to more precipitating factors (problems to be coped with).

Physical illness may be related to depression because it produces actual helplessness or at least feelings of loss of control. The high level of depression in the young, and especially among students, is more difficult to explain. It is supported by other recent surveys (Benfari, Beiser, Leighton, and Mertens, 1972; Berkman, 1971) and suicide rate data (Seiden, 1969). This age group may be faced with problems which are more difficult for them to solve than are the problems faced by older people. A recent survey (ISR, 1979) found a large increase from 1957 to 1976 in worry and anxiety in younger age groups. In discussions with the author, high school and college students expressed feelings of helplessness and lack of control. More work is needed to explore this issue.

The sex-marital-status patterns can be explained in several stages. First, as it will be shown, women are more likely to have more of the learned susceptibility to depression than men. Second, selectivity in marriage can be hypothesized, so that the less helpless women and the more helpless men would be most likely to stay unmarried long enough to become heads of their own households (see Bernard, 1973). Third, divorce and separation, especially if joined with poverty and responsibility for children, can be seen as stressful situations filled with precipitating factors for depression. Divorced-separated women would be both more susceptible (as are married women) and more likely to have children, low incomes and low-status jobs, or be unemployed. Finally, widowhood can be seen as a more stressful precipitant for men, because they have never been prepared to cope with it in either practical terms (by taking over domestic chores) or psychological terms. There are very few widowed males, and in this sense they are deviates from the norm.

Evidence that the learning history of women is more likely to lead to the component of susceptibility to depression, which is due to a lack of instrumental coping, has been reviewed elsewhere (Radloff & Monroe, 1978). Only a brief summary and a few examples will be given here.

The most plentiful evidence comes from studies of sex role stereotypes. Stereotypes reflect what we expect from people. Studies have consistently found that people expect females, even healthy, newborn babies, to be weaker, less able to get what they want by their own actions, and therefore more in need of help and protection than males. What people expect of a person is likely to influence the way they treat him or her and the way he or she behaves. There is evidence that girls are more likely to have things done *for* them, while boys are shown how to do things for themselves.

In the studies of childrearing practices reviewed by Maccoby and Jacklin (1974), only one consistent sex difference is found: The actions of boys more frequently *have consequences* than do the actions of girls. Granted, the boys are often punished especially for aggression, but both rewards and punishments depend on the boys' behavior. Boy's can therefore learn to control rewards and punishments by their own actions. In contrast, an observational study of nursery schools (Serbin, O'Leary, Kent & Tonick 1973) found that girls received fewer reactions from adults for all behaviors, including aggression. The authors describe, for example a small girl who struck out aggressively in anger and was totally ignored. Even her worst temper tantrum had no effect on her environment. That is the ultimate in helplessness, and is reminiscent of clinical descriptions of the impotent rage of the angry depressive.

For males in our culture, achievement and competence are clearly rewarded. For females, they receive mixed results. Some studies found that females who displayed competence were simply ignored. For example, studies of small group problem-solving found that females were less listened to, were more often interrupted and has less influence on the group decisions. An extreme example is found in a study where females were given the right answer ahead of time, but still could not get the group to accept it (Altmeyer & Jones, 1974).

Other studies found that competent females sometimes got rewards, but were often also punished, especially be social rejection. The "fear of success" studies illustrate this. When a female was portrayed as successful especially in achievement-oriented ways, people predicted many bad consequences of her success. In another study, male and female actors portrayed assertive and nonassertive roles. The assertive females were rated by observers as less likeable and more in need of psychotherapy than nonassertive females; the reverse was true for male actors (Costrich, Feinstein, Kidder, Marecek, and Pascale, 1975).

Other studies, (reviewed by Frieze, 1975) have found that females who succeeded in a task were more likely than males to attribute their success to luck or other factors which would not allow them to take credit for their achievement. This could produce a cognitive barrier to learning, by blocking the effectiveness of positive reinforcement. Females were less likely than males to expect to succeed in the future, and were less likely to *attempt* to succeed in the future. Recently, it has been found that depressed people are likely to have a similar "attribution style." When they do well at something they attribute it to luck; when they fail, they take all the blame (Rizley 1978). This attribution could be described as a generalized expectancy of failure to cope.

Many studies have found that work produced by females was rated as less significant, and was less rewarded by pay, promotions, and status than comparable work produced by men (e.g. see Huber, 1973; Safilios-Rothschild, 1972). "Women's work" is sometimes defined as "pleasing other people." Success in pleasing people is unpredictable, and the rewards are very intangible.

In summary, for "competent behavior" which, in our culture is highly praised, females, as compared to males, have been found to get fewer rewards, have less control over their rewards, and more often see their rewards accompanied by punishment, producing conflict, which interferes with learning. Women have also been instructed by the stereotypes that competent instrumental behavior is not expected of them. That this "training in helplessness" has been effective is shown by their attribution style-taking less personal credit for success—and their low expectations of success. the behavioral effect is seen in their reduced rates of attempting to solve problems.

It is suggested that depression is a special problem for women not because they are biologically female nor only because they are exposed to greater numbers of stress-inducing situations, but because they have learned to be more susceptible to depression. There are many sources of learned susceptibility which would affect both sexes equally, but stereotyped sex-role socialization is an added source of susceptibility to depression for women. The implications for treatment and prevention are obvious.

REFERENCES

Altemeyer, R., & Jones, K. Sexual identity, physical attractiveness and seating position as determinants of influence in discussion groups. *Canadian Journal of Behavior*, 1974, *6*, 357–375.

Beck, A. T. *Cognitive therapy and the emotional disorders*. New York: International Universities Press, 1976

Benfari, R. C., Beiser, M., Leighton, A. & Mertens, C. Some dimensions of psychoneurotic behavior in an urban sample. *Journal of Nervous and Mental Diseases*, 1972, *155*(2), 77–90.

Berkman, P. L. Measurement of mental health in a general population survey. *American Journal of Epidemiology*, 1971, *94*, 105–111.

Bernard, J. *The future of marriage*. New York: Bantam Books, 1973.

Brenner, B. Depressed affect as a cause of associated somatic problems. *Psychological Medicine*, 1979, *9*, 737–746.

Comstock, G. W., & Helsing, K. J. Symptoms of depression in two communities. *Psychological Medicine*, 1976, *6*, 551–563.

Costrich, N., Feinstein, J., Kidder, L., Marecek, J., & Pascale, L. When stereotypes hurt: Three studies of penalties for sex-role reversals. *Journal of Experimental Social Psychology*, 1975, *11*, 520–530.

Frieze, I., Fisher, J. McHugh, M., & Valle, V. Attributing the causes of success and failure: Internal and external barriers to achievement in women. Paper presented at conference *New Directions for Research on Women*, Madison, Wisconsin, 1975.

Guttentag, M., S. Salasin, & D. Belle (Eds.). *The Mental Health of Women*. New York: Academic Press, 1980.

Huber, J. (Ed). Changing women in a changing society. Chicago: University of Chicago Press, 1973.

Institute for Social Research Newsletter. Americans seek self-development, suffer anxiety from changing roles. *Institute for Social Research Newsletter*. The University of Michigan, 1979, *5*(winter), 4–5.

Klerman and Weissman see Guttentag, et al.

Maccoby, E. E., & Jacklin, C. N. *The Psychology of sex differences*. California: Stanford University Press, 1974.

McLean, P. Therapeutic decision-making in behavioral treatment of depression. In Davidson P. O. (Ed.), *The behavioral management of anxiety, depression and pain*. New York: Brunner/Mazel, 1976.

Radloff, L. S. Sex differences in depression: The effects of occupation and marital status. *Sex Roles*, 1975, *1*(3), 249–265.

Radloff, L. S. The CES-D scale: A self-report depression scale for research in the general population. *Journal of Applied Psychological Measurement*, 1977, *1*, 385–401.

Radloff, L. S. Depression and the empty nest. *Sex Roles*, in press.

Radloff, L. S., & Monroe, M. M. Sex differences in helplessness: With implications for depression. In Hansen, L. S., & Rapoza, R. S. (Eds.), *Career development and counselling of women.* Springfield, Ill.: Charles C. Thomas, 1978.

Radloff, L. S., & Rae, D. S. Susceptibility and precipitating factors in depression: Sex differences and similarities. *Journal of Abnormal Psychology.* 1979, *88*(2), 174–181.

Safilios-Rothschild (Ed) *Toward a sociology of women.* Lexington, Mass. Xerox Coll. 1972.

Rizley, R. Depression and distortion in the attribution of causality. *Journal of Abnormal Psychology,* 1978, *87,*32–48.

Seiden, R. H. Suicide among youth: A review of the literature. 1900–1967. *The Bulletin of Suicidology,* National Institute of Mental Health, December 1969, 1–62.

Seligman, M. E. P. *Helplessness: On depression, development, and death.* San Francisco: W. H. Freeman, 1975.

Serbin, L. A., O'Leary, K. D., Kent, R. N., & Tonick, I. J. A comparison of teacher response to the preacademic and problem behavior of boys and girls. *Child Development:* 1973, *44,* 796–804.

Silverman, C. *The epidemiology of depression.* Baltimore: The Johns Hopkins Press: 1968.

Weissman, M. M., & Paykel, E. *The depressed woman: A study of social relationships.* Chicago: University of Chicago Press, 1974.

Weissman, M. M., Sholomskas, D., Pottenger, M., Prusoff, B. A., & Locke, B. Z. Assessing depressive symptoms in five psychiatric populations: A validation study. *American Journal of Epidemiology,* 1977, *106,* 203–214.

PART IV

BIOMEDICAL APPROACHES

Somewhat different criteria had to be employed to select the articles for this section. The articles that were chosen were written by recognized authorities and summarize current knowledge of some important biomedical aspects of depression. They are not classics in the sense that that term might be applied to Freud's "Mourning and Melancholia." It would have been difficult to find a biomedically oriented article written at the same time as the Freud article that had anything but historical interest today. An excerpt from the writings of Kraepelin might have been included. Yet, beyond his drawing of the still useful distinction between dementia praecox and manic-depressive psychosis, he was a product of his age and tended to lapse into dogmatic and unscientific assertions about disease entities and elusive predispositions and constitutional defects.

The development of a biomedical perspective with a solid basis for its claims to a scientific status has depended upon both serendipitous findings about drug effects and tremendous technological advances in the fields of anatomy, neurophysiology, and biochemistry. For example, current interest in electrolyte metabolism in depression can be traced to Cade's attempts in the late forties to induce mania in animals with urea (Whybrow, Akiskal, & McKinney, 1984). He employed lithium urate because of it solubility. Although he did not find support for his hypothesis that urea acted as a toxic agent in the onset of mania, he did discover the therapeutic potency of lithium. Success in treating mania in humans led to an extensive research program, but development of our current state of knowledge about electrolyte metabolism in affective disorders depended upon the more recent availability of isotope-dilution techniques. Similar patterns of serendipitous findings about drug effects, followed by a close collaboration between clinical and basic scientists that depended upon technological advances followed upon the discoveries of reserprine-precipitated depressions and the antidepressant effects of imipramine.

The biomedical perspective has undergone rapid changes in the past few decades, and obsolescence comes quickly to ideas. Statements made in the early sixties about the role of amines in depression would be rejected as simplistic today. As Baldessarini (this volume) points out, any hypothesis is now suspect that posits that a single amine is responsible for the full range of biological depressive phenomena.

Technological advances have meant that the evidence that can be cited is much less circumstantial than it was only two decades ago, but the enormous complexity of biomedical aspects of depression is also being appreciated. There is a consensus that some depressions have stronger biological components than others, but we are far from any "gold standard" for the identification of such depressions. Numerous biological markers have been proposed, but it is generally unclear whether they identify the same, overlapping, or quite different groups of patients (Clayton & Barret, 1983).

There is ambiguity, confusion, and controversy within the biomedical perspective, and yet there is an overwhelming sense of progress. The nature of this progress is quite different than that within psychological and social perspectives, where—although there is undeniably an accumulation of new research data—the assension of one theory over another is more often a conceptual rather than an empirical matter.

Winokur opens the section with a fresh discussion of the old controversy of how best to draw distinctions among types of unipolar depressions. He acknowledges that the endogenous-reactive distinction is an imprecise one, but suggests that this does not rule out that there might be a kernal of truth in it. Yet anyone who is going to argue that the distinction is valid has to contend with accumulated research findings that (1) whether a precipitating event is present has not proven to be a good discriminator, and (2) symptoms and other clinical features work somewhat better but are still far from satisfactory (Fowles & Gersh, 1979). Part of Winokur's solution to these problems is to rely on family background and laboratory tests. However, Winokur argues also for the importance of considering whether a patient has had a "stormy" life-style or personality prior to becoming depressed—a history of marital and sexual problems and lifelong irritability. This, he argues, is a better predictor of response to treatment than is precipitating stress.

Winokur goes on to validate the use of a stormy life-style as a discriminator using family background and laboratory tests. Much of the past research on the family background of depressives has centered on the presence or absence of affective disorder among first-degree relatives. However, Winokur also attends to whether there is a family history of antisocial personality or alcoholism. Next he shows that the discrimination that he has made also predicts response to what is becoming a standard laboratory test in depression, the dexamethasone suppression test. (See the discussion below and Baldessarini for a description of this test.) Winokur concludes that there is converging evidence for the usefulness of this distinction, but that further research is needed.

The logic of Winokur's arguments is consistent with other developments in the diagnosis and classification of depression. It is clear that symptoms do not by themselves provide an adequate basis for distinguishing among unipolar depressed patients and that new categories will need to be developed on the basis of the convergence of symptoms with family history and laboratory test results. Yet, as in Winokur's data, there is also some slippage when multiple perspectives are combined, and it is unlikely that the resulting distinctions that can be drawn will be sharp ones.

The second diagnostic question that Winokur addresses is whether there are differences between persons in the community who are diagnosed as depressed on the basis of symptoms and those who are hospitalized. Family background data discriminate well between these groups. Depressed people in the hospital are more likely to have relatives who committed suicide than do community-residing persons who are identified as depressed. He concludes that there is evidence that important differences in the two populations do exist but that they remain to be described more fully.

Winokur is clear in his assumption about the stronger biological basis for the "familial pure depressive disease" than for the "depressive spectrum disease" or "sporadic depressive disease," as well as for hospitalized versus community-residing depressed persons. However, some cautions are in order. As noted in the Introduction, we should reject the dualism and reductionism involved in any strict dichotomizing of biological versus nonbiological depressions. We should not prematurely close discussions about either the psychosocial features of supposedly biological depressions or the biological aspects of depressions that do not have identified familial or laboratory-test correlates. The separation of a subgroup of depressed persons who have a stormy life-style definitely does not in any way rule out the likelihood that psychological and social factors influence the onset, clinical features, and course of the "pure" depressives who lack such a background. The findings concerning the difference between hospitalized and community-residing depressed persons raises some fascinating questions about the social processes by which the hospitalized group are identified as different from other seriously depressed persons and face the outcome that they do. How does the community identify and extrude them?

Finally, it should be noted that the population studied by Winokur is a severely depressed hospitalized group, and one must be cautious about making overgeneralizations about less disturbed outpatient populations. Klerman (1971) has noted that the bulk of biomedically oriented research is conducted with severely disturbed hospitalized patients, even though the bulk of current clinical experience is with less disturbed, noninstitutionalized patients.

Dunner (this volume) discusses progress in the study of the genetics of depression. He notes the types of evidence that can now be mustered as evidence for a genetic component in depression: the clustering of depression in families; differences between monozygotic and dizygotic twins; rates of depression among the offspring of depressed parents who have been adopted by foster parents without a history of depression; and the linking of depression to a specific gene. Of these types of evidence, the first three are strongest; yet, the last remains most crucial, and the findings thusfar remain the weakest and most controversial.

Reviewing some recent large scale studies, Dunner concludes that the risk for affective disorders among the relatives of unipolar and bipolar depressed persons is about 15–20 percent. The lower figure comes from a New York study in which patients were drawn from an outpatient population, whereas the higher figure comes from hospitalized samples. Apparently, there is a weaker genetic component to the less severe depression found in clinic and community samples (Leckman et al., 1984a). The lower figure of 15 percent is large enough to establish a genetic component to at least some depressions, but the higher figure is still small enough to suggest that other factors are involved.

The study of the genetics of depression remains in its infancy. Further advances are going to require better ways of subtyping affective disorders and the discovery of biological markers that are not state dependent, that is, tied to whether someone is currently disturbed. Dunner describes some of the distinctions that he and his colleagues have drawn for bipolar disorder, in terms of the severity of manic and depressive phases (e.g., whether one or both require hospitalization). It is probably true that bipolar disorder is more homogeneous and has a stronger genetic component than unipolar depression, and because of this, Dunner suggests that that is more likely to yield advances in the near future. Some researchers are attempting to identify subtypes of unipolar depression that "breed true," such that the relatives of depressed persons who have a particular pattern of symptoms will themselves show this pattern if they become depressed. There have been some promising findings with concomitant appetite disturbance and excessive guilt (Leckman et al., 1984b), but any substantial advances are going to depend ultimately upon the identification of genetic markers that have thus far proven elusive. Rieder and Gershon (1978) have noted that such markers will need to be stable, heritable, and state independent; capable of differentiating persons with an affective disturbance from persons drawn from the general population; and among the relatives of depressed persons, capable of identifying those who develop affective disturbance from those who do not.

Baldessarini reviews a full range of developments in our understanding of biomedical aspects of severe depression: diagnosis, genetics, endocrinology, and neurophysiology. He notes how technological advances are allowing the field to move beyond its previous reliance upon studies of drug effects make inferences about the role of neurotransmitters in mood disturbance. The hypotheses that could be tested in this manner were always imprecise and oversimplifed. Available drugs generally had multiple effects on diverse transmitters, and evidence of any specific effect was always indirect (Montgomery, 1985). Furthermore, as Baldessarini notes, such research was often used to make unwarranted inferences about the underlying biochemical basis for mood disturbance. By analogy, the effectiveness of aspirin in relieving a headache does not necessarily imply that an aspirin deficiency is implicated in the causes of headaches.

Baldessarini indicates how there has long been a belief that there is some disruption of hormone secretion in severe depression and that one part of this is an excessive secretion of cortisol. The dexamethasone suppresion test that he describes as particularly promising has seemed to be an excellent tool for investigating cortisone secretion, but in the past 18 months, it has become the object of considerable controversy. Baldessasrini and Arana (1985) are among the many researchers producing discouraging data concerning its utility.

The ideal test for some specific disregulation in a particular type of depression has not yet been discovered, but it would have 100 percent *specificity* in not falsely identifying someone as having the mood disturbance who did not, and 100 percent *sensitivity* in identifying everyone who did have the mood disturbance. Initial results with the dexamethasone suppression test indicated that it had a high degree of specificity (90–96 percent) and at least a moderate level of sensitivity for endogenous-melancholic depression (40–67 percent). Thus, these results suggested that the test might be quite revealing when positive, although less so when negative. Almost all positives would be endogenous melancholics, but about half of all endogenous melancholics would test negative. The test is simple, painless, and inexpensive enough to become the first generally used clinical test in psychiatry.

The test became widely accepted immediately, and when some researchers failed to obtain such striking results, the failure was first ascribed to problems in the administration of the test and the fuzziness of the existing criteria for endogenous-melancholic depression. It is certainly true that current diagnostic criteria are problematic, and some still hold to this explanation (Carroll, 1985). However, others are reporting that 15–19 percent of normal volunteers test positive and that factors such as upper respiratory tract infections, moderate weight loss, and aging might produce false positives (Amsterdam, et al., 1982; Brown, et al., 1985). Baldessarini and Arana (1985) concluded from their results that the dexamethasone suppression test has limited power in differentiating major depressive disorders from other acute and severe illnesses. The fabled "gold standard" thus has not been found. Yet Baldessarini and Arana (1985) note the enduring significance of the dexamethasone suppression test. Work on the DST has sharpened the focus on current diagnostic problems and encouraged a further search for simple tests of biological markers. In the article in this volume, Baldessarini has noted some of the current leads that are being pursued.

REFERENCES

Amsterdam, J. D., et al. (1982). The dexamethasone suppression test in outpatients with primary affective disorder and healthy control subjects. *American Journal of Psychiatry*. 139:287–291.

Baldessarini, R. J., and Arana, G. W. (1985). Does the dexamethasone suppression test have clinical utility? *Journal of Clincial Psychiatry*. 46:25–30.

Brown, W. A., et al. (1985). The dexamethasone suppression test and pituitary-adrenocortical function. *Archives of General Psychiatry*. 42:121–123.

Carroll, B. J. (1985). Dexamethasone suppression test: A review of contemporary confusion. *Journal of Clinical Psychiatry*. 46: 13–24.

Carroll, B. J., et al. (1981). A specific laboratory test for the diagnosis of melancholia. *Archives of General Psychiatry*. 38:15–22.

Clayton, P. J. and Barrett, J. E. (Eds.) (1983). *Treatment of Depression: Old Controversies and New Approachess*. NY: Raven Press.

Fowles, D. C. and Gersh, F. S. (1979). Neuotic depression: The endogenous-reactive distinction. In R. A. Depue (Ed.) *The Psychobiology of Depressive Disorders*. NY: Academic Press.

Klerman, G. L. (1971). clinical research in depression. *Archives of General Psychiatry*. 24:304–319.

Leckman, J. F., et al. (1984a) Subtypes of depression *Archives of General Psychiatry*, 41:833–838.

Leckman, J. F., et al. (1984b). Appetite disturbance and excessive guilt in major depression. *Archives of General Psychiatry*, 41:839–844.

Montgomery, S. A. (1985). Development of a new treatment for depression. *Journal of Clinical Psychiatry*. 46:3–4.

Reider, R. O. and Gershon, E. S. (1978). Genetic strategies in biological psychiatry. *Archives of General Psychiatry*, 35:866–873.

Whybrow, P. C., Akiskal, H. S., and McKinney, W. T. (1984). *Mood Disorder: Toward a New Psychobiology*. NY: Plenum Press.

15. Controversies in Depression, or Do Clinicians Know Something After All?

George Winokur

In two extremely lucid efforts, Kendall has reviewed both the historical background of the controversies over classification of depressive illnesses as well as the contemporary viewpoints (7,8). To now attempt a dreary recounting of something like Kraepelin noted, Lange delimited, Gillespie observed, Mapother challenged, Buzzard responded, and Lewis asserted would be reminiscent of the biblical chronicles which noted that Elezarb begat Phinebas, Phinebas begat Abisua, Abisua begat Bukki, and Bukki begat Uzzi, etc. Further, this would not solve the issue. Kendall presents nine different contemporary classifications, mainly based on clinical background. To these we may add others that would be more biological. For instance, some suggest that abnormalities in excretion of MHPG might be used to separate depressions. Response to lithium could separate depression. Response to lithium and prevention of illness with lithium could separate depressions. Abnormal non-suppressor status in the dexamethasone suppression test may be useful in classification, as might 5-HIAA in spinal fluid. All of these biological measures could be related to an entire new set of classifications. The methods that are used vary from simple clinical description and follow-up to cluster analysis, factor analysis, and discriminant function analysis.

However, if we may be allowed to switch simile to metaphors in midstream, we would like to cut the Gordian knot. What seems necessary now is to determine whether any particular classification may be validated by its relationship to other classifications. In other words, if two classifications were compared to each other, would they have a great deal in common? If so, it would indicate some validity in both of them, even though the starting points of the classifications were different.

Clinicians have considered two major groups of depression, endogenous-psychotic and reactive-neurotic. The endogenous-psychotic group shows such symptoms as severe depression, social incapacity, feelings of worthlessness, retardation, terminal insomnia, anorexia, and marked suicidal intent. The reactive-neurotic group is typified by a less severe depression, a neurotic or stormy life prior to the depression, and a relationship to precipitating factors. In fact, the term "reactive" is somewhat misleading. It is fairly clear from the superb studies of Clayton and her colleagues that even a simple bereavement is related to a reactive depression in fully a third of widows and widowers (3). Bereavement is a normal response to a death of a close relative or friend. Although it manifests itself by a definable depression and is associated with a precipitating factor, there is no reason to believe that people who suffer from a bereavement depression are those with a stormy history. Therefore, it will not be considered further in this chapter.

Klerman et al. have presented the criteria for neurotic depression and what is important is the fact that the definition varies from study to study (10). They point out that neurotic depressions may be defined six different ways. They may be less socially incapacitating or they may be nonpsychotic (i.e., no delusions or hallucinations) or they do not present such endogenous symptoms as early morning awakening, weight loss, retardation, or they may follow a stressful event (in which case they would be considered reactive), or they may be a consequence of a longstanding maladaptive personality pattern (i.e., a stormy personality), or finally they may be the result of unconscious conflicts. In any case, they should be considered as a mixed group when clinicians make the diagnosis. The fact that there is no great precision in the diagnosis does not mean that there may not be a kernel of truth in the separation of endogenous-psychotic form of depression from the reactive-neurotic form. In this paper, we will approach this clinical separation by evaluating it against a classification from an entirely different viewpoint, namely a separation on the basis of family background. Although this deals with an old controversy in psychiatry, it is still an active one, and one which is very meaningful to clinicians.

Finally, we will present data on a new controversy in depression which is currently waiting in the wings for a major appearance. This controversy has to do with the diagnosis of depression in the community versus the diagnosis in a psychiatric setting.

THE DIFFERENTIATION OF ENDOGENOUS-PSYCHOTIC FROM NEUROTIC-REACTIVE DEPRESSION

At the outset, let us state that we will not deal with bipolar patients, only unipolars. Further, there is a problem with the differentiation between primary and secondary depression. Secondary depression is a simple depression that occurs in the context of another psychiatric illness, such as alcoholism or antisocial personality, hysteria, or anxiety neurosis. It is entirely conceivable that some patients called reactive-neurotic in fact have secondary depression and their primary diagnoses would be some other psychiatric illness. For the purposes of the present discussion, we will consider only reactive-neurotic patients who have primary depressions.

First, we need to look at circumstances which predate the depression for which the patient is treated. There are only three possibilities for this: precipitating factors, premorbid personality, and a positive family history. Some data exist on the follow-up and perhaps these data might also separate the two groups. It is conceivable that some circumstances which involve the use of laboratory tests might separate the two groups and we will explore that. After we deal with that in the reactive-neurotic, endogenous-psychotic dichotomy, we will examine another method of classification, namely a familial classification, and note any overlap in the findings.

THE CHARACTERISTICS OF NEUROTIC DEPRESSION AND ENDOGENOUS DEPRESSION

In a systematic study of symptoms and other types of clinical data, Kiloh and Garside (9) looked at a variety of items. They evaluated 92 patients who had clinical diagnoses of neurotic depression or endogenous depression. Table 1 shows a variety of clinical features evaluated in the Kiloh and Garside study that correlate with one or the other diagnosis at a significant level ($p<0.05$).

The simple presentation of these features that were correlated with the clinicians' diagnoses does not prove that the two illnesses exist. What it may prove is the certain features may have been uppermost in the minds of the clinicians when they made these diagnoses and these features were the found in retrospect. To assume that this proves the

Table 1. Some clinical features that correlate with diagnosis in decreasing size of correlations

Neurotic depression	Endogenous depression
Reactivity of depression	Early awakening
Precipitation	Dirunal variation
Self-pity	Retardation
Hysterical features	Concentration difficulties
Immaturity	Significant weight loss
Inadequacy	Previous episodes
Irritability	
Hypochondriasis	

existence of these symptoms as separate entities would be circular. The authors then subjected the data to a factor analysis. Two factors were extracted. With further statistical manipulation, it was found that the data could not be produced by a single depressive condition but had to be explained by the presence of two separate conditions. In another publication, Carney et al. examined a group of endogenous and neurotic patients and subjected the clinical features to a multiple regression analysis (4). The distribution of the scores were shown to be bimodal rather than unimodal and this also suggested the presence of two distinct illnesses. Kendall published material using discriminant function analysis and was unable to find the same kind of bimodality; he suggested a continuum rather than separate illnesses (8).

If we look at Klerman's description of the various ways in which a diagnosis of reactive-neurotic depression is made, two major points stand out. These are relevant to the presence of precipitating factors and the presence of a premordid stormy personality. Such features are seen in Table 1. If one peruses Kendall's material, it is clear that such items as childhood neurotic traits, previous hysterical symptoms, previous subjective tension, always ailing, and previous demonstrative suicidal attempts are more likely associated with the diagnosis of neurotic depression than endogenous depression. This is also true as regards precipitating factors, though in both groups, endogenous and neurotic, a majority of patients have precipitating factors (8). However, these clinical features may have been simply the reason for the clinician's diagnosing neurotic depression.

Paykel et al. have shown some relatively weak but significant correlations between life event scores and symptoms in depression, as well as neuroticism scores on the Maudsley Personality Inventory and depressive symptoms (13). Anxiety is positively correlated with the neuroticism scores, as are irritability, obsessional symptoms, and feelings of helplessness. These would be symptoms that would be seen in a reactive-neurotic type of depression. As regards recent life events, these are correlated positively with irritability but negatively with diurnal variation, anorexia, and retardation. The problem seems simple enough. In any large group of patients who are called reactive-neurotic depressive, the two defining characteristics of precipitating factors and a stormy life background will be found. However, it is hardly an invariable finding. Such circumstances are also found in patients who are called depressed for endogenous reasons.

Should one want to determine which is the better of the two criteria, either precipitating factors or a stormy life-style, some data on treatment might be useful. DeCarolis presented material on ECT in 437 patients who suffered from depression (1). Electroconvulsive therapy is more effective in endogenous depression than reactive-neurotic depression. After ECT in the total group of depressives, 72% were considered as improved. On the other hand, of 31 patients who had reactive-neurotic depressions, only 26% were improved as opposed to 85% of the patients who were considered to have endogenous depressions. What is most interesting, however, is that the precipitating event used as a means of separating patients was less useful than the diagnosis of reactive-neurotic depression. Thus, of 111 patients with precipitating events, 62% were considered improved versus 84% of 79 patients with no precipitating event. Clearly, the diagnosis of reactive-neurotic depression is a more useful separator, at least as regards response to treatment, than is the simple assessment of whether a precipitating event was associated with the depression. Presumably, the stormy life-style was more useful as a predictor than the presence of life events.

Of some interest is the study by Mendels who looked at a group of 100 depressed patients and noted that the presence of such reactive symptoms as neurotic traits in childhood and adulthood, precipitating factors, inadequate personality, and emotional liability separated patients into two groups better than such endogenous items as a family history of depression, feelings of self-reproach, diurnal variation, delusions, and early morning awakening (11). He also found that there

Table 2. Outcome in patients with "endogenous" syndrome versus those with "neurotic" syndrome

	"Endogenous" syndrome	"Neurotic" syndrome
n	31	
Recovered on leaving hospital	22 (71%)	12 (31%)[b]
Readmission in follow-up	15 (48%)	9 (23%)[a]
Prolonged ill health	7 (23%)	16 (%)

[a] $p < .05$
[b] $p < .005$

was a poor clinical response to electroconvulsive therapy if the patient showed neurotic traits in childhood, precipitating factors, inadequate personality, and emotional lability. There was a good response to ECT if the patient showed psychomotor retardation.

Probably the most important set of studies in differentiating the endogenous psychotic from the reactive-neurotic groups are the follow-up studies. In a 5–7-year follow-up of 104 cases, Kay et al. showed that immediate recovery was more likely in the endogenous than in the neurotic group (p<0.05) (6). In the follow-up, though there are clearly more readmissions for the endogenous group, the neurotic group is more likely to show prolonged ill health. This is an interesting difference and would suggest a more episodic course with recovery and exacerbations in the endogenous group and a more constant course of morbidity in the neurotic group. A course of prolonged ill health was to some extent predicted by "neurotic" syndrome and somatic complaints. Table 2 presents these data. Paykel et al. also have reported on a follow-up, in this case 10 months (12). In general, endogenous depressives showed a better prognosis. However, the findings were somewhat different from those of the previous study. Patients with remissions and subsequent relapses in that short period of time tended to be more neurotic than patients with remission and no subsequent relapse who tended to be more endogenous. In this study, however, relapse did not necessarily mean readmission. Also, the difference in length of follow-up may not make the studies comparable. Though not all studies are consistent in their results, it seems fairly clear that some patients come into the hospital with a lot of precipitating factors and a life history of stormy problems. Thus, there is some reason to believe that there are a number of patients with these features who may be different from

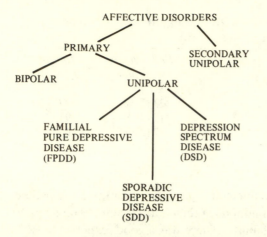

Figure 1. Classification of primary and secondary depressions.

the endogenous group; however, there is a considerable overlap in symptomatology. The question that arises is whether such findings, though not perfect, indicate a meaningful differentiation of specific illnesses within the large rubric of depressive illness.

CROSS VALIDITY USING A DIFFERENT METHODOLOGY FOR SEPARATION OF DEPRESSIVE ILLNESS

There is another way to classify patients who enter the hospital with primary unipolar depressions, namely, by family background. Figure 1 shows a separation of primary and secondary depressions. Secondary depressions are those depressions which occur in the context of another psychiatric illness, such as alcoholism, antisocial personality, anxiety neurosis, and obsessional neurosis. Because secondary depressions may show a "neurotic" background, it is likely that in many studies they overlap to some extent with reactive-neurotic depressions.

The unipolar primary depressives suffer one or more depressions and may be divided on the basis of family background. There are three types. One of these is depression spectrum disease (DSD) which is an ordinary depression occurring in a person who has a first-degree family member who shows alcoholism and/or anti-Social personality. Another first-degree family member may or may not show depression. The second type is familial pure depressive disease (FPDD) which is an

Table 3. Significant differences between female depression spectrum disease and familial pure depressive disease patients

Clinical features	Depression spectrum disease	Familial pure depressive disease
Loss of interest in usual activities	61%	80%
History of sexual problems	32%	15%
History of divorce or separation	20%	8%
Lifelong irritability	20%	8%
Previous episodes of depression/ person	0.66	1.12
At least one relapse in depression at follow-up	21%	49%
Subsequently hospitalized	26%	44%
Final clinical diagnosis of reactive depression	32%	17%

ordinary depression in an individual who has a first-degree family member with depression but no alcoholism, antisocial personality, or mania. The third type is sporadic depressive disease which is an ordinary depression in an individual who has a negative family history for alcoholism, antisocial personality, depression, or mania.

The major differentiating factor in these three groups is age of onset which, for the sporadic group, is far older, close to 10 years, than in either the depression spectrum or the familial pure depressive disease group (19). There is a problem with the definition of an illness such as sporadic depressive disease which is made on the basis of an absence of some specific family history. It is quite possible that there are a number of false negatives in this group; and, therefore, though the group is useful and should be separated from the other two groups, it still has to be studied as an illness on its own. However, it is possible to compare the familial pure depressive disease with the depression spectrum group.

When this is done, there are some interesting differences. The age of onset in the two groups is similar. However, if one looks at a group of female patients and compares the ones with depression spectrum disease to those with familial pure depressive disease, it is clear that there is a larger set of personal problems in the group with depression spectrum disease (17,19). Table 3 presents the clinical features that are significantly different between the groups. What is interesting is that

Table 4. Preliminary data on differences between depression spectrum and familial pure depressive disease patients

	DSD	FPDD
n	35	22
% Female	77	55
Age at index	32.5	40.0
Proportion separated or divorced of those ever married	31%	31%
Proportion with greater than three marital problems of those currently married	61%	36%

the one symptom difference which separates them is one that has usually been considered associated with endogenous depression, namely loss of interest in usual activities. This is seen more frequently in the familial pure depressive disease group. On the other hand, marital and sexual problems which would indicate neurotic difficulties in the past are more frequently seen in depression spectrum disease. The data in Table 3 should be compared with those in Tables 1 and 2 which showed differences between reactive-neurotic depression and endogenous-psychotic depression. The findings are quite similar. Of importance is the fact that although stormy life-styles separate DSD from FPDD, precipitating factors were seen equally in both groups.

Table 3 also shows follow-up material in two groups of women, one with depression spectrum disease and one with pure familial pure depressive disease. The patients with familial pure depressive disease are more likely to have had episodes prior to entering the hospital for an index admission and in the course of the follow-up are more likely to have had subsequent hospitalizations. Thus, the data look rather similar to the material in the Kay et al. (6) follow-up study.

In an attempt to look at these kinds of problems in a new group, we have examined patients with depression spectrum disease and familial pure depressive disease that have been collected locally at the University of Iowa as part of an NIMH Collaborative Depression Study. Table 4 shows these preliminary data. There are more marital problems among the group with depression spectrum disease than one sees in the familial pure depressive disease group. In fact, if one looks at the mean number of symptoms in the two groups together, one finds that there is 3.0 martial problems in the combined groups. Thirty-six percent of the familial pure depressives have greater than three problems, whereas

Table 5. Family history of alcoholism in depression

	Reactive depression	Manic depressive and psychotic depression
Probands (n)	75	212
Alcoholic fathers	13%	9%
Alcoholism in sibships	11%	3%

61% of the depression spectrum disease patients have greater than three marital problems. Of course, this only deals with those people who are currently married. Both groups contain the same number of people separated and divorced, 31%; but as the depression spectrum patients are 7.5 years younger at index, they have had far less time to go through and accumulate separations and divorces.

It would seem clear that many of the qualities that are seen in neurotic depressive patients are also seen in depression spectrum patients and many of the qualities seen in endogenous patients are seen in familial pure depressive disease patients. The thing that is interesting is that the separation adds another dimension to classification. It is done by the presence of the family history rather than by the presence of specific clinical symptoms.

FURTHER DATA SHOWING AN ASSOCIATION BETWEEN FAMILIAL SUBTYPING AND THE ENDOGENOUS-NEUROTIC CONTINUUM

Most studies of the endogenous-psychotic, reactive–neurotic dichotomy, when they have used family history for a separation, have only looked at family history of depression. What seems important is to look at the other possibility which is the family history of alcoholism. In Table 3, a clinical diagnosis of reactive depression is shown to be related to depression spectrum disease which is diagnosed because a person has a family history of alcoholism. In this study of 289 depressed women, 104 had a family history of alcoholism and showed a clinical diagnosis of reactive-neurotic depression in 32%; of 184 with a lack of familial alcoholism, 15% were diagnosed as reactive-neurotic depression ($\chi^2 = 10.7$, d.f. $= 1$, $p < 0.005$) (19). Table 5 shows the results of another study in which the family history of alcholism was compared in "reacative" depression versus manic-depressive disease (20). Significantly more alcholism was found in the sibships of reactive depres-

Table 6. Results of dexamethasone suppression test in different types of unipolar depressions

	n	% abnormal (nonsuppressors)
Endogenous	35	51
Depressive neurosis	18	0
Familial pure depressive disease	50	76
Depressive spectrum disease	41	7

sions. This finding once again makes one believe that there is a clear overlap between depression spectrum disease and reactive-neurotic depression.

Perhaps the most important support for an association between the two classification systems are the dexamethasone test data. Table 6 shows a series of findings on different diagnoses. Carroll has presented data separating endogenous depressives from neurotic depressives; abnormal dexamethasone nonsuppressor status is seen in endogenous depression but a normal status is seen in reactive depression (5). Schlesser et al. have looked at the same test but used a familial classification (14). The familial pure depressive patients are likely to show an abnormal nonsuppressor status whereas the depression spectrum patients are usually quite normal as regards their suppressor status. Again, this shows a real association between the old clinical endogenous-neurotic classification and the familial classification of patients.

There are few data on treatment and subclassification but it is interesting to note that depressives with one or more episodes prior to the index admission are far less likely to respond with marked improvement to antidepressant drugs than those admitted for the first time (2). In a sense this is opposed to the clinical wisdom which indicates that patients with endogenous depression (who may have more episodes than neurotic depressions) are the ones who respond to tricyclics; in fact, what this may indicate is that patients with reactive-neurotic or depression spectrum disease might be somewhat more likely to respond to the antidepressant drugs. This, of course, needs to be investigated further. In any event, on the basis of similarities in stormy premorbid life-style, course of illness, a family background of alcoholism and dexamethasone suppressor status, depression spectrum disease and reactive-neurotic depression appear to overlap, as do endogenous-psychotic depression

Table 7. Affective disorders in a control population in Iowa

	n	%
People examined personally	85	
Diagnosis		
Bipolar	2	2.4
Major depressive disorder, primary	16	18.8
Minor depressive disorder	2	2.4
Total	20	23.5

and familial pure depressive disease. This is of special interest in that it is possible to find some validation of an old classification by the use of a new classification. The common background of alcoholism in re-active-neurotic depression and depression spectrum disease suggests the possibility of a genetic factor in this type of illness.

AN EMERGING CONTROVERSY IN DEPRESSION

It is clear that we are identifying a large number of patients in the community who meet lenient research criteria for depression, either major or minor depression (18). It seems unlikely that this is all one illness. An evaluation of a normal control group in Iowa shows also a large amount of illness in the population. This is noted in Table 7. About 24% of the population is likely to suffer or have suffered from some kind of primary depressive illness which meets the same research cri-teria. Today, it is inconceivable that we would diagnose anybody as depressed who did not meet reasonable research criteria, but it is pos-sible that many people who do, do not necessarily have a depression or at least the same kind of depression as those patients who are hospitalized for a depressive illness.

The questions which arise are whether these patients need to be treated, whether all of them have a similar kind of illness, and for that matter whether they have any illness at all. To obtain an answer, we have used a relative ratio methodology. It is possible to use information from a family study and family history study to assess this. In the Iowa 500 about twice as many relatives of depressives and manics showed an affective illness as was found in a control population (Table 8). However, about eight to nine times as many of the deceased relatives in the families of the affectively ill index cases showed a chart for

Table 8. Relative ratios (clinical affective disorder: controls) on two measures of family psychopathology

	Personal exam measure			Psychiatric records on deceased relatives		
	Relatives at risk	Relatives with mania or depression	Ratio	Deceased relatives	Number of records	Ratio
Controls ($n = 160$)	344	26 (7.6%)	1.7	332	2 (0.6%)	8.5
Manic + depressives ($n = 325$)	500	65 (13%)		918	47 (5.1%)	

Comparisons: controls versus manics and depressives
Personal exam measure ($\chi^2 = 5.72$, d.f. $= 1$, $p < 0.025$)
Psychiatric records measure ($\chi^2 = 12.04$, d.f. $= 1$, $p < 0.001$)
Deceased relative/control $= 2.0$, deceased relative/affective disorder patient $= 2.8$

hospitalization for severe psychiatric illness. Though a higher proportion of relatives of affective disorder probands than control relatives was deceased, this did not account for the increased ratio. Further, in Fig. 2 which shows these ratios graphically, we also find that in a follow-up five to six times as many affectively ill probands died by suicide as did the controls. Thus again the relative ratio comparison favors a difference between the depressive in the population versus the depressive who is hospitalized. What I am suggesting is that the question of severity and the question of medical treatment may really be tapping an entirely different set of people than are found by the simple examination which leads to meeting research criteria. It may be that the community separates out seriously ill people, forces them into treatment, and that these are qualitatively different from those patients who are simply diagnosed in the general population. If severity were not of importance, why would the ratio of deceased relatives with psychiatric records (relatives of ill probands: relatives of controls) be a more discriminating measure of familial pathology than the personal examination data? Neither increased mortality in affectively ill people nor differential emigration rates from the state account for these differences (15,16,21). Further, the suicide differences are also indicative of the importance of severity.

What do these ratios indicate? They support the idea that severity as

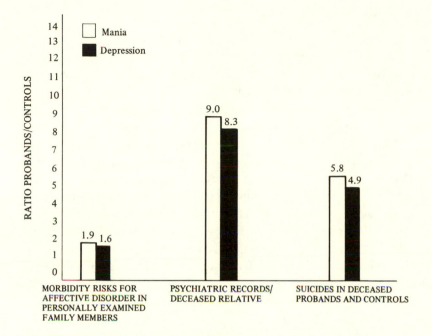

Figure 2. Relative ratios, probands to controls, on measures of serious family psychopathology and suicide.

defined by treatment, particularly treatment in a mental hospital, and the outcome by suicide defines an entirely different population from that which is obtained by patients meeting the criteria for depressive illness in the community. If this statement were not so, we would expect the ratios for suicide in follow-up and psychiatric records per deceased relative to be equal to the ratios of morbidity risks for affective disorder in personally examined family members. That severity as defined by treatment and suicide outcome is important should not surprise us. The studies on bereavement have already suggested this. Bereavement frequently manifests itself similarly to clinical depression, but it does not necessitate treatment. It is simply not enough to accept the clinical picture as a diagnosis. What is necessary is some assessment of seriousness or severity which leads to major or incapacitating consequences. What is necessary are more specific criteria. No doubt this will occur in the course of time.

DISCUSSION

We probably are entering a new era in the investigation of depressive illnesses. We are beginning to develop some laboratory tests which are meaningful, as well as new possibilities for epidemiological evaluations. It seems reasonable that we might separate out an illness which would be similar to depression spectrum disease or reactive-neurotic depression which would manifest itself by the following criteria. The patients would have a series of major personal problems; they would be quite responsive to stress; they would be normal responders in the dexamethasone suppression test; and they would have a family history of alcoholism. The biggest problem here is to systematically define a neurotic or stormy life-style. This is something that ought to be able to be put in a systematic form though it will require effort. These patients should be compared to those patients with a lack of alcoholism in their family, a presence of familial depression, a lack of stormy problems in their lives, and an abnormal dexamethasone suppression test. These criteria would take all of the material that shows an association between the old clinical dichotomy and the familial separation and put them together. It is quite conceivable that such a set of criteria would offer us some increased precision in diagnosis and ultimately also in treatment. It seems doubtful that a simple effort to separate the patients on the basis of their clinical picture is going to lead to anything very productive at the present time. The relative ratio data make the diagnosis based simply on clinical picture suspect. The clinical picture has been around a long time and has served its purpose, but now it is necessary to look at things which have not been exploited as much, namely the genetic or family background and a set of laboratory tests.

REFERENCES

1. Avery, D., and Lubrano, A. (1979): Depression treated with imipramine and ECT: The DeCarolis study reconsidered. *Am. J. Psychiatry,* 136:559–562.
2. Avery, D., and Winokur, G. (1977): The efficacy of electroconvulsive therapy and antidepressants in depression. *Biol. Psychiatry,* 12:507–523.
3. Bornstein, P., Clayton, P., Hallikas, J., Maurice, W., and Robins, E. (1973): The depression of widowhood after 13 months. *Br. J. Psychiatry,* 122:561.
4. Carney, M., Roth, M., and Garside, R. (1965): The diagnosis of depressive syndromes and the prediction of ECT response. *Br. J. Psychiatry,* 111:659–674.
5. Carroll, B. (1978): Neuroendocrine procedures for the diagnosis of depression. In

Depressive Disorders, edited by E. Lindenlaub, pp. 231–236. F. K. Shattaner Verlag, Stuttgart.

6. Kay, D., Garside, R., Roy, J., and Beamish, P. (1969): "Endogenous" and "neurotic" syndromes of depression: A 5- to 7-year follow-up of 104 cases. *Br. J. Psychiatry,* 115:389–399.
7. Kendall, R. (1968): *The Classification of Depressive Illnesses,* pp. 1–102. Oxford University Press, London.
8. Kendall, R. (1976): The classification of depressions: A review of contemporary confusion. *Br. J. Psychiatry,* 129:15–38.
9. Kiloh, L, and Garside, R. (1963): The independence of neurotic depression and endogenous depression. *Br. J. Psychiatry,* 109:451–463.
10. Klerman, G., Endicott, J., Spitzer, R., and Hirschfeld, R. (1979): Neurotic depressions: A systematic analysis of multiple criteria and meanings. *Am. J. Psychiatry,* 136:57–61.
11. Mendels, J. (1968): Depression: The distinction between syndrome and symptoms. *Br. J. Psychiatry,* 114:1549–1554.
12. Paykel, E., Klerman, G., and Prusoff, B. (1974): Prognosis of depression and the endogenous-neurotic distinction. *Psychol. Med.,* 4:57–64.
13. Paykel, E., Prusoff, B., and Klerman, G. (1971): The endogenous-neurotic continuum in depression: Rater independence and factor distributions. *J. Psychiatr. Res.,* 8:73–90.
14. Schlesser, M., Winokur, G., and Sherman, B. (1980): Hypothalamic-pituitary-adrenal axis activity in depressive illness. *Arch. Gen. Psychiatry,* 37:737–743.
15. Tsuang, M. (1978): Suicide in schizophrenics, manics, depressives, and surgical controls. *Arch. Gen. Psychiatry,* 35:153–155.
16. Tsuang, M., Woolson, R., and Fleming, J. (1979): Long-term outcome of major psychoses. I. Schizophrenia and affective disorders compared with psychiatrically symptom-free surgical conditions. *Arch. Gen. Psychiatry,* 36:1295–1301.
17. VanValkenburg, C., Lowry, M., Winokur, G., and Cadoret, R. (1977): Depression spectrum disease versus pure depressive disease. *J. Nerv. Ment. Dis.,* 165:341–347.
18. Weissman, M., and Meyers, J. (1978): Affective disorders in a U.S. urban community. *Arch. Gen. Psychiatry,* 35:1304–1311.
19. Winokur, G., Behar, D., VanValkenburg, C., and Lowry, M. (1978): Is a familial definition of depression both feasible and valid? *J. Nerv. Ment. Dis.,* 166:764–768.
20. Winokur, G., and Pitts, F. (1964): Affective disorder. I. Is reactive depression an entity? *J. Nerv. Ment. Dis.,* 138:541–547.
21. Winokur, G., Tsuang, M., and Crowe, R. (1981): The Iowa 500: Family and follow-up findings in bipolars, unipolars, and controls. *Psychopharmacol. Bull.,* 17:78–80.

OPEN DISCUSSION

Dr. Hagop Akiskal: I found Dr. Winokur's reformulation of the clinical and research controversies in the classification of depressive disorders to be both interesting and challenging. I would like to suggest several modifications with respect to the question of the "stormy life-style" that occurs in the context of affective syndromes. First of all, this can occur as a result of cyclothymic and bipolar II disorders. It can also occur in some patients with high frequency episodic depressions. The remissions are so short and the interpersonal consequences of the illness so prominent that these conditions are often confused with a chronic personality disorder. As shown by our group (*Am. J. Psychiatry* 134:1227, 1977; *Arch. Gen. Psychiatry* 37:777, 1980), in all of these recurrent subaffective and affective disorders the affective condition is concealed by the stormy life-style. Thus, characterologic disturbance can "mask" affective symptoms very much like somatic complaints masking underlying depression. Indeed, we have shown that a substantial proportion of patients labeled "neurotic" or "characterologic" depressions do progress upon prospective follow-up into full-blown melancholia. The biological markers described are of great help in diagnosing these masked melancholic, or subaffective, illnesses.

My second point is that there exists another group of individuals with stormy life-style and depression whose primary pathology is characterologic. Even in your own studies the "depression" of this group has been shown to occur in the setting of pre-existing and lifelong characterologic disturbance, as well as family history of alcoholism rather than affective illness. It would seem to me that the designation of "character spectrum disorder" or "characterologic dysphoria"—as proposed by us—is terminologically more descriptive than "depression spectrum," the term preferred by your group.

Dr. George Winokur: I was reading Dr. Akiskal's paper on the train down from Providence to New York, and I think he showed very well that the group of "neurotic-reactive" patients is a mixed group. I would have no problem at all with the way he suggested separating them. The thing that particularly intrigued me in his paper is that a large number of patients who meet that sort of clinical picture are secondary depressives as well. This is a problem, and the group does have to be divided.

Dr. John Rice: Care must be taken when interpreting a ratio of the rate in relatives of affected individuals to the population base rate. There is a measurement, the K-ratio, proposed in the genetics literature by Penrose in the early 1950s. This K-ratio now appears to have limited utility in quantifying familial resemblance. More importantly, the magnitude of the K-ratio depends on how rare the disease is. If the prevalence of a disease is 25%, the largest the K-ratio can be is 4 (with all relatives affected), whereas if the prevalence was 1%, the K-ratio would be, say, 10 if 10% of the relatives were affected. Accordingly, it is not clear if higher K-ratios with severe (i.e., rare) illness can be interpreted as a higher degree of family resemblance.

Dr. Winokur: How would you correct for that?

Dr. Rice: I prefer to think in the context of genetic models based on a continuous underlying liability scale with affected individual corresponding to individuals having values above a certain threshold value. The estimate of the underlying correlation is given by the tetrachoric correlation coefficient and would be invariant under different threshold points so that cutoffs corresponding to different population prevalences can be compared. Thus, comparison of tetrachoric r's could be used to disentangle the effects due to different degrees of family resemblance and due to different population rates.

Alternatively, the 2 × 2 table of disease state in an individual and disease state in a relative could be analyzed using, say, an odds ratio. However, this approach might require the rates of illness in the relatives of unaffected individuals. Also, the 2 × 3 table of mild/severe illness in the proband, and unaffected/mild/or severe illness in the relative might be interesting to look at.

Dr. Barney Carroll: George, I really want to thank you for putting the searchlight on this whole issue of criteria in relation to diagnosis. If I can summarize what I think you have said, it is that criteria are necessary for diagnosis of depression, but that they are probably not sufficient in and of themselves and that some other discriminative ingredient goes into declaring an individual as a case rather than a noncase, and that this is a discriminative judgment that goes beyond the simple application of criteria.

This is the problem we have always had attempting to explain to other people and to funding agencies the way we do things in our own unit where we say that the person must meet criteria for endogenous depression, but in addition the clinicians have to agree that this is a genuine case. I think these figures really support the way we have been going about it.

The other comment I would like to make is a further extension of what you said about individuals identified in the population simply by criteria. I think it is a very important one for people engaged in research. In some centers, subjects for research studies are recruited by newspaper advertisements; they are, in effect, symptomatic volunteers who are then entered into research studies. I have always had a great deal of skepticism about the validity of that procedure. I think you just contaminate your research groups with subjects who are not real cases in the sense in which the community or a psychiatrist would identify them, despite the fact that they meet criteria. So, I think that your data today can serve as a very serious warning against contaminating research studies with symptomatic volunteer subjects.

Dr. Lothar Kalinowsky: Just one brief question. How would you classify those cases which Sargant described as atypical depressions and which responded to MAO inhibitors better than to tricyclics and to ECT?

Dr. Winokur: How would I describe them? Well, that would depend on which definition I used. We are going to have a series of papers on atypical depression here. If you say that these are patients with marked personal problems and a lot of anxiety symptoms and hysterical symptoms, I would diagnose them as primary affective disorder, unipolar if they meet the criteria, and not if they don't. Now, if they meet the criteria for anxiety neurosis, I would diagnose them as anxiety neurosis. I think one of the problems is that a lot of the patients who have been called atypical depressives, in fact, are secondaries, but I think we probably will hear a little bit more about that today in this meeting.

Dr. Hans Huessy: One of my associates, Dr. Stephen Cohen, recently did a study of adults meeting rigid criteria for the diagnosis of depression. He divided them into those who had a history with aggression in the past and those without aggression in the past. They were matched as to age and sex. What he found was that, of the people who had depression with a history of aggression, there was a total remission of symptoms in 7 days in 100% of the cases. In the depressives without such a history, 0% showed that kind of remission. The two groups differed dramatically in their past histories, making one speculate that these two groups of patients are very different and that the aggressive depressives very likely are grown-up hyperkinetics. Often the response to medication is almost immediate and clearly involves a different biochemical effect than in the usual endogenous depression. The definition of reactive depression then would include a large number of grown-up hyperkinetics. Since childhood hyperkinetics do respond to small doses of tricyclics immediately, and we have also demonstrated that the same is true for grown-up hyperkinetics, I believe it is crucial that we separate this group of patients from our usual diagnostic category of depressive illness.

Dr. Frederic Quitkin: I want to support the suggestion that what is considered a neurotic depression is probably several different groups of depression. We have done two studies with two types of antidepressants in two separate samples of approximately 100 consecutive patients who had Hamilton depression scores of less than 18, and in both studies we defined a group we called chronic dysphorics. It is a term proposed by Don Klein and essentially describes patients who say they are chronically unhappy. Temporarily they may have a better mood, but most of the time they are unhappy. In any event, we thought those patients would not respond to drug or placebo, and we were wrong. They have a higher placebo response rate than patients we call endogenous or endogenomorphic. But, more surprising, in both studies they have drug-placebo differences; with a big enough sample the drug-placebo difference probably would be statistically significant. About 50% of the patients responded to antidepressants as opposed to about 25 or 30% to placebo. This suggests to me that included there are at least two groups of patients—those who are responding to placebo, and those who have a specific drug effect. At present I do not know how to identify these groups prospectively.

Dr. Joseph Zurbin: I think this is the most thought provoking paper I have heard recently, and it really raises fundamental questions. I have only one particular point to raise: What is the implication of the fact that one group is an old, long ago group going back several generations and the other is a current one?

Dr. Winokur: Actually, there is no marked difference in age. The groups are essentially controlled for age, and so are the family members, and there is not enough difference in mortality to account for differences. We are really studying proportionally the same groups from each epoch of time. That is not a problem. In other words, there were the same proportions of relatives of controls who were at risk for hospitalization in an Iowa state hospital as there were for relatives of depressives and manics.

Dr. Zubin: You had to treat them with reference to the customs and practices, the expectations and attitudes, of earlier epochs.

Dr. Winokur: It was certainly different in those days, but the thing is that both groups had equal numbers of people at risk in those days, both the control and the sick groups. We are dealing with groups of people who were living at the same time and were at risk for hospitalization. It is true that those who are alive at the present time are living in a different milieu, and should have a higher amount of illness. This should be true in both the control relatives as well as the relatives of the manics and depressives. In fact, all do. The use of just the interviews makes them all higher than the records, but the relatives are controlled for age and time of ascertainment.

Dr. Craig Nelson: People have turned to other markers for classifying depression because use of symptoms alone has often been disappointing and it is sometimes difficult to agree on the symptoms that a presenting patient has.

It certainly makes sense to consider family history of illness, but isn't it even more difficult to agree on the symptoms or the classification of a family member who had an episode in the past? I thought your approach to this question suggests one alternative—that hospitalization may be a useful marker. I was curious about your experience with this question and whether you think there are other markers for classifying depression in family members.

Dr. Winokur: For practical purposes one of the things we do is diagnose a person as having affective disorder on the basis of a remitting illness. The individual has been well most of his life, but had an illness during which he was incapacitated and then got well. That kind of data is possible to obtain from a family member because, interestingly enough, when you do a family history you get a follow-up on the family member. Most of the family members are not ill at the time of interview. So what you can get is reliable. We have tested that out; Bill Coryell and I have tested reliability by looking at the same family histories to see whether we agree on remitting illness versus chronic illness (which we thought was schizophrenia), and we were in good agreement. It depends to a large extent on a family member having a remitting illness from which he gets well ultimately. If at all possible we like to see somebody say that he was despondent or had depressive symptoms. But sometimes you have to just go on the remitting illness versus the chronic illness.

16. Recent Genetic Studies of Bipolar and Unipolar Depression

David L. Dunner

Classifying depressed patients into bipolar and unipolar subtypes was first proposed in 1962 by Leonhard et al., based on the clinical differentiation of depressed patients with and without mania.[1] Family history studies noted that patients with bipolar illness had more psychosis and suicide among their relatives than patients with unipolar illness. Since 1962, several studies in Europe and the United States have refined and extended this original observation. More importantly, a model for investigation in psychiatry has been developed to the point that genetic data are important for validating clinical diagnosis in psychiatry, particularly among the affective disorders.

This chapter will review data supporting evidence for genetic factors in the etiology of affective disorders, the development of methodology for genetic studies, and the resulting classification systems. We will highlight data from three recently completed large American studies of the genetics of bipolar and unipolar depression. We will review the current status of biological markers for affective disorders and finally present some areas of interest for future research.

EVIDENCE FOR GENETIC FACTORS

Several lines of evidence suggest that some forms of depression may have an etiology on a genetic basis. In order for a genetic etiology to be proven, several factors should be evident. First of all, the disorder should cluster within families; patients with the illness should have relatives who also demonstrate the illness. Second, studies of twins should show that the illness is more prevalent among monozygotic than dizygotic twins. A third line of evidence would come from adoption studies. Adoption studies are designed to differentiate environmental from genetic factors. Data from such studies should reveal that subjects who have a biological parent with illness but who were raised in a foster home develop the illness nevertheless; whereas subjects whose biological parents do not have the illness but who were raised in a home where there is affective disorder, do not develop affective disorder in excess of controls. Fourth, the illness could be shown to be linked to a gene of known Mendelian transmission.

Affective disorders, particularly manic-depressive illness, are familial. The evidence that bipolar illness clusters in families was reported by Leonhard et al.[1] Perris and Angst both suggested that affectively ill relatives of bipolar patients tended to have bipolar and not unipolar disorders, whereas affectively ill relatives of unipolar patients tended to have unipolar illness and not bipolar illness.[2,3] In the 1960s the Washington University group published a series of familial studies in manic-depressive illness, particularly bipolar disorders.[4,5] These studies showed a high familial risk for affective disorder in relatives of manic patients. Second, a very comprehensive family study of affective disorder suggested that manic-depressive illness may be linked to a gene transmitted on the X-chromosome.[5] subsequent studies in the late 1960s from the National Institute of Mental Health (NIMH) also showed a differential familial loading for relatives of patients with bipolar compared with unipolar disorders.[6] Relatives of bipolar patients had elevated morbid risks for bipolar illness, unipolar illness, and suicide, compared to relatives with unipolar patients.

Few twin studies of affective disorder appear in the literature of the last 10 years or so. Kallmann's study is still considered the definitive work, showing very high concordance rates for bipolar illness in monozygotic compared to dizygotic twins.[7]

The adoption technique, utilized in the Danish studies of schizophrenia, has been tried in studies of bipolar illness. Data from adoptees in Iowa indicated that primary affective illness may have a familial factor.[8] Another study of adoptees from manic-depressives also supports the concept of a genetic factor in the etiology of affective disorders.[9]

In the search for genetic linkage of affective disorders, the studies of Winokur et al. pointed toward a genetic factor on the X-chromosome.[5] Attempts to extend and replicate these findings have resulted in considerable controversy. Mendlewicz and coworkers showed linkage of bipolar affective disorder with two markers on the X-chromosome, color blindness, and XG blood type.[10,11] Gershon et al. were unable to replicate these findings and subsequently criticized the data from the Mendlewicz studies on methodological grounds.[12,13]

In summary, the separation of bipolar affective disorder as a distinct subtype has resulted in a clearer definition of the genetic factors that may be involved in the etiology of affective disorders. Most studies attempting to assess genetic factors in affective illness that have separately considered bipolar patients have resulted in positive results. The relatives of bipolar patients show a higher genetic loading and particularly more bipolar illness than relatives of other affectively ill patients. Clearly, unipolar illness as presently defined is a much more heterogeneous collection of disorders than bipolar disorder. Attempts to find subtypes of unipolar disorder using a genetic classification have not been particularly successful. However, Winokur's group separated unipolar patients into women with an early age of onset (depressive spectrum disease) whose relatives showed depression and alcoholism, and depressed men with a late age of onset (pure depressive disease) whose relatives showed depression only.[14]

METHODOLOGY FOR FAMILY STUDIES

The renewed interest in the genetics of bipolar and unipolar depression in the late 1960s and the interest in defining these disorders led to several family studies in the 1970s. The simplest method, the so-called family history method, was to ask patients about illness in their relatives. This tends to underestimate illness in relatives. An interview (Schedule for Affective Disorders and Schizophrenia—SADS) developed early in the 1970s was used to document illness in relatives.[15] Interviewing relatives directly (the "family study" method) led to greater precision regarding the diagnosis of illness in relatives. In a refinement of this technique, relatives are interviewed blind to the proband diagnosis in order to decrease investigator bias. Most of the recent genetic studies conducted in the United States employed a blind family study method, wherein relatives were interviewed with a standardized instrument with the interviewer unaware whether the person being interviewed was the patient, relative, or a control.

CLASSIFICATION OF AFFECTIVE DISORDER

Early genetic studies supporting the separation of bipolar from unipolar patients were based on studying families of patients who had been hospitalized for affective disorders. For the most part, patients considered bipolar manic-depressive had been hospitalized for at least one manic episode, whereas patients considered unipolar had at least one episode of depression. In the Perris study, three episodes of depression were required for a patient to be called unipolar.[2] In 1970 we proposed a classification for affective disorder.[6] Knowing that some depressions occur in the course of other psychiatric disorders and thus might be viewed as complications of these primary disorders, we required that patients have a primary affective disorder according to the criteria of Feighner et al.[16] In reviewing the patients in our sample it was apparent that two groups of patients had manic symptoms. One group of patients had manic symptoms resulting in hospitalization specifically for mania; these patients were termed Bipolar I. These patients were congruent with prior American and European genetic studies of affective disorders by Perris, Angst, and Winokur.[2,3,5] However, there remained a group of patients who had manic symptoms that did not result in hospitalization specifically for mania. These patients had depressions requiring hospitalization and hypomania; we classified them separately from other unipolar and bipolar patients and termed them Bipolar II. It is likely that many other studies of affective disorders had included such Bipolar II patients as unipolar.

We later extended this classification to include subjects who had never been hospitalized for affective disorder but who had received outpatient treatment.[17] Thus our classification system proposed that bipolar patients might be separable into four types: Bipolar I, subjects who have been hospitalized specifically for mania; Bipolar II, subjects with depression and hypomania who had been hospitalized specifically for depression; Bipolar Other, those who had depression and hypomania and who had received outpatient treatment for affective disorder; and a group we term Cyclothymic Personality, referring to subjects who had bipolar affective symptoms but who had not been treated. For Unipolar patients we required at least on depressive episode that met criteria for primary affective disorder and that resulted in either hospitalization or treatment for depression.

The group termed Bipolar I seems to be relatively homogeneous when data from clinical, biological, pharmacological, and genetic studies are evaluated.[18] Bipolar II patients tend to have the clinical appearance of unipolar patients but tend to be pharmacologically and biologically similar to Bipolar I patients. The Bipolar Other group seems to be congruent with Akiskal's cyclothymic patients.[19] Subsequent studies suggest that Bipolar I subjects may well be indistinguishable from Bipolar II subjects.[20] In our classification system the group termed Cyclothymic Personality was reserved for diagnosing relatives of subjects in our genetic studies.

The classification system is not entirely congruent with *DSM III*. The bipolar affective disorder of *DSM III* would include most Bipolar I patients, some Bipolar II patients, and some patients whom we term Bipolar Other. Approximately a third of patients we classified as Bipolar I had mood incongruent delusions and would be Atypical Bipolar disorder or Atypical Psychosis in *DSM III*.[21] Furthermore, although the term Atypical Bipolar disorder specifically mentions Bipolar II illness, many Bipolar II patients will meet *DSM III* criteria for bipolar affective disorder. The group classified as Cyclothymic disorder in *DSM III* is seemingly not congruent with our Bipolar Other or Akiskal's Cyclothymic disorder in that such patients meet criteria for more severe disorders in the *DSM III* nomenclature.[19] The group we considered Unipolar disorder meets the *DSM III* criteria for major affective disorder. However, major affective disorder in *DSM III* includes both primary and secondary depressions and thus represents a population of depressed patients of greater heterogeneity than we had proposed and studied. *DSM III* will be the standard for diagnosis of the 1980s, but the clinical and genetic studies of the 1970s used slightly different concepts of affective subtypes.

RECENT FAMILY STUDIES OF BIPOLAR AND UNIPOLAR DEPRESSION

Three large American studies of the genetics of affective disorders have been recently reported. The New York study was a prospective investigation of approximately 400 patients who met criteria for Bipolar I, Bipolar II, and Unipolar disorders.[22] Diagnosis of the probands was confirmed by SADS-L interviews of about 90% of the living relatives available for interview. Diagnosis of relatives was blind to proband diagnosis and confined to data form the SADS-L. Morbid risks, calculated according to the method of Strömgren, used ages at risk from the New York clinic population. Data regarding ages at risk are presented for first degree relatives age 18 and older. These data were available for approximately 2,000 first degree relatives.

The NIMH sample was also a prospective study consisting of 171 probands separated into Bipolar I, Bipolar II, and Unipolar types.[23] Eleven patients termed schizoaffective were also included. Probands had been hospitalized on the research wards of the NIMH and relatives of these subjects were given a structured interview. Data were available for approximately 1,000 first degree relatives.

The Iowa study was a retrospectively obtained sample of 100 bipolar patients, 225 unipolar patients, and 160 surgical controls.[24] Patients had been hospitalized at the Iowa Psychopathic Hospital 30 to 40 years ago. Approximately 1,600 first degree relatives of these subjects were evaluated blind to proband diagnosis using a structured interview similar to the SADS. In contrast to the New York and NIMH samples, most of the relatives of the Iowa sample who were actually interviewed were siblings and children because the probands' parents were for the most part deceased. Furthermore, the Iowa group did not separate probands into Bipolar I and Bipolar II types, although it could be assumed that most of their bipolar probands were Bipolar I.

Results of these studies are summarized in Table 1. In general, the risk for a first degree relative to have an affective disorder is approximately 15–20%. Second, there is a general consistency in these three studies in that an increased morbid risk for mania (Bipolar I illness) is shown for relatives of Bipolar I patients as compared to relatives of Unipolar patients. Third, the risk for Unipolar illness exceeds that for bipolar illness in relatives of bipolar patients. Additionally, relatives of bipolar patients generally have about the same rate of unipolar illness as relatives of unipolar patients.

The Iowa study did not provide a separate comparison of relatives of Bipolar II subjects. In the New York and NIMH data, relatives of Bipolar II patients tend to have an excess of bipolar illness (types I and II) compared to relatives of unipolar patients. This rate of bipolar illness approximates the combined rate of bipolar illness for relatives of Bipolar I patients.

Table 1. Morbid Risk of Affective Disorder in Relatives of Bipolar and Unipolar Patients

	Patient Diagnosis	Relative Diagnosis		
		Bipolar I	Bipolar II	Unipolar
New York	BPI	2.8	4.6	6.4
	BPII	.8	6.0	10.6
	UP	.2	3.0	8.4
NIMH	BPI	3.5	3.3	10.8
	BPII	2.1	3.7	13.6
	UP	1.2	1.2	13.2
Iowa	BPI	5.3		12.4
	UP	3.0		15.2

Note: Data are morbid risk (%). Morbid risks were calculated by dividing the number of ill subjects by the total number of subjects after the latter were corrected for age of risk for the various disorders.

Certain methodological differences in these studies should be noted. The New York study was entirely prospective and was based on an outpatient sample who came to three outpatient research centers. Criteria for determining that a relative was ill required that the relative have treatment or hospitalization for psychiatric illness. The NIMH sample was derived from an inpatient population. Criteria for illness in relatives included illness causing social disability in addition to treatment and hospitalization. This may explain why the rates for affective illness in the NIMH sample are slightly higher than the New York sample. For the Iowa sample, the probands were obtained retrospectively and the data reported were for those relatives actually interviewed or for whom medical charts were available to indicate psychiatric disorder. Thus, whereas the data in the New York and NIMH samples are for all relatives, the data for the Iowa sample pertain to only approximately 40% of the total number of relatives because many were deceased.

In spite of these methodological differences, the three studies provide a strong data base for an understanding of the genetic contributions to bipolar and unipolar affective disorder. Approximately 400 bipolar probands were studied and the data reflect an analysis of approximately 3,000 first degree relatives. These data clearly demonstrate an increased morbid risk for mania among relatives of manic depressive patients.

Attempts to analyze the genetic data from the New York sample for chromosomal linkage using a Mendelian model were not positive. It should be noted that the hypothesis for an X-linked dominant gene as a major genetic factor in bipolar disorder was not supported by data from the New York sample. Furthermore, the data from these three studies do not clearly support a specific mode of inheritance for bipolar illness.

BIOLOGICAL MARKERS

Research into biological factors associated with affective illness in the 1970s was largely concentrated on attempts to relate biological factors, such as the activities of blood enzymes or concentrations of catecholamine metabolites in cerebrospinal fluid and urine, to depression. The search for biological markers for a genetic disorder should be predicated on the notion of discovering trait rather than state associations. Thus the marker should be present in the well state as well as in the ill state and should be clustered in ill relatives of subjects with the disorder and observed less frequently among well relatives of patients or among controls. Recent reviews indicate that in general there is no satisfactory marker for bipolar and unipolar affective disorders at this time.[18,25] Attempts to demonstrate such markers have been extensive over the past 10 years and have produced a strategy for studying relatives of subjects with affective disorder. Not only are standardized interviews used to establish diagnosis, but also blood tests or provocative tests are made to determine if a biological marker is associated with vulnerability to the illness. Some markers that have been studied and found not to be satisfactorily related to affective disorders include the activities of catecholamine metabolizing enzymes, such as monoamine oxidase and catechol-O-methyltransferase. More recently, cholinergic supersensitivity has been suggested as a possible trait marker for affective illness.[26] Further studies of this system in affectively ill patients are awaited with interest.

SUGGESTED AREAS FOR FUTURE RESEARCH

A very pertinent research area for the 1980s is the so-called high risk study wherein children of subjects who have a familial psychiatric disease are studied in order to determine the antecedents of the illness.

The characteristics required for a high risk study include that the disease be familial, such as bipolar manic-depressive illness, and that the proband diagnosis be satisfactory so that the adult probands can be classified in a relatively homogeneous way. the disorder should become clinically evident early in life so that one might have the opportunity of following children into the age of risk. This is particularly true of bipolar disorder, where at least half of the patients have been hospitalized by the age of 30. A high risk study is dependent on a thoughtful assessment of relevant markers to the illness.

The identification of a trait marker for affective disorder is a goal for research in the 1980s. Bipolar affective disorder is a suitable clinical substrate for such research.

REFERENCES

1. Leonhard KI, Korff I, and Schultz H. Die temperamente in den familien der monopoluren and bipolaren phasischen psychosen. *Psychiat Neurol* 143:416–34, 1962.
2. Perris C. A study of bipolar (manic-depressive) and unipolar recurrent depressive psychoses. *Acta Psychiat Scand* 42(Suppl 194):1–188, 1966.
3. Angst J. "Zuratiologie und Nosologie Endogener Depressiver Psychosen." In *Monographien aus dem Gesamtgebeite der Neurologie und Psychiatrie.* Berlin: SpringerVerlag, 1966, No. 112
4. Clayton PJ, Pitts FN Jr., and Winokur G. Affective disorder: IV Mania. *Compr Psychiatry* 6:313–22, 1965.
5. Winokur G, Clayton J, and Reich T. *Manic Depressive Illness.* St. Louis: C.V. Mosby Co., 1969.
6. Dunner DL, Gershon ES, and Goodwin FK. Heritable factors in the severity of affective illness. *Biol Psychiat* 11:31–42, 1976.
7. Kallmann FJ. "Genetic Principles in Manic-depressive Psychosis." In *Proceedings of the American Psychopathological Association,* edited by Zubin J and Hoch P. New York: Grune and Stratton, 1954.
8. Cadoret RJ. Evidence for genetic inheritance of primary affective disorder in adoptees. *Amer J Psychiat* 135:463–66, 1978.
9. Mendlewicz J and Rainer JD. Adoption study supporting genetic transmission in manic depressive illness. *Nature,* London. 268:327–29, 1977.
10. Mendlewicz J, Fleiss JL, and Fieve RR. Evidence for X-linkage in the transmission of manic-depressive illness. *JAMA* 222:1624–27, 1972.
11. Mendlewicz J and Fleiss JL. Linkage studies with X-chromosome markers in bipolar (manic-depressive) and unipolar (depressive) illness. *Biol Psychiat* 9:261–64.
12. Gershon ES et al. Color blindness not closely linked to bipolar illness: Report of a new pedigree series. *Arch Gen Psychiat* 36:1423–30, 1979.
13. Gershon ES. Nonreplication of linkage to X-chromosome markers in bipolar illness. *Arch Gen Psychiat* 37:1200, 1980.

14. Baker M et al. Depressive disease: Classification and clinical characteristics. *Compr Psychiatry* 12:354–65,1971.
15. Endicott J and Spitzer RL. A diagnostic interview: The schedule for affective disorders and schizophrenia. *Arch Gen Psychiat* 35:837–44, 1978.
16. Feighner JP et al. Diagnostic criteria for use in psychiatric research. *Arch Gen Psychiat* 26:57–63, 1972.
17. Fieve RR and Dunner DL. "Unipolar and Bipolar Affective States." In *The Nature and Treatment of Depression*, edited by Flack FF and Draghi SC. New York: John Wiley & Sons, 1975. pp. 145–66.
18. Dunner DL. "Unipolar and Bipolar Depression: Recent Findings from Clinical and Biological Studies." In *The Psychobiology of Affective Disorders*, edited by Mendels J and Amsterdam JD. Basel: S. Karger, 1980. pp. 11–24.
19. Akiskal HS et al. Cyclothymic disorder: validating criteria for inclusion in the bipolar affective group. *Amer J Psychiat* 135:1227–33, 1977.
20. Dunner DL et al. Classification of bipolar affective disorder subtypes. *Compr Psychiat*, in press.
21. Rosenthal NE et al. Toward the validation of RDC schizoaffective disorder. *Arch Gen Psychiat* 37:704–810, 1980.
22. Dunner DL, Go R, and Fieve RR. A family study of patients with bipolar II illness (Bipolar depression with hypomania). Presented at the annual meeting, American College of Neuropsychopharmacology, San Juan, Puerto Rico, Dec. 1980. (Abstracts p. 25).
23. Gershon ES et al. Clinical, biological and linkage data in affective disorders pedigrees. Presented at the annual meeting, American College of Neuropsychopharmacology, San Juan, Puerto Rico, Dec. 1980 (Abstracts p. 26).
24. Tsuang MT, Winokur G, and Crowe RR. Morbidity risks of schizophrenia and affective disorders among first degree relatives of patients with schizophrenia, mania, depression and surgical conditions. *Brit J Psychiat* 137:497–504, 1980.
25. Gershon ES. "The Search for Genetic Markers in Affective Disorders." In *Psychopharmacology: A Generation of Progess*, edited by Lipton MA, DiMascio A, and Killam KF. New York: Raven Press, 1978. pp. 1197–1212.
26. Sitaram N et al. Faster cholinergic REM sleep induction in euthymic patients with primary affective illness. *Science* 208:200–2, 1980.

17. A Summary of Biomedical Aspects of Mood Disorders

Ross J. Baldessarini

INTRODUCTION

Historical Background

The severe disorders of mood or effect are among the most common of the major psychiatric syndromes. Lifetime expectancy rates for such disorders are between 3 and 8% of the general population.[1-3] Only a minority are treated by psychiatrists or in psychiatric hospitals and about 70% of prescriptions for antidepressants are written by nonpsychiatrist physicians.[4] These and other modern medical treatments of severe mood disorders have contributed to a virtual revolution in the theory and practice of modern psychiatry since the introduction of mood-altering drugs three decades ago.[4-7] These agents include lithium salts (1949), the antimanic and antipsychotic (neuroleptic) agents such as chlorpromazine (1952), the monoamine oxidase (MAO) inhibitors (1952), and the tricyclic or heterocyclic (imipramine-like) antidepressant agents (1957).[6] In addition, electroconvulsive therapy (ECT) continues to have a place in the treatment of very severe and acute mood disorders, especially life-threatening forms of depression.[8]

The development of these modern medical therapies has had several important effects. First, these agents have provided relatively simple, specific, effective, and safe forms of treatment with a profound impact on current patterns of medical practice. for example, many depressed or hypomanic patients can be managed adequately in outpatient facilities to avoid prolonged, expensive, and disruptive hospitalization which were formerly common. Second, partial understanding of the pharmacology of the new psychotropic drugs has led to imaginative hypotheses concerning the pathophysiology or etiology of severe mood disorders. These, in turn, have encouraged a revolution in experimental psychiatry in which the hypotheses have been tested in clinical research. Many of the earlier hypotheses have been found wanting or simplistic. nevertheless, they have led to increased understanding of the diagnosis, biology, and treatment of mood disorders and to newer research that represents a third level of development. This level is the focus of the present summary as it promises to have practical clinical benefits now and in the near future.

Diagnosis and Terminology

For the purposes of orientation, a few comments on psychiatric nosolgy and the nature of theorizing in biological psychiatry may be helpful. The diagnosis of the severe mood disorders is complicated by a number of sometimes confusing terms and associated concepts. The first important step was that of Kraepelin a century ago who boldly lumped a bewildering series of syndromes into the two major categories: manic-depressive illness (MDI) and dementia praecox (schizophrenia). The first syndrome (MDI) included all of the severe mood disorders (mania and melancholia), with or without an intermittent pattern of excitement alternating with depression.[2,9] The MDI concept survives today as a generic term for severe mood disorders. Recent diagnostic schemes have led to several ways of subdividing depressions. Most systems recognize some illnesses that are relatively minor ("neurotic," "reactive") and others currently referred to in the 1980 diagnostic Manual of the American Psychiatric Association as "major." The latter include severe depressions (with or without episodes of mania) marked by striking biologic signs and symptoms (such as loss of energy, libido, sleep, appetite, and intestinal function—all, typically, with some degree of diurnal rhythmicity), a tendency to remit and reoccur spontaneously, and apparent relative autonomy from life-events or stresses. Often (but not always) other psychiatric or medical illnesses are not present and there is a relatively high incidence of similar disorders among close family members. These characteristics have supported the use of such terms as "endogenous," "endogenomorphic," "vital," "psychotic," or "melancholic" depressions. It is this subgroup of severe idiopathic illnesses that is most likely to respond favorably to modern medical treatments.

The apparently biological, vital, endogenous or autonomous and severe forms of depression must be differentiated from patterns of illness and demoralization that are commonly encountered in serious medical disorders, especially chronic infections, tumors, hepatic or renal failure, brain syndromes, intoxications, and metabolic or endocrine disorders (especially of the thyroid, parathyroid, and adrenal glands). In addition, a concept has arisen from a research need to define relatively homogeneous groups of depressed patients with "primary" depressions, that is, mood disorders without additional complicating medical or other psychiatric disorders.[8] Clinically, the value of this concept (except as a reminder to consider fresh cases of mood disorders with a medical differential diagnostic approach) is somewhat limited since some cases of "secondary" depression have striking endogenomorphic or vital characteristics and respond well to antidepressants.

Yet another diagnostic dimension that is useful clinically and in research derives from the concept of "bipolar" vs "monopolar" mood disorders introduced by Leonhard[10] as a way of subdividing MDI syndromes into those without a strong past and family history of psychotic or manic episodes. For etymologic consistency, the latter term has been changed to "unipolar" in the United States. The bipolar (BP/UP) dichotomy is now considered to represent recurrent alternations of mood from normal euthymia into depression or into excited, manic, dysphoric, or psychotic states, vs recurrent depression alone. It is recognized that some BP patients move from depression into mania (the so-called "switch process") only on exposure to antidepressant drugs or ECT,[11] and that still others (so-called BP-Type II disorder) manifest mild, spontaneous *sub*clinical euphoria or hyperactivity alternating with clinical depression.[12] Since the evaluation and management of these two main subgroups of MDI (BP vs UP) are dissimilar, and since their understanding can now be enriched by a consideration of recent genetic and biochemical findings, these will be summarized.

First, however, it may help orientation to reiterate that a major thrust of psychiatric research in severe mood disorders over the past 30 years has been to define biological characteristics of MDI patients that are diagnostically useful, which can help to optimize treatment, and which might even point the way toward the pathophysiology or even the causes of these idiopathic conditions. While there has been considerable progress toward a biologically and clinically robust diagnostic scheme, and in understanding some characteristics that can help to guide treatment,

Table 1. Family History in Bipolar (BP)and Unipolar (UP) Manic-Depressive Illness (MDI)

Illness in the I° Relatives	Rates in Relatives by Diagnosis in Index case		
	BP	UP	(Ratio)
Mood disorder[18,25]	19	13	(1.5)
Mania or affective psychosis[10,16,25]	9.3	2.7	(3.4)
Bipolar MDI[13]	6.8	0.4	(17)
Unipolar MDI[13]	8.3	6.0	(1.4)

Data are pooled from the reports and reviews cited above. Note, for comparison, that a control population had only a 5.5% rate of mood disorders among first degree (I°) relatives, compared with 10% for relatives of index cases with MDI.[25] Since the rates of mood disorders vary markedly among studies, comparisons above are best made between columns, as is indicated by the BP:UP ratios. Note also that about half (40 to 70%) of mood disorders among relatives of *BP* index cases are *depression* only.[24]

search for primary causes has been unsucessful so far. Indeed, virtually all of the biological characteristics of MDI patients that have been defined are "state-dependent" (that is, they disappear with recovery) and not stable biological traits or markers of a possible heritable defect.[13] Thus, while such state-dependent biological alterations can be most useful for diagnosis and for guiding therapy, from a theoretical perspective they may merely be concomitant variations or secondary changes within the MDI syndrome.

GENETICS

Family and genetic studies support both the search for biological explanations of MDI and for improved biomedical diagnostic and therapuetic evaluations of MDI patients. This approach indicates a strong genetic contribution in MDI generally, and provides especially strong support for the BP/UP distinction.[13-25] Thus, as a general rule, family histories of severe mood disorders (manic or depressive) tend to be stronger among first-degree relatives of BP patients. Recent family studies indicate that rates of mood disorders among first-degree relatives of BP cases are about twice those of relatives of UP depressives[18,25] (Table 1) These morbid risk rates for UP depression are, in turn, at least two or three times above those of the general population, in which clinically significant mood disorders occur in about 3 to 5% of men and perhaps 6 to 8% of women over a lifetime,[3,25] although published prevalence rates of mood disorders have varied widely with diagnostic criteria and methods of ascertainment.[1] Studies by Winokur and his colleagues in the US Midwest indicated that risk rates exceeded 25% if a sibling and one parent were affected and exceeded 40% if a sibling and both parents had MDI;[21] rates among close relatives tended to rise when the proband or index case had a UP depression of relatively early age of onset (below 40 years), and especially high morbid risk rates were found among relatives of BP or UP cases of the same sex.[19,25] In UP depression, female probands with an early onset tended to have an excess of female relatives with depressions, while male probands tended to have an excess of relatives not only with mood disorders, but also of male relatives with sociopathic traits or alcoholism.[12] These various details can be diagnostically helpful in evaluating cases of mood disorder.

The Polarity Hypothesis

The early work of Leonhard that led to the current BP/UP concept was based mainly on the observation of an excess of psychosis in the family backgrounds of BP cases.[10] There are now several additional studies that can be added to Leonhard's which support the conclusion that there is a more than threefold excess in rates of affective psychosis among first-degree relatives of BP over UP patients[10,16,25] (Table 1). Leonhard also suggested that there may be familial differences in personality types in which close relatives of BP patients seem to have an excess of excited or hypomanic traits, while relatives of UP patients may have more depressive traits.[10]

Not only do psychoses appear more frequently among close relatives of patients with BP-MDI, but severe psychiatric syndromes tend to "run true" in families. Thus, while the morbid risk of severe mood disorders (in a large series of hundreds of cases and family members evaluated "blindly" by Winokur and his colleagues) among relatives of MDI patients (UP or BP) was 10%, such illness appeared among only 3% of relatives of schizophrenic index cases—a rate that is similar to the value of 5.5% for relatives of normal subjects.[25] Another clinically important point derived from follow-up studies is that the BP/UP distinction remains clinically robust over time. For example, the rates of altered diagnosis were only 3 to 5% whether comparisons were made

Table 2. Twin Concordance Rates in MDI

	Concordance Rates by Index Diagnosis (%)	
Group	BP	UP
DZ	14	11
MZ	72	40
MZ:DZ Ratio	5.1	3.6

Data are pooled from reviews of nine published reports.[15,17,22,25] Overall concordance rates for MDI, irrespective of polarity are 68% and 19% for MZ and DZ twin pairs, respectively (MZ:DZ ratio = 3.6).[25] The groups above include over 100 twin pairs. Among the rare instances (12 pairs) of MZ twins reared separately, the concordance rate for MDI was 75 per cent.[15]

after only a month of followup, or between a first and a second episode of illness, or after more than 10 years of follow-up.[25]

While not specifically a genetic point, there are also compelling data that describe the natural history of recurrent manic-depressive illnesses from long-term follow-up studies.[26,27] For either BP or UP-MDI, the mean cycle-length *decreases* approximately logarithmically, from about three years from the initial episode, to about a year after the fourth or fifth, and to less than a year after the sixth or seventh. Put in other terms, the risk or recurrence within two years is about 50% in a 50 to 60-year-old UP, or a 40 to 50-year-old BP patient, but only about 20 to 30% for those in their twenties. That is, the risk of relapse in MDI (BP or UP) tends to *increase* with age.

Twin and Adoption Studies

A second important class of genetic data is derived from twin studies. Table 2 summarizes data from nine modern studies reviewed by several authors,[15,17,22,25] which indicate much higher concordance rates between identical (monozygote, MZ) twins than between fraternal (dizygote, DZ) twins. In addition, the MZ/DZ ratio tends to be higher for BP illness than for UP cases. These data not only provide additional support for inherited contributions to risk for both BP and UP illness, but also suggest that this contribution may be stronger in BP-MDI (or that UP-MDI is a more heterogeneous cluster of syndromes).

A third important genetic technique that is aimed at separating contributions of environmental factors, learning, or experience (the "nature vs nurture" issue) is the adoption method. One of the few available studies of this type in MDI is that of Mendelwicz and Rainer.[28] They found a marked excess of mood disorders among the *biological* parents of the adopted proband cases (31% prevalence) over the adopting parents (12%). In contrast, adoptive and biological parents control adoptees without MDI, or parents of offspring with a chronic neurological disorder, had similarly low prevalence rates for MDI (6 to 10%), close to those expected in the general population, while the parents of *non*-adoptive manic-depressives had an expected high rate of MDI (26%). When all psychiatric diagnoses were included, the rates were 40% vs 16% for biological vs adopting parents of MDI index cases. Another study[29] found a 38% prevalence of primary depressions among a small number of adoptees, a biological parent of whom had such a disorder, compared with only 7% among a larger number of adoptees without such a parental history of mood disorder. Still other preliminary data from a study of Danish adoptees[30] indicates a 6.5-fold excess of suicides among biological over adoptive relatives of 70 depressed adoptees. Again, strong support is provided by these several approaches for a familial, and probably an inherited contribution to the risk of MDI.

AMINE HYPOTHESES

The next question that arises is what the nature of the genetic contribution to risk of MDI might be. In short, this is not known, although the genetic data just reviewed encourage the search for biological as well as putative developmental or psychosocial factors in MDI. The most prominent of the hypotheses that have been considered over the past two decades have implicated altered function of one or more monoamines acting as synaptic neurotransmitters at nerve terminals in the central nervous system (CNS). About the earliest formulations of such amine-based hypotheses concerning the biology of mood disorders were made by Everett and Tolman[31] and by Jacobsen[32] in 1959, although clinical studies of amine metabolism in MDI patients had been carried out by Weil-Malherbe[33] even earlier in that decade. The most often mentioned amines have been the catecholamine norepinephrine (NE)[34] or the indoleamine serotonin (5-hydroxytryptamine, 5-HT).[35] In addition, there have been considerations of altered function of acetylcholine (ACh)[36] as well as of the catecholamine dopamine (DA),[37] a transmitter in its own right as well as the immediate precursor of NE. All of these substances are known to be synthesized, stored in, and released from

Table 3. Effects of Drugs on the Metabolism of Amines in the CNS

Type of drug	Drug	Action	Behavioral effects
Precursors	L-Dopa	DA increased	Agitation
	Tryptophan (TRY)	5-HT increased	Sedative usually, antimanic (?)
	Choline or lecithin	ACh increased	Depressant(?), antimanic (?)
Inhibitors of synthesis	α-Me-p-Tyrosine (AMPT)	Blocks tyrosine hydroxylase, lowers CA levels	Sedative, antihypertensive
	α-Me-dopa (Aldomet)	Blocks decarboxylase	Sedative, antihypertensive, depressant
	Disulfiram, fusaric acid	Block β-hydroxylase, lower NE, raise DA	Little effect, some depression, some excitement on withdrawal
	p-Cl-Phenylalanine (PCPA)	Blocks tryptophan hydroxylase, lower 5-HT	Aggression, hypersexuality, insomnia
Decrease retention	α-Me-dopa[a]	False transmitter replaces endogenous CA	Sedative, antihypertensive, depressant
	Reserpine,[a] tetrabenazine	Block storage in vesicles, lower amine levels	Sedative, depressant, antihypertensive
Alter membrane crossing	Amphetamines	Increase release, decrease reuptake (some MAO-inhibition)	Stimulant, anorexic, psychotogenic
	Cocaine	Decreases reuptake	Stimulant, euphoriant
	Heterocyclic antidepressants	Mainly block reuptake (weak MAO-inhibition), increase sensitivity of 5-HT, and α-NE receptors and decrease that of β-NE receptors	Antidepressant
	Lithium salts	Decrease release of NE and DA	Antimanic, mood-stabilizing

	Agent	Mechanism	Effect
Block receptors	Neuroleptics	Mainly DA-receptor-blockade	Antimanic, antipsychotic sedative
	Methysergide	Mainly indoleamine-receptor-blockade	Weakly antimanic (?), anti-depressant (?)
	Atropine	Blocks muscarinic receptors	Intoxicant
Inhibitors of catabolism	MAO-inhibitors	Block MAO, increase amine levels	Antidepressant, euphoriant
	Polyphenols (e.g. butylgallate)	Block COMT	Little effect or toxic
	Physostigmine	Block cholinesterase	Depressant (?), antimanic (?)

Abbreviations and symbols used: DA: dopamine; NE: norepinephrine; CA: catecholamine; Me: methyl; MAO: monoamine oxidase; COMT: catechol-O-methyltransferase; 5HT: serotonin; 5HTP: 5-hydroxytryptophan.

[a] Note that depression associated with antihypertensive (anticatecholamine) agents is a problem in clinical practice. About 15% of patients on reserpine (especially those with a past history of MDI) reportedly become significantly depressed (timing is *unpredictable*).

specific neuronal fibers in the brain, spinal cord, or peripheral nervous system. These systems have been well-characterized and their detailed biology is reviewed elsewhere.[38-40]

They are especially well-suited, theoretically, to involvement in mood disorders. Thus, the CNS monoamine systems are widely and diffusely distributed and appear to subserve tonic background activities that occur over a long time base and include regulation of autonomic functions, arousal, sleep, sex and aggression, movement, diurnal cycles, and hypothalamic-pituitary function.

The Pharmacologic Basis of Amine Hypotheses

Support for this class of hypotheses derives mainly from the analysis of the differential actions of drugs on behavior in experimental animals and mood in patients or other human subjects. This pharmacologic literature is large and complex[34, 39-41] and the essence of it is summarized in Table 3. The main idea that arises from these observations is that treatments which deplete, inhibit the synthesis of, or block the actions of monoamines (notably, the catecholamines, CAs) tend to induce depression in susceptible subjects,[42] or at least to induce sedation, behavioral underarousal, or antiautonomic effects; treatments that increase the availability or actions of the CAs have stimulating or arousing actions. The effects of increasing or decreasing the actions of 5HT or ACh tend to be opposite to those of NE or DA. That is, enhanced 5HT or ACh effects tend to be similar to diminished CA effects. This reciprocal tendency may seem confusing since most of the available metabolic support for amine hypotheses in MDI, while suggesting a deficiency of CAs or an excess of ACh function, also suggests a deficiency of 5HT in depression. Perhaps the most reasonable way in which to consider such ideas is to suspect that any single-amine hypothesis that would account for the entire complex of signs and symptoms in MDI is almost certainly oversimplified, while altered function of individual amine systems might contribute to specific features of the syndrome. For example, it is not unreasonable to suppose that increased function of DA might lead to mania or psychosis,[43] while a lack of DA might lead to anhedonia and psychomotor retardation; that a deficiency of NE might lead to anergy and anhedonia too, or that its excess might contribute to agitation or mania; a lack of 5HT might also contribute to

Table 4. Actions of Heterocyclic Antidepressants

Acute (hours)
- Block uptake of NE or 5HT*[41]
- Reduce turnover of NE or 5HT[44]
- Reduce firing rates of NE or 5HT
- Block 5HT, ACh (muscarinic), NE (α_1), and histamine ($H_1 >> H_2$) receptors[46-49]

Later (weeks)
- Block uptake of NE or 5HT
- Return of NE turnover and firing rates[44]
- Decrease NE (β) and NE (α_2, presynaptic) receptor sensitivity[50,52]
- Increase NE release[50] (α_2 effect?)
- Increase $5HT_2$ and NE (α_1) receptor sensitivity[51]

(*) Not true of certain experimental antidepressants, notably iprindole, while some receptor changes can occur with iprindole.

agitation and insomnia; that an excess of ACh might add to psychomotor retardation and depressed mood; and that dysfunction in any of these systems might contribute to altered biorhythms that are now increasingly documented in MDI.

It is important to realize that this way of developing biological hypotheses in psychiatric research has been dominant in the past 20 years. Despite the attractiveness and seeming rationality of this inductive approach, it suffers from potentially fallacious logic when applied to pathophysiology or etiology. Thus, a typical proposition is that if antidepressant treatments tend to increase the function of NE or 5HT[44-52] (see Table 4), and antimanic treatments tend to diminish the function of CAs,[7] then their opposite might reflect the pathophysiology of the illness under treatment. While such notions might be heuristic or experimentally testable, they may be no more logical than to assume a penicillin deficiency state in general paresis (even though the drug helps the illness), or a renal tubular defect in congestive heart failure (even though thiazide diuretics remove edema). Moreover, they are based on a still very incomplete understanding of the actions of mood-altering agents.

One additional curious effect of the amine hypotheses has been their interaction with the process of developing potential new mood-altering agents. In general, there have been remarkably few fundamentally new medical treatments for MDI since the somewhat fortuitous clinical

Table 5. Clinical Strategies to Test Amine Hypotheses in MDI

1. Interpretation of differential drug responses (improvement vs worsening)*
2. Precursor loading (tryptophan, 5-hydroxytryptophan, dopa)*
3. Metabolite excretion vs. clinical state or treatment (esp. urinary 5-hydroxy-indoleacetic acid [5HIAA] or 3-methoxy-4-hydroxy-phenethylene-glycol [MHPG])
4. CSF metabolites (basal or after probenecid to block removal) vs. diagnostic or clinical state (5HIAA, MHPG, vanillylmandelic acid [VMA], or homo-vanillic acid [HVA])
5. Neuroendocrine responses that may be secondary to altered amine function (cortisol or ACTH, growth hormone, prolactin)
6. Postmortem levels of brain metabolites (DA, NE, 5HT, MHPG, HVA, 5HIAA), esp. in suicides
7. Enzyme activities (brain, plasma, platelets, rbc) (tyrosine hydroxylase, dopamine-β-oxidase [DBH], MAO, catechol-O-methyltransferase [COMT])

*As in Table 3.

discovery of the antidepressant effects of MAO inhibitors (MAOIs) and imipramine, or of the antimanic actions of lithium salts and chlorprom-azine—all prior to 1960.[6] A partial understanding of the actions of these agents focussed attention on their interactions with the monoamines (Table 4), and may have contributed to screening tests that have led to ever-larger numbers of similar agents, as well as a possibly excessively narrow focus on such amines in the pathophysiology of MDI. Most of the newer antidepressants have been discovered by screening compounds for blocking actions against CA-uptake (eg, amoxapine, trimi-pramine, maprotiline, mianserin, nomifensin, viloxazine, and metabo-lites of clomipramine), 5HT-uptake (eg, clomipramine, femoxetine, trazodone, and zimelidine), or MAO activity (eg, chlorgyline).[53,54] Iprin-dole may be a notable exception, although its efficacy in severe endog-enous depressions is not well established.[54]

The attempt to test the amine hypotheses of MDI in clinical experi-ments has led to much work using several clever clinical research strategies that are summarized in Table 5. Most of this work has in-volved tests of a CA or a 5HT hypothesis.[33–36,39,42,55–59]

Comments on Amine Hypotheses

Overall, the *clinical* research evidence favoring amine deficiency or excess hypotheses in MDI is weak. The effects of experimental phar-macologic interventions (Table 3, excluding accepted standard treatments with heterocyclic antidepressants (HCAs), MAOIs, Li[+], and neuroleptics) do not provide compelling support. For example, loading patients with amino acids that are precursors of amines[55,60,61] or trials of inhibitors of amine synthesis[59,62] are both known to alter amine turnover in human CNS, based on studies of CSF metabolites.[62]

Yet, they have not provided a useful antidepressant or antimanic treatment to date. Stimulants such as amphetamines provide a most interesting *model* of MDI as intoxication in stimulant abusers results in lithium-sensitive[63] euphoria, followed by agitation and paranoid psychosis (as in mania), followed by depression ("crashing").[58,64-66] Nevertheless, their effects in clinical depression are, at best, transitory in most cases, and they worsen agitation in many cases.[67,68] In mania, stimulants or DA agonists can even induce a paradoxical beneficial effect.[69,70] Interesting preliminary suggestions of benefits have recently been obtained with the 5HT agonist fenfluramine in mania and depression[57] and the DA agonist piribedil in depression,[62] and with the NE-α agonist clonidine[71] and anticholinesterase physostigmine,[72] as well as the ACh precursor choline (or lecithin) in mania.[73,74] These observations have arisen directly from attempts to test amine hypotheses. It is also important to realize that certain antihypertensive (antisympathetic, or anti-NE) agents such as reserpine and α-methyldopa (Aldomet) are associated with clinically significant depression.[42,59]

In metabolic tests of amine hypotheses, the CAs (Table 6) and sertonin (Table 7) are, by far, the most extensively evaluated. Data for Tables 6 and 7 were obtained from previous reviews concerning CAs,[34,58] 5HT,[35,57,75] or both.[37,39,56,59,62] As these tables illustrate, the data supporting a deficiency of CAs or 5HT in depression and the opposite in mania are, frankly, meager and inconsistent. One of the few repeatedly observed relationships is a fall in urinary MHPG with depression and its return to normal values with recovery[58] or switch[11] into mania. There are also suggestions that low MHPG may be more characteristic (or more easily observed) in BP depression.[58] There are several reports of attempts to predict reponses to specific types of heterocyclic antidepressants (HCAs) from initial values of urinary MHPG excretion. The idea has been that low MHPG may predict responsiveness to drugs with relatively strong effects on NE neurons (desipramine or imipramine), whereas higher values may predict responsiveness to HCAs more selective for 5HT systems (clomipramine or amitriptyline).[76]

Table 6. Clinical Guidance Concerning a Catecholamine Hypothesis

Measure	Available Studies (N)	Proportion Supportive	Comments
1. Postmortem Regional Brain Chemistry			
A. NE	3	33%	
B. DA	3	33%	
C. HVA	1		Regions inconsistent; one study found HVA higher.
2. Urinary MHPG			
A. All depressed	11	82%	Most studies are from three labs with small N and much overlap in small decreases among Dx groups and controls.
B. BP vs. UP	3	100%	All three found BP 30% lower; two also found depressed schizoaffectives (?BP) lower than UP (36%), but these differences are similar to interlab. differences in same Dx groups.
C. To predict TCA response	9	67%	Most studies dealt with few variables, with small mean N = 12; two other studies unable to draw conclusions due to high response rates or high MHPG variance.

3. CSF Metabolites (Depression)			
A. [MHPG]	5	40%	Poor correlation with urine MHPG; cannot use
B. [MHPG]	1	0%	probenecid for MHPG; probably unchanged in mania but not adequately studied.
C. [VMA]: Basal	12	67%	UP tend to have lower VMA; with probenecid, not all significantly
Probenecid	9	67%	lower; suggest sub-groups.
4. CSF Metabolites (Mania)			
Basal	6	0%	All studies found low or normal VMA; one found increased rise of
Probenecid	3	33%	VMA.
5. Enzyme Activities			
A. Platelet MAO	7	14%	Four studies suggest low MAO: in BP two found lower, one higher than UP.
B. RBC COMT	5	20%	Two studies found low COMT; another suggested better response to HCA with lower COMT.
C. Plasma DBH	6	20%	One study found low DBH (in UP cases).

(*)Note that the illustrative summaries in Tables 6, 7, and 8 are not exhaustive reviews of every study reported; abbreviations are explained in Table 3.

Table 7. Clinical Evidence Concerning a Serotonin Hypothesis in MDI

Measure	Available Studies (N)	Proportion Supportive	Comments
1. Postmortem Regional Brain Chemistry			
A. 5HT	7	57%	Only 10% mean decrease in most studies.
B. 5HIAA	5	40%	Only 15% mean decrease, but very inconsistent among CNS regions.
2. [5HT] or [TRY] in Plasma or CSF	5	20%	Small changes, highly inconsistent.
3. CSF [5HIAA] in Depressions			
A. Basal	15	47%	Up to 70% decrease in four studies; trend to decrease in 12, but increases in two studies; *subgroup* suggested.
B. Probenecid	9	67%	Up to 60% less accumulation.
4. CSF [5HIAA] in Mania			
A. Basal	3	67%	Decreased in *UP* only
B Probenecid	3	33%	Decreased in *BP* only; these results contradictory, but 3/6 do suggest ca. 30% decrease in UP + BP series.
6. Effects of TCAs on CSF [5HIAA]	8	100%	All find decreases of 10–49% in basal and 31% less rise after probenecid.
7. TRY or 5HTP as Antidepressant	10	40%	Only one double-blind pos. study but 40% suggest some possible benefits alone or with HCA, MAOI or ECT; CSF 5HIAA does rise.
8. PCPA as Antimanic (blocks 5HT synthesis)	1	0%	Not effective in mania; effects in depression poorly evaluated.

However, these ideas are based on the study, to date, of a total of only 71 low MHPG cases and 53 with high MHPG; and at least four recent studies have failed to support the predictions (see ref. 77) or produced equivocal results.[78] Futhermore, the marked interindividual and interlaboratory variance in MHPG assays suggests that this approach may not lead readily to practical routine clinical methods.[79] Indeed, the diurnal variance (ratio of standard error to mean) in MHPG excretion is about 30%-40% in normals and MDI patients, while the mean difference between controls and BP or UP depressed cases is only about 20%-40%.[80] Other recent findings, furthermore, cast doubt on the idea that urinary MHPG levels may selectively reflect NE metabolism in the CNS in that much of MHPG is converted to VMA, and 20% or less of urinary MHPG may derive from central NE metabolism.[81]

Among studies of indoleamine metabolism, some encouragement has come from studies of cerebrospinal fluid (CSF) levels of the main 5HT metabolite, 5HIAA (Table 7).[57,62,75] These results suggest that a *subgroup* may be defined by low 5HIAA levels among MDI cases. These patients may be either UP or BP and are not readily separable by other clinical characteristics. One intriguing proposal emerging from the work of Åsberg, Van Praag, Maas, and Goodwin and their colleagues is that low CSF levels of 5HIAA may correspond with normal levels of urinary MHPG (serotonin deficiency, or in Maas' terminology, "Type-B" depression), and correlate with selective responsiveness to 5HT-enhancing agents such as precursor amino acids or clomipramine or amitriptyline (see refs. 76,82). Conversely, normal CSF levels of 5HIAA and low urinary MHPG (NE deficiency or "Type A") may define a group of endogenous depressions who respond selectively to drugs that selectively enhance NE transmission (eg, desipramine, imipramine)— an effect that may be predicted by an acute activating effect of a test dose of *d*-amphetamine.[68] The proportion of low to normal CSF 5HIAA cases (Types B:A) is about 1:4, based on limited available data.[76] Unfortunately, this approach may not be practical for routine clinical application, due again to the variance of the MHPG measurement, as well as the variance in 5HIAA values (ca. 30%, or about the same as the mean difference between levels in HCA-responsive vs nonresponsive depressed patients), as well as the impracticality of routine lumbar punctures.[62]

Urinary assays of 5HIAA have been found not to be a useful alternative.[57,75] In addition, there is a suspicion that much of the apparent bimodality of distribution of CSF levels of 5HIAA may be due to the inexact matching of groups by sex (males tend to have lower values).[62] If a biologically and clinically meaningful subgroup can be defined by such an approach (regardless of applicability to clinical practice), much more study will be required. One other result of studies of CSF metabolites is that there is now strong agreement (all of eight studies) that HCA treatment regularly leads to decreases of 5HIAA,[62] a result that accords well in theory with recent evidence that HCAs increase sensitivity of central 5HT receptors[51] (Table 4). There is also weak evidence that ECT may also lower CSF levels of 5HIAA,[62] and MAOIs, of course, directly prevent formation of this deaminated metabolite.

NEUROENDOCRINE FINDINGS

It has been known or suspected for many years that the regulation of hormone metabolism is altered in severe psychiatric illnesses. More recently, several specific abnormalities have been described that are apparently characteristic of MDI.[83-87] Some of these have been studied in the context of seeking metabolic signs of putative abnormalities of amine functions in the limbic system and hypothalamus that may lead to dyscontrol of the release of hormones from the anterior pituitary. This approach has also encouraged clinical investigators to evaluate pathophysiologic features of MDI for their own sake, and without the necessity of testing a preconceived body of theory. Simultaneously, there has also been increased interest in the clinical utility of endocrine measurements as laboratory tests to aid in diagnosis and treatment of patients. Several of the well-evaluated or still preliminary endocrine findings in MDI are summarized in Table 8, based on the reviews already cited[83-87] and studies cited below.

The Hypothalamic-Pituitary-Adrenal Axis

It has been known for more than a decade that severe depression is associated with excessive secretion of cortisol from the adrenal cortex. Sachar and others applied the technique of 24-hour sampling of blood through an indwelling venous catheter to permit detection of "spikes" of release of cortisol and evaluation of their diurnal rhythm.[88] This

Table 8. Neuroendocrine Responses in MDI

Hormone	Change	UP vs BP	Data Quality
Cortisol			
Basal	increase	BP = UP	good
Rise with ACTH	increase	?	good
Brain cortisol	decrease	?	weak
DST: depressed	breakthrough	BP ≥ UP (?)	very good
manic or euthymic	suppressed	—	good
ACTH level	(?)	(?)	poor
Growth Hormone			
Basal	none	—	fair
Stimulated (by insulin or CA agonists)*	decrease	UP > BP	good
TSH			
Basal	none	—	fair
TRF-Stimulated: depressed	decrease	I° UP ≥BP (?)	fair
manic	decrease	—	fair
Prolactin			
Basal: mean	decrease or no change	BP > UP	fair
rhythm	diminished	BP = UP	weak
Dopa (decrease)	normal	—	weak
Morphine (increase)	less	BP = UP (?)	fair
Luteinizing Hormone			
Basal	small decrease	UP = BP	weak
Testosterone			
Basal	none	—	weak

(*)amphetamines, dopa, clonidine, desipramine have all been used as NE agonists. See text for references.

approach revealed that spikes were higher and more frequent, and that the normal day-night rhythm was less obvious in depression. Although this markedly increased release of cortisol was at first thought to reflect psychotic disorganization in severe MDI,[83,88] Carroll and colleagues found that similarly agitated and disorganized schizophrenic subjects failed to show a similar high output of cortisol.[89,90] More recently his group and several others have virtually abandoned the use of simple measures of cortisol level in plasma or urine in favor of a *dexamethasone suppression test* (DST), which has recently been established as a relatively simple diagnostic test of great specificity and power, comparable to, or exceeding in clinical utility, many laboratory tests that are considered standard in clinical pathology and medical practice.[87,91]

The DST has been standardized as follows:[87] The synthetic glucocorticoid is given in an oral dose of 1.0 mg at bedtime on day *one*. On day *two,* plasma samples are collected at 4:00 and 11:00 PM for inpatients, or sometimes for simplicity and convenience for outpatients, at 4:00 only. Normally, adrenal function is strongly suppressed by dexamethasone through hypothalamic-pituitary mechanisms that inhibit release of ACTH for up to 48 hours. In endogenous depressions, the suppressing effect is incomplete and short-lived. A criterion of 5 µg/dl (50 ng/ml) has been established as a cut-off, *above* which the DST is said to be *positive*. The use of the afternoon and evening samples can detect about 98% of all positive results, while the afternoon sample, by itself, finds about 79%. While the test is highly selective for primary endogenous depressions (few false positive results), it confirms the diagnosis in only about 60% of cases. Only about 4% of normal persons have a false positive DST result. While the test detects UP and BP cases, rates of positive DST are somewhat higher in BP cases and a family history of a major mood disorder can increase the rate of positive tests to 80–90%.[86,92] Perhaps the greatest power of the DST lies in *negative* results, which almost certainly *exclude* the diagnosis of MDI.

The DST effect in depression is not due to abnormal metabolism of dexamethasone, nor is it related in an important way to age (age accounts for only 2% of the variance).[87] While there had been suggestions that severity of depression may contribute to changes of a positive DST, this is now thought not to be an important factor. Thus, groups of patients with primary vs. secondary depressions of well-matched severity were clearly distinguished by DST. In addition, the correlation between severity of depression as assessed by standardized rating scales and 4:00 PM cortisol levels the day after a dose of dexamethasone is reportedly very weak (r = +0.20). The use of DST under standardized conditions similar to those outlined above has recently been well replicated in several American and European psychiatric centers in studies involving nearly 1,000 depressed patients.[87,92–94]

Potential problems in applying the DST can occur[87] during pregnancy, the use of high doses of estrogens (ordinary menopausal replacement therapy and the use of contraceptive steroids are not a problem), Cushing's disease, corticosteroid therapy, uncontrolled diabetes, use of reserpine or narcotics, severe weight loss, serious medical illness, and some organic mental syndromes. Ordinary doses of antidepressants, lithium salts, and neuroleptics seem not to produce problems, while high doses of benzodiazepines and use of sedatives and anticonvulsants (induce hepatic drug- and steroid-metabolizing enzymes) can all produce spurious results.

While theory indicates that the DST phenomenon in depression is due to dyscontrol of ACTH release, there has been little direct evaluation of plasma ACTH in depression. It is also suspected that NE and 5HT play important roles in the control of ACTH release at the level of the limbic system and hypothalamus. Nevertheless, the precise role of monoamines in the control of ACTH in man remains unclear due to some pharmacologic effects in primates or man that seem *not* to fit models derived from laboratory animals indicating an inhibitory control of corticotropin (ACTH) releasing factor (CRF, a peptide hormone produced in hypothalamus) by NE-α or DA effects, and facilitation of CRF release by 5HT.[84]

The DST phenomenon is clearly state-dependent as cortisol levels tend to fall with treatment and recovery, and they are not elevated in mania. There have, as yet, been few studies attempting to correlate the DST with other biological measurements in depression, but several are currently under way. Also, provocative preliminary attempts to use DST as a predictor of response to HCAs or of risk of relapsing[95] have so far been somewhat inconsistent and require further study.[87]

Other Neuroendocrine Response

Other endocrinologic characteristics of depressed patients are much less well evaluated than is cortisol and the DST, although their highlights are summarized in Table 8. Growth hormone (GH) is known to be released by NE-α, DA and 5HT agonists, but again comparisons between lower animals and primates or man are uncertain.[84] Several laboratories have reported that while basal levels of GH are normal in depression, their response to a variety of NE agonists is low (see ref. 87). These state-dependent differences do seem to differentiate primary endogenous depressed from neurotic patients and normals, but so far do not differentiate UP from BP MDI; mania has not been evaluated adequately. GH responses to NE agonists yielding plasma levels below

4 ng/ml are reported to differentiate primary from secondary depressions fairly well in nearly a dozen studies, although low values have been found in about one-third of normals or patients with secondary depressions. Nevertheless, a high value can rule out endogenous primary depression in 70% to 90% of cases. Among the problems associated with GH response tests in depression are invalidation by the HCAs, and spurious results by the mere insertion of a venous catheter, or if the patient falls asleep during a test.[87]

While most thyroid function tests are in the normal range in MDI, several laboratories have reported diminished elevations of thyroid stimulating hormone (TSH) by intravenous injections of thyrotropin (TSH) releasing hormone (the peptide, TRH) in severe depression, and possibly also in mania.[85] Release of TRH from the hypothalamus may be stimulated by NE and DA and inhibited by 5HT but not by ACh.[84] Results are conflicting, or very preliminary, whether the TRH-TSH test may help to differentiate UP from BP cases (TSH responses may be slightly more blunted in UP-MDI),[96,97] or to separate mania and schizoaffective illness (which may be closely related to. if not synonymous with, MDI) from chronic schizophrenia, which reportedly has normal TSH responses to TRH.[98] To some extent the TSH response may be confounded by interactions of high cortisol levels.[87] A potentially important recent observation is that the blunted TSH response to TRH in primary UP depression may, to some extent, represent a *trait*, as it persisted following recovery in 69% of a small group of patients.[99]

Release of prolactin (PL) is known to be inhibited by DA, and facilitated by 5HT[84] as well as opiates.[100] While there are few studies of PL in depression, there are recent suggestions that BP depressed patients may have somewhat lower basal plasma levels of PL and a blunted release during sleep,[101] and that depressed patients generally may have a blunted PL release in response to infusion of an opiate.[100]

NEUROPHYSIOLOGICAL FINDINGS

Patients with MDI have altered sleep EEG patterns, as might be anticipated in view of classic alterations in sleep behavior. It was reported by Kupfer in the early 1970s that key features in severe depression are a shortened latency between first falling asleep and the start of the first period of rapid-eye-movement (REM) or "dreaming" phases of sleep,

Table 9. REM Sleep Latency in Psychiatric Disorders

Diagnosis	REM Latency (Min ± SEM)
Controls	109 ± 12
Schizophrenics	95 ± 12
Neurotics	87 ± 5
UP-MDI	45 ± 5*
BP-MDI	43 ± 6*

Severe depression was associated with latency as short as 18 min. Schizoaffective cases were indistinguishable from MDI.
From Kupfer et al. [102,103]
(*)Significant

and increased REM activity throughout the night.[102] These characteristics can now be used successfully to differentiate primary endogenous depressions from secondary depressions associated with other medical or psychiatric illnesses, or from other forms of insomnia, in over 80% of cases.[102-104] This observation has been replicated by several investigators and appears to rest on solid ground. Some typical values for changes in REM latency are summarized in Table 9.

This test does not seem to differentiate UP from BP MDI. It is not yet adequately evaluated in mania (technically very difficult), but is clearly state-dependent and to some degree reflects the severity of depression. It has been reported that ACh agonists can mimic the changes found in depression (shorten REM latency in normals).[104] Other pharmacologic observations include indications that initial REM latency per se does not help to predict responsiveness to antidepressant therapy. On the other hand, Kupfer and colleagues found that the degree of prolongation or suppression of REM onset during the first two nights following test doses of a HCA predicted the clinical response to a month of treatment,[105] and correlated significantly with plasma levels of the drug, but poorly with urinary MHPG excretion.[106] Further studies are under way in which several metabolic and hormonal variables are evaluated along with sleep EEG patterns.

These studies on the tendency for REM sleep to be increased in depression, and for antidepressants to suppress or delay REM sleep[105-107] lead to the hypothesis that REM-suppression or other sleep-altering effects of antidepressant treatments may be an important clue to their mechanism of action.[108] These concepts have been given further support by recent provocative claims of antidepressant effects of selective deprivation of REM sleep by deliberately awakening patients[108] or, more paradoxically, by brief partial deprivation of all phases of sleep.[109]

One other EEG characteristic that has been suggested by Buchsbaum and his colleagues as capable of differentiating UP from BP cases of MDI is the pattern of response of EEG potentials evoked by sensory stimuli of increasing intensity (the average evoked response, AER test).[110] BP cases are said to tend to increase EEG amplitudes with increasing stimulus intensity ("augmenters"), while UP cases have an opposite response, at least at strong stimulus intensity ("reducers"). This test has not yet been widely evaluated by other investigators and its significance and possible utility remain unclear. In general, EEG and sleep EEG techniques are not readily available in clinical practice, but for those with access to clinical or research sleep laboratories, the REM latency test can be helpful in evaluating complex or confusing cases.

OTHER APPROACHES

There is now a large literature and clinical experience with the use of chemical assays of blood levels of HCAs to aid in providing optimal treatment regimens for depressed patients. These can be quite helpful in the management of patients with atypical responses (no response or toxicity) or at high risk of intoxication (especially the elderly or cardiacs). In general, blood levels of the parent compound and its major metabolite above 100 ng/ml are associated with favorable antidepressant effects, while levels above 500 ng/ml present high risk of intoxication. This topic has been reviewed elsewhere recently.[111] One additional use of blood drug assays is to predict individual requirements for a TCA. Thus, several groups have found, for example, very high correlations ($r > + 0.90$) between plasma levels of antidepressant 24 hours after a single test dose and those found after several weeks of treatment of the same patient with a therapeutic dose.[112–114]

An additional biological measurement that can be helpful in defining an effective dose of an antidepressant is the criterion of inhibiting blood platelet MAO activity by $> 80\%$, during treatment with phenelzine (Nardil).[115,116] The observed correlations between strong inhibition of platelet MAO and optimal clinical antidepressant effects have encouraged use of larger doses of phenelzine (45 to 90 mg/day) than were common in the past.[116] Whether similar correlations will hold up for other MAOIs is not certain. Some preliminary data suggest that this approach may be feasible with isocarboxazid (Marplan), but probably not with tranylcypromine (Parnate), as the latter produced strong MAO inhibition at clinically ineffective doses[117]

Surprisingly few studies have aimed at evaluating CA hypotheses by measuring cardiovascular responses to infusions of NE agonists, and the few which have been done have, inconsistently, suggested lesser[118] or greater[119] responses in depressed patients than in normals; the possible influence of prior antidepressant treatment in these studies is unknown. There are several intriguing recent reports of altered indices of CA receptor function in blood cells in MDI as well. These include reports of diminished binding of ^{3}H-dihydroalprenolol (which labels β receptors), or of responses of isoproterenol-sensitive (β-receptors) adenylate cyclase in platelets or leucocytes from depressed or manic patients.[120,121] These changes are believed to be state-dependent and not to be artifacts of drug treatment.[121] In addition, the binding ^{3}H-imipramine to platelet membranes is reportedly diminished in MDI, although the significance of this form of "receptor" labeling is not yet clear.[122] Still other uses for blood cells have also been reported. There have been repeated suggestions that erythrocytes (rbc) from BP-MDI patients are dissimilar to UP or normal subjects in their ability to transport monovalent cations, notably Li$^+$, in that a high ratio of rbc:plasma Li$^+$ concentration might predict clinical responses to lithium therapy,[123,124] or that defective Na$^+$/Li$^+$ exchange processes may be inherited characteristics of MDI patients and their first-degree relatives (enduring traits).[125] Unfortunately, these leads have not held up well to critical attempts at replication.[124–126] One other lead concerning altered electrolyte metabolism in MDI is the suggestion made by Coppen and his colleagues in the 1960s that "residual" or intracellular levels of sodium may be increased.[127]

Another emerging strategy in biological research in MDI is to measure a variety of physiological and biochemical changes in patients as a functon of time of day, as it has long been recognized that altered diurnal rhythmicity is a hallmark of the syndrome. Wehr, Goodwin and colleagues have been using this approach intensively and found recently that depression is associated with temporal *delays* in the diurnal peak (acrophase) of body temperature, motor activity, and MHPG excretion.

These peaks are delayed by perhaps 1.5 hours in depression, and even longer (about two hours) in mania.[80] They suggest that dyscontrol of diurnal rhythms may be an essential feature of the pathophysiology of MDI and that mania and depression may not be biological "opposites." In addition, recent experimental therapeutic interventions aimed at altering the timing of sleep and activity in depressed patients[108,109,128] may be effective by their interactions with altered regulation of diurnal bodily rhythms.[128]

For the future, there is a new class of techinical advances which will almost certainly have a profound impact on research and clinical evaluations of the CNS in psychiatric and neurological illnesses. These include improved methods of evaluating cerebral flow in man, which are beginning to suggest regionally selective decreases in depression.[129] Thus far, computer-assisted x-ray tomography (CT scanning) of the brain has not been fruitful in MDI, but still newer scanning methods are just starting to emerge. These include methods for evaluating regional differences in the rate of glucose utilization, the application of positron-emission tomography (PET), and the use of nuclear magnetic resonance (NMR) scanning methods.[130] These new techniques promise to revolutionize the clinical investigation of the abnormal structure and function of the intact human brain.

CONCLUSIONS

For the present, it is clear from the material reviewed above that there have been remarkable advances in the application of biomedical methods to the evaluation of patients with severe manic-depressive illnesses. There has been a trend to move away from attempts to support or refute biological hypotheses derived inductively from a partial understanding of the effects of psychotropic drugs, toward a more neutral and descriptive approach. This approach has provided powerful and compelling support for genetic and metabolic characterization of the MDI syndrome and of its unipolar and bipolar variants. A summary of these characteristics is provided in Table 10. In addition, biological strategies have helped considerably to sharpen our ability to provide more nearly optimal application of available, though imperfect, antidepressant, antimanic, and mood-stabilizing medical therapies as improved treatments

Table 10. Clinical Features of BP/UP MDI

Feature	BP	UP
Mania, hypomania	+ + + +	0
Family History of psychosis or mania	+ + +	+
Mood switches (spont. or Rx-induced)	+ + + +	0
Median onset (yrs)	26	40
≥ 5 episodes (%)	18	6
F/M sex ratio	1.4	1.9
Psychomotor retardation	+ +	+
Hypersomnia	+ +	+
Insomnia	+ + +	+ + +
Diurnal changes	+ + +	+ +
Agitation	+	+ + +
Anger in depression	+	+ + +
Somatic or neurotic sx	+	+ + +
Reduced REM latency	+ +	+ +
DST nonsuppression	+ + +	+ +
Low urinary MHPG	+	±
Li as antidepressant	+	± ?
Prophylaxis	Li	TCAs
Average evoked EEG response	augmentation (?)	reduction (?)

are being sought, as will be discussed further in a future issue of this Journal.

A general criticism of the field is that the practical application of some of the better clinical tests has been remarkably slow. Some (notably the DST and blood antidepressant assays) are adequately developed for routine clinical use. Other endocrine measures and the REM-latency test can be applied almost routinely in advanced treatment and teaching centers. It is also remarkable that more cross-validation among tests and clinical data in the *same patients* at the same time has not been undertaken.

SUMMARY

Severe mood disorders are among the most common major psychiatric disorders in medical practice, with risk rates of about 5 per cent. Theory and management of manic-depressive illnesses (MDI) has virtually been revolutionized with the development of psychopharmacology since 1950. Effective short-term and preventive treatment of depression is afforded by heterocyclic and experimental antidepressants as well as monoamineoxidase inhibitors; neuroleptic agents are highly effective in mania and lithium salts are especially useful in long-term management of MDI. The action mechanisms of these agents have become increasingly rich and complex in recent years, with much current focus on their ability to alter catecholamine and indoleamine receptors in brain tissue; late effects are typically dissimilar to immediate actions. Theories concerning the pathophysiology of MDI have in the past been heavily, perhaps unduly, influenced by such partial understanding of drug actions. The resulting *inductive* approach to formulation and testing of hypotheses has enriched psychiatric research and supported progress in pharmacology. Nevertheless, searches for direct metabolic support for amine hypotheses of MDI in clinical studies have led to an ambiguous and inconclusive literature. Recent trends in MDI research have moved beyond the testing of amine hypotheses to enrich the clinical descriptive, diagnostic, genetic, endocrinologic and neurophysiologic understanding of the syndromes of MDI. These approaches have led to compelling support of bipolar and unipolar subtypes of MDI, to diagnostic laboratory tests at least as robust as those used in general medicine, and to unprecedented enlightenment in the clinical management of manic and depressed patients. These developments represent the most substantial contributions of a biomedical approach to psychiatry to date, and support the clinical and scientific value of the approach.

REFERENCES

1. Silverman C: The Epidemiology of Depression. Baltimore, John Hopkins Press, 1968
2. Winokur G, Clayton P, Reich T: Manic-Depressive Disease. St. Louis, Mosby, 1970
3. Slater E, Cowie V: The Genetics of Mental Disorders. London, Oxford Univ Press, 1971
4. Hollister LE: Tricyclic antidepressants. New Eng J Med 299:1106–1109; 1168–1172, 1978
5. Baldessarini RJ: Mood drugs. Disease-A-Month 11:1–65, 1977
6. Baldessarini RJ: Chemotherapy in Psychiatry. Cambridge, Harvard Univ Press, 1977
7. Baldessarini RJ: Drugs and the treatment of psychiatric disorders. *In* The Pharmacological Basis of Therapeutics. Ed. VI. (Gillman AG, Goodman LS, Gilman A, (eds.) New York, MacMillan, 1980, pp 391–447
8. Fink M: Convulsive Therapy: Theory and Practice. New York, Raven, 1979

9. Kraeplin E: Manic-Depressive Insanity and Paranoia. (Barklay M, Robertson GM, eds.) Edinbugh, Livingston, 1921
10. Leonhard K, Korff I, Shulz H: Die Temperamente in den familien der monopolaren und biopolaren phasischen Psychosen. Psychiat Neurol 143:416–434, 1962
11. Bunney WE Jr, Goodwin FK, Murphy DL: The "switch process" in manic-depressive illness. Arch Gen Psychiat 27:295–3117, 1972
12. Fieve RR, Kumbaraci T, Dunner DL: Lithium prophylaxis of depression in bipolar I, bipolar II, and unipolar patients. Am J Psychiat 133:925–929, 1976
13. Gershon ES: The search for genetic markers in affective disorders. In Psychopharmacology: A Generation of Progress. (Lipton MA, DiMascio A, Killam KF, eds.) New York, Raven, 1978, pp 1197–1212
14. Perris C: Genetic transmission of depressive psychosis. Acta Psychiat Neurol Scand Supp 203:45–52, 1968
15. Price JS: The genetics of depressive behavior. In Recent Developments in Affective Disorders. (Coppen A, Walk A, eds.) Brit J Psychiat (Special Publication No. 2) Kent, Headley-Ashley, 1968, pp 37–54
16. Von Trostorff S: Über die hereditäre Belastung bei den bipolaren und monopolaren phasischen Psychosen. Schweiz Arch Neurol Neurochir Psychiat 102:235–240, 1968
17. Zerbin-Rüdin E: Zur Genetik der depressiven Erkrankungen. In Das Depressive Syndrom. (Hippius H, Selbach H, eds.) Munich, Urban And Schwarzenberg, 1969, pp 37–56
18. Cadoret RJ, Winokur G, Clayton P: Family history studies: VII. Manic-depressive disease versus depressive disease. Brit J. Psychiat 116:625–635, 1970
19. Winokur G, Cadoret RJ, Dorzab J et al: Depressive disease: A genetic study. Arch Gen Psychiat 24:135–144, 1971
20. Cadoret R, Winokur G: Genetic studies of affective disorders. In The Nature and Treatment of Depression. (Flach FF, Draghi SC, eds.) New York, Wiley, 1975, pp 335–346
21. Tsuang MT: Genetics of affective disorder. In The Psychobiology of Depression. (Mendels J, ed.) New York, Spectrum, 1975, pp 85–100
22. Allen MG: Twin studies of affective illness. Arch Gen Psychiat 33:1476–1478, 1976
23. Gershon ES, Bunney WE Jr, Lehman JF, et al: The inheritance of affective disorders: A review of data and hypotheses. Behav Genetics 6:227–261, 1976
24. Mendlewicz J: Application of genetic techniques to psychiatric research. In Biological Bases of Psychiatric Disorders. (Frazer A, Winokur G, eds.) New York, Spectrum, 1977, pp 79–88
25. Winokur G: Mania and depression: Family studies and genetics in relation to treatment. In Psychopharmacology: A Generation of Progress. (Lipton MA, DiMascio A, Killam KF, eds.) New York, Raven, 1978, pp 1213–1221
26. Grof P, Angst J, Haines T: The clinical course of depression. In Classification and Prediction of Outcome of Depression. (Hoechst Symposia Medica, Vol.8) New York, Schattauer, 1974, pp 141–148
27. Zis A, Grof P, Webster M, et al: Prediction of relapse in recurrent affective disorders. Psychopharmacol Bull 16:47–49, 1980
28. Mendlewicz J, Rainer JD: Adoption study supporting genetic transmission of manic-depressive illness. Nature 268:327–329, 1977
29. Cadoret RJ: Evidence for genetic inheritance of primary affective disorder in adoptees. Am J Psychiat 135:463–466, 1978

30. Kety SS, Rosenthal D, Wender PH, et al: (Unpublished observations cited at a McLean Hospital Seminar, 1980.)
31. Everett GM, Tolman JEP: Mode of action of rauwolfia alkaloids and motor activity. *In* Biological Psychiatry. (Masserman J. ed.) New York, Grune and Stratton, 1959, pp 75–81
32. Jacobsen E: The theoretical basis of the chemotherapy of depression. *In* Depression. Proceedings of a symposium at Cambridge, MA, September 1959. (David EB, ed.) New York, Cambridge Univ Press, 1964, p 208
33. Weil-Malherbe H: The biochemistry of the functional psychoses. Adv Enzymol 29:479–553, 1967
34. Schildkraut JJ: Neurospsychopharmacology and the Affective Disorders. Boston, Little Brown, 1970
35. Van Pragg HM: Amine hypotheses of affective disorders *In* Handbook of Psychopharmacology. Vol. 13. (Iversen, LL, Iversen SD, Snyder SH, eds.) New York, Plenum, 1978, pp 187, 297
36. Janowski DS, EL-Yousef MK, David JM: Acetycholine and depression. Pschosom Med 36:248–257, 1974
37. Sjöström R, Roos B-E: 5-Hydroxyindoleacetic acid and homovanillic acid in cerebrospinal fluid in manic-depressive psychosis. Eur J Clin Paharmacol 4:170–176, 1972
38. Baldessarini RJ, Karobath M: Biochemical physiology of central synapses. Ann Rev Physiol 35:273–304, 1973
39. Baldessarini RJ: Biogenic amine hpotheses in affective disorders. *In* The Nature and Treatment of Depression. (Flach FF, Draghi S, eds.) New York, Plenum, 1979, pp 347–385
40. Cooper JR, Bloom FE, Roth RH: The Biochemical Basis of Neuropharmacology. Ed III. New York, Oxford Univ Press, 1979
41. Glowinski J, Baldessarini RJ: Metabolism of norepinephrine in the central nervous system. Pharmacol Rev 18:1201–1238, 1966
42. Goodwin FK, Ebert MH, Bunney WE Jr: Mental effects of reserpine in man. *In* Psychiatric Complications of Medical Drugs (Shader R, ed.) New York, Raven, 1972, pp 73–101
43. Meltzer HY, Stahl SM: The dopamine hypothesis of schizophrenia: A review. Schizophrenia Bull 2:19–76, 1976
44. Schildkraut JJ, Roffman M, Orsulak PJ, et al: Effects of short- and long-term administration of tricyclic antidepressants and lithium on norepinephrine turnover in brain. Pharmacopsychiat 9:193–202, 1976
45. Svenssen TH, Usdin E: Feedback inhibition of brain noradrenaline neurons by tricyclic antidepressants: α-receptor mediation. Science 202:1089–1091, 1978
46. Fuxe K, Ogren S-O, Agnati L, et al: On the mechanism of action of the antidepressant drugs amitriptyline and notriptyline. Evidence for 5-hydroxytryptalmine receptor blocking activity. Neurosci Letters 6:33–343, 1977
47. Snyder SH, Yamamura H: Antidepressants and muscarinic acetylcholine receptor. Arch Gen Pschiat 34:236–239, 1977
48. U'Prichard D, Greenberg DA, Sheen PP, et al: Tricyclic antidepressants; Therapeutic properties and affinity for α-noradrenergic receptor binding sites in the brain. Science 199:197–198, 1978
49. Richelson E: Tricyclic antidepressants and histamine H_1 receptors. Mayo Clin Proc 54:669–674, 1979
50. Crews FT, Smith CB: Presynaptic alpha receptor subsensitivity after long-term antidepressant treatment. Science 202:322–324, 1978
51. Wang RY, Aghajanian GK: Enhanced sensitivity of amygdaloid neurons to ser-

otonin and norepinephrine after chronic antidepressant treatment. Comm Psychopharmacol 4:83–90, 1980

52. Vetulani J, Stawarz RJ, Dingel JV, et al: A possible common mechanism of action of antidepressant treatments. Naunyn-Schmeideberg's Arch Pharmacol 293:109–114, 1976

53. Pinder RM: Antidepressants. Ann Reports Med Chem 15:1–11, 1980

54. Zis AP, Goodwin FK: Novel antidepressants and the biogenic amine hypothesis of depression. Arch Gen Psychiat 36:1097–1107, 1979

55. Carroll BJ: Monoamine precursors in the treatment of depression. Clin Pharmacol Ther 12:743–761, 1971

56. Baldessarini RJ: The basis for amine hypotheses in affective disorders; A critical evaluation. Arch Gen Psychiat 32:1087–1093, 1975

57. Murphy DL, Campbell IC, Costa JL: The brain serotonergic system in the affective disorders. *In* Progress in Neuropsycopharmacology. Vol. 2. Oxford, Pergamon, 1978, pp 5–31

58. Schildkraut JJ: Current status of the catecholamine hypothesis of affective disorders. *In* Psychopharmacology: A Generation of Progress. (Lipton MA, DiMascio A, Killam KF, eds.) New York, Raven 1978, p 1223–1234

59. Garver DL, Davis JM: Biogenic amine hypotheses of affective disorders. Life Sci 24:383–394, 1979

60. Cole JO, Hartmann E, Brigham P: L-trytophan: Clinical studies. McLean Hospital J 5:37–71, 1980

61. Van Pragg H, de Haan S: Depression vulnerability and 5-hydroxytryptophan prophylaxis. Psychiat Res 3:75–83, 1980

62. Post RM, Goodwin FK: Approaches to brain amines in psychiatric patients: A reevaluation of cerebrospinal fluid studies. *In* Handbook of Psychopharmacology. Vol. 13. (Iverson LL, Iversen SD, Snyder SH, eds.) New York, Plenum, 1978, pp 147–185

63. Angrist B. Gershon S: Variable attenuation of amphetamine effects by lithium. Am J Psychiat 136:806–810, 1979

64. Angrist, B, Shopsin B, Gershon S. et al: Metabolites of monoamines in urine and cerebrospinal fluid after dose amphetamine administration. Psychopharmacologia 26:1–9, 1972

65. Ellinwood EH Jr. Sudilowsky A, Nelson L: Behavioral analysis of chronic amphetamine intoxication. Biol Psychiat 4:215–230, 1972

66. Watson R, Hartmann E, Schildkraut JJ: Amphetamine withdrawal: Affective state, sleep patterns, and MHPG excretion. Am J Psychiat 129:263–269, 1972

67. General practitioner research group: Report No. 51: Dexamphetamine compared with an inactive placebo in depression. Practitioner 192:151–154, 1964

68. Van Kammen DP, Murphy DL: Prediction of imipramine antidepressant response by a one-day d-amphetamine trial. Am J Psychiat 135:1179–1184, 1978

69. Corsini GU, Del Zompo M, Manconi S, et al: Sedative, hypnotic, and antipsychotic effects of low doses of apomorphine in man. *In* Advances in Biochemical Pharmacology. Vol 16 (Costa E, Gessa GL, eds.) New York, Raven, 1977, pp 645–648

70. Brown WA, Mueller B: Alleviation of manic symptoms with catecholamine agonists. Am J Psychiat 136:230–231, 1979

71. Jouvent R, Lecrubier Y, Peuch AJ, et al: Antimanic effect of clonidine. Am J Psychiat 137:1275–1276, 1980

72. Janowsky DS, El-Yousef MK, Davis JM, et al: Parasympathetic suppression of manic symptoms by physostigmine. Arch Gen Psychiat 28:542–547, 1973

73. Davis KL, Berger PA: Pharmacological investigations of the cholinergic imbal-

ance hypothesis of movement disorders and psychosis. Biol Psychiat 13:23–49, 1978

74. Lipinski JF: Personal communication, December, 1980
75. Murphy DL, Campbell I, Costa JL: Current status of the indoleamine hypothesis of the affective disorders. *In* Psychopharmacology: A Generation of Progress. (Lipton MA, DiMascio A, Killam KF, eds.) New York, Raven, 1978, pp 1235–1247
76. Goodwin FK, Cowdry RW, Webster MH: Predictors of drug response in the affective disorders: Toward an integrated approach. *In* Psychopharmacology: A Generation of Progress. (Lipton MA, DiMascio A, Killam KF, eds.) New York, Raven, 1978, pp 1277–1288
77. Spiker DG, Edwards D, Hanin I, et al: Urinary MHPG and clinical response to amitriptyline in depressed patients. Am J Psychiat 137:1183–1187, 1980
78. Hollister LE, Davis KL, Berger PA: Subtypes of depression based on excretion of MHPG and response to nortriptyline. Arch Gen Psychiat 37:1107–1110, 1980
79. Hollister LE, Davis KL, Overall JE: Excretion of MHPG in normal subjects: Implications for biological classification of affective disorders. Arch Gen Psychiat 35:1410–1415, 1978
80. Wehr TA, Muscettola G, Goodwin FK: Urinary 3-methoxy-4-hydroxyphenylglycol circadian rhythm: Early timing (phase-advance) in manic-depressives compared with normal subjects. Arch Gen Psychiat 37:257–263, 1980
81. Blombery PA, Kopin IJ, Gordon EK, et al: Conversion of MHPG to vanillylmandelic acid: Implications for the importance of urinary MHPG. Arch Gen Psychiat 37:1095–1098, 1980
82. Maas J: Biogenic amines and depression: Biochemical and pharmacological separation of two types of depression. Arch Gen Psychiat 32:1357–1361, 1975
83. Sachar EJ: Neuroendocrine dysfunction in depressive illness. Ann Rev Med 27:389–396, 1976
84. Ettigi PG, Brown GM: Psychoneuroendocrinology of affective disorder: An overview. Am J Psychiat 134:493–501, 1977
85. Prange AJ Jr, Lipton MA, Nemeroff CB, et al: The role of hormones in depression. Life Sci 20:1305–1318, 1977
86. Carroll BJ, Feinberg M, Greden JF, et al: A specific laboratory test for the diagnosis of melancholia. Arch Gen Psychiat 38:15–22, 1981
87. Carroll BJ: Implications of biological research for the diagnosis of depression. *In* New Advances in the Diagnosis and Treatment of Depressive Illness. (Mendelwicz J, ed.) Amsterdam, Elsevier, 1981 (in press)
88. Sachar EJ, Hellman L, Roffwarg H, et al: Disrupted 24-hour patterns of cortisol secretion in psychotic depression. Arch Gen Psychiat 28:19–24, 1973
89. Carroll BJ: Limbic system-adrenal cortex regulation in depression and schizophrenia. Psychosom Med 38:106–121, 1976
90. Carroll BJ, Curtis GC, Mendels J: Neuroendocrine regulation in depression. Arch Gen Psychiat 33:1039–1058, 1976
91. Editor (anon): The dexamethasone test and depression. Lancet 2:730, 1980
92. Schlesser MA, Winokur G, Sherman BM: Hypothalamic-pituitary-adrenal axis activity in depressive illness. Arch Gen Psychiat 37:737–743, 1980
93. Brown WA, Shuey I: Response to dexamethasone and subtype of depression. Arch Gen Psychiat 37:747–751, 1980
94. Nuller JL, Ostroumova MN: Resistance to inhibiting effect of dexamethasone in patients with endogenous depression. Acta Psychiat Scand 61:169–177, 1980

95. Goldberg IK: Dexamethasone suppression test as indicator of safe withdrawal of antidepressant therapy. Lancet 1:376, 1980

96. Bjørum N, Kirkegaard C: Thyrotropin-releasing-hormone test in unipolar and bipolar depression. Lancet 2:694, 1979

97. Gold MS, Pottash ALC, Ryan N, et al: TRH-induced TSH response in unipolar, bipolar, and secondary depressions: Possible utility in clinical assessment and differential diagnosis. Psychoneuroendocrinology 5:147–155, 1980

98. Extein I, Pottash ALC, Gold MS, et al: Differentiating mania from schizophrenia by the TRH test. Am J Psychiat 137:981–982, 1980

99. Asnis GM, Nathan RS, Halbreich U, et al: TRH tests in depression. Lancet 1:424–425, 1980

100. Gold MS, Pottash ALC, Martin DA, et al: Opiate-endorphin test dysfunction in major depression. Neuroscience Abstracts 6:759, 1980

101. Mendlewicz J, VanCauter E, Linkowski P, et al: The 24-hour profile of prolactin in depression. Life Sci 27:2015–2024, 1980

102. Kupfer DJ, Foster FG: Interval between onset of sleep and rapid eye movement sleep as an indicator of depression. Lancet 2:684–686, 1972

103. Kupfer DJ, Foster FG, Coble P, et al: The application of EEG sleep for the differtial diagnosis of affective disorders. Am J Psychiat 135:69–74,1978

104. Gillin JC, Duncan W, Pettigrew KD, et al: Successful separation of depressed, normal and insomniac subjects by EEG sleep data. Arch Gen Psychiat 36:85–90, 1979

105. Kupfer DJ, Foster FG, Reich L, et al: EEG sleep changes as predictors in depression. Am J Psychiat 133:622–626, 1976

106. Kupfer DJ, Spiker DG, Coble P, et al: EEG sleep and affective disorders: What can it predict? *In* Catecholamines: Basic and Clinical Frontiers. Vol 2 (Usdin E, Kopin IJ, Barchas J, eds.) New York, Pergamon 1979, pp 1920–1922

107. Gillin JC, Wyatt RJ, Fram D, et al: The relationship between changes in REM sleep and clinical improvement in depressed patients treated with amitriptyline. Psychopharmacology 59:267–272, 1978

108. Vogel GW, Vogel F, McAbee RS, et al: Improvement of depression by REM sleep deprivation. Arch Gen Psychiat 37:247–253, 1980

109. Schilgen B, Tolle R: Partial sleep deprivation as therapy for depression. Arch Gen Psychiat 37:267–271, 1980

110. Buschbaum M, Landau S, Murphy D, et al: Average evoked response in bipolar and unipolar affective disorders: Relationship to sex, age of onset, and monoamine oxidase. Biol Psychiat 7:199–212, 1973

111. Baldessarini RJ: Status of psychotropic drug blood level assays and other biochemical measurements in clinical practice. Am J Psychiat 136:1177–1180, 1979

112. Cooper TB, Simpson GM: Prediction of individual dosage of nortriptyline. Am J Psychiat 135:333–335, 1978

113. Brunswick DJ, Amsterdam JD, Mendels J, et al: Prediction of steady-state imipramine and desmethylimipramine plasma concentrations from single-dose data. Clin Pharmacol Ther 25:605–610, 1979

114. Potter WZ, Zavadil AP III, Kopin IJ, et al: Single-dose kinetics predict steady-state concentrations of imipramine and desiprimine. Arch Gen Psychiat 37:314–320, 1980

115. Murphy DL, Brand E, Goldman T, et al: Platelet and Plasma amine oxidase inhibition and urinary amine excretion changes during phenelzine treatment. J Nerv Ment Dis 164:129–134, 1977

116. Robinson DS, Nies A, Ravaris CL, et al: Clinical pharmacology of phenelzine. Arch Gen Psychiat 35:629–635, 1978
117. Giller E Jr, Lieb J: MAO inhibitors and platelet MAO inhibition. Comm Psychopharmacol 4:79–82, 1980
118. Prange AJ Jr, McCurdy RL, Cochrane CM: The systolic blood pressure response of depressed patients to infused norepinephrine. J Psychiat Res 5:1–13, 1967
119. Friedman MJ: Does receptor supersensitivity accompany depressive illness? Am J Psychiat 135:107–109, 1978
120. Pandey GN, Dysken MW, Garver DL, et al: Beta-adrenergic receptor function in affective illness. Am J Psychiat 136:675–678, 1979
121. Extein I, Tallman J, Smith CC, et al: Changes in lymphocyte beta-adrenergic receptors in depression and mania. Psychiat Res 1:191–197, 1979
122. Briley MS, Langer SZ, Raisman R, et al: Tritiated imipramine binding sites are decreased in platelets of untreated depressed patients. Science 209:303–305, 1980
123. Ramsey TA, Frazer A, Dyson WL, et al: Intracellular lithium and clinical response. Brit J Psychiat 128:103–104, 1976
124. Cooper TB, Simpson GM, Lee JH: Thymoleptic and neuroleptic drug plasma levels in psychiatry: Current status. Int Rev Neurobiol 19:269–309, 274–278, 1976
125. Pandey GN, Dorus E, Davis JM, et al: Lithium transport in human red blood cells. Arch Gen Psychiat 36:902–908, 1979
126. Cohen B, Aoba A: Lithium transport in erythrocytes of manic-depressives (unpublished observations, 1980)
127. Coppen A: Mineral metabolism in affective disorders. Brit J Psychiat 111:1133–1142, 1965
128. Wehr TA, Wirz-Justice A, Duncan W, et al: Phase advance of the circadian sleep-waking cycle as an antidepressant. Science 206:710–713, 1979
129. Mathew RJ, Meyer JS, Francis DJ, et al: Cerebral blood flow in depression. Am J Psychiat 137:1449–1450, 1980
130. Phelps ME, Mazziotta JC, Kuhl DE, et al: Metabolic mapping of the visual cortex with and without usual stimulation in volunteers and patients with visual deficits. Neurology 30:432, 1980

Name Index

Head, R., 347
Heckhausen, H., 224, 236, 283
Heider, F., 261, 266, 267, 277
Heller, K., 340
Hellman, L., 476, 477
Helsing, K. J., 406
Henry, W., 170
Heraey-Baron, J., 8
Hersen, M., 207
Hewson, D., 342
Higgins, E. T., 147
Hinchcliffe, M., 8
Hiroto, D. S., 184, 185, 186, 187, 190,
   195, 208, 259, 261, 262, 278
Hirsch, B., 342
Hirsch, K. A., 268
Hirschfeld, R., 429
Hoberman, H. M., 142
Hoch, P., 84
Hokanson, J. E., 350
Hollingshead, A. B., 384
Hollister, L. E., 459, 475
Hollon, S., 222, 290, 295, 339, 346, 354,
   355
Honig, W. H., 197
Hops, H., 304
Horney, K., 72
Hornstra, R. K., 312, 319, 324
House, J. S., 342, 343
Howes, M. J., 350
Hubbard, B., 193, 208
Hubir, J., 418
Huessy, H., 446
Hughes, L. A., 347
Humphrey, G. L., 184, 259
Hurvich, M. S., 193

Inhelder, B., 241

Jacklin, C. N., 417
Jackson, B., 233
Jacobs, M., 340
Jacobs, P. D., 195, 259
Jacobson, E., 8, 66, 72, 90, 317, 320, 465
James, W. J., 283
Janowsky, D. S., 193, 208, 465, 470, 471
Johannson, S. L., 150, 164, 165
Johnson-Laird, P. N., 241, 246

Jones, K., 417
Jourent, R., 471

Kahn, J., 5, 9, 303, 356
Kahn, M. W., 187
Kahn, S., 342
Kalinowsky, L., 446
Kallmann, F. J., 450
Kanfer, F. H., 144, 223, 224, 225, 228,
   236
Kanner, A. D., 336
Karobath, M., 466
Karoly, P., 223, 228, 230
Kasl, S. V., 336, 355
Kastenbaum, R. A., 156
Katsev, R. D., 184
Katz, M. M., 240
Kaufman, I. C., 204
Kay, D., 433, 435
Keller, M. B., 355
Kelley, H. H., 232, 266, 267, 277
Kelly, G. A., 241, 242, 376
Kemler, D., 201
Kendall, P. C., 346
Kendall, R. E., 14, 428, 431
Kennelly, K. J., 268
Kent, R. N., 417
Kessler, M., 357
Kessler, R. C., 308, 351
Ketterer, T., 187, 259
Kety, S. S., 465
Khatami, M., 222, 232, 355
Kidder, L., 418
Killian, D., 169
Kiloh, L. C., 201, 430
Kilpatrick-Tabak, B., 260, 280
Kirkegaard, C., 480
Klein, D. C., 143, 186, 190, 191, 192,
   195, 203, 207, 208, 209, 221, 222, 232,
   240, 245, 259, 261, 262, 278, 279, 282,
   283, 284, 285, 290
Klein, M., 64, 93–97, 99, 103, 122
Klerman, G. L., 5, 193, 240, 307, 327,
   351, 352, 403, 411, 424, 429, 432, 433
Klinger, E., 205
Kopin, I. J., 475, 482
Korff, I., 450, 461, 463, 471
Kovacs, M. J., 6, 16, 29, 145, 184, 187,
   206, 211, 222, 240–56, 295, 354, 355

Subject Index